Springer Texts in Business and Economics

More information about this series at http://www.springer.com/series/10099

Efraim Turban • Judy Strauss • Linda Lai

Social Commerce

Marketing, Technology and Management

 Springer

Efraim Turban
Pacific Institute for ISM
University of Hawaii
Honolulu, HI, USA

Judy Strauss
Managerial Sciences Department
University of Nevada
Reno, NV, USA

Linda Lai
School of Business
Macao Polytechnic Institute
Rua Luis Gonzaga Gomes, Macao

ISSN 2192-4333   ISSN 2192-4341   (electronic)
Springer Texts in Business and Economics
ISBN 978-3-319-17027-5   ISBN 978-3-319-17028-2   (eBook)
DOI 10.1007/978-3-319-17028-2

Library of Congress Control Number: 2015939078

Springer Cham Heidelberg New York Dordrecht London

Printed on acid-free paper

Springer International Publishing AG Switzerland is part of Springer Science+Business Media (www.springer.com)

To Daphne and Sharon with love

Efraim Turban

To my lovely daughters, Cyndi and Malia

Judy Strauss

To my parents for their love, support, and encouragement

Linda Lai

Preface

Social commerce, also known as social business, is an emerging field driven by the explosive growth of the social Web and social media. The field includes social network services such as Facebook, Twitter, and LinkedIn; user-generated content networks such as YouTube and Pinterest; products and services review sites (e.g., Trip Advisor); and social shopping sites (e.g., Groupon, Polyvore). Social commerce (SC) can be viewed as a subset of electronic commerce where the electronic transactions and associated product conversations are conducted on social networks and other social media platforms.

To date, major activities of social commerce are facilitated by marketing communication, online sales transactions, and customer service areas. There are also significant activities in the areas of collaboration, recruiting, and problem solving within organizations (known as Enterprise 2.0). Social commerce networks also benefit organizations by moving them closer to their markets for collaboration and research purposes that often result in product innovation and greater customer value.

SC is expected to maintain its rapid growth, disrupting several current business models in the process. An understanding of the strategies and tactics in this field is critical for the future of any organization. This book is a snapshot of SC in 2015/2016, and it includes many resources and references so the reader can learn about the state of the art and monitor current strategies and tactics.

THE PURPOSE OF THIS BOOK

This book was written as a multidisciplinary textbook by leading authors of e-commerce and e-marketing textbooks, with contributions by several industry experts. It is the first comprehensive textbook and resource collection ever written on this topic and it can be used in one or more of the following ways:

(a) Textbook for an elective course at the undergraduate or graduate levels (including MBA and executive MBA programs).
(b) Supplementary text in marketing, management, or information systems disciplines.
(c) Material for training courses in industry.
(d) Support resources for researchers and practitioners in the fields of marketing, management, and information management.

Multidisciplinary Approach

Social commerce is a multidisciplinary field combining marketing, IT, management, sociology, behavioral sciences, and more.

FEATURES OF THIS BOOK

Several features are unique to this book. It includes both management and theoretical approaches to improve business strategies and tactics.

Managerial Orientation

Social commerce can be approached from two major viewpoints: technological and managerial. This text uses the second approach. Most of the content is about SC applications and implementation. However, we do recognize the importance of the technology and present technological topics as needed. In addition, we provide many technology resources.

Real-World Orientation

Extensive, vivid examples from large corporations, small businesses, governments, and non-profit agencies from all over the world make concepts come alive. These examples show the readers the capabilities of SC, its cost and justification, and the innovative ways these entities are using SC in their operations.

Solid Theoretical Background

Chapter 3 is dedicated to the theoretical foundations necessary for understanding SC, ranging from consumer behavior to social influence. Furthermore, we provide website resources, many exercises, and extensive references to supplement the theoretical presentations.

Most Current Leading-Edge Topics

The book presents the most current topics related to SC, as evidenced by many recent sources. Topics such as crowdsourcing, social CRM, reputation management, social games, mobile social, the Hype Cycle, social analytics, and sentiment analysis are presented from the theoretical point of view as well as from the application perspective.

Global Perspective

The importance of global competition, partnerships, and trade is increasing rapidly. Social commerce can facilitate global collaboration, the management of multinational companies, and electronic trading around the globe. International examples are provided throughout the book, including some from developing countries.

Links to Resources

Several hundred links to research reports, companys' products, books, guides, free e-books, etc. are provided.

Note #1. We do not mark a www. in front of the URLs. If the page is not loaded try to add
            www.
Note #2. The dynamic nature of the field makes some of the links obsolete.
Note #3. In many cases, we provide only the name of a company or its URL, but not both.

User-Friendliness

While covering all major SC topics, this book is clear, simple, and well organized. It provides all the basic definitions of terms as well as logical conceptual support. Furthermore, the book is easy to understand and is full of interesting real-world examples that maintain the readers' interest.

ORGANIZATION OF THE BOOK

The book is divided into 11 chapters grouped into four part (see Fig. 1.6). In addition, there are two primers, one on e-commerce and one on e-marketing, which provide the foundations needed as prerequisites to a course on social commerce. An appendix to the book lists dozens of SC-oriented websites.

COURSE SYLLABUS AND LEARNING OUTCOMES

Per the request of many instructors, we provide the following suggested course description, learning outcomes, and student learning strategies.

Course Description

Social commerce is an introductory course in an emerging, quickly developing field, which utilizes social media, including Web 2.0 tools and social network sites, to conduct e-commerce, e-marketing, and other e-business activities. The course covers the areas of buyer behavior, social media marketing, social enterprise (Enterprise 2.0), social government, social CRM, crowdsourcing, social entertainment and gaming, social strategy, market research and analytics, and several other critical topics. The course is managerially oriented, and includes many social media applications and assignments. The prerequisites are: basic knowledge of introduction to MIS, marketing, and e-commerce.

Learning Outcomes

Upon completion of this course, the student will be able to:

1. Understand the essentials of social commerce and its strategic value.
2. Define social media and describe its composition and tools.
3. Explain the major supporting theories behind social commerce.
4. Describe the components of social commerce.
5. Explain how social media is used in marketing communication (including advertising, reputation management, and company-owned social media content).
6. Discuss how social media can engage customers in social commerce activities.
7. Describe the major models of social shopping.
8. Explain social CRM and the use of social media to support it.
9. Describe the content of social enterprise (Enterprise 2.0) and its benefits and business models.
10. Explain crowdsourcing and collective intelligence and relate them to social commerce activities (e.g., idea generation).
11. Be familiar with many applications of social commerce such as social entertainment, social government, and social learning.

12. Describe social strategy and performance and analytics, including competitive strategy and innovation applications.
13. Assess the implementation and deployment issues involved in social commerce.

Student Learning Strategies

- Learn the important terminology for this emerging field, as presented in the book's extensive glossary.
- Follow links within each chapter to learn many of the topics more thoroughly.
- Read case histories within each chapter and answer challenging questions about the company's social media strategies.
- Study the end-of-chapter review questions that can help self-assessment of knowledge learned.
- Engage in social commerce topics with end-of-chapter activities: discussion, debates, and Internet exercises.
- Watch videos and answer relevant questions about them.
- Delve more deeply into chapter topics with end-of-chapter team assignments and activities.
- Solve interesting, current case problems and video cases introduced in each chapter.

PEDAGOGICAL FEATURES

The text offers a number of learning aids for the students:

- **Book's Learning Outcomes.** The book's learning outcomes are included in the proposed course syllabus.
- **Chapter Outlines.** A listing of the main headings ("Content") at the beginning of each chapter provides a quick overview of the major topics covered.
- **Chapter's Learning Objectives.** Learning objectives at the beginning of each chapter help readers focus their efforts and alert them to the important concepts to be discussed. The summaries at the end of each chapter are organized to correspond with the learning objectives.
- **Opening Cases.** Each chapter opens with a real-world example that illustrates the major topics to be covered in the chapter. Following each case, a short section titled "Lessons Learned from the Case" links the important issues in the opening case to the subject matter of the chapter. Questions for the opening cases are provided in the "Team Assignment" section at the end of each chapter.
- **Application Cases and Examples.** In-chapter cases and numerous examples highlight real-world SC solutions used by organizations. Questions follow each application case to help direct students' attention to the implications of the case material.
- **Exhibits.** Numerous attractive exhibits (both illustrations and tables) extend and supplement the text discussion.
- **Chapter Summary.** The chapter summary is linked one-to-one with the learning objectives introduced at the beginning of each chapter.
- **Review Questions.** Each chapter ends with a series of review questions. These are intended to help students summarize the concepts introduced and understand the essentials of each section before proceeding to another topic.
- **End-of-Chapter Exercises.** Different types of questions measure students' comprehension and their ability to apply knowledge. "Topics for Class Discussion and Debates" are intended to develop critical thinking skills. "Internet Exercises" are challenging assignments that require students to use the Internet and apply what they have learned. More than 100 hands-on exercises direct students to interesting websites to conduct research, investigate applications, download demos, watch videos, or learn about state-of-the-art

technology. The "Team Assignments and Projects" exercises are challenging group projects designed to foster group collaboration.
- **Glossary and Key Terms.** Each key term is defined in the text when it first appears. In addition, an alphabetical list of key terms appears at the end of each chapter and a glossary with the definitions of all terms are available at the end of the book.

SUPPLEMENTARY MATERIALS

The following support materials are also available.

- **PowerPoint Lecture Notes.** These notes, developed by Judy Lang and Efraim Turban, are oriented toward text-learning objectives on a chapter-by-chapter basis.
- **Instructor's Manual.** The Instructor's Manual includes answers to all review and discussion questions, exercises, and case questions written by Jon Outland (Online Colleges and Universities).
- **Test Bank.** A comprehensive test bank was developed by Jon Outland.
- **Online Tutorials**. We provide five technology-related online tutorials. The following tutorials are not related to any specific chapter. They cover the essential of SC technologies and provide a guide to relevant resources.
  T1—e-CRM
  T2—EC Technology: EDI, Extranet, RFID, and Cloud Computing
  T3—Business intelligence and Analytics, Data, Text, and Web Mining
  T4—Competition in Cyberspace
  T5—E-Collaboration
- Two authors' websites
  1. Judy Strauss's site (**judystrauss.com/socialcommerce**) includes valuable additional content to supplement the book material.
  2. Efraim Turban's site (**social-commerce-textbook.com**) includes tutorials and online files.

ACKNOWLEDGMENTS

Many individuals helped us create this text. Faculty feedback was solicited via reviews and through individual interviews. We are grateful to this faculty for their contributions.

The following individuals made useful contributions that assisted us in the process of creating this book.

- Deborrah C. Turban (University of Santo Tomas, Philippines) contributed material to several chapters via her Internet search efforts. She also supported the writing of most chapters, checked the references, and helped with many other tasks.
- Judy Lang (Lang Associates) formatted the manuscript and provided valuable suggestions for its improvement.
- Cyndi Jakus (Truckee Meadows Community College) assisted with referencing issues.
- Ivan C. Seballos II (De La Salle Lipa, Philippines) and Stanley Myles C. Seballos (COC-PHINMA Education Network) drew the figures and helped with research and development for the book.
- We also recognize the various organizations and corporations that provided us with useful content. These include Fabio Cipriani (Brazil), who gave us permission to use his slides with their supporting text. We also recognize the practitioners who helped us to gain valuable insights in the social commerce field: Brian Solis (**briansolis.com**), Matthew Tommasi

(the Social Media Guide; socialmediaguide.com.au), and Brian Smith (the global social director of Useful Social Media; **usefulsocialmedia.com**).

- We thank these contributors for their dedication and superb performance shown throughout the writing of the manuscript.

Finally, we appreciate the assistance provided by the Springer team under the leadership of Neil Levine, Matthew Amboy, and Christine Crigler.

Honolulu, HI   Efraim Turban
Reno, NV   Judy Strauss
Gonzaga Gomes, Macao   Linda Lai

Contents

Part I The Foundations

1 Introduction to Social Commerce 3
    Opening Case: Starbucks Goes Social 3
    1.1   Social Computing and the Social Web 5
          Social Computing 5
          The Social Web 6
          Some Interesting Statistics About the Social Web and Social Media 6
    1.2   Fundamentals of Web 2.0 and Social Media 7
          What Is Web 2.0? 7
          What Is Social Media? 8
    1.3   Social Commerce: Definitions and Evolution 8
          Definitions and Characteristics 8
          The Evolution of Social Commerce 9
    1.4   The Content of the Social Commerce Field 10
          The Landscape and Major Components of the Field 10
          Social Media Marketing 11
          Enterprise 2.0 12
    1.5   The Benefits and Limitations of Social Commerce 13
          Benefits to Customers 14
          Benefits to Retailers 14
          Benefits to Other Types of Enterprises 14
          The Social Business: An IBM Approach 15
          New or Improved Business Models 15
          Concerns and Limitations of Conducting Social Commerce 16
    1.6   The Process of Conducting Social Commerce and Suggested
          Research Topics 16
          The Process of Conducting Social Commerce 16
          Illustrative Research Issues 17
    1.7   The Content and Organization of the Book 18
    Summary 18
    References 21

2 Tools and Platforms for Social Commerce 23
    Opening Case: Pinterest—An Innovative Social Commerce Platform 23
    2.1   Social Media: The Basics 26
          Social Media: Many Definitions 26
          The Landscape of Social Media 27
    2.2   Web 2.0 and Its Major Characteristics 29
          Representative Characteristics of Web 2.0 29
          User-Generated Content 29

2.3   The Major Social Media Tools: From Blogs and Microblogs
       to Wikis and Support Technologies 30
       Blog (Web Log) 30
       Microblogging and Twitter 31
       Wikis 32
       Other Useful Tools and Apps.. 32
2.4   Social Networks and Social Networking Sites and Services........... 33
       Social Network Services (Sites)... 33
       The Major Capabilities and Services Provided by Social Network Sites........ 35
       Business-Oriented Social Networks 35
       Enterprise Social Networks... 36
2.5   Mobile Social Commerce 36
       Mobile Social Networking 36
2.6   Crowdsourcing and Crowdfunding: An Introduction 37
       Crowdsourcing.. 37
       Crowdfunding 39
2.7   Virtual Worlds as a Social Commerce Platform 39
       Major Features 39
       Avatars 39
Summary 40
References.. 43

3   **Supporting Theories and Concepts for Social Commerce** 47
     Opening Case: Netflix Increases Sales Using Movie Recommendations
     by Customers 47
     3.1   Learning About Online Consumer Behavior 49
            A Model of Consumer Behavior 50
            The Major Influential Factors 51
     3.2   The Consumer Purchasing-Decision Process 52
            Generic Purchasing Decision-Making Phases:
            A Managerial Decision-Making Approach 52
            The Consumer Brand Decision-Making Process Models............... 53
            The AIDA Model 53
            Consumer Behavior in Social Media and Commerce.................... 55
     3.3   Personalization and Behavioral Marketing................................... 55
            Personalization in Social Commerce 55
            Behavioral Targeting and Collaborative Filtering......................... 56
     3.4   Word of Mouth in Social Commerce 57
            What Is Word of Mouth (WOM)?.. 58
            Using Word of Mouth in Social Commerce.................................. 58
            The Power of WOM.. 58
            The Major Types of WOM 59
            Viral Marketing and Social Networking....................................... 59
     3.5   Consumer Engagement in Social Commerce 60
            Engagement in Social Commerce 60
            Case 3.1 How Whole Foods Engages Its Customers 61
            Facebook Presence... 62
            Engagement on Twitter and by Blogging 62
            Why Engagement.. 62
     3.6   Social Psychology Theories, Social Network Analysis,
            and the Social Graph.. 63
            Social Psychology and Social Commerce..................................... 63
            Social Network Theory and Analysis.. 64
            The Social Graph 65

3.7 Social Influence, Social Capital, and Social Support.................................... 66
  Social Influence... 66
  Social Capital in Social Commerce 66
  Social Support in Online Communities 67
Summary 67
References 70

Part II Social Media Marketing

4 Marketing Communications in Social Media... 75
Opening Case: Johnson & Johnson Uses New Media Marketing............................ 75
  4.1 Getting Started with Social Media Promotions 78
    Listening to Customers 78
    Developing Market Communication... 78
    Social Media Target Markets 79
    Social Media Communication Objectives 79
    Identify Social Media Hangouts 80
  4.2 Promotional Tools: Definitions and Use 81
  4.3 Social Media for Social Commerce Communication 82
    Social Media Platforms... 83
    Owned, Paid, and Earned Social Media.. 83
  4.4 Owned Social Media.. 85
    Controlling Social Media 85
    Types of Owned Social Media... 85
    Focus on Pinterest 86
    Focus on Twitter and Other Microblogging...................................... 86
    Other Types of Owned Social Media 87
    Making Press Relations Social Media Friendly 88
  4.5 Paid Social Media: Advertising 88
    Advertising Formats.. 90
    Video Advertising 91
    More Social Media Advertising Examples 92
    Advertising Pricing Models 94
  4.6 Coordinating Social, Internet, and Traditional Media Promotion Plans.......... 94
Summary 95
References 97

5 Customer Engagement and Metrics... 99
Opening Case: Häagen-Dazs Viral Video Creates a Buzz 99
  5.1 Earned Media 101
  5.2 Social Media Engagement Levels.. 101
  5.3 Engaging Consumers to Produce Earned Media 103
    Who Should a Company Engage? 104
  5.4 Engagement Techniques 104
    Viral Marketing.. 105
    Ratings, Reviews, Recommendations and Referrals 107
    Collaborative Content Creation by Consumers 109
    How Do Companies Entice Engagement?... 110
  5.5 Reputation Management in Social Media... 112
    Which Reputations Matter? 114
    Build, Maintain, Monitor, Repair, and Learn................................... 114
    Reputations Management Systems 115
  5.6 Search Engine Optimization 116
  5.7 Monitor, Measure, and Refine: SM Metrics 118
    Awareness/Exposure Metrics.. 119

Brand Health Metrics 119
Engagement Metrics 120
Action Metrics 120
Innovation Metrics 120
Measurement Tools 120
Summary 121
References 124

6 **Social Shopping: Concepts, Benefits, and Models** 127
   Opening Case: Groupon—Will the Company Prosper? 127
   6.1 Definitions, Drivers, Concepts, and Benefits of Social Shopping 131
        Definitions 131
        Concepts and Content of Social Shopping 132
        The Benefits of Social Shopping 133
   6.2 Components and Models of Social Shopping 133
        What Components to Expect in a Social Shopping Site 133
        The Major Social Shopping Models 134
        Traditional E-Commerce Sites with Social Media Additions 134
   6.3 Group Buying and Deal Purchasing 135
        Group Buying in China 135
        Group Buying and Flash Sales on Facebook 136
        Deal Purchases (Flash Sales, Daily Deals) 136
   6.4 Shopping Together: Communities and Clubs 136
        Online Social Shopping Communities 137
        Case 6.1 Polyvore: A Trendsetter in Social Shopping 137
        Kaboodle: A Unique Social Shopping Community 138
        Private Online Shopping Clubs and Retail by Invitation 139
        Shopping Together Sites 139
   6.5 Social Shopping Aids: From Recommendations, Reviews,
        and Ratings to Marketplaces 139
        Recommendations in Social Commerce 139
        Other Shopping Aids and Services 142
        Social Marketplaces and Direct Sales to Customers 143
   6.6 Innovative Shopping Models and Sites and Virtual Goods 144
        Examples of Innovative Social Shopping Ideas and Sites 144
        Shopping Without Leaving Facebook and Other Social Networks 146
        Shopping for Virtual Goods in a Virtual Economy 146
        Real-Time Online Shopping 147
        Auctions in Social Shopping 148
        B2B Social Networking 148
        Virtual Visual Shopping 148
        Social Shopping in the Near Future 149
        Activities on Twitter 149
   Summary 149
   References 152

7 **Social Customer Service and CRM** 155
   Opening Case: How Sony Uses Social Media for Improving CRM 155
   7.1 Definitions and Concepts of CRM, E-CRM, and Social CRM 156
        How Social Networks Empower Customers 157
        Defining CRM and E-CRM 158
        What Is Social CRM? 158
   7.2 A CRM Model for Customer Interactions 160
        The Patricia Seybold Group Model for Customer Interactions 160

Customer-Facing Applications... 161
Case 7.1 iRobot Uses Social Media for Multichannel CRM........................... 161
7.3 The Evolution of Social CRM 162
Cipriani's Multidimensional Presentation... 162
Understanding the Social CRM Evolution 166
7.4 How to Serve the Social Customer... 166
The Social Customer.. 166
Implementation of Social Customer Service and CRM................................... 167
How Social CRM Works: Problems and Solutions 167
Some Social CRM Tools.. 168
Automated Response to E-Mail (Autoresponder)... 169
Automated Live Chat... 169
Using Microblogging 169
Product Review Sites 169
7.5 Social CRM in the Enterprise 170
Social CRM in the Enterprise and B2B Environments.................................... 170
Salespeople Benefit from Social Media 171
7.6 Special Applications and Issues in Social CRM... 172
Social Networking Helps Customer Service in Small Companies 172
Customer-Touching Applications 173
Customer-Centric Applications... 173
7.7 Strategy and Implementation Issues of Social CRM 174
Social CRM Strategy 174
Summary 175
References... 177

Part III   Social Enterprise, Other Applications

**8   The Social Enterprise: From Recruiting to Problem Solving
and Collaboration** 181
Opening Case: How a Private Enterprise Network Transformed
CEMEX into a Social Business 181
8.1 Social Business and Social Enterprise... 182
Definitions: Social Business and Social Enterprise 182
Business Networks.. 183
The Benefits and Limitations of Enterprise Social Networking....................... 184
How Web 2.0 Tools Are Used by Enterprises.. 184
8.2 Business-Oriented Public Social Networking.. 185
Case 8.1 Linkedin: The Premier Public Business-Oriented
Social Network... 185
Networks for Entrepreneurs 187
8.3 Enterprise Social Networks... 187
Taxonomy of Social Enterprise Applications 188
Characteristics of Enterprise Social Networks 188
How Enterprise Social Networking Helps Employees and Organizations....... 188
Support Services for Enterprise Social Networks... 189
How Companies Interface with Social Networking 189
8.4 Online Job Markets and Training in Social Networks 190
Social Recruiting.. 190
Virtual Job Fairs and Recruiting Events 191
8.5 Managerial Problem Solving, Innovation, and Knowledge Management........ 192
Idea Generation and Problem Solving... 192
Knowledge Management and Social Networks.. 193

Online Advice and Consulting 194

8.6   Crowdsourcing: Collective Intelligence for Problem Solving
      and Content Creation 194
      Crowdsourcing as a Distributed Problem Solving Enabler 194
      The Process of Crowdsourcing 195
      Successfully Deployed Crowdsourcing Systems:
      Some Representative Examples 196
      Tools for Crowdsourcing 196
8.7   Social Collaboration (Collaboration 2.0) 197
      Supporting Social Collaboration 197
Summary 199
References 201

**9   Innovative Social Commerce Applications: From Social Government
     to Entertainment and Gaming** 205
Opening Case: Justin Bieber—The Ultimate Story of Social Media Fame 205
9.1   Social Media and Commerce in E-Government 207
      Definition and Scope of E-Government 207
      E-Government 2.0 (Social Government) 207
      Case 9.1 Social Networking Initiatives by the New Zealand Government 207
      The Benefits of Government 2.0 209
      Applications and Resources 210
9.2   B2B Social Networking 210
      E-Communities in B2B 210
      The Major Opportunities and Benefits of Social Commerce in B2B 210
      Specific Social Networking Activities in B2B 211
      Using the Major Social Networks in B2B 212
      B2B Success Stories 213
      B2B Virtual Trade Shows and Trade Fairs in Virtual Worlds 213
      Strategy for B2B Social Networking 214
      The Future of B2B Social Networking 215
9.3   Social Commerce: Applications in Virtual Worlds 215
      The Features and Spaces of Virtual Worlds 215
      The Landscape of Virtual World Commercial Applications 215
      The Major Drivers of Social Commerce in Virtual Worlds 216
      The Major Categories of Virtual World Applications 216
      Concerns and Limitations of Commercial Activities in Virtual Worlds 219
9.4   Social Entertainment and Social TV 219
      Entertainment and Social Networks 219
      Multimedia Presentation and Sharing Sites 220
      Internet TV and Internet Social TV 221
      Social Television (TV) 221
      Internet Radio and Social Radio 222
9.5   Social Games, Gaming, and Gamification 222
      Games on Social Networks 222
      The Business Aspects of Social Games 223
      Educational Social Games 223
      Gamification 224
9.6   Socially Oriented Online Person-to-Person Activities 224
      P2P Lending 224
      Social Money Lending 225
Summary 225
References 228

Part IV   Strategy and Implementation

10   Strategy and Performance Management in Social Commerce 233
Opening Case: Social Media-Based Market Research Helps
Del Monte Improve Dog Food 233
 10.1 The Strategy-Performance Cycle 235
    Types of Social Media Projects 236
 10.2 Organizational Strategy and Strategic Planning for Social Commerce 237
    Porter's 5 Competitive Forces Model and Related Strategies 237
    The Key Elements of a Strategic Planning Process 239
    Strategy Implementation in Social Commerce 239
    A Strategy for Successful SC Implementation 240
 10.3 Justification and ROI in Social Commerce 241
    An Overview of Justification 241
    The SC Justification Process 242
    Difficulties in Conducting Cost–Benefit Analysis and Justification 242
    Incorrectly Defining What Is Measured 242
    Intangible Cost-Benefit Analysis 242
    The Use of Gartner's Hype Cycle 243
    Risk Analysis 244
    Conclusion 244
 10.4 Market Research in Social Commerce 245
    Why Conduct Market Research? 245
    E-Marketing Research in Brief 245
    Using Social Networking for Qualitative Market Research 245
    The Process of Conducting Qualitative Market Research
    for Social Commerce 246
    Learning from Customers: Conversational Marketing 246
    Conducting Market Research Using the Major Social Network Sites 247
 10.5 Metrics and Monitoring Performance 249
    Performance Monitoring and Analysis Cycle 249
    Using Metrics in Performance Assessment 250
    Using Metrics in Social Commerce 251
    Balanced Scorecards (BSC) 253
    Metrics and Measurements for Social Influence 253
    Monitoring the Social Media Field 254
 10.6 Social Media Analytics and Sentiment Analysis 255
    Definitions, Importance, and Applications 255
    Social Media Analytics 255
    Tools for Mining Social Media Activities 256
    Sentiment Analysis and Web 2.0 256
    Dashboards in Social Commerce 256
 10.7 Improving Performance via Innovation and Competitive Analysis 257
    Competitive Intelligence for Improving Performance 257
    Innovation in Social Commerce 257
 Summary 258
 References 260

11   Implementing Social Commerce Systems 265
Opening Case: Domino's Employees Post Vulgar Videos on YouTube 265
 11.1 Social Commerce Implementation Issues 267
    What Is Implementation? 267
    The Implementation Process and Its Major Issues 267
 11.2 Security and Fraud Protection in Social Commerce 268
    Social Engineering and Fraud 268

	Social Phishing..	269
	Social Media Makes Social Engineering Easy	270
	Defending Social Commerce Systems..	271
	Protection Against Spam..	272
	Fraud in Social Commerce...	272
11.3	Issues of Legality, Privacy, Cyberbullying, and Ethics....................	272
	Legal Issues...	272
	Case 11.1 Internet Blackout against Anti-Piracy Laws......................	273
	Privacy Issues in Social Commerce...	274
	Cyberbullying	275
	Ethics in Social Commerce..	275
11.4	Technological Issues	276
	Social Commerce Systems Integration	276
	Social Commerce Tools	276
	Acquisition of Social Commerce Systems..	277
11.5	Employee-Related Implementation Issues..	278
	Non-work-Related Use of Social Media..	278
	Employee Reluctance or Resistance to Participate	278
	Quality of Content and Biases of User-Generated Content	278
	Data Leakage and Loss of Data	278
	Social Media Management at Work...	278
11.6	Organizational Issues and the Impacts of Social Commerce............	279
	Improving Marketing and Sales Revenue...	279
	Transforming Organizations and Work...	279
11.7	Other Implementation Issues	281
	Implementation Issues in SMEs...	281
	Some Strategy Issues for SMEs...	282
	Risk Factors and Analysis..	282
11.8	Successes, Failures, and Lessons Learned	283
	A Strategy for Social Commerce Implementation Success	283
	Some Policies and Guidelines..	283
	Learning from Failures	283
	Adoption Strategies..	283
	Revenue Generation Strategies in Social Commerce	283
11.9	The Future of Social Commerce	284
	Creation of Jobs	284
	IBM's Watson, Smart Computing and Social Commerce..................	284
	Conclusion	284
	Summary	285
	References...	287

Appendix: Recommended Resources for Social Commerce 291

Primer A: E-Commerce Basics.. 293

Primer B: E-Marketing Basics 305

Glossary 313

Index... 319

About the Authors

Linda Lai has been an Associate Professor at the Macao Polytechnic Institute of China since September 2006. Prior to her current position, she undertook remits as academic and administrator at the City University of Hong Kong for 15 years. She had also worked as a business professional in Hong Kong and England for more than 6 years. Dr. Lai holds two research degrees from Lancaster University, UK—one in the area of IT applications and the other focusing on wider management issues. Her research interests include decision science, knowledge management, and electronic commerce. Dr. Lai has published more than 40 high impact articles and a book on Chinese e-business entrepreneurship within recent years.

Judy Strauss is Associate Professor of Marketing, emerita at the University of Nevada, Reno. She is an international speaker, seminar leader, entrepreneur, and previous Marketing Director of two companies. She is an award-winning author of 4 books (in 14 editions) and numerous scholarly articles on internet marketing topics, co-authoring Radically Transparent: Monitoring and Managing Reputations Online and E-Marketing—the first textbook on internet marketing (translated into Japanese and Chinese). At UNR, she taught marketing communication, international marketing, internet marketing, and strategy topics—including co-advising the national winners in the AAF National Student Advertising Competition. She still teaches an online Principles of Marketing course and in Germany: Brand Management. She has won two teaching awards and a lifetime achievement in marketing award from the American Marketing Association. Strauss earned a doctorate in marketing at Southern Illinois University, and finance MBA and marketing BBA at University of North Texas.

Efraim Turban, M.B.A., Ph.D. (University of California, Berkeley) is a visiting scholar at the Pacific Institute of Information System Management, University of Hawaii. Prior to this, he was on the staff of several universities, including City University of Hong Kong; Lehigh University; Florida International University; California State University, Long beach; Eastern Illinois University; and the University of Southern California. Dr. Turban is the author of more than 110 refereed papers published in leading journals, such as Management Science, MIS Quarterly, International Journal of Electronic Commerce, Journal of MIS, and Communication of the ACM. He is also the author of 22 books, including Electronic Commerce: A Managerial Perspective, Business Intelligence, Decision Support Systems, and Information Technology for Management. He is also a consultant to major corporations and universities worldwide. Dr. Turban's current interest is social commerce. He is the coeditor of 2011/2012 special issue on the topic in the International Journal of Electronic Commerce, and the author of several related papers in referred journals.

Part I

The Foundations

Introduction to Social Commerce

Contents

Opening Case: Starbucks Goes Social 3

1.1   Social Computing and the Social Web 5

1.2   Fundamentals of Web 2.0 and Social Media 7

1.3   Social Commerce: Definitions and Evolution 8

1.4   The Content of the Social Commerce Field 10

1.5   The Benefits and Limitations of Social Commerce 13

1.6   The Process of Conducting Social Commerce
      and Suggested Research Topics 16

1.7   The Content and Organization of the Book 18

References 21

Learning Objectives

Upon completion of this chapter, you will be able to:

1. Define social computing and the Social Web.
2. Describe the Social Web revolution.
3. Describe the essentials of Web 2.0 and social media.
4. Define social commerce and describe its roots and evolution.
5. Describe the content of the social commerce field.
6. Define social media marketing.
7. Describe Enterprise 2.0.
8. Summarize the benefits and limitations of social commerce.
9. Understand the process of conducting social commerce.
10. Find research opportunities in social commerce and learn about related resources.

OPENING CASE: STARBUCKS GOES SOCIAL

Starbucks Corp. ("Starbucks") is the world's largest coffee house chain. As of October 2014, the company has over 21,000 stores in 66 countries (per **starbucks.com**). In addition to its coffee houses, Starbucks sells coffee and related products from its online store (**store.starbucks.com/**). In 2012, Starbucks began turning itself into a digital and social company (Van Grove 2012 and case study at **storify.com/ MerMaeMarNat/starbucks-social-media-case-study**).

The Problem

Starting in 2007, the company's operating income declined sharply (from over $1 billion in 2007 to $504 million in 2008 and $560 million in 2009). This decline was caused by not only the economic slowdown, but also by the increased competition (e.g., from Green Mountain Coffee Roasters), which intensified even during the recession.

Electronic supplementary material The online version of this chapter (doi:10.1007/978-3-319-17028-2_1) contains supplementary material, which is available to authorized users.

The Solution: Going Social

Starbucks is a tech-savvy company. As such, the company has one of the best social media programs (see Moth 2013). Social media are Internet-based systems that support social interactions and user involvement (see Sect. 1.2). The company's focus is geared toward developing relationships based on the needs, wants, and likes of existing and future customers.

Starbucks' major social media activities include My Starbucks Idea (a community of about 300,000 members that cast over 1,000,000 votes by 2014), a Facebook page, and a presence on all other major social networks (see Moth 2013).

Exploiting Collective Intelligence: My Starbucks Idea

My Starbucks Idea (**mystarbucksidea.force.com**) is a platform in which consumers and employees can make suggestions, vote on the suggestions, ask questions, collaborate on projects, and vent their frustrations (see York 2010). The consumer-generated ideas (70,000 in its first year; 150,000 by 2014) range from thoughts on rewards cards and elimination/recycling of paper cups to ways to better serve customers. The site acts as a place for open dialogue and collaborative environment and a place for sharing ideas and information.

The company also interacts with the community via its 'Ideas in Action' blog. The blog provides statistics on the ideas generated, by category (e.g., product ideas, service ideas), as well as their status (under review, reviewed, in the works, and launched). The company may provide monetary incentives for certain ideas. For example, in June 2010, Starbucks offered $20,000 for the best ideas concerning the reuse of its cups.

Starbucks' Activities on Facebook

Starbucks maintains a strong social media presence on Facebook (**facebook.com/Starbucks**), with over 38 million "Likes" (as of December 2014). Their Facebook page encourages consumers to drop by for conversation and share ideas, feedback, and constructive criticism.

The millions of people who 'like' Starbucks on Facebook verify that the company has one of the most popular fan pages (see current statistics at **fanpagelist.com**). Starbucks is offering one of the best online marketing communication experiences on Facebook to date, along with mobile commerce engagement. For example, users can pay for coffee with their smartphones.

Starbucks posts diversified information (e.g., news, discussion) on its Facebook "wall," whether it is content, questions, or updates. The company also advertises on Facebook (e.g., contests, events, new products) and posts job openings.

Starbucks' Presence on LinkedIn and Google+

Starbucks has profiles on LinkedIn and Google+ sites with millions of followers. It provides business data about the company, shows employee profiles, and advertises available jobs. Note that Starbucks is regularly assessing the cost-benefit of advertising on social networks.

Starbucks' Activities on Twitter

In December 2014, Starbucks had over seven million followers (Follow@starbucks) on Twitter (**twitter.com/starbucks**), organized in lists (e.g., @starbucks/friends). Each 'list' has its own followers and tweets. Whenever the company has a new update or campaign (e.g., discounted drinks) it posts a tweet. By July 2013, Starbucks was the number one retailer to follow on Twitter.

Starbucks' Activities on YouTube, Flickr, Pinterest, and Instagram

Starbucks runs ad campaigns and has its own channel on YouTube (**youtube.com/user/starbucks**) and a "group" for fans on Flickr (**flickr.com/groups/starbuckscoffeecompany**), with fans sharing over 12,000 photos and videos. For details on these and other networks, see Moth (2013).

Early Adoption of Foursquare—A Failure

Not all Starbucks social media projects have been a success. For example, the company decided to be an early adopter of geolocation by working with Foursquare. The initiative simply did not work, and the project ended in mid-2010. As an early adopter, Starbucks did not fully understand how to use the site effectively for its social media needs (see Teicher 2010 for an analysis). With the general lack of interest in geolocation, it looks like Starbucks may stop using this technology.

Social Media Marketing

According to Gibb (2013), Starbucks excels at social media marketing because:

- It has "super influencers"
- It encourages sharing
- It customizes the experience
- Its causes are timely and consistent
- It uses social cross-promotion to reach new audiences
- Its mission is "to inspire and nurture the human spirit one person, one cup, and one neighborhood at a time."

Starbucks Digital Network

When customers are at Starbucks, they have more than Wi-Fi, they get access to the Starbucks Digital Network from all major mobile devices, including tablets and smartphones (see **starbucks.com/coffeehouse/wireless-internet/starbucks-digital-network**). The Network, in partnership with Yahoo!, features free premium online content, such as news, entertainment, business, health, and even local neighborhood information channels. In 2014, Starbucks switched to Google Wi-Fi, instead of AT&T, to give their customers faster Wi-Fi and network speeds.

The Results

Starbucks turned sales around by effectively integrating the digital and the physical worlds. In 2010, its operating income almost tripled ($1.437 billion versus $560 million in 2009) and so did its stock price. In addition, earnings doubled from 2010 to 2013. In 2013, the operating income reached $2.68 billion. Sales are lifting due to digital and social media promotions (see York 2010).

The company's social media initiatives are widely recognized. In 2012, Starbucks was listed by *Fortune Magazine* as one of the top ten social media stars (per **archive.fortune.com/galleries/2012/fortune/1205/gallery.500-social-media.fortune/5.html**), and in 2008, it was awarded the 2008 Groundswell Award by Forrester Research. Starbucks attributes its success to ten philosophical precepts that drive its social media efforts (see Belicove 2010).

Sources: Based on Loeb (2013), Belicove (2010), Van Grove (2012), Moth (2013), Allison (2013), Schoultz (2013), Teicher (2010), **mystarbucksidea.force.com**, **blogs.starbucks.com/blogs/Customer**, and **starbucks.com** (accessed June 2015).

LESSONS LEARNED FROM THE CASE

The opening case illustrates how a large company uses both an enterprise and a public social network. In addition, the company uses social media platforms and Web 2.0 tools to connect and build relationships with its customers for advertising and customer service. At the same time, a central activity is to involve customers in improving the company's operations by soliciting and discussing ideas. It is a large "electronic suggestion box," but it is visible to everyone using the company's in-house enterprise social network. The major objective is to increase the flow of visitors to the physical stores as well as to the online sites. Using special promotions and rewards, Starbucks has attracted a record number of visitors, considerably improving its revenue and profits.

In this chapter, we cover the essentials of social commerce and describe the content of this book.

1.1   SOCIAL COMPUTING AND THE SOCIAL WEB

The first generation of e-commerce (EC) involved mainly e-trading, e-services, and corporate-sponsored collaboration. We are now in the middle of the seconds generation of EC, which includes what we call *social commerce*. It is based on the emergence of social computing and on a set of tools, marketplaces, infrastructure, and support theories, all of which are socially-oriented (see Meeker and Wu 2013).

In this chapter, you will discover the importance of social commerce to customers, retailers, and other organizations.

Social Computing

Social computing is a type of computing that includes an interaction of computers and social behavior. It is performed with a set of social media tools that includes blogs, wikis, social network services (see Chap. 2), and social marketplaces. For details, see **en.wikipedia.org/wiki/Social_computing**.

In social computing, individuals produce information, which is available to all, usually for free. For an interesting study about social computing, see Ericson (2011). Many universities and corporations (e.g., IBM, Microsoft, Intel, HP and Carnegie Mellon University) have centers for social computing.

The Social Web

According to Appelquist et al. (2010), the term **Social Web** "is a set of social relationships that link together people over the [World Wide] Web." For details, see **en.wikipedia.org/wiki/ Social_web**. The Social Web is quickly changing work, entertainment, learning, and human interactions. According to **weblogs.about.com/od/bloggingglossary/g/SocialWebDef. htm**, the Social Web, is "the seconds generation of the World Wide Web which focuses heavily on user-generated content, communities, networking and social interaction."

Welcome to the Social Web Revolution

Social computing interrelates with social consumers. Many experts have found that the Social Web is transforming people's individual and group behaviors as well as the power structure in corporations and marketplaces. This change is very rapid and significant, so we can classify it as a *revolution*. For an overview of this revolution, read Fraser and Dutta (2008) and watch the video titled "Social Media Revolution" (4:22 minutes) at **youtube.com/watch?v=sIFYPQjYhv8**. For a description of this change, see Amerland (2011). The major social network that is currently changing the world and business is Facebook.

F-Commerce

A major force in the Social Web revolution is Facebook, which, in late 2014, had over 1.35 billion monthly active users worldwide. Facebook is considered the "king" of social networks and the implementer of many commercial innovations what is known as F-commerce (see Shih 2011; Kirkpatrick 2010, and **facebook.com/commerce**). For additional details, see **webopedia.com/TERM/F/f-commerce.html**.

Some Interesting Statistics About the Social Web and Social Media

There are many sources of statistics about social commerce and media. A good place to start is with the "100 Fascinating Social Media Statistics and Figures From 2012" posted by Honigman on *Huffington Post*, and corresponding infographic, for 2013 (with recapping statistics from 2012) at (**digitalbuzzblog.com/infographic-social-media-statistics-for-2013**). For social media and video statistics for 2014, watch the video at **youtube.com/watch?=QfVVfB_ UHeA**. See also Pant (2013). Note: These statistics are dynamic, changing with time.

The following examples were compiled from **bazaarvoice. com/research-and-insight/social-commerce-statistics** and **pewinternet.org/2013/12/30/social-media-update-2013**.

- It was predicted that Internet use will quadruple in size from 2011 to 2015 (Goldman 2011), with much of the expected growth attributed to *social networking activities*.
- Since March 2010, there have been more Internet visits to Facebook than to Google.
- As of December 2014, Facebook hosts pages for over 30 million businesses, and has more than 1.5 million advertisers (per **techcrunch.com/2014/07/23/ facebook-usage-time**).
- The first 'Funny or Die' comedy user-generated video, "The Landlord," had 70 million viewers in its first 6 months.
- In March 2011, a teenager from New South Wales had to cancel her 16th birthday party after she posted an invitation on her Facebook page, intending to invite people in her class only. The invitation went viral and close to 200,000 people replied that they were attending, prompting her to cancel the party. (See **news.com.au/national/ chatswood-girl-cancels-facebook-party-after-20000-said-they-would-attend/story-e6frfkwi-1226021517747**).
- The Internet start-up Groupon, a leader in daily deals social shopping, had annual revenues of $500 million in its seconds year of operations. This prompted Google to offer $5.4 billion to acquire the site in October 2010. Groupon rejected the offer and went public with an IPO in 2012 (see opening case to Chap. 6).
- Among the Y generation, 96 % have joined a social network.
- Of the 77 % of American adults who surf the Internet, more than 67 % are members of social networks. The time spent social networking by Internet surfers is growing rapidly. According to comScore Media Metrix, in 2013, the world spent more than 120 billion minutes using social networks and blogs each month, which totaled 24 % of all the time spent online. These numbers are growing over time.
- In July 2014, over 645 million active users worldwide were on Twitter (more than 255 MAUs), sending about 500 million tweets every day (**statisticbrain. com/twitter-statistics**; **about.twitter.com/ company**). Note that these numbers may differ

depending on the source consulted (see, e.g., Craig Smith's "By the Numbers" post [last updated December 21, 2014] at **expandedramblings.com/index.php/march-2013-by-the-numbers-a-few-amazing-twitter-stats/#.U9FtuvldWSo**; not all of Twitter's registered users use the service with any consistency; see **venturebeat.com/2013/09/16/how-twitter-plans-to-make-its-750m-users-like-its-250m-real-users**).

- Before making a purchase, about 90 % of customers conduct research online after they get recommendations from family or friends (July 2014).
- 30 % of big companies offer customer service on Twitter (per Dougherty 2013).
- Over 72 % of adult Internet users in the U.S. use Facebook at least once a month (per **marketingpilgrim.com/2014/03/google-plus-cant-beat-facebook-but-can-it-win-seconds-place.html**). Again, this data can fluctuate depending on the source.
- Microsoft paid $250 million for a 1.6 % ownership of Facebook in 2011. Many people thought that the price paid was too high. However, based on its stock price in July 2014, the valuation of Facebook was estimated to be $180 billion, making Microsoft's investment worth $2.6 billion, an ROI of over 1,000 % in 3 years—not bad!

For Facebook's Q3 2014 earnings (posted October 28, 2014), see **techcrunch.com/2014/10/28/facebook-q3-2014**; for the Quarterly Earnings Slides and accompanying webcast (posted October 28, 2014), see **media-server.com/m/p/22wd72e4**.

For additional statistics and discussion of the social media revolution, see **factbrowser.com/tags/social_commerce**, **pewinternet.org/data-trend/social-media/social-media-use-all-users**, Bullas (2013), Meeker and Wu (2013), and Young (2013).

By the time you read this book, Facebook may have 1.5 billion members, which is over 40 % of all Internet users worldwide and over 20 % of the world population.

1.2 FUNDAMENTALS OF WEB 2.0 AND SOCIAL MEDIA

The Social Web is based on the concept of Web 2.0. These two terms are often used interchangeably, although some experts define them differently.

What Is Web 2.0?

O'Reilly Media introduced the term **Web 2.0** in 2004. O'Reilly viewed this term as describing a seconds generation of Internet-based tools and services. Some properties cited by O'Reilly were: user-generated content, online collaboration and information, and sharing data interactively. For comprehensive coverage, see **en.wikipedia.org/wiki/Web_2.0** and McDonald (2010). In 2006, O'Reilly updated his definition of Web 2.0.

Note that the term is defined in several ways.

O'Reilly (2006) expanded and clarified his 'What is Web 2.0' article (O'Reilly 2005), dividing Web 2.0 into the following four levels ("a hierarchy of 'Web 2.0-ness'"):

1. Level 3 applications, the most 'Web 2.0' oriented, exist only on the Internet, deriving their effectiveness from (interpersonal) connections and from the network effects that Web 2.0 makes possible, are growing in effectiveness as people make more use of them. O'Reilly cited eBay, Craigslist, Wikipedia, Delicious, Skype, Dodgeball, and Google AdSense as examples of level 3 applications.
2. Level 2 applications can operate offline but gain advantages from going online. O'Reilly cited Flickr, as an example, which benefits from its shared photo database and from its community-generated tag database.
3. Level 1 applications operate offline but gain features online. O'Reilly cited examples such as spreadsheets, and iTunes (because of its music store).
4. Level 0 applications work as well offline as they do online. O'Reilly gave the examples of Google Maps, Yahoo! Local, and MapQuest.

Karakas (2009) categorizes Web 2.0 into five shifts, which define the new global landscape of business, technology, and innovation: "a) creativity, b) connectivity, c) collaboration, d) convergence, and e) community…."

The major characteristics and tools of Web 2.0 are presented in Chap. 2 and the applications are described in most of the other chapters. Web 2.0 is considered a platform for running social media. For a summary of Web 2.0 definitions, explanations, and applications, see **en.wikipedia.org/wiki/Web_2.0**.

What Is Social Media?

Many people equate the terms Web 2.0 and social media and use them interchangeably; however, a deeper understanding of the differences helps improve academic and practical research and corporate implementation strategies. While social media uses Web 2.0 and social computing tools and technologies, the social media concept includes the *philosophy* of connected people, the interactions among them, the social support provided, the digital content, and other properties that contribute to successful applications. In essence, it is a product of the *social economy* (see Chui et al. 2012).

Social media can be defined as online text, image, audio, and video content created by people using Web 2.0 platforms and tools for social interactions and conversations, mainly to share opinions, experiences, insights, and perceptions. They also generate content. The key is that *users*, in addition to organizations, generate, control, use, and manage content, often at little or no cost. Social media "is the collective of online communications channels dedicated to community-based input, interaction, content-sharing and collaboration. Websites and applications dedicated to forums, microblogging, social networking, social bookmarking, social curation, and wikis are among the different types of social media" (per **whatis.techtarget.com/definition/social-media**, which also offers examples).

Kaplan and Haenlein (2010) define social media as "a group of Internet-based applications that build on the ideological and technological foundations of Web 2.0, and that allow the creation and exchange of user-generated content." For definitions, examples, and infographics, see **boundless.com/marketing/social-media-marketing/introduction-to-social-media-digital-marketing/what-is-social-media**. In Chap. 2, we discuss several other definitions of social media. For a 2013 infographic by Altimeter, see **slideshare.net/Altimeter/infographic-29122697**. For comprehensive videos, see "The Social Media Revolution 2014" (2:31 minutes) at **youtube.com/watch?v=DYedZth9ArM** and "#Socialnomics 2014 by Erik Qualman" (3:19 minutes) at **youtube.com/watch?v=zxpa4dNVd3c**. New versions of both videos are created annually.

Social media/Web 2.0 are key drivers of social commerce. For the effect of social media on commerce, see the infographic by Pant (2013), the discussion by Solis (2011), and the Slideshare presentation by Solis and Li (2013). There is also a summary of Solis's report available at **briansolis.com/2013/10/altimeter-groups-state-of-social-business-2013-report**. A video titled "Social Media Video 2013," which describes the state of the field, is available at **youtube.com/watch?v=QUCfFcchw1w**. For comprehensive social media statistics for the call center, see Fonolo (2013). For a guide to using social media for small businesses, see Gratton and Gratton (2012).

For the differences between social media and social networking, see **conversationalmarketinglabs.com/blog/2014/04/about-incept/the-difference-between-social-networking-vs-social-media**. For the difference between social networking sites and social media (including infographics), see **blog.referralcandy.com/2013/11/18/difference-between-social-networks-and-social-media**. For using social media vs. social networking as a content marketing strategy, see **searchenginejournal.com/social-media-versus-social-networking-content-marketing-strategy/94867**.

1.3 SOCIAL COMMERCE: DEFINITIONS AND EVOLUTION

As it is a new field that involves several academic and professional disciplines, there is no agreed-upon definition or description of the content and boundaries of the social commerce area. The following are some working definitions.

Definitions and Characteristics

Social commerce (SC) refers to e-commerce transactions delivered via social media. (For a primer on e-commerce, see Online Appendix A.) Some consider social commerce to be a subset of e-commerce. More specifically, it is a combination of e-commerce, e-marketing (for a primer on e-marketing, see Online Appendix B), the supporting technologies, and social media content. This definition is illustrated in Fig. 1.1. The figure shows that social commerce is created from the integration of e-commerce and e-marketing using Web 2.0/social media applications. The integration is supported by theories such as social capital, social psychology, consumer behavior, and online collaboration, resulting in a set of useful applications that drive social commerce.

The social commerce field is growing rapidly; from 2011 to 2015, it was projected to rise to $30 billion in revenues, according to Booz & Co. (reported by Cuccureddu 2011). For the impact of the technology, see ShopSocially (2013). The magnitude of the field can be seen in the statistics and infographic provided by Bennett (2013). For other interesting social commerce statistics, see **bazaarvoice.com/research-and-insight/social-commerce-statistics**.

Wang and Zhang (2012) provide a list of 11 definitions, including that of Stephen and Toubia (2010), who define SC as "a form of Internet-based 'social media' that allow[s] people to participate actively in the marketing and selling of products and services in online marketplaces and communities." They distinguish *social shopping* that connects customers, from *social commerce* that connects sellers. Dennison et al. (2009) provide an IBM definition: "…social commerce is [the concept of] *word of mouth*, applied to e-commerce." (Emphasis added.) Marsden (2011) collected 24 different definitions of SC that include several of SC's properties (such as word of mouth, trusted advice, and buying with the opinions and assistance of friends).

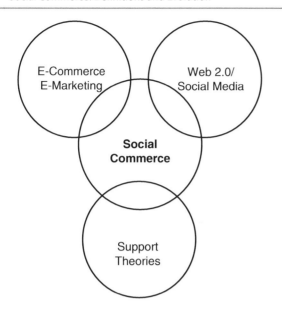

Fig. 1.1 The foundation of social commerce

For additional discussion, see **bazaarvoice.com/research-and-insight/social-commerce-statistics** and Baekdal (2011). Note that social business is about a large collection of tools that need to be assembled in the right way and tied to underlying business processes and strategies (Greengard 2014).

Social Commerce and Social Business

The term social commerce is frequently confused with the term *social business*. The problem is that there are several definitions and explanations of social business. Here are four:

1) Social Commerce Is the Same as Social Business
The two terms are often used interchangeably.

2) The Business That Addresses a Social Problem
The term social business was first defined by Nobel Peace Prize Laureate Prof. Muhammad Yunus. He described the framework of social business as being based on seven principles (see **muhammadyunus.org/index.php/social-business**). According to Yunus, "social business is a non-loss, non-dividend company dedicated entirely to achieve a certain goal" (per **forbes.com/2010/06/15/forbes-india-muhammad-yunus-social-business-opinions-ideas-10-yunus.html**) and should be self-sustainable (attempting to avert losses).

3) IBM's Definition
Any business that embraces networks of people to create business value (see description in Sect. 1.5; for a comprehensive discussion, see the IBM White Paper titled 'The Social Business' at **ibm.com/smarterplanet/global/files/us__en_us__socialbusiness__epw14008usen.pdf**).

4) Our Working Definition
We define social business as any business that uses social media extensively in most or all of its operations. Such businesses also promote the social dimension in their operation. Many companies are transforming themselves to become social businesses. According to this definition, social commerce can be viewed as a subset of social business. Namely, a company that conducts extensive social commerce can be labelled a social business. This definition is close to that of Enterprise 2.0, which is presented later in this chapter and in Chap. 8.

For other working definitions of social business, see **socialenterprisecanada.ca/learn/nav/whatisasocialenterprise.html**.

The Evolution of Social Commerce

In Fig. 1.1, we illustrated the essential idea of social commerce. Let us look at this idea in more detail.

Social commerce emerged from the integration of several fields, which are shown in Fig. 1.2. For example, Marsden and Chaney (2013) show how social media contributes to sales, making it a social commerce application. Spenser et al. (2013) describe how social commerce increases sales and brand reach.

The development of Web 2.0 technologies comes with social computing. With these technologies came commercial applications, which included activities in social networks and the use of social software such as blogs and wikis. A major driver of SC is the globalization of business. This prompted the *need* for collaboration of employees, business partners, and customers. Web 2.0 applications created an efficient and effective platform for such collaboration.

The development and rapid growth of mobile computing and smartphones has also facilitated social commerce. Mobile commerce is the basis for SC models such as location-based applications, virtual communities, virtual worlds, and consumer/company networking. Social commerce also relies on communication and collaboration theories.

A major emphasis of SC is its marketing orientation. Traditional marketing activities were applied to Internet marketing in the mid-1990s, when companies began building websites and using e-mail only to advertise their products for sale offline. As the Web developed, marketers applied the Internet to facilitate e-commerce *transactions*. Until that point, marketers controlled brand messages and continued their advertising and other communication monologues to customers and potential buyers (prospects). With the emergence of social media, marketing communication changed to a dialog with Internet users, and many marketing strategies evolved or completely transformed to support social commerce.

Fig. 1.2 The major roots
of social commerce

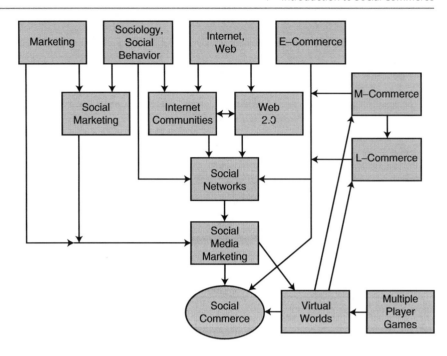

Table 1.1 The major differences between E-commerce and social commerce

Property	E-commerce	Social commerce
Major objective	Transactions	Social interactions
Major activity	Publishing	Engagement
Content	Company generated	User generated
Problem solving	Company experts, consultants	Crowdsourcing
Collaboration	Traditional, unified communications	Web 2.0 tools
Product information	Product descriptions on websites	Peer product reviews
Marketplaces	E-tailers (e.g., Amazon.com) and direct from manufacturers' stores (e.g., Dell)	Social networks (f-commerce), collaborative markets
Targeting	Mass marketing, segmentation	Behavioral targeting, micro segmentation
CRM	Seller/manufacturer support	Social support by peers and by vendors and employees
Online marketing strategy	Selling online	Multi-channel, direct at social network sites
Integration	System integration	Mashups and system integration
Data management	Reports and analytics	Analytics

Note: The original term *social marketing* referred to the application of marketing strategies and tactics to social causes, such as the American Heart Association. This concept was not related to marketing activities in social media. Today, however, many practitioners and academicians use the term *social marketing* to describe *social media marketing*.

Marketing, technology, consumer, and management evolutions paved the way for SC, just as they prompted e-commerce development. The major differences between social commerce and e-commerce are illustrated in Table 1.1. Huang and Benyoucef (2013) describe the evolution to SC by looking at design features.

For a chronicle presentation and infographic of historical milestones in the development of social commerce, see **socialtimes. com/social-commerce-infographic-2_b84120**. For a study of the development of social business, see Solis and Li (2013).

1.4   THE CONTENT OF THE SOCIAL COMMERCE FIELD

The content of the SC field is very diversified.

The Landscape and Major Components of the Field

The landscape of social commerce is multidisciplinary (see Marsden (2009)) "Simple Definition of Social Commerce With Word Cloud and Definitive Definition List. [Updated January 2011]; and Liang and Turban (2011/2012). Most of the activities center around e-marketing conducted using social media, particularly marketing communication, advertising techniques, sales promotions, and public relations usually expressed as *social media marketing* activities. However, several other areas are emerging in the field, especially activities within organizations that are referred to as *social enterprise or Enterprise 2.0.* Liang and Turban (2011/2012) illustrate the social commerce landscape in Fig. 1.3. Discussions of the other activities of the figure are provided throughout the book. Note that, the term *non-Internet* refers to other electronic systems, such as intranets and private networks.

For additional descriptions of some SC elements, see "The 2010 Social Business Landscape" by Hinchcliffe at **enterpriseirregulars.com/23628/the-2010-social-business-landscape**. For a detailed discussion, see the slide presentation by Marsden (2011) titled "Social Commerce Opportunities for Brands" at **digitalintelligencetoday.com/new-presentation-social-commerce-opportunities-for-brands**. For use of social commerce and statistics, see "Social Commerce Statistics" at **bazaarvoice.com/research-and-insight/social-commerce-statistics**. Finally, view the slide show by Appelo (2010) and see Altimeter Group's infographic of the state of social business at **slideshare.net/Altimeter/infographic-29122697**.

The two major elements of social commerce, social media marketing and Enterprise 2.0, are described next.

Social Media Marketing

Social media marketing (SMM) is the use of social networking and social media as marketing communication and other marketing tools (per McAfee 2009). Social media mar-

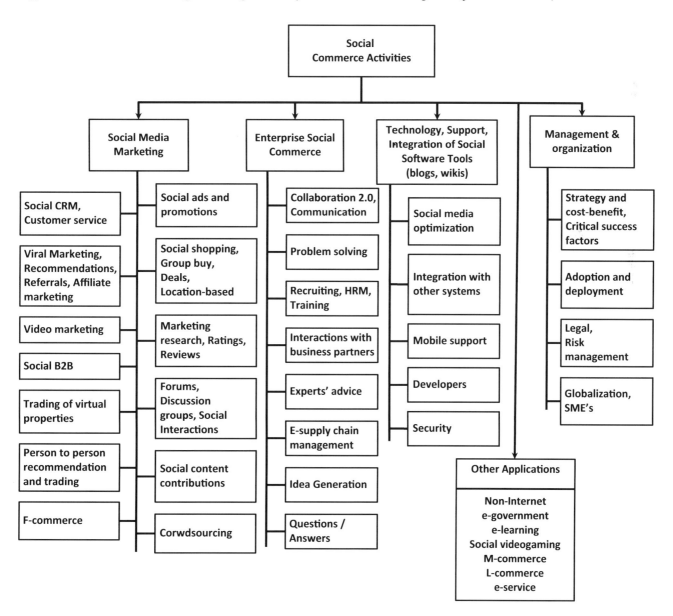

Fig. 1.3 The major dimensions of social commerce

keting facilitates social commerce, increases brand exposure, repairs brand reputation damages in social media, and fosters long-term customer relationships, among other things.

Today, integrated marketing communications is the application of the traditional marketing tools in innovative ways, integrating them with social media, such as in viral marketing. (See Chaps. 4 and 5 of this book for more details.) For additional information and a free toolkit titled "Social Media Marketing 101," see **act-on.com/resources/social-media-marketing-toolkit.**

The emergence of Web 2.0 allows marketers to connect directly with increasingly smaller target markets, including a single individual. For example, savvy marketers now build brands and respond to questions and complaints on social networks instead of (or in addition to) sending press releases to traditional journalists. They can also build social interactions with customers and conduct market research. (For five ways for managing feedback and complaints on social media, see **surveymonkey.com/blog/en/blog/2014/03/11/feedback-complaints-social-media/**.) The various topics of social media marketing communication are described in Chaps. 4–7, by Singh and Diamond (2012), and through various e-books at **salesforcemarketingcloud.com/resources/ebooks**. For an infographic, see Wood (2014). For a description of visual social marketing, see Neher (2014). For marketing tips, see McCarthy (2013) and Walker (2014). Finally, for the future of social media marketing, watch "The Future of Social Media Marketing w/ Gary Vaynerchuk" (28:55 minutes) at **youtube.com/watch?v=0Qy9aLqhxcc**.

Examples of Social Commerce Applications in Marketing

Marketing-related applications in public social network sites include the following examples:

- In March 2010, Dell claimed that it made $6.5 million by selling computers on Twitter since 2007 (see Nutley 2010).
- In 2013, Disney allowed people to purchase tickets on Facebook (without leaving the social network).
- Mountain Dew attracts video game lovers and sports enthusiasts via "Dewmocracy" contests. The company also entices the most dedicated community members to contribute ideas. The company uses Facebook, Twitter, and YouTube to encourage consumers with common interests to participate in the contests.

- Levi's enabled consumers on Facebook to place orders based on what their friends might like. There was also a video "Social Shopping Comes to Levi's" to educate consumers on how to use Facebook to shop for Levi's with the preference of their friends at **youtube.com/watch?v=Ed5vJeaEuzA**. This service was discontinued.
- Wendy's used Facebook and Twitter to post videos they created that are so funny, customers must talk about them. (See **forbes.com/sites/caroltice/2013/10/28/wendys-social-media-success-secretmassive-stupidity**).

Social commerce also occurs in companies' internal (private) social networks, which are known as *enterprise social networks*. In such a case, we refer to the networks as 'social enterprise' or 'Enterprise 2.0.'

Enterprise 2.0

The seconds major type of social commerce is *Enterprise 2.0* (see Fig. 1.3, p. 11), which is used by an increasing number of companies to conduct several social media and social commerce activities inside the enterprise (e.g., idea generation, problem solving, joint design, and recruiting).

There are several definitions of **Enterprise 2.0.** The term "Enterprise 2.0" was first coined by McAfee (2006). The initial definition connected the term to Web 2.0 and collaboration. McAfee revised his definition several times. His refined definition ("Enterprise 2.0, Version 2.0"), as posted on his blog, is "…the use of *emergent social software platforms within companies, or between companies and their partners or customers*" (per **andrewmcafee.org/2006/05/enterprise_20_version_20**); see also McAfee (2009). McAfee further revised his definition to include the "why" of Electronic Commerce 2.0 to "…*the use of emergent social software platforms by organizations in pursuit of their goals*" [emphasis added] (per **andrewmcafee.org/2009/08/defining-moment/**; see also McAfee 2009). A similar definition says that Enterprise 2.0 is a social software platform that helps employees, customers and partners to share, collaborate, innovate, and communicate.

Note: For more definitions and concepts of Enterprise 2.0 technology, see the slide presentation titled "What is Enterprise 2.0?" at **slideshare.net/norwiz/what-is-enterprise-20**. For other definitions, see **erp.asia/enterprise2.asp** and **whatis.techtarget.com/definition/Enterprise-20**. Several Enterprise

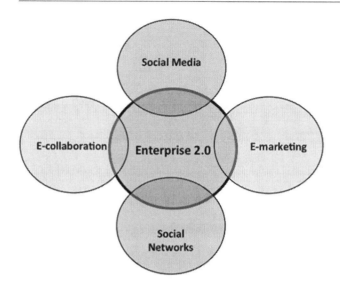

Fig. 1.4 The foundation of Enterprise 2.0

2.0 conferences are held every year, some providing additional definitions that may even change with time (e.g., see **e2conf.com**). For example, e2conf.com provided a white paper (see Enterprise 2.0 Conference 2009) in which it compared Enterprise 2.0 to Enterprise 1.0, listing the following as some of the characteristics of Enterprise 2.0: ease of information flow, agility, flexibility, user-driven technology, bottom up communication, global teams, fuzzy boundaries, transparency, folksonomies (rather than taxonomies), open standards, and on-demand (rather than scheduled) activities. In addition, important characteristics are flat organizations (rather than hierarchical) and short time-to-market cycles.

The benefits of Enterprise 2.0 (social enterprise) are similar to those of social commerce (see Sect. 1.5).

For an extensive slide presentation titled "What Is Enterprise 2.0?," see **slideshare.net/norwiz/what-is-enterprise-20**. Enterprise 2.0 can be viewed as being the intersection of social media, e-marketing, social networks, and e-collaboration (see Fig. 1.4).

For more on Enterprise 2.0, see Chap. 8 and Chui et al. (2013).

Simply put, Enterprise 2.0 means using Web 2.0 tools in the workplace. For a comprehensive discussion of the state of Enterprise 2.0, with a history and infographics, see Hinchcliffe (2007).

For comprehensive coverage of Web 2.0 in the Enterprise, see **msdn.microsoft.com/en-us/library/bb735306. aspx#jour12web20ent_topic1**.

Examples of Social Enterprise Applications

Some examples of social enterprise applications include the following:

- Dell, Starbucks (see opening case), IBM, and many other companies solicit ideas from large groups of employees, customers, and business partners on how to improve their business operations (e.g., Dell's IdeaStorm site).
- More than 50 % of medium and large corporations use LinkedIn and Facebook to announce available positions and to find potential employees.
- Best Buy provides state-of-the-art customer service via Twitter. They also have an idea generation forum on their website called "Best Buy Unboxed."

For a comprehensive study on the benefits and inhibitors of social commerce in the enterprise, see Forrester Consulting (2010).

1.5   THE BENEFITS AND LIMITATIONS OF SOCIAL COMMERCE

According to many practitioners and researchers, social commerce is making significant impacts on organizations and industries (e.g., ShopSocially 2013). For example, a major impact has been seen in the fashion industry (e.g., see Little 2013).

Several surveys have confirmed that social commerce results in significant monetary and strategic benefits to businesses (e.g., Leggatt 2010). See also success stories at IBM (2011b) and 67 case studies that prove social media ROI at **barnraisersllc.com/2010/10/33-case-studies-prove-social-media-roi**. See also Butlion (2013).

SC benefits are organized here in three categories: benefits to customers, benefits to retailers, and benefits to other types of enterprises.

Benefits to Customers

The success of social commerce depends mostly on its benefits to customers. The major benefits appear in the following list:

- It is easy to get recommendations from friends and other customers (e.g., via Twitter, in social media discussion groups, and on product review sites). Recommendations result in more confidence and trust, helping customers decide about purchasing products and services.
- Customers are exposed to special deals (e.g., via Groupon and messages from friends on Facebook) for large savings.
- Purchases can be matched with specific needs, wants, tastes, and wishes of customers (e.g., see the Netflix case in Chap. 3); this increases satisfaction and reduces product selection decision time.
- It is easy for customers to use the social commerce technology.
- Social commerce fits the mobile device lifestyle well.
- Increased trust of customers in vendors (via closer relationships).
- Social commerce allows customers to help other customers (social support).
- Customers can get better customer service from vendors (see Chap. 7).
- Customers can make new friends (e.g., for travel) and socialize online.
- Customers can get rich social context and relevancy during their purchase decision-making process.
- Customers can connect with individuals and businesses who otherwise are inaccessible to them.

Benefits to Retailers

Retailers are also major benefactors of social commerce. For example, Leggatt (2010) reported that over 40 % of businesses globally find new customers via social networks (in 2015, the figure is higher). In addition, over 27 % of companies invest in social networking in order to acquire and retain customers.

Retailers may benefit from social commerce in the following ways:

- Consumers can provide feedback on market communication strategy and on product (service) design.
- Vendors get free word-of-mouth marketing (see Chaps. 3 and 4).
- Increased website traffic (recall the Starbucks opening case), which increases revenue and sales.
- Increased sales when social influence methods (see Chap. 3) are used.

Example

Popular firearms manufacturer Beretta Inc. increased its revenue in 2013 by 15 % by introducing social commerce into its e-commerce store, using ShopSocially's SC platform. For details, see **digitaljournal.com/pr/1655392**.

For a comprehensive presentation of social commerce benefits and impacts on retailing, see Dennison et al. (2009).

Benefits to Other Types of Enterprises

In addition to increased sales and revenue, enterprises can benefit from social commerce in several ways (see Chap. 8):

- Conduct faster and less costly recruitment with larger reach to a large number of candidates.
- Reduce costs via innovative methods such as using the collective intelligence of employees and business partners (see crowdsourcing, Chap. 8).
- Foster better external relationships; for example, with partners and channel distribution members.
- Increase collaboration and improve communication within the enterprise and with business partners (e.g., by using blogs, microblogs, wikis; see McAfee 2009).
- Foster better internal relationships (e.g., by increasing employee productivity and satisfaction).
- Give free advice to small enterprises from other enterprises and by experts (e.g., via LinkedIn groups).
- Understand that it is usually not expensive to install and operate SC systems.
- Locate experts quickly, both internally and externally, whenever needed (e.g., see **guru.com**).
- Conduct market research quickly and inexpensively and get feedback from customers, employees, and business partners (see Chap. 10).

- Increase market share and margins (see survey results in Bughin and Chui 2010).
- Build brands through conversations and social media promotions.
- Create small customer segments for reaching very small markets with brand offerings at a low cost and price.
- Manage company and brand reputations online.
- Build brand communities for positive word-of-mouth online.
- Enhance customer service and support.
- Increase traffic and sales at the company website and at the physical stores.
- Facilitate market research by monitoring conversations online.
- Increase company and brand rankings on search engine results pages.

The potential benefits in the previous list may result in: increasing productivity and value (Chui et al. 2012), providing a *strategic advantage* (Bauer 2011), and encouraging companies to at least experiment with social commerce. Successful applications are introduced in Chaps. 4–8, and a comprehensive list is available on Bazaarvoice. Note that the use of social media and commerce is turning out to be a global phenomenon (e.g. see Ran 2012).

The Social Business: An IBM Approach

The previously noted benefits to enterprises make it desirable for enterprises to transform themselves to what IBM calls a *social business*. A **social business** is "a business [that] embraces networks of people to create business value" (IBM 2011a). Many consider this term equivalent to social commerce and use the two interchangeably. However, IBM is more concerned with the structure and operations of enterprises. IBM and many other companies (notably Intel) are becoming social businesses. (For how IBM evolved into a social business, see Traudt and Vancil 2011.) IBM (2011b) sees the following three goals for social businesses:

1. *Enable an effective workforce.* Functional departments can increase overall employee productivity and job satisfaction through improved knowledge capture, expertise location, and collaboration. Travel, training, and teleconferencing expenses can be reduced. In addition, better and faster recruitment can be done inexpensively.

2. *Accelerate innovation.* Product research and development teams can invoke and accelerate idea generation, information, discovery, and strategy sharing by employees. Companies can gather feedback and ideas from key customers and business partners.

3. *Deepen customer relationships.* With easy and fast access to content and expertise, customer service representatives can work faster and more efficiently and provide higher-quality service. Marketing and sales teams can have more time to spend with customers and concentrate on customer-focused initiatives, thus, strengthening relationships with customers.

In addition, IBM strategically integrates social media into various business processes (e.g., procurement) and is developing an organizational culture to support the integration process for delivering rapid and impressive outcomes. For details, see IBM (2011a) and IBM Social Business (**ibm.com/social-business/us/en/solutions.html**).

Examples of Social Business Implementation

IBM has developed several social business tools (e.g., *SmartCloud Engage*) which are used in many organizations. For an example of how Wakefern Foods uses IBM's social business tools in their workforce, watch the 2013 video (2:44 minutes) at **youtube.com/watch?v=bt3_hGaUjX8**.

New or Improved Business Models

A **business model** describes the method (or plan) implemented by a company to meet the customer's needs, and by which a company generates revenue and creates value. Note that, the January–February 2011 issue of *Harvard Business Review* is dedicated to business model innovations (five articles), including several topics related to social commerce. For a presentation of the models' structure and a list of e-commerce models, see Online Primer A. For a comprehensive business model presentation titled "What is a Business Model?" see **slideshare.net/Alex.Osterwalder/what-is-a-business-model**.

Social commerce provides innovative e-commerce business models. Some are new, while others are improvements of regular EC models (e.g., group buying). A large number of

SC models are in the area of social shopping, as described in Chap. 6. Several other new models are in the area of enterprise commerce (Chap. 8). Here are some brief examples:

- Shopping business models include items such as widgets and "buy now" buttons on social media sites.
- Online software agents that connect buyers and sellers, such as when TripAdvisor refers travelers to providers of travel services.
- Content sponsorship—selling advertising on a site that supports content development (e.g., YouTube).
- Crowdsourcing models that allow companies to better design their products or logos by involving their customers.
- Sales promotions conducted in social networks that drive traffic to the company's site, such as contests, discounts, and offering free music and software to download.
- Recruiting in social networks, as exemplified by LinkedIn and Facebook job markets (Chap. 8).
- Collaboration models that are facilitated by blogs, wikis, and crowdsourcing (see examples in Chap. 8).

Many start-ups have invented these and other business models. For example, some companies offer person-to-person (P2P) services that send broadcast-quality videos over the Internet (see Chap. 9). Webkinz (**webkinz.com**) created a huge business around a virtual pet world for kids, and IZEA Inc. (**izea.com**), the pioneer of Social Sponsorship, created a marketplace for connecting social media creators of content (e.g., bloggers) with the world's biggest brands.

Several of these start-up companies are so prosperous that they went public on stock markets. Well-known companies are Pandora, LinkedIn, Twitter, Yelp, Trip Advisor and Zillow.

The potential for profitable social business models is very large. For example, **wikia.com** is using a crowdsourcing community in an attempt to develop a superior search mechanism. If it can create a successful one, Google may be in trouble. For the opportunities for businesses created by social commerce, see Moontoast (2011). For new business models in the fashion industry, see Knopf (2012), and **businessof-fashion.com**. For a discussion on the strategic power of social media, see Bauer (2011).

Concerns and Limitations of Conducting Social Commerce

Although social commerce presents many opportunities for organizations, its implementation may involve some potential risks, and possibly complex issues such as the integration of new and existing information systems. Representative risk factors are: difficulties in justification of SC initiatives to upper management, security and privacy concerns, possibilities of fraud, legal concerns, quality of UGC, and time wasting by employees during work hours. Companies also risk loss of control over their brand images and reputations in social media conversations and product review sites, which can affect product sales. According to the Enterprise 2.0 Conference (2009), the major barriers to adoption of Enterprise 2.0 are resistance to change, difficulty in measuring ROI, and difficulties of integration with existing IT systems and security. For details, see Chap. 11. A 2011 survey, "Social Business Shifting Out of First Gear," reported by Burnham (2013), ranks the top concerns in deployment of social business as: (1) security and liability exposures, (2) doubts about ability to govern effectively, (3) poor systems integration, (4) doubts about ROI/value, and (5) poor organizational technology adoption. We expand on some of these issues in Chap. 11.

1.6 THE PROCESS OF CONDUCTING SOCIAL COMMERCE AND SUGGESTED RESEARCH TOPICS

This section of Chap. 1 deals with the process of conducting social commerce that drives the content and the structure of this book.

The Process of Conducting Social Commerce

Social commerce can be conducted in different ways, depending on the application and circumstances. However, some general activities exist in most cases. These activities are illustrated in Fig. 1.5.

Starting on the left side are the three components illustrated earlier in Fig. 1.1 (pg. 9).

Next, companies and individual customers become engaged in various social media activities and platforms (see description in Chaps. 2 and 3).

Enterprises monitor communication and other activities and engagements (sometimes referred to as *listening*). This action is done by using monitoring devices. For example, Google Alerts or other applications for scanning tweets and blogs are used to search for a specific company's name on the Web. Monitoring can be done by direct communication with consumers, by listening to online conversations, and so forth (see more in Chap. 10).

The collected information, including those portions that are visible in the direct communication to consumers, are examined via social analysis methods (Chap. 10), and are used as input for managerial decision making regarding marketing communication (such as advertising, pricing, competitive strategy, product design, or problem identification).

Fig. 1.5 The process
of conducting social commerce

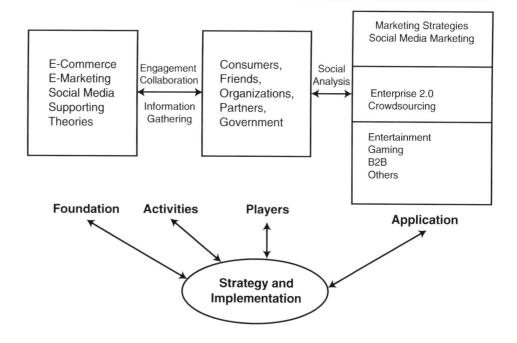

Some of these are intended to influence consumer purchasing decisions (see social influence, Chap. 3). Influencing consumers' decision making can be done via reviews, recommendations, and discussions. This influence can be explained via social and behavioral theories and marketing communication models. The non-marketing activities include mostly social enterprise activities (such as collaboration, problem solving, or recruitment) and activities in other areas such as government, business-to-business, virtual worlds, person-to-person, and entertainment.

Example:

IBM provides several products and platforms to enable social media applications and implementation. Such systems collect and analyze data and process them to enable predictions, recommendations, and strategy. For details, watch the 2013 IBM Smarter Commerce video, "Advanced Social Analytics Platform" (3:44 minutes), at **youtube.com/watch?v=AxzqyMx0Mm8**.

Note that enterprise activities and applications in other areas may include some marketing/advertising actions. All of these issues need to be embedded in strategy, justification, and planning. Finally, a slew of issues may surface during the implementation of social commerce. These range from adoption strategy and software selection to corporate policies. Successful implementation depends on the appropriate selection of social network services and sites. In May 2014, the leading B2C social platforms were Facebook, Twitter, Pinterest, LinkedIn, Google+, YouTube, and others, while

B2B favored social platforms were LinkedIn, Facebook, Twitter, followed by blogging, Google+, YouTube, and others. (From **blog.percolate.com/2014/05/b2b-vs-b2c-marketing-social-media-blurred-lines**, referencing Stelzner 2014.)

Illustrative Research Issues

As a new discipline, social commerce is gradually attracting the attention of researchers worldwide. The number of papers delivered in scientific conferences and published in professional journals is increasingly rapidly. In addition, a large number of books about conducting social commerce are appearing in specific social networks, mostly Facebook, Twitter, LinkedIn, and Pinterest.

A comprehensive framework of social commerce was proposed by Wang and Zhang (2012). According to this framework, SC research was categorized into people, management, technology, and information. A historical recount of the field, from 2005 to 2011, was conducted according to these four categories. Within each category, Wang and Zhang (2012) identified application areas (e.g., social shopping, business models and so forth). The researchers also provided several possible directions for future research.

Aral et al. (2013) developed a framework for research in the area of social media and business transformation, referencing the fact that social media is fundamentally changing the way we communicate, collaborate, consume, and create.

Liang and Turban (2011/2012) developed a research framework for social commerce. They presented an organization framework with a representative list of topics. The framework includes four major areas: social media marketing, enterprise management, technology support and management, and organization. Each area is divided into subtopics suitable for research (e.g., viral marketing in SC). The framework also includes relevant theories (e.g., social support), outcome measures of success, social media tools, and platforms and adaptation of traditional MIS research themes (e.g., user behavior).

In the remaining chapters of this book, we provide representative examples of relevant research issues.

Finally, in Online Appendix C to this book, we provide a comprehensive list of resources that can be used by both researchers and practitioners.

1.7   THE CONTENT AND ORGANIZATION OF THE BOOK

We end this chapter by providing a visual summary of the book's composition.

The book is composed of four major parts that contain 11 chapters. In addition, there are three online appendices.

Figure 1.6 displays the book's chapters (their titles are abbreviated) and the way they are organized in parts.

SUMMARY

In this chapter, you learned about the following SC issues as they relate to the chapter's learning objectives.

1. **Social computing and Social Web.** This emerging computing approach is situated at the intersection of technology and social behavior. Social computing is done with Web 2.0 tools; when done on the Internet, it is referred to as the *Social Web*. Its major objectives are improved collaboration and social interactions. It is based on user-generated content, controlled by users, and intended for users. It is also based on social support of people to each other and lately it is being used commercially (e.g., for advertising).

2. **The Social Web revolution.** The emergence of the Social Web is considered a revolution due to the speed and magnitude of the changes introduced by the technology. One measure is the size of many social networks. The impacts on work, services, entertainment, collaboration, communication, social interactions, and so forth, are significant in many areas, as are the changes in the way that many companies treat their employees and customers. Marketing, for example, is centered around the social customer, and consumers are treated

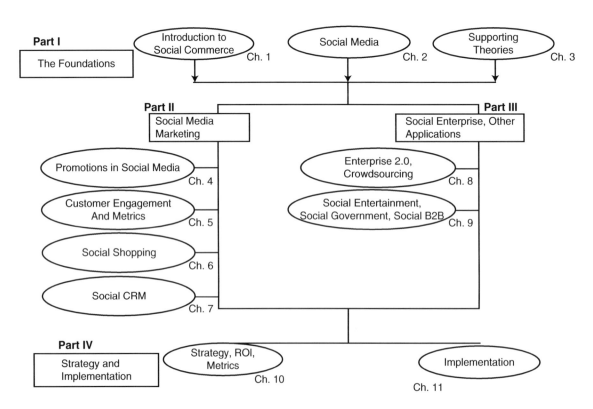

Fig. 1.6 The content and organization of the book

with social CRM. Social games are attracting many millions of participants and trust and loyalty is increasing rapidly in marketplaces. Finally, many companies are transformed into social businesses.

3. **The Web 2.0 revolution and social media.** Web 2.0 refers to a new way of using the Web. It is a trend that makes use of the Web by people and for people. For example, user-created content, the use of social software, and the rise of social networking are major characteristics of Web 2.0. Social media implements Web 2.0 tools for social interactions, conversations, engagement, and sharing ideas in many different ways.

4. **Social commerce evolution.** Social commerce (SC) can be viewed as a subset of EC where activities are done in social networks and/or by using social media tools. SC operates at the intersection of social media, EC, e-marketing, and supporting theories from several disciplines, including social psychology, marketing, sociology, and information technology. SC is able to add value to the performance of organizations, while at the same time increase the satisfaction and the added value to employees and customers. The main activities and content of social commerce are in the areas of social media marketing, social enterprise, and social games and entertainment.

5. **The content of the social commerce field.** Social commerce refers to conducting e-commerce in social networks and using social media tools, such as blogs. It is a comprehensive field comprised mostly of social media marketing (advertising, market research, and customer service) and social enterprise (problem solving, recruiting, and collaboration). It also includes social entertainment, social games, and crowdsourcing. Social commerce is driven by the existence of giant social networks, Web 2.0 infrastructure tools, and the emergence of social customers.

6. **Social media marketing.** This is an umbrella name for the major marketing activities conducted via social networking. Most notable are marketing communication and advertising, social shopping, market research, and social CRM. It is an integrated, multifaceted marketing and advertising practice.

7. **Enterprise 2.0.** Using social media technologies and Web 2.0 tools within an organization is called *Enterprise 2.0,* or *social enterprise.* It is based upon social media activities, such as publishing, sharing, collaborating, and creating knowledge. The major practical applications are: social media assist in recruitment, idea generation via crowdsourcing, and collaboration via blogs, wikis, and other Web 2.0 tools.

8. **Benefits and limitations of social commerce.** A large number of benefits are available for customers, retailers, and other businesses. Customers can get better prices and customer service, and also receive social support (e.g., product recommendations) from friends. Users can meet new people and establish new contacts. Retailers can reach more customers, get feedback quickly, improve relationships with customers, go global, and use free word-of-mouth marketing communication. There are also benefits to businesses. Businesses can conduct fast and inexpensive market research, recruit employees from all over the globe, innovate, collaborate, and locate experts when needed. Companies can receive help from other companies, sometimes at little or no cost. The major limitations are the possible invasion of privacy of the participants, the difficulty justifying the investment in SC, the possibility of poor quality of UGC, and the difficulty of integration of SC , EC, and IT.

9. **The process of conducting social commerce.** The process depends upon the application of concern. In marketing-related applications, vendors monitor information flow to and within social networks and attempt to structure market communication strategy accordingly (e.g., ad campaigns, coupon distribution, special sales). In the social enterprise, companies use the wisdom of the crowd to solve problems via crowdsourcing and to reach potential job seekers via social networking. In addition, internal and external collaboration is a by-product of the SC process.

10. **Research topics in social commerce.** Given that this field is new, there are many evolving research opportunities, yet not much has been done. Some suggestions are provided in subsequent chapters.

KEY TERMS

Business model	15
Enterprise 2.0	12
Social business	15
Social commerce (SC)	8
Social computing	5
Social media	8
Social media marketing (SMM)	11
Social Web	6
Web 2.0	7

REVIEW QUESTIONS

1. Define social computing and the Social Web.
2. List the major properties of the Social Web.

3. Explain why many consider the Social Web/media as a revolution.
4. Define Web 2.0 and describe its major properties.
5. Define social media, social networks, and social networking.
6. Define social commerce.
7. List some major origins of social commerce.
8. List the major building blocks of social commerce.
9. List five benefits of social commerce to consumers and five to retailers.
10. Define social media marketing.
11. Describe Enterprise 2.0.
12. What is a social business (per IBM)?
13. List some limitations of social commerce.

TOPICS FOR DISCUSSION AND DEBATES

1. Discuss the differences between social media and Web 2.0.
2. Relate social media to collaboration.
3. Describe five properties of Web 2.0 and discuss how they differ from those of Web 1.0.
4. Discuss the major benefits of social commerce to consumers.
5. Review any two Socialcast customer case studies related to social commerce at **socialcast.com/customers#case-studies** and discuss the following:
   (a) What benefits have the companies that embraced Socialcast realized?
   (b) What are the major lessons learned from these cases?
6. Debate: Are the benefits of social networking large enough to compensate for its negatives? Start with the article titled "The Great Debate: Social Networking" at **thesnapper.com/2011/09/22/the-great-debate-social-networking**.
7. Watch the video (4:07 minutes) about Bumbu Desan Restaurant Group at **enterpriseinnovation.net/article/video-bumbu-desa-restaurant-group-taps-social-optimize-communications-1159410969** and answer the following questions:
   (a) What motivated the restaurant chain to become a social business?
   (b) What were the benefits to the customers?
   (c) What kinds of management reports are available?
   (d) What are the benefits to the company? How has its competitive advantage increased?

INTERNET EXERCISES

1. Enter a social network (e.g., Google+ or Facebook). Create a homepage. Make at least five new friends.

2. Enter **mashable.com** and review the latest news regarding social networks and network strategy. Write a report.
3. Enter **bazaarvoice.com**. Summarize its major services. Examine Bazaarvoice Connections (**bazaarvoice.com/solutions/connections**) in particular.
4. Enter LinkedIn and join a group related to social marketing. View the activities conducted there. Prepare a report.
5. Enter **socialmediatoday.com**. Examine the content on the site, especially content related to social commerce. Write a report.
6. Enter **bestbuy.com** and find their social commerce activities. Write a report.
7. Enter Amazon.com and find out how shopping is done with smartphones using the Amazon mobile app. Write a report.

TEAM ASSIGNMENTS AND PROJECTS

1. **Assignment for the Opening Case**
   Read the opening case, find some new material about Starbucks and social commerce, and answer the following questions:
   (a) Why is Starbucks putting such an emphasis on social media?
   (b) List the specific social networking activities done by the company.
   (c) What are the differences and similarities between Starbucks' own social network and its pages on Facebook, LinkedIn, and other social networks?
   (d) Why did Starbucks fail with Foursquare? (Consult Teicher 2010)
   (e) How are ideas generated at My Starbucks Idea? By whom?
   (f) What did you learn about social media strategy?
2. Watch the video titled "Expert Views on the Social Purchase Journey" (5:45 minutes) at **youtube.com/watch?v=yx4Rh8snQDE**, and answer the following questions:
   (a) How does multichannel marketing fit social purchasing?
   (b) What mobile applications are described in the video?
   (c) What did you learn about customer experiences, customer purchasing decisions, and customer engagement?
   (d) What else did you learn from this video?
3. Social commerce is rapidly changing the fashion industry (e.g., see Knopf 2012, Little 2013, and **bussinessoffashion.com**). Prepare a list of all fashion 2.0 business models, leading companies, benefits, success stories, and concerns. Write a report.

REFERENCES

Allison, M., "Starbucks Presses Social Media Onward." April 27, 2013. **seattletimes.com/html/businesstechnology/2020862483_starbuckssocialxml.html** (accessed December 2014).

Amerland, D. "How Social Media Is Changing the World." August 25, 2011. **socialmediatoday.com/content/how-social-media-changing-world-0** (accessed December 2014).

Appelo, J. "Social Commerce – What Are We Waiting For?" May 20, 2010. **slideshare.net/jurgenappelo/social-commerce-what-are-we-waiting-for** (accessed December 2014).

Appelquist, D., et al. "A Standards-Based, Open and Privacy-Aware Social Web: W3C Incubator Group Report." December 6, 2010. **w3.org/2005/Incubator/socialweb/XGR-socialweb-20101206** (accessed December 2014).

Aral, S., et al. "Introduction to the Special Issue -- Social Media and Business Transformation: A Framework for Research." *Information Systems Research*, Vol. 24(1) pp. 3-13. March 2013. (Published online January 14, 2013.) [DOI: http://dx.doi.org/10.1287/isre.1120.0470]

Baekdal, T. *Social Commerce...It Is a Completely New Playing Field!* Kindle edition. New York: Baekdal Media, 2011.

Bauer, R. "Discover the Strategic Power of Social Media." August 11, 2011. **information-management.com/newsletters/social_BI_ROI_search_data_management_analytics-10020948-1.html** (accessed December 2014).

Belicove, M. "How Starbucks Builds Meaningful Customer Engagement via Social Media." *American Express Open Forum*, April 1, 2010. **americanexpress.com/us/small-business/openforum/articles/how-starbucks-builds-meaningful-customer-engagement-via-social-media-1/** (accessed December 2014).

Bennett, S. "The Rise of Social Commerce –Incredible Statistics, Facts, & Figures." July 10, 2013. **mediabistro.com/alltwitter/social-commerce_b46141** (accessed December 2014).

Bughin, J., and M. Chui. "The Rise of the Networked Enterprise: Web 2.0 Finds Its Payday." *McKinsey Quarterly Insights & Publications*, December 2010. **mckinsey.com/insights/high_tech_telecoms_internet/the_rise_of_the_networked_enterprise_web_20_finds_its_payday** (accessed December 2014).

Bullas, J. "21 Awesome Social Media Facts, Figures and Statistics for 2013." May 5, 2013. **jeffbullas.com/2013/05/06/21-awesome-social-media-facts-figures-and-statistics-for-2013/** (accessed December 2014).

Burnham, K. "How to Beat Top Social Business Obstacles." *Information Week Government*, July 18, 2013. **informationweek.com/how-to-beat-top-social-business-obstacles/d/d-id/1110808** (accessed December 2014).

Butlion, J., "The Many Benefits of Social Commerce." April 9, 2013. **blog.yotpo.com/2013/04/09/the-many-benefits-of-social-commerce** (accessed December 2014).

Chui, M., et al., "Building the Social Enterprise." *McKinsey Quarterly Insights & Publications*, November 2013. **mckinsey.com/insights/organization/building_the_social_enterprise** (accessed December 2014).

Chui, M., et al. "The Social Economy: Unlocking Value and Productivity through Social Technologies." *McKinsey Global Institute Insights & Publications*, July 2012. **mckinsey.com/insights/high_tech_telecoms_internet/the_social_economy** (accessed December 2014).

Cuccureddu, G. "Social Commerce to Rise Six Fold to $30 Billion in 2015, According to Booz & Co." February 3, 2011. **appmarket.tv/news/1021-social-commerce-to-rise-six-fold-to-30-billion-in-2015-according-to-booz-a-co.html** (accessed December 2014).

Dennison, G., S. Bourdage-Braun, and M. Chetuparambil. "Social Commerce Defined." IBM White Paper #23747, IBM Corporation, Research Triangle Park: NC, November 2009.

Dougherty, J. "30% of Big Brands Now Have Customer Service on Twitter." September 16, 2013. **socialmediatoday.com/content/30-big-brands-now-have-customer-service-twitter** (accessed December 2014).

Enterprise 2.0 Conference. "Enterprise 2.0: What, Why and How?" White Paper, e2conf.com, May 2009. Boston, MA, June 22-25, 2009. Available for download at **informationweek.com/whitepaper/Internet/enterprise-2-0-what-why-and-how--wp1366879055?articleID=191708382** (accessed December 2014).

Ericson, J. "Exclusive Research: The Social Business Technology Horizon." August 31, 2011. **information-management.com/news/-10021052-1.html** (accessed December 2014).

Fonolo. "25 Social Media Statistics for the Call Center." eBook (Free); Toronto: Fonolo Corp., 2013. Available for download at **fonolo.com/ebook-25-social-media-statistics-for-the-call-center/** (accessed December 2014).

Forrester Consulting. "Social Networking in the Enterprise: Benefits and Inhibitors." White Paper, June 2010. [A commissioned study conducted by Forester Consulting on behalf of Cisco Systems] **cisco.com/web/offer/gist_ty2_asset/SocMednInhib/SocNW_En_TLP.pdf** (accessed December 2014).

Fraser, M., and S. Dutta. *Throwing Sheep in the Boardroom: How Online Social Networking Will Transform Your Life, Work, and World.* Hoboken, NJ: Wiley & Sons, 2008.

Gibb, C. "6 Ways Starbucks Excels at Social Media Marketing." February 13, 2013. **prdaily.com/Main/Articles/6_ways_Starbucks_excels_at_social_media_marketing_13814.aspx** (accessed December 2014).

Goldman, D. "The Internet Is Expanding at Breakneck Speed." June 1, 2011 (Updated). **money.cnn.com/galleries/2011/technology/1105/gallery.cisco_visual_networking_index/index.html** (accessed December 2014).

Gratton, S. J., and D. A. Gratton. *Zero to 100,000: Social Media Tips and Tricks for Small Businesses.* Indianapolis, IN: Que, 2011 and Pearson Education 2012.

Greengard, S. "The Social Business Gets Results." June 19, 2014. **baselinemag.com/messaging-and-collaboration/the-social-business-gets-results.html** (accessed December 2014).

Hinchcliffe, D. "The State of Enterprise 2.0." October 22, 2007. **zdnet.com/blog/hinchcliffe/the-state-of-enterprise-2-0/143** (accessed December 2014).

Huang Z., and M. Benyoucef. "From E-Commerce to Social Commerce: A Close Look At Design Features." *Electronic Commerce Research and Applications*, July-August 2013.

IBM. "The Social Business: Advent of a New Age." White Paper, February 2011a. **ibm.com/smarterplanet/global/files/us__en_us__socialbusiness__epw14008usen.pdf** (accessed December 2014).

IBM. "The Compelling Returns from IBM Connections in Support of Social Business: Five Stories." White Paper #EPW14010-USEN-01. Somers, NY: IBM Corp. Software Group, December 2011b.

Kaplan, A. M., and M. Haenlein. "Users of the World, Unite! The Challenges and Opportunities of Social Media." *Business Horizons*, vol. 53, no. 1, 59-68, February 2010. [doi:10.1016/j.bushor.2009.09.003]

Karakas, F. "Welcome to World 2.0: The New Digital Ecosystem." *Journal of Business Strategy*, (30)4, pp. 23-30, 2009. [doi: http://dx.doi.org/10.1108/02756660910972622]

Kirkpatrick, D. *The Facebook Effect: The Inside Story of the Company That is Connecting the World.* New York: Simon and Schuster, 2010.

Knopf, E. "E-Commerce Week/The Rise of New Business Models." January 18, 2012. **businessoffashion.com/2012/01/e-commerce-week-the-rise-of-new-business-models.html** (accessed December 2014).

Leggatt, H. "Survey: Small Businesses Find Success with Social Networking." July 9, 2010. **bizreport.com/2010/07/survey-small-**

businesses-find-success-with-social-networking.html (accessed December 2014).

Liang, T-P., and E. Turban. "Introduction to the Special Issue: Social Commerce: A Research Framework for Social Commerce." *International Journal of Electronic Commerce*, vol. 16, no. 2, Winter 2011-12. pp. 5-14. [doi>10.2753/JEC1086-4415160201]

Little, K. "Models on Twitter: Tech Hits the Runway." February 11, 2013. **cnbc.com/id/100449013** (accessed December 2014).

Loeb, W. "Starbucks: Global Coffee Giant Has New Growth Plans." January 31, 2013. **forbes.com/sites/walterloeb/2013/01/31/starbucks-global-coffee-giant-has-new-growth-plans** (accessed December 2014).

Marsden, P. "Simple Definition of Social Commerce (With Word Cloud & Definitive Definition List). [Updated January 2011]." November 17, 2009. **digitalinnovationtoday.com/social-commerce-definition-word-cloud-definitive-definition-list/** (accessed December 2014).

Marsden, P. "Speed Summary: Wired (Feb 2011) Cover Story on Social Commerce." January 6, 2011. **digitalintelligencetoday.com/speed-summary-wired-feb-2011-cover-story-on-social-commerce** (accessed December 2014).

Marsden, P., and P. Chaney. *The Social Commerce Handbook: 20 Secrets for Turning Social Media Into Social Sales*, New York: McGraw-Hill, 2013.

McAfee, A. P. "Enterprise 2.0: The Dawn of Emergent Collaboration." *MIT Sloan Management Review*, vol. 47, no. 3, 21-28, Spring 2006.

McAfee, A. *Enterprise 2.0: New Collaborative Tools for Your Organization's Toughest Challenges*. Boston: Harvard Business School Press, 2009.

McCarthy, A. *500 Social Media Marketing Tips*, Andrew McCarthy, 2013.

McDonald, D. D. "On Attempting an Updated Definition of 'Web 2.0.'" June 28, 2010. **socialmediatoday.com/content/attempting-updated-definition-web-20** (accessed December 2014).

Meeker, M., and L. Wu. *Internet Trends Report* 2013. *Internet Trends D11 Conference*, May 29, 2013. **slideshare.net/kleinerperkins/kpcb-internet-trends-2013** (accessed December 2014).

Moontoast, *The Social Commerce Opportunity: How Brands can Take Advantage of the Next Evolution in Commerce* (A free e-book), Boston: Moontoast, 2011. **moontoast-wordpress-dev.s3.amazonaws.com/wp-content/uploads/2011/11/Moontoast_The_Social_Commerce_Opportunity.pdf** (accessed December 2014).

Moth, D. "How Starbucks Uses Pinterest, Facebook, Twitter and Google+." March 6, 2013 **econsultancy.com/blog/62281-how-starbucks-uses-pinterest-facebook-twitter-and-google#i.1k5vbfsm0ndjpt** (accessed December 2014).

Neher, K., *Visual Social Marketing For Dummies*, Hoboken, NJ: John Wiley & Sons, 2014.

Nutley, M. "Forget E-Commerce; Social Commerce Is Where It's At." July 29, 2010. **marketingweek.co.uk/forget-ecommerce-social-commerce-is-where-its-at/3016388.article** (accessed December 2014).

O'Reilly, T. "What Is Web 2.0: Design Patterns and Business Models for the Next Generation of Software." September 30, 2005. **oreilly.com/pub/a//web2/archive/what-is-web-20.html** (accessed December 2014).

O'Reilly, T. "Levels of the Game: The Hierarchy of Web 2.0 Applications." July 17, 2006. **radar.oreilly.com/2006/07/levels-of-the-game-the-hierarc.html** (accessed December 2014).

Pant, R. "Social Currency: The Effect of Social Media on Commerce [Infographic]." July 12, 2013. **socialmediatoday.com/content/social-currency-effect-social-media-commerce-infographic** (accessed December 2014).

Ran, Y. "Social Networking Sends a Message to Business." November 26, 2012. **usa.chinadaily.com.cn/epaper/2012-11/26/content_15958935.htm** (accessed December 2014).

Schoultz, M. "Starbucks Marketing Makes Social Media a Difference Maker." June 15, 2013 **digitalsparkmarketing.com/creative-marketing/social-media/starbucks-marketing/** (accessed December 2014).

Shih, C. *The Facebook Era: Tapping Online Social Networks to Market, Sell and Innovate*, 2nd ed. Upper Saddle River, NJ: Prentice Hall, 2011.

ShopSocially. "Social Commerce is Making an Undeniable Impact in 2013." July 31, 2013. **prweb.com/releases/2013/7/prweb10980191.htm** (accessed December 2014).

Singh, S., and S. Diamond. *Social Media Marketing for Dummies*, 2nd ed. Hoboken, NJ: Wiley & Sons, 2012.

Solis, B., *Engage!: The Complete Guide for Brands and Businesses to Build, Cultivate, and Measure Success in the New Web*. Hoboken, NJ: Wiley & Sons, 2011.

Solis, B., and C. Li. (With J. Groopman, J. Szymanski, and C. Tan). " The State of Social Business 2013: The Maturing of Social Media into Social Business." *Altimeter Group Network on Slideshare*, October 15, 2013. **slideshare.net/Altimeter/report-the-state-of-social-business-2013-the-maturing-of-social-media-into-social-business** (accessed December 2014).

Spenser S., et al. *Social eCommerce: Increasing Sales and Extending Brand Reach*. San Jose, CA: O'Reilly Media, 2013.

Stelzner, M.A. "2014 Social Media Marketing Industry Report: How Marketers are Using Social Media to Grow Their Businesses." May 2014. **socialmediaexaminer.com/SocialMediaMarketingIndustryReport2014.pdf** (accessed December 2014).

Stephen, A. T., and O. Toubia. "Deriving Value from Social Commerce Networks." *Journal of Marketing Research*, Vol. 47, No. 2, pp. 215-228. April 2010. [doi: http://dx.doi.org/10.1509/jmkr.47.2.215]

Teicher, D. "What Marketers Can Learn from Starbucks' Foursquare Stumble." July 27, 2010. **adage.com/article/digitalnext/marketers-learn-starbucks-foursquare-stumble/145108** (accessed December 2014).

Traudt, E. and R. Vancil. "Becoming a Social Business: The IBM Story." IDC White Paper, Doc# 226706. January 2011.

Van Grove, J. "How Starbucks is Turning Itself into a Tech Company." June 12, 2012. **venturebeat.com/2012/06/12/starbucks-digital-strategy** (accessed December 2014).

Walker, S., *Social Media Marketing Tips*, Seattle, WA: CreateSpace Independent Publishing Platform, 2014.

Wang, C, and P. Zhang. "The Evolution of Social Commerce: The People, Management, Technology, and Information Dimensions." *Communications of the Association for Information Systems (CAIS)*, vol. 31, article 5, 2012. [DOI: http://aisel.aisnet.org/cais/vol31/iss1/5]

Wood, T. "The Marketers Guide to the Social Media Galaxy (Infographic)." January 2, 2014. **business2community.com/infographics/marketers-guide-social-media-galaxy-infographic-0729381** (accessed December 2014).

York, E. B. "Starbucks Gets Its Business Brewing Again with Social Media." February 22, 2010. **adage.com/article/special-report-digital-alist-2010/digital-a-list-2010-starbucks-brewing-social-media/142202** (accessed December 2014).

Young, S. "28 Must See Social Media Statistics." August 11, 2013. **socialmediatoday.com/content/28-must-see-social-media-statistics** (accessed December 2014).

Tools and Platforms for Social Commerce

Contents

Opening Case: Pinterest—An Innovative Social
Commerce Platform... 23

2.1 Social Media: The Basics 26

2.2 Web 2.0 and Its Major Characteristics............. 29

2.3 The Major Social Media Tools: From Blogs
    and Microblogs to Wikis and Support Technologies....... 30

2.4 Social Networks and Social Networking Sites
    and Services.. 33

2.5 Mobile Social Commerce 36

2.6 Crowdsourcing and Crowdfunding: An Introduction 37

2.7 Virtual Worlds as a Social Commerce Platform.............. 39

References.. 43

Learning Objectives

Upon completion of this chapter, you will be able to:
1. Describe the major basics of social media.
2. Describe Web 2.0 and its major characteristics.
3. List the major social media tools and their uses in SC.
4. Describe social networks.
5. Describe mobile social commerce.
6. Understand the essentials of crowdsourcing.
7. Describe virtual worlds.

OPENING CASE: PINTEREST—AN INNOVATIVE SOCIAL COMMERCE PLATFORM

Pinterest is an innovative fast-growing social bookmarking website where users 'pin' related images and content on a virtual pinboard. The company started in 2010, creating a new opportunity for social commerce. (See a guide by Leland 2013, statistics in Smith (2014a), and **pinterest.com/pinnablebiz/pinterest-statistics**.)

For a free e-book about using Pinterest for business, see Georgieva (undated). For infographics, search Google Images for 'Pinterest.' For Pinterest "facts, stats, and rules," including case studies, see **pinterest.com/wglvsocialmedia/pinterest-facts-%2B-stats-%2B-rules**.

The Opportunity

Pinterest's roots relate to social bookmarking images, which have been used globally for several years. The company's founders saw the business potential and the success of similar companies in Brazil and China. Furthermore, Pinterest succeeded in attracting initial venture capital to expand the business.

Electronic supplementary material The online version of this chapter (doi:10.1007/978-3-319-17028-2_2) contains supplementary material, which is available to authorized users.

The Solution

Pinterest is a provider of virtual pinboards that allow users to organize and share images found on the Web (referred to as pins). The pinned images are organized by topic (theme or category). For example, one can collect pictures of sailboats and pin them on one pinboard, with appropriate text explanation. You can collect decorations for your home on another pinboard, and you can collect Chinese recipes on a third pinboard. Millions of people create pinboards and anyone can search and view them (see Engauge 2012). People use Pinterest for many different reasons. It is an app for saving and organizing images and sharing those images with others. Users can add friends to their account and can 'follow' them. The company's goal is to connect people according to common interests and do it while making profit. For a large number of infographics, search Google Images for 'Pinterest Infographics.'

Having many visitors and a rapid growth rate are necessary, but not sufficient, for social commerce success. Viable business and revenue models are also needed.

The Business and Revenue Models

Pinterest's revenue model is based on charging for advertising. (The company is privately held and it does not have to report its revenue to the public.) It looks as though the company's current priority is, according to CEO Ben Silbermann, "to turn the site into a viable business" (see MacNeil 2014). To learn more about how the company aims to become a viable business, and to read an interview with the CEO, see MacNeil (2014). Nevertheless, many people try to speculate about (or suggest) revenue opportunities for the company (e.g., see Leland 2013), some of which are provided next. In May 2014, Pinterest began selling advertising ("promoted pins") to selected marketers. These ads will show up in Pinterest's search and category feeds (see **techcrunch. com/2014/05/12/pinterest-launches-paid-ads-with-select-brands-in-form-of-promoted-pins**). In June 2014, according to Pinterest's product manager, Pinterest began adding "do it yourself" advertising to Promoted Pins, which are available on a cost-per-click basis, allowing businesses of all sizes to "promote their Pins to reach more people and get visits back to their website" (see Stone 2014). Pinterest is also adding updated analytics (see **business.pinterest. com/en/blog/new-tools-businesses**). In August 2014, Pinterest expanded the Promoted Pins platform to more businesses (see **techcrunch.com/2014/08/13/pinterest-expands-self-serve-promoted-pins-to-more-businesses**). For more about Promoted Pins and how they work, see **ads. pinterest.com**.

Yang's Suggestions

Quora Inc. (**quora.com**) posted a question on its website: "How does Pinterest generate revenue?" One of the most comprehensive answers received was provided by Yang (2012) who presented 13 *potential* monetization opportunities in four categories: charging advertisers (e.g., see Dembosky 2013); charging e-commerce partners; charging users; and charging B2B partners. Most of these opportunities have existed in EC for years (e.g., charging for premium services, creating an online retail shop, using an affiliate program, and building a comprehensive advertising scheme).

Selling Data for Market Research and Analysis

Brave (2012) suggested selling customer data available on Pinterest to retailers who can use analytics, including data mining (or mining "affinity data"), to conduct market research using this data. Customer data may reveal important statistical associations and relationships between consumer behavior, content (e.g., product recommendations, personalization, ads), and services and products provided. These associations can be used for one-to-one relationships and segmentation, as well as for marketing promotions and advertisements. Retailers can use *affinity modeling* and analysis to ascertain relationships so retailers can better understand consumer purchasing behavior. This enables optimal marketing *communication strategies*. Brave also noted that by pinning and repinning on Pinterest, consumers show their affinity for certain themes or for specific products.

Other Suggestions for Doing Business on Pinterest

Many consultants offer suggestions about doing business on Pinterest:

- Hemley (2012) provides 26 different suggestions in an A-Z guide (e.g., A=Add a Pinterest "Follow" and/or "Pin it" Button; B=Brands and Pinterest; C=Crowdsourcing, and so forth).
- HubSpot offers a free e-book titled "How to Use Pinterest for Business" (see **offers.hubspot.com/how-to-use-pinterest-for-business**). It includes suggestions such as how to create Pinterest business accounts and how to drive traffic and leads to companies' website using Pinterest.
- Mitroff (2012) suggests the approach that Zappos Corporation uses. This approach, which is called *PinPointing*, involves product recommendations based on what customers pin. Pinterest may collaborate with

retailers such as Zappos to jointly create product recommendations.

- Green (2013) suggests that businesses pin and repin. She also offers the following: making boards for anything (e.g., boards for inbound marketing, social media); pinning images (e.g., photos with text, infographics); and finding people to follow and getting followers.

For more suggestions, see **realbusiness.com/2013/12/a-pinterest-guide-for-your-business**. PinAlerts (**pinalerts.com**; not affiliated with Pinterest) provides a comprehensive Pinterest business library with many boards and thousands of pins to help businesses market on Pinterest (see **pinterest.com/pinnablebiz**). For comprehensive coverage, see MacNeil (2014).

Using Pinterest for Advertising, Marketing, and Other Business Activities

Most of the suggestions cited above, as well as suggestions by others, concentrate on advertising and marketing opportunities. For comprehensive coverage, see Macarthy (2013), MacNeil (2014), Cario (2013), Hayden (2012), and Miles and Lacey (2013). For how retailers use Pinterest, see Jopson and Kuchler (2013) and Greer (2013).

For a free e-book on how to use Pinterest for business, see Leaning (2013).

Results and Managerial Issues

According to ShareThis (as reported by *Business Insider*), as of Q3 2013, Pinterest was the fastest growing content-sharing platform (see **businessinsider.com/pinterest-is-fastest-growing-content-sharing-platform-2013-11**). As of September 2014, Instagram is now the fastest growing content sharing platform (per **socialmediatoday.com/content/instagram-fastest-growing-social-network-4-brands-riding-wave**). Also according to eBizMBA.com (August 2014 data), Pinterest is the fourth most popular social networking site, behind Facebook, Twitter, and LinkedIn (**ebizmba.com/articles/social-networking-websites**).

As of July 2013, the total number of users worldwide is 70 million (**smallbusiness.yahoo.com/advisor/30-reasons-market-business-pinterest-2014-infographic-184545665.html**). In December 2014, the number topped 70 million. For comprehensive 2014 statistics, see Smith (2014a).

Similar reports on this amazing growth rate and popularity are provided by comScore and other reporting companies. This growth attracted over $200 million in venture capital in 2012 and 2013 and it has generated many suggestions on money-making possibilities with Pinterest (e.g., see Leaning 2013; Loren and Swiderski 2012).

In October 2014, the valuation of Pinterest was about $5 billion (up from $3.8 billion in late 2013). Should the company be able to generate significant revenue, it probably will go the IPO route, in which case the valuation may be much higher. (The company plans to have an IPO in 2015). Let us look now at some managerial issues facing the company.

Legal Concerns

Many people collect images from the Internet to build their pinboards (and possibly a brand) without asking permission from the content creators, giving them an attribute, or compensating them. Some of the collected material is formally copyrighted; other material may be considered copyrighted. A similar problem exists with material used on Facebook or by bloggers. According to Pinterest's 'Terms of Service,' members are "solely responsible for" the content they post on Pinterest. Furthermore, users must have explicit permission from the owners of the content to post them. According to Shontell (2012), one lawyer deleted all her Pinterest boards out of fear of copyright violations. Note that Pinterest places all blame and potential legal fees on its users (who also may pay the legal fees incurred by Pinterest). Pinterest has taken several steps to alleviate the legal concerns of users (e.g., see Hempel 2012). The company is continuously adding measures to minimize the legal problems (see **en.wikipedia.org/wiki/Pinterest**). For example, in May 2012, the company added automatic attribution of credit to content creators. For a discussion, see Hornor (2012). Finally, legal concerns may include dealing with the spammers who are busy on the site.

Pinterest's Competition

The popularity of Pinterest has resulted in many attempts to clone the company. Since the core concept is basically image sharing, it may not be patentable. Competitors are emerging in niche markets. For example, TripAdvisor concentrates on travel; Gentlemint.com focuses on "manly things" (e.g. cars, world news, fitness); and Dribbble.com is for designers to share their creations. An emerging competitor to Pinterest is **fancy.com**, which partnered with Google+ in February 2013. **Boxnutt.com** is very similar to Pinterest, but concentrates on funny images and clips. Indirect competitors include several Chinese companies that operate in a culturally different environment, (see McKenzie 2012). Companies such as Facebook and Google may initiate a competitive service. According to Hempel (2012), Pinterest is more business oriented than Facebook or Twitter, and visitors tend to buy more there, although Facebook and Twitter drive more visitors to their sites.

Conclusion

It seems that Pinterest has some potential benefits for small businesses (e.g., designers). Many companies already use Pinterest to derive benefits (e.g., see Etsy.com and Volpe 2012). However, these applications do not provide any revenue to Pinterest at the moment. The success of Pinterest will be determined by its revenue model and the company's profitability.

Sources: Based on Brave (2012), Carr (2012), Jopson and Kuchler (2013), MacNeil (2014), MacMillan (2014), Hempel (2012), Loren and Swiderski (2012), Yang (2012), and Volpe (2012).

LESSONS LEARNED FROM THE CASE

Pinterest is a unique platform for conducting social media and e-commerce activities. The participants form a social network which connects people who find interesting images on the Web and organize them by topic. Pinterest is also a platform on which several activities of SC can be supported. For example, companies can build pinboards that promote their brands. Pinterest can be used as a platform for facilitating innovations via idea-generation and sharing. Pinterest is a derivative of Web 2.0 and social media, and as such, it is a new mechanism for supporting social commerce. Other mechanisms covered in this chapter are social networks, crowdsourcing, and virtual worlds. Note: In addition to the tools and platforms described in this chapter, social commerce requires the generic tools of e-marketing and e-commerce.

2.1 SOCIAL MEDIA: THE BASICS

In this book we use the word *media* to mean digital text, sounds, pictures, and videos that are shared via the Internet or other computing systems. Social media, like all media, delivers content to audiences for marketing, entertainment, learning, collaboration, for other purposes. Let us first define social media.

Social Media: Many Definitions

The term *social media* was defined in Chap. 1 as: online media content using Web 2.0 tools and platforms conducting social interactions and conversations. These can be sharing opinions, creating content, providing recommendations, and so forth.

Social media is a powerful force of socialization, enabling interactions, communication, and collaboration on a massive scale. For a comprehensive description, see Kaplan and Haenlein (2010), who define social media as "a group of Internet-based applications that build on the ideological and technological foundations of Web 2.0, and that allow the creation and exchange of user-generated content."

Here are some additional definitions of social media adopted from Kawasaki and Fitzpatrick (2014), Safko (2012), and Luttrell (2014):

- Any website that utilizes Web 2.0 concepts. This includes microblogs, blogs, wikis, social videos, and so on.
- Software tools that enable people to generate content (text, video, audio, etc.) and engage in person-to-person sharing, publishing, conversations, and dissemination of content in a social environment.
- Media that is frequently designed by users and is disseminated through social networking.

Note: Tommasi (2011) provides 50 different definitions of social media. This is typical in a developing interdisciplinary field. (Available for viewing as part of a Datasift SlideShare presentation (posted April 3, 2012), titled "Follow the Content": see **slideshare.net/datasift/follow-the-content**.)

A common thread running through all the definitions of social media is that they are a blend of technology, content, and social interactions for the co-creation of value. For details about social media, see **en.wikipedia.org/wiki/Social_media**, Kaplan and Haenlein (2010), and Kawasaki and Fitzpatrick (2014). For a critical history of social media see Van Dijck (2013). For a brief history of social media (1969–2014), references, news and more, see **uncp.edu/home/acurtis/NewMedia/SocialMedia/SocialMedia**

History.html). For free e-books, see **hongkiat.com/blog/ free-ebooks-social-media**.

The complexity and richness of the social media field can be seen in the *social media map* available at **social mediatoday.com**, in Kaplan and Haenlein (2010), and in Safko (2012). A comprehensive slide show (115 slides) on social media implementation is available at **slideshare.net/ fated82/social-media-implementation-slides**. For a report on the state of social media, see Eitel (2015).

It is useful to organize the diversified content of social media into a framework or model that enables the organization of the content as illustrated next.

The Landscape of Social Media

Social media can be viewed as containing three major types of entities: (1) application tools for media components for applications (e.g., text, images, audio, and videos); (2) delivery platforms, mainly social network sites and services; and (3) social media activities such as conversations, sharing, and recommendations. These three parts are illustrated in Fig. 2.1 (the corners of the large triangle), and they are interconnected by a networked community of people, organizations, society, and technology. For comprehensive coverage, see Divol et al. (2012). For social media statistics, see Pring (2013) and Wallace (2013). For 2014 major social network statistics, see **mediabistro.com/alltwitter/social-media-statistics-2014_b57746**. For 2014 social media statistics

with an interactive infographic, see **c4lpt.co.uk/ blog/2014/06/07/social-media-2014-statistics-interactive-infographic**. For a video on the social media revolution (2013), see **youtube.com/watch?v=QUCfFcchw1w**.

The Major Parts of Social Media

The details of the three parts of social media are:
1. *Media components and applications.* These include text, audio, images, and video. Social media uses a wide variety of content presentations, known as *rich media.*
2. *Social network sites and services.* These are websites that are platforms for social media. They enable people to meet in communities of shared interests, hobbies, or causes; these are referred to as **social network sites**. Starting with well-known names such as Facebook and LinkedIn, there are thousands of social network sites around the globe (e.g., see Van Belleghem et al. 2011). According to Webopedia, a social networking site is "any website that enables users to create public profiles within that website and form relationships with other users of the same website who access their profile" and are "community-based" (see **webopedia.com/TERM/S/social_networking_site. html**). Several different types of these services are described in Sects. 2.4 and 2.5. These sites enable the third part of our model (Fig. 2.1), social media activities.
3. *Social media activities.* Many activities can be performed using social media. The major ones are:

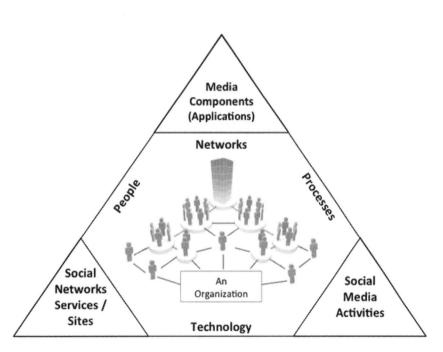

Figure 2.1 The components of social media

Functional Building Blogs

In what they describe as the "jungle of social media," Kietzmann et al. (2011) identify seven social media functionalities that they consider the *building blocks* of the field.

The building blocks are:

- **Sharing:** Sharing content among users (e.g., in discussion forums, chats, or video and photo exchanges; e.g., on Snapchat). It is the extent to which users exchange, distribute, and receive content.
- **Presence:** Finding where your friends are at a given time. It is the extent to which users can know if others are accessible.
- **Conversations:** There are many ways to have conversions using social media tools, ranging from Twitter to Facebook to Whatsapp. It is the extent to which users communicate with other users in a social media setting.
- **Relationships:** Users can relate to each other in many ways. For example, you can join a group in LinkedIn or follow somebody on Twitter. It is the extent to which users can be related to other users.
- **Reputation:** Users like to know the social standing of others. For example, endorsements at LinkedIn. It is the extent to which users can identify the standing of others, including themselves, on a social media setting.
- **Identity:** Disclosing who you are is an integral part of many social networks. Having a profile is essential to build relationship. It is the extent to which users reveal their identities in a social media setting.
- **Groups:** Given the large size of social networks, many social media platforms offer smaller communities. It is the extent to which users can form communities and sub-communities. On LinkedIn you can join professional groups, and on Facebook and Twitter you have friends and followers.

A large number of social media guides for some of the above activities, for social network sites, and for the major social media tools are provided (some for free) on the *Social Media Examiner* website. For the impact of social media on commerce, see the infographic, at **staging.socialmediatoday. com/ritu-pant/1586661/social-currency-effect-social-media-commerce**, Wildfire, Inc. (2012), and Kaplan and Haenlein (2010). For a framework for research, see Aral et al. (2013). Schaefer (2014a) explains the business trend of social media.

Social Media Marketing (SMM)

A major area of application of social media is **social media marketing (SMM)**, which is the process of conducting marketing activities, such as marketing communication, engagement, and advertising. The major objective of SMM is to attract the attention of potential buyers through social media tools and platforms (Media 2014). In SMM, marketers create content for this purpose by themselves, or by using user generated content. In addition, by using social media tools and platforms, marketers try to have the created content shared over the Internet. For 500 social media marketing tip, see Macarthy (2013). Also, see the tips and strategy suggested by Walker (2014). For a list of successful campaigns, see **en.wikipedia. org/wiki/social-media-marketing**. Many of SMM activities are done in the major social networks (see Macarthy 2013).

Details of SMM are presented in Chaps. 4 and 5.

Web 2.0 Tools and Applications

The social media tool kit includes a large number of tools, and these can be defined and categorized in several different ways. Popular tools are blogs, wikis, and RSS feeds. The tools' capabilities are ever changing.

In Table 2.1, we provide a fairly comprehensive list of social media tools. We describe some of these tools in Sect. 2.3.

Software Applications (Apps)

Software applications (abbreviated as "apps") are closely related to, and frequently confused with, social media tools. A **software application (app)**, also known as *Web application*, is a piece of software (usually small) that is run on the Internet, or on an intranet on your workplace computer, or on your wireless device, such as a smartphone or tablet. Apps are designed for end-users.

Numerous apps are available for social media. For example, Facebook offers Facebook Local Currency Payments—a payment application that offers a method of paying for digital and virtual goods in games and apps used across Facebook. Unfortunately, the distinction between software tools and apps is not always clear. This may not be an important issue for users, but it is important for developers.

A list of the top 1,000 Web 2.0 tools and applications in 60 categories is available at **sites.google.com/a/vmbulldogs. com/van-meter-secondary-library-voice/web-2-0-tools**. A similar list of Web 2.0 tools and applications is provided at **go2web20.net**. A comprehensive resource with links to Web 2.0 tools is provided at **xmarks.com/site/www. web20searchengine.com/web20/web-2.0-list.htm**.

Table 2.1 Social media software tools and services

Tools for online communication
- Blogs, vlogs (video blogs), microblogs (e.g., Twitter)
- Wikis
- Instant messaging and VoIP (Voice over Internet Protocol)
- Internet forums
- Text chat
- Collaborative real-time editors

Platforms and applications for support
- Social networks general services
- Commercial and professional social networks
- Social search engines
- Enterprise social networks
- Social guides
- Multimedia sharing sites (e.g., YouTube) and photos (e.g., Flickr)
- Article sharing
- Social bookmarking
- Social citations
- Social libraries
- Social cataloging
- Virtual worlds and massively multiplayer online games (MMOGs)
- Crowdsourcing and idea generation
- Social games in networks (e.g., Zynga, Electronic Arts)
- Content management tools

Emerging technologies
- Peer-to-peer social networks for selling and bartering
- Virtual presence
- Mobile tools for Web 2.0
- Productivity and support tools

Tools for individual users
- Personalization tools
- Customization
- Search in blogs, in all types of media
- Clipping tools
- RSS
- File-sharing tools

Web 2.0 development tools
- Mashups
- Web services

The three parts shown in Fig. 2.1 are interconnected by people (individuals, groups), organizations, and communities, and are enabled by Web 2.0 tools and applications and their characteristics (i.e., the technology and processes). Social media is recognized today as an effective tool with proven ROI. For 166 case studies and a free e-book, see Petersen (2011).

2.2 WEB 2.0 AND ITS MAJOR CHARACTERISTICS

In Chap. 1, we introduced the essentials of Web 2.0. Web 2.0 is a major element of social media because it provides the tools people use when engaging in social media activities. The terms

Web 2.0 and *social media* are frequently used interchangeably to describe the same things. However, many treat Web 2.0 as tool-oriented technology only, and social media as a broader concept of innovative applications, tools, content, and strategy (e.g., see Edwards 2013). For a comprehensive handbook of research on Web 2.0 (47 chapters), see Murugesan (2010).

Representative Characteristics of Web 2.0

The major characteristics of Web 2.0 are presented in Table 2.2.

Of these characteristics, here we will discuss only the topic of user-generated content. Other characteristics are described in various chapters of this book (e.g., new business models were described in Chap. 1).

User-Generated Content

User-generated content (UGC), also known as *consumer-generated media (CGM)*, refers to media content that is produced by end-users and is publicly available. It is also used

Table 2.2 Major characteristics of Web 2.0

The following are representative characteristics of Web 2.0:

User-created content (self-publishing)
- The ability to tap into the collective intelligence of users. The more users who contribute, the more popular and valuable a Web 2.0 site becomes
- Unique communication and collaborative environment
- Making data available in new and innovative ways
- Web 2.0 data that can be remixed or "mashed up," often through Web services interfaces, much like the way a dance-club DJ mixes music
- The presence of lightweight programming techniques and tools that lets nearly anyone act as a developer (e.g., wikis, blogs, RSS, and podcasting)
- The virtual elimination of software-upgrade cycles that makes everything a perpetual beta, or work in progress, and allows rapid prototyping using the Web as a platform
- Unique sharing of content of all types
- Networks as platforms, delivering and allowing users to use applications entirely through a browser
- Open source architecture, which makes connectivity to computing resources simple
- Users own the data on the site and exercise control over that data
- An architecture of participation and digital democracy that encourages users to add value to the application as they use it
- Creation of new business models
- A major emphasis on social networks
- A rich, interactive, user-friendly interface based on Ajax or similar frameworks. Ajax (Asynchronous JavaScript and XML) is a Web development technique for creating interactive Web applications
- More productive organization communication due to improved search, links, user authority, and so on
- Global spread of innovation. As soon as a successful idea is deployed as a website in one country, similar sites appear worldwide

to describe a wide range of applications, content creation, and other activities. Examples include reviews, recommendations, problem solving, marketing communication (such as user-generated ads), news, word of mouth, and entertainment. Some social media sites are entirely populated by UGC, such as YouTube (videos), Flickr (photos), Meetup (network of local groups), LinkedIn, Google+, Twitter, Instagram, and other social networks. Note that, according to research reported by Knoblauch (2014), millennials trust UGC 50 % more than they trust other content.

For details about UGC, including its limitations and legal concerns, see **en.wikipedia.org/wiki/User-generated_content**. Regarding commercial applications, UGC is used in writing Wikia and Wikipedia entries and similar collective intelligence projects. It is also used to engage an organization's markets by preparing (or contributing to the preparation of) ads, encouraging comments to blog entries, and soliciting product improvement recommendations (such as My Starbucks Idea). Sites entirely populated by UGC, such as YouTube, attract a multitude of visitors and thus provide revenue through an advertising business model.

With an increase in user-generated content on the Web, the user (or consumer) is largely in control of brand conversations. As a result, traditional marketing strategies (such as banner ads) may not work as well in social media environments.

Following the traditional word of mouth, consumers want to be associated with, and receive, product recommendations from friends and family. They want to visit and participate in online "environments" where trust, interest, and knowledge is shared by communities. Web 2.0 technologies allow consumers to listen and contribute to UGC on a large scale. However, some major issues related to UGC include its quality, fairness, how current the content is, and the potential invasion of privacy of those cited in specific UGC. This is inevitable in an environment where everyone is a publisher with little editing control; however, several commercial systems are in place to moderate online discussions and other UGC (see reputation management systems in Chap. 5).

As stated earlier, social media activities are enabled by a set of tools that are referred to as Web 2.0 or *social software*. These are described next.

2.3 THE MAJOR SOCIAL MEDIA TOOLS: FROM BLOGS AND MICROBLOGS TO WIKIS AND SUPPORT TECHNOLOGIES

Social software encompasses a range of software tools that allow users to interact and share data and other media. The major social software tools were listed in Table 2.1. For comprehensive coverage, see **social7.org**. For comprehensive coverage of social media tools, tactics, platforms, and strategies, see Safko (2012).

Many of the applications performed with social media tools share the common characteristics described earlier, as well as having the ability to easily upload data/media. Major advocates of using social media tools believe that they are the backbone needed for creating online innovative communities and applications.

Note that these tools are also popular in social networks. For example, photo sharing and blogging are integral parts of many social networks. However, several of the tools are also written in traditional information systems such as blogs in corporate portals.

In this section, we will cover only representative tools that are used more extensively in social commerce: blogs and microblogs (e.g., Twitter), wikis, and social search.

Blog (Web Log)

The Internet offers the opportunity for individuals to *publish* on the Web using a technology known as *Web logging*, or *blogging*. A **blog** is a personal website, or part of a website, open to the public, where the owners express their thoughts and opinions, and provide information and expertise. Blogs are "a publicly accessible personal journal" and "new content is published by the author on a regular basis" (per **etc. usf.edu/techease/mac/internet/what-is-blogging-and-how-can-i-use-it-as-a-classroom-activity**). Blogs can become a two-way communication that may facilitate collaboration. Blogs can be used on the Internet or internally within the enterprise on intranets. The totality of blogs is known as the *blogosphere*. For comprehensive coverage of blogs, see **en.wikipedia.org/wiki/Blog**. Blogging is probably the most popular Web 2.0 tool among the largest U.S. corporations. For the top ten business blogs for entrepreneurs (in 2013), see **onlinebusiness.volusion.com/articles/best-business-blogs**. For the top 50 business blogs (Blog Rank), see **blogmetrics.org/Business**.

Many blogs provide commentaries on a particular subject; others function mostly as personal online diaries. A typical blog includes text, videos, images, and links to relevant sources. A **video blog (vlog)** is a blog with video content. Because it is getting easy to embed videos in blogs many blogs are changing to vlogs. According to WP Virtuoso, in November 2013, there were over 152 million blogs on the Internet, with a new blog created somewhere in the world every half seconds (172,800 per day; per **wpvirtuoso.com/how-many-blogs-are-on-the-internet**, which also provides an infographic with interesting facts about blogs). Note that almost 10,000 fake or spam blogs are each created daily (out of 150,000–200,000 total). Most blogs are written in English. Note that, while most blogs are written by one individual, there are some blogs that are written by two or more people (sometimes by many employees of a company).

Building Effective Blogs

It is becoming much easier to build blogs. Programs from Google (**blogger.com**) and other vendors (e.g., **typepad.com**) are very user-friendly, allowing blog authors to write directly on theirs or on any other website (e.g., when they write for a vendor). Blog space is free; the goal is to make it easy for users to create their own blogs. *Bloggers* (the people who create and maintain blogs) invite others to their blogs. Blogs can easily be edited and forwarded. Blogging platforms, such as **wordpress.org** or **movabletype.org**, have more complex features and also allow users to host their blogs at a third-party site, such as **godaddy.com** or directly on WordPress. Bloggers also use special terminology, such as 'blog storm,' where thousands of bloggers in the blogosphere write about the same topic, event, or activity in order to push the story to mainstream news. See **whatis.techtarget.com/reference/Blog-terms-Glossary** for a glossary of blog terms. For building effective blogging business for profit see Murdoch (2014).

To review the legal and social consequences of blogs, including the dangers of defamation or liability, political dangers, issues in relation to employment, and court cases, see **en.wikipedia.org/wiki/Blog**. For the potential impact of blogs on the reputation of brands or organizations, see Chap. 5. For EFF's Legal Guide for Bloggers, see **eff.org/issues/bloggers/legal**.

Commercial Uses of Blogs

The blog concept has transferred quickly and extensively to the corporate world. For coverage, see Rich (2014) and Schaefer and Smith (2013). Typical applications include:

- Building brands.
- Demonstrating company or individual expertise to attract clients.
- Attracting many readers for the purpose of selling advertising on the blog.
- Providing customer support for problem resolution, interactions, and encouragement of customer engagement.
- Using search engines to increase traffic to the owner's other sites.
- Setting up blogs for partner and customer feedback.

Example: How Stonyfield Farm Uses Blogs

Stonyfield Farm (**stonyfield.com**) makes the number-one selling brand of organic yogurt and is the third largest overall yogurt company in the U.S. The company's core values are promoting healthy food (organic) and protecting the environment. The company guarantees the use of only natural ingredients in its products and it donates 10% of its profits each year to environmental non-profit groups (see their videos at **youtube.com/user/stonyfieldorganic/videos**).

The company uses word-of-mouth marketing approaches that are compatible with its grassroots "people-friendly" image. As of 2007, Stonyfield has turned to blogs to further personalize its relationship with its customers and connect with even more people. The blogs provide the company with what the management calls a "handshake" with customers. Stonyfield publishes six different categories of blogs on its website, including "on the farm," "at home," and "in the cup." Each category includes sub-categories.

Stonyfield hires bloggers to post new content to each of the blogs on a regular basis. When readers subscribe to the blogs, they receive automatic updates, and they can also respond to the postings. The blogs have created a positive response for the Stonyfield brand by providing readers with topics that inspire them and pique their interests. The blog readers are encouraged to try Stonyfield products. Management believes that blogs are an excellent method of communication with the customers, as well as for public relations.

Microblogging and Twitter

Microblogging is a form of blogging that allows users to write short messages, post an image, or embed a video, and then publish them on a forum. These messages can be delivered as text messages from mobile devices, as instant messaging, through e-mail, or just posted on the Web. The messages are delivered in real-time or close to it (e.g., commentary during a sporting event).

The content of a microblog differs from that of a regular blog due to the limited amount of characters per message (e.g., Twitter has a limit of 140 characters on any device).

The most popular service is Twitter, although in 2014, there were hundreds of competitors (e.g., **tumblr.com** and see Frasco 2013). A very large and popular microblog service in China is Sina Weibo (**us.weibo.com/gb**). Note that many of the microblogging sites include social media and social networking functionalities.

Twitter and Tweeting

Twitter is a microblogging service with some social network features, that enables its users to send messages and read other users' messages and updates, otherwise known as **tweets**, which are short text-based posts. Tweets can be read directly online or delivered to users (followers) who sign up to read them. Twitter can be viewed as a social media platform for broadcasting information and opinions. According to Twitter's homepage, "Twitter is a service … to communicate and stay connected through the exchange of quick frequent answers to one simple question: 'What are you doing?'" However, the service additionally includes social networking capabilities, such as user profiles, lists of friends, and dozens of applications, so Twitter can also be considered a social network. For capabilities and details, see Collier (2014), Fitton et al. (2014), and **tweeternet.com**. Twitter and its business applications are described in detail on **business. twitter.com/basics** and by Schaefer (2014b). The shares of the company are publically traded and their price advanced rapidly (in 2014). Also see **twitter.com/101Guide**. The latter is also a guide to using Twitter for business.

As of August 2014, Twitter claims to have more than 271 million monthly active users (per **about.twitter.com/company**). For 250 amazing statistics see Smith (2014b). Twitter is used by customers and it is also becoming a useful enterprise tool. Socialtext (**socialtext.com**) is a social software company that offers functionality including a Twitter-like service for the enterprise (see **en.wikipedia.org/wiki/Socialtext**).

Twitter is an important social commerce tool because it:

- Enables the contribution of information by people whose opinions are important to a company and its management. This includes idea generation and improved innovation.
- Helps rapid dissemination of information and news and consequently is facilitating word-of-mouth information, so it is can be used as a marketing communication tool.
- Allows people to interact with others, which helps them find business partners and sales leads.
- Helps employees find colleagues, understand what their colleagues are doing and share advice and get help.
- Helps with customer care and problem resolution.

For Twitter statistics, see **statisticbrain.com/twitter-statistics**, and Smith (2014b).

For the benefits of using Twitter for business, see Dessau (2013), and Bennett (2014).

Wikis

A **wiki**, also called a *wikiblog*, is a tool that enables users to jointly create digital documents. According to Wikipedia, Wikis are powered by wiki software. They also are deployed via corporate intranets and in knowledge management systems (e.g., create and update knowledge).

A wiki can be viewed as a continually revised, multi-authored blog. Whereas a blog usually is created by an individual (or maybe a small group) and frequently has an attached discussion board or a continuous list of comments, a wiki essentially is a blog that enables anyone to participate as a co-editor. Any user may add, delete, edit, or change content. (In contrast, content blogs cannot be changed by anyone but the original poster.) A wiki is like a loose-leaf notebook with a pencil and eraser left in a public place. Users can read it, scrawl notes, tear out a page, add an image, and so on. Wikis can be implemented in many ways. One way is through contributions by many, as in the case of Wikipedia (see Waters 2010). A similar concept is employed by sites such as **investopedia.com**. For a comprehensive list of wikis, see **wikiindex.org**. For characteristics, e-commerce applications, resources, and more, see **en.wikipedia.org/wiki/Wiki**. For collaborative wiki types, see **pbworks.com** and WikiHub (**getwikihub.com**).

Business Applications of Wikis

Wikis are becoming an important enterprise collaboration tool. Even universities use them for project collaboration, such as working on accreditation materials for business schools. An interesting example is Wind River (**windriver. com**), a software company that uses wikis extensively to support teamwork (see details at **twiki.org/cgi-bin/view/Main/TWikiSuccessStoryOfWindRiver**).

Other Useful Tools and Apps

Hundreds interesting tools can be classified as social media tools. Here are few representative examples:

- **Snapchat**—A mobile photo messaging app used for taking photos, videos and drawings, and sending them to recipients on a desired list.
- **WhatsApp**—A free cross-platform messaging exchange app for smartphones that allows users to send SMS messages at no charge (a Facebook company).
- **Ortsbo**—Enabler of real-time conversational translation mainly in social media settings.
- **DROTR** (Formerly Droid Translator)—Translates voice, videos calls, and chats into 29 different languages. The program has been upgraded and is now a completely separate VoIP service for mobile devices. See Petroff (2014) and **droid-translator. tiwinnovations.com**.

- **Tagged**—A maker of *social discovery* products. It enables people to meet and socialize with other people through advanced browsing and matching features, shared interests, etc.
- **Viber, Line, etc.** Several new companies are centered on mobile devices. For example, providing mobile apps for free texting, free phone calling, photo messages, and location sharing with others. Line Inc. also provides stickers and the latest news and coupons. As social networks, these companies allow creation of reviews, etc. See Macarthy (2013). Several companies provide free voice and video calls for mobile devices and desktops (e.g. Viber for Desktop).
- **Hashtags**—Enables users to click on a hashtag on Facebook and see all public content related to a specific keyword. Also enables users to join any public conversation related to a posted hashtag (see Vandermeersch 2013).
- **Google+ Hangouts**—Google's Messaging and chatting tool for the mobile environment (see Tech2 News Staff 2014 and **plus.google.com/hangouts**).
- **We Chat**—A popular mobile text, images, video and voice messaging communication service; now with real-time location service (owned by Tencent Holdings of China). It is similar to WhatsApp (see Tech2 News Staff 2014).

Social Search

Searching information available in social networks can be improved with tools such as "Graph Search" from Facebook. The tool is integrated with Facebook's *Social Graph* (see Chap. 3). Social Graph can process information available in natural language, including queries. Social search discovers social connections and much more. For details, see **facebook.com/about/graphsearch**. Graph Search ads provide income to Facebook. Google also incorporates social features to its standard search engine.

Specialized Search Engines for Social Networks

Several search engines are designed specifically for searching social networks and networking. Representative examples are: **pipl.com**, **wink.com**, **peekyou.com**, **yoname.com**, and **zabasearch.com**. For ways to make it easier for people to find others online, see Cockburn (2014).

For a comprehensive beginner's guide to social media, see **moz.com/beginners-guide-to-social-media**.

Using Multiple Tools to Improve Performance

Many companies combine Web 2.0 tools to improve performance.

Now that you have an idea about social media tools, we can move on to the seconds of our framework (see Fig. 2.1, p. XX), describing social networks.

2.4   SOCIAL NETWORKS AND SOCIAL NETWORKING SITES AND SERVICES

There are several definitions of the basic concepts related to social networks.

First, there is a community of people with common interests that exist online and are referred to as a *virtual community*. (For example, Trimdownclub.com is a community of people that are interested in reducing their weight.) A community is using a website to communicate and share ideas, etc. Such a website is referred to as a *social network site* (or *service*).

A **social network**, in general, is a structure that describes social relationships and flows of information and activities among the participants in a community. The structure is made of nodes that describe the participants (people, computers, other objects). These nodes are connected by lines that describe the relationships and activities in the community. The nodes in a network are connected by one or more interdependencies, such as ideas, values, visions, ideologies, financial interest, friendship, or similar interests. The structures can range from simple to very complex.

In its simplest form, a social network can be described by an image of all relevant connections among the nodes. The network can also be used to determine the social capital (see Chap. 3) of individual participants. These concepts are often displayed in a social network diagram, where nodes are the objectes and participants, and the lines are the ties.

Social Network Services (Sites)

Social network services (SNSs) (also known as social network sites), such as LinkedIn or Facebook, provide and host a free Web space for people to build their public profile. They also provide communication and support tools (e.g., blogs, forums, polling, e-mail, and chatting capabilities), and apps that enable different activities. Social networks are people-oriented. Today, corporations have a great interest in the business aspect of social networks, for professional reasons as well as for networking and for promoting products and services. An example is **linkedin.com**, the largest business-oriented social network that connects professionals and businesses by industry, functions, geography, and areas of interest (see Chap. 8).

The following are some examples of representative social network services.

- **Facebook.com**. The largest and the most visited social network service.

- **YouTube.com** and **metacafe.com**. Users can upload and watch video clips at these sites.
- **LinkedIn.com**. The largest network for professional people and for recruiting.
- **Pinterest.com**. The most popular pinboard-based network.
- **QQ.com**. China's Tencent QQ, with over 800 million active IM users. The site has some social network capabilities (e.g., online social games, music), and it is the largest online chat community in the world. An English version is **imqq.com**. QQ International, which is distributed through an English-speaking portal, provides non-Mandarin speakers the ability to connect with other QQ users. It also provides a non-Mandarin interface to access Qzone, China's largest social media network.
- **Plus.google.com**. A social network designed to be the social extension of Google that may rival Facebook and/or LinkedIn. (See Meyer 2013 for an infographic; for a 2014 infographic on how to improve engagement on Google+, see **thehubcomms.com/infographic-how-to-improve-engagement-on-google/article/354606**.)
- **Flickr.com**. A photo-sharing service; share and connect with the community.
- **Hi5.com**. A popular global social network for meeting new people through games, shared interests, and more. Acquired by Tagged in 2011.
- **Habbo.com**. A global entertaining virtual world-based site.
- **MySpace.com**. Social network focusing on music.

For a list of the major sites, including the number of users, see **en.wikipedia.org/wiki/List_of_social_networking_websites** and **ebizmba.com/articles/social-networking-websites**. For a 2014 social media infographic with statistics and other information, see **blog.digitalinsights.in/social-media-users-2014-stats-numbers/05205287.html**.

Social Networking

It is useful to distinguish between *social networks* and *social networking*. **Social networking** refers to the execution of any social media activity listed in Sect. 2.1, including having a presence in social networks. It is the act of exchanging information, private or public, through various forms of network technology, such as the Internet, cellphones, and other devices and services, using social media tools, apps, or networks.

Social networking includes all social media activities, regardless if they are done in social networks or in any other website (e.g., corporate portal).

Social networking is viewed as being all about people and relationships, basically describing the activities conducted in social network sites.

The Social Networking Landscape

The social networking landscape can be categorized as follows:

- **Leisure-oriented sites.** Socially focused public sites are open to all users. However, companies also use these for promoting their products. For example, Facebook, hi5, and Google+. MySpace is known as a place where musicians sell their music.
- **Professional networking sites.** Sites focusing on business networking. Examples: LinkedIn, Xing, and Biznik.
- **Media sharing sites.** Sites that enable focusing on the display and sharing of user-generated multimedia content, such as video and photos. Examples: YouTube, Flickr, and Instagram.
- **Virtual world sites.** 3D virtual worlds built and owned by their residents (the users). Examples: Second Life, Webkinz, and Hobbo.
- **Communication sites that possess social networking capabilities.** Many socially oriented websites facilitate communication. For example:
  - Microblogging/presence applications, such as Twitter, Plurk, and Sina Weibo
  - Unified communication products such as Microsoft's SharePoint, Salesforce's Chatter, Microsoft's Yammer, and IBM Connections (formerly Lotus Connections) empower and enable communication, conversations, collaboration, and other social networking activities.
  - **Enterprise-owned sites.** These are *private* sites owned by companies. Examples include: Starbucks, Disney, or Dell.

For a comprehensive list of social network websites, see **en.wikipedia.org/wiki/List_of_social_networking_websites**.

Note that, in each of the social network sites, you may find social software tools and socially oriented applications (apps). Also note that, thanks to mashups, it is possible to have content from several sites combined. For instance, a Facebook page might include photos from Flickr, videos from YouTube, and news from Twitter. Social media and networking are becoming new communication venues that impact the manner in which people interact. Finally, note that the capabilities and business models of social network sites are changing constantly (e.g., regarding Facebook, see Hutchinson 2013). For a comprehensive guide to social networks, including social networking basics, and different categories of social networks, see **webtrends.about.com/od/socialnetworking/u/list-of-social-networks-guide.htm**.

A Global Phenomenon

Although Facebook, Twitter, and LinkedIn attract the majority of media attention in the United States, in general, many other social network sites are proliferating and growing in popularity worldwide (e.g. see **emarketer.com/Article/Which-Social-Networks-Growing-Fastest-Worldwide/1009884**).

For popularity around the world, see **royal.pingdom.com/2013/01/16/internet-2012-in-numbers** (2012 data); Alexa's top 500 (**alexa.com/topsites/global**); and **statista.com/statistics/272014/global-social-networks-ranked-by-number-of-users**. (However, it is important to note that rankings differ depending on the source and manner of calculation and fluctuate between dates.) For example, **renren.com**, Qzone (**qzone.qq.com**), and **weibo.com** are premier social networking services in China. **Mixi.jp** has attained widespread adoption in Japan, **tuenti.com** in Spain, studiVZ (**studivz.net**) in Germany, and Vkontakte (**vk.com**) in Russia. In Poland one can find Nasza-Klasa (**nk.pl**). **Hi5.com** has been adopted globally. Additionally, previously popular communication services have begun implementing social networking features. For example, the Chinese QQ (an instant messaging service), cited earlier, instantly became one of the largest social networking services in the world once it added profiles and made friends visible to one another. Note that international entrepreneurs, inspired by the success of the largest social network sites in the USA and their capabilities, have created their own local knock-offs. Information about social networks is changing rapidly; therefore, to get the most up-to-date data, go to **alexa.com**, **expandedramblings.com**, or **comscore.com**.

For a comprehensive slideshow about the spread of social media globally, see Van Belleghem et al. (2011).

The Major Capabilities and Services Provided by Social Network Sites

Social network sites provide many capabilities and services such as:

Although not all networks have all these capabilities, some have even more. These capabilities can make social networks useful for consumers (see Zeisser 2010).

- Users can construct a Web page where they are able to present their profiles to the public.
- Users can create a circle of friends who are linked together.
- The site provides discussion forums (by subgroup, by topic).
- Photo, video, and document viewing and sharing (streaming videos, user-supplied videos) are supported.
- Wikis can be used to jointly create documents.
- Blogs can be used for discussion, dissemination of information, and much more.
- Some social network sites offer community e-mail and instant messaging (IM) capabilities.
- Experts (including paid and non-paid) can be made available to answer members' queries.
- Consumers can rate and comment on products and services.
- Online voting may be available to poll members' opinions.
- Some sites provide an e-newsletter.
- Some sites support conference (group) chatting, possibly combined with (document and image) sharing.
- Users can chat both by text (Instant Messaging) and voice.
- Message and bulletin board services are available for posting information.
- Some social network sites provide storage for content such as photos, videos, and music.
- Users can bookmark their self-created content.
- Users can find what is going on in others' networks, or in topics of interest.
- Users can shop, relying on advice received from friends and other shoppers.

To learn about Facebook and its capabilities, see the free tutorial at **gcflearnfree.org/facebook101**.

Business-Oriented Social Networks

Business-oriented social networks, also known as *professional social networks*, are networks whose primary objective is to facilitate business activities and connections. The prime example here is **linkedin.com**, which provides business contacts and interactions and enables job searching and recruiting (see Chap. 8).

Businesses increasingly use business social networks for building professional networking, and introducing themselves online. Social networks also make it easier to keep connected globally.

Example of a Business-Oriented Social Network: XING

Originated in Germany, XING (**xing.com**) is a business network for business professionals—job seekers, recruiters, salespeople and managers from many countries, mostly in Europe (mostly German-speaking countries; see details at **corporate.xing.com/no_cache/english/company/xing-ag**). The site offers secure services in 16 languages serving 200 countries. Users can visit the site to:

- Establish new business contacts and find sales leads.
- Expand and manage their contact with networks of professionals.
- Promote themselves to employers in a professional business context.
- Find experts that can give advice on any topic (for fee or for free).
- Organize professional conferences and related events.
- Control the level of privacy and ensure that their personal data are protected. (XING handles members' data in accordance with strict German data protection regulations.) This is especially important in the European Union, where data privacy issues are more important and legislated than in the United States and most other countries. See **security.xing.com** for more about their trust and security policies.

For more on XING, see **xing.com/help**. Services also are available for mobile devices.

Enterprise Social Networks

Business-oriented social networks can be *public*, such as LinkedIn. They are usually owned and operated by independent companies. Another type of business-oriented social network is *private*, owned by corporations and operated inside them. These are known as *enterprise social networks*, such as My Starbucks Idea. They can be available to customers, or solely to the company's employees (see Chap. 8).

2.5 MOBILE SOCIAL COMMERCE

Mobile computing is growing faster than any other type of EC computing. According to Cisco Systems' 2014 Visual Networking Index (as reported by Sartain 2014), global mobile data traffic increased by 81% (from 820 petabytes per month in 2012) to 1.5 exabytes per month in 2013. (To access Cisco's White Paper, see **cisco.com/c/en/us/solutions/collateral/service-provider/visual-networking-index-vni/white_paper_c11-520862.pdf**.) This growth clearly facilitates global mobile commerce. According to a survey conducted by eDigital Research and Portaltech Reply (as reported by *The Retail Bulletin* 2012) 64% of smartphone consumers use mobile devices to shop online, a fourfold increase since 2010). For research regarding the explosion of mobile social media, see Redsicker (2013). In subsequent chapters, we will discuss many mobile applications. Here we present the basic definitions, technologies, and a few examples.

Mobile Social Networking

Mobile commerce is spreading very rapidly in social media and social commerce applications (Redsicker 2013).

Mobile social networking refers to social networking where members chat and connect with one another using any mobile device. Most major social networking websites now offer mobile services. By Q1 2014, Facebook had over 1 billion mobile monthly active users out of a total 1.28 billion monthly active users (see **techcrunch.com/2014/04/23/facebook-passes-1b-mobile-monthly-active-users-in-q1-as-mobile-ads-reach-59-of-all-ad-sales**. Some social networking sites offer mobile-only services (e.g., **path.com** and **in-galaxy.com**).

Mobile social networking is especially popular in Japan, South Korea, and China, generally due to better data pricing (flat rates are widespread in Japan).The network can be only mobile or the site can offer both mobile and non mobile access. In Japan and South Korea, where 4G networks offer more bandwidth, the leaders in social networking are **mixi.jp** and game-centric Mobage by DeNa (**mbga.jp**) in Japan, and **cyworld.com** in South Korea. For an infographic of 2013 mobile growth statistics, see **digitalbuzzblog.com/infographic-2013-mobile-growth-statistics**.

Experts predict that mobile social networks will experience explosive growth, as evidenced since 2012. For how social platforms are powering mobile commerce, see Gupta (2011). For opportunities of mobile social networks see Wu and Wang (2014).

Video Sharing

Mobile video sharing, which sometimes is combined with photo sharing, is a relatively new technological and social trend. Mobile video-sharing portals are becoming popular (e.g., see **vimeo.com**). Many social networking sites offer video sharing features (e.g., see **mfubo.com**).

Examples of Social Mobile Commerce Applications

There are several types of social mobile applications. Illustrative examples are provided next.

Example 1

IBM is a leader in social commerce adoption of mobile devices. Following are some examples of IBM's initiatives according to Taft (2011):

- **IBM Mobile Connect**. This is a mobile version of IBM Connections (formerly Lotus Connections; social media and social networks building software). Customers can get immediate access to blogs, wikis, and other tools. They can also share photos, videos, and files on major mobile devices (e.g., Android, Blackberry, Apple).
- IBM Connections allows people to create business value. For example, employees can use the Ideation Blog to generate and vote on ideas at work (see **ibm.com/connections/blogs/SametimeBlog/?lang=en**).
- The new capabilities in IBM Connections 4.5, such as the Moderation application, or Ideation Blogs, enable workers to embrace networks of engaged people.

Example 2

A poll conducted by TravelClick in October 2011 revealed that half of the participating hoteliers around the globe are investing in mobile technologies to support social commerce (see **bizreport.com/2011/10/travelclick-hotels-to-invest-more-in-mobile-social-marketing.html**).

With the current technology, we also see a trend toward the sophisticated mobile interactions of Internet social networks with images, voice, and videos. This is expected to be a powerful managerial and marketing feature in the near future.

Experts predict that mobile access to social networks will experience explosive growth. For the connection between mobile computing and social media marketing, see Sanovy (2013).

Mobile Community Activities

In many mobile social networks, users can utilize their mobile devices to create their profiles, make friends, create and participate in chat rooms, hold private conversations, and share photos, videos, and blogs. Some companies provide wireless features that allow their customers to build their own mobile community (e.g., using **sonopia.com**).

2.6 CROWDSOURCING AND CROWDFUNDING: AN INTRODUCTION

Crowdsourcing and crowdfunding are relatively new platforms for conducting social commerce.

Crowdsourcing

Crowdsourcing is a platform for using collective intelligence for conducting social decision support and other social commerce activities (see **crowdsourcing.org**). Crowdsourcing is usually managed over the Internet. Here we present the essentials of the technology. In Chap. 8 we present the applications that are based on this technology.

Definitions and Major Concepts

The term *crowd* refers to any group of people, (usually large one) such as a group of consumers, employees of a corporation, or members of a social network, who usually possess expertise, when used for crowdsourcing.

Crowdsourcing utilizes the wisdom of crowds to collectively execute tasks such as solving problems, innovating, or completing large projects by dividing the work among many people. The term was coined by Jeff Howe in a June 2006 *Wired* article (Howe 2008). In the crowdsourcing process, the initiator recruits a crowd (e.g., customers) to create content, accomplish a cumbersome task (e.g., additions to Wikipedia), or conducting research and development. This is based on the idea that many heads are better than one. The collective intelligence of large groups is assumed to be able to solve complex problems at low cost (see Sherman 2011; Brabham 2013).

The basic elements of crowdsourcing are illustrated in Fig. 2.2. Three elements are involved: the task(s) to be carried out, the *crowd*, which is used to work on the *task*, and the *tools and processes* used by the crowd to execute the task. These elements are connected by features related to the task(s) and the crowd (such as the composition or size of the crowd), the technologies used (such as idea generation and voting), and implementation issues such as incentives paid to the participants.

The Process of Crowdsourcing

Crowdsourcing can be viewed as a collective problem-solving or a work-sharing process and usually is conducted on the Web. In a typical example of crowdsourcing, problems are broadcasted either to a known crowd (e.g., employees or business partners) or to an *unknown* group of participants (e.g., expert problem solvers or consumers). The communication usually starts as an open call for solutions (see first step in Fig. 2.3). The members of the crowd are organized as online communities, and members submit individual solutions. The crowd may also discuss the solutions and may vote for a final short list. (The short list can be prioritized [e.g., ranked].) The final selection can be made by the crowd or by management (Fig. 2.3). The winning individuals in the crowd are compensated, either monetarily or with special recognition or acknowledgement of a job well done. In other cases, the only rewards may be the intellectual satisfaction.

Example

In 2008, Starbucks introduced My Starbucks Idea (**mystarbucksidea.force.com**), a social media site designed to solicit ideas and feedback from Starbucks' customers (see opening case in Chap. 1). The site was built around three key themes: 1) ideas are user generated, 2) users can vote to short list the submitted ideas, discussing them before and/or after the

vote, 3) company employees act as "idea partners,'" providing answers to questions and leading discussions.

The process is visible to the entire community. The members can see the status of each proposal.

Note that crowdsourcing focuses on innovation, creativity, and the problem-solving capabilities of a crowd organization. An overview of crowdsourcing is provided in videos about crowdsourcing at **youtube.com/watch?v=F0-UtNg3ots**, at **crowdsourcing.org**, and by Sherman (2011). Crowdsortium (**crowdsortium.org**) sees crowdsourcing as a network of specialists. These specialists have developed best practices for the industry.

Benefits of Crowdsourcing

The major perceived benefits of crowdsourcing include the following:

- Problems can be analyzed or solved at comparatively little cost. (Payment can be determined by the results; however, sometimes there is no monetary payment, just praise or accolades).
- Solutions can be reached quickly since many people work on the needed research. In addition, product designs may be expedited.
- The contributing crowd may reside within the organization, so talents may be discovered.
- By listening to the crowd, organizations gain first hand insight into their customers' (or employees') desires. There is built-in market research when the crowd is composed of customers.
- Crowdsourcing can tap into the global world of ideas. The crowd may include business partners, customers, academicians, etc.
- Customers tend to be more loyal if they participate in a company's problem solving process.

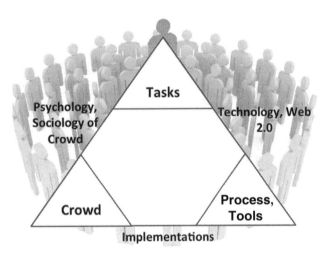

Fig. 2.2 The basic elements of crowdsourcing

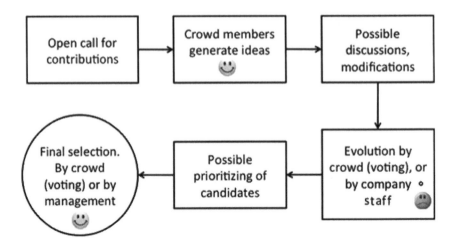

Fig. 2.3 A typical crowdsourcing process

Uses of Crowdsourcing in Social Commerce

There are several social commerce applications used in crowdsourcing—notable are idea generation, such as used by Starbucks and the creation of Wikipedia. Sherman (2011) presents many other successful applications; the major ones are described in Chap. 8.

Crowdfunding

Crowdfunding is an Internet platform for collecting small amounts of money from many individuals (a crowd). The money is collected for several possible purposes. Most common ones are:

- **Equity funding.** This is one way for funding start-ups. The contributors get shares of the company. For an overview see Lennon (2014). The recipient of the funds can get an idea off the ground very quickly (see examples in Chap. 8). Equity funding is done by intermediaries such as Kickstarter.
- **Rewards crowdfunding.** According to **en.wikipedia. org/wiki/crowdfunding**: "entrepreneurs pre-sell a product or service to launch a business concept without incurring debt or sacrificing equity/shares."
- **Contribution to a cause.** People raise money as a philanthropy activity for individuals in need and for civic projects.

For further discussion, examples of application see Chap. 8 and the Wikipedia entry.

2.7 VIRTUAL WORLDS AS A SOCIAL COMMERCE PLATFORM

A **virtual world** is a site for online communities situated in a computer-generated setting, where users socialize and work with one another through the use of avatars. Objects, jobs, homes, and businesses are created in a 3D environment, and are owned by the residents. It is an interactive environment, which is fun and satisfying. Virtual worlds (also referred to as *digital worlds* or *metaverse*), usually structured as interactive 3D virtual environments, and are created for users to inhabit and interact. Users feel as if they are actually within the environment because they have the ability to control certain features of the virtual world. Virtual worlds, according to Wikipedia, initially appeared in massively multiplayer online games; however, they are not limited to games. Players can create a character that travels between buildings, towns, and even planets and stars, as well as conduct activities there. In a virtual world, you can be anyone you want. You can build a dream house, decorate it, have a

job, or fly a spaceship. For a comprehensive overview, see Malaby (2009). For research issues see Wasko et al. 2011. To learn more about Seconds Life, see **wiki.secondlife.com/ wiki/Video_Tutorials**, and the video titled "Philip Rosedale: Seconds Life, Where Anything Is Possible" (28:31 minutes) at **youtube.com/watch?v=lHXXsEtE3b4**.

Major Features

There are several different types and purposes of virtual worlds; however all share the following features (compiled from The Virtual Policy Network's 'A Virtual Worlds Primer' (**virtualpolicy.net/resources/virtual-worlds-primer**), and the authors' experiences:

- The worlds can be used by many users who access them via an online interface.
- The interface is mostly 3D, which is more engaging than 2D.
- All interactions are in real time from anywhere.
- Most of the content is user-generated. It is facilitated by tools provided on the sites.
- The virtual world is always in motion, regardless of the presence of its residents.
- Socialization is encouraged. Tools are provided for engagement and for creating groups and socially-oriented activities.
- Communication among users can include text, graphical icons, visual gestures, video clips, sound, and so forth.
- Use of avatars is a common way to represent the residents of the virtual worlds.

Avatars

Residents of virtual worlds can represent themselves by 2D or 3D images known as avatars. **Avatars** are interactive, animated, computerized characters that are graphical images designed to look like people and are programmed to exhibit human behavior. Avatars have unique names and can move around. Advanced avatars can "speak" and display behaviors such as emotions, gestures, and facial expressions. They can be fully automated to act like robots. Avatars are designed to gain the trust of users. Many companies use avatars as tour guides or to staff virtual reception desks. For a demonstration of avatars in action, see **meez.com**.

The purpose of avatars is to make the human–computer interface more realistic. Thus, they are sometimes referred to as interactive *conversational characters*. They are being used extensively to support users' Internet chat with companies (e.g., Live Chat), representing the company's employees or "help desk." A popular use is the live chat with avatars. You ask questions and the avatar, using natural language processing, attempts to understand your questions. The avatar then matches an answer from a database to each question. For an example, see "Ted" at TD Ameritrade (**tdameritrade.com**). Instant-messaging programs such as **google.com/hangouts** use avatars (e.g., see **hangoutapps. com**). Avatars can improve customer satisfaction and retention by offering personalized, one-to-one service. They also can help companies get to know their customers in order to better design promotions. For more on avatars, you must see the 2009 movie *Avatar*.

Example 1: Jetstar Airline

According to *Business Wire* (2013), Nuance Communications, Inc. announced that Jetstar "has launched a new virtual assistant called 'Ask Jess,' which is based on Nuance Nina Web, an intelligent virtual assistant that delivers a human-like, conversational customer service experience. Customers simply type their request to Jess, and Jess provides the answers. The new Ask Jess virtual assistant draws on Nuance Nina, an intelligent virtual assistant that leverages innovative technology for natural language understanding and delivers a conversational interface to Web visitors which stimulates human conversation. By understanding what customers want, Ask Jess makes getting information on booking, baggage, and seating easier than navigating pages on a website. Jetstar's 'Ask Jess' virtual assistant is also fully integrated with the company's existing live chat service." (To ask Jess a question, see **jetstar.com/au/en/customer-service**.)

Example 2: Market Research

Starwood Hotels constructed a prototype of its Aloft brand hotels before they were built in 2008. People using Seconds Life were asked to view the prototype and give the company their opinions on the model. Using the feedback, the company completed the design and built the hotels.

Example 3

Avatars guide and advise passengers in airports. As of 2012, you can see human-sized avatars acting as greeters in many airports in Europe (e.g., Paris) and the U.S. (New York), that are there to help passengers by giving them information about ground transportation, etc. (see **abcnews.go.com/ Travel/york-airports-introduce-avatars-assist-passengers/ story?id=16957584**). For a demonstration of the avatars in the New York airports, watch WNYC's video titled "Airport Avatar Demonstration" (47 sec.) at **youtube.com/ watch?v=tI3YBf36twk**. Advanced avatars can conduct vocal conversations with passengers (sometimes in several languages). Similar avatars act as guides in some companies, universities, and tourist attractions. New York airports are developing interactive avatars that allow customers to ask questions about the airport (see **digitaltrends.com/cool- tech/new-york-airports-are-installing-virtual-avatars- to-help-visitors**).

Virtual Shopping

You can go shopping with friends while each shopper is located at his or her individual home. You enter a virtual store in the virtual mall and find jeans on sale. Your avatar tries on the jeans (the avatar's body's size is the same as yours) and displays it to your friends. They provide an assessment. Then, if you like it, you may buy the pants online or visit the physical store later. Virtual shopping is gaining popularity (see Chap. 6).

SUMMARY

In this chapter, you learned about the following SC issues as they relate to the chapter's learning objectives.

1. **Define the landscape of social media.** Social media is composed of three parts. First, there are Web 2.0 tools, such as blogs or mashups. In addition, there are applications that act in a similar fashion to the tools, enabling different activities. Seconds, there are social network sites and services, notably Facebook and LinkedIn. They are equipped with the tools and apps. In this seconds category, we also find social networks that enable users to conduct many activities, including media sharing (such as YouTube), or support communication (such as Twitter). The third category is the activities people conduct with the help of social media and its tools, such as sharing, interacting, recommending products, and connecting with people.

   The previously noted parts are interconnected via networks of people, organizations, technology, and society.

2. **Web 2.0 characteristics.** Web 2.0, the seconds generation of the Web, is based on social computing. It is all about people and their interactions and relationships. A major characteristic is the generation of content by users and for users. These users are engaged in many activities that increase trust and loyalty. Web 2.0 also enables the wisdom of crowds and several other business models. Notable activities are reviews and recommendations, as well as the ability to post questions and get answers from friends and other people. The many characteristics enable the creation of online communities where people with similar or shared interests can congregate and act. Web

2.0 operates in an open source technological environment, and it is flexible and inexpensive, or completely free.

3. **The major social media tools.** Blogs and wikis are probably the most mature tools of social media. Other well-known tools are microblogging, file sharing, idea generation (ideation), social search engines, recommendation engines, and voting (polling) tools. Web 2.0 tools can be combined (e.g., via mashups), and are embedded in many social networks. They are also used extensively inside enterprises (e.g., blogs in a company's portal).

4. **Social networks.** Social networks are websites for large Internet communities. The networks enable sharing of content including text, videos, voice, and photos. Social networks promote online socialization and interaction. Many thousands of networks are popping up around the world, some of which are global. These social networks compete for advertising money. Millions of corporations advertise, entertain, and even sell on social networks.

Business-oriented communities concentrate on business issues, either in only one country or worldwide (e.g., conducting recruiting, finding business partners). Social marketplaces meld social networks and some aspects of business. Notable business-oriented social networks are LinkedIn and XING. Some companies use their own private social networks, whereas others conduct business in public social networks, such as Facebook. Enterprise social networks are those owned and operated inside one company. Their members usually are present and former employees. Business networks are used mainly for collaboration, recruiting, personal networking, knowledge creation preservation and sharing, training, and socialization. Many large companies have such networks (e.g., IBM, Wells Fargo, Starbucks, Coca-Cola, and Disney).

5. **Mobile social commerce.** Many users of social networks are also users of wireless technologies. Therefore, conducting business as mobile commerce is exploding in social networks and in mobile applications in the enterprise. In addition, there is an explosive growth in social entertainment and gaming, part of which is commercial. All major social networks enable wireless activities. In fact, some social business models (notably location-based services) are delivered mostly wirelessly. Social and business connections can be made in real time or close to it (e.g., via Twitter).

6. **Crowdsourcing.** Crowdsourcing is a process of outsourcing work, including problem solving to large communities (a crowd). The community members can be chosen based on the nature of the tasks to be performed. The technology is used for idea-generation, performing large tasks, social collaboration, and facilitating engagement. It is considered a social commerce activity because certain applications, such as team problem solving, and crowdfunding involve social interactions. Crowdfunding involves raising small amounts of money from a group of individuals for purposes such as funding a start-up company or contributing to a cause. Crowdfunding is usually done on the Internet.

7. **Virtual worlds.** Virtual worlds provide entertainment and education through trading virtual properties, discussion groups, learning, training, and much more. Everything in a virtual world is simulated, animated, and supported by avatars. Starting with playing 3D games, people can create imaginary worlds where they can do almost anything they like. They can build virtual houses, cities, schools, or factories, and then do almost anything they can imagine there. Thousands of companies have established presences in virtual worlds, especially in Seconds Life, which also offers dissemination of information and advertising.

KEY TERMS

Avatars	39
Blog	
Business-oriented social networks	35
Crowdfunding	39
Crowdsourcing	37
Microblogging	31
Mobile social networking	36
Social media marketing (SMM)	28
Social networks	35
Social network sites	35
Social network services (SNSs)	33
Social networking	34
Social software	30
Software application (app)	28
Tweet	31
Twitter	31
User-generated content (UGC)	29
Virtual world	39
Video blog (vlog)	30
Wiki (wikilog)	32

REVIEW QUESTIONS

1. What is social media?
2. What are the three major components of social media?
3. Snapchat is a very popular photo sharing application. Compare its capabilities to those of Instagram. Comment on why it is so popular (start by reading Leahey 2013).
4. Describe user-generated content. What is its importance?
5. List five major Web 2.0 tools.
6. View IBM's video "IBM Customer Testimonial: Wakefern Foods Uses Social Business Tools to Activate

Their Workforce" at **youtube.com/watch?v=tI3YBf36 twk**. Identify the social business tools used by the company.

7. Define social networks as compared to social network services (sites).

8. Describe the major capabilities of social network sites.

9. What is an enterprise social network? List some of its major capabilities.

10. What are the critical features that distinguish a blog from a user-produced regular Web page?

11. Define crowdsourcing (see Howe 2008).

12. List the elements of crowdsourcing and describe the process.

13. What are the benefits of crowdsourcing?

14. What is social mobile networking?

15. Describe the major types of crowdfunding.

16. Define virtual worlds and list their characteristics.

17. Describe avatars. What are they used for?

TOPICS FOR DISCUSSION AND DEBATES

1. Discuss the differences between a wiki and a blog. Are there any similarities?

2. Discuss how wikis, blogs, forums, social networks, crowdsourcing, and virtual worlds can be used to facilitate collaboration.

3. Discuss some reasons why Twitter is so popular.

4. What are the major differences between physical and virtual communities?

5. How do business-oriented networks differ from regular social networks such as Facebook?

6. What are the major characteristics of Web 2.0? What are some of the advantages of using Web 2.0 applications?

7. Debate: Blogs and wikis are going to eliminate e-mail. Yes or no?

8. Compare Twitter, Tumblr, and Plurk.

9. What type of social network is Quora (**quora.com**)? Is Keek (**keek.com**) considered a video-based social network? Compare it to YouTube.

10. It is said that social media and mobile computing facilitate each other. Discuss.

11. What are the social elements of crowdsourcing?

12. Is Google+ a social rival to Facebook? (Start by reading **readwrite.com/2013/07/18/watch-out-facebook-why-google-and-pinterest-are-gaining-as-social-rivals**). Debate the issue.

13. Discuss the differences and similarities between crowdfunding and person-to-person money lending (Chap. 8).

14. Read "Social Media 101" at **socialquick.com/content/1-why_social_media_marketing** and discuss the major areas of activities. Prepare a report.

INTERNET EXERCISES

1. Enter **google.com** and find the services offered to bloggers by software vendors (e.g., look for Blogger.com). Write a report.

2. Enter **anshechung.com** and see Saenz (2011) and prepare a report on Anshe Chung's empire.

3. Enter *Web 2.0 Journal* at **web2.sys-con.com** and find recent material on wikis, blogs, and Twitter. Write a report.
   (a) Find out what any three companies are doing on the site.
   (b) Choose two universities and find out what they are doing on Seconds Life.
   (c) Write a report.

4. Register at **secondlife.com** and enter the site.

5. Enter **socialmediatoday.com**. Find five articles or blog posts related to one topic of this chapter. Write a summary.

6. Enter **communityroundtable.com**. Make a list of activities conducted there that are related to the content of this chapter. Describe what you see there.

7. Enter **paperbackswap.com**. What kind of a community is it? Who can use it? Why?

8. Enter **sunzu.com**. What kind of social network is it? Why?

9. Enter **scholarpedia.org**, **softpedia.com**, **webopedia.com**, and **investopedia.com**. Relate their attributes to social media.

10. Enter **metacafe.com**. What is offered at the site? What type of social media is used? Why?

11. Enter **facebook.com** and identify the different Web 2.0 tools available on the site.

12. Go to **kylelacy.com/25-case-studies-using-twitter-to-increase-business-and-sales**. Select five cases out of the 25 provided, and find additional information on each. Write a summary.

TEAM ASSIGNMENTS AND PROJECTS

1. **Assignments Related to the Opening Case**
   (a) Why is Pinterest considered a social network?
   (b) What are the company's business and revenue models?
   (c) How can manufacturers advertise on Pinterest?
   (d) Compare and contrast Pinterest and We Heart It. Pay attention to the business models.
   (e) Pinterest has a large amount of money. How does it use this money on its website to increase its competitive advantage?

2. Watch the video "Online Communities: The Tribalization of Business (Part 1)" (6:15 minutes); (Parts 2 and 3 are optional), at **youtube.com/watch?v=qQJvKyytMXU** and answer the following questions:

(a) Why is the term *tribalization* used?

(b) What are virtual communities?

(c) How can traditional businesses benefit from online communities?

(d) What is the value of communities for the customers?

(e) Compare social vs. marketing frameworks.

(f) How are virtual communities aligned with businesses?

(g) Discuss the issues of measurements, metrics, and CSFs in social networks.

3. The teams concentrate on new tools and apps that can support social commerce. Start with **whatsapp.com**, **snapchat.com**, **hshtags.com**, **wechat.com/en**, and **plus.google.com/hangouts**. Describe the support they can provide. Give presentations to the class.

4. Conduct a comparative analysis of three to five major microblogging sites (e.g., **twitter.com**, **tumblr.com**) revenue models, growth rates, and competitive features. Each group can concentrate on one topic, or on one company.

5. Enter **socialmedia.org**, **ecommercetimes.com**, **socialmediatoday.com**, and similar sites and find ten case studies regarding business applications of social commerce technologies. Distribute the ten cases to team members and search for more information on each case. Write a report.

6. What is social bookmarking? How it can be used? How can it facilitate social networking?

REFERENCES

Aral, S., C. Dellarocas, and D. Godes "Social Media and Business Transformation: A Framework for Research." *Information Systems Research*, 3-13, March 2013.

Bennett, S., *140 Twitter Marketing Power Tips: How to get More Followers, Generate Leads and Grow Your Business with Twitter*, Seattle, WA: Shea Bennett Pub., 2014.

Brabham, D. C. *Crowdsourcing*. Cambridge, MA: The MIT Press, 2013.

Brave, S. "Pinterest, We've Got a Business Model for You." March 24, 2012. **gigaom.com/2012/03/24/pinterest-weve-got-a-business-model-for-you** (accessed January 2015).

Business Wire. "Jetstar Selects Nuance's Nina Web for 'Ask Jess' Virtual Assistant." December 16, 2013. **businesswire.com/news/home/20131216005468/en/Jetstar-Selects-Nuance's-Nina-Web-"Ask-Jess"#.VAB-TfldWSo** (accessed January 2015).

Cario, J. E. *Pinterest Marketing: An Hours a Day*. Hoboken, NJ: Sybex, 2013.

Carr, K., *Pinterest for Dummies*. Hoboken, NJ: For Dummies, 2012.

Cockburn, S. "6 Easy Ways to Help People Find You Online." June 26, 2014. **growingsocialbiz.com/6-ways-to-make-it-easier-for-people-to-find-you-on-social-networks** (accessed January 2015).

Collier, M. *Facebook & Twitter for Seniors for Dummies*. Hoboken, NJ: For Dummies, 2014.

Dembosky, A. "Pinterest Takes New Tack with Advertising Launch." *Financial Times*, September 20, 2013.

Dessau, L. "What Twitter Can Do For Your Business Blog - Before You Even Tweet." September 3, 2013. **socialmediatoday.com/content/what-twitter-can-do-your-business-blog-you-even-tweet** (accessed January 2015).

Divol, R., D. Edelman, and H. Sarrazin. "Demystifying Social Media." *McKinsey Quarterly*, April 2012. **mckinsey.com/insights/marketing_sales/demystifying_social_media** (accessed January 2015).

Edwards, S. *Web 2.0 Guide - Tools and Strategy for the New Internet Wave* [Kindle Edition]. Seattle, WA: Amazon Digital Services, 2013.

Eitel B. "State of Social Media in 2015." Pew Research Center. January 9, 2015. **faniq.com/article/100003128** (accessed January 2015).

Engauge. "Pinterest: A Review of Social Media's Newest Sweetheart." (2012). **engauge.com/assets/pdf/Engauge-Pinterest.pdf** (accessed January 2015).

Frasco, S. "A Quick and Dirty Guide to Tumblr." September 4, 2013. **socialmediatoday.com/content/quick-and-dirty-guide-tumblr** (accessed January 2015).

Fitton, L., A. Hussain, and B. Leaning. *Twitter for Dummies*, 3rd ed., Hoboken, NJ: For Dummies, 2014.

Georgieva, M., *An Introduction to Pinterest for Business* (free e-book), **offers.hubspot.com/hs-fs/hub/53/file-291768926-pdf/offers/An_Introduction-To-Pinterest-for-Business.pdf** (accessed January 2015).

Green, M. "How to Use Pinterest for Business." November 16, 2013. **socialmediafuze.com/introduction-pinterest-for-business** (accessed January 2015).

Greer, R. *Pinterest Marketing Made Easy*, [Kindle Edition]. Seattle, WA: Amazon Digital Services, 2013.

Gupta, A. "How Social Platforms Are Powering Mobile Commerce." September 1, 2011.**socialmediatoday.com/content/how-social-platforms-are-powering-mobile-commerce** (accessed January 2015).

Hayden, B. *Pinfluence: The Complete Guide to Marketing your Business with Pinterest*. Hoboken, NJ: Wiley, 2012.

Hemley, D. "26 Tips for Using Pinterest for Business." February 27, 2012. **socialmediaexaminer.com/26-tips-for-using-pinterest-for-business** (accessed January 2015).

Hempel, J. "Is Pinterest the Next Facebook?" March 22, 2012. **fortune.com/2012/03/22/is-pinterest-the-next-facebook** (accessed January 2015).

Hornor, T. "Pinterest Legal Concerns: What is Lawful to Pin?" June 26, 2012. **socialmediatoday.com/content/pinterest-legal-concerns-what-lawful-pin** (accessed January 2015).

Howe, J. *Crowdsourcing: Why the Power of the Crowd Is Driving the Future of Business*. New York: Crown Business, 2008.

Hutchinson, A. "What Becomes of Facebook in 2014?" December 28, 2013. **socialmediatoday.com/content/what-becomes-facebook-2014** (accessed January 2015).

Jopson, B., and H. Kuchler. "Retailers Pin Festive Hopes on Pinterest." *Financial Times*, November 26, 2013.

Kaplan, A. M., and M. Haenlein."Users of the World, Unite! The Challenges and Opportunities of Social Media." *Business Horizons*, vol. 53, no. 1, 59-68, 2010.

Kawasaki, G., and P. Fitzpatrick. *The Art of Social Media: Tips for Power Users*. New York, NY: Portfolio Hardcover, 2014.

Kietzmann, J. H., K. Hermkens, I. P. McCarthy, and B. S. Silvestre. "Social Media? Get Serious! Understanding the Functional Building Blocks of Social Media." *Business Horizons*, vol. 54(3), 241, May-June 2011.

Knoblauch, M. "Millennials Trust User-Generated Content 50% More Than Other Media." April 9, 2014. **mashable.com/2014/04/09/millennials-user-generated-media** (accessed January 2015).

Leland, K. *Ultimate Guide to Pinterest for Business (Ultimate Series)*. Irvine, CA: Entrepreneur Press, 2013.

Leahey, C. "The Real Reason Why Millennials Love Snapchat." December 23, 2013. **fortune.com/2013/12/23/the-real-reason-why-millennials-love-snapchat** (accessed January 2015).

Leaning, B. "How to Optimize and Measure your Pinterest Business Account." 2013. **cdn1.hubspot.com/hub/53/Guide_To_Pinterests_New_Business_Accounts_Final.pdf** (accessed January 2015).

Lennon, P. *The Crowdfunding Book: A How-to Book for Entrepreneurs, Writers and Investors*, Seattle, WA: Difference Press, 2014.

Loren, J., and E. Swiderski. *Pinterest for Business: How to Pin Your Company to the Top of the Hottest Social Media Network (Que Biz-Tech Series)*. Indianapolis, IN: Que Publishing, 2012.

Luttrell, R. *Social Media*. New York, NY: Rowman and Littlefield Pub., 2014.

Macarthy, A. *500 Social Media Marketing Tips*. UK: CreateSpace Independent Publishing Platform, 2013.

MacMillan, D. "Pinterest CEO Lays Out Growth Plan, Sees Revenue in 2014." *The Wall Street Journal*, January 21, 2014.

MacNeil, L. *Pinterest Ultimate Guide: How to use Pinterest for Business and Social Media Marketing [Pinterest Guide, Pinterest for Business], (Pinterest Marketing, Pinterest Tutorial, Social Media Marketing)*, [Kindle Edition]. Seattle, WA: Amazon Digital Services, 2014.

Malaby, T. *Making Virtual Worlds: Linden Lab and Seconds Life*. New York: Cornell University Press, 2009.

McKenzie, H. "Here's a Social Shopping Site that Could Undermine Pinterest." May 22, 2012. **pando.com/2012/05/22/heres-a-social-shopping-site-that-could-undermine-pinterest** (accessed January 2015).

Media, F. R., *Social Media Marketing Successfully for Beginners: Create Successful Campaigns, Gain More Fans and Boost Sales from Any Social Network (Social Media Series... Marketing, Instagram, Youtube, Marketing)*, [Kindle Edition], Seattle, WA: Amazon Digital Services, 2014.

Meyer, M. "Google Plus versus Facebook?" [Infographic] September 5, 2013. **socialmediatoday.com/content/google-plus-versus-facebook-infographic** (accessed January 2015).

Miles, J., and K. Lacey. *Pinterest Power: Market Your Business, Sell Your Product and Build Your Brand on the World's Hottest Social Network*. New York: McGraw Hill, 2013.

Mitroff, S. "How Zappos Could Help Pinterest Pin Down a Business Model." August 30, 2012. **wired.com/2012/08/pinterest** (accessed January 2015).

Murdoch, R. *Blogging Business: The Ultimate Guide to Building a Successful Blogging Business (Blogging, Blogging for Profits, Blogging for Business)*, [Kindle Edition]. Seattle, WA: Amazon Digital Services, 2014.

Murugesan, S. *Handbook of Research on Web 2.0, 3.0 and X.0: Technologies, Business, and Social Applications (Advances in E-Business Research Series (AEBR) Book Series)*. Hershey, PA: Information Science Reference, 2010.

Petersen, R. *166 Case Studies Prove Social Media Marketing ROI*, free e-Book and Infographic. 2011. **barnraisersllc.com/2012/07/166-case-studies-prove-social-media-marketing-roi-free-ebook** (accessed January 2015).

Petroff, A. "Want to Chat in 29 Languages?" January 2, 2014. **money.cnn.com/2014/01/02/technology/translation-service-app** (accessed January 2015).

Pring, C. "103 Crazy Social Media Statistics to Kick off 2014." December 5, 2013. **thesocialskinny.com/103-crazy-social-media-statistics-to-kick-off-2014** (accessed January 2015).

Redsicker, P. "Mobile Social Media Exploding According to New Research." December 3, 2013. **socialmediaexaminer.com/mobile-social-media-trends-research** (accessed January 2015).

Rich, J. R. *Start Your Own Blogging Business (StartUp Series)*. Irvine, CA: Entrepreneur Press, 2014.

Saenz, A. "Entrepreneur Anshe Chung Makes a Fortune Selling Virtual Land, Banking and Fashion." August 23, 2011. **singularityhub.com/2011/08/23/entrepreneur-anshe-chung-makes-millions-selling-virtual-land-banking-and-fashion** (accessed January 2015).

Safko, L. *The Social Media Bible: Tactics, Tools and Strategies for Business Success*, 3rd ed. Hoboken, NJ: Wiley, 2012.

Sanovy, L. "Social Media Marketing Is Boosting Mobile Commerce." July 29, 2013. **mobilecommercepress.com/social-media-marketing-is-boosting-mobile-commerce** (accessed January 2015).

Sartain, J. D. "Global Mobile Data Traffic to Surpass 15 Exabytes by Per Month by 2018." *CIO*, March 27, 2014.

Schaefer, M. W., and S. Smith. *Born to Blog: Building Your Blog for Personal and Business Success One Post at a Time*, New York: McGraw-Hill, 2013.

Schaefer, M. W. *Social Media Explained: Untangling the World's Most Misunderstood Business Trend*, New York: Mark W. Schaefer Pub., 2014a.

Schaefer, M. W. *The Tao of Twitter*, 2nd edition. New York: McGraw-Hill, 2014b.

Sherman, A. *The Complete Idiot's Guide to Crowdsourcing*. New York: Alpha, 2011.

Shontell, A. "A Lawyer Who Is Also a Photographer Just Deleted All Her Pinterest Boards Out of Fear." February 28, 2012. **business insider.com/pinterest-copyright-issues-lawyer-2012-2** (accessed January 2015).

Smith, C. "By the Numbers: 120 Amazing Pinterest Statistics." August 16, 2014a (updated periodically). **expandedramblings.com/index.php/pinterest-stats/** (accessed January 2015).

Smith, C. "By the Numbers: 250 Amazing Twitter Statistics." Periodical updating, last: October 29, 2014b. **expandedrambling.com/index.php/march-2013-by-the-numbers-a-few-amazing-twitter-stats** (accessed January 2015).

Stone, G. "Pinterest Adds "Do-It-Yourself Advertising to Promoted Pins: Brands Test New Tools." *Ad Week*, June 5, 2014.

Taft, D. K. "Enterprise Mobility: 10 Ways IBM Is Pushing Social Business Adoption on Mobile Devices." *eWeek*, September 2, 2011.

Tech2 News Staff. "App Updates This Week: IFTTT for Android, Hangouts, Truecaller, WeChat and More!" April 25, 2014. **tech.firstpost.com/news-analysis/app-updates-this-week-ifttt-for-android-hangouts-truecaller-wechat-and-more-222528.html** (accessed January 2015).

The Retail Bulletin. "M-Commerce Quadruples in Two Years." May 24, 2012. **theretailbulletin.com/news/mcommerce_quadruples_in_two_years_24-05-12/** (accessed January 2015).

Tommasi, M. "50 Definitions of Social Media." January 9, 2011. **slideshare.net/datasift/follow-the-content** (accessed January 2015).

Van Belleghem, S., M. Eenhuizen, and E. Veris. "Social Media around the World 2011." Report and slide show, InSites Consulting, September 14, 2011. **slideshare.net/stevenvanbelleghem/social-media-around-the-world-2011** (accessed January 2015).

Vandermeersch, A. "Hashtags on Facebook: What Does It Mean for You?" June 21, 2013. **socialmediatoday.com/content/hashtags-facebook-what-does-it-mean-you** (accessed January 2015).

Van Dijck, J. *The Culture of Connectivity: A Critical History of Social Media*. Boston: Oxford University Press, 2013.

Volpe, M. "7 Examples of Brands that Pop on Pinterest." February 4, 2012. **socialmediatoday.com/content/7-examples-brands-pop-pinterest** (accessed January 2015).

Walker, S. *Social Media Marketing Tips: Essential Strategy Advice and Tips for Business: Facebook, Twitter, Google+, YouTube, LinkedIn,*

Instagram, and Much More! [Kindle Edition]. Seattle, WA: Amazon Digital Services, 2014.

Wallace, B. "Top Social Media Stats of 2013." [Infographic] December 27, 2013. **socialmediatoday.com/content/top-social-media-stats-2013-infographic** (accessed January 2015).

Wasko, M., R. Teigland, D. Leidner, and S. Jarvenpaa. "Stepping into the Internet: New Ventures in Virtual Worlds." *MIS Quarterly Special Issue*, 645-652, September 2011.

Waters, R. "Wikipedia: Fact and Friction." *Financial Times*, January 1, 2010.

Wildfire, Inc. "Measuring the Business Impact of Social Media." [Infographic] January 18, 2012. **wildfireapp.blogspot.com/2012/01/measuring-business-impact-of-social.html** (accessed January 2015).

Wu, J., and Y. Wang. *Opportunistic Mobile Social Networks*. Boca Raton, FL: CRC Press, 2014.

Yang, J. "Pinterest: How Does Pinterest Generate Revenue? What is the Company's Business Model?" 2012. **quora.com/Pinterest/How-does-Pinterest-generate-revenue-What-is-the-companys-business-model** (accessed January 2015).

Zeisser, M. "Unlocking the Elusive Potential of Social Networks." *McKinsey Quarterly*, June 2010. **mckinsey.com/insights/marketing_sales/unlocking_the_elusive_potential_of_social_networks** (accessed January 2015).

Supporting Theories and Concepts for Social Commerce

Contents

Opening Case: Netflix Increases Sales Using Movie
Recommendations by Customers 47

3.1   Learning About Online Consumer Behavior 49

3.2   The Consumer Purchasing-Decision Process 52

3.3   Personalization and Behavioral Marketing 55

3.4   Word-of-Mouth in Social Commerce 57

3.5   Consumer Engagement in Social Commerce 60

3.6   Social Psychology Theories, Social Network
Analysis, and the Social Graph 63

3.7   Social Influence, Social Capital, and Social Support 66

References 70

Learning Objectives

Upon completion of this chapter, you will be able to:

1. Describe the factors that influence online consumer behavior.
2. Understand the decision-making process of online consumer shopping.
3. Explain how consumer behavior can be analyzed for creating personalized services.
4. Describe online word of mouth and its benefits.
5. Define online engagement and describe its influence on social trust, loyalty, and satisfaction.
6. Describe social psychology theories relevant to social commerce, social network analysis, and the social graph.
7. Describe social influence, social capital, and social support.

OPENING CASE: NETFLIX INCREASES SALES USING MOVIE RECOMMENDATIONS BY CUSTOMERS

Netflix (**netflix.com**) is the world's largest online movie and TV show (streaming library) rental company, with more than 57 million paid subscribers worldwide (Q4 2014). Netflix's customers receive DVDs either by mail from an extensive selection or by streaming media (of selected titles) over the Internet to PCs, tablets, smartphones and TVs, allowing consumers to watch them immediately. Netflix also offers original series (e.g. *House of Cards*, *Orange is the New Black*), which are very successful. Among the ever-expanding base of devices compatible for streaming, Netflix includes game consoles (e.g., Microsoft's Xbox 360, Nintendo's Wii, and Sony's PS3 and PS4); Blu-ray disc players; HD TVs; Apple's TV, iPhone, and iPad; set top boxes (e.g., Roku); and handheld devices (e.g., Amazon's Kindle, Barnes & Noble's

Electronic supplementary material The online version of this chapter (doi:10.1007/978-3-319-17028-2_3) contains supplementary material, which is available to authorized users.

Nook). In all, more than 200 devices can stream Netflix. The company's success is built on providing a large selection of DVDs, an easy to navigate catalog, recommendations of what to view based on users' taste preferences, and fast, free delivery. Netflix distributes millions of video programs each day. The growth history of Netflix is described by Gallaugher (2008) and Smith (2014).

The Problem

Because of the large number of available titles, customers often have difficulty deciding what they want to watch. Often, customers choose the most recent and popular titles, which means that Netflix has to stock many copies of the same title to send via postal mail. In addition, some less popular titles do not rent well, even though they could match many customers' preferences. For Netflix, it is critical to best match titles with customers' profiles, yet maintain a reasonable level of DVD inventory.

A seconds major problem facing Netflix is the competitive nature of the movie rental business (e.g., see **us-dvd-rental-websites.no1reviews.com**). Netflix competes against several online rental companies (e.g., Café DVD), as well as against companies such as Amazon Instant Video and Hulu and Hulu Plus that offer movies, TV shows, and videos to download and watch instantly. DVD rentals, at prices as low as $1/day (e.g. Redbox), are also being offered from kiosks located at supermarkets and malls. In 2008, Blockbuster started offering online movie rental subscriptions, but shut down this service in 2013. In 2013, Blockbuster started a video streaming service called Blockbuster On Demand (**blockbusternow.com**), offering thousands of movies available on devices such as PCs, tablets, and Roku. (Blockbuster closed its physical stores in 2013.) Other online content providers such as Apple iTunes, the television broadcast companies, and Google Play have also become direct competitors. HBO is planning a streaming service in 2015, but Netflix believes that both companies will prosper since they have different shows; however, according to Morgan Stanley, increased competition from Amazon, Hulu, and HBO GO "could take away Netflix's ability to grow its subscriber base in 2014" (see **forbes.com/sites/maggiemcgrath/2014/01/07/amazon-and-hulu-could-slow-netflix-growth-in-2014-morgan-stanley-says**). Another issue is that there is a clear trend for more and more viewers to watch videos online (some for free). Hence, in 2008, Netflix decided to bring a "watch instantly" service to attract Internet subscribers. Netflix wants to rid itself of the DVD business since online streaming has no shipping costs. Redbox started an online streaming service, but it was not successful.

The Solution

Netflix reacted successfully to the issue of matching viewers and movies and the competitive pressure with a recommendation service that was called *Cinematch* (it is now referred to as "*recommendation algorithm*"). This service uses data mining tools to analyze more than three billion film ratings made by customers, as well as through histories of customers' rentals. Using proprietary algorithms, the system recommends to customers what titles to watch. It is a personalization service similar to the one offered by Amazon.com that recommends books to customers. The recommendation is accomplished by comparing an individual's preferences with people that have similar tastes, by using the *collaborative filtering* software (described later in this chapter).

For the accuracy of their matching algorithms, Netflix started a contest in October 2006, offering $1 million to the first person or team to write a computer program that would beat Cinematch's prediction accuracy by 10 %. The company understood that this would take quite some time; therefore, it offered a $50,000 Progress Prize each year the contest ran. After more than 2 years of competition, the grand prize of $1 million went to "BellKor's Pragmatic Chaos," a 7-member team. Netflix's recommendation system is constantly changing and improving. For example, in 2013, Netflix introduced "Max," a new personal recommendation system that talks back to the user (for use with PlayStation, but will roll out to other devices [e.g., iPad] in the future). For a description of "Max" and how it works, see **blog.netflix.com/2013/06/let-max-be-your-netflix-guide-on-ps3.html**.

Netflix subscribers can also invite one another to become "friends" and make movie recommendations directly to each other, view one another's rental lists, and share movies rating using a social network called *FriendsSM*. All of these personalized functions make the online rental store very customer friendly.

In March 2013, Netflix unveiled a sharing program called "Netflix Social." You can connect your Netflix account with Facebook to connect you with your friends that use Netflix. Social features include sending recommendations to Facebook friends, and sharing what you watch with them automatically. For information, see **slashgear.com/netflix-introduces-netflix-social-to-share-favorite-movies-and-shows-with-friends-13273705** and **help.netflix.com/en/node/464**. For a demonstration, see **blog.netflix.com/2013/03/introducing-netflix-social.html**. For comprehensive coverage, see O'Neill et al. (2014). In September 2014, Facebook and Netflix created a new, private recommendation system that allows users to recommend videos to friends without publicly posting on their wall.

The Result

Netflix has seen very fast growth in sales and membership. The benefits of the algorithms-based recommendation system include the following:

- **Effective recommendations.** Approximately 60 % of Netflix members select their movies based on one-to-one movie recommendations.
- **Customer satisfaction.** Before 2011, more than 90 % of Netflix members said they were fully satisfied with Netflix. Customer satisfaction dropped significantly in 2011 when Netflix hiked up their prices for instant streaming service and divided DVDs by mail in to a separate service. (Satisfaction picked up as of 2013.)
- **Finance.** Netflix has experienced a significant growth in membership and financial performance.
- **Ratings.** Netflix has more than 3.5 billion movie ratings from members in their database. (Each member has rated about 200 movies.)
- **Rental habits.** Members rent twice as many movies per month as they did prior to getting the recommendations. As a result, the rental queues (movies members want to rent) grew rapidly.
- According to the *Huffington Post*, 75 % of what people watch on Netflix comes from the site's recommendations (**huffingtonpost.com/2013/08/07/netflix-movie-suggestions_n_3720218.html**).

Netflix advertises extensively on the Web using several promotional techniques. Primarily, it places static banner ads on high-traffic sites, but it also uses permission-based e-mail marketing, blogs, social networks, classifieds, Really Simple Syndication (RSS) feeds, and more. The domain **netflix.com** attracted over 34 million unique visitors in October 2014, according to Compete.com (go to **siteanalytics.compete.com/netflix.com/#.VFao0vnF-So** for more information).

The recommendation system has become the company's core competency. Netflix's future depends heavily on this system making accurate recommendations and subscribers accepting them, which is why Netflix strives to increase the system's accuracy. For the science behind these algorithms, see Vanderbilt (2013).

Sources: Based on O'Neill et al. (2014), Vanderbilt (2013), Poggi (2013), Smith (2014), and **netflix.com** (accessed June 2015).

LESSONS LEARNED FROM T...

This case illustrates the use of the so... ence customers. In particular, Netfl... intelligent agents in its recommend... gain a substantial advantage over its competitors by making personalized movie recommendations to influence its members to rent DVDs that they might possibly like, based on previously viewed films. Netflix's recommendation algorithms are designed to increase customer satisfaction and loyalty. The algorithms use several theories to create recommendations; one is influencing consumer behavior via other customers' reviews and recommendations, another one is by checking what customers with similar profiles are ordering, and inferring from that data what a specific customer may like; and yet another is using a large number of reviewers to build a knowledge base and use it for an input to the recommendation algorithms.

Several consumer behaviors and other theories are related to social commerce. In this chapter, we will deal mainly with those relating to influencing people's buying decisions. These include consumer behavior models (generic), online consumer behavior, consumer behavior in social commerce, word of mouth, social psychology, online collaborative filtering, ratings, reviews and recommendations, social influence, social capital, and social support.

3.1 LEARNING ABOUT ONLINE CONSUMER BEHAVIOR

Companies are operating in an increasingly competitive environment: therefore, sellers must try to understand customers' needs and influence them to buy their products and services. Customer acquisition and retention are key success factors, both offline and online. This is particularly important for online businesses, as most interactions with their customers are online. For a summary of factors affecting consumer behavior, see **aipmm.com/html/newsletter/archives/000434.php**.

For a large collection of pins on online and offline consumer and buyer behavior, see **pinterest.com/thewebchef/consumer-behavior**. For a 2014 infographic showing online consumer shopping habits and behavior, see **business2community.com/infographics/online-consumer-shopping-habits-behavior-0952526**.

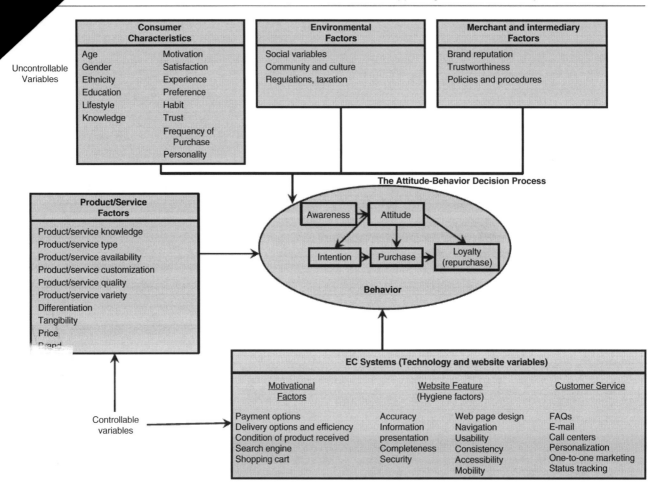

EC consumer behavior model

A Model of Consumer Behavior

For decades, market researchers have tried to understand consumer shopping behavior, and develop various models to summarize their findings.

Consumers can be divided into two groups: individual consumers and organizational buyers, including governments, private corporations, resellers, and nonprofit organizations. These two types of buyers tend to have different purchasing behaviors and usually are analyzed differently. In this chapter, we focus on individual buyers.

An individual consumer behavior model often includes *influential internal and external factors* that affect the buyer's *decision process* and the process for making a purchasing decision.

This section is divided into three parts: First, we introduce the generic topic of consumer behavior. Then, we move to online behavior, and finally, we present consumer behavior in the social commerce environment.

Figure 3.1 shows a consumer behavioral model, which is divided into the following two parts:

- **Influential factors**. Factors influencing purchasing decisions fall into five major dimensions. They are: *consumer characteristics, environmental factors, merchant and intermediary factors, product/service factors* (which include market stimuli), and *EC selling systems*. The first three dimensions are not controllable by the sellers, while the last two are mostly controlled by the sellers. The dimensions are shown in Fig. 3.1. The influential factors affect the buyers' decision process. (For more about factors that influence the online shopping experience, see **blog.profitero.com/competitor-monitoring-what-factors-influence-the-online-shopping-experience-comscore**, and Perreau 2013).

- **The attitude-behavior decision process**. The influential factors affect the buyers' decision process. The seconds part of a consumer behavior model is the decision-making process, which usually starts with an awareness of the situation and a positive attitude, and ends with the buyer's decision to purchase and/or repurchase (see the oval part in Fig. 3.1). A *favorable attitude* would lead to a stronger *buying intention*, which in turn would result in the *actual purchase and repurchase behavior*. Previous research has shown that the links between attitude, purchase intention, and actual purchase and repurchase behavior are quite strong.

The Major Influential Factors

Major influential factors of consumer purchasing behavior fall into the following categories:

Consumer Characteristics

Consumer (personal) characteristics, which are shown in the top-left portion of Fig. 3.1, refer to *demographic* factors, individual *preferences*, and *behavioral* characteristics (e.g., social psychological variables). Several websites provide information on online customer buying habits (e.g., **emarketer.com**, **clickz.com**, and **comscore.com**). The major demographics that such sites track are gender, age, marital status, race, educational level, and occupation (some are listed in Fig. 3.1), which can be correlated with Internet usage and SC data. For example, both males and females have been found to perceive market information differently, depending on their levels of purchase, confidence, and internal knowledge. Several studies show that shopping experience has a significant effect on consumer attitude and intention to purchase and repurchase online (e.g., Crespo and del Bosque 2010; Chiu et al. 2014).

Marketers also study psychological variables, such as personality and lifestyle characteristics. These variables are briefly mentioned in several places throughout this book. To read about the impact of lifestyle differences on online shopping, see Wang et al. (2006).

Merchant and Intermediary-Related Factors

Online transactions may also be affected by the merchant that provides the product/service. This group of factors includes merchant reputation, size of the transaction, trust in the merchant, and so on. For example, people generally feel more secure when they purchase from Amazon.com (due to its reputation) than from an unknown seller. Other factors such as marketing strategy and advertising can also play a major role.

Product/Services Factors

Another group of factors is related to the product/service itself. The consumer's decision to make a purchase is affected by the nature of the product/service in the transaction. These factors may include the price, appearance, quality, design, brand, and other related attributes of the product.

EC and/or Social Commerce Trading Systems

The EC (and SC) platforms for online transactions (e.g., security protection, payment mechanism, and so forth) offered by the merchant and the type of computing environment (e.g., mobile vs. desktop) may also have effects. EC design factors can be divided into payment and logistics support, website features, and consumer services. Liang and Lai (2002) classified them into *motivational* and *hygiene* factors and found motivational factors to be more important than hygiene factors in attracting online customers. Another factor that we include here is the type of EC. For example, consumer behavior in m-commerce may be unique and so is behavior during social shopping.

Motivational Factors
Motivational factors are functions available on the website to directly support the purchasing process (e.g., search engine, shopping carts, multiple payment methods).

Hygiene Factors
Hygiene factors are functions available on the website. Their objective is to make the website functional and serviceable (e.g., ease of navigation, show items added to the cart); their main purpose is to protect consumers from risks or unexpected events in the transaction process (e.g., security breaching and site technical failure).

Environmental Factors

The environment in which a transaction consumer's purchase decision. As show ronmental variables can be grouped i categories:

Social Variables
People are influenced by family members, friends, coworkers, and current styles. Therefore, social variables (such as customer recommendations, word of mouth) play an important role in SC. Of special importance in SC are social networks and discussion groups, where people communicate via chat rooms, electronic bulletin boards, tweeting, and newsgroups. A study by Liang et al. (2011/2012) shows that social support in online communities significantly enhances the intention to purchase online.

Cultural/Community Variables

The influence of culture on buying behavior varies between countries and regions (e.g., rural vs. urban areas). For example, the purchases made by consumers in California's Silicon Valley will likely be different from those made by individuals who live in the mountains in Nepal. Bashir (2013) conducted a comprehensive study about online shopping for electronics in Pakistan.

Other Environment Variables

These include aspects such as available public information, government regulations, legal constraints, and situational factors. For example, tax rates (Chap. 11) may affect online shopping (see Einav et al. 2014).

Note that this model may be somewhat different in the mobile environment. For information on mobile marketing, browse **mashable.com/category/mobile-marketing**.

We now turn to the process that buyers use while making product-purchasing decisions (the center of Fig. 3.1) and its relevant models.

3.2   THE CONSUMER PURCHASING-DECISION PROCESS

In Sect. 3.1 we described the factors influencing the consumer purchasing decision. Here, we describe the process of purchasing.

Several models were developed in an attempt to understand and explain the consumer's purchasing process decision. We will describe two major categories of these models. The first is a model developed from the perspective of managerial decision making. The seconds is a model developed from the marketing management perspective.

The purchasing decision process is another major element in analyzing consumer behavior. It is composed of several phases, as discussed next. A generic model is introduced below.

Generic Purchasing Decision-Making Phases: A Managerial Decision-Making Approach

From the consumer's perspective, a generic purchasing-decision model for decisions involving financial, social, or other factors (e.g., high involvement) consists of a sequential process of five major phases (Hawkins and Mothersbaugh 2012). In each phase, we can distinguish several activities and, in some, more than one decision. The five phases are (1) *need identification*, (2) *information search*, (3) *evaluation of alternatives*, (4) *purchase and delivery*, and (5) *post-purchase activities*. Although these phases offer a general guide to the consumer decision-making process, one should not assume that every consumer's decision-making process necessarily

proceeds in this order. In fact, some consumers may proceed to a specific decision point and then revert to a previous phase, or they may skip a phase altogether. The five phases are discussed next in more detail.

1. **Need identification.** The first phase in the purchasing process is for a customer to recognize a need. This occurs when a consumer is faced with a gap between the current state of what the customer has and the desired state (e.g., his mobile phone needs a useful new feature, such as a bigger screen). A consumer can recognize a need in different ways (e.g., by internal stimuli, hunger or thirst; or external stimuli, exposure to an advertisement). A marketer's goal is to get the consumer to recognize such a gap and then convince the consumer that the product or service the seller offers will fulfill the need.

2. **Information search.** Once the need has been recognized, the customer seeks information on how to fulfill that need. Here, we differentiate between two decisions: what product to buy (*product brokering*) and from whom to buy it (*merchant brokering*). These two decisions can be separate or combined. The consumer's search for information, catalogs, advertisements, promotions, and reference groups could influence decision making. During this phase, online product searches and comparison engines can be very helpful. See examples at **shopping.com**, **pricegrabber.com**, and **mysimon.com**, as well as discussions in some social networks.

3. **Evaluation of alternatives.** The information search usually yields a few feasible options. From these, the would-be buyer will further evaluate the alternatives and, if possible, negotiate terms. In this phase, a consumer needs to generate and rank criteria for making the final choice. For online consumers, the criteria may include product prices, payment terms, and product features.

4. **Purchase and delivery.** After evaluating the alternatives, the consumer will make the purchasing decision, arrange for payment and delivery, purchase warranties, and so on.

5. **Post-purchase activities.** The final phase in the process is a post-purchase phase, which consists of customer service and evaluation of the usefulness of the product. Customer service and consumer satisfaction will result in a positive experience and positive word of mouth and/or positive written reviews (e.g., "This product is really great!" or "We really received good

service when we ████████████████ ███ er is
satisfied with the ████████████████ will
increase, repeat ████████████████ customer will reco ████████████████ thers.
Alternatively, unsatisfied customers may disseminate negative word of mouth (see the discussion of
reputation management in Chap. 5).

For more about online consumer behavior, see van Bommel et al. (2014). For more related information, see Amo (2014). For online consumer behavior future trends see **corra.com/news/consumer-insights-on-what-drives-online-shopping**. Also, for consumer purchasing decision making see **slideshare.net/saphniemachado/consumer-behaviour-9852224**.

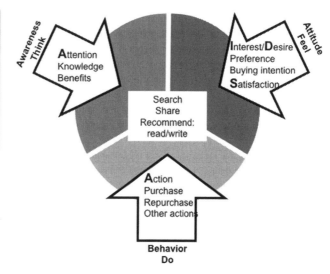

Fig. 3.2 Social commerce brand decision process

The Consumer Brand Decision-Making Process Models

Marketers often view the purchasing decision model as a three-phase process, which they use for designing marketing communication strategies and tactics. These phases are:

1. *Awareness* and knowledge of the product's features and benefits. This is a cognitive stage happening inside the consumer's mind.
2. *Attitude* about the product (positive or negative). This stage is about the consumer's feelings, such as liking, disliking, or preferring the product and post-purchase satisfaction level.
3. *Behavior* involves the consumer actually doing something, such as purchasing, repurchasing, writing an online product review, or visiting a website.

If the consumer forms a positive attitude, it may transform a *buying intention* into an actual purchase. Marketing research has shown that the linkages among these three phases are quite strong. Therefore, developing a positive consumer *attitude* about the product and website experience plays a central role in the final purchase decision.

This decision-making model, displayed in a circular fashion in Fig. 3.2, reflects the idea that consumers can begin activities at any point on the circle and not necessarily proceed in any regular order, as previously mentioned. The following sections describe two variations of this model.

The AIDA Model

The *Attention-Interest-Desire-Action (AIDA)* model describes a common set of events that may occur as a reaction to an advertisement. (Some add "S" for satisfaction, to form AIDAS.) The model is commonly used by advertisers to create messages that influence a buyer's awareness, attitude, or behavior (see **mindtools.com/pages/article/AIDA.htm** and **en.wikipedia.org/wiki/AIDA_(marketing)**). This model argues that consumer processing of an advertisement or other promotional message includes the following events or stages:

1. *A—Attention* (awareness). The first step is to get the customer's attention (e.g., be quick and direct; use powerful words or phrases to catch a customer's eye). This is done usually by advertising.
2. *I—Interest.* By demonstrating features, advantages, and benefits, the customer becomes interested in the product (e.g., engage the customers by getting them interested).
3. *D—Desire.* After evaluation, the consumer generates a desire to acquire the product or service (e.g., build the reader's interest and create a desire in them—a motivation to act).
4. *A—Action.* Finally, the consumer will take action toward purchasing (e.g., act on their desires and buy the product/service).
5. *S—Satisfaction.* Customer post-purchase satisfaction will generate higher loyalty and lead to repurchase after using a product/service.

A recent version of AIDA is the AISAS model proposed by the Dentsu Group, **dentsu.com/crossswitch/dictionary/index.html** that is tailored to online behavior. The model replaces *desire* with *search* and adds *share* to show the increased word-of-mouth effect on the Internet. It indicates that consumers go through a process of *Attention-Interest-Search-Action-Share* in their online decision process. The model, which is particularly suitable to social commerce, is described next.

Social Commerce Brand Decision Process

The Dentsu Group model is particularly suitable for social commerce, so we have integrated it into the appropriate areas in Fig. 3.2. The center of this model reflects actions particular to social commerce. Buyers use Google and other search engines during their information search and product evaluation stages. They share this information with others before, during, and after their purchase. Marketers make sharing easy by providing "like" buttons, comment boxes, and several other tactics (discussed throughout this book). Finally, consumers read and write recommendations on product review sites, social networks, and other online sites. For a video from Reevoo regarding these and other consumer SC shopping habits, titled "Consumer Research on Social Commerce" (3:06 minutes), see **vimeo.com/25357746**. For consumer behavior in social media, see Heinonen (2011).

Players in the Consumer Decision-Making Process

Several different people may play roles in various phases of the purchasing decision process. In B2B, they usually act as a team to make the buying decision(s). The following are five major roles:

1. **Initiator.** The person who recognizes and suggests the need to buy a specific product or service.
2. **Influencer.** A person who tries to convince other people to make a purchase.
3. **Decider.** The person who makes the final buying decision.
4. **Buyer.** The person who purchases the product or service and pays for it.
5. **User.** The customer who uses the product.

The roles apply both to the organizational and to the individual consumer buying process. For example, a recent college graduate (initiator, decider, and buyer) considered buying a car for his mother (user), and his father and friends (influencers) offered brand suggestions. Finally, he took his father's advice and purchased the car.

The sellers need to decide which of the roles is more important to be influenced and try to do it. Sellers should use the most beneficial role to influence the buyer based on each situation.

In social media, we can use a variation of these roles that include:

1. **Followers.** These are social media users (the majority) who seek advice from others and are influenced by the advice.
2. **Influencers.** These are people who have large networks of followers, or have reputations as being experts and fair (e.g., bloggers, review writers).
3. **Advocates.** These are usually loyal customers who are satisfied with certain products or services and are willing, when asked, to provide testimonials to this effect.

Example: Influencers at Sony

Dragon (2014) describes Sony's *Sony Club*, an annual program for recruiting successful bloggers to act as influencers. The selected bloggers need to have a natural affinity for the brand. The bloggers, who are not paid for their time (but are reimbursed for all expenses), attend a 3-day conference where they are provided with Sony products. After the conference, the bloggers share their experience and review the products.

Note

A study conducted in April 2013 by First Direct (**firstdirect.com**) found 12 social media personalities: the dippers, the ultras, the deniers, the virgins, the lurkers, the peacocks, the ranters, the changelings, the ghosts, the informers, the quizzers, and the approval seekers. For definitions of these and more details, see **newsroom.firstdirect.com/press/release/the_ranters_and_peacocks_-_new** and for a related infographic, see **cliveroach.tumblr.com/post/48414019461/12-personality-types-in-social-media-revealed**. See also "A New Breed of Social Media Personalities" at **pinterest.com/pin/16888567325374584**.

When more than one individual is involved in the buying process, it becomes more difficult to properly target social commerce marketing communications strategies. Different marketing efforts may be designed to target people who are playing different roles. This is especially true when those responsible for the buying decision in a business are considering purchasing online. Note that major enterprise purchases are being made by several users, influencers, buyers, and so on. In such cases, there is a group decision process.

Corporate Buyers' Behavior and the Players in the Buyer Decision Process

Buyers for businesses and governments are also influenced by most of the factors in Fig. 3.1. The main difference is that corporate buyers' characteristics do not play as big a role; nevertheless, the buyers are often motivated by personal desires for promotion, pay increases, and career marketability—for example, getting a great bargain with an online purchase can help the buyer's reputation as an efficient employee.

Consumer Behavior in Social Media and Commerce

Understanding both online and offline consumer behavior can be helpful, but in social commerce, we are especially interested in knowing about consumer behavior in social media systems, and particularly in social networks. One issue is that many people come to social networks to socialize and not to conduct business. However, this situation is changing. More users come to social networks for both "pleasure and business." For example, rating and recommendations for products (Chap. 6) have become popular. One issue for sellers is to identify the specific behavior relevant to their customers' social commerce activity. According to Rayson (2013), vendors can enhance their social media strategy if they know the various personalities and roles of their customers. For more information, see **conversionxl.com/how-to-use-social-media-to-drive-sales**.

One of the major social networks that increases its commercial activities by learning and manipulating consumer behavior is Facebook. For example, in 2013 the company stopped direct sales of real products, concentrating on selling virtual products. Many researchers and consultants have investigated this topic, ranging from how social media influences purchasing behavior (Peneycad 2013), to using social media to market to women (Walter 2013). For other aspects, see Lee (2012).

The Shop.org Study

A joint study conducted in 2011 by Shop.org, comScore. com, and Social Shopping Labs found some interesting facts about consumer behavior in social commerce. Partial results were reported by Grannis (2011). The results include data in how customers interact with Facebook, Twitter, and registered blogs. The study also surveyed group-buying and location-based sites.

What Prompts Users to Share on Social Media

Sharing content is a major behavior on social media. One reason is that sharing helps define the user's personality. Another reason is "to promote an issue." For finding your social media personality, see **pinterest.com/pin/16888567325446527** and Exercise #9 in "Topics for Discussion and Debates" at the end of this chapter.

3.3 PERSONALIZATION AND BEHAVIORAL MARKETING

A major characteristic of Internet-based social commerce (as well as with many offline purchases) is that consumers are influenced by recommendations made by family, friends, other customers, and experts. Such recommendations can be general to all buyers (e.g., service or product ratings/reviews), or they can be targeted to a specific individual, such as in the Netflix case.

There are several major ways that recommendations can be done online. First, customers may initiate a request to friends or other consumers (e.g., via e-mail, text message, tweet, or post a query on Yahoo! Answers). Seconds, companies (e.g., as done by Netflix and Amazon.com) may attempt to make individually tailored recommendations based on a specific consumer's social interactions or preferences, or based on that of similar customers. For example, vendors can integrate Facebook Platform (formerly Facebook Connect) with a user's profile to connect to a site, or they can use 'social sign-on,' also known as 'social login,' which is a single sign-in using existing information from a social networking site like Facebook. This means that brands can access users' social activity to present them with the products or services that are tailored to their tastes. Most large online retailers have already implemented social sign-on into their sites.

In this section, we will address three key methods relating to social commerce: *personalization*, *behavioral targeting*, and *collaborative filtering*. All these methods intend to influence customers to buy.

Personalization in Social Commerce

Personalization refers to the matching of services, products, and/or marketing communication content to individuals, based on their preferences. The matching process is based on what a company knows about the individual user. This knowledge usually is expressed in a *user profile*. The **user profile** describes customer preferences, behaviors, and demographics. It can be created by getting information directly, by observing the user's online clicking behavior (i.e., what people are doing online), or by asking customers to fill in a questionnaire. Another way for vendors to create profiles is through the use of software tools such as a cookie (also known as an HTTP cookie, web cookie, or browser cookie), which is a data file that is placed, without the knowledge of a user, on the user's hard drive. For details about 'cookies,' see **en.wikipedia.org/wiki/HTTP_cookie** and **searchsoftwarequality.techtarget.com/definition/cookie**. In addition, profiles can be built from previous purchase patterns. Finally, vendors can build profiles by conducting marketing research (as in the Netflix case) or by making inferences from information known to them about similar customers.

Once a customer profile is constructed, a company can match the profile with a database of products, services, or marketing promotions. Manual matching is a time-consuming and expensive process; therefore, the matching process is usually done by software (intelligent) agents. One-to-one matching can be implemented by using one of several different methods. One well-known method is *collaborative filtering* (discussed later in this section).

Many vendors provide personalization tools that help in customer acquisition and retention. Examples of such vendors are Sidecar (**hello.getsidecar.com**) and Magnify360 (**magnify360.com**). For a comparison of personalization done in e-commerce and social commerce see Li and Karahanna (2012).

Web Cookies in Social Commerce

Cookies are small files sent from a website and stored in a designated area in your computer. They allow companies to save certain information for future use. According to Webopedia, "the main purpose of cookies is to identify users and possibly prepare customized Web pages for them" (per **webopedia.com/TERM/C/cookie.html**).

The use of cookies is a well-known method of monitoring consumers that enables the identification of a customer during future visits to the same computer (see **whatarecookies. com**). Are cookies bad or good? The answer is "both." When users revisit Amazon.com or other sites, they are greeted by their first name. Amazon.com knows a user's identity by using cookies. Vendors can provide consumers with considerable personalized services if they use cookies that signal a consumer's return to a site. Cookies can provide marketers with a wealth of information, which can then be used to target specific ads to customers. The vendors can then recommend products similar to what the customer previously purchased. A variation of cookies is known as *e-sugging* ("SUG-ing," from "selling under the guise of research").

Thus, marketers get higher rates of "click-throughs," and customers can view information that is most relevant to them. Cookies can also prevent repetitive ads because vendors can arrange for a consumer to not see the same ad twice. Finally, advanced data mining companies (e.g., such as SPSS and Sift) can analyze information collected and stored in cookie files so vendors can better meet their customers' needs.

However, some people object to cookies because they do not like the idea that "someone" is watching their activity on the Internet. Users who do not like cookies can disable them. On the other hand, some consumers may want to keep the "friendly" cookies. For example, many sites recognize a person as a subscriber by accessing their cookies so that they do not need to re-register every time they visit the site.

Cookies can be removed if the user does not like them. For instructions on deleting cookie files from your Internet browser (e.g., Internet Explorer, Google Chrome, Firefox), see **whitecanyon.com/delete-cookie**.

Using Personalized Techniques to Increase Social Commerce Activities

It has become common practice for vendors to provide personalized services to customers in order to increase customer satisfaction and loyalty. A prime example is Amazon. com, which provides many personalized services, the most common one being product recommendations. Amazon. com automatically generates such recommendations based on the buyers' purchasing and browsing histories, and upon the purchasing history of other customers with similar purchasing histories.

Personalized services can be facilitated when the companies know more about their customers. Information for personalization is provided by vendors such as TowerData.com (**towerdata.com**; formerly Rapleaf), which offers a service that helps businesses learn more about their customers so they can personalize content (go to **intelligence.towerdata. com/developers/personalization-api**). For a free e-book about the 40 best ways to personalize your website, see **qub-itproducts.com/content/40-best-ways-to-personalize**.

Laengin (2013) provides a slide presentation on personalization and social commerce. For a vendor that specializes in e-commerce personalization and social shopping, see Barilliance (**barilliance.com**).

Behavioral Targeting and Collaborative Filtering

A major goal of marketing is to enhance customer value through delivering the right product or service to the customer. One of the most popular ways of matching ads with customers is *behavioral marketing*, which is identifying a specific customer behavior on the Web and designing a marketing plan for this customer accordingly.

Behavioral Targeting

Behavioral targeting uses consumer browsing behavior information and other information about consumers, to design personalized ads that may influence consumers better than mass advertising does. It also assumes that users with similar profiles and past shopping behavior may have similar product preferences. Google tests its "interest-based advertising" to make ads more relevant and useful. Representative vendors of behavioral targeting tools are PredictAd (**predictad.com**), Boomerang Digital Marketing Solutions (**boomerang.com**), Criteo (**criteo.com**), and Conversant (**conversantmedia.com**).

Behavioral targeting refers to the one-to-one targeting of ads to consumers base on individuals' Web-browsing behavior, such as search history. Many vendors believe that this approach can help them deliver more accurate online advertisements to consumers, influencing the consumers to buy their products. A well-known example is Google AdWords (**google.com/adwords**), which presents ads to users on the search engine results pages based on the key words typed into the search engine (called "sponsored links"). Behavioral targeting can be used on its own or in conjunction with other forms of targeting, such as using the customers' real time location, their demographics, or the content they are interested in. Google is offering its "interest-based advertising," in its Display Network (**google.com/ads/displaynetwork**) to make ads more relevant and useful. For social media behavioral targeting, see Lee and Kotler (2011) and for additional information, see Hiam (2014). A major method of behavioral targeting is *collaborative filtering*.

Collaborative Filtering

When (or even before) new customers come to a business, it would be useful if a company could predict what products or services are of interest to them without asking them or viewing their previous records. A method that attempts to do just that is **collaborative filtering**. Using proprietary formulas, collaborative filtering automatically connects the preferences and activities of many customers that have similar characteristics to predict the preferences of new customers

and to recommend products to them. For a free tutorial of 119 slides about collaborative filtering from Carnegie Mellon University, see Cohen (undated). Many commercial systems are based on collaborative filtering.

Amazon.com's "Customers who bought this item also bought…" is a typical statement generated by collaborative filtering, which intends to persuade a consumer to purchase the recommended items.

For a comprehensive discussion and more information about data collection, targeted advertising, and 105 companies that catch data, and so forth (including an infographic), see Madrigal (2012).

Legal and Ethical Issues in Collaborative Filtering

A major issue in using collaborative filtering for personalization is the collection of information from users without their consent or knowledge. Such a practice is illegal in many countries (e.g., the U.S.) because of the violation of privacy laws. Permission-based practices solve this problem. In fact, empirical research indicates that permission-based practices are able to generate better positive attitude in mobile advertising (Tsang et al. 2004). The negative effect of behavioral targeting can be seen in the case of Facebook. In June 2014, Facebook made a major shift in the way it collects consumer data, by announcing that they would now include members' Internet behavior to fine-tune its interest-based advertising. This means that Facebook collects their members' *external* Web surfing behavior and compare it with their members' *internal* behavior on Facebook. This will help advertisers better understand users' interests and provide members with more relevant ads (see **ghosteryenterprise.com/facebooks-new-behavioral-targeting-program-internet-advertising-hits-high-ghostery-dispatch**). Since there are many members who believe their privacy is being violated, Facebook is providing them with stronger privacy controls, and a way to opt-out of the program by visiting a website built by the Digital Advertising Alliance, which lets Facebook and other companies know that users do not want to receive these specially targeted ads.

3.4 WORD OF MOUTH IN SOCIAL COMMERCE

As you may recall from Chap. 1, IBM's definition of social commerce states that it is an application of word of mouth. Therefore, it follows that a basic understanding of word of mouth may be a useful precondition for building a social commerce strategy.

What Is Word of Mouth (WOM)?

According to Investopedia, **word of mouth** refers to oral communication that passes information from person to person. An important area of marketing is called *word-of-mouth marketing (WOMM)*, also known as *viral* marketing, which, according to Wikipedia, relies on the added credibility of person-to-person communication (e. g., a personal recommendation). Marketers do not have control over this form of communication as they do with company-generated marketing tactics; however, they try to stimulate positive WOM and monitor to see if it works. There are several variations of this method. For more about word-of-mouth marketing, see **investopedia.com/terms/w/word-of-mouth-marketing. asp**, **entrepreneur.com/encyclopedia/word-of-mouth-advertising**, and **businessdictionary.com/definition/word-of-mouth-marketing.html**. For use of word of mouth in business, see Sernovitz (2012).

What Makes Content Go Viral?

According to Horton (2013), "content goes viral if it spreads very fast on the Internet." An infographic from Mashable. com shows that content will go viral if it is hilarious, provokes emotional responses (positive or negative), is thought-provoking and ready for good gossip. For more information, see **mashable.com/2011/12/03/viral-infographic**.

Using Word of Mouth in Social Commerce

Word-of-mouth marketing (WOMM) is a subset of electronic WOM, whose major subject is marketing. According to *Entrepreneur*, word-of-mouth advertising (marketing communication) is "an unpaid form of promotion in which satisfied customers tell other people how much they like a business, product, or service" (per **entrepreneur.com/encyclopedia/word-of-mouth-advertising**). WOMM is a powerful promotional tool and should be considered as a part of almost every business marketing strategy.

WOMM is highly valued by vendors, social media users, and performance marketers (this is called "earned media" in Chap. 5). It is transmitted via e-mail, videos (e.g., see **mashable.com/2011/01/26/viral-videos-infographic**), and discussions in social networks, etc. Marketing strategies use WOMM to increase credibility and trust. Research has revealed that customers are inclined to believe WOM rather than company-generated promotions. The consumer tends to believe that users who deliver WOM are not receiving a benefit from the company. According to Nielsen's 2013 "Global Survey of Trust in Advertising," 84 % of consumers worldwide say they trust word-of-mouth recommendations from their trusted friends and families (per **mediapost.com/publications/article/209286/ nielsen-consumers-trust-wom-over-other-messaging. html#axzz2gntQPihd**). Word-of-mouth content depends on both the extent of customer satisfaction with a product or a service and the degree of the perceived value of the WOM. To promote and manage word-of-mouth communications, marketers can focus on *brand advocates*, the people who are the most brand-loyal and proactively recommend their favorite brands and products online and offline without being paid to do so (such as people who own iPads). *Influencer marketing* is WOMM used to target key individuals who have authority and a high number of personal connections (the influencers). Chapter 5 describes several WOMM techniques in social media (see **forbes.com/sites/kimberlywhitler/2014/07/17/ why-word-of-mouth-marketing-is-the-most-important-social-media**).

Viral content spreads fast in social commerce due to the large number of contacts and connections in social networks. In addition, microblogging, such as posting on Twitter, accelerates the spread of WOM.

The Process of Digital WOM

Digital WOM is a cyclical process whereby messages are transmitted electronically, starting with one person who sends the message to his friends on his network. Some of the friends then send the message to their friends on different networks, and from there the messages are spread to more and more people. The process is described in Fig. 3.3. Digital WOM is sometimes laughingly called "Word of Mouse."

The Power of WOM

Several studies show the power of WOM. For example, Bazaarvoice provides detailed statistics on WOM at **bazaarvoice.com/research-and-insight/social-commerce-statistics**; including the following (you will see varying findings of these stats in later chapters):

- Close to 90 % of online customers trust recommendations from people they know.
- 70 % of online customers trust recommendations from other customers that they do not know.
- 67 % of shoppers spend more money online because of recommendations from friends.
- 53 % of people on Twitter recommend products and/or vendors on their tweets.
- 80 % of all recommendations in bazaarvoice.com are positive (four or five stars).
- 44 % of all online purchases of consumer electronics are influenced by WOM.

Fig. 3.3 The process of digital WOM

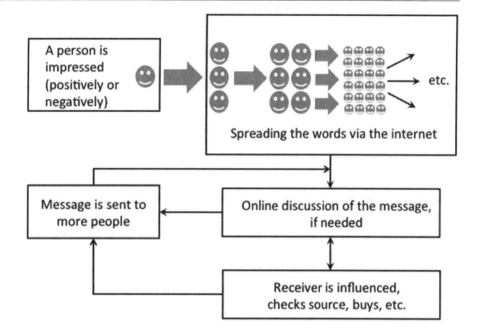

For a slideshow on the power of e-WOM, see **slideshare. net/fbarrenecheaf/the-power-of-eword-of-mouth- adding-social-media-to-the-marketing-mix**. For WOM as a facilitator of customer driven innovation, see G. Brown (2014).

For factors influencing the adoption of WOM (such as gender, age, type of product, etc.) in online shopping in general, see Cheung et al. (2008).

The Major Types of WOM

There are two major types of WOM: (1) *Analog:* This is person-to-person, face-to-face communication, as well as the traditional written, printed, and telephone media. (2) *Digital:* Information is digitized and possibly stored in a format that can be sent and re-sent electronically.

The digital format is used in social media marketing. You tell something to your network, then people in your network tell people in their networks, and it continues to expand exponentially. Web 2.0 tools and social networks such as Facebook, Twitter, and YouTube make the spread of information easy and fast. A practical issue is what channels should one use to entice information dissemination. This topic will be discussed in Chap. 5.

Consultants help companies improve WOM. For example, in order to draw attention to their products or help build a mailing list, a vendor may offer a gift giveaway of a new game or video that people will like and probably share with their friends. Companies can also hold contests, giving away a game or video and advertise on social networking sites. Vendors can use e-mail, Facebook, or Twitter for the initial

dissemination and information about the product based on a deep knowledge of the brand's target market. According to Marketing Made Simple, a message spread through YouTube can be much faster than face-to-face communication (see **marketing-made-simple.com/articles/word-of-mouth- advertising.htm**).

Viral Marketing and Social Networking

Viral marketing refers to a word-of-mouth method by which people tell others (frequently their friends) about a product they like or dislike. Viral marketing and advertising has many variations and it plays a major role in e-commerce and social commerce (see Logan 2014).

Viral marketing is especially popular among young adults and on Facebook and Twitter. Thus, information (good or bad) can spread quickly to millions with minimal cost to the companies' advertisers. For example, when YouTube first started, the site conducted almost no traditional advertising in its first few months, but millions joined because of WOM. For the "power of WOM," see **ama.org/publications/MarketingNews/ Pages/The-Power-of-Word-of-Mouth.aspx**. For comprehensive coverage, see Wilde (2013).

Viral Blogging

Many retailers are capitalizing on WOM marketing by using bloggers. See some examples at **buildabetterblog.com/ business-blogging-articles-to-get-you-started.html**. (This is known as *blogger outreach.*) When viral marketing is done by bloggers, it is ⬚⬚⬚⬚⬚⬚⬚⬚⬚⬚⬚⬚⬚⬚ ʒing. Viral blogging can be very effec⬚⬚⬚⬚⬚⬚⬚⬚ ɔls such as Twitter (e.g., see **slidesh**⬚⬚⬚⬚⬚⬚⬚ **how-dell-is-using-social-media-to-d**⬚⬚ **⬚⬚ustomer-relationships-and-build-trust**). For a video describing a viral blogging system, see Payne (2013).

Note: A collection of videos tagged "viral blogging system" is available at **vimeo.com/tag:viral+blogging+system**.

Example

PayPerPost (**payperpost.com**) runs a marketplace where advertisers and bloggers, video bloggers, online photographers, and podcasters can connect with each other. Those who need services describe what they want and how much they are willing to pay. Providers then bid on the jobs.

PayPerPost checks the reputation of the bloggers and matches them with the advertisers' requirements. PayPerPost also arranges payment to the bloggers. Note that the PayPerPost bloggers are required to disclose that they are being paid for their postings. (For details, see **payperpost. com/bloggers/blogger-how-it-works** and **payperpost.com/ advertisers/how-it-works**).

Viral Videos

A **viral video** is a video that is spread rapidly through the process of online information sharing. These videos become popular when they are circulated via e-mail, SMSs, social networks, microblogging, blogs, discussion forums, and so forth. This way, people share videos that receive more attention, sometimes drawing millions of viewers in a short time. Popular sites that are used for sharing viral videos include YouTube and VEOH. For the top viral video ad campaigns, see **www.visiblemeasures.com/insights/charts/adage**.

Viral videos are liked (or disliked) so much that viewers send them to others, spreading the word about the videos quickly across the Internet. Marketers are using viral videos by inserting ads in videos or by using ads as pop-ups prior to the start of presentations; see **adage.com/section/the-viral-video-chart/674**. Note that, if the reactions to a video are positive, the buzz can be useful, but negative reactions can hurt the brand (see the discussion on reputation systems in Chap. 5). *Baseline* magazine periodically provides a list of the ten best viral marketing videos. For viral video marketing case studies (the best virals of 2013), see **digitalstrategy-consulting.com/intelligence/2013/12/viral_video_market-ing_case_studies_the_best_virals_of_2013.php**.

Consumer-Generated Videos

Many companies are utilizing user-generated videos for their online ads and even for their TV commercials.

YouTube is the largest advertising platform for video ads. It has billions of videos and is growing rapidly. YouTube permits selected marketers to upload videos with ads to the site. Google's AdSense ad distribution network also offers ad-supported video clips. Another way for advertisers to use viral videos is by creating contests (see **onlinevideocontests. com** and **onlinevideocontests.com**).

Example: Crash the Super Bowl

Doritos runs an annual online contest, inviting fans to create their own Doritos ads. The winners get a bonus prize of up to $1 million and their ad airs during that year's Super Bowl. In 2010, Doritos invited Pepsi Max to be a part of their fourth contest, receiving over 3,000 entries. In 2013, the contest was moved to Facebook, attracting over 3,500 submissions and over 100 million views. In 2013, for the first time, Doritos took its contest globally, opening it to fans worldwide. This resulted in a sizable advertising effect.

Other Viral Marketing Methods

Viral marketing is done in most social networks through e-mail, messaging, and forwarding of videos, stories, and special offers. In addition, there are other innovative ways to go viral. Carter (2013) provides 15 examples of viral marketing mostly related to social commerce.

Note: An interesting question was raised by Seraj (2012): "Does electronic word of mouth in social media help or confuse?" Extensive research was conducted by Seraj, who provided a conceptual model of how electronic WOM affects the buying decisions of customers and what the role of social media is in influencing buying decisions.

3.5 CONSUMER ENGAGEMENT IN SOCIAL COMMERCE

Several interdependent social behavioral theories are related to *engagement*. We will describe the essentials of engagement in this section.

Engagement in Social Commerce

Today's customers are socially-oriented and engaged. One of the most talked about concepts in social media is *customer engagement* (see Sherman and Smith 2013). Unfortunately, there are many definitions for this umbrella term.

Definitions of Engagement

En.wikipedia.org/wiki/Customer_engagement)　　defines **customer engagement (CE)** as "the engagement of customers with one another, with a company, or a brand. The initiative for engagement can be either consumer- or company-led and the medium of engagement can be on or offline."

According to Wikipedia, **online customer engagement** refers to:

1. "A *social phenomenon* enabled by the wide adoption of the Internet in the late 1990s and taking off with the technical developments in connection speed (broadband) in the decade that followed. Online CE is qualitatively different from the engagement of consumers offline.
2. The *behavior of customers* (who) engage in online communities revolving, directly or indirectly, around product categories (cycling, sailing) and other consumption topics. It details the process that leads to a customer's positive engagement with the company or offering, as well as the behaviors associated with different degrees of customer engagement.
3. *Marketing practices* that aim to create, stimulate, or influence CE behavior. Although CE-marketing efforts must be consistent both online and offline, the Internet is the basis of CE-marketing.
4. *Metrics* that measure the effectiveness of the marketing practices which seek to create, stimulate, or influence CE behavior."

Rhoads and Whitlark (2008) define engagement as "the emotional bond or attachment that a customer develops during the repeated and outgoing interactions accumulated as a satisfied, loyal, and influencing customer." To show the diversity of definitions, you may want to watch the video: "How Do You Define Engagement?—Social Media Camp 2011 Ep#36" (6:26 minutes) at **youtube.com/watch?v=sF0U-OYuKFU**. According to **staging.socialmediatoday.com/heatherrast/324809/brand-interest-not-outdone-brand-engagement**, no one can pinpoint what engagement really means. However, despite the lack of an agreed upon definition and the skeptics that call it a fad and buzzword, the majority of people agree that it is a useful concept. We view engagement as a link between a company and customers, as illustrated in Fig. 3.4.

For many visual examples of various types of engagement, search Google Images for: 'engagement in social media.' For an interesting infographic that shows the potential complexity of value chains needed for customer engagement, see **customerengagementagencies.com/business-case/value-chains**.

The Benefits of Engagement

The following are the major benefits of customer engagement:

- Optimize online customer interaction and increase awareness.
- Leverage customer contributions to lead to competitive advantage.
- Leverage employee engagement for competitive advantage.
- Enable organizations to properly and quickly respond to the fundamental changes in consumer behavior on the Internet.
- Overcome the ineffectiveness of the traditional advertising broadcasting model.
- Overcome the decreasing brand loyalty trend, increasing brand loyalty and a company's reputation.
- Help companies provide an effective communication agenda.
- Help maximize customer value across all online channels.
- Increase sales.
- Decrease operating cost.

For additional benefits, see Sherman and Smith (2013) and Barnes and Kelleher (2015). Epstein (2013) describes how 14 companies benefit from engagement. Wikipedia also sees loyalty as a contributor to strengthen customer relationships that emotionally tie them more closely to companies. Wikipedia also connects engagement to satisfaction, WOM, awareness, trust, loyalty, and helping customers engage and assist each other.

For how to boost engagement in LinkedIn, see Ahmad (2014). For an example, see Case 3.1.

Case 3.1
SC Application

How Whole Foods Engages Its Customers

Whole Foods Market (**wholefoodsmarket.com**) is operating in a very competitive industry. To succeed, the company is constantly looking for innovations. Therefore, it has become a first mover in its industry, embracing social media to build a closer relationship with its customers (e.g., see Moth 2013

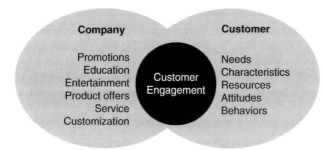

Fig. 3.4 Customer engagement

and **media.wholefoodsmarket.com/fast-facts**). Also see the slideshow at **slideshare.net/JenniferKesik/wholefoods-social-media-marketing-31878552**.

In order to engage its customers, the company is successfully using social networks. Here are some examples:

Facebook Presence

The central feature of Whole Foods Market's social media campaign is its presence on Facebook (**facebook.com/wholefoods**). It not only has a central Whole Foods Fan Page where the company runs campaigns and contests, posts recipes and product information, and supports customers' conversations, but all of the local outlets also maintain an individual fan page, which is controlled and updated mostly by the individual store.

Engagement on Facebook

To encourage easy customer engagement, according to Loayza (2010), Whole Foods:
(a) Assigned and trained "a specific employee at each store to become the Community Manager (CM)" (per Loayza (2010)).
(b) Created guidelines so that the CM knows what content can be posted and what content must be avoided.
(c) Developed moderation rules and guidelines to be used in case there are any belligerent fans on their Facebook wall.
(d) Recommended FB post-tree items to keep the CM organized and keep the content on the wall alive and fresh. (A post-tree can be health tips, career opportunities, and so forth.)

The campaign's objective, according to Loayza (2010), is to provide a platform that allows the community to interact and become engaged with their local Whole Foods store. The brand's goal is to "belocal."

For how Whole Foods marketing uses social media to its advantage, see **digitalsparkmarketing.com/creative-marketing/social-media/whole-foods-marketing**.

Engagement on Twitter and by Blogging

In addition to its company website, Whole Foods has a company blog (**wholefoodsmarket.com/blog/whole-story**) and a Twitter account (**twitter.com/wholefoods**).

Why Engagement?

According to Loayza (2010), "Whole Foods interacts with consumers and provides them with relevant content. News features are posted on the FB Fan Page and receive more feedback and shares from the FB Fan Page than on the actual blog. The FB Community Manager doesn't just post the link and let it happen, the CM actually takes the time to write a descriptive paragraph describing what the post is about…. Furthermore, Whole Foods has not linked the blog to its Notes feed of the Facebook fan page. Instead, they only post highly relevant posts that their FB community would like to read."

For how Whole Foods creates customer engagement by providing a unique experience, see **linkedin.com/pulse/20141124223243-43172975-how-to-create-customer-engagement-by-providing-a.unique-experience**.

As of 2012, Whole Foods uses Pinterest for customer engagement (Drell 2012).

Involvement with Whole Foods Employees

Finally, according to Loayza (2010), "Whole Foods embraces transparency, and features real-life employees in its videos to support the campaigns that it is holding. Again, this is in line with the 'Local' brand and allows FB Fans to see the real people that make Whole Food[s] happen."

For more about Whole Foods Market's use of social media, see Moth (2013).

Sources: Based on Loayza (2010), Stanchak (2011), Stelzner (2010), Drell (2012), Moth (2013), and **fr.slideshare.net/socialtech/whole-foods-social-media-case-study**.

Questions
1. Enter **facebook.com/wholefoods**. What kinds of engagement activities are available there?
2. Find information about the Whole Foods Market "Love Local" Facebook page related to the nearest store to you. Identify all SC-related activities.
3. Examine **twitter.com/wholefoods**. Identify their engagement activities.
4. How does the company use their blog to engage with customers?
5. Find out how the company is using Pinterest.

Mobile Engagement

A major trend in social engagement is to use mobile devices and mobile commerce systems. Each interaction channel that is used by customers provides for different experiences and opportunities. According to IBM (2014), none of the communication channels is as personally and effectively engaging as the mobile channels. Mobile channels allow companies to engage with their customers regardless of location. Therefore, it can be most beneficial for companies to interact with customers with the right messages in the right place and time, by using the right business processes, creativity, and technology (which IBM and other vendors provide). To learn more about how this is done, see IBM (2014). Also, see Adobe (2013).

The Measure of Engagement

Since there are many ways for customers to be engaged, there are different measurements and metrics that companies can use to gauge engagement. The following are some commonly used measures of engagement:

- *Methods.* What types of engagement are used (e.g., blog, video, wiki)?
- *Frequency.* How often does a member visit?
- *Duration.* How long do members stay on the site when they visit?
- *Recency.* When was the last visit?
- *Virality.* How often do members share content on the site? In addition, how much is their sharing amplified throughout social networking?
- *Activity level.* How active are visitors?
- *Community.* What kind of community are they in?
- *Category.* What activity (e.g., communication, collaboration, rating, sharing, etc.) does it fit?
- *Ratings.* How often do members rate content on the site?

Papworth (2011) relates the measurement of engagement to the seven stages in the following list, starting from shallow engagement (e.g., photo sharing) to deep engagement (e.g., collaboration).

1. Internal/enterprise (e.g., wiki, sharing photos)
2. Monitoring (e.g., management listening to employees)
3. Broadcasting (Twitter, bulletin board, news, RSS)
4. Viral (see Sect. 3.4, all types)
5. Campaigns (see Chaps. 4 and 5)
6. Collaboration (internal and external; see Chap. 8)
7. People powered (crowdsourcing, questions and answers, social support)

For details on the levels of engagement, see Papworth (2011). Another measure of engagement level is the ratio of brands engaged to those not engaged. See Chap. 5 for another engagement categorization system. A special social engagement index for buyers was developed by Zambito (2011). For tools to monitor and analyze engagements, see Radian6 (a SalesForce company). Finally, there is an interesting aspect of engagement—psychology (see Solis 2012 and the next section).

Note: In addition, to customer engagement, one should consider employee engagement (see Kelleher 2013).

3.6 SOCIAL PSYCHOLOGY THEORIES, SOCIAL NETWORK ANALYSIS, AND THE SOCIAL GRAPH

Given the strong influence of friends, family, and other customers on consumers' purchasing decisions, it is useful to explore some of the supporting behavioral and social theories behind this influence.

Social Psychology and Social Commerce

There are many definitions of the term *social psychology.* According to the Merriam-Webster dictionary, **social psychology** is "the study of the manner in which the personality, attitudes, motivations and behavior of the individual influence and are influenced by social groups." Our interest here is the study of influences that are related to social commerce in general and online shopping in particular. There are many theories and studies about social commerce psychology (e.g., see Marsden 2009; Solis 2012; DeLamater and Ward 2013). Here, we present only some of the theories.

Social Commerce Psychology

Social shopping relies on social psychology that "harnesses the human capacity for *social learning,* learning from the knowledge and experience of others we know and/or trust. This social learning faculty is part of our *social intelligence,* the ability to understand and learn from each other and profit from social situations. However, social shopping tools also work at a more fundamental level, by playing to cognitive biases in how people are influenced by other people when shopping" (Marsden 2009).

Note: A cognitive bias, according to Princeton University, is "a pattern of deviation in judgment that occurs in particular situations."

For more on social commerce psychology, see **aimclearblog.com/2012/03/20/social-commerce-psychology-the-whys-hows-of-consumer-behavior-sesny** and DeLamater and Ward (2013). For a video on social psychology and shopping carts, see **youtube.com/watch?v=YWaEGkbQ2XQ**.

Cognitive Styles and Morphing in Behavioral Marketing

Cognitive styles that define how people process information has become a subject of research in Internet marketing and advertising. The underlying rationale is that people with different cognitive styles have different preferences in website design and marketing messages. Specifically, an attempt is made to connect the Web with users in their preferred cognitive style. This can make one-to-one advertising messages more effective. MIT designed an empathetic Web that is utilized to figure out how a user processes information and then responds to each visitor's cognitive style. For a comprehensive description, see Urban et al. (2009).

The topic of social influence (Sect. 3.7) is closely related to social psychology.

The Universal Heuristics of Shopping

Research has found that shoppers do what is popularly known as "thinslicing" when they are out shopping (see Marsden 2009). *Thinslicing* is a style of thinking (psychologists call it *heuristic-thinking* and marketers call it *decision heuristics*). This style of thinking involves ignoring most of the information available, and instead "slicing off" and using a few salient information cues, often social in nature, along with a set of simple, but usually smart mental rules of thumb (heuristics) to make intuitive purchasing decisions. According to Marsden (2009), psychologists have identified six universal heuristics developed by Robert Cialdini (2008, 2001a, b) that shoppers use to process thinsliced information: *social proof* (follow the crowd), *authority* (follow the authority), *scarcity* (scarce products must be good), *liking* (follow those you like), *consistency* (be consistent), and *reciprocity* (repay favors). For extensive coverage, see Goleman (2006). Social shopping tools are powerful because they harness these heuristics to make purchase decisions more likely. For example, the "Black Friday" online retailer discounts, good only on the day after Thanksgiving, evokes the scarcity principle. (However, the deals are now offered online for weeks prior to the Thanksgiving holiday and afterwards.)

Social Network Theory and Analysis

To apply social commerce properly, it may be helpful to learn about the foundation of social network sites. Two major topics are described here: social network theory and social network analysis.

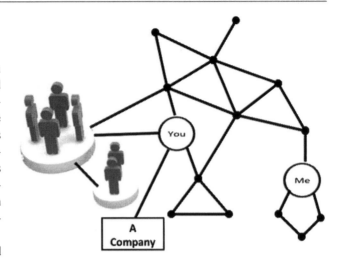

Fig. 3.5 A simple social network structure (there are only three connections between you and me)

Social Network Theory

According to Wikipedia, a **social network** "is a social structure made up of a set of social actors (such as individuals or organizations) and a set of the dyadic ties between these actors. The social network perspective provides a set of methods for analyzing the structure of whole social entities as well as a variety of theories explaining the patterns observed in these structures." The social actors (nodes) are connected by lines (the dyadics) that signify relationship (and contacts) such as friendship, kinship, common interest, financial exchange, dislikes, beliefs, or related knowledge.

A *social network structure* can be illustrated by a graphical display of specific connections (also known as ties, edges, or links) between the nodes of the network as illustrated in Fig. 3.5. The network can also be used to measure *social capital*—the value that an individual gets from a social network (to be described later).

Figure 3.5 is simplified. Using computerized drawings, one can show hundreds, or even thousands, of nodes and links in one diagram. A sample of many networks, known as *sociograms,* is shown in Google's search results of images for sociograms. Note that the connecting lines are not always presented as arrows. This may mean that the connections are not known or they are bidirectional. A unidirectional arrow signifies one-way messaging.

The theory of social networks was developed by sociologists, starting in 1950, by looking at one individual and his relationship with 100–150 other individuals. On the Web, *social network sites*, such as Facebook, have expanded the concept to include organizations and their environment (e.g., customers, society, suppliers, or government). The theory enables social network sites to allow many users to publish their own content for their friends and others to see. Social networks also help site users to display their professional profiles. The sites provide tools for sharing features, communication capabilities, and more. The graphical display of the relationships is the basis for social network analysis.

Social Network Analysis

Social network analysis (SNA) is a method for analyzing social networks (see Scott and Carrington 2011). It involves the mapping and measuring of both relationships and information flows among groups, organizations, and other connected entities in social networks. SNA provides a visual analysis of human relationships that is both quantitative and qualitative. In the business world, this is sometimes called *organizational network analysis.*

The use of SNA depends on the availability of data that describe the latest in social networking.

One of the methods of SNA is based on finding the center point in the network. This information gives us insight into the operation of the network, such as who are the players, who are the leaders and what subgroups exist. For details, see **orgnet.com/sna.html**.

The Benefits of Social Network Analysis

The following are the major benefits of SNA that relate to social commerce:

- Leverage peer support
- Facilitate innovation and learning
- Identify the individuals, teams, and subgroups who play the influencers roles in social networks.
- Find information flow problems and identify those who are not getting information properly as a result of the problems
- Help in refining social commerce strategies.

For comprehensive coverage of SNA, see Scott and Carrington (2011).

The Social Graph

A **social graph** is a diagram that illustrates the interconnections among people, groups, and organizations in a social network (see **whatis.techtarget.com/definition/social-graph**).

Mark Zuckerberg, co-founder and CEO of Facebook, used the term initially to refer to the networks and relationships among Facebook users. This definition was expanded later to refer to a social graph of all Internet users. A social graph can be described as a *"global mapping of everybody and how they're related"* (per **cbsnews.com/news/facebook-one-social-graph-to-rule-them-all**). The term was used to explain the Facebook Platform (**facebook.com/platform**), which was introduced in 2007.

The Facebook social graph describes the relationships between individuals online. This is in contrast with social network analysis, which describes connections and relationships in the real world. The two concepts are very similar. However, the social graph is digital; while social network analysis is mostly quantitative. In addition, relationships are defined by the social graph more explicitly.

Facebook helps people and websites with the construction of the social graph. For details, see **en.wikipedia.org/wiki/Social_graph**. The Facebook Graph Search algorithm finds information from within a user's network of friends. See **search.fb.com** displays a Facebook ad created from an individual's information and sent to other members using a social graph.

A social graph is exemplified by a sociogram similar to that of social networks (as illustrated earlier in Fig. 3.5). The diagram depicts all personal relationships of an individual with others. By searching Google Images for 'social graph and Facebook,' one can find hundreds of visual images of social graphs.

Graph Search

A Graph Search is Facebook's search engine, which is integrated with the Social Graph. It can process natural language queries to return information from social networking. It also helps to find people and things. It is used for advertising on Facebook (see Constine 2013). For how marketers can leverage Facebook's Graph Search, see **socialmediaexaminer.com/facebook-graph-search-marketing**. In 2014, Facebook brought Graph Search for mobile systems. For details, see **recode.net/2014/12/08/facebook-finally-brings-graph-search-to-mobile**.

The Power of the Social Graph

According to Whitney (2010), the "Social Graph is a way to model social networks and help make the connections between people in those networks clearer. It [is] an extremely powerful tool for understanding the connections between people. The question is, how much information does [a company's] brand get from the Social Graph? The answer is, as much as the social network owners and participants of the social network allow (the brand) to have." Several companies help retailers utilize the power of the social graph. For an example of the powers and limitations of the social graph, see **psfk.com/2013/01/social-graph-search-facebook.html**. For a study on the relationship between social graph, consumer behavior and online shopping, see Guo et al. (2011).

3.7   SOCIAL INFLUENCE, SOCIAL CAPITAL, AND SOCIAL SUPPORT

Of the several social theories that are related to social commerce, here we present only three.

Social Influence

As described earlier, one objective of SC vendors is to influence consumers. When the influencers are friends, or socially connected, the influence may be stronger. For details, see Singh and Diamond (2012). To some extent, "everyone is an influencer on something" (see Kramer 2013).

There are several definitions of social influence. For example, according to Changing Minds.org, **social influence** "is the change in behavior that one person causes in another, intentionally or unintentionally, as a result of the way the changed (persons) perceive themselves in relationship to the influencer, other people and society in general" (see **changingminds.org/explanations/theories/social_influence. htm**). According to **qualities-of-a-leader.com/personal-mbti-type-analysis**, "Social influence occurs when one's thoughts, feelings, or actions are affected by others. Social influence takes many forms and can be seen in conformity, socialization, peer pressure, obedience, leadership, persuasion, sales, and marketing." (See **en.wikipedia.org/wiki/ Social_influence**.) It is also one of the social psychology heuristics for consumer decision making, as previously mentioned. Vendors use social influence theories, such as communicating about the large number of people who purchase a product, to *persuade* people to purchase online (see Lee et al. 2006). Note that social influence may be the result of social engagement (e.g., see Hall 2013). Social influence is important in e-commerce (Grimes 2013). For mobile social influence, see Martin (2013).

Types of Social Influence

Several areas of social influence are distinguished (per Wikipedia, based in part on Herbert Kelman):

1. *Identification* is when people are influenced by someone who is liked and respected, such as a famous celebrity.
2. *Internalization* is when people accept a belief or behavior established by those people or groups who are influential to them.
3. *Conformity* is changing how you behave to be more like others.
4. *Compliance* refers to a case in which people publicly appear to conform to the majority, but keep their real feelings and beliefs private.
5. *Obedience* is a form of social influence that is derived from an authority figure.

Social Media Influence

In social commerce, vendors and other organizations tend to influence consumers mainly by conformity and voluntarily compliance. Social psychology, for example (Sect. 3.6), includes several different methods of social influence. One, the *social exchange theory*, explains social exchange as it relates to benefits and rewards. This theory is used by vendors who provide rewards for social-based actions (such as a discount for writing a product review). Companies such as Groupon and Foursquare utilize this theory in their SC strategy.

Persuasion, according to Wikipedia, is also "a form of social influence. It is the process of guiding oneself or another toward the adoption of an idea, attitude, or action by rational and symbolic (though not always logical) means." For details and tactics of influences in general, see Harvard Business Essentials (2005). Note that social media is used also to influence the influencers (see **socialbro.com/blog/make-friends-influence-the-influencers-using-social-media**). For an infographic showing how social media influences business, see **go-gulf.com/blog/social-media-influence-businesses**.

The presence of social networks is changing people's shopping habits. For a study, see Bowling (2012).

Tracking and Measuring Social Media Influence

Vendors may be interested in measuring the effect of social media influence so they can evaluate the success of their social commerce strategy. For a coverage of tools, see Hall (2013). For a further discussion, see McCue (2013).

Social Capital in Social Commerce

Social capital refers to the value created by connections among individuals and within social networks. It highlights the value of social relations and the role of cooperation. It also helps to get economic results. Like any other economic capital, people can save and spend social capital. The term *social capital* is frequently used in different interpretations depending on the perspective.

There are several definitions of social capital that share the idea that social networks have or facilitate value (social capital). The concept is similar to that of *human capital* and *physical capital*. Social contacts, for example, can affect the productivity of individuals, teams and organizations. For details, see **go.worldbank.org/C0QTRW4QF0**. For social capital research activities, see **facebook.com/social.capital. research**.

An example of using social capital theory for explaining customer information sharing in social communities is provided by Liu et al. (2013).

Effects of Social Networking on Social Capital

Social networking activities can positively affect an organizations' social capital. In our book, social capital refers to the network of social connections that exist between people and their shared values. That is, social networks have value and social capital refers to the collective value in the network. For example, using network sites, crowdsourcing, and information sharing may increase innovation, which increases social capital. The ability for a quick connection (e.g., via Twitter) facilitates social interactions and collaboration.

Impact on Sales and Marketing

Social capital theory, if properly used, can increase reputation and sales. The concept of *brand* can be facilitated by using social capital. Vendors can use social capital to *influence* consumers (e.g., see McCue 2013).

Social Support in Online Communities

As indicated earlier, social networking facilitates social interactions and brings social values to its users (e.g., see Bambina 2007). This facilitates social support.

Social support refers to one's perception of being cared for, receiving responses, and being helped by people in their social group. Social support can also be viewed as a vehicle for satisfying one's psychological needs. Users can obtain social support from an online community. For a discussion, see Huang et al. (2010) and Hampton et al. (2011). For how social support facilitates e-commerce, see Liang et al. (2011/2012).

Social support can help a person feel better, by providing direct assistance to solve personal problems when they occur. Therefore, such good experiences may make people more satisfied with social interactions. For a guide to social support in social commerce see Strother (2014).

Since interactions on the Internet are virtual in nature, online social support can help social media users, usually in intangible ways, such as giving informational and emotional support (Huang et al. 2010). For a study about the linkage between social support and intention to conduct social commerce, see Liang et al. (2011/2012).

SUMMARY

In this chapter, you learned about the following SC issues as they relate to the chapter's learning objectives.

1. **Factors influencing online consumer behavior.** Consumer behavior in SC is similar to that of any consumer behavior, but it has some unique features. It can be described by several decision models that are influenced by factors including the consumer's personal characteristics, environmental characteristics, product/service features, merchant and intermediary, and SC systems (logistics, technology, and customer service). All of these characteristics may influence the consumer purchasing decision. A major objective of social commerce is to influence consumers by using social theories, relationships, and connections.

2. **The online consumer decision-making process.** A major objective of marketing research is to understand the consumers' online decision-making processes, and formulate strategies accordingly to influence the consumers' buying decisions. For each of the five steps in the traditional process, sellers can develop appropriate strategies. Another model, the Attention-Interest-Desire-Action (AIDA) model, can help design ads and marketing campaigns. The Attention-Interest-Search-Action-Share (AISAS) model is tailored to the online behavior in the decision process. This model is particularly suitable for social commerce. Social media tools can be used in each step of the process. For example, friends can help with need identification, information search, and product evaluation (see Chaps. 4 and 5).

3. **How consumer behavior can be analyzed for creating personal services.** Consumer behavior can be observed (e.g., via cookies or monitoring browsing history), or it can be derived from questionnaires. Given the information about the consumers, vendors can create a consumer profile where they try to infer what the consumer likes and/or needs. Consumer behavior can

also be predicted by having information about other consumers with similar profiles or shopping habits. Given the availability of such information, vendors can tailor ads or messages targeted to individual consumers on a one-to-one basis. The analysis and targeting is done by using proprietary formulas based on theories such as collaborative filtering.

4. **Word of mouth online.** The information in online WOM travels via electronic communication channels such as e-mail, blogs, notes on pages of social networks, tweets, or other social media tools. It also can be transmitted via videos, photos, sounds, or any other communication device.

   The benefit for the receivers is that they get information that may add value to them. WOM may result in conversations and discussions that clarify issues and reduce ambiguity. WOM increases interactions and engagement.

   Vendors may get free publicity that can travel very fast. They also may get information on what needs to be corrected (see reputation management in Chap. 5). Furthermore, vendors can devise marketing strategies based on what they hear through WOM, so that they can improve marketing plans.

5. **Define online engagement and describe its influence on trust, loyalty, and satisfaction.** Engagement describes the various social networking activities used by customers, employees, and others on social networks, and in participating in social networking (e.g., writing blogs). This includes activities that involve sharing videos and stories, using WOM, reviewing, voting, discussing, recommending, collaborating, posting questions, answering questions, and more. By engaging in these activities, people increase the bond with participants, including vendors, governments, and service providers. The relationships and contacts generated by social media engagement facilitate trust (in others, including vendors), increased loyalty to brands and products, and elevated customer satisfaction, thus influencing them to buy more products and services.

6. **Social psychology, social network theory, and social graph.** Social psychology, as it relates to consumer behavior online, is a prime supporting theory in social commerce. The issue is how to influence consumers to shop for certain brands. A primary approach is via social networks. This involves collecting consumer data and the analysis of the structure and operation of social communities and networks. Facebook's social graph is also a useful theory in social commerce. Social graph theory was created initially in order to help people with social networking. Later, the social graph was also used to facilitate social influence.

7. **Social influence, capital, and support.** The theories that are well-known in social psychology can be used in social commerce to influence and assist consumers. People can be influenced by other people who they may know or be connected to. Social capital reflects the value added to people as a result of social interaction and engagement. Social capital, like human capital, can be preserved and used by vendors to influence people. Finally, social networks and engagement can provide support to individuals and facilitate their shopping decisions.

KEY TERMS

Behavioral targeting	57
Collaborative filtering	57
Cookie	56
Customer engagement (CE)	60
Online customer engagement	61
Personalization	55
Social capital	66
Social graph	65
Social influence	66
Social network	64
Social network analysis (SNA)	65
Social psychology	63
Social support	67
User profile	55
Viral blogging	60
Viral marketing	59
Viral video	60
Word of mouth (WOM)	58

REVIEW QUESTIONS

1. Describe the major components and structure of the online consumer purchasing behavior model (see Fig. 3.1).
2. List some major personal characteristics that influence online consumer purchasing behavior.
3. List the major environmental variables of the purchasing environment.
4. List and describe five major merchant-related variables.
5. List the five phases of the generic online purchasing-decision model.
6. Provide an example to explain the five phases of the generic purchasing-decision model.
7. Describe the AIDA and AISAS models and analyze their differences in illustrating online purchasing behavior.
8. Describe the major players in an online purchasing decision.
9. Define personalization and list some of its benefits.
10. Define cookies and explain their use in influencing customers.
11. Define behavioral targeting and describe how it is used.

12. Describe collaborative filtering.
13. Describe how social psychology and cognitive style influence shopping decisions.
14. What is social influence? Why is it so important?
15. Define social network theory.
16. Define WOM and list its advantages.
17. What are the benefits of social network analysis (SNA)?
18. Define the social graph and Facebook's Graph Search.
19. Define social capital and compare it to human capital.
20. Describe social support as it relates to social commerce.
21. Describe engagement in social media.

TOPICS FOR DISCUSSION AND DEBATES

1. How can you describe the process of the purchase decision when the customer is online and looking for an iPhone? What can an online store do to attract this customer to purchase an iPhone from them?
2. Why is personalization becoming an important element in SC?
3. What techniques can be used to learn about online consumer behavior?
4. Distinguish between social network theory and social network analysis (SNA).
5. Discuss the role of social capital in social commerce.
6. Debate: Some say that people come to social networks to socialize, and they will not accept ads or conduct trading there. Others say that people do not mind the ads, but may ignore them.
7. Debate: Netflix.com, Amazon.com, and others use customers' historical purchases as a part of their recommendation systems. Is this an invasion of privacy?
8. McCafferty (2011) claims that the influence of social media on purchasing is overrated. View his slide show and gather additional information. Debate the statement.
9. Enter **pinterest.com/pin/16888567325446527**. Try to match the suggested personalities to several students. Comment on the value and accuracy of the suggested personalities.
10. Some claim that social influence can be negative. Discuss the issue and how empowered consumers may not always be swayed by the decisions of others (e.g., see Brooks 2013).
11. C. Brown (2014) claims that customers do not want to be "one," but prefer to be one out of the "many." Debate this issue.

INTERNET EXERCISES

1. Enter **whattorent.com** and compare its recommendation system to that of Netflix. Write a brief report.

2. Enter **exacttarget.com/products/predictive-intelligence** and identify information about social influence on online shopping.
3. Enter **infosys.com/edge** and check their EdgeVerve platforms. Make a list of all social commerce activities that can be facilitated with the software.
4. Enter **clickz.com** and **bazaarvoice.com** and find recent material on online trust and loyalty.
5. Enter **walmart.com**. Compare their customer comments to that of Amazon.com.
6. Enter **retailsystemsresearch.com** and find recent research on three of the theories presented in this chapter. Write a report.
7. Enter **resourcenation.com/blog/category/social-media**. Find recent material related to the topics discussed in this chapter. Write a report.
8. Find Carter's (2013) examples of viral marketing and analyze the following examples: Honda, Dove, and Grey Poupon Society of Good Taste. Write a report on their use of social media.

TEAM ASSIGNMENTS AND PROJECTS

1. **Assignment for the Opening Case**
   Read the opening case and answer the following questions:
   (a) In your opinion, is recommending videos a major success factor for Netflix? Why or why not?
   (b) Netflix is moving on to streaming movies, instead of physical shipping of DVDs. However, by doing so, the company faces more competition. What are some critical success factors for Netflix in this area?
   (c) Netflix uses traditional banner ads for the mass audience. Is this wise? Any suggestions for improvement?
   (d) Visit Netflix and identify all major social media applications.
   (e) Examine Netflix's major competitors. Start with Hulu Plus (**hulu.com/plus**). Read **heavy.com/tech/2014/07/Netflix-vs-hulu-plus-whats-the-best-app-to-stream-tv-shows-and-movies**.
2. Research sources that discuss consumer behavior in social media and social commerce (e.g., **onlineconsumers.wordpress.com**, **socialmediatoday.com**, **brandprotect.com/social-media-monitoring.html**, and **pinterest.com/thewebchef/consumer-behavior**. Prepare a report divided into most cited categories.
3. Does eWOM in social media help or confuse? Debate.
4. Watch the 6:24 minutes video posted by Payne (2013). Answer the following questions:
   (a) How can a social network facilitate viral blogging?
   (b) What are the major benefits of viral blogging?
   (c) What are the major limitations?

REFERENCES

Adobe. "Enriching the Mobile Customer Experience." *Peppers & Rogers Group*, White Paper, 2013.

Ahmad, I. "How to Boost LinkedIn Engagement [Infographic]." January 3, 2014. **socialmediatoday.com/content/how-boost-linkedin-engagement-infographic** (accessed December 2014).

Amo, C., "Online Consumer Behavior Trends in 2014." November 10, 2014. **retailonlineintegration.com/article/online-consumer-behavior-trends-2014/1** (accessed December 2014).

Bambina, A. *Online Social Support: The Interplay of Social Networks and Computer-Mediated Communication*. Amherst, NY: Cambria Press, 2007.

Barnes, R., and B. Kelleher, *Customer Experience for Dummies*, Hoboken, NJ: J. Wiley & Sons, For Dummies, 2015.

Bashir, A. Consumer behavior towards online shopping of electronics in Pakistan. Thesis, University of Applied Sciences, Seinäjoki, Winter 2013. **theseus.fi/bitstream/handle/10024/53661/Thesis.pdf** (accessed December 2014).

Bowling, D. "Facebook, Twitter Influence Psychology of Online Shopping." March 2, 2012, **webpronews.com/facebook-twitter-influence-psychology-of-online-shopping-habits-2012-03** (accessed December 2014).

Brooks, C. "Empowered Consumers Resist Social Media Influence." July 29, 2013. **businessnewsdaily.com/4828-empowering-customers-resist-social-media.html** (accessed December 2014).

Brown, C. "44 Facts Defining the Future of Customer Engagement." October 6, 2014 **forbes.com/sites/sap/2014/10/06/44-facts-defining-the-futire-of-customer-engagement** (accessed December 2014).

Brown, G., *Many to Many: Word of Mouth Marketing, Customer Driven Innovation and the End of the Middle Man*, [Kindle Edition], Seattle, WA: Amazon Digital Services, Inc., 2014.

Carter, C. "15 Viral Marketing Examples Over the Past 5 Years." *Ignite*, September 18, 2013. **ignitesocialmedia.com/social-media-examples/15-viral-marketing-examples-campaigns-past-5-years** (accessed December 2014).

Cheung, C. M. K., M. K. O. Lee, and N. Rabjohn. "The Impact of Electronic Word-of-Mouth: The Adoption of Online Opinions in Online Consumer Communities." *Internet Research*, vol. 18, no. 3, 2008 pp. 229-247. (DOI: **dx.doi.org/10.1108/10662240810883290**)

Chiu, C.-M., et al. "Understanding Customers' Repeat Purchase Intentions in B2C E-Commerce: The Roles of Utilitarian Value, Hedonic Value and Perceived Risk," *Information Systems Journal*, 24 (1), 2014. [doi: 10.1111/j.1365-2575.2012.00407.x] (Article first published online on July 15, 2012.)

Cialdini, R.B. *Influence: Science and Practice*, 5th edition, Upper Saddle Valley, NJ: Pearson, 2008.

Cialdini, R.B. "The Science of Persuasion." *Scientific American*, February 2001a. pp. 76-81.

Cialdini, R.B. "Harnessing the science of persuasion." *HBR OnPoint*, October 2001b pp. 72-80.

Crespo, A. H., and I. R. del Bosque. "The Influence of the Commercial Features of the Internet on the Adoption of E-Commerce by Consumers." *Electronic Commerce Research and Applications*, vol. 9, no. 6, November-December 2010. [DOI: 10.1016/j.elerap.2010.04.006]

Cohen, W.W., "Collaborative Filtering: A Tutorial," *Carnegie Mellon University* (undated). Available for download at **cs.cmu.edu/~wcohen/collab-filtering-tutorial**.

Constine, J., "Graph Search Ads Could be a Goldmine for Facebook." January 15, 2013 **techcrunch.com/2013/01/15/graph-search-ads** (accessed December 2014).

DeLamater, J. and A. Ward (Eds.), *Handbook of Social Psychology*, 2nd ed. New York: Springer, 2013.

Drell, L., "What Marketers Can Learn from Whole Foods' Organic Approach to Pinterest." February 23, 2012, **mashable.com/2012/02/23/pinterest-whole-foods** (accessed December 2014).

Dragon, R. "The Big Brand Theory: Sony Influencer Program." February 11, 2014. **socialmediatoday.com/content/big-brand-theory-sony-influencer-program** (accessed December 2014).

Einav, L., D. Knoepfle, J. Levin, and N. Sundaresan. "Consumer Behavior in Online Shopping is Affected by Sales Tax." *London School of Economics and Political Science*, January 14, 2014. **blogs.lse.ac.uk/usappblog/2014/01/14/sales-tax-internet** (accessed December 2014).

Epstein, J., "How 14 Leading Brands Are Doing More Social Engagement With Less." August 14, 2013. **sprinklr.com/social-scale-blog/how-14-leading-brands-are-doing-more-social-engagement-with-less/** (accessed December 2014).

Gallaugher, J., "Netflix Case Study: David becomes Goliath." 2008. Viewed at **flatworldknowledge.com/node/19553** (accessed December 2014).

Goleman, D. *Social Intelligence*: *The New Science of Human Relationships*. New York: Bantam Books, 2006.

Grannis, K. "New Study Evaluates Consumer Behaviors, Attitudes Toward 'Social Commerce'." *National Retail Federation Press Release*, May 27, 2011.

Grimes, T. "Social Influence: The Next Step for E-Commerce." February 27, 2013. **econsultancy.com/us/blog/62240-social-influence-the-next-step-for-ecommerce** (accessed December 2014).

Guo, S., et al. "The role of social networks in online shopping: information passing, price of trust, and consumer choice." *EC 11 Proceedings of the 12th ACM Conference on Electronic Commerce*. New York, NY: 2011, pp. 157-166. (doi: 10.1145/1993574.1993598)

Hall, S. H., "Don't like Klout? 12 Other Ways to Track Social Media Influence and Engagement." June 4, 2013 **blog.crazyegg.com/2013/06/04/dont-like-klout** (accessed December 2014).

Hampton, K., L. S. Goulet, L. Rainie, and K. Purcell. "Social Networking Sites and Our Lives." *Pew Internet & American Life Project*, June 16, 2011. **pewinternet.org/Reports/2011/Technology-and-social-networks.aspx** (accessed December 2014)

Harvard Business Essentials. *Power, Influence, and Persuasion: Sell Your Ideas and Make Things Happen*, Boston: Harvard Business Review Press, 2005.

Hawkins, D. I., and D. L. Mothersbaugh. *Consumer Behavior: Building Marketing Strategy*, 12th ed. Boston: McGraw-Hill, 2012.

Hiam, A. *Marketing for Dummies, 4th ed*. Hoboken, NJ: John Wiley & Sons, 2014.

Heinonen, K. "Consumer Activity in Social Media: Managerial Approaches to Consumers' Social Behavior." *Journal of Consumer Behaviour*, November/December, 2011.

Horton, C. "Social Media Marketing 101: What Makes Content Go Viral?" August 1, 2013. **socialmediatoday.com/content/social-media-marketing-101-what-makes-content-go-viral** (accessed December 2014).

Huang, K-Y., P. Nambisan, and O. Uzuner. "Informational Support or Emotional Support: Preliminary Study of an Automated Approach to Analyze Online Support Community Contents." *International Conference on Information Systems (ICIS 2010 Proceedings)*, St. Louis, Missouri, December 12–15, 2010.

IBM. "5 Keys Strategies for Successful Mobile Engagement." *IBM Software Smarter Commerce*, Publication #UVM12345USEN, 2014.

Kelleher, B., *Employee Engagement for Dummies*, Hoboken, NJ: For Dummies, 2013.

Kramer, B. "Everyone Is an Influencer on Something." September 4, 2013. **socialmediatoday.com/content/everyone-influencer-something** (accessed December 2014).

Laengin, S. "Real Time Personalization & Social Commerce." A SlideShare presentation. March 5, 2013. **slideshare.net/Adtelligence/real-time-personalization-social-commerce-by-stefan-laengin** (accessed December 2014).

Lee, M. K. O., C. M. K. Cheung, C. L. Sia, and K. H. Lim. "How Positive Informational Social Influence Affects Consumers' Decision of Internet Shopping?" *HICSS, Proceedings of the 39th Annual Hawaii International Conference on System Sciences*, Kauai, HI, January 4-7, 2006. [doi:10.1109/HICSS.2006.204]

Lee, N. and P. Kotler, *Social Marketing: Influencing Behaviors for Good, 4th Edn.*, LA: Sage Publications, 2011.

Lee, S., "Consumer Behavior." *A Prezi Presentation*, December 4, 2012. **prezi.com/usalu3pmcfbq/consumer-behavior** (accessed December 2014).

Li, S., and E. Karahanna. "Peer-Based Recommendations in Online B2C E-Commerce: Comparing Collaborative Personalization and Social Network-Based Personalization" 45th Annual *Proceedings Hawaii International Conference on System Science (HICSS)*, Maui Grand Wailea, January 4-7, 2012.

Liang, T.-P., and H.-J. Lai, "Effect of Store Design on Consumer Purchases: An Empirical Study of On-Line Bookstores." *Information & Management*, 39, no. 6, May 2002.

Liang T.-P., et al. "What Drives Social Commerce: The Role of Social Support and Relationship Quality." *International Journal of Electronic Commerce*, vol. 16, no 2, pp. 69-90,, 2011/12.

Liu, I.L.B., C.M.K. Cheung, and M.K.O. Lee. "Customer Information Sharing Behavior in Social Shopping Communities: A Social Capital Perspective." *PACIS 2013 Proceedings*, 2013. Jeju Island, Korea. June 18-22, 2013. **aiselle.aisnet.or/pacis2013/227** (accessed December 2014).Loayza, J. "Social Media Case Study: Whole Foods." *Viralogy*, January 15, 2010.

Loayza, J. "Social Media Case Study: Whole Foods." *Viralogy*, January 15, 2010

Logan, N., *GoViral!: The Most Effective Viral Marketing Strategies To Launch Your Online Business* [Kindle Edition] Seattle, WA: Amazon Digital Services, Inc., 2014.

Madrigal, A. C. "I'm Being Followed: How Google—and 104 Other Companies—Are Tracking Me on the Web." February 29, 2012. **theatlantic.com/technology/archive/2012/02/im-being-followed-how-google-151-and-104-other-companies-151-are-tracking-me-on-the-web/253758/** (accessed December 2014).

Marsden, P. "How Social Commerce Works: The Social Psychology of Social Shopping." December 6, 2009. **digitalintelligencetoday.com/how-social-commerce-works-the-social-psychology-of-social-shopping** (accessed December 2014).

Martin, C., *Mobile Influence: The New Power of the Consumer*, New York, NY: Palgrave Macmillan, 2013.

McCafferty, D. "Social Media Influence on Purchasing Overrated." September 7, 2011. **baselinemag.com/c/a/Intelligence/Social-Media-Influence-On-Purchasing-Overrated-660095** (accessed December 2014).

McCue, T.J. "Social Capital is Path to Social Selling," June 30, 2013. **forbes.com/sites/tjmccue/2013/06/30/social-capital-is-path-to-social-selling** (accessed December 2014).

Moth, D. "How Whole Foods Market Uses Facebook, Twitter, Pinterest and Google+." September 25, 2013. **econsultancy.com/blog/63471-how-whole-foods-market-uses-facebook-twitter-pinterest-and-google** (accessed December 2014).

O'Neill, M., et al. *The Ultimate Netflix Guide: Everything you Wanted to Know About Netflix but were Afraid to Ask*, [Kindle Edition], Colchester, UK: MakeUseOf, 2014. [Also available as a free e-book to download at **makeuseof.com/tag/ultimate-netflix-guide-everything-wanted-know-netflix-afraid-ask/**] (accessed December 2014).

Papworth, L. "7 Levels of Social Media Engagement." March 11, 2011. **socialmediatoday.com/laurelpapworth/277499/7-levels-social-media-engagement** (accessed December 2014).

Payne, K. "Inside The Viral Blogging System." December 4, 2013. **youtube.com/watch?v=Oj28cieWlJs** (accessed December 2014).

Peneycad, M. "Unignorable Stats About How Social Media Influences Purchase Behaviour." June 13, 2013. **socialmediatoday.com/rgb-social/1532766/unignorable-stats-about-how-social-media-influences-purchase-behaviour** (accessed December 2014).

Perreau, F. *The Forces that Drive Consumer Behavior: And How to Learn from it to Increase Your Sales.* [Free e-book.] (2013). Retrieved from **theconsumerfactor.com/en/download-the-ebook-forces-drive-consumer-behavior** (accessed December 2014).

Poggi, J. "Data-Mining Boosts Netflix's Subscriber Base, Showbiz Clout." September 2, 2013. **adage.com/article/special-report-marketer-alist-2013/data-mining-boosts-netflix-s-subscriber-base-showbiz-clout/243759/** (accessed December 2014).

Rayson, S. "Four Ways Personalities Can Enhance Your Social Media Strategy." eptember 9, 2013. **socialmediatoday.com/content/four-ways-personalities-can-enhance-your-social-media-strategy** (accessed December 2014).

Rhoads, G., and D. Whitlark. "Discover Engagement: what is engagement and why is it one of the most powerful emerging business concepts of the 21st century." 2008. **allegiance.com/documents/AllegianceDiscoverEngagement.pdf** (accessed December 2014).

Scott, J., and P.J. Carrington (eds.), *The SAGE Handbook of Social Network Analysis.* Thousand Oaks, CA: SAGE Publications, Ltd., 2011.

Seraj, M. "Electronic Word-of-Mouth in Social Media: It Helps or Confuses?" (2012) **scribd.com/doc/212201273/Mina-Seraj-ewom-pdf** (accessed November 2014).

Sernovitz, A. *Word of Mouth Marketing: How Smart Companies Get People Talking*, 3rd Edn. Austin, TX, Greenleaf Book Group Press, 2012.

Sherman, A., and D. E. Smith. *Social Media Engagement for Dummies (For Dummies (Business & Personal Finance Series))*, Hoboken, NJ: John Wiley & Sons, 2013.

Singh, S., and S. Diamond. *Social Media Marketing for Dummies*, 2nd ed. Hoboken, NJ: John Wiley & Sons, 2012.

Smith, C., "By the Numbers: 40 Amazing Netflix Statistics and Facts," *Digital Marketing Ramblings,* October 24, 2014 **expandedramblings.com/index.php/Netflix_statistics-facts/** (accessed December 2014).

Solis, B. "The 6 Pillars of Social Commerce: Understanding the Psychology of Engagement. April 5, 2012. **socialmediatoday.com/briansolis/484521/6-pillars-social-commerce-understanding-psychology-engagement** (accessed December 2014).

Stanchak, J. "How Whole Foods Market Uses Social Media to Keep Its Marketing Fresh." July 25, 2011. **smartblogs.com/social-media/2011/07/25/how-whole-foods-markets-uses-social-media-to-keep-its-marketing-fresh** (accessed December 2014).

Stelzner, M. "Reaching Millions with Twitter: The Whole Foods Story." February 9, 2010. **socialmediaexaminer.com/reaching-millions-with-twitter-the-whole-foods-story** (accessed December 2014).

Strother, E., "5 Steps to Superior Social Support." March 8, 2014. **business2community.com/customer-experience/5-steps-superior-social-support-0803919** (accessed December 2014).

Tsang, M. M., S-C. Ho, and T.-P. Liang. "Consumer Attitudes Toward Mobile Advertising: An Empirical Study." *International Journal of Electronic Commerce*, Spring 2004. Vol. 8, No. 3, pp. 65-78.

Urban, G. L., J. R. Hauser, G. Liberali, M. Braun, and F. Sultan. "Morph the Web to Build Empathy, Trust and Sales." *MIT Sloan Management Review*, vol. 50, no. 4, pp. 53-61, (2009). **web.mit.edu/hauser/**

www/Papers/Urban-Hauser-et-al_Empathetic_Web_SMR09. pdf (accessed December 2014).

van Bommel, E., et.al. "Digitizing the Consumer Decision Journey." *McKinsey & Company Insights &Publications*, June 2014. **mckinsey.com/insights/marketing_sales/digitizing_the_consumer_decision_journey** (accessed December 2014).

Vanderbilt, T. "The Science Behind the Netflix Algorithms That Decide What You'll Watch Next." August 7, 2013. **wired.com/2013/08/qq_netflix-algorithm/** (accessed December 2014).

Walter, E., "Marketing to Women: How To Get It Right." September 2, 2013. **socialmediatoday.com/content/1708156/marketing-women-how-get-it-right** (accessed December 2014).

Wang, E. T. G., H.-Y. Yeh, and J. J. Jiang. "The Relative Weights of Internet Shopping Fundamental Objectives: Effect of Lifestyle Differences." *Psychology and Marketing,* 23, no. 5, 353-367, (2006).

Whitney, M. "The Eve of the Social Commerce Era." September 3, 2010. **blog.moontoast.com/the-eve-of-the-social-commerce-era** (accessed December 2014).

Wilde, S. *Viral Marketing Within Social Networking Sites: The Creation of an Effective Viral Marketing Campaign* (Google eBook). Munchen, Germany: Diplomica Verlag, 2013.

Zambito, T. "The Social Buyer Engagement Index." *iMedia Connection*, October 5, 2011. **blogs.imediaconnection.com/blog/2011/10/05/the-social-buyer-engagement-index** (accessed December 2014).

Part II

Social Media Marketing

Marketing Communications in Social Media

4

Contents

Opening Case: Johnson & Johnson Uses New
Media Marketing 75
4.1   Getting Started with Social Media Promotions 78
4.2   Promotional Tools: Definitions and Use 81
4.3   Social Media for Social Commerce Communication 82
4.4   Owned Social Media 85
4.5   Paid Social Media: Advertising 88
4.6   Coordinating Social, Internet, and Traditional
Media Promotion Plans 94
References 97

Learning Objectives

Upon completion of this chapter, you will be able to:
1. List and define the six social media promotion steps.
2. Identify the key social media communication objectives.
3. Explain how to select social media tools and platforms to achieve campaign objectives.
4. Compare and contrast the essentials of owned, paid and earned media.
5. Give examples of several owned social media channels and tactics.
6. Explain the advertising formats for social media.

OPENING CASE: JOHNSON & JOHNSON USES NEW MEDIA MARKETING

The Problem

Johnson & Johnson is the world's largest health care, medical devices, and diagnostics company. It has more than 128,000 employees worldwide (2014 data). A major problem facing the company is that its production and marketing must comply with strict global government regulations. With high Internet and mobile usage, it is important for companies to use online communication tools to reach and support its customers. Moreover, the company has about 30,000 Internet domains. In the past several years, Johnson & Johnson has applied Internet media extensively, and as a result, achieved significant performance improvement.

Using Internet Media Channels

Using social media, Johnson & Johnson has grown in online strategies over the years. The following include some of its strategies.

Electronic supplementary material The online version of this chapter (doi:10.1007/978-3-319-17028-2_4) contains supplementary material, which is available to authorized users.

E. Turban et al., *Social Commerce: Marketing, Technology and Management*, Springer Texts in Business and Economics,
DOI 10.1007/978-3-319-17028-2_4, © Springer International Publishing Switzerland 2016

Web 1.0 Stage

In 1996, for the first time in the company's history, Johnson & Johnson launched its first website, **jnj.com**, and began advertising in the cyberworld. This Web 1.0 website presented a simple online brochure to promote the company's products.

Web 2.0 Stage

Several activities were conducted:

1. *Kilmer House (First Blog)*. In 2006, the company introduced its first Web 2.0 promotional tools after using Web 1.0 for over 10 years. Kilmer House was named after the company's first science director, Dr. Frederick Barnett Kilmer. The goal for the blog was to "offer a way to tell some of the stories about the early days and history of Johnson & Johnson, and the people who worked here." The blog was a perfect way for the company to enter the Web 2.0 era.
2. *JNJ BTW (The Corporate Blog)*. In 2007, the company launched its seconds blog. This blog promised to become "the voice for the company." JNJ BTW became a place where the company joined the online conversation about subjects that are related to Johnson & Johnson, and it became a great venue to offer public education about health care. More recently, the company added a blog for parents, called "JNJ Parents Blog." (**jnjparents.com**). A blog for parents by parents, it covers a multitude of topics, from family safety and wellness to social responsibility and holiday celebrations.
3. *JNJ Health Channel on YouTube*. Through the company's first three new social media channels, Johnson & Johnson gained the experience of producing good content without violating regulatory rules. In May 2008, the company launched two JNJ health test videos on YouTube: "Ask Dr. Nancy—Prostate Cancer" and "Obesity and Gastric Bypass Options." In mid-2014, Johnson & Johnson had over a hundred videos with over ten million views and 10,570 subscribers. The content covers a wide spectrum from health and wellness stories to innovations, company news, philanthropy, and sustainability.
4. *Twitter and Facebook*. In March 2009, the company launched its Twitter channel, monitored and updated by Marc Monseau, the editor of the former JNJ BTW blog. J&J now has several Twitter accounts. Their "Johnson & Johnson Cares" Twitter account currently has 34,900 followers and the company is excellent at posting frequent tweets, videos, and images. JNJ Cares uses the hashtag: #howloveworks. Its "J&J News" account posts updates and information for the media, and has over 69,000 followers. In April 2009, the company created its first Facebook page (**facebook.com/jnj**), which, as of mid-2014, had over 624,000 "likes." The page contains a company overview, biographical information and focuses on "caring for the world, one person at a time." Twitter and Facebook also serve as "bridging communicative tools" to integrate viewers into JNJ BTW for further details about Johnson & Johnson. The company's Facebook page has links to some of its various websites including the J&J Channel.
5. *Other social media channels*. Johnson & Johnson also maintains a Foursquare presence. People can check in when they visit the worldwide headquarters in Brunswick, New Jersey. In June 2013, Johnson & Johnson teamed up with the company (RED) to raise AIDS awareness. J&J donated $1 to the Global Fund to Fight Aids for every person who shared on social media (retweeting, pinning, etc.). J&J made a specially created infographic, which documents the progress the world has made fighting AIDS since 2003 (see **mashable.com/2013/06/10/share-red-campaign**).

Mobile Advertising Campaigns

In a classic example, Johnson & Johnson also integrated several mobile promotional campaigns from 2007 to 2009.

1. *Johnson & Johnson ACUVUE campaign with IM*. J&J in Singapore, Hong Kong SAR, and Taiwan wanted new vibrant methods of engaging potential target consumers, and helped them understand the benefits of the product (ACUVUE Moist Disposable Contact Lenses). In response to research showing that 85 % of daily contact lens wearers use instant messaging (IM) to stay in touch with their friends via chat throughout the work day, and their target audience would be "highly attracted" to images that are "friendly, cute, and fun," the company worked with Microsoft Digital Advertising Solutions in 2007 to come up with a three-way strategy using linked components. They created a game called Saving Momo (hosted within Windows Live Messenger), a Theme Pack to be added to IM, and Windows Live Alerts. The theme pack included branded wallpapers, display pictures, and emoticons that enabled users to express their feelings while chatting. The "Saving Momo" game hinged on stopping the cartoon figure Momo from getting dry eyes by giving him Acuvue, while they ran promotional banners on Hotmail Live and Messenger. All three strategies highlighted the Johnson & Johnson's ACUVUE brand of contact lenses. J&J was pleased with the results of the campaign (see **docstoc.com/docs/9919750/Industrial-Marketing-Report-Update-johnson-and-johnson-company**).
2. *Using a multichannel mobile campaign*. In 2008, the company used in-call audio ads (ads played while people

are on hold on the phone), SMS, and mobile websites to create a new way to send out promotional messages to its target audiences. The company used VoodooVox In-Call Networks to attract target audiences to fill out a form on the company's Wireless Application Protocol (WAP) page. Once an audience user fills out the form, MindMatics, a German mobile services provider, alerts VoodooVox on the behalf of J&J, and it sends a free trial offer of One-Day ACUVUE Moist Lenses for consumers to try.

3. *Johnson & Johnson's Zyrtec and iPhone 2.0.* Zyrtec is an over-the-counter allergy medication that generated $315.9 million of sales in 2008. In 2009, Johnson & Johnson conducted a mobile advertising campaign with The Weather Channel (TWC), putting a banner ad on TWC promoting a free application for iPhone users to download. TWC reaches more than 38 million users online each month, and it is the most popular online weather source in North America. The special feature is that it when the consumer clicks on the banner ad (giving an option to click on the "try it free" icon), it expands to take up most of the screen without closing the Weather Channel app. Therefore, the mobile advertising created a win-win situation for both the consumers and the brand, combining the latest forecast with an increased awareness of the Zyrtec brand.

Social Networks

Johnson & Johnson is very active in the use of social media. For example, on the company's main Facebook page **facebook.com/jnj**, the company provides a link to its YouTube channel (J&J Channel), which offers extensive health information. The Facebook page has over 625,000 million 'Likes' and the most engaged city is São Paulo, Brazil (August 2014 data). J&J's most active Twitter account is its @JNJNews. Finally, J&J is using social media to save lives (the "RED" AIDS awareness campaign discussed above; see Olenski 2013).

The results of an IMS Health Report (January 2014) revealed that J&J Pharma is #1 for social media engagement. Of the ten pharmaceutical companies that were active on Facebook, Twitter and YouTube, Johnson & Johnson came out on top—by a wide margin (see Munro 2014). In June 2014, the FDA issued proposed social media guidelines for the pharmaceutical and medical devices industry. The guidelines proposed by the FDA include restrictions on product advertising on platforms with character limitations, such as Twitter, and require companies to post the risks and benefits associated with a product (for more details, see **medcitynews.com/2014/06/fda-finally-proposes-social-media-guidelines-pharma-medical-device-makers**).

Results

The intensive campaigns on various new social media platforms have resulted in significant financial and managerial performance improvements.

1. Robert Halper, director of video communication for Johnson & Johnson, explained the ROI (return on investment) of using new media: "There is certainly a subjective ROI in terms of our reputation. Look at some of the comments on our Nursing videos…Management that I report to is extremely positive about the channel, particularly the large amount of views (over 700,000) and cost (essentially $0)." Halper goes on to state, "YouTube provides an excellent metric, including views over time, trends, most popular videos, even viewer retention rates. I provide this data to senior management in my department, and sometimes to the operating companies, when applicable" (See Ploof 2009).

2. Mobile advertising has shown positive results with minimum effort over the years. In 2007, ACUVUE's 1-month campaign recorded nearly 300,000 Theme Pack downloads and 200,000 game plays of Saving Momo. The campaign drove sales, improved the brand engagement within the target markets and had a positive viral impact on the brand. In 2008, Johnson & Johnson used the In-Call Network as another option to engage consumers, which made it easier for users to get a free trial of ACUVUE.

3. The Zyrtec campaign achieved more than three million downloads in the first 3 months after it was launched, and The Weather Channel remained the number one download for iPhone users in the Apple Store. Mobile advertising has been seen as "a real medium with real reach" because of its direct interaction between the brand and consumers (per Butcher 2009).

Sources: Based on: Butcher (2008, 2009), Microsoft (2009), Ploof (2009), and Sernovitz (2011).

LESSONS LEARNED FROM THE CASE

The opening case illustrates how Johnson & Johnson, a very large company, uses several social media tools to increase its customers' awareness, positive attitude, and trial of its brands. The company started to communicate with its customers in blogs, later adding all major social media tools and social networks. The company runs several well-known campaigns with financial, administrative, and social-related success. We explain here, and in the rest of the chapter, how companies can use the above tools strategically.

4.1 GETTING STARTED WITH SOCIAL MEDIA PROMOTIONS

The first step in effective and efficient social media marketing communication is to identify and gain a good understanding of an organization's target markets and their social media use and behavior (see Fig. 4.1).

Listening to Customers

This involves listening to customers, both collectively and individually. *Collective listening* occurs through quantitative and qualitative primary market research and social media monitoring via live dashboards. Johnson & Johnson hit gold when research revealed the high use of instant messaging (IM) among contact lens users and then used this information to design the Saving Momo game (hosted within Live Messenger). *Individual listening* occurs through participation in social media conversations and by monitoring these conversations through various techniques discussed in this book.

How does this listening to customers aid promotion strategy and tactic selection? It helps businesses understand the characteristics, decision-making processes, behavior of target markets, and effectiveness of marketing stimuli to ultimately increase sales and customer satisfaction, as discussed in Chap. 3. In particular, marketers want to know three critical things that relate to a consumer's experience with the AIDA model (Attention, Interest, Desire, and Action; see Chap. 3):

1. What proportion of their target markets is aware of the company's brands and individual products (attention)?

2. Are the attitudes of the markets positive or negative toward these brands (desire, interest)?

3. What proportion of the market purchases the products and how frequently do they make repeat purchases (action)?

Developing Market Communication

Once marketers understand their consumer and business or government buyer markets on these dimensions, they can develop marketing communication goals for their social media campaigns. For example, if no one is aware of a new product or the features of a current product, the need to build market awareness will guide the communication message. If the blogosphere is active with product criticism, the goal will be to join the conversation with accurate information and genuine concern. For companies like Coca-Cola with nearly 100 % awareness of the Coke product worldwide, the communication goals shift to the action realm—how to motivate purchase among non-users or how to increase purchase amounts and occasions among users (such as Coke's campaigns to drink the product for breakfast).

Example
IBM believes it has a larger number of employees involved in social media than does any other corporation. It has over 394,000 employees on LinkedIn, over 17,000 "likes" on its official "Greater IBM Connection" Facebook page (global community of current and former employees), 89,000 members in its LinkedIn Group and over 10,000 followers on Twitter. The official Twitter page has 110,000 active followers, while the official FB page has over 531,000

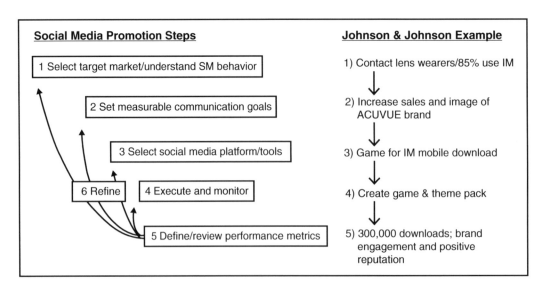

Fig. 4.1 Social media promotion steps and examples

"likes." These social media participants present themselves as topic area experts—positioning IBM as the agenda setter, listening to local market discussions, gaining market insight, and finding opportunities to add positive and helpful comments to the social media conversations (Sysomos 2011). "We educate our sales force to be actively involved with social media; to make fewer calls per day, and spend the other time participating in conversations on LinkedIn, Twitter, etc. We've been able to create new leads that way and validate that time investment. We don't host the parties—we need to find them and invite people back to ours," according to IBM Social Media Marketing Manager, Delphine Remy-Bautang. This social media involvement aids social commerce—in a survey of 2,300 employees, IBM found that its social media participation increased sales by 60 %, customer satisfaction by 42 %, personal reputation by 64 %, and productivity by 74 %. Furthermore, the company expected to generate $4.8 billion in revenue in 2012 due to social media participation (Remy-Boutang 2014).

For the top 25 social media listening aids to increase your hearing (2014), see **biznology.com/2014/04/25-social-media-listening-aids-to-increase-your-hearing**.

However, customers and prospects are not the only target markets for social media communication campaigns, as discussed next.

Social Media Target Markets

In the IBM example, social media participation increased employee productivity while working with customers. However, social media communication tactics often target an organization's employees for the purpose of recruiting, information sharing, idea generation, or morale building.

Examples

Sharpe HealthCare posted a video on YouTube that featured employee interviews at a recruiting fair in San Diego. One employee said: "Passion, purpose, and possibility and that is why I've been here for 7 years" (see "Sharp Employees Talk About The Sharp Experience" at **youtube.com/watch?v=25Ik9rAoQEs**). In another example, the employees of Connected Ventures created a humorous video: a "Lip Dub" version of the song "Flagpole Sitta" by Harvey Danger. It featured all the employees lip-syncing the song in the company offices. The video made Connected Ventures look like a really fun place to work. The company posted the video on Vimeo in 2007 (which went viral) with a last slide: "We're hiring: **connectedventures.com/jobs.php**." Kevin Rose of Digg posted the video link on his Tumblr microblog, and many others sent tweets about it, resulting in over 200 candidate applications in a very short time (see **vimeo.com/173714**).

In another interesting example, Orabrush created a humorous YouTube video about the benefits of using its tongue cleaners. After it experienced 39 million views, the company spent only $28 on Facebook ads directed at Walmart retail buyers, which resulted in the distribution of the tongue cleaners to 3,500 Walmart stores (Neff 2011).

Starcom MediaVest Group (SMG) is a Marketing & Media Services company with approximately 8,000 employees in 67 countries. SMG's officers went on a global tour with key partners: Google, Facebook, and MSN, and wanted to let SMG employees participate by providing meeting updates and answering questions while on the tour. Using the Yammer private enterprise social network, SMG benefited by leveraging collective employee expertise, finding key emerging topics and empowering and engaging the 1,549 employees who followed the 3 day management dialogue (for more examples, see Yammer.com case studies at **about.yammer.com/customers**).

Social media also connects business partners and distribution channel members for increased social commerce activity.

One important feature of social media communication is that, with their messages, companies can effectively and efficiently target markets as small as one person. Called *micro-targeting*, this is not possible to do with traditional media, except via direct postal mail, but information technology allows inexpensive automated messages to be sent to very small markets that share similar interests.

Social Media Communication Objectives

For companies, commerce is the ultimate goal of social media communication with customers and prospects, as mentioned previously. Organizations set very specific, measurable objectives before beginning any communication campaign, thus, helping to determine the budget/staff time. Companies then monitor the campaign with performance metrics to see if it is successfully accomplishing the objectives (discussed in Chap. 5). An example commerce objective is to generate a 5 % increase in sales within 12 months. Companies can also set tactical objectives to support sales goals, such as increasing conversations, driving traffic to the website, gaining a large number of "likes" on Facebook, or changing negative views of the brand. The following specific, general, and tactical objectives leading up to purchase will help guide communication messages or promotional offers, and move customers and prospects to the ultimate social commerce act:

- **Current customers:** Build brand loyalty, entice customer advocacy about the brand in social media, retain the customer's business and build the purchase frequency and quantity over time for all the company brands (more about this in Chap. 7: Social CRM).
- **Prospects:** Increase brand awareness, build interest and desire for the product and move to initial purchase or other actions (such as registering in a social network or following the company's Tweets and Vine Videos).
- **Both customers and prospects:** Engage customers through social media content by consuming information, commenting or reviewing products, creating content, such as videos to upload and collaborating by posting innovative suggestions to improve the brands.

Examples of Goals and the Social Media Platform/Tool Tactics to Accomplish Them

Following steps 2 and 3 in Fig. 4.1, we present the following:

- **Product Awareness:** Sick Puppies is an Australian band that posted a YouTube video entitled "Free Hugs Campaign" and received over 75 million views in the 8 years since its 2006 upload.
- **Interest and Desire:** In 2010, Dunkin' Donuts ran a Facebook campaign that invited followers to design a new donut, with the 12 finalists receiving a prize of $1,200 worth of free donuts for life, and the winning entry to go on sale at the U.S. stores that autumn. Dunkin' Donuts received 90,000 entries, tripling their Facebook fan base and gathering 53,000 Twitter followers. WaveMetrix measured the conversation sentiment and discovered a substantial amount of positive conversation: 44 % regarding the promotion, 38 % discussing the great taste and nearly 20 % expressing love for the brand. The negative comments centered on lack of availability, inconvenient store locations and poor product taste (see **wave.wavemetrix.com/content/dunkin-donuts-uses-social-media-drive-positive-brand-engagement-00107**).
- **Purchase:** Ticketmaster created an interactive social seat map for over 9,000 events. When people want to buy tickets to an event, they can check in from their Facebook account and view a seat map that shows where their Facebook friends are sitting. "Once people purchase their tickets, they can share their seat tag with friends, triggering a post about the seats on Facebook." Their friends can then purchase a ticket with a reserved seat nearby. This great new idea increased traffic to Ticketmaster by 33 % (see **facebook-successstories.com/ticketmaster** for more information).

Objectives in Non-profit and Government Organizations

Non-profit and government organizations also set goals for social media communication. Most seek to communicate with constituents for sharing information (such as "warning signs of heart disease"), promoting ideas (such as "stop smoking"), learning about constituents' needs, and capturing innovations.

Examples
Doctors Without Borders (**doctorswithoutborders.org**) has a Facebook page with news, photos and videos of its work around the world. The page has over 702,000 Facebook "likes" as of July 2014 (see Shih 2011 for a full chapter on non-profit and government uses of social media).

In another government example, GovLoop, with over 100,000 members, is a social network for any member of the government community, as well as students and others interested in working for the government, working on community service projects, or contracting for profit (see **govloop.com**). Specific branches of the government also correspond with the public via social media (e.g., Facebook, Twitter, blogs). For example, the TSA blog is "sponsored by the Transportation Security Administration to facilitate an ongoing dialogue on innovations in security, technology and the checkpoint screening process" (see **blog.tsa.gov**).

As seen in previous examples, companies set communication goals for employees and partners as well, such as sharing information, retaining employees, brainstorming and fostering creativity. The remainder of this chapter focuses on social media communication tools/platforms used to connect with a company's selected consumer target markets.

Identify Social Media Hangouts

It can take a lot of time to monitor social media, so how does one know which tools and platforms are most effective for social commerce promotions? The answer: Go where the company target markets congregate. Facebook is an obvious solution because of its huge market penetration among Internet users. However, there are some people who are either too young or who do not use technology on a regular basis, and if they are a company's market, it is time for these marketers to stop reading this book. Low technology use occurs in some international markets, because only 2.9 billion people of the world's 7.1 billion population had Internet access in 2014, so nearly 60 % of the world is not on Facebook or other social media sites—primarily in developing countries (see numbers of users by specific country at **internetlivestats.com**).

What about Twitter? Nearly 16 % of Twitter users were active in 2014, according to research firm **statista.com**. Thus, a company will definitely use Twitter if its customers and prospects are in the elite 16 %. For example, the singer, Beyoncé, recorded a new album and posted videos of herself and the album cover on Instagram. Within 12 hour there were 1.2 million tweets about the album and more than 430,000 copies were sold on iTunes within 24 hour (Tracy 2013).

Discovering the Best Social Media to Use

There are three ways to discover which social media sites the target markets frequent. First, following the traditional media model, check with each social media property to get statistics on user profiles to see the proportion of overlap with the company's target market(s). If there is significant presence in that medium, this is an effective place to participate. For example, marketers can visit the Facebook advertising section, select the specific market profile desired, and find the number of users in that market. Figure 4.2 displays a Facebook ad for a music event narrowly targeted to 2,520 local residents, with interests that make them an ideal target market, as listed in their profiles. When placing the ad, the company was able to

Ad Preview

Edit

Gong Concert Feb. 26 @ UNR

Pathtobliss.com

Experience the soothing Vibrations as 5 gong Mystique memebers play Sixteen finely tuned Gongs and more at UNR On 2/26 @ 7:30 pm.

Fig. 4.2 Facebook Ad for a Gong Concert. *Source*: Owned by one of the book authors

specify exactly which Facebook users would be shown the ads on their home pages. After selecting the geographic, psychographic, and demographic criteria, Facebook presents advertisers with the number of users in the target who will see the ad on their home pages. In this example, the advertiser selected characteristics based on the following user profiles presented by Facebook when creating the ad:

- Live in the United States and within 50 miles of Reno, Nevada
- Eighteen years of age or older
- Have the following interests in their profiles: Buddhism, Deepak Chopra, meditating, metaphysics, Power Now, Reiki energy, sound healing, spirituality, tai chi, or yoga (Facebook presented options and the advertiser simply selected them).

The seconds way to discover the best social media for reaching a desired target market is to survey the company's customers to see which social media they use and assume that prospective customers with similar characteristics are also using that medium. The third way is to participate in social media that seem appropriate and to see if customers and prospects engage in this content. Be careful with this experimental approach, however, because you do not want to spend too much time with trial and error if it does not help to achieve the social commerce objectives. In contrast, sometimes the social media chooses the company because employees may detect conversation about the brands, executives, or company itself in a medium previously unused by the company and will want to participate in that discussion.

If the company detects many effective social media, then the decision is based on efficiency: Do the company's employees have time to communicate in them all, or if the company is buying advertising, which ones are the least expensive to reach the market? Advertising pricing models will be discussed in more detail later in this chapter.

The final consideration involves platforms preferred by target customers. For instance, there are many effective and efficient applications and other tools for mobile phone users that are not available on computers, and if that is where a company's target market spends time, promotions should be tailored for the mobile phone format.

After the groundwork for successful promotional campaigns is completed, companies will select the social media tools used for social commerce.

4.2 PROMOTIONAL TOOLS: DEFINITIONS AND USE

Consumers tend to think that everything with a company name on it, from a Facebook contest or YouTube video to an iPhone application, is "advertising." In contrast, marketers have specific definitions of the five key marketing communication tools they use (often called the "promotion mix"). These definitions help when selecting the appropriate tool(s) to create the desired effect in the target market. Following are definitions from the best-selling textbook, *Principles of Marketing* (Kotler and Armstrong 2013), along with social media platform examples that the company controls (versus user generated content):

- **Advertising**: "Any paid form of non-personal presentation and promotion of ideas, goods, or services by an identified sponsor." Social media examples: Paid message placed in a YouTube video, Facebook or LinkedIn ad, Google AdWords, promoted Tweets, paid product placement in virtual worlds or online games, and ad sponsored content delivered to mobile phones.
- **Public relations**: "Building good relations with the company's various publics by obtaining favorable publicity, building up a good corporate image, and handling or heading off unfavorable rumors, stories, and events." Social media examples: Company-created multimedia content (e.g., online videos, blogs, wikis, photos, book/product reviews, podcasts and answering questions on sites such as eHow and Yahoo! Answers), social media press releases, viral videos and other content, social media events, participation in virtual worlds, social bookmarking and tagging, conversation/commenting on other people's content about brands, social media apps for mobile phones.
- **Sales promotion**: "Short-term incentives to encourage the purchase or sale of a product or service." Social media examples: Groupon shared discounts, free sampling of digital products (e.g., music, software, research, or news stories), contests/sweepstakes, games (e.g., advergames, where the product is featured in the game can be a combination of advertising and sales promotion).
- **Direct marketing**: "Direct connections with carefully targeted individual consumers, to both obtain an immediate response and cultivate lasting customer relationships—the use of direct mail, the telephone, direct response television, e-mail, the Internet, and other tools to communicate directly with specific customers." Social media examples: The entire Internet and social media might be considered direct marketing; however, specific social commerce examples falling only in this category [a]re text messaging with offers from companies,

behavioral targeting (displaying ads based on user behavior online), location based systems, and RSS feeds of content to individuals who opt in to receive the data.
- **Personal selling**: "Personal interactions between a customer and the firm's sales force for the purpose of making sales and building customer relationships." Social media examples: Chat bots that allow for conversation on a website (also called virtual agents/assistants) and sales lead generation tools.

In general, marketers have the least control over the advertising tool because they are placing messages on someone else's social media platform, and the medium will have technical, legal, content, and ad size requirements. In addition, companies must develop the advertising content and also pay for the space, whereas the other tools only require staff time or technology costs to develop the content. In addition, note that marketers combine many of these tools for increased social commerce effectiveness, such as when an advertisement carries a sales promotion discount offer or link to a public relations content (such as a video). For example, an ad intended to build awareness of a new product will more likely compel users to purchase if the ad also carries a link to the product and a limited time discount offer.

In the spirit of social media transparency, we also want to point out that these tools have been used for decades in traditional media (such as television, radio, magazines, newspapers, and outdoor spaces), but social media opportunities are really pushing marketers to redefine and upgrade these tools.

We now move to social media carrying the marketing communication messages via these promotion mix tools.

4.3   SOCIAL MEDIA FOR SOCIAL COMMERCE COMMUNICATION

Media are communication channels used to disseminate news, information, entertainment and promotional messages. Like all media, social media can take many different forms, including text, images, audio, or video, as discussed in Chap. 2. Social media are one type of media, with two differentiating characteristics: (1) they consist of online platforms and tools; and (2) they blend technology and social interactions for the co-creation of value. That is, people use social media for social interactions and conversations (refer to Chap. 2). In this definition, "people" collectively refers to organizations, their employees, customers, and prospects and the general population of Internet users.

Social Media Platforms

Marketers place multimedia content in many types of social media platforms. These platforms facilitate social actions, such as interaction and conversation. Following are representative platforms used for social commerce, as was discussed in Chap. 2, and in more detail later in this chapter and Chap. 5.

- Article sharing (e.g., Delicious bookmarking, Digg social tagging)
- Blogs and microblogs (e.g., Blogger, Tumblr, Twitter)
- Mobile Apps (e.g., company-specific apps and many other dedicated apps like Foursquare that are available for both mobile and Web platforms)
- Multimedia sharing sites (e.g., Photo sharing: Flickr, Photobucket, Video sharing: Vimeo, YouTube, Vine, and audio sharing: e.g., iTunes, Pandora, Spotify)
- Messaging and chatting: WhatsApp, Viber, Line, Google+ Hangouts, WeChat
- Peer-to-peer consumer product selling and bartering (e.g., Craigslist, peer-to-peer lending institutions online)
- Public and private communities (e.g., Google Groups, Wikipedia, and a company's private community)
- Search engine rankings (e.g., Google, Bing; Wink, PeekYou—for social media)
- Social networks (e.g., Facebook, Twitter, dating sites and many more/Wikipedia lists over 100 social networks)
- Virtual worlds (e.g., Seconds Life, Webkinz)
- Wikis (e.g., Wikipedia, wikiHow)
- Mashups (e.g., Facebook Places, Google Places)

Owned, Paid, and Earned Social Media

Over 46 % of companies reported that social media drove business sales in 2013, according to *Forbes* (Makovsky 2013). *Forbes* also reported that the following proportions of businesses use these social media: Facebook (89 %), Twitter (88 %), LinkedIn (78 %), YouTube (71 %) and corporate blogging (51 %). How do they select from among this plethora of social media tools to achieve social commerce goals within their selected target markets? To help companies sort out the opportunities, Forrester Industry Analyst Sean Corcoran developed a rubric to classify all media into three categories (earned, owned, and paid), giving an explanation of the roles, definitions, benefits, and challenges of each type (traditional, Internet, and social; Corcoran 2009). The Interactive Advertising Bureau Social Media Committee revised this rubric to classify only social media into the same three categories:

1. **Owned media** carry communication messages from the organization to Internet users on channels that are owned and, thus, at least partially controlled by, the company.
2. **Paid media** are when the brand pays to leverage social media properties. These are properties owned by others who are paid by the organization to carry its promotional messages (e.g., advertising). The company controls the content; however, the media have content and technical requirements to which the advertisers must adhere.
3. **Earned media** are when customer conversations become the channel: Messages about a company that are generated by social media authors (such as bloggers), traditional journalists on media websites, and by Internet users who share opinions, experiences, insights, and perceptions on social media sites and mobile applications. Companies have the least amount of control over this media channel; however, they respond to customer conversation and try to guide it toward their positive brand messages (earned media are discussed in Chap. 5).

Table 4.1 summarizes the roles, benefits, and challenges of social media. Effective social commerce campaigns will have both owned and paid media components as their foundation in order to achieve earned media objectives—such as a YouTube video it creates (owned) and an ad in a related YouTube video (paid). These, in turn, will help motivate earned media components, such as when consumers comment on the videos or pass the video link along on their Facebook pages and other media.

Social Media Content

Content generated by sellers drives owned, paid, and much of the earned media (see Fig. 4.3 for an overview). **Content marketing**, as defined by the Content Marketing Institute, is "a marketing technique of creating and distributing valuable, relevant, and consistent content to attract and acquire a clearly defined audience – with the objective of driving profitable consumer action…. It is an *ongoing process* that is best integrated into your overall marketing strategy, and it focuses on *owning media*, not renting it" [emphasis in the

Table 4.1 Roles of earned, owned, and paid social media

	Owned social media	Paid social media	Earned social media
Definition	• Channel a brand partially controlled	• Brand pays to leverage social media platforms	• When customers become the channel
Examples	• Corporate and micro sites with social hooks • Facebook fans • Twitter • Branded channels • Communities • E-mail • CRM	• Installs (cost per install—CPI) • Social actions (cost per action—CPA) • Social engagement (cost per engagement—CPE) • Sponsorships	• WOM (Word of Mouth) • Buzz • Viral
Role	• Build "social CRM" channels for longer-term relationships with consumers	• Ability to reach consumers in social platforms and act as catalyst that feeds owned and earned media	• Social media as earned media is often the result of a well-executed and well-coordinated owned social and paid media
Benefits	• Engagement with consumers at various stages of purchase funnel • Multiple social channels/touch points • Each fan/follower can influence one-to-many via social graph • Increased targeting • Builds customer loyalty	• Targeting • Immediacy • Scale • Peer to peer social distribution • Branded content • Measurable • Brand safe (moderation) • Brand directed	• Peer to peer/social • Brand can direct message in paid/owned media • Transparent • Consumer voice • Measurable • Spreads quickly via social graphs
Challenges	• Multiple channels to build/maintain • Ongoing interaction • Content controlled/not distributed platform • Public CRM	• Industry standards in early stages • Pricing models evolving • Rapidly changing environment	• Active brand involvement • Consumers can ignite positive or negative conversation quickly

Source: Interactive Advertising Bureau. "Social Media Guide." February 2010. **iab.net/media/file/IAB_SocialMedia_Booklet.pdf** (accessed August 2014). Used with permission

Fig. 4.3 Owned, paid, and earned media are all content driven. *Source*: E-marketing, Strauss and Frost (2014)

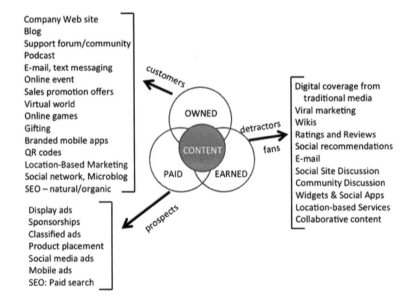

original quote] (see **contentmarketinginstitute.com/what-is-content-marketing**). This is an interesting and huge trend, in which companies are organizing themselves as online media publishers. Marketers have long created content offline when they create paper flyers, newsletters, brochures, catalogs, infomercials, and DVDs ("interrupt" marketing). What is new is that marketers now use digital content as inbound marketing that attracts customers and prospects. It is about having content available to inform, entertain, and engage users when they seek the company—and most Internet users in both B2B and B2C markets do searches and come across this material when researching or shopping. For example, instead of placing a banner ad that might receive as little as a 0.5 % click though, many companies create video content that entertains, engages, and entices users to visit the company website to learn more. Some companies publish small items, such as videos, online press releases and blog posts. Others create lengthy white papers, infographics, and e-books. For example, we received e-mails about white papers on various social commerce topics and clicked through to download the papers as research for writing this book.

Next, we will discuss various social platforms and tools used for owned and paid media. Chapter 5 addresses how owned and paid media result in earned media to motivate social commerce. Keep in mind that no categorization scheme is perfect, and many tools can be used for more than just one goal.

4.4 OWNED SOCIAL MEDIA

In this section, we discuss some of the social media channels that are partially controlled by the organizations that create the lion's share of the multimedia content. The primary goals are to (1) engage consumers with the positive brand content, (2) entice them to pass this content along to others (earned media), and (3) build social CRM (customer relationship management). All of these goals attempt to increase social commerce initial and repeat purchases. Companies often inform consumers of sales promotion offers using some of these channels (such as discount offers, contests/sweepstakes or free product samples).

Controlling Social Media

Note that companies can monetize their owned media content in three important ways. First, they can sell digital content on their social media properties, such as white papers, music, software, or online Webinars (and many other products). In addition, the Shopify.com shopping cart service now offers a Facebook webstore option for selling tangible products. Seconds, they can accept Google's Ad Sense or other types of ads and receive payment when users click on these ads. These ads can appear on a company's own website or blog, and also in multimedia content it uploads elsewhere, such as ads shown in their own YouTube videos (in this case, the company shares revenue with the site owner, YouTube). The third way is to become an affiliate of another website, such as Amazon. Companies receive revenue when users click on a book or other product featured on their blogs or other social media property and subsequently purchase it on Amazon (for example, see **pathtobliss.com/books.html**).

It is important to include visuals, such as videos and images, in all owned media (and paid media). This is because the human brain processes visuals much faster than it does text, (60,000 times faster) and posts with visuals increase content engagement by 180 %. Finally, the target market spends 100 % more time on sites that contain videos (Walter and Gioglio 2014). This partially explains the rapid growth of Pinterest, YouTube, and Instagram. Bottom line: Storytelling through words and images is critical to capturing the user's attention.

Types of Owned Social Media

Chapter 2 described most of the following types of owned media and the following expands on some of them:

- *Websites dedicated to gathering customer opinions.* Some sites exist for consumers to provide new product ideas. For example, Starbucks has a site that encourages people to post and comment on new products, experiences, or community involvement suggestions. As of August 2014, the site had received over 198,000 suggestions (see **mystarbucksidea.force.com**). Dell's IdeaStorm invites product suggestions and comments and votes from users. Dell personnel respond with a section called "Implemented Ideas" (see **ideastorm.com**). Providing company feedback encourages users to submit ideas.
- *Online public and private communities.* Companies create spaces for consumers, prospects and business customers to discuss topics of interest or seek company support with technical or product issues (among other goals). These include social networks such as Facebook, LinkedIn, Twitter, Pinterest, and numerous special interest-based networks and online classified sites (e.g., Craigslist). Organizations create profiles and pages in these networks and post content to start conversations.
- *Blogs and microblogs.* Individuals in sponsoring organizations create blogs to express opinions, discuss product uses, and share information in sites such as Blogger, Tumblr, and the WordPress publishing platform. Twitter started as a microblogging site that turned into a social

network, so it spans both categories. Blogs can be added to a company's Facebook page (and other social networks), as well as to the company's own website. Sometimes blogs are authored by many employees, such as Kodak's "A Thousand Words," where employees share personal stories, illustrated with images they took using Kodak cameras (see **1000words.kodak.com**).

- *Multimedia sharing sites.* These include photographic image sharing (e.g., Flickr, Pinterest, Instagram, and Photobucket), video sharing (e.g., YouTube, Vine, and Vimeo), and podcast (audio) sharing (e.g., iTunes and Sound Cloud). Sellers can bring their products to life and improve their visitors' experiences by adding video or audio content to their product pages on social networks or their corporate portals. They can further increase their Google search presence by uploading business photos to a Flickr stream, and use an app to bring the stream onto their website.
- *Virtual worlds.* Companies can create a presence in metaverses such as Seconds Life, or create their own virtual world to support commerce, such as Webkinz. On Webkinz children enter a key code from a stuffed Webkinz animal they purchased at a brick and mortar retailer, then create a life online for their animal, while connecting with others doing the same (see **webkinz.com**). In Seconds Life, companies can create a virtual webstore, multimedia event or talk/lecture, contest, and can also create blogs. They can publish a URL containing streaming audio or video content and publish it, so that other Seconds Life residents will view their content and subscribe. Companies can also participate in Seconds Life media, such as providing content for the in-world radio and television stations. Obviously, all of this content must be enticing enough for in-world residents or it will not be consumed. Other interesting tactics include offering visitors branded items, such as clothing containing logos (every avatar wants that Calvin Klein Beanie hat!). Finally, some companies use their avatars as promotional vehicles, engaging other avatars in conversation about the brand and offering sales promotions such as coupons. For example, the Nesquik Bunny avatar hops around Seconds Life, attending various events (for more information see **wiki.secondlife.com/wiki/Advertising_in_Seconds_Life**).
- *Company-hosted virtual events.* Organizations host Webinars and online events that attract participants who can send questions and chat with each other during the event.
- *Mashups.* These include many types of website combinations to engage consumers. One notable example is Google Places for Business, which allows business owners to list their business name and location so that mobile and computer users can find the business location on a Google Map. Lil' Piddlers Pet Grooming & Boutique in

Oakland Park, Florida realized a 30 % increase in sales within 5 years of using Google Places (search for "places for business success stories" at **google.com** for more).

Focus on Pinterest

Pinterest (see Chap. 2 opening case) is responsible for 23 % of all social commerce sales (Bobowski 2014). Sellers build business by creating Pinterest boards of new products, best-selling products, gift ideas and promotional offers. Forever 21 ran a contest that encouraged Pinterest users to build boards with Forever 21 products and win a chance to get a $1,000 gift card. In July 2013, Shopify, a leading commerce platform for over 100,000 stores, recently added Pinterest's "rich pins," making it easier for shoppers to discover things they like and purchase from those stores directly (see **business.pinterest.com/en/blog/welcome-shopify-stores-pinterest**). These pins include meta data taking Pinterest users directly to posted products. Shopify reported a 70 % increase in click throughs from Pinterest to its merchants, based on rich pins. Shopify noted that Pinterest is a better marketing communication tool than Twitter or Facebook (see **shopify.com/blog**).

Focus on Twitter and Other Microblogging

Twitter and other microblogging social network sites allow sellers to create text, video, or image-based content of interest for followers. Companies can tweet about their business and product offerings, announce sales promotions, and entice Twitter followers (as well as their own followers) to visit the virtual or brick and mortar store. For example, in 2010, Virgin America gave away free flights to tweeters with a large number of followers who would entice conversation and a lot of traffic about the company's new destination, Toronto, Canada. The social commerce software suites (e.g., from 3dCart) help merchants reach their Twitter followers by posting "tweets" when the merchants add new products or create new promotions.

It is extremely important to send interesting and informational posts on a microblog and not use a "hard sell" as the major topic of the tweet. People on Twitter want to know "what are you doing?" and "what can you tell me?" and not "what are you selling?" A smart marketer will conceal the promotional message in the post or comment. A very smart marketer will present him or herself as a subject area expert who happens to work at a particular company in a specific field. Note that only one of Twitter's competitors is really successful. It is an Asian mobile microblogging platform, "migme" (formerly Mig33; see **mig.me**).

The following are ways to use Twitter for successful promotional campaigns (see **business.twitter.com**):

- Industry analysts, journalists, bloggers, and other influencers from most sectors of the economy are well-represented on Twitter. Smart companies tweet interesting content (i.e., not just marketing materials) and engage in dialog to get consumers talking, tweeting, and blogging about the company.
- Staying in touch with customers on Twitter is not only more real-time than many other techniques, it is also far more cost-effective than direct mail, attending trade shows, phoning, or even maintaining a customer newsletter. It is not that Twitter can replace other touch points completely, but it can reduce the required cost and frequency of high-touch interactions.
- It is very likely that customers, prospects, and key influencers are already having conversations about an industry, or the company and its competition on Twitter. If companies are not participating in that conversion, they are missing valuable intelligence, business opportunities, and possibly even the opportunity to prevent potential damage to the firm's reputation. For example, American Apparel uses Twitter to solicit and discuss ideas for ads, posts flash sales, and do holiday campaigns to give away free costumes (see **blog.twitter.com/2014/influencer-qa-with-ryan-holiday-american-apparel-sold-50k-in-an-hours-on-twitter**).
- Hashtags continue to grow in popularity on Twitter and in other social networks. They are used to spread and categorize information. On Twitter, #hashtags are also used to categorize posts into "trending topics."

Other Types of Owned Social Media

There are many other important owned social media properties to support social commerce activities. For example, company employees can establish expertise in their industries by answering questions on Yahoo! Answers or eHow, or by reviewing books at Amazon.com and other booksellers on topics related to their product categories. In the following sections, we will discuss four important avenues: Online gaming, gifting, branded apps and the social media press release.

Online Games and Advergaming

Games can be played on three types of hardware: Consoles, PCs, and portable devices. Zynga, Inc. produces online games and sells virtual products to players who use real currency to buy them. In "FishVille," for example, the company successfully sells a virtual fish for $3 to $4 each. Som lars a month on virtual sk nary chickens in "FarmVi players do not purchase amount of monthly users ple who buy these "ima generate "big bucks" for

Advertisers sometime available at Yahoo!, ESP sports fans (e.g., fans of jor League Baseball). Onlir ons of visitors every month.

Advergaming (in-game advertising) refers to (1) games featuring a company's product, or (2) the integration of advertisements into video games, especially computer-based ones: both promote a company's product or a service. Video games are popular in social networks and give advertisers a chance to reach millions of game players. For an example, see Intel's gaming page "IT Manager Duels" (**itmanagerduels.intel.com**). *Enter the Matrix*, the first video game based on *The Matrix* series of films, is one such game that includes hyperlinks for players to click on to learn more about the plot of the next level. Advergames are unabashedly commercial by nature, but if they are fun and exciting, players will enjoy them and tell their friends. Advergames create brand awareness and viral marketing: word-of-mouth.

During the fall back-to-school season in 2008, JC Penney created an online game for girls on Facebook called Dork-Dodge. Players had to navigate their way past undesirable boyfriends to get to their dream date. The retailer also had an interactive video (a modern-day take on the movie *The Breakfast Club*) where users could choose clothes from JC Penney for the actors.

For details on advergaming, see **adverblog.com/category/advergames**. Camaret (2013) provides several definitions of social and other types of advergaming, along with some examples of successful advergames.

Online Gifting

GroupCard's application (acquired by InComm) allows retailers to sell group gift cards on their own websites and social networking pages. What is unique about this app is that the customer who creates the card can circulate it to many others, who then can add additional personalized messages and contribute a dollar amount via PayPal. GroupCard also offers collaborative gifting so that a group of people can combine funds for a gift certificate at the merchant's own Web properties (see **groupcard.com**).

JibJab (**jibjab.com**) allows users to create videos and eCards using images of friends or family. Consumers upload a headshot from their computers and drag it into the hilarious and charming videos, then send the link to the person in the headshot or post it on a social network. These can quickly go viral, and more people visit the site to pay $1.99 to download the video or $18 a year to make more eCards and videos in a premier account.

Branded Apps

Many companies create branded online applications and widgets that support social interactions and user contributions. "**Widgets** are mini Web applications that are used to distribute or share content throughout the social Web, downloaded to a mobile device or desktop, or accessed on a website or blog," according to the "Social Media Buyer's Guide" (Interactive Advertising Bureau 2010). The content in widgets can be branded information, games, or other types of interactive content.

For example, Nike+ iPod Sports Kit is a sensor application that measures the distance and pace of a user's walk or run in the physical world. It uses a unit embedded in the shoes that communicates with any iPod. Nike+ has many such apps. Facebook features hundreds of thousands of third-party software applications on its site. One popular application allows companies to run contests on Facebook and collect user e-mails and other information.

Making Press Relations Social Media Friendly

The traditional press release is a typed document that includes the "what, when, where, who, and why" of something newsworthy the company sends to journalists for possible inclusion in print or online media (e.g., a new product announcement). Many companies include these text heavy press releases as links on their websites, or worse, as PDF files for download. This is changing. Now bloggers and other social media journalists want to gain quick bits of information and expert quotes on topics they are writing about. Because they want to include images, video, and text information for articles, news releases are beginning to become social media friendly. Figure 4.4 is an updated social media press release template created by Shift Communications (2012), to be used on company websites. Following is the key to the numbered features on this outstanding press release template (Social Media Press Release 2.0):

1. **Sharing tools** (previously "simple sharing buttons") allow users to share specific content from the release.
2. Shift recommends that **headlines** contain fewer than 55 characters for mobile-friendliness and easy retweeting and resharing in social networks.

3. It is important to include a link to a **YouTube video** because this platform is mobile-friendly, has the largest video audience online that loves to share, and nearly every social network recognizes YouTube URLs.
4. It is good to have an audio service like **SoundCloud** because this platform is mobile-compatible and shareable.
5. **Photo galleries** are key, with Flickr being an excellent choice due to its high sharing ability and defense of intellectual property.
6. **Social commenting** allows for integrating social discussions into Facebook and other systems.
7. Use **selected contact information** based on particular social media, which the company uses actively.
8. While not displayed here, the **entire press release is embedded inside a marketing automation system**. This allows the company to see who has shared the release.

The large PR firm, Edelman, uses social media press releases, along with traditional releases. This new form of press release includes the important facts and is largely interactive, providing links to company-created multimedia and white papers. It is especially social media friendly because it allows for easy pass along with social media buttons. This press release is the brainchild of Shift Communication's Todd Defren, who also created a social media newsroom template for company websites, similar to what is being used by Google and other companies.

4.5   PAID SOCIAL MEDIA: ADVERTISING

As previously mentioned, social media sites sell space to advertisers who wish to reach the site's audience. Paid media can engage target markets, moving them to owned media and resulting in social media conversation (earned media). Great content will not stay trapped in owned media but will spread (such as videos or white papers). Paid media often also carries sales promotions, such as discounts. This cycle of owned, paid, and earned media can also result in increased e-commerce sales.

In this section, we discuss the purchasing of advertising space on these sites. The findings of a 2012 Nielsen study conducted by Digiday concluded that marketers will use more social media advertisements in 2013. According to the survey, 75 % of advertisers and 81 % of ad agencies invest in paid social media advertising. Furthermore, 64 % of those advertisers said they plan to spend more on social advertising in the future (Nielsen 2013). Marketers use social media advertising to achieve the following objectives:

- Create positive brand images
- Build brand awareness
- Generate video views

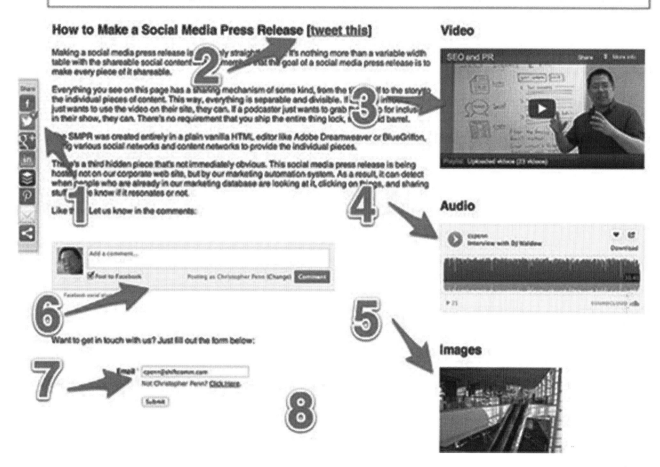

Fig. 4.4 Social Media Press Release 2.0. *Source*: Reprinted with permission from Shift Communications (**shiftcomm.com/2012/12/ social-media-press-release-2-0**)

- Generate leads/build database
- Gain feedback about products
- Support product introductions
- Drive traffic to an online destination
- Increase size of community (friends, followers, fans)
- Engage existing customers in conversation
- Sell products (the ultimate goal)

Thus, paid social media are for building awareness, creating positive brand attitudes; collecting valuable information about customers; and motivating actions such as joining a community, clicking through to a site, and purchase. To drive sales, users require a compelling reason to click. For example, the fast-food chain Chick-fil-A ran a successful Facebook free-sample sales promotion engagement ad campaign; clicking on the ad revealed a form to receive a mail-in coupon.

Advertising is the major current revenue source for social commerce media companies. Advertisers are willing to pay a great deal for placing ads and running promotions in social networks because of the large number of visitors in the networks and the amount of time they spend there. Consider these statistics:

- Online advertising in 2013 hit $42.8 billion, which is 25 % of all advertising expenditures (both on- and offline; Interactive Advertising Bureau 2014a).
- Some of the ad formats in 2013 that support social commerce include: Search marketing (43 %), display/banner advertising (19 %) and mobile ads 17 % of the $42.8 billion total, (Interactive Advertising Bureau 2014a).
- Facebook has over one million advertisers who spent $2.59 billion on Facebook advertising in 2013. Mobile ad revenue was 53 % of that total (Edwards 2014).

Like other SC activities, advertising is placed both in public as well as in private company-owned social networks. Before discussing a few examples of advertising in social media, it is important to understand how advertising is created and purchased: The formats and pricing models.

Advertising Formats

Anything goes with paid media online: text—from a sentence to pages of story—graphics, sound, video, hyperlinks, or an animated car driving through a page. A paid search ad, prompted by keywords, is the most important technique. Mobile advertising is the fastest growing category. Many of these also have interactive capability—involving mutual action between consumers and producers. This occurs when the advertiser provides a link, game, or direct purchase shopping cart within the ad, and the consumer can click on the ad to activate a drop down menu or other interactive feature. For example, Virgin America created an interactive ad that allows users to vote for their favorite in-flight feature: (a) Electrical plugs at every seat, (b) MP3s, movies and TV or (c) fresh food, mixed drinks. The bottom of the ad indicated the number of people voting and if the ad is used in a social network, how many of the voters are the user's friends.

Advertisers use social media to build brand awareness, engage existing customers, increase size of community (friends, followers, fans) and drive traffic to an online destination. Advertisers also use social media to introduce new products, build databases, and gain feedback from users. Next, are some examples.

Display Ads

These use text and graphics, as well as the company's logos and contact information/Web links. Display ads are popular offline in billboards, the Yellow Pages, and movies. Internet display ads come in many different sizes, the most popular of which are banners, buttons, rectangles, and skyscrapers (tall and narrow) ads. See the Interactive Advertising Bureau for definitions of standard display advertising units and many other new creative "rising star" formats (go to **iab.net/guidelines/508676/508767/ad_unit**). All major search advertising companies (e.g., Google, Yahoo!, Microsoft's Bing) gain revenue by selling their huge audience's attention to advertisers via display ads. Display ads also appear as overlays on videos; however, these only account for a small portion of all online advertising. The reason for this may be that social media marketing is more effective (consumers are tired of seeing display ads), according to a survey of 10,000 brand marketers, social media consultants, and influencers (Denny 2013).

Classified Ads

These usually use text, but may also include photos. The ads are grouped according to classification (e.g., cars, rentals), and tend to be the least expensive format.

Classified ads can be found on dedicated sites (e.g., **craigslist.org** and **superpages.com**), as well as online newspapers, exchanges, and Web portals. In many cases, posting regular-size classified ads is free, but making them larger, in color, or with some other noticeable features is done for a fee.

Choose-Your-Own-Ad Format

Hulu "Ad Selector" is an online video format created in 2010, which lets users choose their own ads. The AdSelector allows consumers to select what ads they like to view prior to streaming content (they are presented with two or three options). This model has been in use mostly for online videos with Hulu. Publishers like Yahoo! and CBS use the Ad Selector. For details, see Learmonth (2010). For an interactive demonstration of how Ad Selector works, see **hulu.com/watch/76466**.

Social Ads

A **social ad** is "an online ad that incorporates user interactions that the consumer has agreed to display and be shared. The resulting ad displays these interactions along with the user's persona (picture and/or name) within the ad content" (Interactive Advertising Bureau 2009). A social ad has three criteria: Ad content customization based on profile data, targeting information, and social interaction functionality. Data to create these ads comes from the user's profile data, social data (connections between individuals), and interaction data (data about the user's online interaction with friends). For example, Fig. 4.5 displays an ad that was created from Judy's Facebook profile, indicating she watched a cool new movie (movie title deleted in this example). The ad is then presented to the Facebook friends that she selected to view it and thus, share her excitement

Fig. 4.5 Social ad. *Source*: Adapted from Strauss and Frost (2014)

about this new movie (or product). A social ad also can include interactive features such as polling, votes, sharing, and other types of user engagement.

In general, when companies incorporate social networks into ads, Facebook advertising is quite effective. One study of more than 800,000 Facebook users and ads of 14 different brands showed a big increase in ad recall, awareness, and purchase intent—this occurred when the home-page ads mentioned the friends of users who were already fans of the advertised brand (Neff 2010). In 2012, Facebook began to generate billions of dollars from advertising. For example, users' "Likes" can appear in ads targeted to friends. For 45 'tips and tricks' for mastering Facebook marketing, see Marrs (2014).

Video Advertising

Video advertising refers to the insertion of video ads into regular online content. The Internet Advertising Bureau (IAB) believes in the importance of video ads, and created a guide on the topic; see **slideshare.net/hardnoyz/iab-guide-to-video-advertising-online** and the accompanying document transcript. Video ads are common in Internet TV programs and YouTube videos.

Video ads are growing rapidly, mainly due to the popularity of YouTube and similar sites. A 2013 IAB report shows a growth of digital video ads revenue from 731 million in 2012 to 807 million in 2013 in the United States (Interactive Advertising Bureau 2014b). Online video is growing nearly 40 % annually while TV viewing continues to fall. For monthly statistics, see **marketingcharts.com**.

Video ads appear all over the Web, both as unsolicited pop-ups, or when you give permission to see a demo or information about a product. Video ads have become very popular in the Web 2.0 environment and in social networking.

The major reason for the popularity of videos is that almost everyone who uses the Internet now watches online videos. Videos are also viewed on all mobile devices (e.g., smartphones, tablets) and they can be posted on social networks (e.g. Twitter). Social media and the accessibility to increased broadband mobile access are also reasons for the growth of online video usage. Another reason is the power of visualization and the popularity of social networking (e.g., see Walter and Gioglio 2014).

Behaviorally Targeted Ads (Also Called Contextual Ads and Remarketing)

Advertising networks track user click behavior, usually through cookie files placed on the user hard drive and then present ads to the user based on their previous behavior.

For example, when you search for a particular CD on Amazon, an ad for that CD might appear on Amazon.com or another site on a subsequent visit. This is accomplished via ad networks that maintain a large number of website clients and use the cookie data to present ads to appropriately targeted users on one of their sites. The largest ad networks are search engines—e.g., the Google AdWords has a network that reaches 67 % of Internet users (Google's overall market share). For example, the BMC Music Source, a music store in Connecticut, used AdWords, and by selecting appropriate search key words, increased sales significantly (see **google. com/adwords/success-stories.html** for more success stories). Google's AdSense program also uses behavioral targeting to display appropriate ads on someone else's website or mobile application. The website owner gets paid when the targeted ads appear on its site. Finally, Google+ enters this scene when users search for a retailer or restaurant and get an AdWord that also displays a friend's face or comments from Google+. This happens because the Google+ friend previously endorsed the ad.

Sponsored Content

Sponsorships integrate editorial content and advertising based on either underwritten (someone else's content) or advertiser-created content. These can include content features or functions in social media stand-alone micros or other websites or interactive functions, associating the sponsor's brand with the content. The IAB has observed the following types of sponsorships: content creation, mobile/Web applications, branded interaction, contests/sweepstakes, games, podcasts, polls/surveys, and trivia.

For example, a food company might pay for space on a cooking blog or wiki to insert recipes using its products as ingredients. This looks like content from the site, but is actually paid space. Companies also can pay bloggers directly to endorse products by writing positive reviews. A problem with sponsored content, however, is that bloggers are not required to disclose that they are being paid (or receiving gifts) for their endorsements. However, if they do not tell and are found out, they can be exposed with a huge and negative amount of discussion online. In an example taken from the early days of blogging, a couple named Laura and Jim created a blog about their journey across the U.S. in an RV ("Walmarting Across America"). They stayed overnight in Walmart parking lots and wrote about their experiences on the road. Other bloggers believed that the blog was misleading, noting that that the Laura and Jim never said a bad word about Walmart, and on further digging, discovered that their trip was actually sponsored by PR firm Edelman on behalf of their client, Walmart. This fake blog ("flog") created a huge negative backlash for the authors, Edelman, and Walmart, who did not follow their own rules for transparency (see **businessweek.com/stories/2006-10-17/wal-mart-vs-dot-the-blogosphere businessweek-business-news-stock-market-and-financial-advice**).

A sponsored content intermediary, PayPerPost (**payperpost.com**) runs a marketplace where advertisers can find bloggers, video bloggers, online photographers, and podcasters who are willing to endorse advertisers' products. A company with a product or a service to advertise registers with PayPerPost and describes the type of endorsement it wants and how much it is willing to pay. A sneaker company, for example, might post a request for people willing to write a 50-word blog entry about their shoes or upload a video of themselves playing basketball wearing the sneakers. The company also describes what it is willing to pay the bloggers for such posting. Bloggers create the blog post (or whatever content is requested) and inform PayPerPost, which checks to see that the content matches what the advertiser asked for, and PayPerPost arranges payment. Note that the PayPerPost Marketplace *requires* full disclosure by all participants (per **payperpost.com/terms_and_conditions**).

Product Placement

Advertisers can deeply embed products or ads in TV shows or films. Game publishers are now using the same tactic—product placement in online multiplayer games or videos. This is similar to movie product placement offline. For example, the online music video game Guitar Hero often has advertisements on the stage behind the musicians. Game players enjoy this kind of advertising because it makes the games seem more realistic, given that there are ads in live offline concerts too.

Text Link Ads

Link ads are ads that are simply a hyperlink placed in specific text in a blog post or other social media content—including content downloaded by mobile phone users. In a hypothetical example, a flower shop might buy a specified number of links for the word "rose" on many blog sites, and these would have a hyperlink to the flower shop's website. The goal of these ads is to raise a site's rankings in search engines. For example, a furniture store bought three key words in a large number of related websites and in over a 1 year period, the store moved from a rank of 97 to 4 in a Google Search Engine results page for those three key words (see **textlinkbrokers.com/client-rankings.html** for other client success stories).

More Social Media Advertising Examples

Paid messages can be placed in another company's online content, using any of the social media platforms listed previously, either on the Web or delivered to mobile phones. Social networks provide huge advertising opportunities because of their rapid user growth. According to one source, social media advertising totaled $6.2 billion in 2013 and is still growing rapidly (13.9 % of all online advertising; PR Newswire 2014). The following are some good examples of social network ad campaigns.

Facebook Advertising

By advertising on Facebook, advertisers can reach over 1.28 billion members (with 829 million active daily users), with over 63 % of users logging in on any given day, according to Latka (2014). However, most advertisers prefer narrower targeting to reach their well-defined markets, and this can easily be done via member profile information (as seen in Fig. 4.2, p. 79). When placing the ad, the marketer selects the desired target profile. For this ad in, Fig. 4.2, the criteria were Facebook users with the following information in their profiles:

- Live in the United States,
- Live within 50 miles of Reno, NV,
- Are age 18 and older, and
- Like meditation, tai chi, Reiki, power now, sound healing, metaphysics, meditating, Buddhism, Deepak Chopra, spirituality or yoga (as mentioned in their profiles).

This narrow targeting resulted in 4,980 Facebook users, who were presented the ad on their walls and would likely be interested and able to attend the Reno gong concert. The cost for the ad was based on the number of people clicking on it, at a rate of 88¢ per click.

Facebook advertising is important for global advertisers because Facebook is available in more than 70 different languages on the site, and over 81 % of active users live outside of the United States and Canada. Facebook ads can include interactive features, links to other brand content, and are very easy to create. Advertisers simply upload an image and type the text right into the Facebook template. Facebook offers excellent metrics to see how many people were presented the ad, and whether or not they took an action, like clicking on a link. Furthermore, advertisers can choose to pay either by using the CPM (cost per thousand views) or CPC (cost-per-click on the ad) pricing models by setting a maximum daily budget.

Here are some additional interesting ways to advertise on Facebook:

- **Boosted Posts.** For a $5 fee, users can boost a Facebook post so more people will see it. A boosted post can reach friends of your friends or new audiences. This is good for promoting special events, offers and company news.
- **Facebook Offers.** These involve posting special promotions or product discounts. Viewers on Facebook can click on the "get offer" button to claim the offer or share it with other friends.
- **Facebook Exchange.** This is a form of remarketing that allows advertisers to "reach people on Facebook who have expressed an interest through their online behavior (e.g., visiting your site) so you can reach them with a similar product or service" (per **facebook.com/business/a/online-sales/facebook-exchange**).

For going global using Facebook, see Adobe (2012).

Twitter's "Promoted Tweets," "Trends," and "Accounts"

Barking at Facebook's heels, Twitter is a strong competitor for advertisers' dollars. According to Learmonth (2011), Twitter launched its first ad product—*promoted tweets*—in 2010 and netted $45 million in ad dollars. That was due in part to the enthusiasm among brands like Virgin America, Coke, Ford, and Verizon to give the untried format a whirl. *eMarketer* estimates the promoted tweet ad revenue to be $540 million in 2014, with 90 % coming from U.S. companies (reported by Indvik 2012). Promoted tweets are ads purchased by advertisers that appear as content at the top of a Twitter search page or within a user's timeline. They can be targeted to Twitter users by geographic location and by whose Twitter streams users follow. Users can interact with promoted Tweets just as they can with organic Tweets. *Promoted trends* are ads placed on hot topics in Twitter that are presented near a user's timeline. *Promoted accounts* invites targeted Twitter users to visit brand accounts that may be of interest to them. These ads help companies attract more users. (See **business.twitter.com/ad-products** for more about Twitter ads.)

LinkedIn Advertising

The LinkedIn social network is great for advertising to narrowly targeted business professionals. Advertisers can use the LinkedIn Ads product to target by (1) job title and function, (2) industry or company size, (3) company seniority or age, or (4) LinkedIn Group membership. Advertisers have the choice of paying for the number of impressions or clicks (see more in the pricing model discussion below). According to Matt Johnson of uTest, "50 % of our paid inbound leads come from LinkedIn. LinkedIn is our most cost-effective online marketing channel" (see **linkedin.com/ads** for more information).

Advertising in Seconds Life

Interestingly, it is possible to advertise in virtual worlds. For instance, in Seconds Life, companies can pay virtual clubs, stores, or malls to put up posters or kiosks featuring brand information and links, and can even provide "teleports" to the company's virtual property.

Mobile Advertising

Mobile advertising is a rapidly developing area, with a global expenditure increase of 105 % in 2013, and is predicted to increase another 75 % in 2014 (Schmidt 2014). Mobile advertising refers to advertisements on smartphones and other wireless mobile devices, such as tablets (e.g., iPad). The competition for mobile ad revenue is intensifying, especially with the increased use of cell phones with Internet access. Recently, watching video clips has become popular on smartphones. Advertisers are starting to attach ads to these video clips. Finally, advertisers use microblogging, especially Twitter, to reach large audiences with short messages (SMS) ads via mobile devices. According to Patel (2011), a Nielsen study of iPhone users compared Apple's iAds involving Campbell Soup Company as an advertiser against similar TV ads. The study found that those exposed to one of Campbell's iAd campaigns had higher brand recall than those who had seen similar TV ads: The 5-week study showed that consumers shown an iAd remembered the brand "Campbell's" five times more often than TV ad respondents, and the ad messaging three times more often. For details about this study, see Patel (2011).

As seen in the table below, mobile ads were found to create the greatest advertising opportunity versus Internet or traditional ads, as suggested in research from Meeker (2014). It is notable that advertisers spend more on media that are not consumed as often by their markets.

Medium	Proportion of time spent by users (%)	Proportion of money spent by advertisers
Print	5	19 %
Radio	12	10 %
Television	38	45 %
Internet, in general	25	22 % ($43 billion)
Mobile	20	4 % ($7.1 billion)

For news, statistics and more about mobile advertising, see **mashable.com/category/mobile-advertising**.

Location-Based Ads

Delivering location-based ads to mobile devices is becoming popular. Location-sensitive businesses can take advantage of this feature to deliver location-based ads. A good example is a Google Map that can show nearby convenience stores, gas stations, hotels, and restaurants when a location is searched. Some of these are paid ads (see Chap. 5 for details).

Advertising Pricing Models

Social media price their advertising space using many different models. Cost per thousand impressions (CPM) and cost per click (CPC) are the two most commonly used models for all Internet advertising and are also used by social media properties. Cost per action (CPA) includes social actions, such as the number of chocolate gifts sent to friends (from an ad), number of posts to a profile, number of comments to a blog, number of users who play a game or watch a video trailer, or number of fans as a result of an advertisement. Cost per install (CPI) is the cost charged for a unique installation of a widget or other application included in a social media page. Finally, cost per engagement (CPE) is the cost of each user-defined engagement, such as submission of branded content generated by the user, contest entries, votes/polls, reviews or comments, ratings, engagement or replies to interactive ads, to, clicks or favorites, a Promoted Tweet or other social actions (clicking on "Like" button or a "thumb up/down" icon). Download the "Social Media Buyer's Guide" at **iab.net/guidelines/508676/801817/sm_buyers_guide** for definitions and more examples.

In one interesting example, JC Penney hired Gigya to create a widget that allowed its teen market to add hats, mustaches, and other fun things to photos of their friends using a social network application. Called "Stuck on You," the campaign paid the social media property using a CPI model, with a goal of 2.9 million starts by users in 2008–2009. The result was over 43 clicks for every widget install (engagement), and an average of 22 friends was reached in addition to the original install (Interactive Advertising Bureau 2010). In Chap. 5 you will learn all about these performance metrics and other measures of success for social media marketing communication campaigns.

Finally, there is one burning issue asked by all marketers: How does one integrate these new media into traditional marketing communication plans?

4.6 COORDINATING SOCIAL, INTERNET, AND TRADITIONAL MEDIA PROMOTION PLANS

The primary goal of marketers has always been to become monomaniacally customer driven and build long term relationships that bring revenue to the company. This all starts with customers and discovering their needs and wants—discussion and listening via social media is a great way to do that. Many online media do not allow for social interactions, such as some traditional websites and e-mail campaigns. Traditional marketing communication media only allow one-way communication, yet these are still important for building brand awareness (e.g., an ad in the SuperBowl that reaches 60 % of the U.S. population), creating desire and interest, and moving prospects and customers to purchase (e.g., a coupon or calendar event listing in the Sunday print newspaper). Yet, marketing is moving more to the concept of **inbound marketing**: a strategy that has as its objective to bring customers to a company's website, instead of "interrupt" marketing (distracting them with one-way communication, such as advertising, while they are engaged in viewing content—such as watching a television program or reading a story on a website). Inbound marketing entices customers with relevant content and earns their attention. Although it may still be sponsored content, paid for by an advertiser, it is in a more relevant context that attracts viewers.

According to a Marketing Sherpa survey of 3,300 marketers, roughly 25 % extensively integrated social media with both offline and online tactics (see **marketingsherpa.com/article/chart/social-media-integration**).   Research from a 2011 survey by the Pivot Conference and Brian Solis found that 70 % of marketers who use social media campaigns noted that they mostly integrate social advertising at the campaign planning stage to drive engagement (*eMarketer* 2011).

These marketers face a mashup of new and traditional media that can carry the promotional tools of advertising, sales promotion, direct marketing, public relations and personal selling. The guiding force for selecting appropriate tools and media is the communication objectives in desired target markets. For example, if a company's goal is to sell its new software package to accountants, it could do any of the following: (1) use PR by describing the software on its own website and with a social media press release, (2) use Twitter to talk about software needs in the industry and offer codes for free sample downloads (sales promotion), (3) include recommendations from current customers on a LinkedIn page, (4) upload a video demonstration with software tutorials, or (5) advertise in a traditional print accounting industry magazine and on the industry's website (including testimonials from the LinkedIn pages). All this could direct prospects to a website where they can download a free sample and purchase the product after a 30 day trial. This would be much more effective than giving away free iPads on Facebook, because that tactic does not align with the campaign goals or target market.

Below is another example of how to drive traffic to both digital sites and physical retailer stores, as described in the Starbucks' opening case of Chap. 1. 3dCart (**3dcart.com**) lists the following:

- Use a Facebook Page for your company and add a Facebook Store. Customers will become "fans" of your business to check on updates and meet others with similar interests.
- Tweet about the business and any promotions/new products, etc.
- Blog to your customers to keep them updated about new products, etc.
- Integrate videos (e.g. YouTube) on your website.
- Add social bookmarking to your product's page for easy return.
- Embrace mobile apps.
- Add a Facebook "Like" button with its sponsored story to your product (e.g., Gatorade brand scored 1.2 million conversations in 6 months using their 'Mission Control' campaign).

For more details, see **blog.3dcart.com/7-social-commerce-tools-to-increase-traffic**.

There are many other tactical ways to integrate marketing communications media, and they primarily involve providing links to all the Web and social media sites in all promotional media and integrating positive conversation into various appropriate media.

The main thing to remember is that the traditional and some Internet media carry corporate monologues, while social media contain dialogs with target markets. Both play a role, but the dialog is becoming much more important and is more true to the well-accepted company goal of customer-driven marketing. This is the subject of Chap. 5.

SUMMARY

In this chapter, you learned about the following SC issues as they relate to the chapter's learning objectives.

1. **List and define the six social media promotion steps.** The first step in effective and efficient social media marketing communication is to identify and gain a good understanding of the organization's target market(s) and its social media use and behavior. Seconds, companies develop marketing communication goals for their social media campaigns, and third, they select the social media platforms, such as Facebook or YouTube videos, and tools (such as advertising or sales promotion). The fourth step is to execute and monitor the campaign, and fifth is to define/review performance metrics (such as number of clicks on an ad). Finally, the marketer refines the other five steps based on how well the campaign is working.

2. **Identify the key social media communication objectives.** The key communication objectives include building awareness, interest, desire and action (AIDA). Other important objectives are building brand loyalty and purchase frequency/quantity over the customers' lifetime and engaging customers and prospects in social media content.

3. **Explain how to select social media tools and platforms to achieve campaign objectives.** Selection among the communication tools of advertising, sales promotion, public relations, direct marketing, and personal selling depends on the communication objective in the target market. The most important criterion for platform selection is to find which social media are used most by the company's target markets. Companies achieve this by getting user statistics from the social media company, surveying customers, or experimenting to see if a site's users want to engage in the company's content.

4. **Compare and contrast the essentials of owned and paid media.** Owned media includes content that is partially controlled by the company, such as a Facebook page. It serves to build longer-term relationships with customers. Paid media is space the company buys in someone else's medium, such as an ad on a YouTube video. It acts as catalyst that feeds owned and earned media. Companies must create the content for both types of media; however, they pay additional money for paid media when buying the space.

5. **Give examples of several owned social media channels and tactics.** Exemplary channels include online public and private communities (e.g., a company's Facebook page), blogs (e.g., a company executive writes a blog) and microblogs (e.g. Twitter), multimedia sharing sites (e.g., a company creates a video about its products and uploads it to YouTube), virtual worlds (e.g., the company creates a virtual webstore in Seconds Life), company-hosted virtual events (e.g., an online Webinar), and mashups (e.g., businesses list their name and location on Google Places). Other important owned media are online games, online gifting, branded apps and social media press releases.

6. **Explain the advertising formats for social media.** Display ads use text and graphics, as well as the company's logos and contact information/Web links. Classified ads can be found on dedicated sites, such as Craigslist. Social ads incorporate user interactions that the consumer has agreed to display share, such as a profile picture and

name. Behaviorally targeted ads present ads to the user based on their previous behavior. Sponsored content integrates editorial content and advertising based on either underwritten (someone else's content) or advertiser-created content. Product placement embeds products or ads in online multiplayer games or videos (as well as traditional media). Text link ads include a hyperlink placed in specific text in social media content.

KEY TERMS

Advergaming (in-game advertising)   87
Advertising   88
Content marketing   83
Direct marketing   82
Earned media   83
Inbound marketing   94
Owned media   83
Paid media   83
Personal selling   82
Public relations   82
Sales promotion   82
Social ads   90
Widgets   88

REVIEW QUESTIONS

1. Describe the six steps of social media promotion.
2. Identify several social media markets.
3. What are the main communication objectives companies seek to achieve with customers and prospects?
4. List and define the five traditional promotional tools.
5. What is the most important criterion used by companies to select appropriate social media platforms for communication?
6. Define owned, paid, and earned social media.
7. Define all the types of owned social media.
8. What are the key advertising formats used in social media to aid commerce?
9. How is Facebook used for advertising?
10. How do marketers integrate online and offline communication plans?

TOPICS FOR DISCUSSION AND DEBATES

1. Is there a large risk for bloggers who accept sponsored content? Debate this issue.
2. If you were running a social media campaign for Nike, how would you allocate your advertising budget among social media platforms, and why?

3. How can a social media marketer use Facebook to reach international markets?
4. What are the advantages and disadvantages of using social media compared to using a company's own website?
5. Which would be the best social media for advertising the college book store to students at your university? Explain and defend your answer.
6. Compare and contrast the use of a blog instead of a Facebook page for social commerce.
7. Which social media platform(s) would be best for a sales promotion tactic, such as a coupon or contest? Why?
8. Discuss the potential business use of Twitter for social commerce.
9. What are the advantages of a social media press release, and why would a company use that instead of a traditional release?
10. The Pivot Conference research found only 9 % of respondents using social media to sell products (see **pivotcon.com/wp-content/uploads/2013/07/RotSA2011.pdf**). Why use social media if this is not the goal?
11. Do you think that social ads have any privacy risks for Facebook page owners? Why or why not?

INTERNET EXERCISES

1. Visit Wikipedia and search for the article about your university. Register and edit the article to make it more accurate and engaging. Make a copy of the before and after pages and write a short report discussing the process you used.
2. Find three social media display ads that you think are ineffective and explain why, describing how you would improve the ads.
3. Visit the Interactive Advertising Bureau (**iab.net**) and read the 2013 study on mobile advertising (**iab.net/ovumstudy**). What are the key findings and future outlook for mobile ads?
4. Visit **us.coca-cola.com/home** and **facebook.com/cocacola** and compare and contrast, explaining what you think are the objectives of each.
5. LinkedIn is growing rapidly. Visit **linkedin.com/about-us** read about it. Do you think business networks like this will ever draw more traffic than other social networks, such as Facebook? Why or why not?
6. Visit Twitter.com and read some of the tweets. If you were an entrepreneur with a new product, how could you use Twitter to build awareness and increase social commerce (sales)?
7. Enter **advertising.com**. Find and describe the innovative/scientific methods that are offered and related to social commerce.

8. Visit Google and do a search for your favorite car. What sponsored ad appeared on the results page? Now, do a search for your favorite music group. What sponsored links appeared on the results page? What conclusion can you draw about targeted advertising?

TEAM ASSIGNMENTS AND PROJECTS

1. Review the opening case and answer the following questions:
   (a) Identify the online promotional actions adopted by Johnson & Johnson and relate them to the methods described in the chapter.
   (b) Search the Internet to find more details about Johnson & Johnson's marketing activities on YouTube.
   (c) Search the Internet to find more details about Johnson & Johnson's marketing activities on Facebook and Twitter.
   (d) Search the Internet to find more details about Johnson & Johnson's marketing activities on mobile devices.
   (e) Outline the major benefits from Johnson & Johnson's online marketing activities.

2. Each group is assigned a social network that has business activities (e.g., LinkedIn, Xing, Facebook, Twitter, Seconds Life, etc.). Each group will identify all paid and owned social marketing communication on the sites. Write a report and deliver a class presentation.

3. Facebook is increasingly offering new marketing tools (e.g., Open Graph, Social Plugins). Identify all the tools offered. Each group will concentrate on the implication in one of the following areas: owned media, advertising, shopping, market research, customer service, CRM, and others. Present your findings to the class.

4. Each group will adopt one or two of the following companies that actively promote their products on Facebook and Twitter: Coca-Cola, Starbucks, Ford, Pepsi, Disney, Victoria Secret, iTunes, Toyota, Sony, or P&G. Find what methods they use and how they run their campaigns. Present your findings to the class.

REFERENCES

Adobe. "Going Global in a Social World: Promoting Global Brands Using the Facebook Page Structure." A White Paper by Adobe Systems Inc., #91069096, March 2012. **marketingpedia.com/ Marketing-Library/Social%20Media/Adobe_Going_Global_ Social_World.pdf** (accessed August 2014).

Bobowski, K. "How to Convert Pinterest Traffic into Sales." April 3, 2014. **imediaconnection.com/content/36287.asp** (accessed August 2014).

Butcher, D. "Johnson & Johnson Breaks Multichannel Mobile Campaign." November 10, 2008. **mobilemarketer.com/cms/news/ advertising/2075.html** (accessed August 2014).

Butcher, D. "Johnson & Johnson's Zyrtec Runs Mobile Banner Campaign on App." March 31, 2009. **mobilemarketer.com/cms/ news/advertising/2938.html** (accessed August 2014).

Camaret, V. "Advergaming: The New Advertiser's Toy?" September 4, 2013. **digi- vibes.com/advergaming-new-advertisers-toy** (accessed August 2014).

Corcoran, S. "Defining Earned, Owned, and Paid Media." December 16, 2009. **blogs.forrester.com/interactive_marketing/2009/12/ defining-earned-owned-and-paid-media.html** (accessed August 2014).

Denny. "Social Media Marketing Outperforms Display Ads." December 31, 2013. **mobilecommercepress.com/social-media-marketing- outperforms-display-ads/8510163** (accessed August 2014).

Edwards, J. "Facebook Shares Surge on First Ever $1 Billion Mobile Ad Revenue Quarter." January 29, 2014. **businessinsider.com/ facebook-q4-2013-earnings-2014-1** (accessed August 2014).

eMarketer. "Advertisers Begin to Look Beyond Facebook and Twitter." August 1, 2011. **emarketer.com/Article/Advertisers-Begin-Look- Beyond-Facebook-Twitter/1008520** (accessed August 2014).

Indvik, L. "Twitter to Top $1 Billion in Ad Revenue in 2014 [Report]." June 1, 2012. **mashable.com/2012/06/01/twitter-ad-revenue** (accessed August 2014).

Interactive Advertising Bureau. "2013 Internet Ad Revenues Soar To $42.8 Billion, Hitting Landmark High & Surpassing Broadcast Television For The First Time—Marks a 17% Rise Over Record- Setting Revenues in 2012." April 10, 2014a. **iab.net/about_the_ iab/recent_press_releases/press_release_archive/press_release/ pr-041014** (accessed August 2014).

Interactive Advertising Bureau. "Social Advertising Best Practices." May 2009. **iab.net/media/file/Social-Advertising-Best- Practices-0509.pdf** (accessed August 2014).

Interactive Advertising Bureau. "Social Media Buyer's Guide." February 2010. **iab.net/media/file/IAB_SocialMedia_Booklet.pdf** (accessed August 2014).

Interactive Advertising Bureau, *IAB Internet Advertising Revenue Report: 2013 Full Year Results.* April 2014b. [Conducted by PwC and sponsored by IAB]. **iab.net/media/file/IAB_Internet_Advertising_ Revenue_Report_FY_2013.pdf** (accessed August 2014).

Kotler, P., and G. Armstrong, *Principles of Marketing, 15th Ed.* Upper Saddle River, NJ: Pearson Education, Inc. 2013.

Latka, N. "25 Facebook Facts and Statistics You Should Know in 2014." July 29, 2014. **jeffbullas.com/2014/07/29/25-facebook- facts-and-statistics-you-should-know-in-2014** (accessed August 2014).

Learmonth, M. "Study: Twitter Ad Revenue Grow to $150M in 2011." *AdAge*, January 24, 2011.

Learmonth, M. "Vivaki Predicts $100M Market for Choose-Your- Own-Ad Format." *AdAge*, May 24, 2010. May 24, 2010.

Makovsky, K. "A Snapshot of Social Media 2013." *Forbes*, November 7, 2013. Marrs, M. "45 Fabulous Facebook Advertising Tips & Magic Marketing Tricks." January 30, 2014. **wordstream.com/ blog/ws/2014/01/30/facebook-advertising-tips** (accessed August 2014).

Marrs, M. "45 Fabulous Facebook Advertising Tips and Magic Marketing Tricks." January 30, 2014. **wordstream.com/blog/ ws/2014/01/30/facebook-advertising-tips#.** (accessed December 2014).

Meeker, M. " Internet Trends 2013: Code Conference." May 28, 2014. **amazonaws.com/kpcbweb/files/85/Internet_Trends_2014_ vFINAL_-_05_28_14-_PDF.pdf?1401286773** (accessed August 2014).

Microsoft. "Johnson & Johnson Acuvue Case Study." Compendium 2009. [Greater Asia Pacific] **advertising.microsoft.com/asia/ WWDocs/User/Asia/ResearchLibrary/CaseStudy/GAP%20 Case%20Study%20Compendium_2009_Final.pdf** (accessed August 2014).

Munro, D. "New Study Ranks Johnson &Johnson #1 in Pharma for Social Media Engagement." *Forbes*, January 21, 2014.

Neff, J. "How Orabrush Got National Walmart Deal with YouTube Videos, $28 in Facebook Ads." *AdAge*, September 20, 2011.

Neff, J. "Nielsen: Facebook's Ads Work Pretty Well." *AdAge*, April 19, 2010.

Nielsen. "Getting Socially Minded: Marketers to Up Their Social Media Ads in 2013." *Newswire*, January 29, 2013. **nielsen.com/us/en/insights/news/2013/getting-socially-minded-marketers-to-up-their-social-media-ads-in-2013.html** (accessed August 2014).

Olenski, S. "How Johnson & Johnson is Using Social Media to Save Lives." *Forbes*, July 10, 2013.

Patel, K. "Apple, Campbell's Say iAds Twice as Effective as TV." *AdAge*, February 3. 2011.

Ploof, R. *Johnson & Johnson Does New Media*. e-book, June 15, 2009. **ronamok.com/ebooks/jnj_case_study.pdf** (accessed August 2014).

PR Newswire. "Databook Q1 2014: Social Media Advertising Spend in the US." July 17, 2014. **marketwatch.com/story/databook-q1-2014-social-media-advertising-spend-in-the-us-2014-07-17** (accessed August 2014).

Remy-Boutang, D. "Social Media and the Employment Relationship." Presentation at Social Media and the Employment Relationship, Grange Holborn Hotel, London, UK March 3, 2010. **slideshare.net/delphRB/ibm-swg-social-media-marketing-delphine-remy-boutang-3rd-march-3467701** (accessed August 2014).

Schmidt, S. "5 Mobile Advertising Trends for 2014." *MMA*, April 14, 2014. **mmaglobal.com/articles/5-mobile-advertising-trends-2014** (accessed August 2014).

Sernovitz, A. "How Johnson & Johnson Uses Social Media in Highly Regulated Industries." February 4, 2011. **smartblogs.com/social-media/2011/02/04/andys-answers-how-johnson-johnson-uses-social-media-in-highly-regulated-industries** (accessed August 2014).

Shih, C. *The Facebook Era: Tapping Online Social Networks to Market, Sell, and Innovate*, 2nd *Edition*, Upper Saddle River N.J: Pearson Education, Inc. 2011.

Strauss, J., and R. Frost. *E-Marketing*. Upper Saddle River, NJ: Pearson Education, 2014.

Sysomos. "Extend the Depth of Your Marketing and Promotional Campaigns Using Social Media." A White Paper (2011). **social-media-monitor.co.uk/resources/whitepapers//Sysomos-Extend-Your-Campaigns.pdf** (accessed August 2014).

Tracy, A. "Beyoncé Shows How Social Media is Changing Marketing." last updated December 16, 2013. **inc.com/abigail-tracy/beyonce-shows-the-true-power-of-social-media.html** (accessed August 2014).

Walter, E., and R. Gioglio. *The Power of Visual Storytelling: How to Use Visuals, Videos and Social Media to Market your Brand*. New York: McGraw-Hill, 2014.

Wingfield, N. "Virtual Products, Real Profits." September 9, 2011. **online.wsj.com/news/articles/SB10001424053111904823804576502442835413446** (accessed August 2014).

Customer Engagement and Metrics

5

Contents

Opening Case: Häagen-Dazs Viral Video Creates a Buzz....... 99

5.1   Earned Media... 101

5.2   Social Media Engagement Levels.................................... 101

5.3   Engaging Consumers to Produce Earned Media............ 103

5.4   Engagement Techniques... 104

5.5   Reputation Management in Social Media 112

5.6   Search Engine Optimization.. 116

5.7   Monitor, Measure, and Refine: SM Metrics................... 118

References.. 124

Electronic supplementary material The online version of this chapter (doi:10.1007/978-3-319-17028-2_5) contains supplementary material, which is available to authorized users.

Learning Objectives

Upon completion of this chapter, you will be able to:

1. Describe the five levels of user engagement (5 Cs).
2. Describe the major engagement techniques in social commerce and implementation issues.
3. Express the role of trust in social commerce.
4. Provide examples of collaborative content creation by consumers.
5. Describe how a company can build, maintain, monitor, and repair its reputation in social media.
6. Identify several ways companies can improve their brand positions on search engine results pages.
7. Define performance metrics used to monitor, measure, and refine social commerce goals and tactics.

OPENING CASE: HÄAGEN-DAZS VIRAL VIDEO CREATES A BUZZ

Häagen-Dazs (a Nestlé-owned company), whose brand dates back to the early 1920s, was established in 1961 and opened its first store in 1976 in New York with chocolate, vanilla, and coffee flavors. It was later purchased by Pillsbury, which was subsequently bought by General Mills. In the U.S., the ice cream products are produced by the Nestlé subsidiary, Dreyer's, although General Mills still owns the brand name. Häagen-Dazs is served in over 900 franchises and company owned shops in 50 countries. Häagen-Dazs maintains a website, a Facebook page with over 1.2 million likes (**facebook. com/HaagenDazsUS**) and several other Facebook pages for various countries (e.g., Malaysia, Singapore), as well as an interactive microsite and videos dedicated to the honey bee crisis. From the beginning, Häagen-Dazs ice cream sought to innovate and bring new frozen dessert experiences to its customers, including distinctive flavors such as vanilla Swiss almond, butter pecan, and Dulce de leche, to name just a few. Häagen-Dazs was also the first to introduce the world to ice cream bars for a grown-up palate, with the introduction of the Häagen-Dazs brand ice cream bar line in 1986. Other super-premium innovations followed, such as frozen yogurt in 1991 and sorbet in 1993.

The Problem

In 2006, Häagen-Dazs (H-D) discovered that the world's honey bee populations were quickly disappearing due to a phenomenon called Colony Collapse Disorder (CCD): when honey bees mysteriously desert their hives and die. This was a problem for the brand because bees pollinate the flowers of one-third of all the food we eat—including pears, strawberries and raspberries—all important ingredients in the company's ice creams, sorbets, frozen yogurts, and bars. Häagen-Dazs estimated that 30 of the 73 flavors contain ingredients pollinated by honeybees.

The Solution

Haagen-Dazs saw this as an important opportunity to initiate its first "cause marketing" campaign for the brand. For starters, they partnered with leading research facilities to donate over $1 million to honey bee research. Their funds are used to help support the largest agricultural facility in the U.S., located at U.C. Davis in California. The H-D Honey Bee Haven was planted in 2009 next to the Honey Bee Research Facility at Davis (**beebiology.ucdavis.edu**). H-D then used traditional and social media to raise awareness and motivate support for the disappearing honey bee cause. The company created educational websites (e.g., **beebiology.ucdavis.edu/ HAVEN/index.html**) with links to bee news, information and "how you can help." There were television ads, documentaries, and a video produced for the Internet, entitled "Bee-Boy Dance Crew" (for the story behind the video and to watch the video, see Yoerg 2008). The video targeted a young 18–24 year old market ("youth thirsty for honey") with a hip-hop interpretation of how a honey bee "dances" when alerting hive mates to a newly found source of nectar. The video garnered two million views (on YouTube) within 2 weeks, while "visits to "Haagen-Dazs' 'Save the Bees Site' spiked, reflecting heightened interest in the bee issue" (Yoerg 2008). The strategy: this market was more likely to send the video link to friends, thus raising awareness for the cause. The company also created a designated cause Web microsite, which allowed users to watch the video, explore the panoramic fields by clicking the mouse, and create and send a virtual bee to friends. The site also engaged users by accepting donations online, asking for support for reinstatement of the Boy Scout Beekeeping Merit Badge, and providing downloadable instructions on how to plant a bee-friendly garden.

H-D hired an online marketing firm, Feed Company, to promote the Bee-Boy video. It sent creative messages to narrowly targeted online media, including influential bloggers (such as *Huffington Post* writers). The message varied depending on the media outlet. For example, "green" blogs received information on the environmental impact of the disappearing bee population, and entertainment outlets received references to the pop culture value of the Bee-Boy video. As the buzz increased, Feed Company gained coverage in more mainstream online media sites and offline broadcast and print media.

Other Social Media Activities

Häagen-Dazs operates in a very competitive environment (e.g., Ben & Jerry's) and therefore the company's strategy aims at increasing brand awareness and loyalty. The company is extremely active in using social media tools and platforms. Here are a few examples:

- Engagement and word-of-mouth (WOM). Kolah (2013) reports on activities on the company's Facebook page in the UK and creating WOM buzz around the brand and with brand advocates on Twitter. The objective is to increase customers' loyalty. The company wanted to increase consumer engagement on its Facebook page and build awareness and bookings for a campaign they were running targeted at women for a "girls' night."
- The company is active in amplifying social presence via mobile campaigns on Facebook (see Kats 2012).
- For a social media campaign case study on how the company increases customer engagement, see **slideshare.net/ QubeMedia/qube-casestudy-hdboudoir**.

Results

Within 2 weeks of the campaign's July 15, 2008 start, the following results began to emerge:

- The 'Bee-Boy Dance Crew' video received over two million views, primarily on YouTube, but also on Yahoo, Vimeo, and Daily Motion. CNN wrote about the story, which resulted in 1.3 million video views; it was covered in over 150 blogs (Yoerg 2008).
- Many high visibility blogs covered the cause. For example, the 6.9 million readers of the *Huffington Post* and 1.6 million TreeHugger viewers were exposed to the story.
- There was a high level of user engagement with this campaign: over 3,500 YouTube comments, 5,850 ratings of the video (averaging 4.5 stars and considerable positive feedback), and 11,024 discussions by users in forums, blogs, and other social networking sites.

- Since 2008, Häagen-Dazs donated $620,000 to two universities and $1 million to University of California at Davis for honey bee research (Yoerg 2008).

In total, the campaign generated over two million video views, thousands of conversations, and many impressions. By August 2009, the University of Illinois scientists had discovered the cause of CCD, and the HD honey bee site continued to report on the disappearing bee population and search for a solution (see the H-D site).

Sources: Based on Goodby et al. (2008), Kats 2012, Kolah (2013), Yoerg (2008) **en.wikipedia.org/wiki/Häagen-Dazs**, **haagen-dazs.us**, and **facebook.com/HaagenDazsUS** (all accessed August 2014).

LESSONS LEARNED FROM THIS CASE

Dreyer's and its Häagen-Dazs brand connected with a cause that threatened the brand. The passion for the disappearing honey bee cause subsequently attached to the brand as well. The company astutely identified its target market (18–24 year olds) and through its agency, created social media to attract and engage the market. H-D placed the information and video on social media sites which the target would see, and that drove brand engagement and viral activity. This is an example of owned media that resulted in widespread positive earned media: the goal of every company. You will learn more about these techniques in this chapter.

This chapter discusses many important types of earned media: how a company can encourage positive user-generated content (UGC) and protect its reputation in an uncontrollable social media conversation, and concludes with the ways to monitor and measure all three types of media (owned, paid, and earned) for social commerce effectiveness.

5.1 EARNED MEDIA

Well-executed owned and paid social media can drive prospects and customers through the steps from awareness to product purchase, repurchase, and into long-term customer loyalty. However, earned media have a multiplier effect (e.g., $1+1=5$), intensifying and spreading the communication messages far and wide in social media—as experienced by H-D in its "Save the Honey Bee" campaign. "Whatever your methods, find a way to incorporate a social element into every marketing campaign you run by finding compelling reasons for people to share. That'll make every dollar you spend on marketing look like two" (Dhalokia 2011; Marketo

2011). Recall from Chap. 4 that earned media occurs when "customer conversations become the channel" on blogs, product review sites, Facebook, news sites, many other places, and in comments on owned media pages everywhere they are allowed (see Fig. 5.1).

Earned media is often initiated by the company through branded (owned) content distribution, such as entertaining YouTube videos about the product, social media press releases (public relations), or other activities intended to engage users, such as placing social hooks on company brand sites and microsites (e.g., Facebook register, subscribe or "like," Digg, Pinterest, Delicious, RSS, and other buttons). Companies also put "follow us" links to these social sites on their Web pages and in e-mail messages sent to customer or prospect databases. Earned media can have a direct cost associated with it, such as when the company sponsors a contest or creates content that spreads, but there is no financial cost when it is simply user conversation. By definition, others create earned media, and companies have little to no control over this user-generated content (UGC). This communication can get ugly very quickly—and often does when people criticize brands online. Professional and citizen journalists share their own opinions and experiences all over the social media via computers and mobile phones, even at times when companies are not monitoring these posts.

Before discussing how owned and paid media generate earned media, it is important to learn the possible levels of social media engagement.

5.2 SOCIAL MEDIA ENGAGEMENT LEVELS

Social media engagement occurs among customers and between the company and Internet users who are actively discussing the brand (Chap. 3). This is compared to traditional media, which only allows passive exposure, such as when a consumer is watching television. Occasionally, however, traditional media will prompt engagement when (1) the consumer writes an e-mail or letter to the editor, (2) telephones a broadcast station, or (3) posts a reaction on their own or the company's Facebook or Twitter page. Traditional media can also prompt communication to companies about their brands when designed for this purpose, such as awarding a prize to the first 100 people that send a text message to a company. However, it is not as easy for consumers to engage when they receive the information via traditional media and must access their computer, tablet, or mobile device to respond.

There are many levels of online user engagement. It is important for a company to understand its social commerce objectives and what proportion of its customers and prospects operate at each level, so that it can use social media for

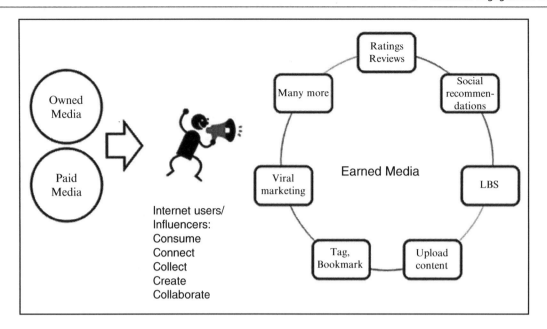

Fig. 5.1 Owned and paid media drive earned media. *Note*: figure in middle is free clip art

positive discussion online and collaboration with customers. Forrester's Social Technographics™ framework includes seven levels of participation, and this company has data about the entire Internet population that companies can use for comparison with their consumer activity levels: "inactives, spectators, joiners, collectors, critics, conversationalists and creators" (Band et al. 2010; **blogs.forrester.com/ gina_sverdlov/12-01-04-global_social_technographics_ update_2011_us_and_eu_mature_emerging_markets_ show_lots_of_activity**). Evans and McKee (2010) also suggest a four-level engagement ladder that moves engagement beyond simple owned and paid media consumption. Figure 5.2 displays an iteration of these ideas, displaying the levels of engagement from least to most.

1. The least engaged Internet users *consume* online content only. They only read blogs, watch videos, look at photos, listen to podcasts, and read the reviews and opinions expressed by others occupying higher levels of engagement on websites and forums.

2. At the next level, users *connect* with others by creating a profile on a social network, such as "friending" on Facebook or joining TripAdvisor or other sites that require registration to access the social media content. These consumers do not post anything, however. Connecting is a low-risk level of engagement that allows people to participate in small steps. Another way to connect is through a social gathering, happening either on or offline. This is often facilitated by a site that allows groups to coordinate these meetings. For example, in 2010, St. Supéry winery (**stsupery.com**) used **meetup. com** to create an online global celebration of a wine—they called it #Cabernet Day ("on social media sites" (the

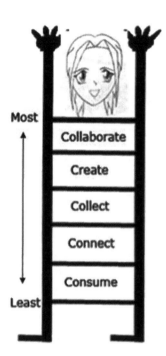

Fig. 5.2 Five stages of social media engagement

"#" is a Twitter hash tag). In a 24-hour time period, over 1,000 people online and 75 in real life met to celebrate and purchase and drink the wine. Many messages were also posted on social network sites and YouTube, and there were even check-ins at Foursquare (Bakas 2010).

3. Consumers who *collect* information go through a process of filtering content and tagging what they find valuable in social media sites. This could include Delicious for bookmark sharing and Flickr or Facebook for photo tagging or

"liking" someone else's content. Collectors might also subscribe to RSS feeds on blog sites so that they can actively read content of interest. Finally, collectors show their preferences by voting in polls online. For example, collector shoppers at Sears.com have the option of sharing prom dresses they like with their Facebook friends using a feature called "Prom Premier 2011." Sears supplemented the option with an ad campaign placed on Facebook.

4. Moving up the engagement ladder, *creators* actually write or upload original multimedia content to websites, such as videos to YouTube, pin boards on Pinterest, or music and podcasts to iTunes. This involves creating content, which is a higher level than simply voting on someone else's content. These consumers write product reviews/ratings, create their own blogs/Web pages and comment on other people's blogs, contribute to wiki sites (e.g., eHow, Wikipedia), and generally add much more to the social media content.

5. Finally, the most engaged customers *collaborate* with the company when they work with others in discussion to find ways to improve products. CNN offers iReporter, where users send in videos of breaking news, which can result in CNN sending a company reporter to the event for a story. Another example is Dell's IdeaStorm site (**ideastorm.com**), where users post questions and product problems and others view and vote the posts as important concerns or not. Dell then responds on the status of each idea ("under review" or "implemented"). As we are writing this, one of the top ideas that Dell implemented was use biodegradable packaging material for shipping (posted by a collaborator and voted on by 202 "collectors"). Finally, Twitter's hash tag (#), marking keywords and topics in Tweets, was actually created by Twitter users. This type of collaboration helps companies and bloggers improve products.

According to the Pew Internet Project, as of January 2014, 74 % of online adults and 89 % of 18–24 year olds used social media (**pewinternet.org/fact-sheets/social-networking-fact-sheet**). According to its Q2 2014 financial report, as of June 30, 2014, Facebook had 1.32 billion monthly active users worldwide. For an infographic listing Facebook statistics from 2004 to 2014 ("10 years of Facebook"), see **cnn.com/2014/02/03/tech/social-media/facebook-graphic**. In the next sections, you will see how companies engage customers to create earned media product discussion and multimedia content uploading.

5.3 ENGAGING CONSUMERS TO PRODUCE EARNED MEDIA

When a couple becomes engaged to be married, they are expressing their trust, commitment, and caring for each other—this is also true when a brand seeks this kind of love from its markets and wants them to talk about the products. Wikipedia defines **customer engagement (CE)** as "the engagement of customers with one another, with a company or a brand. The initiative for engagement can be either consumer- or company-led, and the medium of engagement can be on or offline" (see **en.wikipedia.org/wiki/Customer_engagement**). The essentials of customer engagement are covered in Chap. 3. For a free e-book on more effective social media engagement, see Brusselmans (2014).

Trust is a key component of word-of-mouth communication resulting from customer engagement. Edelman, the world's largest public relations firm, found that 65 % of respondents across 25 countries trust a "person like yourself" for credible information about a company (Fig. 5.3). This is in contrast to the only 43 % who trust the company CEO (do a Google search for "Edelman trust barometer

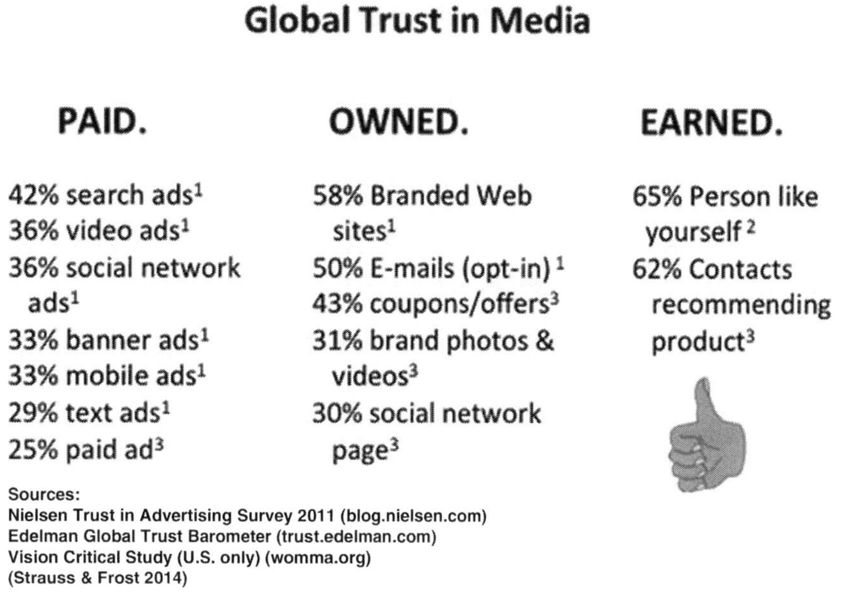

Fig. 5.3 Proportion of consumers expressing trust in media

Global Trust in Media

PAID.

42% search ads[1]
36% video ads[1]
36% social network ads[1]
33% banner ads[1]
33% mobile ads[1]
29% text ads[1]
25% paid ad[3]

OWNED.

58% Branded Web sites[1]
50% E-mails (opt-in)[1]
43% coupons/offers[3]
31% brand photos & videos[3]
30% social network page[3]

EARNED.

65% Person like yourself[2]
62% Contacts recommending product[3]

Sources:
Nielsen Trust in Advertising Survey 2011 (blog.nielsen.com)
Edelman Global Trust Barometer (trust.edelman.com)
Vision Critical Study (U.S. only) (womma.org)
(Strauss & Frost 2014)

2014," and see the results in a slideshare presentation at **edelman.com/insights/intellectual-property/2014-edelman-trust-barometer/about-trust/global-results** for more information). "A person like yourself" is someone who shares similar interests or friends in a social network. For example, when planning trips or on the road, many travelers will visit the largest travel site, TripAdvisor, to check out the over 170 million reviews and opinions of hotels and sites in 43 countries, which are written by travelers across the world. Thus, when people post opinions about products, over half of the readers are likely to believe what they say, which will influence their purchase decisions. In general, the data show that people trust earned media more than owned or paid media. This indicates the huge advantage to earned media.

We now turn to a discussion of the "who, what, how, and where" to engage customers in conversation about a company and its brands.

Who Should a Company Engage?

It is not effective, efficient, or likely possible to get the entire Internet universe talking about an organization and its products. As discussed in Chap. 4, the company will identify its target markets and objectives before developing an engagement campaign. For example, Hagen-Dazs selected the 18–24 year old market, as you read in the opening case example. Another tactic used by H-D and many other companies is to target influential bloggers and members of social networks, such as Arianna Huffington's *The Huffington Post*, with its 50,000 bloggers and over 78 million global unique visitors (Business Wire 2013). For ways that how bloggers can catch and keep their readers' attention, see Ahmad (2013).

Companies identify social media influencers in two ways. First, they can observe and participate in conversations in social media platforms where people discuss their industries. This will help them see who is active and has the most Facebook fans or friends, Flickr comments, Tumblr or Twitter subscribers, or simply the most comments on user posts. For example, the eMarketing Association Network group in LinkedIn has over 586,000 members, and by clicking on the "members" tab, members can see the list of "This Week's Top Influencers." These contributors, along with the group creator owner (Robert Fleming, who is the CEO/founder of the eMarketing Association), are members who start a discussion and comment on other group members' discussions. Under the "Pulse" tab on the member's Home page, you can see the "top posts" for the day, week, of all time, and the most recent posts. On the "pulse" page, you can also search and find the "top influencers" and "most searched influencers." (*LinkedIn Today*, *Influencer Posts*, and *Channels* - Move your cursor over *Interests* at the top of your homepage and select *Pulse*.)

For a B2B company selling products to eMarketers, this is an ideal source for building a buzz with influential social media participants.

The seconds way to find influentials is to use a service such as Klout, Inc. (**klout.com**). Klout measures over 400 variables from 8 different networks for each of over 620 million social network participants and ranks them based on (1) number of people they reach, (2) how much influence participants have on their followers (e.g., number of "likes" or "retweets"), and (3) how influential the person's network members are. The result is a Klout Score from 1 to 100, with the top scored people having the most social media influence. According to Klout, "We measure multiple pieces of data from several social networks, and also real world data from places like Bing and Wikipedia. Then we apply them to our Klout Score algorithm, and then show the resulting number on your profile. The higher your Klout Score, the tougher it becomes to increase" (per **klout.com/corp/score**). Klout also lists the topics these influencers write about and their social media style (e.g., broadcaster or specialist). Klout also has a "perks" program that offers free products and discounts from over 500 companies to high-Klout score users/the influentials with brands they are likely to care and write about, such as Starbucks, Audi, Virgin America, and Dove. People with scores over 55 even get free access to the American Airlines Admirals Club lounges in selected cities worldwide. The benefit to companies is that they can pay to gain access to high Klout score individuals/influentials (see **klout.com**). In 2011, Canadian pop/R&B singer, songwriter and actor Justin Bieber was the only person with a perfect 100 Klout score, while President Barak Obama had a score of 99. In 2012, Klout changed its scoring algorithm (to the current 400 metrics from the previous 100 metrics); as of August 2014, Bieber's score has fallen to 92, while President Obama's is 99 (both of their Klout scores fluctuated within the years). To raise your Klout score, see the example provided by Kamboe (2014). For further discussion, see Chap. 10.

5.4   ENGAGEMENT TECHNIQUES

Most social media provide space and tools for earned media content. You have read about many of them in this book, such as sites that allow multimedia content uploads (YouTube, Flickr, Vine), comments, bookmarking (Delicious), tagging (Flickr, Facebook), reviews, recommendations and more (recall Fig. 5.1). Both websites and mobile apps offer tools for these connections and conversations. In the following sections, we focus on just a few important or new techniques not fully described in other chapters.

Sales funnel   **Viral funnel**

Fig. 5.4 Viral marketing turns the sales funnel upside down

Viral Marketing

Viral marketing is a bad name for a great technique. **Viral marketing (viral advertising)** "is any marketing technique that induces websites or users to pass on a marketing message to other sites or users, creating a potentially exponential growth in the message's visibility and effect" (see **whatis. techtarget.com**). This marketing technique uses social networks to produce exponential increases in brand recognition or to achieve other marketing objectives (such as product sales) through self-replicating viral processes. This is analogous to the spread of physical or computer viruses (see **onbile.com/info/mobile-viral-marketing**). It is the opposite of the marketing sales funnel, which starts with many prospects and then narrows as prospects drop off to fewer customers, as shown in Fig. 5.4. The viral funnel does the reverse because it increases the number exposed to brand messages as content circulates.

Viral marketing can be delivered by offline word of mouth or enhanced by the network effects of the Internet. Viral marketing can occur when users forward e-mail, send text messages, or share images and videos on Facebook, interactive Flash games, advergames, e-books, brandable software, and images. The founder of Hotmail, a free e-mail service that grew from 0 to 12 million subscribers in its 18 initial months, and to more than 50 million subscribers in about 4 years, used viral marketing. Each e-mail sent via Hotmail carried an invitation for free Hotmail service.

According to a 2010 survey conducted in Chinese markets, word of mouth has become an important factor in consumers' purchasing decisions. In 2010, 64 % of respondents said that word of mouth influenced their purchasing decisions, increasing from 56 % in 2008 (Atsmon et al. 2010). Well-executed viral strategies work because individuals trust their acquaintances and family to help them with their choices (Atsmon et al. 2010).

As with all engagement strategies, the ultimate goal of marketers interested in creating successful viral marketing programs is to create content (1) that appeals to individuals with high social networking visibility and (2) that has a high probability of being presented and spread quickly by these individuals and their friends in their communications with others.

Viral marketing has long been a favorite strategy of online marketers pushing youth-oriented products. For example, marketers might distribute a small game program or a video embedded within a sponsor's e-mail that is easy to forward. By releasing a few thousand copies of the game to select consumers, vendors hope that it is spread quickly to reach hundreds of thousands of others. Also known as *advocacy marketing*, viral marketing, if properly used, can be effective, efficient and relatively inexpensive—as experienced by H-D in the opening case. eWOM platforms can also influence consumer product judgment (see Lee and Youn 2009). For further details, see **en.wikipedia.org/wiki/Viral_marketing** and **wisegeek.net/what-are-the-different-types-of-viral-marketing-campaigns.htm**. For a scientific take on viral marketing with examples, see **helpscout.net/blog/viral-marketing**. For five great viral marketing campaigns and how they worked, see **creativeguerrillamarketing.com/viral-marketing/5-great-viral-marketing-campaigns-worked**.

Every company wants to create content that goes viral, but few accomplish this feat. The content has to be entertaining or mysterious, match popular culture and gain user attention. In a sea of online content and information overload, sometimes even the best content does not go viral.

The term "viral marketing" has also been used pejoratively to refer to stealth marketing campaigns or the unscrupulous use of online astroturfing—the attempt to create an impression of widespread support for a policy, individual, or product, where little such support exists by misleading the public into believing that the position of the astroturfer is the commonly held view. Tactics include multiple online identities or a reviewer or commentator being paid by a company to post an opinion or mention a brand or product on Twitter or blogs (see **theguardian.com/commentisfree/2012/feb/08/what-is-astroturfing**). Another downside of a viral strategy is that several e-mail hoaxes have been spread this way. Viral marketing has also been criticized by consumers due to a concern over unsolicited e-mails, which many see as an invasion of privacy. For more details about viral marketing, see McColl (2010).

Examples of Viral Campaigns

Viral marketing is often very successful with entertaining videos (especially from YouTube) that are spread via e-mail, Facebook sharing, and by microbloggers (e.g., Twitter). Following are some successful viral campaigns:

- Burger King's "The Subservient Chicken" campaign, running from 2004, was an extremely successful example of viral marketing from a microsite with an interactive video **subservientchicken.com** of a man dressed in a chicken costume. The chicken video had received over 450 million views as of 2011. It is particularly relevant and appropriate for the brand because users could type a command, such as "dance," and the chicken will dance in the video—supporting Burger King's "Have it your way" advertising slogan. Then the chicken video disappeared and in April 2014, Burger King posted on its Twitter page: "We Miss You Subservient Chicken. #TBT pic.twitter. com/msrZqeX0PH." The company also posted ads in the style of "missing persons" bulletins ("Have you seen this chicken"?) in many newspapers, such as *The New York Times*, while online the hashtag #FindTheChicken appeared. Burger King issued a press release in April 2014 (the tenth anniversary), that they would reintroduce the Subservient Chicken alongside the Chicken Big King Sandwich (Burger King 2014). On the **subservientchicken.com** site in 2014, Burger King showed an empty couch with the missing chicken with the line: "Help. There's a chicken on the loose and we are desperately trying to find him" (Morrison 2014). On the "resurrected" site, Burger King also posted a video of the adventures the chicken had for the last 10 years, asking viewers to share the video using the hashtag "#ChickenRedemption," Burger King is also encouraging people to use the hashtag "#FindTheChicken" to promote the campaign, which is for the new Chicken Big King sandwich (**time.com/79309/burger-king-subservient-chicken-missing**; includes the picture of the "Have you seen this chicken?" poster). This clever campaign will boost the viral nature of this site once again. Based on Chithra (2012), Burger King (2014), Morrison 2014, **time.com/79309/burger-king-subservient-chicken-missing/**; and **subservientchicken.com** (both accessed August 2014).
- In December 2009, podcasters of The Mike O'Meara Show launched a viral marketing campaign on Facebook to encourage others to download the show.
- Between December 2009 and March 2010, a series of seven videos were posted to YouTube under the name "iamamiwhoami" which led to speculation that they were a marketing campaign for a band by that name. In March 2010, an anonymous package was sent to an MTV journalist claiming to contain a code, which if cracked, would give the identity of the artist. The seventh video, entitled 'y,' appears to feature the Swedish singer Jonna Lee.
- On July 14, 2010, Old Spice launched the fastest growing online viral video campaign ever, garnering 6.7 million views after 24 h, ballooning to over 23 million views after 36 h. Old Spice's agency created a bathroom set in Portland, OR and had its TV commercial star, Isaiah Mustafa, reply to 186 online comments and questions posted on websites like Twitter, Facebook, Reddit, Digg, YouTube, and others. The campaign ran for 3 days.

Viral Blogging

Viral blogging is when bloggers conduct viral marketing activities by leveraging the power of the blog community to spread content. Viral blogging can be very effective with the use of tools such as trends on Twitter. Many retailers entice WOM marketing by bloggers. For example, Paramount wanted to build awareness and box office sales for a sneak preview of the modestly budgeted "Super 8" science fiction film, which opened on June 10, 2011. Paramount sent a single Tweet and purchased advertising on Twitter via two Promoted Trends—one a day before the premier and one on the day of the premier. The "Twitter exclusive" sneak previews generated $1 million in box office sales, and the opening weekend for the film surpassed Paramount's goals by 52 % (see **business.twitter.com/success-stories/paramount-pictures**).

Stormhoek Vineyards (**stormhoek.com**) initiated successful viral marketing on social networks. The company first offered a free bottle of wine to bloggers. Within 6 months, about 100 of these bloggers voluntarily posted comments about the winery on their own blogs. Most had positive comments, which were read by their readers and other bloggers. The Stormhoek example raises an interesting question: Can bloggers be bought? The criticism is that bloggers have not been required to disclose that they are being paid (or receive gifts) for their endorsements. Companies can pay bloggers directly to endorse products, or do so via an intermediary, such as PayPerPost (as discussed in Chap. 4). However, the U.S. Federal Trade Commission requires disclosure from all bloggers who receive gifts or cash for promoting products. The FTC does not monitor bloggers so this practice of not revealing the pay or gifts continues with some bloggers.

Viral Videos and Video Ads

According to Techopedia, a **viral video** is "any clip of animation or film that is spread rapidly through online sharing" (per **techopedia.com/definition/26863/viral-video**). These videos become popular when they get circulated via e-mail, texting, blogs, Facebook, discussion forums, and so forth. This way, people share videos that receive more attention, sometimes drawing millions of viewers in a short time. Popular sites that are used for sharing viral videos include YouTube (**youtube.com**) and Vimeo (**vimeo.com**).

Mobile Viral Marketing

Viral marketing is often deployed to mobile platforms. This is called *mobile viral marketing*. A typical approach is to develop and distribute apps for mobile devices. A successful example involves the "Get Your Island On" Malibu Bowling Game, a campaign launched by Pernod Ricard rum in 2009 to support the launch of a new flavor. Their 2009 multi-channel campaign included a free bowling game called "Get Your Island On," available on iPhones and other smart-phones. The game got over two million downloads in the first 6 months. The managing director of the Great Works ad agency, hired by Pernod Ricard, said that a phone app is a perfect way of branding, since the product is featured in the game (the bowling pins are replaced by Malibu rum bottles). For details see **mobilemarketer.com/cms/news/advertising/3178.html.**

Ratings, Reviews, Recommendations and Referrals

Prior to a purchase, consumers like to collect information, such as, what brand to buy, from which vendor, and at what price. Online customers do this via shopping aids (e.g., comparison shopping sites), consulting product review sites such as Epinions, and conducting research at company sites and other sources. Ratings and reviews posted on social networks facilitate social commerce. According to Gartner Inc., the majority of consumers rely on social networks to guide them in purchase decisions (per Gartner, Inc. 2010). In the social commerce environment, shoppers look to their friends, fans, followers, and experienced customers for their opinions and advice. With peer-to-peer engagement through social media and high consumer trust in friends, family, and acquaintances, retailers recognize that their customers' voices can be an extremely strong marketing tool for building sales and improving products. Therefore, retailers want to hear what the customers have to say. A variety of SC models and tools is available for this purpose.

- **Customer ratings and reviews.** This is feedback from real customers, integrated either into an e-commerce product page, a social network page, a customer's review site, or in customer news feeds (e.g., Amazon.com, iTunes, Buzzillions, Epinions). Customer ratings are often summarized by votes or polls.

- **Expert ratings and reviews.** The view from an independent voice of authority, whether professional, or "prosumer" (professional consumer), can be integrated into an e-commerce product page, a social network page, a product review site, an online magazine, and/or in news feeds (e.g., Metacritic and CNET Reviews).
- **Sponsored reviews.** These are paid-for reviews written by either customer bloggers or by experts on social media platforms (e.g., SponsoredReviews, PayPerPost). Expert and sponsored reviews are often generated in video format (see **expotv.com**; sharing "Videopinions" about products and services).
- **Conversational marketing.** People communicate via e-mail, blogs, live chat, discussion groups, and tweets, in both original posts and in comments. Monitoring conversations yields rich data for market research, product improvements (collaboration), and customer service.
- **Customer testimonials.** Customer stories and case studies are often published on a social media site that allows comments and discussion (e.g., Bazaarvoice site reviews).

Ratings and reviews have been the cornerstone of e-commerce since 1995 (e.g., at Amazon.com), and are a great way to boost traffic volume, conversions (from surfing a site to buying), and increase average order value. Reviews may result in word-of-mouth marketing through social influence, promoting purchase decisions with credible information. Bazaarvoice (**bazaarvoice.com**) measured the impact of ratings and reviews as boosting conversion to purchase by up to 25 %. According to a 2012 study by review company Reevoo as reported by Chowney (2012), 30 % of customers who do not see any negative views become suspicious and buyers who seek out and read bad reviews convert 67 % more than the average consumer. Interestingly, negative reviews appear not to have a detrimental effect on sales; we do not live in a five-star world, and apparently, shoppers do not expect this. New developments in ratings and reviews are *review syndications* (to social networks), *contrast reviews* (showing positive and negative reviews), *tagged reviews* (tagging reviews with keywords and hashtags), *video reviews, geotagged mobile reviews,* and story-based *customer testimonials.* For more about the positive impact of negative reviews, see Abel (2014).

Social Recommendations and Referrals

Whereas ratings and reviews are usually visible to all, recommendations and referrals are personal endorsements that have higher value for customers and advocates. The in-store analogy for this strategy is when consumers ask a fellow shopper for advice. Often, social recommendations take the form of online versions of traditional referral-rewards programs (e.g., Sky TV's "Introduce a Friend"), but can also use syndication tools via Twitter and Facebook to share recommendations with friends, fans, and followers. These are closely related to ratings and reviews, and are sometimes integrated with them.

Traditional online product review companies such as Amazon.com, Bazaarvoice, and PowerReviews have advised many consumers. Up-and-coming social shopping software such as ShopSocially (**shopsocially.com**), Wanelo (**wanelo. com**), Blippy (**blippy.com**), Swipely (**swipely.com**), and Bee BargainsBeetailer (**beetailer.com**) now enables *conversations* about purchases. The product recommendations come from people consumers know and are arguably trustworthier than reviews by strangers (recall the trust statistics previously mentioned). It will be interesting to see if this kind of model for product reviews will eventually replace traditional company-generated website recommendations.

Many vendors provide infrastructures and services for soliciting recommendations. For example, ThisNext (**thisnext.com**) is a social commerce site where "experts, top bloggers, style mavens, and trendsetters of every kind" *recommend* their favorite products for shoppers to discover (see **thisnext.com/company**). It blends two powerful elements of real-world shopping otherwise lost for online consumers: word-of-mouth recommendations from trusted sources and the ability to browse products in the way that naturally leads to discovery. ThisNext has also developed a suite of distribution tools for bloggers, online communities, and e-commerce sites. Another special site, **productwiki.com**, collects product reviews from people all over the world and any user can write a review. Users can review products, comment on products, and make changes to ProductWiki.

Sometimes, social shopping portals that bundle ratings and reviews with recommendations also provide shopping tools: A prime example is provided in the Kaboodle shopping community. Common recommendation methods follow:

- **Social bookmarking.** Recommended products, deals, and tips are bookmarked and shared with friends, fans, and followers, using social bookmarking sites such as Delicious.com. Members also bookmark many other types of website content.
- **Referral programs.** These involve financial rewards for customers and partners who refer new customers (e.g., Groupon, Gilt). For example, Vente Privee's referral program "Add your referral ad with a referral link." Some of these programs give social media sites the opportunity to make money when a user clicks from the site to the retailer and purchases a product. For example, the Amazon.com Associates program (**affiliate-program. amazon.com**) provides bloggers and others with linking tools for their sites; the social media owner gains revenue by customers making "Qualified Purchases" via clicking on the "Buy from Amazon.com" link. You can find exam-

ples of this on blogs where the authors have a sidebar of "books I like" or simply recommend books on a topic of discussion complete with a link to Amazon.com (e.g., Path To Bliss; go to **pathtobliss.com/books.html**). The first "matchmaking" referral service in the U.S. is ReferAround (**refaround.com**).

- **Social recommendations.** Personal shopping recommendations are based on profile similarities to other customers (e.g., Amazon Recommendations).
- **Other innovative methods.** Companies such as Netflix and StyleFeeder automate personal recommendations based on algorithms, comparing similarities between customer purchasing histories and profiles and movie similarities. Amazon's collaborative filtering software presents product recommendations by displaying additional titles purchased by other consumers who also purchased the same book or CD.

Quick Reference (QR) Codes

QR codes are barcodes that appear as many black modules arranged as a square grid on a white background (see Fig. 5.5). These barcodes were first developed for the automobile industry in 1994 to track inventory, according to Wikipedia; however, they are now an exciting extension of offline paid media that engages Internet users (see **en. wikipedia.org/wiki/QR_code**). Consumers who have the mobile tag reader application on their mobile device can scan a QR code appearing in a print or outdoor advertisement by taking a picture with their phones. This immediately transports the user to a Web or social media site for

Fig. 5.5 QR Code. *Source*: created by Judy Strauss for free at **qrcode. kaywa.com**

more information on the brand, contest, or other information provided by the brand online. QR code scanning can present a user with an online movie trailer, wallpaper for download, text-based information on an event location and time, in a form of dynamic promotions. According to a study by comScore, in June 2011, 14 million users had scanned a QR code from their mobile phones (as reported in **internetretailing.net/2011/08/14m-americans-scanned-qr-and-bar-codes-with-their-mobiles-in-june-2011**) and **qrcodepress.com/qr-codes-are-being-scanned-on-an-increasing-basis/8522600**). Although many people think QR codes are dead (replaced by augmented reality apps and others), we mention them here because they are still a very popular form of user engagement in branded promotional content. At the time of this writing, marketers are beginning to place QR codes on physical objects, such as ads, and by scanning them, consumers will be transported to Facebook and record an immediate "like"—just as would happen when they click the "like" button on a website with a computer mouse. Companies can generate QR codes for free at many websites and incorporate them in printed materials, such as ads and business cards (see for example the **the-qrcode-generator.com**, **beqrious.com**, **unitag.io/qrcode**, or **qrcode.kaywa.com**).

There are many other techniques and examples for successful customer engagement in a brand or organization's messages. Next, we move to the gold at the top of the engagement ladder: user collaboration.

Collaborative Content Creation by Consumers

As previously mentioned, the most engaged customers help the company improve products and promotions because they either care deeply about the brand or are enticed by a successful engagement technique, such as posting product improvement suggestions. In the process of reading customer postings, the company gains market research about the behaviors and preferences of its markets. Collaborative content creation is crowdsourcing at its best.

At the simplest level, when you visit an automobile company's website and click around to change the color of the car, give it leather seats and other options, you are helping the company learn about consumer preferences as it captures your online click stream—and this will guide their future product design.

At a deeper engagement level, The LEGO Group, a toy maker, allows consumers to download software for creating virtual LEGO designs ("build your dream model")—Lego Digital Designs (see **ldd.lego.com/en-us**; previously "Design By Me"). Consumers create cool castles, robots, and other virtual LEGO designs, and then upload their masterpieces to the LEGO gallery online. This is a great way for LEGO to engage customers and to learn which new design kits might sell well in brick-and-mortar stores.

Wikis are a great example of collaborative content creation because users actually create the content of the site. For example, Demand Media Inc.'s eHow has over two million articles and videos created by consumers and professionals covering 30 categories and every topic from house and garden tips to business ideas. All content is created by site users and screened by site editors for quality and value (see **ehow.com**).

Amazon.com, Barnes and Noble, and other online booksellers allow anyone to self-publish content by uploading a digital e-book and selling it for download by iPad, PC, Kindle, and other digital book readers. For example, 26 year old Amanda Hocking could not find a publisher for her young-adult paranormal novels, so she began selling them at online bookstores for $0.99 to $2.99 per digital download of the book. In January 2011, she sold 450,000 copies of the 9 titles (Memmott 2011)! In January 2011, Hocking earned 30 % for every 99¢ book and 70 % of every $2.99 of the sales price for each book she sells. This self-publishing capitalizes on the consumer behavior trend toward more people reading e-books. It also cuts out the book publishing middlemen and allows the online booksellers to offer many products created by consumer authors. Incidentally, Amazon.com also allows users to upload DVD, CD, MP3, and video content created by users for sales on the site.

Many other social media sites benefit by allowing users to upload digital multimedia content. CNN's iReport accepts videos, photos, and audio from citizen journalists who are on the scene of breaking news. The best content is shown on the site, and some receive iReport awards. iTunes and Amazon.com allow musicians to upload digital music files for sale on their sites. Musicians cannot upload music directly, but must go through a distributor, such as CD Baby (the largest indie online music store), who helps them obtain a bar code and ascertains that the intellectual property belongs to said musician. Obviously, YouTube, Flickr, and many other multimedia sites contain only user-created content. Their business models entice users to upload content, draw many eyeballs, and sell advertising.

Many brands invite consumers to create advertising (especially in videos) and upload it to a website for public viewing, voting, and sharing. This UGC is often better than the ads the company or agency would normally produce because the authors often understand the market better than the company.

Example

Beginning in 2010, the Frito-Lay "Crash the Super Bowl" contest offered consumers the chance to create winning 30-s television commercials for the Doritos brand and upload the videos to the contest site (**crashthesuperbowl.com**). In 2014, Frito Lay opened the contest up to contestants worldwide, and received thousands of video ad submissions from over 30 countries. Site visitors vote on the best ad and select two grand prize winners (one voted by site viewers and the other selected by the company). The winners get their creation aired as a commercial during the Super Bowl championship football game in January. The winner does not receive additional money; however, if the spot is awarded one of the top three of the broadcast, according to the USA TODAY ad meter rankings, the grand prize winner receives between $400,000 and $1 million (for the top spot) and a chance to work with professionals to produce another ad. Other brands, such as FootLocker, teaming up with the shoe company Asics, also offer opportunities to win video contests (e.g. see **onlinevideocontests.com** and **filmthenext.com**).

How Do Companies Entice Engagement?

As Oscar Wilde famously noted, "The only thing worse than being talked about is not being talked about." How do companies engage the public, gaining trust and guiding people from passive content consumption, up the ladder to sparking positive brand conversations and viral activity? This involves creating content and promotions that encourage people to interact with the brand and then tag, bookmark or rate the content and share opinions with others via comments and recommendations in social media. Because they can reach millions of people when they share, it is like the old fashioned word-of-mouth on steroids.

As with all effective promotions, three basic criteria must be met—delivering the right message to the right markets in the right environment, Kaplan and Haenlein (2010). Accomplishing this requires a deep understanding of the audience's needs, behaviors, and motivations. In a 2011 ExactTarget study about the "Meaning of Like," a research company found reasons users don't hit the "like" button on a Facebook brand page (eMarketer 2011a):

- 54 % because they do not want to be bombarded with ads or messages,
- 45 % because they do not want companies to have access to profile information,
- 31 % do not want to push things into friends' networks,
- 29 % do not want companies to contact them through Facebook and
- 23 % did not see the benefit of doing so.

In contrast, Facebook members who do "Like" a company or brand have certain expectations: gain access to exclusive content, events, or sales (58 %); receive discounts or promotions through Facebook (58 %); receive updates newsfeeds (47 %). The company can

post updates, photos, or videos on newsfeed (39 %); the name of the company, brand or organization to show up on my profile (37 %); the company will contact me through other channels (24 %); and do not expect anything to happen (37 %) (eMarketer 2011a). For the full report, see **exacttarget.com/resources/SFF8.pdf**.

Thus, social media participants want to be informed, entertained, appreciated, and not bombarded with interruptive brand messages, as seen in the following engagement principles and examples.

Provide High Quality, Timely, Unique, and Relevant Information

When companies like eMarketer, A.C. Nielsen, ComScore, or Forrester release statistics from their primary research, bloggers will write about it, giving their interpretations for readers to comment upon and share. For example, Internet marketing consultant Andy Beal started the Marketing Pilgrim blog in 2005. He began his day in the wee hours by reading his RSS streams from over 100 sites he followed. He then would write a blog post about the latest news announced by Google or another company, and give his expert analysis on what it means to Internet marketers. Beal built his consulting business from his blog followers, sells advertising space on his blog, participates in many interviews with mainstream media, added a team of experts to write articles, and is often in the top ten media and marketing blogs, as rated by *Advertising Age* (see **marketingpilgrim.com**). Robert Fleming, President/CEO of the eMarketing Association in the U.S., wrote a very provocative blog post on the association's website. The article, "Social Media has Ruined Marketing," was posted on LinkedIn, and this quickly received nearly 600 comments, creating a very lively discussion.

Create Entertaining Content

Consumers will watch and share video commercials and other company-created content that is entertaining, irreverent, interesting or unusual. For example, Blendtec created a series of infomercials (called "Will It Blend") showing the power of its new consumer market blenders. The videos showed the company CEO blending everything from a garden rake to golf balls, glow sticks, and an iPad. The iPhone 5 blending video alone received 8.4 million views within 12 months, and the blended iPhone remnants from an iPhone 4 blending received over $900 on eBay in 2007. As of March 2013, the Blendtec video series had received over 294 million views on YouTube, an undetermined amount on the

Willitblend.com microsite, and have had an "amazing impact" on company sales, according to the company CEO, Tom Dickson (see **digitalsparkmarketing.com/creative-marketing/marketing-strategy-creative-marketing/will-it-blend-marketing-campaign** and YouTube for more details).

Offer Competitions

Many people love to compete and win prizes. For example, the Microsoft Windows 7 launch included a "School Pride" sales promotion campaign, asking site visitors to vote on videos created by middle or high school students who hoped to win a computer lab makeover. Microsoft used a social graph that allowed voters to invite friends and followers to vote as well. Microsoft experienced a 75 % increase in traffic during the competition (Marketo 2011). Incidentally, Washington's Whatcom Middle School won the competition, providing another opportunity for social media activity and publicity from Microsoft and its partner, NBC.

Appeal to Altruism

People like to share stories, videos, and other content about social causes, such as experienced by H-D for the Save the Honey Bees campaign. In another example, the American Red Cross ran an article on their website announcing a blood drive to assist residents after the storms that battered the East Coast of the U.S. in 2011. Instead of providing the usual paper sticker for the donor's clothing ("I gave blood"), The Red Cross made a virtual status badge that people could share on their social networks, encouraging friends and followers to also donate blood (see Marketo 2011). In 2010, if blood donors checked in via Foursquare, they could "shout" a 140 character post including the words "Red Cross" "blood" and "donate" to friends that they were currently giving blood and this would unlock a special donor badge that appeared on the user's Foursquare profile and would be automatically sent to a Twitter feed and the user's Foursquare profile (Behlmann 2010)

Make an Exclusive Offer

The social psychology principle of "scarcity" often motivates people to take action immediately (such as "only two left so buy now!"). Artists and movie produces often release songs or trailers for viewing by their fan bases, prior to release to the general public. American rapper, Pitbull, went further when promoting his CD, *Planet Pit*, by telling fans that if they sent an early release online track link to friends,

and three visited the website to listen, the original fan would get to unlock three additional bonus tracks from the CD (Marketo 2011).

Reward Influentials and Fans

Following the famous Pareto principle (the "80-20" rule"), that 80 % of the business comes from 20 % of the customers; most of the buzz about a brand comes from a small number of fans. If Andy Beal or the *Huffington Post* continuously write about a company, they should be rewarded. Rewards of appreciation can take the form of exclusive information, first chance at breaking news, or a free gift—such as the chance to review a new product that they get to keep, an exclusive offer or a special discount. Following the principles of customer relationship management (Chap. 7), a brand will do well to occasionally appreciate its important fans. Foursquare allows this by awarding "mayor" status to the people who check in the most number of days during a 60-day time period at a particular location. Frito-Lay made the Guinness World Records title in April 2011 for the "most fans on Facebook," with more than 1.5 million new "likes" on its Facebook page ("fans"). They rewarded fans by giving away 24,000 bags of chips, via coupons, to the first fans who "liked" the page and registered on a special "giveaway tab" (see **fritolay.com/about-us/press-release-20110428.html**). It didn't stop there: Frito-Lay had 2,356,753 likes as of August 2014.

Incentivize Group Behavior

Following the social psychology principle of reciprocity, customers can be motivated to participate in social media if offered an incentive up front (versus the simple "thank you" type reward just mentioned). For example, Oscar Mayer gave consumers an offline discount coupon to an initial product trial of its Oscar Mayer Selects hot dogs. They added a deal sweetener: share a "Taste-a-Monial" review of the product and receive a seconds coupon. The twist was that for every 5,000 people who shared Taste-a-Monials, the coupon value increased by 50¢ until the consumer could receive a full free pack of the hot dogs. Using the scarcity principle, the offer was limited to a short time period (Dhalokia 2011).

A key principle of enticing engagement is to make it easy for users. For instance, most social media and many websites provide one click buttons for "liking," tagging, bookmarking (e.g., offering a Delicious button), subscribing via an RSS feed button (which can rapidly spread the content) and sharing content on social networks. Many sites also allow users to register with one click, using their Facebook or other social network profile. For example, BostInnovation (now BostsInno) provides information on happenings in the Boston area. The site implemented Gigya's social login application so that users could register and sign in using an existing Facebook, Twitter, etc. account, and comment directly on BostonInnovation's site. This resulted in a 58 % increase in commenting activity, according to BostonInnovation's co-founder Kevin McCarthy (**appsthisway.files.wordpress.com/2012/01/gigya-social-roi-casestudies.pdf**).

Thus far, we have been painting a rosy picture of customer engagement and all the good it can do for a brand or organization. As hard as marketers try to deliver a good product and respect consumer communication preferences, things can quickly go downhill in social media. For example, in 2006, General Motors emulated the Frito-Lay consumer generated ad contest, providing consumers with video, audio, and images to use in constructing commercials for the Chevy Tahoe. It worked well for GM, too; however, there was negative backlash—approximately 20 % of the entries had superimposed text right in the ads mentioning the Chevy Tahoe's part in using up the world's oil and causing global warming. For example, one YouTube video entry had the following text over images of the Chevy Tahoe driving in wilderness: "Like snow? Beautiful landscapes? Be sure to take it all in now because tomorrow this (expletive deleted) SUV will change the world. Global warming isn't a pretty SUV ad. It's a frightening reality." (See **npr.org/templates/story/story.php?storyId=5320442**.) These videos subsequently were posted as ad parodies on YouTube and received a lot of press. Regardless, GM felt the campaign was a huge success because 80 % of the ads were positive about the brand and many people watched them. The moral: in an online environment where everyone is a critic, expect the brand's underbelly to be exposed. This brings us to an important topic: How can a company manage its brand messages and reputation in the "Wild West" environment of social media?

5.5   REPUTATION MANAGEMENT IN SOCIAL MEDIA

In February 2011, Egyptian citizens used social media to organize protests against President Hosni Mubarak, high unemployment, and rising prices. They used Facebook, Twitter, and YouTube until the government blocked all WiFi and cell networks. This didn't stop the people, who then used dial up phone modems to connect and organize protests. Mubarak fell from power. If social media conversation can bring down the government of Egypt, what can it do to a company, brand or CEO?

Kitchen Aid, the appliance producer, found out very quickly in 2012 when the social media manager sent an inappropriate tweet from the company @KitchenAidUSA Twitter account that spoke negatively about then candidate Barack Obama, saying something to the effect that his grandmother died three days before he became president the first time because she knew it wasn't going to go well with him as President. That 140 character message created a fast and huge backlash against the company. Even though the tweet was meant to be sent from someone's personal account, the company sent an apology tweet to the Twitter community and directly to Obama, taking full responsibility for its social media mismanagement (Moore 2012).

Reputation is "the beliefs or opinions that are generally held about someone or something," according the Oxford dictionary. Abraham Lincoln is attributed to saying that "Character is like a tree and reputation like a shadow. The shadow is what we think of it; the tree is the real thing." Thus, an entity's reputation is based on what other people think of it, not what it thinks of itself. With social media, there is plenty of opportunity for consumers to shape the reputation of a company, its brands and its employees. Brands and companies have lost a great deal of control over their images and reputations and must now monitor, engage, and participate in social media conversations or pay the consequences. In a global study of 300 large company executives in 2013, Deloitte found a consensus that reputational risk was among corporate America's greatest challenges. (See the survey results at **deloitte.com/view/en_IQ/iq/press/press-releases/d78b76006de23410VgnVC-M3000003456f70aRCRD.htm**.)

Quality, transparency, and trust principally influence company and brand reputations (according to a recent Edelman annual Trust survey). In order to be trusted, an entity must be reliable, high quality, authentic, transparent, and follow through on its promises. Marketers often describe a brand as a promise to deliver promoted benefits, and if they do not follow through on that promise, they are open to attack in the social media. For example, if an automobile does not get the advertised gas mileage, a customer will lose some degree of trust in the company/brand and likely talk about this gas mileage disparity online on product review sites or in social networks or blogs. Transparency occurs when companies honestly and quickly reveal the truth before or during a reputation crisis. If they hide the truth and later are discovered, the negative social media conversation will escalate. Transparency includes honest conversation in social media and revealing product improvement processes, such as Dell does in its IdeaStorm microsite previously discussed.

Consider the following statistics:

- In 2013, only 58 % of the world trusted businesses to do "what is right" (according to the 2013 Edelman Trust Survey).
- 25 % of searches for the world's twenty largest brands return links to user-generated content (reported by Qualman 2009). Search engines rank as the first place people go for information about a company, according to the Edelman Trust Survey.
- 34 % of bloggers post opinions about product and brands, and these are read by those people who follow and trust the blogs (reported by Qualman 2009).
- Only 14 % of people trust advertisements (Qualman 2009). This is likely because the intent of advertising is to persuade consumers by presenting only the positive about a product (in contrast, recall the high number of people who trust people like themselves).
- Who do consumers trust? According to the 2013 Edelman Trust Survey, most trusted are academics or experts on company issues (68 %), then "a person like you" (60 %), followed by regular employees (49 %) and CEO's (40 %).
- Trust needs repetition: In order to trust a company message, 4–14 % will believe the positive information after hearing it one to two times, and only 35 % will believe it after hearing it three times (according to the 2013 Edelman Trust Survey).

Beyond social media participant responses to company actions, people often write negative posts in the middle of the night, surprising the companies who are the objects of these attacks. This happened to Nestle in March 2010, as discussed in the following example:

Example

Greenpeace UK, the activist not-for-profit organization working for a green and peaceful world, posted a video on both their site and YouTube to build awareness of a perceived problem of the diminishing rainforest and pushing orangutans towards extinction. Nestlé, the maker of Kit Kat candy bars, was purchasing palm oil extracted from forests in Indonesia, thus "trashing the Indonesian rainforests, threatening the livelihoods of local people and pushing orangutans towards extinction," according to the video's description (**greenpeace.org/international/en/campaigns/climate-change/kitkat**). The video on the Greenpeace site, titled: "Need a Break? So Does the Rainforest" and on YouTube, titled: "Have a Break? Greenpeace Campaign against KitKat and Nestle" (**youtube.com/watch?v=VaJjPRwExO8**) shows an office worker taking a break by eating a Kit Kat bar. When he bites into it, blood gushes from the chocolate bar.

The whole series of videos received 1.5 million views by March 2010; however, the damage really escalated on Nestlé's Facebook page. Immediately after the initial March 17, 2010 video post, viewers began complaining about the palm oil harvesting with comments on the company's Facebook page. Some of the protesters created a graphic imitation of the Kit Kat candy bar, replacing the brand name with the word "Killer" in the same font or stamping the package with bloody orangutan footprints. They made this image their profile picture on Facebook so every post on the Nestlé page included this image.

Nestlé responded by saying: "we welcome your comments, but please don't post using an altered version of any of our logos as your profile pic—they will be deleted." This inappropriate response created a blog storm and many more posts, and shifted the conversation away from the core issue of forest destruction and animal extinction to Nestlé's ineptitude in social media. Nestlé debated with commenters, defending its decision to censor profile pictures and then started deleting comments as well. It got very nasty. Eventually, the Nestle executive running the Facebook page posted this comment: "This (deleting logos) was one in a series of mistakes for which I would like to apologize. And for being rude. We've stopped deleting posts and I've stopped being rude."

What is really amazing is the speed at which this happened:

- March 17: Greenpeace posted the video on YouTube. The video was viewed 750,000 times in 1 week. Nestle attempted to have the video removed.
- March 18: 190 Facebook complaints and thousands of Tweets in response.
- March 19 at 2:26 AM: Nestlé responds on Facebook with the plan to delete the "Killer" bar logos and comments.
- March 19 at 1:29 PM: Nestlé apologizes on Facebook and stops deleting the posts.

Several companies analyzed the social media conversations after this incident. One found that social media conversations including both terms "Nestlé" and "Facebook" jumped by 40 % on March 19, 2010, and that 16 % of this conversation was negative, 66 % neutral, and 16 % positive (as measured by the former site, **blog.biz360.com**). For an analysis of Nestlé's social media crisis, see the slideshow at **slideshare.net/ngonza/nestle-greenpeace**.

Sources: youtube.com/watch?v=VaJjPRwExO8; **greenpeace.org/international/en/news/features/Sweet-success-for-Kit-Kat-campaign**;   and   **slideshare.net/ngonza/nestle-greenpeace** (all accessed August 2014).

In Chap. 7, we describe several incidents of how people use social media to publicize their complaints. Notable is the case of 'United Breaks Guitars.'

Note: To learn how to complain effectively in social media, see McGrail (2013) and visit **gripvine.com**, a forum where unhappy customers can connect directly with customer decision makers to get their voices heard and complaints resolved quickly.

Which Reputations Matter?

As previously mentioned, brand and company reputations are very important. Twenty-one percent of company market value on the New York Stock Exchange's S&P is based on corporate reputation (according to a study conducted by intangible asset specialist Reputation Dividend, and reported by the Holmes Report on May 25, 2014; **holmesreport. com/expertknowledge-info/14999/More-Than-20-Percent-Of-SP-500-Value-Attributable-To-Reputation. aspx**). It is very difficult for a company to recover from reputation damage, and according to the experiences of many companies, it can take several years to repair reputation damage.

In an interesting example, Brazilian creative agency, Moma Propaganda, was stripped of two awards and prohibited from entering the Cannes Lions International Festival of Creativity for a year. The agency entered two fake ads for Kia Motors Brazil—"fake" meaning that they created the ads for the competition—but the ads were neither approved by Kia nor run in any traditional or online media. Cannes discovered this when it came across the firestorm of social media conversation, which criticized the campaign for overtones of lust and pedophilia. This incident created reputation-damaging publicity for both the agency and Kia Motors Brazil, until the latter said they had neither seen nor approved the ads (Wentz and Penteado 2011).

The reputation of a company's CEO is linked closely to the reputation of the company. Many PR firms suggest that problems occur when there is negative company or CEO news. Often, the reputations of other company executives also affect the company. For example, the reputations of job recruiters in a company can make a big difference when trying to attract good employees (Shih 2011). Successful recruiters build their reputations on LinkedIn and this helps them build good relationships with previous job candidates and new hires.

Recently, there has been a great deal of talk and information about using social media for personal branding. This especially applies to consultants, salespeople, and other professionals, as well as to college students who are about to enter the job market (see **business.unr.edu/faculty/jstrauss/ personal.htm** for a series of exercises to develop your personal brand).

Build, Maintain, Monitor, Repair, and Learn

The reputation management process includes four steps: build, maintain, monitor, and repair. Many of the techniques for implementing these steps are discussed elsewhere in the book so we just touch upon them here. There are many promotional techniques for *building* a strong reputation, but it all starts with the company's actions. As previously mentioned, most social media reputation crises happen because of something the company does or does not do. Given positive actions, the company can use owned or paid media and join the conversation in earned social media to communicate its benefits to consumers and other stakeholders. This book gives many examples of how companies do this, such as engaging customers and prospects who participate in social media, where they hang out online and using search engine optimization tactics (discussed later in this chapter).

Maintaining positive reputations requires constant Internet and offline media monitoring and then sometimes participating when things go awry. We say "sometimes" because companies decide whether or not to respond based on three factors: (1) how valuable is the poster to the company, (2) how much potential does the comment contain for creating reputation damage, and (3) how widely can the discussion travel in social media (Flynn 2012)? For example, if the comment came from a high value customer or influential journalist, the company will respond immediately, sometimes by direct e-mail to the person who posted the comment. Conversely, if the poster is a low value customer or competitor and it does not seem like a big enough conversation to spread far, the company might ignore the comment. Interestingly, one survey of marketers found that in response to customer complaints or questions, 29 % seldom or never respond to them on Twitter and 17 % said the same for Facebook posts (eMarketer 2011b). These may be low-value complaints, but this same study found that 22 % of companies do not even know if their customers use social media to comment on company products, so we suspect that many reputations are declining unnoticed by marketers.

The Nestlé example shows the need to *monitor* social media conversation 24/7 and assign appropriate personnel to Facebook and other social media for beneficial user interactions. Xbox was found to be the fastest brand to respond to customer queries on Twitter, with an average response time of 2 minutes and 42 second(s), whereas another study found the fastest U.S. retailer responses took over 4 h (Hanger 2011). It is also critically important to understand and fix the underlying problem, if possible, prior to responding to bloggers and other social media detractors. Without substance, responses to a crisis can be seen as empty promises to social media participants.

When a company creates a Facebook business page, by default, it allows other Facebook members—potentially including disgruntled customers or unscrupulous competitors—to post notes on the page, or comment on what the company has posted. However, if the page owner turns off the feature that allows others to write on the Wall, people may wonder what the company fears or is hiding. Turning off the feature also precludes great customer fan conversations and engagement that could promote the products and services better than the company could do (because people trust others like them online). Companies can delete posts, but that may only encourage the poster to scream louder about being censored, as happened in the Nestlé case. Most social media marketing experts advise deleting only the most offensive posts, while trying to address the rest as constructively as possible. In fact, this is how a company can learn things that will improve its products and processes.

For example, Coca-Cola has 88 million fans on its Facebook page worldwide, with 80 % living outside the U.S. (2011 data). The company uses geotags so that fans see relevant posts in their own language, based on the poster's IP (Internet Protocol) address (for example, someone posting from .de would see only German language posts). Coke posted something it thought would appeal to fans—"Student Day:" "Today's the Day of the Student! If you're part of this group [of students], show us by having some fun or posting a comment here. And congratulations" (Creamer 2011). Unfortunately, there was a glitch in the geotagging on Facebook and for 10 minutes U.S. fans saw this post in Portuguese instead of English. This created a firestorm of xenophobic comments from U.S. fans, such as "Speak English or @#* die!" (Expletive deleted). Apparently, U.S. fans think that Coke is an American brand and should stay that way. Many of the comments were in blatant disregard of Coke's Facebook rules, and Coca-Cola removed the Portuguese post and all the offensive comments from its American viewers.

Repairing reputations can take an average of 3.2 years, as previously mentioned. This involves fixing the fundamental problems causing the crisis, communicating the solutions to important stakeholders, and enticing social media participants to spread the conversation. One site to watch is RipOffReport.com, because it allows users to post company/product complaints, scams, reviews or frauds. The post often appears in a Google search for the company or brand. As with most negative posts, the way to bury it into later Google search results pages is to be sure the company has many positive posts and pages that include recent content.

Most good companies *learn* from criticism in social media and act upon what they hear. Negative comments add authenticity in balancing a company's one-sided owned and paid media, and when handled well, can boost reputations and sales. Product reviews, complaints, and positive sugges-

tions help companies improve products, processes, and Web content. The best way to encourage this type of posting is by hosting a conversation on the company's own social media properties so it becomes easier to identify, learn, and then respond that changes have been made (if warranted). This kind of dialog often prevents complaints from going viral as well. For example, My Starbucks Idea (**mystarbucksidea.force.com**) has several hundred thousand users and accepts ideas for product, experience, and involvement categories. **Mystarbucksidea.force.com** lists recent ideas as they are sent via Twitter, Facebook, or posted on the site, and then reports on "ideas in action." Users can click on each idea to see its status and add comments. This is a brilliant way to learn from customers without doing expensive market research, and it yields a lot more actionable data as well (see Chap. 1 opening case for more information). For more information on using reputation management, see **seofriendly.com/tag/reputation-management**.

One important way to avoid unwarranted reputation crises involves building a reputation management system in company owned social media.

Reputations Management Systems

Reputation management systems use various predefined criteria for processing complex data to report reputation. This is a technology solution that helps companies initiate and monitor reputations. One tactic is to design the system properly so that there will be more opportunities for positive comments. A properly designed site will attract the proper visitors and facilitate proper trust and interactions. Thus, instead of looking at negatives, reputation systems should build trust, promote quality, facilitate member matching, and sustain loyalty.

Example
Most social media platforms have a member profile feature, which allows others to see more about who is posting on the medium, and also to view information about some of the member's activities. Furthermore, many social networks require a reply to an automated outgoing e-mail when a user signs up to access that site, so they know the user actually resides at that e-mail address and is not simply a spammer. eBay and other social commerce sites have feedback systems so that buyers can rate sellers for all future buyers to see; buyers have the same system. Similarly, Slashdot (**slashdot.org**) uses a "karma" rating system, and others also have systems where users can rate the reviews and even the ratings of other users. These reputation management systems help build authenticity and trust in contributors to the conversation.

Facebook grew and outdid MySpace partially because of its reputation management techniques. It initially engaged users and built trust through e-mail authentication, privacy settings, building the site around relationships in the offline world (Shih 2011). Facebook started as a site for Harvard University and other Ivy League schools, adding to its credibility.

In another reputation management system example, Rosetta Stone is a maker of software for language translation. It is mostly a B2B organization. To get the most out of social media, Rosetta Stone uses a strategy and software to control its customer interaction on Facebook. The strategy involves both human intervention as well as an investment in software to help monitor its social networking presence. Specifically, the company software helps to monitor Wall posts and respond to them appropriately. Rosetta Stone uses Parature, Inc. software to scan fan Wall posts, add them to a database, and flag those that need a response from the company. This solution is handy because it all occurs on a special Facebook support tab and separates fans chatting among themselves from discussions involving company customer service representatives (Carr 2010). For details, see **facebook.com/RosettaStone**.

5.6 SEARCH ENGINE OPTIMIZATION

Search engine optimization (SEO) is the process of improving the visibility of a company or a brand on the results page displayed by a search engine. Here, we will discuss only a few principles, which relate to social media and positive earned media. The purpose of search engine optimization "is to increase a website's traffic counts, and eventually conversions, by getting higher search engine placement for the keywords in the search query" (per Bruce Clay; see **bruceclay.com/seo/search-engine-optimization.htm**), who provides a free tutorial on SEO).

Search engines rank sites on search engine results pages (SERP) using complicated algorithms partially based on user-inputted key words because the search engines want to present results that are relevant to users. Ideally, the results should be among the top five listings on the first page. Companies often hire search optimizers or try to optimize by themselves. SEO can increase the number of visitors to a website, and therefore companies are willing to pay for this service. To learn how to do this, see Harris (2013). SEO is performed in all types of online searches, including video search, social network search, and image search. Google is well known for using over 200 factors in their algorithm to determine rankings (e.g., social signals, user interaction signals, trust); however, a few important principles regarding SEO and social commerce are discussed below (see Google's Search Engine Optimization Starter Guide for more detail at **static.googleusercontent.com/media/www.google.com/en/**

us/webmasters/docs/search-engine-optimization-starter-guide.pdf). For an infographic and examples of Google's search engine ranking factors (2013), see **searchenginejournal.com/infographic-googles-200-ranking-factors/64316**. We focus on Google in this section because it had a 68.7 % share of the search market in June 2014 (according to comScore's monthly qSearch), while none of the remaining search engines achieved more than a 19 % share (see **comscore.com/Insights/Market-Rankings/comScore-Releases-July-2014-US-Search-Engine-Rankings**). The principles are:

1. **Spread fresh content all over the Web.** The more sites and social media pages a company or brand maintains, the more links will appear on search engine results pages. This is important because when negative content appears in social media, it will briefly appear within the search results but a lot of solid, current Web content, such as images, podcasts, videos, press releases, and articles, will quickly drive the negative content to later pages in the search results. For example, when searching for "Will it Blend," the branded microsite appears first on the results page. This is followed by three YouTube videos, the Blendtec company YouTube channel, a Wikipedia entry, the company's Facebook page, the company's blog, and then two social media columns about the company's blenders and fascinating campaign—one a humorous and positive parody of the viral videos ("will the blender blend itself?"). See Fig. 5.6 for the top five results. Of course, a company will only create content for sites frequented by its target audience and social media influentials.

2. **Relevance and popularity.** Google judges relevance by incoming links to a Web page and the popularity of the site based on clicks from a SERP or number of tweets or "likes" or comments on a company's Facebook page. For example, if it is a musician's site and lots of credible similar sites link to it (such as a radio station blog), Google assumes it is highly relevant and popular, moving it closer to the top of the SERP. Companies seek these inbound links—e.g., one blogger we interviewed for a previous book asked to be linked from our university pages because ".edu" domains have more Google credibility than do ".com" sites. Social media marketers put many cross-links to various sites, such as linking from the microsite to the Facebook page and cross-linking to pages within the site. Google also defines "relevance" as individual-specific using social graphs, so if you search for "the best restaurant" in your town the top result might well be one that your Facebook friends rated highly on Yelp.com, whereas someone else's SERP will reflect what their friends commented upon in other social media sites.

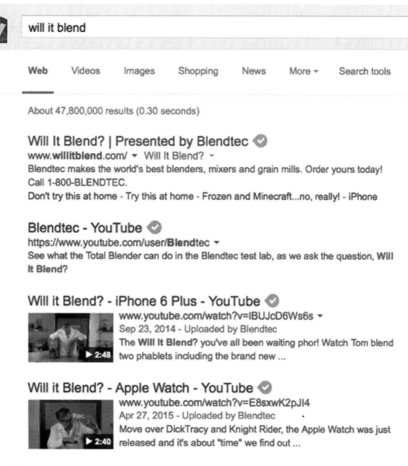

Fig. 5.6 SERP for "Will it Blend". *Source*: Reproduced with permission from © Blendtec and permission standards on **google.com**

3. **Optimize content.** A search engine's automated robots search websites to see which words are the most important, partially by looking at topic headings, page titles (words that appear on the browser tabs), URL names, meta tags (placed in the HTML code for each page), and other things in large fonts. This means that social media marketers must understand their audiences' desired benefits and search habits so they can select key words to populate the sites used by target markets for searching. For example, the "Student LoanDown" blog about student loans and Wells Fargo bank financing uses 29 key words in its meta tag but only 3 of them rank in Google's first SERP but don't rank in Google's first page for 26 of them—these are the ones used in the name of the blog as well (search for **blogs.wellsfargo.com/studentloandown**). This site needs to revise its key words to focus on a smaller number to be used throughout the content.

4. **SEO tactics constantly change.** Google is famous for adjusting its search algorithm (around 500–600 times per year; "major" algorithm changes about once a month), both to improve results and to control site owners from spamming the system (such as putting key words at the bottom of the page in white text all over a white background so search engines are able to read it but users do not; promoting the same piece of content repeatedly; place unneeded words in title tags). Bloggers who partake in spamming can have their blog disappear— "blacklisted"—from Google search. This means that social media marketers must constantly watch developments and change tactics accordingly. We recommend visiting **searchengineland.com/library/channel/seo**, **searchenginewatch.com/seo**, and **moz.com** (formerly SEOmoz), for the latest SEO developments and capabilities. Google provides three free SEO tools: Google Webmasters, Google AdWords Keyword Planner, and Google PageSpeed (see Dawson 2014).

In one example of what not to do, Nevada's former governor, Jim Gibbons, posted images from appearances, a blog, and his authored white papers on the official State of Nevada website (**nv.gov**). When the citizens became critical of his decisions, a search for "Jim Gibbons" showed the **nv.gov** page first on the search results page and then nine links to criticism on other sites. Some of these links to the negative content lasted for several years on the first page of the SERP and could have been bounced to later pages, if the governor had spread fresh content, such as, posting images on Flickr, making a unique URL for his blog, creating Facebook and Twitter accounts, and inserting content in Wikipedia and elsewhere that would appear in the first ten links on the SERP for his name. This action would move the criticism on other sites lower in the SERP in favor of fresh content posted by the governor on many different sites.

Note that, although password protected sites such as Facebook and Twitter are crawled by search engines for public display in the SERP, users have to log onto these sites in order to follow the link. If a company wants its content to appear on Google and be easily viewed, it will create a public page that is available to people who are not required to be logged onto the site. Moreover, Facebook provides its own powerful search engine for users who are logged in, and there are many specialized search engines for social media sites, such as Topsy and Bing Social. For 40 advanced and alternative top search engines, see to **blog.kissmetrics.com/ alternative-search-engines**. Companies work to be sure their content is listed by these specialty companies, who usually allow submissions if the search robots have not yet found the sites.

As with any social strategy, companies working on an SEO program first work to understand the Web behaviors and social sites used by their target market and influentials in terms of publishing and sharing content. They then set SEO goals and monitor the results.

In the next section, you will learn about how companies listen and measure in social media.

5.7 MONITOR, MEASURE, AND REFINE: SM METRICS

A **performance metric** is a measure of the organization's performance on activities designed to achieve specific objectives (also called "Web Analytics" for the online environment). As shown in Fig. 4.1 (in Chap. 4), a company specifies which metrics will be used to measure marketing communication success, then uses these measures as feedback to (1) see if the campaign objectives were met, and (2) continually refine the strategies and tactics to enhance performance. For example, Starbucks wanted to engage customers and learn ways to better meet their needs through product innovation. It created the My Starbucks Idea microsite and can count the number of suggestions, measure the sentiment (as positive/

negative), and identify the number of product changes to see if its engagement and learning goals were achieved. We will discuss strategy, tactics, and measurement more thoroughly in Chap. 10; however, this section includes popular metrics for measuring the success of communication efforts through owned, paid, and earned media.

There are hundreds of possible performance metrics, so it is important to select some that can easily be measured on a continuous basis and directly applied to the organization's social commerce communication objectives. Both Albert Einstein and sociologist William Bruce Cameron have been credited for variations of quote: "Not everything that can be counted counts, and not everything that counts can be counted." Marketers are drowning in metrics and many choose easy metrics, such as number of clicks on a link to a Web page or "likes" on Facebook. It is critical for them to be effective and efficient in metric selection and measurement so that the results of their efforts will help improve marketing communications toward meeting the company's goals.

Figure 5.7 displays five general measurement areas, from awareness through innovation, along with sample metrics used in each area. For the purposes of measurement, see Patterson (2014). For ten online marketing metrics organizations need to be measuring, see DeMers (2014). The pyramid shape represents the fact that the number of consumers acting at each level decreases at higher levels: e.g., (1) the most people will become aware of a Blendtec blender from the viral video, (2) fewer will post comments about it (brand health), (3) fewer still will engage more deeply with the brand by forwarding or using social bookmarking to tag the video (engagement), then (4) even fewer will visit the Blendtec site to read about their blenders and purchase one (action), and (5) the smallest number are loyal customers who post collaborative type comments that Blendtec can use to improve the product (innovation).

We next provide some examples of metrics at each pyramid level. Note that companies also use many of these metrics to monitor their competition.

Awareness/Exposure Metrics

The most accurate way to measure an increase in brand awareness is to conduct survey research using a representative sample from the company's target market. However, this is very expensive and difficult to accomplish due to declining response rates on surveys, so organizations use many other proxy metrics to gain some measure of progress toward this awareness level goal. These metrics assume that if users access an organization's Facebook page or other social media content, they will become aware of the product features discussed in an ad or on the pages:

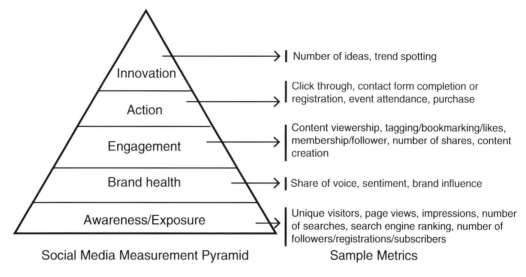

Fig. 5.7   Social media measurement areas. *Source*: created by Judy Strauss

- *Unique visitors* measures the number of visitors—without repetition—who access a site, application, video, or other social media content within a specific period of time. Unique visitors are measured by user registration, cookie files, or by a third party measurement service such as Nielsen or comScore. Unique visitors additionally are categorized as either new or repeat visitors. Search engines also visit these sites, so companies must filter out visits from automated "bots." The number of views of each video on YouTube is posted under the video.
- *Page views* refer to single pages that are viewed on a social media site. For example, one unique visitor can view many different blog entries on one blog site. Obviously, the more pages users view, the longer they are on the site learning about the brand.
- *Impressions* refer to the number of times an ad loads on a user's screen. This metric forms the bases of the CPM (cost per thousand impressions/views) pricing model.
- *Number of searches* measure the number of times users search for the brand, company, or associated key words selected by the organization while typing the key words in a search engine.
- *Search engine ranking* evaluates where the organization's social media content appears in the search engine results pages for desired key words. For instance, if a user types in the name of the company, brands, or executives, ideally the links will appear in the first ten links/page one of the results page.
- *Number of followers, registrations, or subscribers* to the blog, social network page, video channel, or other content. These are also used to measure earned media engagement.

Brand Health Metrics

In this category, companies want to measure the influence their communications have on consumers. Brand health refers to the amount of conversation and what proportion of the sentiment is positive or negative. It also measures the brand importance to consumers and whether or not this translates into purchases. Measures in this area include the following:

- *Share of voice (SOV)* is the proportion of conversations about one brand versus its competitors. In the offline world, SOV measures the weight of advertising space in traditional media, but in social media, it usually is only measured by conversation. In a quantitative example, if your brand "appeared in the media 20 times in 2013 and there were 150 instances of total coverage among your company and its competitors, your quantitative share of voice would be 13.3 % $(20/150 = 0.1333 \times 100 = 13.3)$" (Cramer 2014). Qualitative measures include the level of importance for the site that mentions a brand (e.g., CNN would score higher than an lesser-known local media station). For more details, including a formula for calculating SOV, examples and charts, see **socialmediaexaminer. com/metrics-to-track-your-social-media-efforts**.
- *Sentiment* refers to the proportion of conversation about a brand that is positive, negative, or neutral, whereas SOV is simply about the number of conversations. On August 16, 2014, we typed "Nike" into the social media search box at **socialmention.com** and got the following results (number of mentions): positive (86), neutral (253) and negative (4). The site calculated brand strength at 55 % due to a 22:1 positive to negative con-

versation (sentiment). This site aggregates user generated content "across the universe." It monitors over 100 social media properties and SOV (see **socialmention.com/about**). For six ways to measure social media see Bendror (2013).

- *Brand influence* can include a number of other metrics, including number of inbound links to a social media property, number of Twitter links that are retweeted, number of comments on posts, and number of times content is shared or linked (Jones 2011).

Engagement Metrics

There are many ways to engage social media users, as discussed in this chapter and Chap. 3. Engagement metrics are endless, and the ones companies select depend on the specific content, promotion, or other communication objectives and tactics. Following are some of the most common measures relating to the engagement levels previously discussed:

- *Content viewership* refers to the number of users who consume content, such as reading a blog (page views), watching videos or listening to podcasts, and downloading white papers.
- *Tagging, bookmarking* or "likes" for content that can be counted.
- *Membership/follower* metrics count the number of RSS subscribers, members in a community, such as a LinkedIn or Meetup.com group, or number of followers on Twitter.
- *Number of shares* measures how many times viral content is shared with others.
- *Content creation* counts the number of users who upload ads for a UGC contest, such as the Frito-Lay Super Bowl promotion. Companies can also measure the number of people who rate or review products, write comments on blogs or videos or retweet interesting or humorous tweets, and other content related items measured in previous categories.
- *Virtual worlds:* number of users visiting the company property, how long they stay, and whether or not they interact with the various features.
- *Online games:* number playing, length of time spent in the game, purchase of virtual properties and clicks on game links.

Action Metrics

Although engagement metrics demonstrate actions taken by users, this category takes it to a higher level of action:

- *Click through* to an organization's site. The proportion of all people who are exposed to a communication message and those who click to visit the site measures this.

- *Contact form completion* or *registration*. This allows the company to add the person to their database of names, e-mail addresses, and more.
- *Branded mobile apps:* number of downloads, updates and number of actions that that are built into the app (such as "checking in" with a location-based app or earned media "shares").
- *QR codes:* number of scans and other actions, such as sales, taken at the designated location.
- *Event attendance:* this can be online or offline, based on a social media promotion for a Webinar or other event.
- *Purchase* is the ultimate goal for social commerce. Companies measure conversion rates (proportion of all site visitors who purchase), number of purchases, average order value, and many other metrics that evaluate communication effectiveness toward this goal. Note that, many other factors lead to purchase, such as product quality, price, and availability; however, social media communication (especially discount promotions) can play an important role in motivating purchase.

Innovation Metrics

In this category, companies want to know if their social media communications are driving customers to comment and review in ways that help the company improve its products and services. Many of these metrics are also included in other categories, but we single innovation out because it is a very high level of brand engagement and builds customer loyalty. A few measures include:

- *Number of ideas* shared in a company's social media site (such as Dell's IdeaStorm).
- *Trend spotting* helps companies know what is hot in their target markets. Google Trends displays "hot" search key words and allows users to search trends. Trendsmap tracks and displays real time Twitter trends worldwide, and many blogs and other sites provide word cloud displays of the most popular words in posts. Many other companies report social media trends.

Measurement Tools

Many companies offer excellent tools for measuring the previously mentioned and many other metrics. You can search Google images for "social media dashboards" and see many tools. Companies select from free Google analytics, other paid tools or use more sophisticated analytic dashboards that are continuously populated with metrics of choice. These tools help companies monitor progress toward objectives and tactical effectiveness, and help them catch negative conversations about their products as they occur, which is just as important.

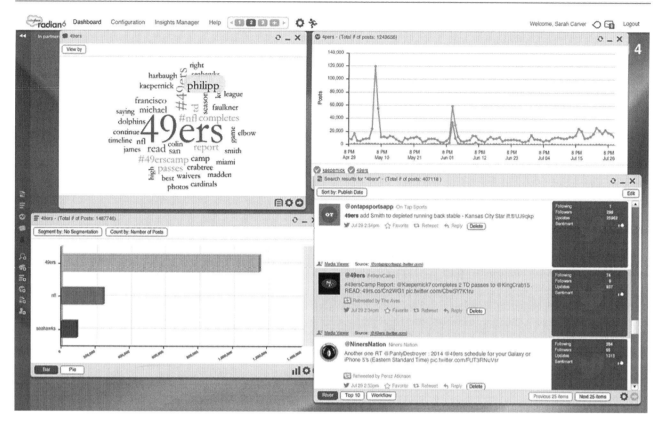

Fig. 5.8 Salesforce Radian6 Social Media Dashboard. *Source*: © Salesforce.com, reproduced with permission

Perhaps the simplest free tool is Google Alerts. Anyone can use this tool by entering the topic for monitoring and which sources (video, blogs, news, or discussions) and Google will send e-mails based on the selected criteria at the requested frequency (real time, daily, weekly). Companies monitor their names, brand names, executive names, and tag lines or slogans in advertising campaigns. Google also provides free website or blog analytics to measure the awareness metrics, such as page views and action level click-throughs. When companies advertise on Facebook, they get metrics about number of impressions and clicks, and more. Many social media sites provide various measures so that organizations can track their users.

Beyond that are complex dashboards, such as those provided for a fee by **sdl.com** (formerly Alterian), **sysomos. com**, Radian6 (**salesforcemarketingcloud.com**), **trackur. com**, and many more. To view many dashboards, simply type "social media dashboard" into a Google image search. Figure 5.8 displays a social media dashboard created by Radian6 (now owned by Salesforce.com) for monitoring social media. The pie chart and graph below display conversation sizes in various segments over time. The top right box shows tweets about the conference, listed in chronological order, and the bottom right dashboard is a word cloud, dem-onstrating the most mentioned terms in the largest font size. Conference planners will be watching the social media conversation on this dashboard as it develops.

For more information on social media metrics, see Altimeter's 2011 white paper (written by Susan Etlinger): *A Framework for Social Analytics* (available at **webtrends. com/files/report/Report-AFrameworkForSocial Analytics-Altimeter.pdf**, and viewed as a SlideShare presentation at **slideshare.net/setlinger/altimeter-social-ana-lytics081011final**). Incidentally, as of mid-August, 2014, the SlideShare presentation has received 131,460 views (over 91,000 on SlideShare), over 10,000 downloads, and 18 comments: a metrics company monitoring itself.

The role that metrics play in social media strategy is covered in Chap. 10, especially in Sect. 10.5.

SUMMARY

In this chapter, you learned about the following SC issues as they relate to the chapter's learning objectives.

1. **Describe the five levels of user engagement (5 Cs).**
   The least engaged Internet users *consume* online content by reading blogs and other text, watching videos and

looking at photos, and listening to podcasts. At the next level, users *connect* with others by creating social network profiles, joining sites of interest, and attending online events. Consumers who *collect* information filter content (e.g., via RSS feeds) and tagging content on blogs or Twitter, "liking" (e.g., on Facebook), or bookmarking what they find valuable on social media sites. *Creators* actually write or upload original multimedia content to websites, such as posting videos on YouTube or music and podcasts on iTunes. The most engaged customers *collaborate* with the company when they work with others and discuss ways to improve products (e.g., Dell's IdeaStorm site).

2. **Describe several important techniques for engaging users in social media.** Companies attempt to use viral marketing through viral videos and viral blogging. They also provide space for consumer created ratings, reviews, testimonials and conversations via chat, e-mail, tweets, blogs, and more. Social recommendations and referrals happen via social bookmarking, referral programs, and other innovative methods. Companies also seek expert ratings and reviews and sponsored (paid-for) reviews from bloggers and others. Finally, quick reference (QR) codes provide offline to online engagement. They entice engagement by providing quality information, creating entertaining content, offering competitions, appealing to altruistic values, making exclusive offers, rewarding influentials and fans, and incentivizing group behavior.

3. **Express the role of trust in social commerce.** Consumers trust other consumer opinions online 65 % of the time and only 43 % trust the company CEO, according to Edelman. Social media takes traditional word-of-mouth communication to a much higher level because people trust product reviews and recommendations from others like themselves much more than they trust company advertisements and other communications. Additionally, a company's reputation is built on trust and when that falls, so do sales.

4. **Provide examples of collaborative content creation by consumers.** Collaborative content creation uses crowdsourcing to gain market research about the behaviors and preferences of its markets for improving products and marketing communication. Examples: LEGO virtual design uploads, wikis, self-publishing content with online booksellers and UGC for advertising creation (e.g., Frito-Lay "Crash the Super Bowl" contest).

5. **Describe how a company can build, maintain, monitor, and repair its reputation in social media.** Quality, transparency and trust principally influence company, brand, executive, recruiter, salesperson, and other employee reputations. A company must be true to its

brand promises and be authentic in social media. The reputation management process involves building via its actions and online content, maintaining its reputation by monitoring and sometimes participating in online and offline conversations and repairing the reputation when things go wrong. Finally, the best companies learn from criticism expressed in social media and use this information to improve operations and marketing. Reputation management systems can help social media keep users honest, positive, and authentic. Finally, companies spread positive content all over the Web and use SEO to increase visibility on the first page of a keyword SERP.

6. **SEO.** This is the process of improving the visibility of a company or a brand on the results page displayed by a search engine. Search engines rank sites on search engine results pages (SERP) using complicated algorithms partially based on user-inputted key words because the search engines want to present results that are relevant to users. To improve a site's SEO, managers (1) spread fresh content all over the Web, (2) be sure their sites are relevant and popular with target markets, (3) optimize content on Web pages and in social media, and (4) monitor Google for changes in the algorithm (this is the way Google decides which sites are highest on results pages).

7. **Define performance metrics used to monitor, measure, and refine social commerce goals and tactics.** There are hundreds of possible performance metrics; therefore, it is important to select some that are easily measured on a continuous basis, and that apply directly to the organization's social commerce communication objectives and refine tactics. They fall into these basic categories: Awareness/exposure metrics (unique visitors, page views, impressions, number of searches, search engine ranking and number of followers/registrations/subscribers to a social media site). Brand Health metrics include share of voice (SOV), sentiment, brand influence, and more. Engagement metrics include content viewership tagging, bookmarking, membership/follower, number of shares, and content creation. Action metrics include click throughs, contact form completion/registration, event attendance, and purchase. Finally, innovation metrics include number of ideas shared and trend spotting measures.

KEY TERMS

Customer engagement (CE)   103
Performance metric   118
QR codes   108
Reputation management systems   115

Search engine optimization (SEO) 116
Viral blogging 106
Viral marketing (viral advertising) 105
Viral video 106

REVIEW QUESTIONS

1. List the five levels of user engagement (5 Cs).
2. Describe viral videos and viral blogging.
3. How do ratings and reviews affect social commerce?
4. Identify several social recommendation tactics.
5. What are seven ways to create content that entices consumer engagement?
6. Why does collaborative content help companies?
7. What creates a solid social media reputation?
8. Which entities should be concerned about their reputations?
9. How can a company repair its reputation online?
10. Define SEO.
11. List six important awareness/exposure metrics.
12. List three important brand health metrics.
13. List four important engagement metrics.
14. List four important action metrics.
15. List two important innovation metrics.

TOPICS FOR DISCUSSION AND DEBATES

1. Do you think that marketers are losing control of brand images due to the social media? What should marketers do to gain more control, or should they give up the cause?
2. How can marketers use social networks for viral marketing?
3. Do you think that user engagement in social media can result in product sales? Explain your answer.
4. Which level of engagement best describes your online behavior? How could your favorite brand move you to a higher level using the principles in this chapter?
5. If you wrote a blog about your experiences at the university you attend in order to help high school students understand what college is like, which metrics would you use to measure the blog's success, and why?
6. Scan a QR code that you find in a print publication and visit the site. Do you think the additional material was worth the effort to find? Why or why not? How could the landing page be improved?
7. Pretend that you are a consultant to your university. Based on the material in this chapter and Chap. 4, what do you think are the best owned and paid media for generating positive earned media about the university?

8. Read Merriman (2011) on handling negative feedback. Discuss the methods described there. How can the feedback be used for improvement?

INTERNET EXERCISES

1. Enter **comblu.com**. Explore its products and discuss the role of a social marketing dashboard.
2. Google the president of your university. Review the top ten links in the SERP and see how his/her reputation is online. Make recommendations for improving it, using SEO and other techniques discussed in this chapter.
3. Create an account at **delicious.com**. Tag an article you like online and then follow the links to others who have also tagged it, seeing what else they have tagged. Write a report about your findings.
4. Enter **usocial.com** and **softcity.com**. Identify all the methods/tools they offer to increase social engagement/marketing communication. Write a report.
5. Imagine you are planning a vacation to Rio de Janeiro, Brazil. Visit **tripadvisor.com** and search for hotels on Copacabana beach. Examine the reviews of five hotels that seem right for you. Do you trust all of these reviewers? Why or why not? Based on the reviews, which hotel would you select, and why?
6. Check out your personal reputation online by searching for your name on Google ("egosurfing"). If you were a job recruiter, would you hire yourself based on what you find? Why or why not? What can you do online to improve your chances in the job market?
7. Search Google images for "social media dashboards." Look at the dashboards and follow their links to the companies that created them. Which one do you think best for a large consumer goods company, such as Coca-Cola? Why do you recommend the one you do?
8. Visit **doritoscrashthesuperbowl.thismoment.com** and view the top videos in the current contest. Then review the article about Chevy Tahoe's negative consumer generated content and write five guidelines companies should use while creating strategies involving consumer generated ads (watch the video "Drew Neisser on Chevy Tahoe Advertising" at **youtube.com/watch?v=1nMRs24Q4oQ**).
9. Read the story about how Mattel used social media to reconcile the relationship between Ken and Barbie (see **blog.bazaarvoice.com/2012/01/03/a-social-love-story-how-ken-won-barbie-and-customers-through-paid-owned-and-earned-media**). Write a report on how Mattel used owned, paid, and earned media to promote the Ken doll and which performance metrics they used to measure the campaign's success. Conclude with your insights: why was this campaign successful?

TEAM ASSIGNMENTS AND PROJECTS

1. Review the opening case and answer the following questions:
   (a) Which principle(s) for enticing consumer engagement did Haagen-Dazs use for the honey bee campaign?
   (b) Watch the "Bee-Boy Dance Crew" video at **youtube. com/watch?v=Wa0db-7bsAo**. Why do you think it was good enough to go viral? Suggest ways for improving the video or tactics that would create more viewership.
   (c) After watching the Bee-Boy video, review the comments. How would you evaluate this "earned media" for enhancing the brand reputation of Haagen-Dazs?
   (d) Select three techniques discussed in this chapter that were not used in the honeybee campaign but which might increase engagement and earn media discussion. Defend your choices.
2. Each member of the team will register with a social bookmarking site, such as **delicious.com**, then research "viral marketing" and bookmark at least five high quality online articles. Follow the links to others who have bookmarked the same articles and see what they have found. Share your findings and report on the usefulness of social bookmarking for researching this topic.
3. Search for more online videos and discussion about the Greenpeace palm oil/Nestle issue, discussed in this chapter (such as Kit Kat Greenpeace 2: Go to **youtube.com**, and search for "Nestle Kit Kat Greenpeace"). Document all the earned media you discover and write a report on this attack against Nestlé's reputation, including your recommendations for actions Nestlé could take to recover from this negative conversation using social media.
4. Develop a reputation management plan for building your own personal brand online so you are attractive to recruiters in the job market. With your team, share your plans and devise a common plan that uses the best from each. Explain why yours is the perfect plan. For more resources, review the personal branding worksheet at **personalbrandingblog.com/your-personal-branding-worksheet**. Also see Chris Brogan's "100 Personal Branding Tactics Using Social Media," at **chrisbrogan.com/100-personal-branding-tactics-using-social-media**.

REFERENCES

Abel, G. "The Positive Impact of Negative Reviews." *G2 Crowd*, May 7, 2014. **about.g2crowd.com/blog/positive-impact-negative-reviews** (accessed August 2014).

Ahmad, I., "Getting Your Readers' Attention [Infographic]" December 21, 2013. **socialmediatoday.com/content/getting-your-readers-attention-infographic** (accessed August 2014).

Atsmon, Y., et al. "China's New Pragmatic Consumers," *McKinsey & Company Insights &Publications*, October 2010. **mckinsey.com/insights/marketing_sales/chinas_new_pragmatic_consumers** (accessed August 2014).

Bakas, R. "How to engage a global audience." October 6, 2010. **rickbakas.com/how-to-engage-a-global-audience** (accessed August 2014).

Band, W., N. Petouhoff, C. Moore & A. Magarie. "Topic Overview: Social CRM Goes Mainstream." *Forrester Research, Inc.*, January 5, 2010 (Updated January 26, 2010). **cdn2.hubspot.net/hub/76666/file-569607040-pdf/Topic_Overview_Social_CRM_Goes_Mainstream.pdf?t=1405608182759** (accessed August 2014).

Behlmann, E. "Red Cross unlocks a blood donor badge on Foursquare." November 17, 2010. **bizjournals.com/wichita/blog/2010/11/red-cross-unlocks-a-blood-donor-badge.html?page=all** (accessed August 2014).

Bendror, Y. "6 Ways to Measure Social Media." February 15, 2013. **webmarketingtoday.com/articles/6-ways-to-measure-social-media/** (accessed August 2014).

Brusselmans, L., "A Practical Guide to More Effective Social Media Engagement." *Engagor*, (2014). **discover.engagor.com/download-free-ebook-a-practical-guide-to-more-effective-social-media-engagement** (accessed August 2014).

Burger King. "The Subservient Chicken Returns." News and Press, April 30, 2014. **bk.com/en/us/company-info/news-press/detail/the-subservient-chicken-returns-2904.html** (accessed August 2014).

Business Wire. "The Huffington Post Announces Record Year in Audience Growth, Video, Native Advertising, and International Expansion." December 16, 2013. **businesswire.com/businesswire.com/news/home/20131216005482/en/Huffington-Post-Announces-Record-Year-Audience-Growth#.U-iEj_ldWSp** (accessed August 2014).

Carr, D. F. "Business Strategy on Facebook." *BaselineMagazine*, February, 2010.

Chithra, M. "Viral Marketing 2012." SlideShare presentation. January 1, 2012. **slideshare.net/vishmitha/viral-marketing-11566632** (accessed August 2014).

Chowney, V. "Bad Reviews Improve Conversion by 67%." January 10, 2012. **econsultancy.com/blog/8638-bad-reviews-improve-conversion-by-67#i.96madn4fqcw3rz** (accessed August 2014).

Cramer, B. "How should you Measure Your Share of Voice?" August 19, 2014. **prdaily.com/Main/Articles/How_should_you_measure_your_share_of_voice_15816.aspx** (accessed August 2014).

Creamer, M. "Even Coke Can't Teach the World to Sing in Perfect Harmony on Facebook." *Ad Age*, August 11, 2011. **adage.com/article/digital/coke-teach-world-sing-perfect-harmony-facebook/229229/** (accessed August 2014).

Dawson, J., "Top Free Tools for SEO Provided by Google." *Social Media Today*, August 3, 2014. **socialmediatoday.com/content/top-free-tools-seo-provided-google** (accessed August 2014).

DeMers, J. "10 Online Marketing Metrics You Need to Be Measuring." Forbes, August 15, 2014. **forbes.com/sites/jaysondemers/2014/08/15/10-online-marketing-metrics-you-need-to-be-measuring/** (accessed August 2014).

Dhalokia, S. "5 ways to encourage customers to share your content." *Mashable*. July 12, 2011. **mashable.com/2011/07/12/encourage-social-sharing/** (accessed August 2014).

eMarketer, "What do Facebook users expect from brands?" *eMarketer*, October 7, 2011a. **emarketer.com/Article/What-Do-Facebook-Users-Expect-Brands/1008630** (accessed August 2014).

eMarketer. "How Well Do Companies Respond to Customer Complaints?" November 10, 2011b. **emarketer.com/Article/How-Well-Do-Companies-Respond-Customer-Complaints/1008686** (accessed August 2014).

Evans, D. & J. McKee. *Social Media Marketing: The Next Generation of Business Engagement*. Indianapolis, Indiana: Wiley Publishing, Inc. (2010).

Flynn, N. *The Social Media Handbook*. Indianapolis, Indiana: Wiley Publishing, Inc. (2012).

Gartner, Inc. "Gartner Says Majority of Consumers Rely on Social Networks to Guide Purchase Decisions." *Newsroom Press Release*, July 26, 2010. **gartner.com/newsroom/id/1409213** (accessed August 2014).

Hanger, L. "Who's Ignoring Their Customers? A Survey of the Largest US Retailers and Their Use of Social Media." *Conversocial Blog.* November 2, 2011 **conversocial.com/blog/whos-ignoring-their-customers-a-survey-of-the-largest-us-retailers-and-their-use-of-social-media#.U_A9UfldWSo** (accessed August 2014).

Harris, C., *SEO Top Secret: How to Get Top Ranking on the First Page of Google by Search Engine Optimization (Simple Online Marketing),* [Kindle Edition], Seattle, WA: Amazon Digital Services, 2013.

Goodby, Silverstein, and Partners. "Case Study: Häagen-Dazs Viral Video Helps Honey Bees Cause." (2008). **feedcompany.com/wp-content/uploads/feed-company-haagen-dazs-bee-case-study.pdf** (accessed August 2014).

Jones, R. "5 Ways to Measure Social Media." *ClickZ*. November 14, 2011. **clickz.com/clickz/column/2102934/measure-social-media** (accessed August 2014).

Kamboe, H., "How I Raised My Klout Score From Less Than 18 More Than 43 in Less Than 90 Days." *Marketing Profs*, July 31, 2014. **articles/2014/25702/how-i-raised-my-klout-score-from-less-than-18-to-more-than-43-in-less-than-90-days** (accessed August 2014).

Kaplan, A.M., and M. Haenlein, "Users of the World, Unite! The Challenges and Opportunities of Social Media." *Business Horizons*, vol. 53, issue 1, 2010.

Kats, R., "Häagen-Dazs Amplifies Social Presence via Mobile Campaign" *Mobile Marketer*, May 30, 2012 **mobilemarketer.com/cms/news/advertising/12946.html** (accessed August 2014).

Kolah, A., "Customer Loyalty Lessons from Häagen-Dazs." *Vocus*, October 31, 2013 **vocus.com/blog/customer-loyalty-lessons-from-haagen-dazs/** (accessed August 2014).

Lee, M. & S. Youn, "Electronic Word of Mouth (eWom): How eWom Platforms Influence Consumer Product Judgment." *International Journal of Advertising*, 28(3), pp. 473-499 (2009).

Marketo. "5 Ways to Encourage Customers to Share Your Content." Marketo e-book (free). 2011. **marketo.com/_assets/uploads/5-Ways-to-Encourage-Sharing.pdf?20130115221621** (accessed August 2014).

McColl, P. *Viral Explosions! Proven Techniques to Expand, Explode, or Ignite Your Business or Brand Online*, Pompton Plains, NJ: Career Press (2010).

McGrail, M. "How to Complain Effectively via Social Media", *Social Media Today*, September 4, 2013. **socialmediatoday.com/content/how-complain-effectively-social-media** (accessed August 2013).

Memmott, C. "Authors catch fire with self-published e-books." *USA TODAY.* February 8, 2011. (Updated February 9, 2011). **usatoday30.usatoday.com/life/books/news/2011-02-09-ebooks09_ST_N.htm** (accessed August 2014).

Merriman, M., "Handling Negative Feedback- A Story of Lip Balm and Soda Pop." *Social Media Today*, November 17, 2011 **socialmediatoday.com/content/handling-negative-feedback-story-lip-balm-and-soda-pop** (accessed August 2014).

Moore, P. *"KitchenAid – Bad Tweets Happen to Good Brands Who Don't Manage Social Media Risk Properly." Marketing Nutz*, October 4, 2012. **pammarketingnut.com/2012/10/kitchenaid-bad-tweets-happen-to-good-brands-who-dont-manage-social-media-risk-properly/** (accessed August 2014).

Morrison, M. "Burger King Resurrects Subservient Chicken." *AdAge*, April 27, 2014. **adage.com/article/news/burger-king-resurrects-subservient-chicken/292902/** (accessed August 2014)

Patterson, L., "What You Should Measure in Your Marketing -- and Why", *Marketing Profs*, July 31, 2014. **marketingprofs.com/opinions/2014/25703/what-you-should-measure-in-your-marketing-and-why** (accessed August 2014).

Qualman, E. "Statistics Show Social Media is Bigger Than You Think." *Socialnomics*, August 11, 2009. **socialnomics.net/2009/08/11/statistics-show-social-media-is-bigger-than-you-think/** (accessed August 2014).

Shih, C. *The Facebook Era: Tapping Online Social Networks to Market, Sell, and Innovate, 2nd Edition*, Upper Saddle River N.J: Pearson Education, Inc. 2011.

Wentz, L. & C. Penteado. "Banned from Cannes." *AdAge*, July 22, 2011. **adage.com/article/cannes-2011/banned-cannes/228883** (accessed August 2014).

Yoerg, A. "'Bee Boy Dance Crew' Spreads Awareness of Bee Crisis." *Osocio*, March 9, 2008. **osocio.org/message/haeagen_dazs_viral_vid_helps_honey_bees** (accessed August 2014).

Social Shopping: Concepts, Benefits, and Models

Contents

Opening Case: Groupon—Will the Company Prosper? 127

6.1 Definitions, Drivers, Concepts, and Benefits
of Social Shopping 131

6.2 Components and Models of Social Shopping 133

6.3 Group Buying and Deal Purchasing 135

6.4 Shopping Together: Communities and Clubs 136

6.5 Social Shopping Aids: From Recommendations,
Reviews, and Ratings to Marketplaces 139

6.6 Innovative Shopping Models and Sites
and Virtual Goods 144

References 152

Learning Objectives

Upon completion of this chapter, you will be able to:

1. Describe social shopping and discuss its drivers.
2. Describe the framework for social shopping, its major participants, its components, and various models.
3. Define group buying and flash sales and explain how they work together.
4. Describe shopping together, shopping communities, and shopping clubs.
5. Describe social recommendations, marketplaces, and other shopping aids.
6. Provide examples of other innovative shopping models.
7. Discuss shopping for virtual goods.

OPENING CASE: GROUPON—WILL THE COMPANY PROSPER?

The name Groupon is a combination of *group* and *coupon*. Groupon was founded in November 2008 and it was considered the fastest-growing company ever in Web history (in terms of revenue and valuation). Initially, Groupon offered both *group buying* and *deal of the day* (one highly discounted deal per day) models in selected metro areas in the United States (**businessinsider.com/companies-revolutionizing-retail-2014-3**). As of December 2014, Groupon does business in over 500 markets worldwide, in 48 countries. According to Groupon's Q3 2014 financial report, the number of customers that have purchased a Groupon deal within the last 12 months grew by 24 % year-over-year, to 52.7 million as of September 2014, with about 23.5 million in North America, 14.9 million in EMEA, and 14.3 million in the rest of the world. Mobile app downloads have increased in Q3 2014, which has been facilitated by recent initiatives taken on their mobile platform. As of Q3 2014, worldwide transactions on mobile devices comprised over half of Groupon's

Elektronisch zusatz-materialien Die online-version dieses kapitels (doi:10.1007/978-3-319-17028-2_6) enthält zusatzmaterial, das für autorisierte benutzer ist.

business and over 100 million people have downloaded Groupon's mobile app. Experts predict that mobile will fuel growth for the company in the future (see **forbes.com/sites/greatspeculations/2014/11/05/groupons-solid-third-quarter-results-drive-stock-price-higher**). For Groupon statistics and facts, see **statista.com/topics/824/groupon.**

The Opportunity

Groupon is a start-up that offers special highly discounted deals, mostly via e-mail. The idea is that when subscribers hear about a big discount, they will forward the news to friends who may also place an order (the 'social' element). Initially, in order to receive the deal, there had to be a minimum number of buyers ("tipping point"), thus creating a group buy. However, this model has been changed, as will be described next.

The Solution

To exploit the chance that people are likely to spread news about bargains to their friends on social networks, Groupon developed a unique business model.

The Business Model and the Strategy

According to Groupon (**groupon.com**), the company, as an intermediary, offers special sales, called "Groupons," in each city that the company serves.

The sales are offered usually by well-known merchants. The advertised deal lasts for a limited time (usually between 24 and 72 h) and becomes available to all registered members. According to Groupon's customer service department, in the past, Groupon's policy was to guarantee participating merchants a certain number of sales. In other words, the customer would only get the discount if enough people (hence, the "group" element) purchased that particular Groupon. If Groupon did not meet that promised quota, there was no need for the seller to honor the deal, nor was any commission paid to Groupon, and the customer was not charged.

Groupon charges advertising and promotion fees, which is usually a percentage of the revenue generated by the sellers. The retailers can use the system to promote their business, gain new customers, and run sales during their slow seasons (e.g., such as liquidation during the late summer). The initial process, a combination of *group buys* and *daily deals*, is illustrated in Fig. 6.1. Today, Groupon is basically a flash (daily or longer) discount deal business and an operator of a marketplace. The reason merchants are willing to offer a 50–90 %

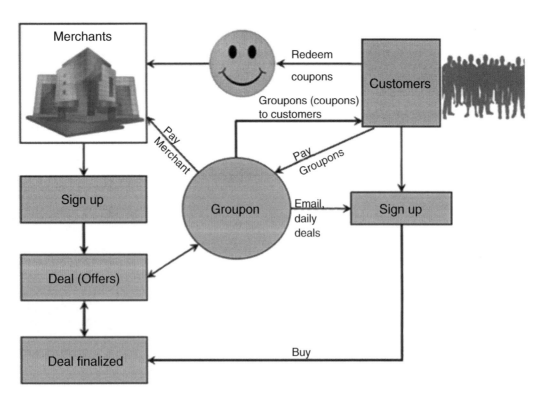

Fig. 6.1 Groupon's business model and process

discount to volume shoppers is that the merchants' marketing and overhead costs are lower, while their market share increases due to the attraction of new customers.

Groupon's business strategy is to work with quality merchants who are willing to provide substantial discounts. Groupon uses both traditional e-mail and social networking (e.g., Facebook, Twitter, Pinterest, etc.) to promote the deals. Deals are e-mailed directly to members when available, but those interested in other products or services can go to Groupon Goods (**groupon.com/goods**) to search for something specific. Groupon also offers a goods "clearance" section; the offers change daily. In addition to their daily deals, Groupon also offers coupons and promotions each month (e.g., Cyber Monday Mania). Groupon offers a "refer a friend" program, where shoppers can earn $10 for every friend they refer who buys their first deal (see **groupon.com/referral**). Note that Groupon changes its business model from time to time. In addition, it provides services to the merchants that simplify the process illustrated in Fig. 6.1. For example, in May 2014, Groupon launched 'Gnome'—a tablet solution that helps merchants manage their business and connect with customers (for details, see **investor.groupon.com/releasedetail. cfm?releaseid=848707**). In October 2014, the company launched "Snap" by Groupon, a free mobile app that pays customers cash to buy featured grocery items (see **investor.groupon.com/releasedetail.cfm?releaseid=874306**).

Benefits and Expansion

The major benefits to customers are:

- Steep discounts (50–90 %).
- Discovery of new/specialized services and products.
- No need to search for deals; Groupon organizes them for you.

The major benefits to merchants are:

- Can sell larger quantities and liquidate merchandise, quickly.
- Save on advertising and marketing expenses (e.g., by using viral advertising).
- Get repeat customers (if they like the deal and the service, customers will return).
- Lower customer acquisition cost.
- Knowledge of, and collaboration with, related vendors in a close geographical area.

Limitations of the Model

Some of Groupon's deals can become too large for vendors to fill. In one example, according to Crum (2011), a restaurant in Tokyo sold 500 Groupons for a traditional New Year's dinner, but the business was unable to process the orders in a timely fashion due to the overwhelming demand. Customers complained about late deliveries and about orders arriving "in terrible condition." A similar problem occurred in India when a high demand for onions caused the Groupon website to crash (see AOL On News 2013).

In response to such a problem, Groupon officials have created formulas to help participating merchants determine how to meet consumer demands, and how many Groupons to offer (capping the orders to a reasonable number).

Another limitation is that some businesses may not make money on the deal and may possibly even suffer a loss (e.g., see Phibbs 2011). Finally, although Groupon and similar companies can generate large revenues, they may have large expenses as a result, and actually lose money by offering more deals. Thus, many question the profitability of the model, especially in light of the strong competition.

Groupon is attempting to become more than just a "deal of the day" business. As part of their branching out, in November 2013, Groupon built a new website and opened an e-commerce deal "marketplace" (online retail site), called Groupon Goods (**groupon.com/goods**), which also offers discounts on various products and services (e.g., beauty, automotive, pet grooming). These deals also have a time limit (ranging from 3 to 7 days) and limited quantities. In Q2 2013, less than 40 % of Groupon's North America revenue came from the company's daily deal e-mails, suggesting the marketplace store (with over 60 % of revenue) is becoming successful (see **usatoday.com/story/tech/2013/11/01/groupon-new-website-marketplace/3319943**). However, as of 2014, the company is still in transition.

The Deal Marketplace is Groupon's shift in strategy from providing one-off "daily deals" to offering longer-running, recurring campaigns. With the launch of the marketplace, local businesses now can offer discounts on their goods and services for an extended period of time.

In 2011, Groupon partnered with **expedia.com** to launch Groupon Getaways (**groupon.com/getaways**), which focuses on discounted travel (hotels, tours, etc.). In February 2014, Groupon created "Deal Builder," a program that allows merchants to build their own Groupon deal. The program is a part of GrouponWorks.

In September 2012, Groupon acquired a company called Savored (**savored.com**), a leading provider of reservations at the best restaurants in the US. Participating restaurants in select cities give diners discounts when they have empty tables. Unlike the usual daily deal where you buy a voucher, with Groupon Reserve, you make a reservation online and show up;

the restaurant will already have your reservation in their books. Customers can make a reservation after they purchase the deal via the Groupon site or via the Groupon mobile app. Groupon Reserve is available for select high end restaurants.

The Competition

There are many companies that are attempting to clone Groupon. Hundreds of Groupon clones exist (between 400 and 600 worldwide, as of 2011, depending on the source), and that number is growing. In addition, software development companies offer Groupon-clone platforms (groupon-clone scripts), such as Oorjit and Agryia. For example, at one time, there were over 1,000 similar companies in China alone, but many did not succeed. (For more about the top ten daily deal sites in China in 2013, see **thenextweb.com/asia/2013/02/18/chinas-daily-deal-market-consolidates-as-top-10-sites-claim-90-revenue-share-report**.) Nevertheless, as of December 2014, Groupon had many competitors, including **livingsocial.com**, sponsored by Amazon.com. Other notable competitors are **giltcity.com**, Gilt Groupe (**gilt.com**), **local.amazon.com**, and **tiprr.com**. For Groupon's top five competitors, see **brandongaille.com/the-top-5-groupon-competitors**. Indirect competition comes from Yipit (**yipit.com**), an e-mail-based "daily deal aggregator" that gathers deals (in your city) from daily deal sites such as Groupon. Tell Yipit what you want, and they will alert you when there are deals that match.

Possible future competitors include Yahoo!, Yelp, local restaurants offer big discounts, and other service providers that advertise special deals digitally and in newspapers. Finally, some major retailers and manufacturers (e.g., Walmart, Home Depot) offer daily deals independently.

In November 2014, Twitter joined the list of Groupon competitors by introducing an online coupon system called Twitter Offers. The new tool is allows merchants to use the platform to advertise their goods and offer discounts to their customers. For more details, see **valuewalk.com/2014/11/groupon-competitors-grows-twitter**. For more details about Twitter Offers, see also **blog.twitter.com/2014/introducing-twitter-offers**.

In 2011, online retail giant Amazon.com jumped on the daily deals "bandwagon" with the launch of Amazon Local, a local daily deals website that offers savings on products and services (for a limited time in limited quantities). To learn more about Amazon Local, go to **local.amazon.com**. Amazon itself offers deals on its main Web page. Amazon also has "Gold Box Deals," which are viewed by clicking on the "Today's Deals" link at the top of most Amazon.com pages or directly at **amazon.com/gp/goldbox**.

Factors in the Competition

It is challenging to compete with Groupon, given its large size and resources. Groupon still controls more than 50 % of all daily deal markets in the U.S. Therefore, competitors use strategies such as concentrating on a niche market, which targets consumers in smaller demographics, such as one product, or one industry (e.g., tickets for travel [**jetsetter.com**; for the military and veteran community at **troopswap.com**]; free software [**giveawayoftheday.com**]; food [**ddfoodoutlet.com**]; and fashion [**polyvore.com**]). In addition, some sites concentrate on a small territory (e.g., a particular [city] where they have a competitive advantage (e.g., see Hot Deals Hawaii [**hotdealshawaii.com**]). Similarly, deals for certain social or professional communities are getting popular, deal sites geared toward mothers and families (**plumdistrict.com**, deal sites geared towards men (**mandeals.com**), religion-based deals (**jdeal.com**), and dog lovers (**doggyloot.com**), may be very successful. For more about niche daily deal sites, see **business.time.com/2012/02/09/a-deal-just-for-you-niche-sites-with-deals-for-moms-dudes-jews-dog-lovers-the-military-more**.

Several sites have either folded (e.g., Facebook Deals) or were acquired by other companies. For example, BuyWithMe was purchased by Gilt Groupe, Buy.com was purchased by Japanese company Rakuten.com Shopping (**rakuten.com**), and private travel site **jetsetter.com** was acquired by TripAdvisor in 2013. As of December 2014, Groupon has acquired 34 sites, including the hotel booking app Blink (**blinkbooking.com**), which is now known as "Blink by Groupon." In January 2014, Groupon announced that it had has acquired 'Ticket Monster,' a Korean e-commerce company (a subsidiary of LivingSocial Korea) and online retail daily deal site Ideel (**ideel.com**).

The Results

In 2010, Groupon rejected a $6 billion buyout offer from Google. Instead, the company went public on November 4, 2011, raising $700 million. Share prices soared 31 % the first day, bringing Groupon's valuation to about $16 billion. Since then, the share price has declined due to concerns about profitability. Groupon lost money until the first quarter of 2013, and in May 2014, share prices were down 40 %. The share price slowly began recovering in late 2014.

Sources: Based on Crum (2011), Sennett (2012), Phibbs (2011), AOL On News (2013), **grouponworks.com/merchant-resources**, and **groupon.com** (both accessed December 2014).

LESSONS LEARNED FROM THE CASE

Groupon's initial business model included *group buying*, which is a social activity. Later, it changed this model, concentrating instead on daily deals. In the daily deals model, we can see how WOM is spreading via social networks, such as notifying friends about Groupon's deals (e.g., sharing on Facebook and Twitter). Group buying is a powerful social shopping model, but it is difficult to implement. This chapter presents group buying and deal of the day social shopping models as well as several others. This chapter also covers social-oriented shopping aids and provides a glimpse into the future of social shopping.

6.1 DEFINITIONS, DRIVERS, CONCEPTS, AND BENEFITS OF SOCIAL SHOPPING

Social shopping has grown very rapidly and may become a major portion of B2C sales in the future. According to Regus (2011), in 2010 about 53 % of companies located in countries with heavy Internet use were using social networks to acquire goods and increase sales. Today, the number is higher (see Stelzner 2014), especially due to the new features such as "Buy" buttons, introduced by Facebook and Twitter. For how to create a Facebook store, watch the video "How to Create a Facebook Store Even If You Are a Beginner" (3:23 minutes) at **youtube.com/watch?v=UWRNVzXXYIM**.

This increase in sales is also due to the new innovative online social shopping opportunities and models. Let us see how social shopping is done. First, you need a webstore (or use someone else's webstore). For example, companies that provide the technology to set up a Facebook store include Ecwid, which provides a free Facebook e-commerce app (see **ecwid.com/facebook-commerce**), and PinnacleCart (**pinnaclecart.com/sell-on-facebook**). Then you start selling.

Definitions

Shopping can be viewed as a social activity. **Social shopping** (also known as *Sales 2.0*) is online shopping with social media tools and platforms and sharing shopping experiences with friends. It is a growing activity in social commerce. Social commerce blends e-commerce and social media. Thus, social commerce takes the key features of social media (e.g., discussion groups, blogs, reviews, etc.) and uses them before, during, and after online shopping. According to

Popilskis (2014), social shopping is facilitated by companies having the capability to sell products using social media platforms (e.g., by creating a storefront on their Facebook page), without requiring the customers to leave the social network to complete the transaction. Note that social shopping is only one activity of social commerce. For the differences between social shopping and social commerce, see **personalweb. about.com/od/socialcommerce/a/Social-Shopping-Definition.htm**.

The Drivers of Social Shopping

An overview of selling on social networks is provided by Shih (2011) and by Singh and Diamond (2012), who cite the following drivers of social shopping:

- The large number of people visiting social networks attracts advertisers.
- Changing customers' shopping habits (see infographic at **visual.ly/social-media-changing-way-your-customers-show-online**).
- The increasing number of recommendations/suggestions made by friends, and the ease and speed of accessing them.
- The pressure from top management to increase effectiveness and efforts to improve overall efficiency of marketing in general.
- The need to compete (e.g., by differentiation) and to satisfy the social customers.
- The emergence of social customers with knowledge and competence in using the Internet (e.g., in finding reviews and comparing prices).
- The need to collaborate with business partners.
- The huge discounts provided by some of the newer business models (e.g., flash sales), causing customers to buy more goods/services.
- The socially-oriented shopping models (e.g., group buying, communities).
- The ease of shopping while you are using social networks (e, g., the Facebook 'Buy' button).
- The ease of communicating with friends in real time using Twitter and mobile devices.

For more on social shopping, see **webtrends.about.com/od/web20/a/social-shopping.htm** and **dbpedia.org/page/Social_commerce**. For an infographic, see Kimball (2013). Note: A considerable amount of information on social shopping is available by searching Google for 'social media marketing' (also see Halligan and Shah (2014).

Concepts and Content of Social Shopping

Social shopping is done through social networks (e.g., Polyvore, Wanelo), in vendors' socially oriented webstores (e.g., Greenberg et al. 2011), in special intermediaries' stores (such as Groupon.com), and more. The buyers are *social customers* who trust and/or enjoy social shopping. As will be seen later in this chapter, there is a wide range of social shopping models that utilize many of the Web 2.0 tools as well as social communities. Finally, an increasing number of B2C marketers offer stores on Facebook and other social networks (see e.g., **heidicohen.com/ b2c-versus-b2b-the-most-important-social-media- platform-research**).

The nature of shopping is changing, especially for brand name clothing and related items. For example, popular brands including the Gap are sold by e-tailers such as Shopbop and InStyle. In addition, fashion communities such as Stylehive and Polyvore help promote the latest fashion collections. Social shoppers are logging on to sites such as Net-a-Porter to buy designer clothes online. Shoppers can log on to sites such as ThisNext, to create profiles and blog about their favorite brands. For practical issues and guides to social shopping, see **digitalintelligencetoday. com/social-shopping-101-a-practitioners-prime**.

Where Is Social Shopping Done?

Most of social shopping today is done in public networks and communities, ranging from Polyvore to Kaboodle. Shoppers can also engage in social shopping through private social clubs and socially-oriented vendors' stores. Furthermore, social shoppers can buy from individual sellers and directly from manufacturers. For 35 companies that are changing the way we shop and eat, see 35 slides by Lutz and Peterson (2014).

There are two basic ways to engage in social shopping:
1. Add social software, apps, and features (e.g., polling) to existing e-commerce sites.
2. Add e-commerce functionalities (e.g., e-catalogs, payment gateways, shopping carts) to social media and social network sites.

Major retailers such as Target and Best Buy are increasingly looking to tap Facebook, Pinterest, and Twitter to drive sales (see Lee 2013).

For more on social shopping sites, see **webtrends.about. com/od/socialshopping/tp/7_essential_social_shopping. htm** and **pcmag.com/article2/0,2817,2424709,00.asp**.

For finding the right social media platform to drive most sales, see Shopify.com's infographic provided by Macdonald (2014).

Why Shoppers Go Social

Many shoppers like to hear from other shoppers prior to purchasing. Therefore, they ask for recommendations from friends, or use the communal shopping method.

Communal shopping (also known as *collaborative shopping*) is a method of shopping where consumers enlist friends and other people they trust to advise them on what products to shop for. This results in more confidence in the decisions they make—whether or not to buy (a phenomenon known as the "bandwagon effect"). For details, watch Bloomberg TV's video titled "New Frontiers in the Communal Shopping Experience" (2:58 minutes) at **bloomberg.com/video/eden-s- communal-shopping-experience-ExvmRAIhTE2AZ apKKd5aVA.html**.

People's Roles in Social Commerce

In 2010, Gartner Inc. conducted a study on social commerce (see **gartner.com/newsroom/id/1409213**), identifying the following roles people play in social media and e-commerce:

- **Connectors.** These are the people with contacts that introduce people to each other. Connectors try to influence people to buy. Consultants and connected people play this role.
- **Salespeople.** Like their offline counterparts, salespeople's major effort is to influence shoppers to buy. They are well connected so they can impress buyers.
- **Seekers.** These consumers seek advice and information about shopping and services from experts, friends, and mavens.
- **Mavens.** Mavens are recognized, but unofficial, experts in certain domains who can provide positive or negative recommendations to people who are seeking advice.
- **Self-sufficients.** These people find information on their own; they do not need or even pay attention to recommendations, and are not influenced by the opinions of others.
- **Unclassifieds.** Most people do not belong to any one of the above categories; some fulfill different roles and others exhibit characteristics of different categories.

The major influencers are friends, other consumers, salespeople, connectors, and mavens (experts). For further details, see Dubey (2010). In addition to roles, personality traits such as 'feeling' and 'thinking' may influence shopping.

The Benefits of Social Shopping

Social shopping influences both buyers and sellers.

Benefits to Buyers

Social shopping can provide benefits to buyers such as:

- Get super deals (50–90 % discounts) via group buying, daily specials, and more. Join Groupon for daily deals.
- Socialize while shopping and receive social support and rewards.
- Discover products/services you never knew existed (e.g., see **thisnext.com**).
- Interact directly with vendor (brand) representatives easily and quickly (e.g., feature available at **stylehive.com**).
- Increase confidence and trust in online shopping by interacting with friends.
- Shop anytime from any place.
- Exchange shopping tips with friends, fans, and others. Therefore, you can learn from other shoppers' experiences.
- Build and share wish and gift lists.
- Shop together with people like you.
- Get simplified comparisons, even in real time.
- Communicate in real time while shopping with friends and others using Twitter and other social media tools.

Kasteler (2009) elaborates on these and other benefits and provides a list of several dozen start-up shopping sites. For an overview and infographic, see **guerillaconnection.com/wp-content/uploads/2012/06/Guerilla-Social-Media-Trends.pdf**.

Therefore, before you go shopping online, it is wise to consult social shopping sources. In addition, visit socially-oriented sites where you can ask questions and get feedback from your friends.

Benefits to Sellers

The seller can:

- Improve overall sales unit productivity (e.g., see Smith and Ballve 2013).
- Increase revenue growth per customer.
- Gain feedback from new customers.

- Learn from customers.
- Increase customer loyalty and trust.
- Quickly liquidate overstocked or obsolete merchandise.

Note that social shopping sites may generate additional revenue from advertising, commission on actual sales, sharing customer information with retailers, and using affiliate marketing.

For more benefits to retailers, watch the video titled "Social Media a Powerful Tool for Online Retailers—Online Retail Expert Tips" (4:08 minutes) at **youtube.com/watch?v=1ByDmQICXs4**. For answers to questions regarding social sales, see Viskovich (2014). For strategy and marketing tips, see Walker (2014).

6.2 COMPONENTS AND MODELS OF SOCIAL SHOPPING

Social commerce features a unique set of components. It also employs distinctive business models. All these are described next.

What Components to Expect in a Social Shopping Site

Depending on the social shopping model, the product offering, related information, and the supportive information systems, one may find a diversity of components on a social shopping site. The following are the major components that help customers make purchasing decisions:

- **Visual Sharing.** Photos, videos, and other images enable shoppers to visually share their product experiences.
- **Online discussions.** Ratings, reviews, interactions, recommendations, blogging, and comments facilitate discussions regarding features and benefits of products.
- **How to use products.** These demonstrate, via videos, blogs, and step-by-step instructions, how to use products.
- **Guides.** Guides are created by user-generated content (UGC). The users can be experienced consumers, experts, or employees. The guides are supported by case studies, testimonials, and videos.

The Major Social Shopping Models

Several social shopping models and strategies have appeared in recent years, many created by start-ups such as Groupon. Some are extensions of EC generic models; others are unique to social shopping. These models can be stand alone, combined, or used within social networks. We have grouped them into the following categories, followed by the location where they are further discussed in this book. The grouping is based on Yin (2010), Strauss and Frost (2014), and the authors' experiences:

- Group buying (Sect. 6.3)
- Deal purchases (flash sales), such as daily special offers (Sect. 6.3)
- Shopping communities and clubs (Sect. 6.4)
- Recommendation sites (Sect. 6.5)
- Marketplaces (Sect. 6.5)
- Innovative models (Sect. 6.6)
- Shopping for virtual products and services (Sect. 6.6)
- Location-based shopping (presented briefly in Chap. 5; see also Zwilling 2011)
- Shopping presentation sites (e.g., on YouTube) and gaming sites (Chap. 9)
- Peer-to-peer models (e.g., money lending; Chap. 9)
- B2B shopping (Chap. 9 and Gillin and Schwartzman 2011)

Note: Both Pinterest and Twitter provide activities that use several of these models, directly and indirectly. For Twitter, see **business.twitter.com**. Note also that public social shopping sites may generate revenue from advertising, commissions on actual sales, shared customer information among retailers, and affiliate marketing.

The major models are illustrated in Fig. 6.2.

To see the diversity of social commerce, see the slide presentation on transforming retail into social commerce at **slideshare.net/oukearts/transforming-retail-into-social-commerce-retail-ceo-briefing-strategy-boutique-thaesis**. See also Shih (2011).

Traditional E-Commerce Sites with Social Media Additions

In addition to pure social shopping sites, there are many traditional e-commerce sites that add social media capabilities. An example from Germany is presented next.

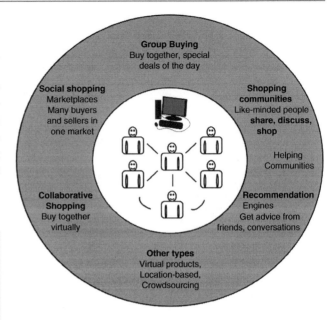

Fig. 6.2 The major categories of social shopping

Example: Nestlé Interactive Social Commerce Site

The global food and beverage manufacturer launched an interactive online social commerce platform in Germany in September 2011 to engage with consumers while providing greater access to its products (**nestle.com/media/newsandfeatures/nestle-marks-largest-ever-investment-germany**). The Nestlé Marketplace ("Marktplatz"; **nestle-marktplatz.de**) website, according to **fdbusiness.com/2011/09/nestle-pilots-social-commerce-with-new-interactive-site**, is the first social commerce platform of its kind in Germany, from a food and beverage manufacturer of Nestlé's size and range. Consumers can purchase products online (including foreign Nestlé products that are not available in most of Nestlé's physical stores or the physical stores of retailers who sell Nestle's products) and also review, rate, recommend, and ask questions about each product. The site supports two-way communication. According to **fdbusiness.com/2011/09/nestle-pilots-social-commerce-with-new-interactive-site**, people can leave ratings and comments about the products. Shoppers can submit suggestions for new products on the site. With more than 2,000 products and 75 different brands available online (February 2014), Nestlé Germany receives an estimated 6,247 unique visitors and 31,235 page views per day (per **whoismachine.com/review/nestle-marktplatz.de**; November 2014 data).

The company wants to enable its customers to engage and help Nestlé Marketplace to prosper.

Visitors to the Nestlé Marketplace can search for products using a variety of detailed criteria, including taste, packaging, color, specific occasions, or diet preferences. Nutritional information can also be found for each product. **Nestle-marktplatz. de** is supported by a Facebook page, which provides a space for discussion about the company's brands, foods, and cooking. For details, see **nestle.com/Media/NewsAndFeatures/Pages/Nestle-pilots-social-commerce-with-new-interactive-site-for-German-consumers.aspx**.To learn about the company's strategies, expectations, and experiences, see **e-commerce-facts.com/background/2012/03/nestle-marketplace**.

Other examples for socially-oriented e-commerce stores are Zappos (app called Ask Zappos; **askzappos.apps.zappos.com**) and Levi's webstore. For a comprehensive comparison of social and e-commerce, see Shen (2012). Bessette (2014) describes how nine companies ('social media superstars') use social media platforms to stay ahead of the competition. For an interesting e-book about the social sales revolution, see Salesforce (2011).

6.3 GROUP BUYING AND DEAL PURCHASING

The group buying model describes a group of people who come together to get a *quantity discount*. The B2C model was unpopular in traditional e-commerce and seldom used in many countries. An exception is a modified group buying method that succeeded in China. The problem with the original e-commerce model was the difficulty in organizing the online groups, even with an intermediary. Furthermore, even if a group was organized, negotiating discounts was often difficult, unless a very large volume was involved. However, in the new model, in order to rally shoppers, sites like Groupon, LivingSocial, and GiltCity (which acquired BuyWithMe), offer large discounts or special offers that are available for a limited time (usually 24–72 h). The social commerce companies act as intermediaries to carefully negotiate the discounts and other terms with vendors. According to Harbison (2010), social media and group buying is a "match made in heaven," since everybody is a winner. For a discussion, see Dugan (2010). Unfortunately, the model is still not so popular in the U.S. and many other countries.

Note: This situation may be changing; see Mander (2014) and discussion later in this chapter.

Customers post daily deals with comments on Facebook and Twitter and other social media sites. This is a good way to find deals without joining any specific daily deals sites.

Group Buying in China

The Chinese created group buying for many products, especially expensive ones (e.g., cars, computers, artwork) even before sites like Groupon existed. Group buying in China ("tuangou" in Chinese) differs from that of other countries due to the Chinese culture. Group buying companies have been active all over China. For example, the giant e-commerce company, Baidu, entered into this business in August 2013 by purchasing a 59 % stake in Nuomi (Renren's group-buying site), and in 2014, agreed to purchase the remaining stock (see Campos 2014). However, according to the research group China e-Business Research Center, in 2012, half of the group buying sites have shut down (see **pcworld.com/article/260892/nearly_half_of_chinas_group_buying_sites_now_closed_amid_heated_competition.html**). According to a report by news portal **Xkb.com.cn**, in 2010, at the peak of the group-buying craze, 5,058 such websites were in the market, but in August 2013, there were only 943. A main reason for this is lack of funding. For more information on the status of group buying websites in China, see **bambooinnovator.com/2013/08/13/group-buying-websites-in-china-face-funding-crisis**.

In Q1 2013, the largest in market shares was Juhuasuan (**ju.taobao.com**; per 2013 research report by Dataotuan, as reported by Techinasia; see **techinasia.com/china-daily-deals-q1-2013-data**); however, as of January 2014, the top daily deals startup is now Meituan, earning almost $500 million in sales annually, roughly double to what it was earning in 2013, and their competitor, Lashou, is valued at $1.1 billion (see Campos 2014). Group buying soared in China between 2010 and 2013. About 83 million people in China used group buying sites in January 2013, up from just 64 million at the end of 2011, according to the China Internet Network Information Center. In 2014, all major Chinese Internet companies have launched, or planned to launch, group buying and flash deal sites. These include Baidu, Sina, Tencent, and Alibaba. For details, see Madden (2010) and watch the video titled "Group Buying in China" (2:10 minutes) at **cnn.com/video/data/2.0/video/business/2011/01/26/yoon.china.coupon.gen.cnn.html**. Note that, in 2014, China's cosmetics deal site Jumei was the first Chinese daily deals site to seek an IPO in the U.S. (see **techinasia.com/china-daily-deals-site-jumei-files-for-400-million-dollars-us-ipo**).

How Group Buying Is Done in China

According to **adage.com/article/global-news/advertising-china-group-buying-discounts-groupon/147641**, "years ago, Chinese Internet users started getting together online to organize as a group to buy the same car from the same dealer in order to get a [quantity negotiated] discount, and this team-buying concept quickly spread to other categories like computers. [To accomplish this], a group leader would coordinate the group's requirements and bargain with prospective dealers to close the sale." Sometimes the leader brings the entire buying group to the face-to-face negotiation (read Eunice Yoon's report and watch the video "Group Buying in China" at **slinkingtowardretirement.com/?p=23479**). In fact, in

2008, according to the *Adage* report, "a group of Ford Focus buyers got into a shoving match at a Ford dealership when the employees reportedly reneged on the agreed price, and the prospective buyers uploaded footage of the melee to video sites" (watch the video at **vimeo.com/8619105**).

Group Buying and Flash Sales on Facebook

Several years ago, it was common to combine group buys with flash sales (also known as daily deals). However, this combination was not too successful and the two models are now used mostly independently of each other. For group buying and daily deals software, see **groupbuyingsite.com**.

Example
Lot18 (**lot18.com**) offers access to fine wines at up to 60 % off. Their team of curators works directly with producers around the world to bring high-quality, hard-to-find products directly to members. They showcase new wines daily, made available in limited quantities for a limited time, or until members have purchased all available quantities. Several new products appear on the site each day. Lot18 uses Facebook to advertise flash deals. Advertising flash sales on Facebook provides an ideal environment for recruiting friends into group-buy deals (members who invite friends to register are rewarded with a Lot18 credit for future purchases after the friend's first order ships). Each member receives a personalized referral link, which he or she can share with friends via e-mail or by posting the link on their Facebook or Twitter pages.

Customers post daily deals with comments on Facebook and Twitter and other social media sites. This is a good way to find deals without joining any specific daily deal sites.

The Future of Group Buying

There are two opinions regarding the future of group buying. Mander (2014) and Lee (2014) report an increase in group buying and flash sales, in Southeast Asia, China, and the U.S. On the other hand, Jingli (2014) reports the opposite about China. One possible explanation is that the companies in these emerging areas are merging into other companies and do not report results for these models anymore.

Deal Purchases (Flash Sales, Daily Deals)

Gilt Group (**gilt.com**) pioneered the online flash sale in the US in 2007. (See **business.time.com/2012/10/25/high-and-low** and Dugan 2010.) There are several definitions of

flash sales. For examples, see **digitalmarketing-glossary. com/What-is-Flash-sales-site-definition** and **senior-planet.org/online-flash-sales-how-to-get-good-deals**. Flash sales are very common offline. These are short term deals that are designed to attract people who are already in a physical store. In addition, "doorbuster" sales between certain hours on a certain day (e.g., Black Friday) also are common offline. There are several variations of flash sales when done online.

The "deal of the day" may be offered only in one city or state, while some are offered nationally. For example, Living Social (**livingsocial.com**) asks people to sign up for a deal at a restaurant, spa, or an event in a particular city. You can click on "today's deals" or browse "all deals." The deals are e-mailed to anyone that signs up with LivingSocial, or you can browse their site for something in particular. If you like it, you click on the "Buy it" icon to purchase the deal. After you buy the deal, you get a unique link to share the deal information with your friends (LivingSocial also has a friend referral program).

A common strategy of flash sale sites is to focus on a particular industry. For example, Gilt.com focuses on designer apparel, jewelry, bags, and upscale home furnishings. iDine (**idine.com**) is a loyalty program that rewards customers with benefits when they dine out at discounted prices in participating restaurants.

Woot! (an Amazon company) offers community information related to its deals. For example, there is a "discussion about today's deal," a Woot! blog, top past deals, deal news, and what percentage of community members bought this product and what quantities of the products were sold. Testimonials by members are also available. Woot! is known as a community for "gadget geeks." Thus, Woot! is not only a brand, but also a culture. See **woot.com**. Other interesting flash sale companies are **jetsetter.com**; acquired by TripAdvisor in 2013) and **ruelala.com**. Companies like Groupon, LivingSocial, and Woot! run promotions for deals in major metropolitan areas. Discounts of 50 % are common, and sometimes they reach 80 %.

6.4 SHOPPING TOGETHER: COMMUNITIES AND CLUBS

Shopping together is an enjoyable activity among many people while in physical stores. Today, due to social software and social media innovations, it is also possible to shop together online. As you may recall, social shopping is a mix of online shopping and social networking. Social shopping is done in two places: community platforms and online clubs, as is described next.

Online communities (and shopping clubs, to be discussed later) are places where people gather to spend time talking about books, investments, wine, and so on, with like-minded people, for different purposes, including shopping.

Online Social Shopping Communities

According to **socialecart.com/social-shopping**, "*shopping communities* bring like-minded people together to discuss, share, and shop" (emphasis added). For customer behavior in social communities, see Liu et al. (2013). The community platforms and forums connect people with each other, with businesses, and with other communities. Many such sites allow users to create custom shopping lists and share them with friends. To date, fashion communities (e.g., Polyvore, StyleFeeder; a Time company, and ShopStyle) are the most popular ones. For some examples of fashion communities and online social networks, see **itsjustpeople.com/2012/03/30/the-top-fashion-communities-and-online-social-networks-find-out-who-they-are-here**. However, other shopping communities are organized around food, pets, toys, and so forth. For example, **listia.com** is an online community for buying and selling used or new items, along with fashion, in online auctions using virtual currency. **Djdoodleville.com** is an online shopping community specializing in arts and crafts.

For a summary of social shopping communities, see **digital-innovationtoday.com/speed-summary-ijec-social-commerce-special-edition-social-shopping-communities**.

Common Features in Communities and Forums

Communities and forums share the following major features (per Marsden 2009; Fisher 2010; [slideshow with transcript], and the authors' experiences):

- **User forums.** Forums are discussion places in social networks where people can meet to discuss issues or to work together to solve problems raised by participants in discussion groups.
- **User galleries.** Galleries are usually hosted by vendors to display images and videos for discussion by viewers such as customers and business partners (e.g., Burberry's Art of the Trench; **artofthetrench.burberry.com**). In January 2013, Twitter added video to its user galleries and is now calling them "media galleries" (see **marketingland.com/twitter-adds-videos-to-user-media-galleries-32095**).

- **Idea boards.** These are usually located inside enterprise networks (e.g., **mystarbucksidea.force.com**; "free crowdsourcing of product ideas," Dell's **ideastorm.com**). This is a crowdsourcing mechanism for idea generation and idea evaluation.
- **Q&A forums.** Online groups where users (e.g., customers) can ask and answer questions about various topics (e.g., a company's products) and be helped by product experts and savvy customers (e.g., Bazaarvoice's "Ask & Answer" or PowerReviews' "Social Answers"). Questions and answers can be organized in Q&A format.
- **Brand communities.** Communities that are organized around a brand (e.g., Sony's MP3) to discuss a product or brand.
- **Comprehensive (multipurpose communities).** Kaboodle is probably the most well-known comprehensive community, while Polyvore is the leading community for fashion (and related products).

Examples of Shopping Communities

There are many sites that can be classified as pure shopping communities. A prime example is Polyvore, which is presented in Case 6.1.

Case 6.1
SC Application
Polyvore: A Trendsetter in Social Shopping
According to Polyvore (**polyvore.com**), the company is a community site for online fashion and style where users are empowered to discover and develop their style and possibly set fashion trends. Users do this by creating "sets," which are shared across the Web. The company collaborates with prominent brands such as Calvin Klein, Lancôme (**lancome-usa.com**), Coach, and retailers such as Net-a-Porter to drive product engagement; the user-generated fashion products on its site are then judged by community members and by celebrities such as Lady Gaga and Katy Perry. Today, the company also uses mobile technologies. For example, it has an app for iPad with many capabilities (see **blog.polyvore.com/2014/02/new-ipad-and-iphone-updates-clip-to.html**).

Note: Some celebrities, such as Lady Gaga, post their own products for sale on the site.

The story of the now-profitable Polyvore is described in detail by Jacobs (2010) and Chaney (2011); see also the infographic provided by Grant (2013). Users create "sets" of their wardrobe designs using a special editor provided free on the site. These "sets" can then be posted and shared on Polyvore's site, Facebook, and Twitter. Merchants (e.g., designers) can use the site for free by (a) creating a profile, (b) uploading existing products, and (c) creating sets.

Once merchants create a profile and upload products, Polyvore encourages them to engage with other community members by reviewing and evaluating the sets. Polyvore believes that the merchants' activity will be reciprocated. To facilitate actual shopping, the sets link to the creators' sites.

Polyvore can be viewed as a *crowdsourcing fashion* business model that reflects the creativity and opinion of many; plus, it can be viewed as expressing current fashion trends (see Wang 2011). They now do the same with interior design, where you can submit your creative room sets (**polyvore. com/polyvore_interior_design_co/group. show?id=29235**). According to Wang (2011), the site provides a new business model for both shopping and product and style discovery, as well as a venue for designers to hone their skills by introducing new fashion items.

In October 2014, Polyvore had over 20 million unique visitors importing 2.2 million items to the site each month, creating about three million fashion sets per month via Polyvore's website and its mobile app. Over 100 million items have been added to the network since its debut. Mobile activity is increasing, with 50 % of sets being created on a smartphone or tablet (per **techcrunch.com/2014/10/07/polyvore-gets-personalized-with-new-iphone-app-featuring-just-for-you-style-suggestions/**). Polyvore also released a "new and improved" iPhone app in July 2014. Users spend hours browsing, following favorite taste streams, asking questions and sharing ideas, which is profitable for businesses (see **corp.wishpond.com/blog/2013/02/05/understanding-polyvore-for-business**). Polyvore is considered by many to be the best place to discover or evaluate fashion trends, which are facilitated by contests managed by the company. For more information, see **venturebeat.com/2012/12/20/polyvore-gets-a-cro.**

Polyvore can be used together with Pinterest to increase traffic to the site (see Mally 2012).

For Polyvore's features, see **microexplosion.com/tips-2/polyvore-the-biggest-site-youve-never-heard-of**. To learn how to use Polyvore to drive traffic and sales for your webstore, see **shopify.com/blog/13815533-how-to-use-polyvore-to-drive-traffic-and-sales-for-your-online-store**.

Sources: Based on Jacobs (2010), Wang (2011), Taylor (2013), **polyvore.com**, and **crunchbase.com/organization/polyvore** (both accessed June 2015).

Questions

1. How can one use the Polyvore Editor to create designs? Watch the short video (2:02 minutes) by Polyvore titled "How to Create a Set in the Polyvore Editor" at **vimeo. com/7800846**.

2. The company added supermodel Tyra Banks as an investor in 2013. Comment on the logic of this.
3. Jacobs (2010) writes, "Polyvore is a lot like playing paper dolls with pictures of real clothes." Discuss.
4. Read Jacobs (2010) and explain what and how people create at Polyvore. Also identify the critical success factors of this site.
5. Explain the statement made by Polyvore's vice president of product management: "Our mission is to democratize fashion."
6. Identify all the features of a shopping community in this case.

Kaboodle: A Unique Social Shopping Community

Kaboodle (**kaboodle.com**) is a large, comprehensive *social shopping community* and network, according to **kaboodle.com/zm/about**. According to **crunchbase.com/product/kaboodle**, "Kaboodle is a free service that lets users collect information from the Web and store it on a Kaboodle list that can be shared with others." The site's primary goal "is to simplify shopping by making it easier for people to find items they're interested in and by allowing users to share recommendations with one another using Kaboodle *lists* and *groups*. Kaboodle lists, however, can also serve a variety of purposes besides just shopping. [For example], they can be used for planning vacations [or parties], sharing research for work or school, sharing your favorite bands with friends, and basically anything else you might want to collect and share information about" (emphasis added).

To learn more about how Kaboodle works, take the Kaboodle Tour at **kaboodle.com/zd/help/getStarted.html**.

Some of Kaboodle's Capabilities

The "Add to Kaboodle" button simplifies the online shopping experience because, once installed, the user can simply click on it whenever a product is selected from any website. Then, a snapshot of the selected item, its price, and other product information is automatically uploaded with a link about where to place it on the user's Kaboodle lists. The user then can find any specific item in the future. Users can also discover deals, find new products, express their unique styles, connect with others, share their discoveries, blog, create shopping lists, and more.

Kaboodle allows the creation of "Top Picks" from the Kaboodle lists based on what members like (e.g., the "top 10 weird and interesting products").

Private Online Shopping Clubs and Retail by Invitation

French e-commerce company Vente-Privee (**us.venteprivee. com**) pioneered the first private online shopping club specializing in "members only" online flash sales. The club concentrates on designer products at discounted prices (up to 80 %). Vente-Privee also sells exclusive designer brands such as fashion accessories, homewares, sports products, consumer electronics, and wine. In general, private shopping clubs run flash sale events featuring luxury brands at huge discounts. Luxury brands use the clubs to liquidate out of style items, overstock, or special samples. Consumers like the clubs due to the steep discounts.

The key to this business model's success is that, in contrast with the Groupon model, *not everyone* is allowed to shop. The *members-only* model serves a myriad of purposes. Partially, it is a marketing device that makes members feel like VIPs, but it also helps the clubs manage healthy growth.

Examples of Private Clubs

Some private (or "members only") clubs are: Beyond the Rack (U.S. and Canada), Gilt Groupe, Rue La La, Amazon BuyVIP (**buyvip.com**; Europe only), Ideel, and BestSecret. For members only clubs around the world, see **members-only-shopping.com**. Note that, to minimize conflict with department stores, some luxury brands now offer selected items at lower prices in stores such as Target Inc.

Shopping Together Sites

Dozens of sites facilitate shopping together activities. For example, Select2gether (**select2gether.com**) is a "virtual room where you can meet and greet your friends, colleagues, customers and prospects. Select2gether allows you to organize and share all the beautiful things you find on the Web. You can browse Meet Rooms created by other people to discover new things and get inspiration from people who share your interests. You can show your stuff to others and get advice and other views from friends and advisors." For details and explanations, see **select2gether.com/about/help**. Select2gether utilizes the WeLiket tool, which lets users "grab" images from any website to add to the Meet Room. The free WeLiket tool is unique to Select2gether. For more about the WeLiket tool, see **select2gether.com/pages/toolbar**.

Coshopping

Coshopping is an IBM software package (feature of the IBM WebSphere Commerce pack) that enables online shoppers to invite friends to a coshopping session. Shoppers and their friends can explore a store, view products, exc sages, and chat about products. Coshopping pro time synchronization of two shoppers' Web bi create a single collaborative shopping session con ∟ by one of the shoppers (with individual's privacy protected).

Coshopping can also facilitate a customer care center's live chat solution by allowing a customer service representative to guide the customer through product browsing and selection on the site. To learn about the features and capabilities of Coshopping, see **ibm.com/support/knowledgecenter/SSZLC2_7.0.0/com.ibm.commerce.coshopping.doc/concepts/csmcoshopping.htm**. For other examples of social shopping networks, see **online.wsj.com/news/articles/SB10001424052970204425904578073320375105606**.

6.5 SOCIAL SHOPPING AIDS: FROM RECOMMENDATIONS, REVIEWS, AND RATINGS TO MARKETPLACES

In addition to the typical e-commerce shopping aids such as comparison engines and recommendations a la Amazon.com style, there are special aids for social commerce.

Recommendations in Social Commerce

Prior to making a purchase, customers tend to collect information that will help them make a decision, such as what brand to buy, from which vendor, and at what price. Online customers do this by consulting shopping aids (e.g., price comparison sites) such as **nextag.com**, product review sites such as **epinions.com**, and researching other sources. Examining and participating in social networking forums is another way to compare prices and read product and service reviews. According to Gartner Inc. (reported by Dubey 2010), the majority of online customers already rely on social networks to guide them in purchasing decisions. A variety of SC models and tools is available for this purpose (e.g., see Dugan 2010). We present two major categories here. For an infographic on what engages millennials and influences their purchasing decisions, see **quicksprout.com/2014/11/14/how-to-influence-purchasing-decisions**.

Ratings and Reviews

Ratings and reviews by friends, even by people that you do not know (e.g., experts or independent third-party evaluators), are usually available for social shoppers. In addition, any user has an opportunity to contribute reviews and participate in relevant discussions. The information about the tools for conducting rating and reviews, which are presented here, is based on Fisher (2010), Rowan and Cheshire (2011), Shih (2011), **bazaarvoice.com/solutions/conversations**, and the authors' experiences. The major types of tools and methods are:

- **Customer ratings and reviews.** Customer ratings are popular. They can be found on product (or service) review sites (e.g., **buzzillions.com**) or independent review sites (e.g., **tripadvisor.com**), and/or in customer news feeds (e.g., Amazon.com, Epinions). Customer ratings can be summarized by votes or polls.
- **Customer testimonials.** Customer experiences are typically published on vendors' sites, and on third party sites such as TripAdvisor. Most sites encourage discussion (e.g., **bazaarvoice.com/solutions/ conversations**).
- **Expert ratings and reviews.** Ratings or reviews can also be generated by domain experts and appear in different online publications.
- **Sponsored reviews.** These are written by paid bloggers or domain experts. Advertisers and bloggers find each other by searching through websites such as **sponsoredreviews.com**, which connects bloggers with marketers and advertisers.
- **Conversational marketing.** People communicate via e-mail, blog, live chat, discussion groups, and tweets. Monitoring conversations may yield rich data for market research and customer service (e.g., Dell's use of their "Social Media Command Center"). See Chap. 10 and **exacttarget.com/sites/ exacttarget/files/10-Examples-of-Social-Media-Command-Centers.pdf** for details.
- **Video product review.** Reviews can be generated by using videos through communities such as Expo (**expotv.com**), where consumers can leave "Videopinions" about products and services. YouTube users can create reviews that are uploaded, viewed, commented on, and shared.
- **Blogger reviews.** This is a questionable method since some bloggers are paid and may use a biased approach. However, many bloggers have a reputation of being unbiased. For a list of 50 product review blogs, see Sala (2012).

Example

Maui Jim (**mauijim.com**) is a company that designs high quality polarized sunglasses. According to *Business Wire* (2010), the company is using Bazaarvoice Ratings & Reviews to enable customers to rate and review the company's entire line of sunglasses and accessories. The company is relying on word-of-mouth marketing to advertise its products and help shoppers. Customers are invited to share their opinions on the style, fit, and quality of specific sunglass models. Maui Jim also sends customers opt-in e-mails asking them to review products. The company lists the reviews with the product listings, and also integrates them in the site search functionality so customers can see its star rating in the search results.

Social Recommendations and Referrals

Recommendation engines allow shoppers to receive advice from other shoppers and to give advice to others.

Social shopping may combine recommendations in a social network platform with actual sales. Social recommendations and referrals are closely related to ratings and reviews and are sometimes integrated with them.

Traditional online product review companies such as Amazon.com and Bazaarvoice have helped traditional consumers, but today's customers like to receive advice from, and give advice to, friends and other shoppers. Sites such as **cnet.com**, Wired Reviews (**wired.com/category/reviews**), **buzzillions.com**, **epinions.com**, **consumerreports.org**, and **thefind.com** can be used for this purpose. Amazon.com also provides reviews on the products they sell.

Example

ThisNext (**thisnext.com**) is a social commerce site where community members *recommend* their favorite products, so others can discover desirable or unique items and decide what to buy. ThisNext uses WOM, social experiences, and personalization to facilitate shopping. To assist with discovery and help finalize shopping decisions, the community includes experts, bloggers, style mavens, and trendsetters. ThisNext has also developed a set of shopping tools for bloggers, designers, and shoppers. For a further description, see **thisnext.com/company**.

It makes sense to combine recommendations with marketing communications and shopping. Recommendation and review sites allow shoppers to receive and provide advice to specific friends, in contrast with traditional online product reviews that include advice provided by unknown shoppers. Furthermore, these sites sell ad space, provide coupons, and some offer automatic cash-back rewards for shopping with local merchants.

A new trend is to encourage conversations around purchases with a shopper's "real life" friends. The sites that include reviews from people one knows are logically more trustworthy than sites that include only the reviews made by strangers.

Sometimes, social recommendations are embedded in social shopping portals that offer shopping tools as well as bundling recommendations with ratings and reviews. A prime example is Kaboodle (described earlier as a shopping community).

Common recommendation methods are:

- **Social bookmarking.** Recommended products, services, etc. are bookmarked so members of social networks can easily find them.
- **Personal social recommendations.** These are based on finding people with similar profiles. By using these customers' actual purchases, conclusions can be reached about general and targeted recommendations (e.g., see Apple's Near Me **[getnearme.com]**; applications that are popular based on a user's current location, Amazon Recommendations, and **snoox.com** "your friends' recommendations, on everything").
- **Referral programs.** Affiliate programs (e.g., **affiliate-program.amazon.com**, **apple.com/itunes/affiliates**) pay people for referring new customers. For more about referral programs, see **slideshare.net/getAmbassador/building-an-effective-referral-program**.
- **Matching algorithms.** Consulting companies and vendors (e.g., Netflix) provide recommendations based on similarity algorithms (as described in Chap. 3).

For more on product reviews, see **buzzilions.com** and **bazaarvoice.com/product-reviews**.

Illustrative Examples of Recommendation Sites

Recommendations, reviews, ratings, and other engagement activities can be done in the communities described in Sect. 6.4. For a list of rating and review websites, see **epower.com/rating-review.php**. However, the *major objectives* of communities like Kaboodle are different because they *concentrate* on recommendations, reviews, and ratings as important shopping aids.

Crowdstorm

According to Chaney (2011), "**crowdstorm.com**" is a *shopping recommendation* website with two goals: (a) [being] a hub for product reviews, and (b) [being] a source where shoppers can find the best online prices for consumer goods such as electronics, sporting equipment, clothing, and jew-elry. The site is fueled by user-submitted product listings and product reviews. However, it also has expert reviews, buyer guides, and question-and-answer sessions. The site promotes an open policy by allowing users to post their reviews to blogs, other reviews sites and online stores" (emphasis added). The site is doing extensive *price comparisons*. The site claims to have over 300,000 visitors a month; however, it does not sell anything—it just aids shoppers. Crowdstorm is also a social shopping experience provider, where shoppers can ask others for recommendations about products they are looking to buy and to find the best online prices for many consumer goods. By adding a social shopping aspect to their website, Crowdstorm is aiming to be much more than simply a price comparison site.

Buzzillions

Buzzillions.com is a user-generated product review site. It gets reviews from its partner company, PowerReviews (acquired by Bazaarvoice), which provides customer review software to e-commerce sites. It also incorporates product reviews from companies that use other third-party providers, or have an in-house review system. The site provides several useful tools for tagging and researching the reviews. It also provides rankings.

Buzzillions' business model is based on selling traffic information, or product leads, from Buzzillions right back to the merchant network that uses PowerReviews. In other words, Buzzillions' users read reviews imported from many other sites, and they can then click on products of interest, giving them the opportunity to read more about these products and possibly purchase them from the seller's site.

The company is unique because:
1. The rankings are based on feedback from customers. The company provides the tools to narrow down the search, but the consumers have to read the reviews to see if the product is right for them.
2. Positive or negative, all reviews are encouraged on Buzzillions. Unless a review is profane or violates the company's terms, it will be shown on the site.
3. Buzzillions does not sell products, although the company has retail partners listed on the site for direct contact by consumers.

Example: How Intuit Corp—Helps Consumers with Recommendations

Intuit's TurboTax program is very popular, with about 20 million users. The company uses a social media recommendation system, called the TurboTax Live Community (**ttlc.intuit.com**). The Live Community has several million questions and answers in their database; it is presented in a Q&A format where you can ask questions and get answers from experts and the community. TurboTax also offers "Customer Ratings and Products Review." The reviews and ratings are available so yours can "read unfiltered reviews from [their] customers…." Searches can be segmented into tax-related categories like 'bought a house' or 'lost my job.' Intuit also made the search function on its site more prominent and easier to use. From the Customer Ratings and Product Reviews page (**turbotax.intuit.com/reviews**), consumers can also click on any rating or review and post it on their Facebook or Twitter page. While on the Customer Ratings and Product Reviews page, users can easily share their reviews on Facebook and Twitter with one click. The Live Community (**ttlc.intuit.com**) consumers doing their taxes can ask a question and get an answer from another customer or a TurboTax support expert.

Concerns About Social Reviews and Recommendations

Some people are concerned about the accuracy of the reported reviews and recommendations. In 2012, Gartner, Inc. predicted that by 2014, 10–15 % of social media reviews would be fake and paid for by companies (**gartner.com/newsroom/id/2161315**). In fact, consumers are skeptical about social media marketing (see **blogs.wsj.com/digits/2014/06/03/amid-fake-reviews-consumers-skeptical-of-social-media-marketing**). For example, see the 'Alleged Manipulation by Yelp' section on Wikipedia at **en.wikipedia.org/wiki/Yelp**. There is also a concern that businesses are paying people money to post favorable reviews and that in cases of a small number of reviewers, a bias (positive or negative) may be shown. Some government agencies are getting involved in dismantling the system of fake reviews. For example, in September 2013, the Attorney General of New York City assessed monetary penalties against 19 companies who created false reviews for products and services (see **nbcnews.com/tech/internet/ny-attorney-general-cracks-down-fake-online-reviews-f4B11235875**).

Other Shopping Aids and Services

In addition to recommendations and marketplaces, there are several sites that provide social shopping aids, as illustrated in the following examples.

Yelp: The Shoppers' Best Helper

Yelp (**yelp.com**) is a company that operates an online urban (local) guide that helps people find services ranging from mechanics to restaurants in a specific city based on reviews and recommendations of local users. In this way, it connects people with great local businesses. Community members, known as "Yelpers," write reviews of the businesses and then rate them. Yelpers also find events and special offers and can "talk" with each other by posting and replying to conversations on different topics (**yelp.com/talk**).

The site is also a place for businesses to advertise their products and services (there is no fee to create a business page; however, there is a fee for business owners to post a "Yelp Deal"). Yelp is also accessible via mobile devices. The site offers several social networking features such as discussion forums, posting photos, and using Facebook to find friends who have Yelp accounts. Yelp has a company blog (**officialblog.yelp.com**), along with a community blog for Yelpers and Elite members worldwide (**communityblog.yelp.com**). Yelpers who frequently become actively involved and engage on the site can apply to become an "Elite Squad" member (see **yelp.com/elite**).

Since its inception in 2004, Yelp operates in major metro cities in the United States, Canada, the United Kingdom, and other countries worldwide. For 2014 statistics, see Smith et al. (2014). As of Q3 2014, Yelp had a monthly average of 139 million unique visitors (as measured by Google Analytics) and Yelpers had written over 67 million rich, local reviews by the end of Q3 2014. Approximately 73 million unique visitors visited Yelp via their mobile device on a monthly average basis during Q3 2014. For more information, see the infographic on Yelp's "Factsheet" at **yelp-press.com/phoenix.zhtml?c=250809&p=irol-press**.

How Yelp Works

Users look for a business in a specific city. Yelp's search engine finds available businesses and presents ratings and reviews as well as accessibility and directions. Yelp connects with Google Maps to show the location of the businesses and further aids in discovering related businesses. (Google was negotiating to buy Yelp in November 2010, but the deal fell through in January 2011.)

Adding social features to user reviews creates a reputation system, whereby site visitors can see both the positive and the negative reviews.

For more about reputation management, see Chap. 5 and **outspokenmedia.com/guides/orm-guide**. Yelp became a major commercial success and was listed on the stock market in March 2012. Its stock price keeps increasing (with pauses).

Most of Yelp's revenue comes from advertising (in 2012, 80 % came from local advertising). For Yelp's business model and an infographic, see **streetfightmag.com/2013/05/06/how-does-yelp-make-money-and-where-is-it-going-next**. For further information, see **yelp.com/faq**.

Note that some shopping aids can be used for both online and offline shopping. One such aid is the touch-screen PC available at kiosks in physical stores (e.g., Kohl's) where you can examine catalogs and place your order while in the store.

Collaborative Reviews

Sites such as **productwiki.com** are structured like a wiki; thus, every user can contribute. The goal is to create a comprehensive resource collection. The companies believe that a need exists for unbiased, accurate, and community-based resources for product information. These sites use *collaborative reviews*, a collection of pros and cons about a product submitted by and voted on by the consumers. The result is a comprehensive review that takes the opinions of many people into account, and highlights the most important aspects of a product. A collaborative review is made up of two things—statements and votes. Community members submit and vote on specific statements that are separated by pros and cons, making it easy to see what is good and bad about each product. For further information on collaborative reviews, see **productwiki.com/home/article/collaborative-reviews.html**.

In March 2013, ProductWiki merged with Bootic (**bootic.com**), which is known as a "wiki of products" (see **bootic.com/_aboutus**). The idea is for ProductWiki to offer a marketplace in addition to product reviews. Bootic is the first marketplace that allows shoppers to express themselves by editing, adding content, and enhancing the overall product description. As a result of this partnership, ProductWiki, like Bootic, will offer a marketplace in addition to product reviews. According to its website, vendors love Bootic's marketplace because "Bootic's e-commerce platform offers a free suite of easy-to-use Web-based tools and technology to help our vendors create their own individualized online shops. Unlike other marketplaces, we don't charge fees. On Bootic, storefronts can quickly get up and running without incurring any set-up costs, listing or on-going transaction fees. Bootic empowers small businesses to enhance their online brand while optimizing a new revenue stream."

Filtering Consumer Reviews

As described earlier, TurboTax, a division of Intuit, also launched a ratings and reviews page (**reviews.turbotax.intuit.com**).This page allows consumers to describe their particular tax situations, and then filter reviews on TurboTax products, to see only those written by "people like them" (similar tax and income situations); then, they can quickly find which TurboTax product best suits their needs.

Dealing with Complaints

As will be seen in Chap. 7, customers have learned how to use social media to air their complaints. For a UK survey that shows that customers are more likely to complain via social media, see **xlgroup.com/press/new-survey-finds-customers-increasingly-likely-to-use-social-media-to-complain**. See also **wptv.com/dpp/news/science_tech/facebook-fb-twitter-twtr-used-to-complain-get-answers**.

Social Marketplaces and Direct Sales to Customers

The term **social marketplace** refers to a marketplace that uses social media tools for enabling shoppers to perform activities, such as the buying and selling of products, services, and resources. As with any other marketplace, a social marketplace brings sellers and buyers together to connect and transact. The social marketplace is an intermediary that provides the infrastructure and procedures for transactions, including display, product discovery, interactions, comparisons, security, and payments (see **affino.com/innovation-features/innovation-features/introduction-to-social-marketplace**).

Ideally, a social marketplace (like Polyvore) should enable the members to market their own creations.

Examples of Social Marketplaces

- **Craigslist.** Craigslist (**craigslist.org**) is considered a social network marketplace because it provides online classified ads in addition to supporting social activities (meetings, dating, events).
- **Fotolia.** Fotolia (**us.fotolia.com**) is a social marketplace for affordable royalty free photos, images, and video clips. By December 2014, there were more than 34 million images available on the site. Fotolia serves a community of artists, designers, and other creative people who express themselves through images, forums, and blogs. Buyers can legally buy images (pay as you go, or a daily/monthly subscription). For details, see **us.fotolia.com/Info/AboutUs**.
- **Flipsy.** According to **applegazette.com/feature/sell-your-apple-device-using-flipsy-and-get-as-much-cash-as-possible**, "Flipsy [**flipsy.com**] is essentially a price comparison site, albeit with a slight twist. Instead of you looking for what others are selling, you are looking for information on the figures that others are willing to pay for the item you are selling…. Using Flipsy is simple enough. You just have to specify the item you are selling, and the site will return offers from various buyback websites." As of 2014, Flipsy does not charge commissions or fees. Since Flipsy does not buy products, payment processing for items purchased is handled by a third party, such as PayPal.

- **Storenvy.** Storenvy (**storenvy.com**) is a global market-place for emerging brands and inspired goods. Businesses can launch a custom store to sell unique goods. At no cost to sellers, a simple way is made available (no programming experience is needed) to create personalized web-stores. Sellers have the ability to make their sites as socially friendly as they wish, giving customers the chance to follow or interact with sellers as well as with other customers.
- **ShopSocially.** ShopSocially (**shopsocially.com**) is a cloud-based social commerce platform, which sells a suite of social apps to retailers to embed on their site. The software package enables the retailers' customers to share shopping experiences via WOM (e.g., recommending products to friends). It offers retailers hundreds of apps such as 'share-a-purchase' and 'shopping community.' ShopSocially combines the concepts of online shopping and social networks, creating a new business model for the retailers that use their products. For example, users can solicit shopping information from friends via Facebook, Twitter, and e-mail. Users can ask shopping questions and get answers. ShopSocially helps companies to turn visitors in sites to fans. For details and benefits to retailers, see **shopsocially.com**.

Example

Firearms manufacturer Beretta Inc. is using ShopSocially's social commerce platform and Facebook to increase customer engagement and sales conversation rate. In addition, it captures customers' delight after a new purchase, and converting it into valuable WOM recommendations that are being shared virally on social networks. As a result, the company has added over 10,000 fans on Facebook, experienced a 15 % increase in sales conversion rate, and gained brand recognition and retention. For details, see **prweb.com/releases/2013/12/prweb11440494.htm**

Some Unique Marketplaces

Chaney et al. (2013) lists the following marketplaces: **Addoway.com**; a site that integrates with Facebook's Social Graph, and enables users to recommend merchants that your friends have purchased from. **Pikaba.com**; works like a reverse auction—you post what you want to buy and merchants will compete to offer the best price. **Buyosphere.com**; fashion marketplace focused on unique designs; a community where you can ask stylists, bloggers, designers, and others where to find something that is right for you. **Officearrow.com**; a B2B marketplace designed to connect buyers and sellers, along with providing unbiased ratings and reviews by community members.

Example: How Musicians Sell Online via Social Networks

Many musicians and other artists used to invest money to make their own CDs, T-shirts, and other items before they sold them. Now there is a free social commerce solution. Audiolife Inc. (acquired by Alliance Entertainment, which was acquired by video distribution company Super D in 2013) provides artists with webstores (one per artist), where artists (sellers) can directly interact with potential buyers. This arrangement also allows artists to sell custom made merchandise.

To entice fans to order products, artists post their own Audiolife selection on any large social network site (e.g., Facebook). Each order, even for one item, is then forwarded to the artist for production. Audiolife arranges payment and shipping to the buyers. By August 2014, Audiolife powered close to 100,000 webstores worldwide, serving 300,000 artists, including those who are already established. For details, see **audiolife.com/about.html** and Billingsley (2010).

6.6 INNOVATIVE SHOPPING MODELS AND SITES AND VIRTUAL GOODS

There are hundreds of start-ups in social commerce. Even Facebook is introducing SC services like "Page post link ads" and the "Buy" button. Twitter began testing a "Buy" button in fall 2014, and will make it available to the general public in 2015. Here we provide some representative examples.

Examples of Innovative Social Shopping Ideas and Sites

Social shopping includes many new and innovative business models. Some were described earlier in the chapter. We include several more models here.

- **Getting help from shoppers via TurnTo Networks.** The TurnTo Networks (**turntonetworks.com**) platform involves partnering with certain websites to have them carry a TurnTo link. TurnTo is a Social Q&A platform for e-commerce sites that enables shoppers to ask questions about products and get answers from other customers. The shoppers' questions are sent out to a select number of customers who have actually bought the merchandise. Their answers are then e-mailed back to the shoppers and displayed on the merchant's product pages for others to read. According to its website, TurnTo's products are designed from the ground up to meet the needs of online retailers.

In October 2013, TurnTo announced a partnership with **needle.com**, a guided shopping platform specializing in live chat and customer engagement strategies. Needle recruits knowledgeable shoppers who are familiar with certain brands and puts them to work chatting with customers and answering questions, making recommendations, or guiding them toward finding the right products. These "Needlers" are independent contractors and are compensated with cash as well as points to redeem for products.

For how the site works, see **turntonetworks.com/ social-commerce-webinar-coffeeforless.com-solves-customer-engagement-challenge-with-social-qa**. Note that Lenovo and Shoes.com use TurnTo for their Q&As. For an infographic of the social Q&A model, see **turntonetworks.com/social-qa-infographic/**.

- **Find what your friends are buying**. Finding what your friends are buying was offered, for example, by **clubfurniture.com**, a North Carolina company that sells online home furnishings at factory prices directly to customers. Note: This service was popular between 2009 and 2011 with several companies, but was discontinued mainly due to privacy concerns.

- **Wanelo.** This popular social shopping network combines bookmarking and product sharing. Members can follow others to find trendy items. For details, see Leahey (2013). According to **bits.blogs.nytimes.com/2013/01/24/a-look-at-wanelo-a-social-commerce-site-for-younger-shoppers/?_php=true&_type=blogs&_r=2**, the company's name is an abbreviation for 'Want, Need, Love,' and is popular with young shoppers. Wanelo (**wanelo.com**) is an online community-based e-commerce site that brings together products from a vast array of stores into one pinboard-style platform. You can browse, save, and buy items, post new products from around the Web, and follow members, stores, or product collections. Catering to both brands and shoppers, members create collections—similar to Pinterest boards—from items onsite or external links. It also has an app on iTunes and Google Play and a Facebook Fan page. For more information about Wanelo, see **pcmag.com/article2/0,2817,2424709,00.asp** and **mashable.com/2013/11/05/wanelo-social-shopping**. For the company's business model, see **businessweek.com/articles/2014-04-24/wanelo-deena-varshavskayas-site-takes-over-social-shopping**. Wanelo is unique since if you see something you like, you can purchase it with one click.

Additional Examples of Social Shopping

There are many other examples. Here are few:

Example 1: Helping Sellers and Bloggers Sell Products

Etsy is a socially-oriented marketplace which helps bloggers and sellers (mostly artists) monetize their businesses by making it easy for them to sell products directly to consumers. Note: A company called OpenSky used to do this; however, they changed their business model. For some new social commerce business models, see Colao (2013).

Example 2: Event Shopping

Thee are many sites that help buyers, with the assistance of their friends, shop for a special event (e.g., a wedding). Many variations of this model exist. For example, in 2010, Wendy's gave away $50 gift cards for boneless wings to 100 consumers who organized viewing parties of that year's NCAA Basketball Championships over Facebook.

Socially-Oriented Person to Person (P2P): Selling, Buying, Renting, or Bartering

When individuals conduct business online, they may do so with some social elements. For example, some consider Craigslist to be a socially oriented virtual community. Here are some more examples:

P2P Lending

P2P money lending is growing rapidly, enabling one person to lend money to another. This is done without a bank but with the assistance of a matching company such as Prosper or Lending Club. There are several other types of P2P lending. Another start-up created a community of people that rent out goods to people, usually for the short term. In P2P landing, people get to know each other (a social aspect).

P2P Sharing (Also Known As Collaborative Consumption)

SnapGoods facilitates P2P sharing. Some other sites, like SwapBabyGoods.com, Swapmamas.com (a social community for moms who want to get to know each other and swap goods they no longer use for things they need) and Neighborhood Fruit (that helps people share fruit that are growing in their yards or find fruit trees on public lands), have a niche market. The sharing and renting trend is booming, especially during the economic recession, and there is a "green" aspect as well—saving resources. There is also the social aspect of sharing, allowing people to make meaningful connections with others (see Walsh 2010 for details).

Several variations of this model exist. Some people share cars, others invite travelers to stay free in their homes, or exchange homes for short periods (e.g., HomeExchange.com; **homeexchange.com**) and much more. Lending Tree (**lendingtree.com**) is another company that allows prospective borrowers to get quick offers from multiple lenders.

In May 2013, Google took a stake in P2P investment site Lending Club (**lendingclub.com**; see Hempel 2013).

Start Ups: Examples

In 2014, Facebook started a program to help startup companies go online using Facebook and its services. Here are a few examples.

Example 1: "Wine Condom" Bottle Stopper

This small start-up (mother-and-son) invented a quality cover for wine bottles. They placed the idea on Kickstarter and raised $9,285 from a community of 311 backers (see **kickstarter.com/projects/1269355871/wine-condoms**). This is an example of *crowdfunding* (see Kavilanz 2014). Once the duo raised the money, they used Facebook as a platform to find customers and distributors. They established contacts with wineries worldwide and connected with cruise ship companies. They use Facebook for advertising campaigns. The wine condoms are sold to both businesses and individuals and are available for $10 a package at **winecondoms.com**.

Example 2: Divas Snow Gear

In order to attract more women to the snowmobile sport, Wendy Gavinski invented attractive and flattering clothing for women. Her problem was that industry magazines and online forums were geared towards men. Gavinski designed one outfit as an experiment, and found a manufacturer to work with her, creating her first sample. Because Gavinski could not find women snowboarders through traditional advertising, she decided to use Facebook ads to advertise her products. She started in 2010 with a Facebook page. Using Facebook, she directed customers to visit retailers and their events. According to Gavinski, Facebook became their primary means of marketing since it is the only channel that allows her company to specifically target women. With over 47,000 'Likes' and the use of other social media channels, the business became profitable in 2014, adding more products and gained market share in the U.S., Canada, Europe, and Russia. For details, see Gavinski (2014), **facebook.com/divassnowgear1**, and **divassnowgear.com**

Shopping Without Leaving Facebook and Other Social Networks

There are several avenues for turning Facebook fan pages into retail outlets, so fans do not have to leave Facebook to shop. However, payment and security are two issues yet to be resolved. In 2011, several large brands (e.g., Gap, Nordstrom, GameStop) closed their shops on Facebook. Companies closed their Facebook stores for a number of reasons, citing that people prefer to shop directly from the stores' website, or on Amazon.com. Some stores wanted to focus on advertising using broader media. According to Ashley Sheetz, VP of marketing and strategy at GameStop, the company did not get enough revenue from using the Facebook webstore. She told Bloomberg that Facebook is "a way we communicate with customers on deals, not a place to sell." However, this situation is changing. In summer 2014, Facebook introduced the "Buy" button to simplify shopping without having the customer leave Facebook. In addition, security and payments improved. A large number of tools and apps facilitate e-commerce activities on Facebook. For example, Soldsie (**soldsie.com**) can help you sell directly to your Facebook fans on Facebook through comments on your page (see **new.soldsie.com/how-it-works**). For a ShopSocially infographic that reveals strategies for profitable social commerce with Facebook, see **blog.shopsocially. com/2014/05/15/facebook-drives-social-commerce/#. VBEksPldWSo**. Small businesses are also opening Facebook stores where customers can buy directly from the "shop" link on their Facebook page. Examples are NutriBullet (**facebook.com/thenutribullet**) and Sweet Blossom Gifts (**facebook.com/SweetBlossomGifts**), who are using Storefront Social to create their stores. (NutriBullet offers a "Buy" now button; Sweet Blossom Gifts offers a "Purchase" button.) Some musicians, including Lady Gaga, Muse, and Greenday have opened Facebook webstores. For an overview, see Porterfield et al. (2013). For how to add a store to a company's Facebook page, see **ecwid.com/face-book-commerce** and watch the video titled "Setting up a Store on Facebook to Sell Products" (7:24 minutes) at **you-tube.com/watch?v=Q9IrJef7zDA**.

Note: Many companies direct Facebook users from their pages to the companies' own websites. Screen Print Designs only does business from their Facebook page (see **facebook. com/screenprintdesigns**).

Shopping for Virtual Goods in a Virtual Economy

An increasing number of shoppers purchase all kinds of virtual products and services online. **Virtual goods** are computer images of real or imaginary goods. These include, but are not limited to, properties and merchandise on Seconds Life (such as virtual mobile phones to equip your avatar), and a large number of items sold in multiplayer games on social networks (e.g., FarmVille on Facebook). According to eMarketer (2011), revenues from virtual goods in social gaming in the U.S. grew almost 60 % from $653 million in 2011 to $792 million in 2012.

According to Wikipedia, "Virtual goods are non-physical objects and money purchased for use in online communities or online games … . Virtual money (or in-game currency) is used to purchase virtual goods within a variety of online communities, which include social networking websites, virtual worlds, and online gaming sites" (see **en.wikipedia.org/wiki/Virtual_goods**).

The Virtual Economy

A **virtual economy** is an emerging economy existing in several virtual worlds, where people exchange virtual goods frequently related to an Internet game or a virtual business. People go there primarily for entertainment. However, some people trade their virtual goods or properties. A virtual property can be any resource that is controlled by virtual objects, avatars, or user accounts. According to Lehdonvirta and Ernkvist (2011), the term "virtual economy" was coined by Edward Castronova, and refers "to artificial economies inside online games, especially when the artificially scarce goods and currencies of those economies [are] traded for real money." For the characteristics of these properties, see **en.wikipedia.org/wiki/Virtual_economy**. For how payments are made for virtual goods, see Takahashi (2011), and for an overview of Facebook Payments, see **developers.facebook.com/docs/payments**. For how one online game developer accepts payments for virtual goods in Bitcoins, see **coindesk.com/online-game-developer-bigpoint-now-accepts-bitcoins-virtual-goods**. In March 2013, Facebook released figures showing that there is a significant increase in the number of people paying to play social games, rising 24 % in 2012. Over 250 million desktop game users were playing games on Facebook, jumping from 235 million in October 2012. Further research showed that in 2012, a total of $2 billion was paid to developers (see Womack 2013).

Why People Buy Virtual Goods

There are several reasons why people buy virtual goods. For example, many people in China buy virtual properties because they cannot afford to buy properties in the real world (**online.wsj.com/news/articles/SB10001424052702304703804579380683402958724**). According to Savitz (2011; in collaboration with Ben Perry), there are four major reasons for such purchases made in any country:

1. **Generating special experiences.** Studies found (e.g., see Markman 2010) that some people can maximize their happiness by spending money on the experience they get in a virtual world rather than when spending money on physical goods. Happiness from a dinner or a movie does not last for a long time, but it makes us happy in the moment. The same is true with virtual goods, since they are experiential in nature, but these can be very imaginative and beautiful, providing much more happiness.

2. **Generating emotions.** Purchasing virtual goods often fills emotional needs. In the virtual world, you can be whatever or whoever you always wanted to be, so people are willing to exchange real money for real emotions they find in the virtual goods.

3. **Small purchases make people happier.** Making small and frequent purchases of virtual goods (for a small amount of money) makes many people happier than making infrequent purchases of larger physical goods.

4. **Virtual goods are low cost and low hassle.** Virtual goods are among the cheapest form of entertainment. There is no need to store virtual goods, maintain them, or be criticized about why you purchased them. In short—there is no hassle as long as one stays within one's budget.

In fact, several real world retailers are promoting their virtual goods in online games.

Real-Time Online Shopping

In real-time online shopping, shoppers can log onto a site and then either connect with Facebook or with another social network instantly from a smartphone or computer, or invite their friends and family via Twitter or e-mail. Friends shop online together *at the same time*, exchanging ideas and comparing experiences (e.g., see Dugan 2010). For example, cosmetics company MAC has a feature called "Shop Together" that lets customers consult with their friends and family online for shopping help. The technology allows customers to shop with friends just like they are in a MAC store, only online. You can invite friends to chat with you at any time via Facebook, Twitter, IM, and e-mail. You can shop and chat at the same time, see what your friends are browsing, and recommend products to each other, all in real time. For more information, see **maccosmetics.com/cms/customer_service/shopto-gether.tmpl**.

Examples of real-time shopping platforms are: BevyUp (see **bevyup.com/about_us.html**) and Samesurf (see (**same-surf.com/about.html**), which empowers multiple users to share their browsing experiences in real time.

Auctions in Social Shopping

There are several e-auction sites for social shoppers. The most well known is eBay (**ebay.com**). Other auction sites are:

Listia

According to Wikipedia, "Listia [**listia.com**] is a free online marketplace for trading goods between individuals, by using a virtual currency instead of real money. The marketplace uses an auction system where users bid on each other's items until the auction ends and the highest bidder wins…. Users earn credits during sign-up and then continue to earn more as they place items in the marketplace. Purchasing credits is also an option, and is Listia's main business model" (**en.wikipedia.org/wiki/Listia**).

Like some other auction sites, Listia experiences both complaints and responses to those complaints about fake bidding and cheating by the sellers, or even by the auction company (e.g., see **ripoffreport.com/auction-liquidators/listia-inc/listia-inc-listia-com-the-auti-fbabc.htm**). For more on Listia, see Chaney (2011).

Tophatter

Tophatter (**tophatter.com**) is an entertaining virtual auction site that conducts live online auctions every day (sellers begin auctions every hour) where buyers and sellers can interact, chat, and transact in many categories. Tophatter sends their members a daily e-mail notifying them when a new auction is starting. For more information on Tophatter, see **techcrunch.com/2013/11/08/tophatter-android** and their Facebook page at **facebook.com/tophatter**.

B2B Social Networking

B2B social marketers must deal with a number of issues. For a comprehensive guide to B2B, see Gillin and Schwartzman (2011). In addition, you can listen to Schwartzman's 2010 podcast on the topic, available at **ontherecordpodcast.com/pr/otro/B2B-social-networking.aspx**.

Example: SAP

SAP (**sap.com**) is a large B2B software company with several million members in its SAP Community Network (SCN). SCN is one of the most successful B2B and B2C enterprise networks for employees, business partners, faculty, students and experts.

As of September 2013, SCN (2014) had over 2,500,000 registered members from 230 countries and territories, over 113,000 contributors, over 30,000 new members per month, 1.1 million newsletter subscribers, 2.1 million unique visitors per month, 110 million page views and contributed content by 400,000 members. The network has over 500 SCN topic spaces, and over 15,000 discussion threads per month.

Zwilling (2011) presents nine location-based service (LBS) opportunities for B2B.

Virtual Visual Shopping

Many consumers are driven to impulse buying when they see interesting or new products in physical stores. Theoretically, online shoppers in 3-D environments might also make such purchases.

One aspect of 3D is its ability to put items into a more physical view than 2D does. A 3-D view of a house interior could help someone shopping for furniture visualize whether a large dining table would fit in the intended space. Consumers can experiment with the location of the virtual table and see how it will fit into their home before they buy it. 3-D platforms could take the guesswork out of buying many types of products online, ranging from furniture to clothes.

Example

Can you imagine looking at a computer screen where you can see yourself wearing a piece of clothing you have selected, exactly as you can in a physical clothing store's fitting room? Now wave your hand and the color of the outfit changes; wave your hand again and a dress will be shorter or longer. Another wave of your hand and another dress is on your virtual body. A dream? Not really, it is already here! To learn about this virtual "try-on" system, see Facecake Marketing Technology's "Swivel" (**facecake.com/swivel**) and watch their video. For an illustration, watch the video titled "Tobi Virtual Dressing Room" (1:14 minutes) at **dailymotion.com/video/xcg18d_tobi-virtual-dressing-room_tech**.

For more information, see **virtwayworld.com/EN_products_3d_virtual_shop.php**.

Social Shopping in the Near Future

Imagine this scenario: A retailer will ask you to log in through Facebook on your mobile device as soon as you step into a physical store. (Many of Facebook's partners have custom Facebook applications (Partner Apps) that users can download (see **facebook.com/mobile**).

In this way, users can receive *customized recommendations* on their mobile phones. What about the risks? Privacy is a concern to many, but less important to millennials who frequently share their experiences with others. In addition, sometimes people do not need to reveal their full identity on an in-store screen. Watch a related video titled "The Future of Shopping" (48 s) at **youtube.com/watch?v=R_TAP0OY1Bk**.

For example, according to Admin (2011), "when you walk into a dressing room [in a department store], the mirror reflects your image, but you also see images of the apparel item [you like] and [certain] celebrities wearing it on an interactive display [in the dressing room]. A webcam also projects an image of the consumer wearing the item on the website for everyone to see. This creates an interaction between the consumers inside the store and their social network [friends] outside the store. The technology behind this system uses RFID [Radio Frequency Identification]." RFID technology has already been tried by the Prada store in New York City for showing customers which shoes and purses would go with the clothes they are trying on in the dressing room. You can watch a video titled "Future Store (Smart Dressing Room)" (2:53 minutes) of how a "smart" dressing room works at **youtube.com/watch?v=0VII-xdg5Ak&feature=related**. Note that, due to privacy concerns, Prada (and other stores) discontinued their RFID systems.

The concept of virtual shopping is expanding. A new Internet of Things technology enables the "smart fitting room." The "Connected Fitting Room," by Microsoft, Accenture, and Avanade, uses smart technology (RFID) to track what the customer tries on. With a push of a button, the customer can call for something else and the clerk will receive notification on his or her mobile device. As of June 2014, the Connected Fitting Room is operating as a pilot program in the U.S. and the UK (see **fastcodesign.com/3031689/microsofts-smart-fitting-room-is-like-a-robo-shop-clerk**). To read more about virtual shopping in the future, see **huffingtonpost.com/2014/05/24/shopping-in-the-future_n_5386395.html**.

Instagram Marketing

According to Offerpop (2014), Instagram is revolutionizing the visual Web. With more than 300 million active monthly users and over 70 million photos shared each day (per **instagram.com/press**), the commercial opportunities are unlimited. For a marketing guide, see Offerpop (2014).

Facebook's Plans

Facebook is expanding its social commerce advertising model to include social shopping. Most notable is the 'Buy' button, which Facebook introduced in 2014. This feature is designed to let shoppers purchase items directly from ads and posts they see on Facebook's news feed and in mobile apps, without leaving Facebook (see Axelrad 2014). In September 2014, the "Buy" button was still in the testing phase. For benefits of the 'Buy' button on Facebook and Twitter, see Bennett (2014).

Activities on Twitter

According to **archive.financialexpress.com/news/coming-soon-to-twitter-facebook-click-to-buy-now/1271913**, "If you see a retailer's tweet promoting a particular product and want to get the deal, you might soon be able to click a button or send a reply to simply add the discount to a stored credit card—without leaving Twitter's site or firing up another app. For the last couple of years, Twitter and American Express have offered AmEx cardholders the ability to load various discounts onto their cards through tweets.

The next logical step would be to allow users to click to buy a product, an idea that Twitter is also exploring, potentially with the payment processing company Stripe."

In May 2014, Twitter also began testing a "Buy" button for its users to make instant purchases (see **nytimes.com/2014/09/09/technology/twitter-begins-testing-buy-button-for-posts.html**). For more on using Twitter for e-business, see Krogue (2013).

SUMMARY

In this chapter, you learned about the following SC issues as they relate to the chapter's learning objectives.

1. **Describe social shopping.** Social shopping refers to online shopping that is supported by social media and involves friends and online social communities. It includes recommendations, group purchasing, clubs, and more. It also includes shopping on social networks, such as Facebook and Kaboodle, and using Web 2.0 tools to aid online shopping. The major drivers are the large number of people who are engaged in social networks, reliance on the recommendations of friends, the possibility

of large discounts to buyers, the potential increase of sale volume for sellers, the socially-oriented shopping models, and the rise of the social customer. It looks as though the future of online commerce is socially oriented.

2. **Framework and models of social shopping.** Social shopping is done in social networks (public and private), social communities, and social marketplaces, as well as in virtual worlds. The shopping mechanisms are similar to those of e-commerce (Turban et al. 2015) and e-marketing (Strauss and Frost 2014). What makes social shopping unique is the social media aspects and the innovative business models. The major models are daily deals, group buying (which may be combined with daily deals); providing reviews, recommendations, ratings, and conversation; shopping clubs and communities; location-based shopping; peer-to-peer trading; Facebook commerce (F-commerce); and shopping while you tweet. Groupon, Gilt, Kaboodle, and hundreds of other start-ups are active participants. Competition is getting stronger, and success is visible mostly on Facebook and Twitter (both sites are just starting to implement the "Buy" button), and Pinterest (which recently partnered with Shopify).

3. **Group buying and deal purchases.** Social media is enabling the revitalization of group buying, which can be combined with the "deal of the day" offer. Buyers are encouraged to tell their friends and recruit them to buy the daily deal(s). If successful, the original buyer will get an even larger discount, and so will the group when it is large enough ("cheaper-by-the-dozen"). This model is mostly successful in China; unfortunately, it has not been yet in the US. The 'daily deals' model, which has many variations and is the backbone of Groupon, is much more popular. Vendors have a chance to boost revenue while buyers enjoy the discounts. The biggest winner is the intermediary. This is why stiff competition is developing among intermediaries such as Groupon. There is intense competition in this area, both from vendors who are selling direct, and from local newspapers, TV, and specialized companies such as iDine (**idine.com**), a loyalty program that rewards consumers with benefits and discounts when they dine out at participating restaurants.

4. **Shopping communities and clubs.** Shopping together in the physical world is a popular activity. Usually, it is done with family members and friends. Online, shopping together can be done in different ways. The most popular method involves communities, managed by an independent company, which provide many services and opportunities. Fashion-oriented communities such as Polyvore are very popular. The communities provide opportunities for designers to create designs and see how much the communities like them.

Social clubs limit membership, but they operate in a similar manner to open communities. Communities and clubs may be structured as marketplaces, or operate as referral services, generating income per click by potential buyers who click on the sellers' logo. They may also receive a commission from actual purchases.

5. **Social recommendations and marketplaces.** Social buyers like *social recommendations* made by friends, family members, and other shoppers. Social shoppers may also like reading negative comments (see reputation management in Chap. 5). Recommendations can be combined with reviews, rankings, price comparisons, and so forth. There are several different ways that recommendations can be made (some in communities, others on special sites). Recommendations are also made by bloggers and may even be posted on sellers' sites (e.g., travel sites, Amazon.com, etc.). In certain cases, recommendations are more trustworthy if made by experts or independent evaluators. Family members and friends are usually the most influencing parties. Recommendation sites use several incentives to attract buyers. This revenue model is frequently sponsored by advertisers (pay for clicks on the sellers' banners) and from commission on actual shopping resulting from the click throughs. Several models exist.

Social marketplaces bring sellers and buyers together and provide the services necessary for conducting transactions. Marketplaces may exist in social communities and on other networking sites. Some marketplaces help sellers create innovative products and services. Marketplaces are sometimes confined to a certain commodity, industry, or profession. They use different support mechanisms as well, including negotiations and auctions. Like communities, marketplaces encourage interaction and building relationships. They also provide shopping aids such as search engines, payment mechanisms, and order fulfillment.

6. **Innovative shopping models.** There are many innovative social shopping models. Notable ones are social auctions, trading for virtual goods, virtual visual shopping, shopping together in real time, crowdsourcing shopping (getting advice from the crowd), selling via blogs, and direct selling by artists.

7. **Shopping for virtual goods.** As social networking games have mushroomed in popularity, people are spending more money on buying virtual goods. The most popular transactions are game-related, such as buying virtual farming tools in FarmVille (a Facebook game) and properties in virtual worlds (e.g., Seconds Life). People of all ages may like virtual goods because of their ability to provide unique experiences, and for their low price (you can buy an island or a factory for

only a few dollars). Furthermore, satisfaction can be great and privacy is usually guaranteed. People can make their dreams come true, quickly and inexpensively. This has created a billion-dollar industry. Legality, taxation, and payments for virtual goods trading are still evolving issues.

KEY TERMS

Communal shopping   132
Social marketplace   143
Social shopping   131
Virtual economy   147
Virtual goods   147

REVIEW QUESTIONS

1. Define social shopping and describe its drivers.
2. List the major benefits of social shopping.
3. List the major models of social shopping. Briefly describe their capabilities.
4. Describe ratings, reviews, and recommendations.
5. How do customers and patrons of establishments conduct ratings and reviews?
6. Relate recommendations to social reviews and ratings.
7. Describe social marketplaces and list their benefits.
8. Define group buying. How does it work with flash sales?
9. Define social communities and social clubs as they relate to marketing. How do they work?
10. Describe Kaboodle and list its major capabilities. Why is it so successful?
11. Define social marketplaces and describe what happens there.
12. Define virtual goods and explain why people buy them.
13. Describe the major shopping aids.
14. Describe social shopping in the near future.

TOPICS FOR DISCUSSION AND DEBATES

1. Compare group buying to shopping together.
2. Enter **socialmediatoday.com**. Choose five articles that are related to this chapter and discuss each briefly.
3. Compare Polyvore to Pinterest.
4. Discuss the benefits and concerns of using Yelp.
5. Discuss the reasons why people buy virtual goods.
6. Discuss the critical success factors of Polyvore.
7. Discuss how traditional online vendors can add social networking capabilities to their sites.

8. Under what circumstances would you trust an expert's recommendation rather than a friend's? What about the opposite?
9. Debate: Is the social media influence on purchasing overrated? Start with the slideshow titled "Social Media Influence on Purchase Overrated" (McCafferty 2011) at **baselinemag.com/c/a/Intelligence/Social-Media-Influence-On-Purchasing-Overrated-660095**. Find similar, newer data.
10. Debate: One day all e-commerce will be social.
11. Daily deals are being advertised today by many offline and online retailers. Internet-only offers are common. Is there a need for intermediaries such as Groupon? Debate the issue.
12. Discuss the role of trust in social shopping. (Consult **bazaarvoice.com/solutions**).
13. Why do you think that Wanelo is so popular with teens?
14. Watch the video titled "SHOP.CA Realizes E-Commerce Vision with Smarter Commerce" (3:00 minutes) at **youtube.com/watch?v=bFjKZmvNcck** and discuss.

INTERNET EXERCISES

1. Enter **thisnext.com**. What are the site's features? What do you like? Dislike? Why?
2. Enter **tkg.com/social-media-marketing**. What social media platforms do they offer?
3. Search Google for "social shopping." Find five articles that relate to this chapter and discuss each briefly. Start with **venturebeat.com/tag/social-shopping**.
4. Enter **select2gether.com**. What services do they offer? What is the WeLiket toolbar and how does it facilitate shopping online with friends?
5. Enter **kaboodle.com**. What are the major benefits you can derive from becoming a member?
6. Enter **blog.360i.com** and find recent material on social shopping; include the 2012 POV report on social shopping. Write a summary.
7. Enter **facebook.com** and find what and how you can buy there while playing social games.
8. Enter **powerreviews.com**. Compare their activities to those offered by similar sites.
9. Enter **socialmediatoday.com** and **hubspot.com/customers**, and find five recent social commerce customer case studies. Summarize in a report.
10. Enter **socialshoppingnetwork.org**. Find material related to Chap. 6. Write a report.
11. Enter **placecast.net**. Explain the features offered.
12. Enter **bazaarvoice.com**, **quora.com**, and **bebo.com**. How can these sites facilitate shopping?

TEAM ASSIGNMENTS AND PROJECTS

1. **Assignment for the Opening Case**

   Read the opening case and answer the following questions:

   (a) It is difficult for merchants to do business with Groupon. A large percentage of merchants' applications to do business with Groupon is dismissed by the company. Why do you think Groupon is so strict and how will this policy affect the competition?

   (b) Some claim that Groupon is an e-mail list that charges advertisers a marketing fee to send out their coupons. Comment. Note that Groupon makes money by charging a marketing fee for advertising and promoting vendors' offers. In most cases, that fee is a percentage of the revenue generated by selling via Groupon. (Start with: **grouponworks.com/articles/ groupon/overview/business-model/how-groupon-makes-money**.)

   (c) Write a short essay on Groupon's chance of survival in the intensely competitive environment. Examine its revenue model and expansion plans. Check stock market analysts' reports about the company.

   (d) Groupon is changing its business model again, moving from coupons to discount sales. Study this business model. Write a report.

   (e) Learn more about Groupon's order fulfillment (e.g., ability to handle volume, control of deliveries, and dealing with marketing and competitors). Write a report.

   (f) Research Groupon's global efforts. Write a report.

   (g) Groupon also deals in B2B. Search the Internet and find out how this is being done and how successful it is.

   (h) Read Phibbs' (2011) book (Kindle edition) and debate the following issues: Are deep discounts good or bad for sellers? What are some of the disadvantages to merchants? What are the advantages?

2. The class will investigate group buying in China and India. What is the prospect for group buying in Asia? (Start with **businesstoday.intoday.in/story/websites-specialising-in-group-buying-deals-future/1/198416. html**). Why are group buying sites in India succeeding?

3. Shopping communities for fashion are exploding on the Internet. Make a list of ten major sites (e.g., Polyvore, ShopStyle, Pinterest, My It Things, etc.). Investigate their activities and list their competitive advantage. Why is this industry a prime setting for social communities? How are they related to Facebook and Twitter? What are their business and revenue models? Write a summary report.

4. Each group will research one publicly traded social commerce company (e.g., Groupon, Pandora, TripAdvisor, Bazaarvoice, Yelp). Check competition, stock perfor-mance, revenue sources, and so forth. Also check the major Chinese companies listed on the US stock exchanges (Alibaba, Tencent, Baidu, etc.). Use information from **finance.yahoo.com**, **google.com/finance**, **bloomberg.com**, and so forth. Write a summary report.

5. The issue of the viability of Groupon and similar sites is highly debatable (e.g., Buehler 2012; Srinivasan 2011). Follow Groupon's financial performance, conduct a literature search, and debate the issue. Read **fool.com/ investing/general/2014/09/08/why-groupon-inc-stock-has-plunged-40-in-2014.aspx**. Write a summary report.

6. Shopping clubs are gaining popularity. Review the list provided at **stream-recorder.com/forum/list-american-private-shopping-clubs-sample-sale-t12846.html**. Visit these and similar sites. Also visit **fivefourclothing.com**. Classify the clubs, and list their major features.

7. Ratings and reviews are popular aids in social shopping. Compare **yelp.com**, **angieslist.com**, **trip advisor.com**, and two other sites of your choice. Concentrate on their capabilities. In addition, find the revenue sources of each site.

8. Learn "How to Create a Facebook Business Page 2014 (Updated)" (17:26 minutes) at **youtube.com/ watch?v=O9SDy58HBYo**. Build a page as a class project.

REFERENCES

Admin. "Social Shopping." January 15, 2011. **socialecart.com/social-shopping** (accessed January 2015).

AOL On News. "Groupon Website in India Crashes After Crazy Onion Deal." September 10, 2013. **on.aol.com/video/groupon-website-in-india-crashes-after-crazy-onion-deal-517928180** (accessed December 2014).

Axelrad, J. "Facebook Rolls Out 'Buy' Button. A Challenge to Amazon? (+ Video)" *The Christian Science Monitor*, July 17, 2014. **csmonitor.com/Innovation/Horizons/2014/0717/Facebook-rolls-out-Buy-button.-A-challenge-to-Amazon-video** (accessed January 2015).

Bennett, C. "Facebook's 'Buy' Button Will Change How Brands Sell Online." July 30, 2014. **entrepreneur.com/article/236046** (accessed December 2014).

Bessette, R. "Social Media Superstars 2014." January 16, 2014. **fortune.com/2014/01/16/social-media-superstars-2014-fortunes-best-companies-to-work-for** (accessed December 2014).

Billingsley, E. "Cash-Strapped Musicians Empowered by Tech Company: Web: Portable Store Allows Artists to Sell Direct." *San Fernando Valley Business Journal*, March 29, 2010.

Buehler, D. "What Groupon, Living Social and Other Group Buying Businesses Are Doing Wrong." *Technorati*, April 15, 2012. (No longer available online.)

Business Wire. "Maui Jim Sees Social Commerce Success with Bazaarvoice." April 5, 2010. **businesswire.com/news/ home/20100405005803/en#.VA0g2_ldWSo** (accessed December 2014).

Campos, A. "Why Baidu Acquired Renren's Group Buying Site." *The Motley Fool*, January 28, 2014. **fool.com/investing/general/2014/01/28/why-baidu-acquired-renrens-group-buying-site.aspx** (accessed December 2014).

Chaney, P. "5 Social Marketplaces for Merchants and Shoppers.", April 2, 2013. **practicalecommerce.com/articles/3970-5-Social-Marketplaces-for-Merchants-and-Shoppers** (accessed December 2014).

Chaney, P. "13 Social Shopping Sites for Ecommerce Merchants." August 1, 2011. **practicalecommerce.com/articles/2947-13-Social-Shopping-Sites-for-Ecommerce-Mechants** (accessed December 2014).

Colao, J. J. "Four Years and $50 Million Later, Has OpenSky Cracked the Code for Social Commerce?" September 18, 2013. **forbes.com/sites/jjcolao/2013/09/18/four-years-and-three-business-models-later-has-opensky-cracked-the-code-for-social-commerce** (accessed December 2014).

Crum, C. "Groupon Apologizes for Deal Gone Bad in Tokyo: Company Didn't Expect Such Quick Growth in Japan." January 17, 2011. **webpronews.com/groupon-apologizes-for-deal-gone-bad-in-tokyo-2011-01** (accessed December 2014).

Dubey, K. "Gartner Analyzes Social Networking Influence on Purchase Decisions." July 31, 2010. **techshout.com/internet/2010/31/gartner-analyzes-social-networking-influence-on-purchase-decisions** (accessed December 2014).

Dugan, L. "The Complete Guide to Social Shopping." October 27, 2010. **socialtimes.com/social-shopping-complete-guide_b25950** (accessed December 2014).

eMarketer. "Marketers Are On Board with Virtual Goods." July 27, 2011. **emarketer.com/Article.aspx?R=1008513&RewroteTitle=1** (accessed December 2014).

Fisher, S. "Creating a Killer Social Commerce Website Experience." February 22, 2010. **slideshare.net/stevenfisher/social-commerce-camp-killer-social-commerce-experience** (accessed December 2014).

Gavinski, W. "Finding the Right Fit for My Specialty Clothing Line with Facebook." September 18, 2014. **huffingtonpost.com/wendy-gavinski/finding-the-right-fit-for_b_5333252.html** (accessed December 2104).

Gillin, P., and E. Schwartzman. *Social Marketing to the Business Customer: Listen to Your B2B Market, Generate Major Account Leads, and Build Client Relationships.* Hoboken, NJ: John Wiley & Sons, 2011.

Grant, R. "A Look at Polyvore's 20m Users [An Infographic]." February 21, 2013. **wearesocial.net/blog/2013/02/polyvores-20 m-users/** (accessed December 2014).

Greenberg, P., et al. (ed.) *The Art of Social Sales.* A comprehensive report sponsored by Oracle, March 2011. **oracle.com/us/products/applications/Siebel/051270.pdf** (accessed December 2014).

Halligan, B. and D. Shah, *Inbound Marketing: Attract, Engage and Delight Consumers Online,* 2nd edn. Hoboken, NJ: John Wiley & Sons (2014).

Harbison, N. "Social Media and Group Buying: Why It's a Match Made in Heaven." September 16, 2010. **thenextweb.com/socialmedia/2010/09/16/social-media-and-group-buying-why-its-a-match-made-in-heaven** (accessed December 2014).

Hempel, J. "Google Takes Stake in Lending Club." May 2, 2013. **fortune.com/2013/05/02/google-takes-stake-in-lending-club** (accessed December 2014).

Jacobs, A. "Fashion Democracy: The World of Virtual Anna Wintours." March 29, 2010. **newyorker.com/reporting/2010/03/29/100329fa_fact_jacobs** (accessed December 2014).

Jingli, S. "Where Have China's Big Group-Buying Websites Gone?" October 27, 2014. **chinadaily.com.cn/bizchina/2014-10/27/content_18804926_5.htm** (accessed January 2015).

Kasteler, J. "Why You Should Get Involved with Social Shopping: E-Commerce 2.0." July 28, 2009. **searchengineland.com/why-you-should-get-involved-with-social-shopping-e-commerce-20-22995** (accessed December 2014).

Kavilanz, P. "Facebook Launched My Startup: 'Wine Condom Bottle Stopper.'" July 16, 2014 (last updated). **money.cnn.com/gallery/smallbusiness/2014/07/16/facebook-twitter-social-media/2.html** (accessed December 2014).

Kimball, M., "Social Media: Changing the Way Your Customers Shop Online [Infographic]." September 10, 2013. **blog.marketmesuite.com/social-media-changing-the-way-your-customers-shop-online** (accessed December 2014).

Krogue, K. "31 Twitter Tips: How to Use Twitter Tools and Twitter Best Practices for Business." August 30, 2013. **forbes.com/sites/kenkrogue/2013/08/30/31-twitter-tips-how-to-use-twitter-tools-and-twitter-best-practices-for-business/** (accessed December 2014).

Leahey, C. "Why Your Teen Loves Wanelo." May 23, 2013. **fortune.com/2013/05/23/tech-star-deena-varshavskaya/** (accessed December 2014).

Lee, E. "2013 China's Group-buying Turnover Rockets 67.7 % to 35.88 Billion Yuan." January 15, 2014. **technode.com/2014/01/15/2013-group-buying-turnover-rockets-68-percent-yoy-in-china** (accessed January 2015).

Lee, T. "With Shoppable Hangout, Best Buy Marries Social Media to Commerce." December 25, 2013 (updated). **startribune.com/business/237205921.html** (accessed December 2014).

Lehdonvirta, V., and M. Ernkvist. "Converting the Virtual Economy into Development Potential: Knowledge Map of the Virtual Economy." Washington, DC: infoDev/World Bank 2011. **infodev.org/infodev-files/resource/InfodevDocuments_1056.pdf** (accessed December 2014).

Liu, I.L.B., C.M.K. Cheung, and M.K.O. Lee. "Customer Knowledge Contribution Behavior in Social Shopping Communities." *Proceedings of the 46th Hawaii International Conference on System Sciences (HICSS)*, January 7–10, 2013, Maui, HI.

Lutz, A. and H. Peterson. "35 Companies That Are Changing the Way We Shop and Eat." March 12, 2014. **businessinseder.com/compnies-revolutionizing-retail-2014-3** (accessed July 2015).

Macdonald, M. "Which Social Media Platforms Drive the Most Sales? [Infographic]." March 10, 2014. **shopify.com/blog/12731545-which-social-media-platforms-drive-the-most-sales-infographic#axzz2vgUrLnVA** (accessed December 2014).

Madden, N. "China Pioneers Group Buying Discounts Without Groupon." December 14, 2010. **adage.com/article/global-news/advertising-china-group-buying-discounts-groupon/147641** (accessed December 2014).

Mally, S. *How to Use the Social Media Sites Pinterest and Polyvore Together to Drive Traffic to Your Website or Blog,* Kindle edition. Seattle, WA: Amazon Digital Services, Inc., 2012.

Mander, J., "The Continuing Rise of Group Buying Sites." March 7, 2014. **globalwebindex.net/blog/group-buying-sites** (accessed January 2015).

Markman, A. "Money Can Buy Happiness If You Spend It Right." May 21, 2010. **psychologytoday.com/blog/ulterior-motives/201005/money-can-buy-happiness-if-you-spent-it-right** (accessed December 2014).

Marsden, P. "The 6 Dimensions of Social Commerce: Rated and Reviewed." December 22, 2009. **digitalintelligencetoday.com/the-6-dimensions-of-social-commerce-rated-and-reviewed** (accessed December 2014).

McCafferty, D. "Social Media Influence on Purchasing Overrated."September 7, 2011. **baselinemag.com/c/a/Intelligence/Social-Media-Influence-On-Purchasing-Overrated-660095** (accessed December 2014).

Offerpop. *The Definitive Guide to Instagram Marketing. eBook,* 2014. **go.offerpop.com/Definitive-Guide-Instagram-Marketing** (accessed December 2014).

Phibbs, B. *Groupon: You Can't Afford It—Why Deep Discounts Are Bad for Business* [Kindle Edition]. United States: Beyond the Page Publishing, 2011.

Popilskis, A. "Is Your Brand at Risk of Missing the Social Commerce Revolution?" January 3, 2014. **business2community.com/social-selling/brand-risk-missing-social-commerce-revolution-0728766#!bPnl0b** (accessed December 2014).

Porterfield, A., et al. *Facebook Marketing All-in-One for Dummies,* 2nd edn. Hoboken, NJ: John Wiley & Sons, 2013.

Regus. "A Social Recovery: A Global Survey of Business Use of Social Networks." June 2011. **regus.com/images/A_Social_Recovery_tcm8-39640.pdf** (accessed December 2014).

Rowan, D., and T. Cheshire. "Commerce Gets Social: How Social Networks Are Driving What You Buy." January 18, 2011. **wired.co.uk/magazine/archive/2011/02/features/social-networks-drive-commerce** (accessed December 2014).

Sala, K. "Top 50 Product Review Blogs." June 25, 2012. **cision.com/us/2012/06/top-50-product-review-blogs** (accessed December 2014).

Salesforce. "Social Sales Revolution: 7 Steps to Get Ahead." (free eBook) 2011. Available to download from **salesforce.com/form/pdf/wp-sales-social-sales-revolution.jsp** (accessed December 2014).

Savitz, E. "Four Reasons Why Virtual Goods Make Us Happy." October 25, 2011. **forbes.com/sites/ciocentral/2011/10/25/four-reasons-why-virtual-goods-make-us-happy** (accessed December 2014). (A guest post written by Ben Perry.)

SCN. "Community Data." September 16, 2014.

Sennett, F. *Groupon's Biggest Deal Ever: The Inside Story of How One Insane Gamble, Tons of Unbelievable Hype, and Millions of Wild Deals Made Billions for One Ballsy Joker.* New York: St. Martin's Press, 2012.

Shen, J. "Social Comparison, Social Presence, and Enjoyment in the Acceptance of Social Shopping Websites." *Journal of Electronic Commerce Research*, vol. 13, no. 3, pp. 198-212, 2012.

Shih, C. *The Facebook Era: Tapping Online Social Networks to Market, Sell, and Innovate,* 2nd edn. Upper Saddle River, NJ: Prentice Hall, 2011.

Singh, S., and S. Diamond. *Social Media Marketing for Dummies,* Seconds edn. Hoboken, NJ: John Wiley & Sons, 2012.

Smith, C. "By the Numbers: 40 Amazing Yelp Statistics." *Digital Marketing Ramblings*, October 29, 2014 (last updated). **expandedramblings.com/index.php/yelp-statistics** (accessed December 2014).

Smith, C., and M. Ballve. "The Rise of Social Commerce—How Tweets, Pins and Likes Are Driving Sales, Online and Offline [Charts]." August 6, 2013. **businessinsider.com/social-commerce-and-retailer-benefits-2013-8** (accessed December 2014).

Srinivasan, R. *To Group Coupon or Not: Quick Start Guide to Groupon, LivingSocial and Other Group Coupon Sites* [Kindle edn.] Seattle, WA: Amazon Digital Services, Inc., 2011.

Strauss, J., and R. Frost. *E-Marketing*, 7th edn. Upper Saddle River, NJ: Pearson/Prentice Hall, 2014.

Stelzner, M.A. "2014 Social Media Marketing Industry Report: How Marketers are Using Social Media to Grow Their Businesses." May 2014. **socialmediaexaminer.com/SocialMediaMarketingIndustryReport2014.pdf** (accessed December 2014).

Takahashi, D. "PayPal: 12 M Monthly Users Are Paying for Virtual Goods (Updated)." August 1, 2011. **venturebeat.com/2011/08/01/paypal-says-there-are-12m-monthly-users-paying-for-facebook-games-exclusive** (accessed December 2014).

Taylor, C. "Polyvore Expands Beyond Fashion (And Into An Older, More Moneyed User Base) With New Home Decor Section." September 13, 2013 **techcrunch.com/2013/09/17/polyvore-for-home** (accessed January 2015).

Turban, E. et al. *Electronic Commerce: A Managerial and Social Networks Perspective,* 8th edn. New York: Springer, 2015.

Viskovich, J. "Your Social Selling Questions Answered." July 31, 2014. **socialmediatoday.com/content/your-social-selling-questions-answered** (accessed December 2014).

Walker, S. *Social Media Marketing Tips: Essential Strategy Advice and Tips for Business: Facebook, Twitter, Google + YouTube, LinkedIn, Instagram and Much More!* [Kindle edn]. Seattle, WA: Amazon Digital Services, 2014.

Walsh, B. "Borrow, Don't Buy: Websites that Let Strangers Share." *Time Magazine*, December 5, 2010. Retrieved from **content.time.com/time/magazine/article/0,9171,2032109,00.html** (accessed December 2014).

Wang, J. "How Polyvore Became a Trend-Setter in Social Shopping." May 24, 2011. **entrepreneur.com/article/219675** (accessed December 2014).

Womack, B. "Facebook Says Gamers Paying to Play Surges 24 Percent." March 27, 2013. **bloomberg.com/news/2013-03-26/facebook-says-tally-of-users-who-pay-to-play-games-has-risen-24-.html** (accessed December 2013).

Yin, E. "Social Shop Till You Drop: A Quick Primer." July 11, 2010. **gigaom.com/2010/07/11/social-commerce** (accessed December 2014).

Zwilling, M. "Location-Based Services are a Bonanza for Startups." January 31, 2011. **forbes.com/sites/martinzwilling/2011/01/31/location-based-services-are-a-bonanza-for-startups** (accessed December 2014).

Social Customer Service and CRM

7

Contents

Opening Case: How Sony Uses Social Media
for Improving CRM 155

7.1 Definitions and Concepts of CRM, E-CRM,
and Social CRM 156

7.2 A CRM Model for Customer Interactions 160

7.3 The Evolution of Social CRM 162

7.4 How to Serve the Social Customer 166

7.5 Social CRM in the Enterprise 170

7.6 Special Applications and Issues in Social CRM 172

7.7 Strategy and Implementation Issues of Social CRM 174

References 177

Elektronisch zusatz-materialien Die online-version dieses kapitels
(doi:10.1007/978-3-319-17028-2_7) enthält zusatzmaterial, das für
autorisierte benutzer ist.

Learning Objectives

Upon completion of this chapter, you will be able to:

1. Define CRM, e-CRM, and social CRM (SCRM).
2. Describe the major types of customer interactions with companies.
3. Describe the evolution of CRM to SCRM.
4. Define social customers and describe how they can be served.
5. Describe how social CRM works inside the enterprise.
6. Describe unique and innovative applications of SCRM.
7. Describe social CRM strategy and implementation issues.

OPENING CASE: HOW SONY USES SOCIAL MEDIA FOR IMPROVING CRM

Sony, the giant consumer electronics producer, has been struggling during the last few years. Now, by using social media improvement is in sight.

The Problem

Sony Corporation (**sony.com**) faces fierce competition from Samsung, Sharp Electronics, LG Electronics, and other large, global companies. This competition has intensified during the economic slowdown in recent years. As a result, total revenues for Sony declined every year from 2008 until 2012. The company suffered heavy losses in 2009 and 2012, causing its share price to drop from $35/share in 2010 and 2011 to $9.57 in late 2012. In 2013 the stock rose mostly due to the recovery in Tokyo's stock exchange. Consumer electronic products are fairly mature, so the differences in quality and prices are not substantial. Therefore, the competitors in the field are promoting their customer service as a strategic differentiator. Sony is trying to do this with the help of their social media communities and initiatives.

The Solution: Social Media Projects

Sony Corporation embarked on social CRM as a vehicle for improving customer service in April 2013. According to Jack (2013), Sony combined a customer support and direct marketing program, mostly using social channels. The various initiatives are managed by Sony's Customer Experience Management Team. The team organized *Sony's Community Site* (**community.sony.com**), which is a central hub for customer information and support. It includes *idea boards, discussion groups, blogs, Twitter feeds*, and other content-generating channels. The site is used also for marketing campaigns.

The following are representative activities, many of which are done at Sony Europe (see Taylor 2013).

- Active social communities; some are for specific products, others are general for the entire Sony brand. The company's staff members and consumers are involved in these communities. Members of these communities are helping each other and providing feedback. Customer service employees are "listening" to the feedback and using the information to improve service.
- YouTube videos provide training for customers on the use of Sony's products.
- Using Lithium Social Web software (a SAP company), relevant sites are monitored for reviews and comments (positive and negative). This allows Sony to improve operations, resolve problems, and capitalize on opportunities.
- There is a special "Customer Relations" tab located on Sony's Community site, the company's central social network, for easy communication.
- The company created a 'Facebook Support Community' (**facebook.com/sony**), Twitter 'Sony Support USA' (**twitter.com/sonysupportusa**), Tumblr 'Sony Support USA' (**sonysupportusa.tumblr.com**), and a YouTube Sony Support Channel 'Sony Listens' (**youtube.com/user/SonyListens**).
- In the communities, the company's staff demonstrates how problems are resolved quickly and efficiently. For example, there is an "Experts" tab for "How To" videos and technical support, and so forth. See **community.sony.com/t5/Meet-Our-Experts/bg-p/experts**.
- Sony is using all its social media channels, including LinkedIn, to proactively engage users and provide customer service in a timely fashion.
- Sony Electronic integrates Pinterest (**pinterest.com/sonyprousa**) to send information about its products to community members (see details in Eckerle 2013 and **ohsopinteresting.com/lessons-from-sony-on-pinterest**).

According to Holland (2011), Sony mines social media conversations and conducts sentiment analysis (Chap. 10) to improve customer service and product improvements and design. Note that Sony is using social media campaigns to engage customers (e.g., 2011 'CatchTheTablet' campaign; see **atomicpr.com/results/sony-catch-the-tablet**). Finally, according to Revoo (2011), software from Reevoo helps Sony automatically translate reviews from one language to another.

The Results

Significant results were realized in 2014 after the deployment of most SC initiatives. However, some improvements have materialized earlier. For example, according to Jack (2013), the improved communication resulted in a 22 % increase in 'clicks' (over 100 % in some cases). Other results are:

- Customers' trust in Sony increased (Jack 2013).
- Page views, conversation volume, and engagement activities (e.g., posting) increased by 100 % (Jack 2013).
- Customer service was combined with marketing promotions, which resulted in new sources of revenue for Sony.
- In March 2014, PlayStation had about 2.5 million followers on Twitter and 35 million fans Facebook.

Sources: Based on Jack (2013), Taylor (2013), Eckerle (2013), Revoo (2011), and **en.wikipedia.org/wiki/Sony** (accessed July 2015).

LESSONS LEARNED FROM THE CASE

The Sony case illustrates that a company can use social media to not only advertise and sell, but also to provide outstanding customer service. Operating in a highly competitive market, customer service can be an important strategic differentiator. Sony has supplemented their traditional customer service with social networks, blogs, Twitter, and a Facebook fan page. They have concentrated on improving communication and interactions with customers. The customer service provided via social media tools and platforms is more interactive, timely, and direct. Furthermore, the system fosters a truly conversation-based communication. This kind of service is important to customers, and contributes to the company's success. In this chapter, we concentrate on social CRM.

7.1   DEFINITIONS AND CONCEPTS OF CRM, E-CRM, AND SOCIAL CRM

It is well known that customers are the revenue engine of most organizations. Without customers, there would be no business. Therefore, customers must receive outstanding service.

In today's world, highly valued customers receive even more attention.

The customer care field is undergoing a significant transformation, both in the way that customer service professionals conduct business and in the way that customers interact with companies that use the Social Web. The implementation of social media has altered both the expectations of customers and the way corporations provide customer service (as the growth of e-mail did many years ago).

At first, one may think that there is not much connection between customer service and social commerce. In fact, the opposite is probably true. For an overview, Lacy et al. (2013).

How Social Networks Empower Customers

It is said that one angry tweet can torpedo a brand, but one sweet tweet can correct a problem (Bernoff and Schadler 2010). According to Sysomos Inc. (2011) and **parature.com/lp/report-2014-state-multichannel-cs-survey-comm.html**, more than 65 % of all customers have ended relationships with vendors due to what they perceived to be poor customer service. Let us examine how one angry customer used Facebook in an attempt to change one company's policy.

Example: How Facebook's Chorus Ended the Instrument Luggage Ban at Qantas Airways of Australia

Qantas Airways had a policy that required large musical instruments to be stored in the cargo hold, which would sometimes cause damage to the instruments. In fall 2010, after suffering $1,200 in damages to her saxophone, Jamie Oehlers of Australia organized a Facebook campaign to persuade the airline to reverse the policy. When one person complains, the company's standard response is to send the customer a letter of apology, but usually the policy does not change. However, more than 8,700 people (including members of the country's symphony orchestras) joined forces on Facebook by posting similar incidents and pictures of damaged instruments and saying they would boycott Qantas if the airline did not change their policy. Qantas announced that they listened to their customers, and in December 2010, amended the policy, allowing any instrument in a hard-shelled case on board, provided it falls within the airline's length and weight restrictions (based on a news item from Staff Writers 2010). Alternatively, one may purchase a seat for a large instrument and carry it as a bulky item. (For information about Qantas's new policy, see **qantas.com.au/travel/airlines/carry-on-baggage/global/en**).

This story is not unique; similar stories frequently appear in the media. A well-known case from 2008 is 'United Breaks Guitars,' the saga of a musician named Dave Carroll who flew United Airlines with his guitar, only to have it broken.

Carroll and his bandmates were sitting at the rear of the aircraft waiting to deplane, when the United baggage handlers threw Carroll's $3,500 guitar, with little care, causing it to break. After nine months of a series of e-mails and telephone calls, the airline's representative told Carroll that United refused to take responsibility. Carroll offered them a settlement of $1,200 in flight vouchers, to cover his salvage costs repairing his guitar, which was rejected. Carroll, however, realized that as a musician and songwriter, he was not without options. He told the United representative that he would be writing three songs about his experience with United Airlines. He would then make videos for these songs and offer them for free download on YouTube and his own website. Carroll's goal was to get one million hits on YouTube, but the first song, titled "United Breaks Guitars," became a viral sensation and surpassed 150,000 views the first day and over three million views in just 10 days. In August 2009, Carroll and his band released "United Breaks Guitars: Song 2" that has surpassed over 1,700,000 views as of January 2014, and in 2010, he released the final chapter, "United Breaks Guitars Song 3: 'United We Stand,'" which has garnered over 672,000 views as of January 2014. The original "United Breaks Guitars" song has been watched by over 13,700,000 people as of January 2014 (see **youtube.com/watch?v=5YGc4zOqozo**).

Since the whole debacle and the release of the songs and videos, Carroll has published a book about his experience and has become a public speaker. (Watch the video from Dave Carroll's presentation given at the Brite 2010 conference titled "Dave Carroll: Lessons from 'United Breaks Guitars'" (20:14 minutes) at **youtube.com/watch?v=_Hd8XI42i2M** to learn more about how United changed its ways, and the lessons for customer service in an age of social media.) Also see **mashable.com/2012/02/02/united-breaks-guitars-gripevine**. In addition, in February 2012, Carroll helped launch a customer service platform called Gripevine (**gripevine.com**); a forum for disgruntled customers to post their complaints and bad experiences they have had with companies. Gripevine's automated response technology notifies the company and invites them to the site to review the gripe, giving both parties an opportunity to work towards a positive resolution.

In another example, a customer named Heather Armstrong complained that Maytag (appliances) customer service was unhelpful about her new broken washing machine. Frustrated with her experience, Armstrong told the unhelpful customer service representative that she has over 10,000 followers on Twitter. They did pay attention to her only after she tweeted about her nightmare experience with the company. Within a day, she received a telephone call from their parent company's corporate office, and the next day her washer was working. In the past, customer complaints usually received little or no attention, even when customers threatened to publish their complaint on the Internet. Armstrong said that "Twitter has become a tool to 'empower' customers like her—once a company figures out she has a listening audience (in this case, her 10,000 Twitter followers), it'll need to listen and act" (see Olson 2009).

These examples show how, at the most basic level of customer service, social media acts as a "social telephone" (see Sysomos Inc. 2011).

Today, when a customer says, "I will organize a campaign against your company on Facebook or Twitter," you can be sure that someone at the company will pay attention. An empowered customer is a major driver of social CRM (Bernoff and Schadler 2010). Chapter 5 reveals how companies handle their reputations when under attack in the social media.

Defining CRM and E-CRM

Three basic concepts are important for an understanding of this chapter: CRM, e-CRM, and social CRM (SCRM).

Customer Relationship Management (CRM)

Customer relationship management (CRM) is an approach that focuses on acquiring customers and building long-term and sustainable relationships that add value to the customers as well as the organizations. There are several other definitions of CRM. For example, according to Greenberg (2009), "CRM is a philosophy and a business strategy, supported by a technology platform, business rules, processes and social characteristics, designed to engage the customer in a collaborative conversation in order to provide mutually beneficial value in a trusted and transparent business environment." Petersen (2012) provides 16 definitions of CRM, by 21 experts, some in words and some in pictures.

Note: CRM is only one way to deal with customer relationship and care. Traditional marketing activities, such as providing promotions, have been used for a long time in business. However, CRM adds functionalities that were not available before.

Characteristics of Customer Relationship Management (CRM)

According to Greenberg (2009), "CRM is an integrated business model and a set of operating practices coordinated and aligned to maximize revenue from targeted customers. CRM is based on the assumption that customers are the core of a business, and that a company's success depends on effectively managing its relationships with them." The term *relationship* is unclear. Does it require an emotional attachment

or bond between the parties in the relationship? Do the parties have to be interdependent on one another? To some degree, the answers are yes. In this chapter, a relationship exists if there are a series of interactive episodes between two or more parties over time.

For more coverage, see **en.wikipedia.org/wiki/Customer_relationship_management** and **management-studyguide.com/features-of-crm.htm**.

Defining e-CRM

Today, most CRM programs, applications, and services depend heavily on IT more than they did prior to the advent of the Web in 1993. The IT-supported programs constitute part of what is known as *electronic CRM* (e-CRM). **Electronic customer relationship management (e-CRM); also known as CRM 1.0**) is the electronically delivered set of tools that helps manage CRM. E-CRM is related to all forms of managing relationships with customers when using information technologies. It arises from the consolidation of traditional CRM with the e-business applications, and it covers the broad range of information technologies used to support a company's CRM strategy. For the difference between CRM and e-CRM, see **en.wikipedia.org/wiki/ECRM** and Beal (undated).

However, since nearly all CRM practices use some IT, the terms *CRM* and *e-CRM* are used interchangeably by many. Numerous CRM software packages are available. For a review of 40 top CRM software packages including cloud-based see **crmsoftwarereview.org/2014reviews**. For the top ten vendors of 2014, see **crm-software-review.toptenreviews.com**. For more in e-CRM, see Online Tutorial T1.

A growing component in e-CRM is social CRM.

What Is Social CRM?

Social CRM is one component of developing a social business. It is practiced very differently by various organizations.

Definition

According to Roebuck (2011), **social customer relationship management (SCRM)** also known as **CRM 2.0**, is CRM supported by social media (e.g., Web 2.0 tools, social network sites, as demonstrated in the opening case), which are designed to engage customers in conversations, sharing, and other interactions in order to provide benefits to all participants and increase trust. SCRM is based on social media, in support of companies' stated goals and objectives of optimizing the customer's experience, and building trust and loyalty, see Huba (2013). Success requires considering people, business processes, and technology associated with the interactions between customers and enterprises.

SCRM is an extension of CRM, not a replacement (see **the56group.typepad.com/pgreenblog/2009/07/time-to-put-a-stake-in-the-ground-on-social-crm.html**). It adds two dimensions: social media and people. It is designed to engage customers in conversations using social media tools. An important goal of SCRM is to add benefits to the sellers (e.g., increased trust, loyalty, and sales from their customers) and to the customers (e.g., better, quicker service; more engagement; product improvements). SCRM is the segment of business strategy that addresses the issue of how companies adapt to the *social customers* and their expectations regarding the companies with which they conduct business. SCRM evolved from CRM (and e-CRM) in a process that is described in Sect. 7.3, and in Chess Media Group (2010; in collaboration with Lieberman). For a detailed presentation of this process and an overview of social CRM, download the free "Guide to Understanding Social CRM" at **chessmedia-group.com/research/white-papers**. For comprehensive coverage of social CRM, see Roebuck (2011), Lacy et al. (2013), and Fagan (2014).

The Elements of Social CRM

The major elements and characteristics of SCRM are shown in Fig. 7.1. As the figure illustrates, the characteristics are the foundations of a social customer who is driven by social networking. As described in Chap. 1, the social customer's needs are different from those of the customer who does not use social media. Social customers, for example, want to communicate with vendors by using the Internet (e.g., see Metz 2011). This communication is provided by social media, which is the major element of social CRM. The social environment is also a major element of social CRM, since it is the source of interactions with the social customer (see Sect. 7.4).

The Benefits of Social CRM

This new breed of customers (the social customer) places new demands on organizations. However, social media tools can meet these demands nicely, usually at a low cost (except for staff time). Social media provides for engagement and collaboration that eventually results in a competitive advantage to the organization if implemented properly.

Social CRM offers the following potential benefits to customers ("c") and enterprise ("e") in the list below.

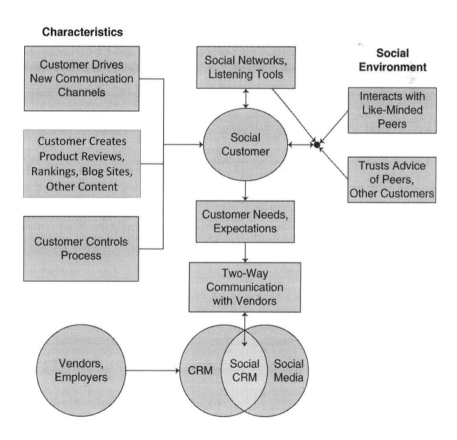

Fig. 7.1 The elements of social CRM

(Note: Several of these are illustrated in Case 7.1 iRobot, presented later in this chapter). These benefits to iRobot are marked with an ("I".)

- Drives quick resolution of customers' problems (c)
- Provides for effective and efficient business—customer collaboration (c), (e)
- Improves the reputation of companies (e), (I)
- Provides better understanding of customer needs and wants (e)
- Provides focused, intuitive, and easy-to-use CRM applications (e)
- Provides better marketing, better targeting, and improved products/services due to customers' creation of content, and WOM (e)
- Provides customer input for market research at a quicker rate and at a low cost for improving products and customer service (e)
- Provides customers with more information about products/services quickly (c), (I)
- Increases trust and loyalty (e)
- Provides a more complete view of the customer than what traditional CRM can provide (e)
- Decreases overall customer care costs (e.g., through self-helping communities) (e)
- Enables salespeople to find sales leads quickly and easily (e)
- Develops new revenue opportunities and turn new customers into repeat customers (c)
- Increases CRM staff productivity by teaching them to use analytics and collaboration 2.0 techniques (e)
- Improves employee performance by benefiting from knowledge sharing gained in social networks (e)
- Improves customer satisfaction by providing them with opportunities for engagement using social media platforms (c), (I)
- Converts leads to opportunities with more effective campaigns (e)

Petersen (2011) illustrates the benefits of social CRM in 16 case studies. Minkara and Pinder Jr. (2014) describe the strategic advantage provided by CRM.

An article by Tiffany Brown (at **tiffanyabrown.word-press.com/2011/10/26/social-CRM-as-a-holistic-marketing-tool**) includes a video which shows the essential elements of the SCRM process.

For additional benefits, see Shih (2011), Fagan (2014), and Ziff Davis (2012).

For more information about social CRM in general, visit **oracle.com/socialCRM** and see Metz (2011). For a comprehensive case study, see Egeland (2009). For an overview of social CRM, see Fagan (2014) and Ziff Davis (2012).

For Petersen's free e-book *166 Case Studies Prove Social Media Marketing ROI*, see **barnraisersllc. com/2012/07/166-case-studies-prove-social-media-marketing-roi-free-ebook**. For the case of OCBC Bank see Hootsuite (2014).

The Projected Growth of Social CRM

The benefits of SCRM and the projected growth of social media in general have led researchers to believe that SCRM will grow exponentially during the next few years. According to Valentine (2011), SCRM IT expenditures grow at an annual rate of 30 %. Gartner Inc. projected that social CRM software, which accounted for merely 5 % of the total CRM software in 2010, will account for 30 % of the total CRM IT spending in 2015.

Enterprises practice SCRM in a variety of ways, including hosting and supporting social communities, monitoring conversations in a social network, and facilitating information sharing in social networks.

A major condition required for this growth to occur is the need to provide clearer and measurable benefits for both customer service and sales. In addition, companies and software vendors need to provide close integration with traditional CRM processes.

7.2 A CRM MODEL FOR CUSTOMER INTERACTIONS

Before we describe the social SCRM field, let us look at the ways that customers interact with CRM applications and with enterprises.

The Patricia Seybold Group Model for Customer Interactions

The Patricia Seybold Group (**customers.com**) focuses on CRM, e-CRM, and social CRM from the customer's point of view, where a customer is viewed as being interested in a simplified, straightforward, honest, consistent interaction and relationship with a company. Toward this end, SCRM focuses on applications used to make it easy for a customer to communicate, engage, and collaborate with a company. The Patricia Seybold Group distinguishes between *customer-facing, customer-touching, customer-centric intelligence,* and *online networking* applications.

1. **Customer-facing applications.** These include all the areas where customers interact with the company: social media channels; call centers, including help desks; sales force automation; and field service automation. Such CRM applications automate information flow and support employees in sales or service while they interact with customers. Web 2.0 tools are used here to facilitate interactions.

2. **Customer-touching applications.** In this category, customers interact directly with the applications, rather than through a company representative. Notable examples are self-service activities, such as using FAQs and involvement in content creation. Several applications in social networks belong to this category. For example, crowdsourcing can be used to create FAQs.

3. **Customer-centric intelligence applications.** These are applications that analyze the results of operations and performance and use the results of this analysis to improve CRM activities and procedures. Web analytics, sentiment analysis, and social analytics (Chap. 10) are the prime tools in this case.

4. **Online networking applications.** Online networking refers to methods that provide the opportunity to build *personal relationships* with a wide range of people. Social CRM support includes chat rooms, blogs, wikis, discussion forums, and social network sites.

(See the Patricia Seybold Group's "An Executive Guide to CRM: How to Evaluate CRM Alternatives by Functionality, Architecture, & Analytics" by Patricia Seybold Group's Executive Series at **crmodyssey.com/Documentation/ Documentation_PDF/An%20Executive%20Guide%20 To%20CRM.pdf**).

The above four categories of applications are used to organize our presentation of applications in the remainder of this chapter. A discussion of the first category follows. For a discussion of the other categories, see the remainder of this chapter and Roebuck (2011).

To learn about the Five Waves of CRM, see **customers. com/articles/the-five-waves-of-crm.**

Customer-Facing Applications

Customer-facing applications make extensive use of social media. For definitions and examples, see **amduus.com/ cms/?q=node/66** and **searchcrm.techtarget.com/definition/ customer-facing**.

A primary application of customer-facing CRM is in *multichannel call centers*, otherwise known as *customer interaction centers*. (See the free e-book titled *25 Social Media Statistics for the Call Center* at **fonolo.com/ ebook-25-social-media-statistics-for-the-call-center**.)

Customer Interaction Centers

A **customer interaction center (CIC)** is a comprehensive customer service entity in which enterprises take care of customer service issues communicated through various contact channels; see **searchcrm.techtarget.com/definition/ contact-center**. These include social media channels such as blogs and forums in social networks. A *multichannel* CIC works like this: (1) A customer makes contact via one or more channels. (2) The system monitors the contacts and integrates than within a database, then determines an appropriate service response. (3) The system directs the customer to self-service, an avatar, or to a live agent. (4) The service is provided to the customer (e.g., the customer's problem is resolved or the question is answered). For images and infographics, search Google Images for: customer interaction center.

An example of a well-managed integrated call center is iRobot's customer support group. The center, which provides a myriad of cross-channel customer touch points, is detailed in Case 7.1. As the case shows, social media provides several channels of customer support. For more examples of CICs and call centers, see **callcenterops.com**.

Case 7.1
SC Application

iRobot Uses Social Media for Multichannel CRM
iRobot (**irobot.com**), which was founded in 1990 by three roboticists at MIT with the vision of making practical robots a reality, designs and builds some of the world's most important robots. According to their website, in 2013, iRobot generated $487 million in revenue and employed more than 500 of the robot industry's top professionals, including mechanical, electrical and software engineers and related support staff. (See **iRobot.com/us/Company/About.aspx**.) iRobot makes robots for the government, defense and security, military and civil defense forces worldwide, commercial applications, industries, and home use. The public is mostly familiar with the Roomba vacuuming robot (see Dignan 2013). Due to the technical nature of its products, the company's customers may require specialized support and service. On their customer care website, the company provides self-diagnosis, support videos, live chat, product FAQs, and more (e.g., see **homesupport.irobot.com**). However, there are home market customers who may need more

technical assistance since many people are new at using robots. The company's objective is to expand the sale of home market products. Therefore, they must provide extensive assistance to inexperienced customers. The company supports a community and provides discussion boards, community search capability, and live chat.

Social CRM: Serve the Customers While Learning from Them

iRobot utilizes a CRM system with the help of Oracle RightNow Inc. (see **oracle.com/us/products/applications/ rightnow/overview/index.html**). The system enables customers to contact iRobot's service group via several different communication channels, including e-mail, live chat, social networks, and Web self-service. This way, iRobot can respond to any online customer communication in a timely manner, regardless of the channel used. All this needs to be done at a low cost; therefore, it is necessary to automate the services as much as possible.

Specific Social Media Activities

iRobot customers can post service and support requests or complaints on **homesupport.irobot.com** or they can contact the help desk. The company monitors these messages and tries to provide immediate responses. iRobot tries to find the identity of the customers that have problems by monitoring relevant conversations in the various social channels (e.g., in forums on social networks conversations). Once identified, iRobot communicates with the customers privately to resolve the issues.

The social media-oriented activities are integrated with documents and videos in a knowledge base managed by RightNow. The company uses RightNow's monitoring tools to identify the customers who post the comments. Some customers may provide their real names. Anonymous customers are encouraged to contact iRobot directly. For how the company listens to social media, see **informationweek.com/software/ social/roomba-robots-listen-to-social-media/d/d-id/1100404?**

Responding to issues quickly is important because, as discussed earlier, customers can attract a considerable amount of attention using Facebook or Twitter (the company runs promotions, such as giveaways and games on Twitter), to publicize their complaints. In addition to problem resolution, the company gets valuable feedback from the customers so it can improve its products and services.

By 2013, iRobot achieved a 97 % Web service rating, realized a 30 % reduction in customer phone calls, and provided improved customer service at a 20 % reduced cost.

iRobot has a presence on Facebook, Twitter, Pinterest, YouTube, and Tumblr. The company uses these sites to disseminate information and collect customer feedback and complaints.

Sources: Based on Carr (2011), RightNow Technologies (2010), Dignan (2013), Oracle (2011), and **irobot.com** (accessed July 2015).

Questions

1. What is meant by the term *multichannel service support*?
2. What are the activities related to social media at iRobot? What are their benefits?
3. Describe how the company listens to their customers' complaints, and how they resolve the problems.

7.3   THE EVOLUTION OF SOCIAL CRM

Now that you have a basic understanding of CRM, e-CRM, and SCRM, we can look at the evolution of SCRM as well as some differences between SCRM and e-CRM. SCRM can be viewed as an extension of e-CRM. Most e-CRM software companies, such as Salesforce Inc. (**salesforce.com**), offer social media features in their products. However, there are some significant differences between e-CRM and SCRM. These differences can be seen at **slideshare.net/ JatinKalra/e-crm-112520123741** and Cipriani (2008).

Cipriani's Multidimensional Presentation

Fabio Cipriani (2008) outlines the difference between CRM and SCRM (referred to as CRM 1.0 and CRM 2.0) along several dimensions. Figures 7.2, 7.3, 7.4, 7.5, and 7.6 show five of these dimensions: landscape, customer touch points, business processing modeling, technology, and organizational mindset.

The Landscape

The landscape describes the difference between CRM 1.0 and CRM 2.0 in the structure, focus, relationship with the community, and value creation, as illustrated in Fig. 7.2.

Notice that in CRM 2.0, the community is larger than in CRM, and it includes interconnections among the customers that were not present online in the early days of CRM.

Touch Points

The term *touch point* refers to any point of interaction a customer has with a brand or seller. Some points are company initiated (e.g., advertising or e-mail discussions) and others are out of the company's control, such as word-of-mouth. CRM 2.0 adds additional touch points, as shown in Fig. 7.3 (all the Web 1.0 tools + Web 2.0 tools). We can add crowdsourcing to this list.

Example: Get Satisfaction for CRM

Get Satisfaction (**getsatisfaction.com**) is a platform where customers can interact with one another and voice their opinions and complaints. Using a forum, they can quickly get resolu-

CRM 1.0

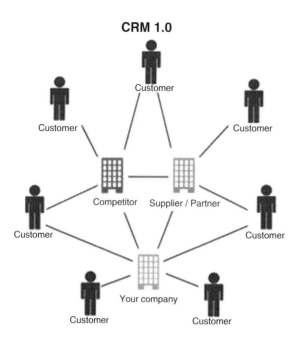

CRM 2.0

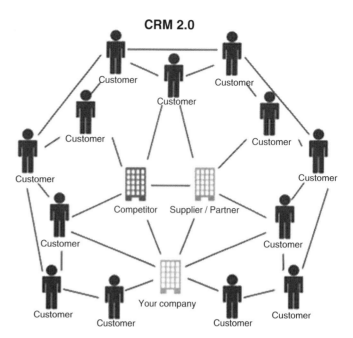

- Focus on individual relationship (company to customer, company to partner, etc.)
- Limited view of the customer and his community preferences, habits, etc.
- Targeted messages generate value

- Focus on collaborative relationship (engaging a more complex relationship network)
- Multiple connections allow better understanding of the customer and his community
- Conversation generates value

Fig. 7.2 The landscape of SCRM vs. CRM. *Source*: Courtesy of F. Ciprianni, "Social CRM: Concept, Benefits, and Approach to Adopt," November 2008. **slideshare.net/fhcipriani/social-crm-presentation-761225** (accessed July 2015). Used with permission

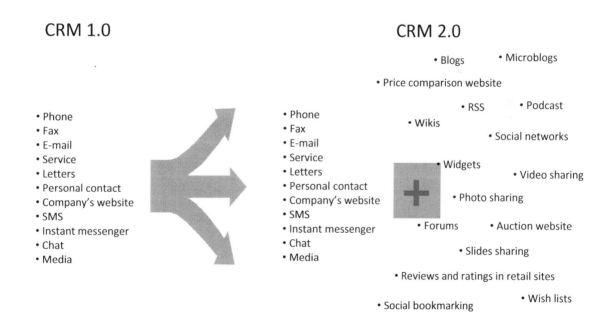

- Single view of the customer based on the interactions history, customer profile data residing in the company's base, and data integration with internal systems.
- Company owns the data but it is limited to previous interactions.

- Single view of the customer is far more complex to achieve. Besides internal information, the company must rely on external information such as customer profiles in social networks and his behavior when participating in a community.
- Customer and other web 2.0 sites own part of the precious data.

Fig. 7.3 Touch points of SCRM vs. CRM. *Source*: Courtesy of F. Ciprianni, "Social CRM: Concept, Benefits, and Approach to Adopt," November 2008. **slideshare.net/fhcipriani/social-crm-presentation-761225** (accessed July 2015). Used with permission

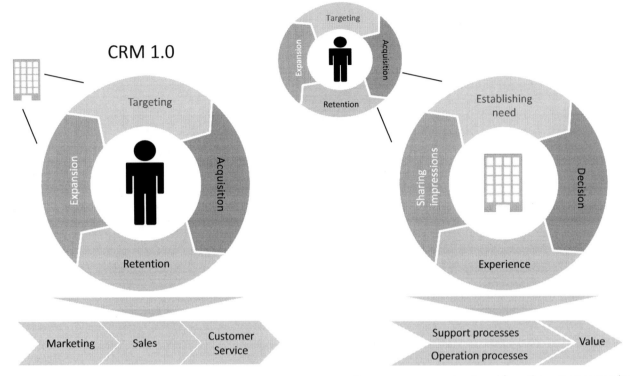

Fig. 7.4 The evolution of business processes in SCRM. *Source*: Courtesy of F. Ciprianni, "Social CRM: Concept, Benefits, and Approach to Adopt," November 2008. **slideshare.net/fhcipriani/social-crm-presentation-761225** (accessed July 2015). Used with permission

tions to their problems. Each community is organized around four topics:

1. **Ask a question**. Customers can answer one another's questions.
2. **Share an idea**. Aggregated feedback is provided from customers (by topic, product, vendor).
3. **Report a problem**. Search to see if anyone posted a similar problem. Post yours.
4. **Give praise**. Customers can praise a product or vendor.

Get Satisfaction provides management of the customers' conversations to interested vendors at no charge. For an example of a Get Satisfaction Support Community, see **get-satisfaction.com/safarichallenge**.

Evolution of Business Processes in CRM

Traditional CRM was a part of a linear process that started with marketing that led to sales and then was followed by customer service (if needed). In CRM 2.0, the process starts with

listening to customers' needs, based on social media conversations, rather than only on traditional market research through quantitative surveys or small scale qualitative research. The objective is to generate value for both the customer and the company. This difference is illustrated in Fig. 7.4.

The Evolution of Technology

Traditional e-CRM focused on automating and supporting the internal business processes that relate to customer service. In CRM 2.0, an attempt is made to provide this same process support, but it is based on community creation and on improved interactions among customers and between vendors and customers, as illustrated in Fig. 7.5.

Organizational Mindset

In CRM 1.0, there is a dialog between one customer service employee and one customer, or between a sales support team

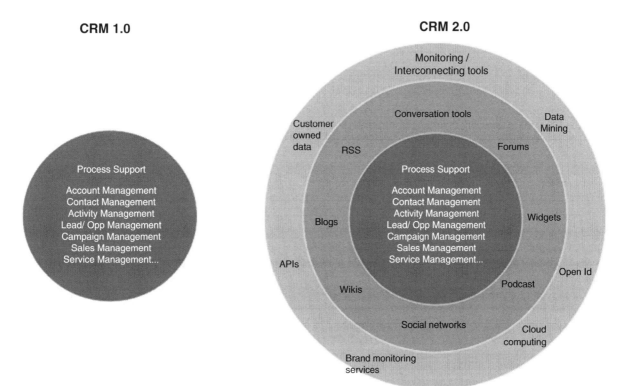

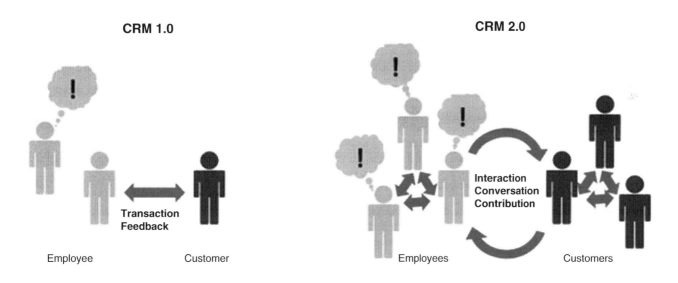

and one customer. Most interactions are routine, with limited innovations. In CRM 2.0, as shown in Fig. 7.6, interactions occur among all employees (as in the Sony opening case) and several customers who also interact with each other (as in the iRobot case). This environment facilitates innovation and increases customer satisfaction.

Conclusions

Incorporating the previous five areas requires empowering the employees, which means that a new set of employee skills is needed. For a long time, marketers have said that everything starts with the needs of consumers. With social CRM and all the social media product discussions, marketers must now learn how to incorporate this philosophy in their strategies.

A complete presentation by Fabio Cipriani (2008) can be viewed at **slideshare.net/fhcipriani/social-crm-presentation-761225**. For an additional presentation on the previous topics, see **slideshare.net/fhcipriani/how-social-crm-can-help-address-changing-consumer-demands**.

Understanding the Social CRM Evolution

A similar description to Cipriani's of the evolution of SCRM from the traditional CRM is provided by Morgan (2010) and Chess Media Group (2010; in collaboration with Lieberman). These authors explain why the revolution happened by citing the following drivers:

- 93 % of Americans want brands to have a presence on social network sites.
- 60 % of Americans regularly interact with companies on social network sites.
- 92 % of Americans prefer to buy from a reputable company.
- 88 % of Americans use recommendations from friends and family to decide which brands to buy.
- 43 % of Americans say that companies should use social networks to solve customers' problems.

For a comprehensive discussion and suggestions, see Boardman (2013).

Finally, Salesforce Inc. provides 18 interesting statistics regarding the changes introduced by social CRM, in a slideshow, that can be viewed at **slideshare.net/Salesforce/18-gamechangin-customer-service-stats**.

7.4 HOW TO SERVE THE SOCIAL CUSTOMER

Once customers are empowered, the question becomes: How does a company serve the social customer?

Companies seek an answer to this question, not only because they are worried about the negative comments posted by social network members, but also because they see an opportunity to involve the customers proactively in product development and problem solving. This can be done in several ways. By listening to social media discussions, companies may be able to find the causes of problems and improve customer service (Parature 2014). Furthermore, companies can increase customer loyalty and get more respect from them, and make their own customer service employees happier. Customer service and CRM are often practiced in organizations by several departments, and these departments need to integrate the social CRM activities with the traditional CRM. See Parature (2014), Bernoff and Schadler (2010), and Fagan (2014). Let us first look at the social customer.

The Social Customer

The Qantas Airways story (Sect. 7.1) shows us that customers and companies' attitudes toward them are changing. In the past, customers were frequently poorly treated. Many are treated better now, because they have *more power* due to social media tools and platforms.

Such empowered customers are referred to as **social customers**. These customers are usually members of social networks. They share opinions about products, services, and vendors; do social shopping; and understand their rights, and they know how to use the wisdom and power of the crowds and communities to their benefit. The highlights of the social customers are shown in Fig. 7.7.

As the figure illustrates, the social customer has new behavior patterns. Social customers are choosing how they interact with companies and companies' brands, which poses challenges to enterprises in regards to handling increased data volume, dynamic channels, and elevated expectations. The customers' new behavior patterns require a new strategy for both marketing communication and customer service (see Chap. 5 for more on new marketing communication strategies). The social customer is not just a purchaser but also an active influencer. Note that individuals are influenced not only by their own friends, but also by friends of their friends. Merchants must understand the difference between these consumers (and their numbers are increasing exponentially) and conventional customers, and therefore provide them with more effective customer service. For an extensive discussion of today's social customer, see Metz (2011) and Shih (2011). Procedures, guidelines, and software are publically available for social CRM (e.g., see Smith et al. 2011). For an overview of the social customer, you can download a free e-book from SAP titled *The Social Contract: Customers, Companies, Communities, Conversations in the Age of the Collaborative Relationship*, available at **thesocialcustomer.com/sites/the-socialcustomer.com/files/TheSocialContract.pdf**. Also, see

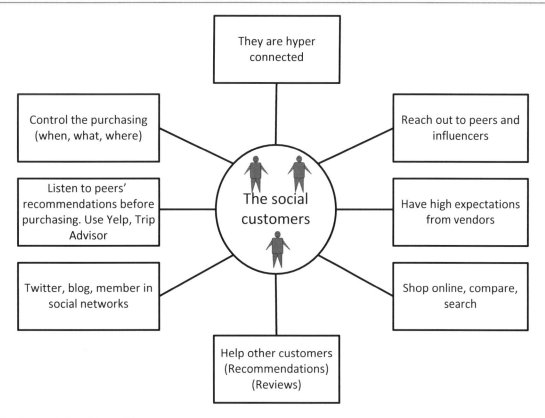

Fig. 7.7 The characteristics of the social customer

socialcustomer.com. For how SCRM adds customer value, see Doligalski (2015).

Implementation of Social Customer Service and CRM

There are several models and methods for implementing social customer service. First, let us look at what Safeway is doing in this area.

Example: How Safeway Provides Social Customer Service

Safeway (**safeway.com**), a large grocery chain, has a virtual customer club. Members can get in-store discounts as well as e-mails with coupons and a list of sale items. An online newsletter with health news and recipes, shopping tips, and so forth is also available to members. To extend this service, Safeway invites their customers to become Safeway Fans on Facebook (**facebook.com/Safeway**) and follow the company on Twitter (**twitter.com/Safeway**. This allows customers/members to know about exclusive promotions, campaigns, and links to recipes. In addition, members can connect and share information with other Safeway shoppers. These are also forums for customers and shareholders to post comments and complaints about products and stores.

In their 'Just for U' program, shoppers can get digital coupons and personalized deals based on their shopping history (see **safeway.com/ShopStores/Offers-Landing-IMG. page**). There is no need to cut coupons anymore. See the video titled "Safeway Just for U™ Shopper Tip: Easy Sign Up" (1:48 minutes) at **youtube.com/watch?v=VaRnJCZV Btw&list=PL2D85D3BE900AA5CB&index=2**.

For an infographic about using social media as a customer service tool, see Smith (2013). For how Nissan Corp. used social media to improve the customer experience see Solis (2012).

How Social CRM Works: Problems and Solutions

The following five real-world examples of how social CRM works are based on **blog.softwareadvice.com/articles/crm/social-crm-ftw-how-realcompanies-are-going-social-and-winning-1111910**.

1. **Chordiant Software (now part of Pegasystems)**
   The Problem: Chordiant, an enterprise software company, needed a better way to find and coordinate the needs of people who are involved in their products' information requirements process.

The Solution: They created an online community where employees, developers, customers, and other partners can collaborate about information needs for product development. The feedback was very positive, resulting in 15 successful collaborative software product releases.

2. **Linksys**

   The Problem: Linksys, a Cisco division, needed to reduce costs while maintaining high levels of customer support.

   The Solution: The company partnered with Lithium (a social CRM consultant) to create an online support community. The deployment of the community increased self-service activities engagement and sharing, which reduced the need for costly phone and other support. Linksys reported savings of millions of dollars.

3. **Enterasys Networks**

   The Problem: Enterasys Networks "has hundreds of employees stationed around the globe." It required a social networking tool that would eliminate geographical boundaries and allow its employees to communicate in real time.

   The Solution: Enterasys decided to deploy Salesforce. com's Chatter application, which includes Web 2.0 tools. "The company experienced improved service performance thanks to real-time collaboration on service issues. Additionally, the sales team was able to work more closely together and completed a record number of sales in the first quarter immediately after implementing Chatter" (per **salesforce.com/chatter/overview**).

4. **H&R Block**

   The Problem: H&R Block wanted to find out what issues their customers were discussing online in order to anticipate problems before they arose.

   The Solution: The company decided to use Radian6's social monitoring technology to achieve H&R Block's goal. The trend analysis tool from Radian6 allowed the company to drill down into community online conversations and see which topics were creating the most buzz. This gave better insight, enabling H&R Block to be more proactive in their customer service. (For more about Salesforce's Radian6, see **salesforcemarketingcloud. com/products/social-media-listening**).

5. **Pepperdine University**

   The Problem: Pepperdine University was looking for a better way to encourage collaboration among its students, staff, and faculty.

   The Solution: The university used Yammer's software (see Chap. 8) "to create a Twitter-like environment where users can interact, communicate in real time, and do so with more transparency. The university saw a significant

increase in community participation" and collaboration. See the video of Pepperdine's Director of E-Learning discussing the university's social network – Yammer (2:21 minutes) at **vimeo.com/68710684**.

Improving the Websites

Social customers like to see user-friendly websites. Indeed, many companies are changing their websites by adding tools for engaging visitors, such as social media hooks (e.g., "Like us," "Bookmark this page") and incorporating better search functionality.

Example

Bloomingdales, the luxury department store that also sells online at Bloomingdales.com, restructured its website. The new site is dynamic, engaging, and easy to browse and search in multiple ways (by product, size, color, material, price, and gender). This enables the company to conduct sophisticated marketing campaigns and then analyze their results.

For more examples on using social CRM for marketing, see Stelzner (2014) and Solis (2012).

Some Social CRM Tools

In the realm of social CRM, a company's customer database can be inundated with information, data, photos, and status updates, which are fed from social network sites and from listening to customers' conversations. Therefore, companies may need some special tools for information processing and analysis.

Here are some representative SCRM tools:

- *Batchbook* (**batchbook.com**) is an inexpensive e-CRM tool for small and medium enterprises.
- *Rapportive* (**rapportive.com**) is a free plug-in, but it works only with Gmail. It will show you details of contacts (such as people's LinkedIn profile, as well as their Twitter stream, Skype handle, or Facebook profile) right inside your inbox.
- *Desk* (**desk.com**; previously Assistly) is a Salesforce customer service application that helps rapidly growing companies deliver effective and efficient customer service. For their capabilities, see **desk.com**.
- *Piksel* (**piksel.com**; previously Kit Social Platform) helps companies maximize reach and return.

For more information about SCRM software, see Jive Software (**jivesoftware.com**).

Automated Response to E-Mail (Autoresponder)

E-mail is a popular traditional online customer service tool. Inexpensive and fast, e-mail disseminates information and sends correspondence on many topics, including responses to customer inquiries. E-mail is available within many social networks between members (e.g., on Facebook) and in IMs (e.g., using Skype).

However, the growth of e-mail messages has resulted in a flood of customer e-mails. Some companies receive tens of thousands of e-mails a week, or even in a day. Answering these e-mails manually would be expensive and time-consuming. However, customers want quick answers, usually within 24 h (a policy of many organizations). Therefore, many vendors offer automated e-mail reply systems known as **autoresponders**, which provide answers to commonly asked questions. Autoresponders, also called *infobots* and *e-mail on demand* (see description in Webopedia.com), are text files that are sent automatically via e-mail, on demand. They can relay standard information for support of customer service and marketing communication (see **egain.com** and **aweber.com**). Many automated responses often do not provide actual answers, but only acknowledge that a query has been received (e.g., "I am out of the office and will return on Monday"). Customer queries are classified in a decision-support repository until a live agent responds. Advance auto responders use FAQs to select proper answers. Even more advanced are systems that use natural language processors to find more accurately what bothers the customers.

Improving the Call Center

Customers who are unsatisfied with a call center's service may post negative comments online about the companies. Therefore, companies know how important it is to have effective call centers.

Several innovations have been introduced by vendors. For example, Fonolo (**fonolo.com**) introduced virtual dialing, virtual queuing, pre-call questions, and smartphone-ready features.

Automated Live Chat

Similar to the advanced autoresponders some companies use an automated 'Live Chat.' There are several types of conversation under this title, some of which are in real time with avatars. The avatars allow you to choose a question from an FAQ menu; the program then provides you with the FAQ answer. Others allow you to use natural language processing, such as the eGain system, to converse with an "intelligent" avatar.

Example

The eGain system looks for certain phrases or key words, such as *complaint* or *information on a product*, and then taps into a knowledge base to generate a canned, matching response. For messages that require attention from a live agent, the query is assigned an ID number and passed along to a customer service representative for a reply. Figure 7.8 shows this process. Note that, the answers and their relationships to problems (questions) are stored in a knowledge database which is updated each time a live agent provides a new solution. Such systems are known as *e-mail response management (ERM)* systems.

Using Microblogging

As the Sony case demonstrated, company microblogging (mostly on Twitter) is becoming very popular in SCRM. Some companies design a special customer care program around Twitter. One example is Yahoo! (**twitter.com/YahooCare**), which is used as a new channel for engaging customers for facilitating problem resolution ("How can we help you today?") and disseminating updates. Their Twitter page also has photos and videos to help customers with troubleshooting.

Product Review Sites

Many customers post product reviews on general sites, such as eBay Commerce Network's Epinions (**epinions.com**; "Unbiased Reviews by Real People"), or on industry (or company-specific) sites. Companies use Web monitoring software, such as Google Alerts, to receive automatic notifications when people post about their products. For example, travel site **tripadvisor.com** has a review forum for guests to review a hotel, vacation, restaurant, or attraction they visited (see **tripadvisor.com/UserReview**). An owner or representative (e.g., hotel manager) is also able to post a response to reviews about their property. They sometimes apologize for a guest's poor experience, and explain what they are doing to remedy the situation. Other times, they thank guests who post positive comments.

For a discussion of the evolution process and the integration of social CRM with e-marketing, see Henschen (2012) and Strauss and Frost (2014).

Monitoring and Analyzing Social Media Reviews

According to their website, Sysomos Inc. (**sysomos.com**) is a company with a comprehensive and "powerful product suite that provides customers with the tools to measure, monitor, understand, and engage with the social media landscape.

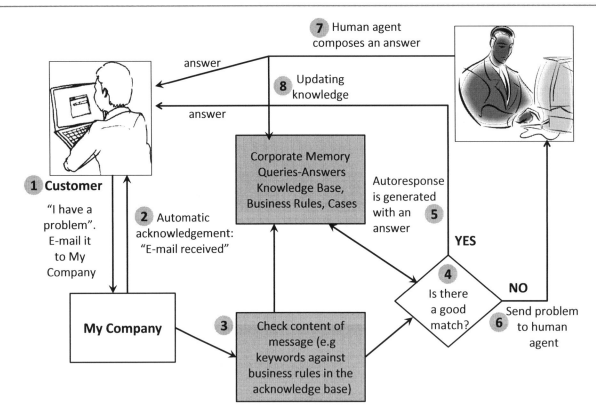

Fig. 7.8 An intelligent autoresponder

Sysomos provides instant access to all social media conversations from blogs, social networks, and micro-blogging services to forums, video sites, and media sources." Sysomos was the first professional tool to manage Facebook fan pages ("Facebook Page Central"). For more information about what they do, see **sysomos.com/products** and **sysomos.com/resources/facebook-page-central**. See Chap. 10 for presentation on this topic.

7.5 SOCIAL CRM IN THE ENTERPRISE

The concept of CRM can be extended from consumer markets (B2C) to the B2B and enterprise environment. Companies sell to other companies (B2B), and these relationships with business partners are very important. In B2B, companies work with distribution channels and other partners or suppliers, this CRM is referred to as *partner relationship management*, or *supplier relationship management*.

Major contacts in B2B are made by corporate salespeople, either individually or in teams. Field service employees also make contact with customers. They can serve both individual customers (B2C) and corporations (B2B). Both groups can benefit from social media, as will be illustrated later in this section and in the annual conference "Dreamforce" (see **salesforce.com/dreamforce**).

Social CRM in the Enterprise and B2B Environments

Facebook, Twitter, and social media tools have changed the way people communicate and collaborate. Today, social media is changing the way salespeople and other B2B personnel collaborate, work, learn, and interact with business customers. For an overview of the challenges salespeople face, the impact of social commerce within the enterprise, and the CRM features that are assisting salespeople, see Fagan (2014).

For a comprehensive case study, see Egeland (2009).

Social CRM offers the following benefits in B2B.

- Enables quick discovery of sales leads while helping convert leads to actual sales (e.g., by using marketing communication that is more effective).
- Enables winning sales deals by sending the right messages to businesses.
- Provides easy and quick access to data and information acquisition and analysis.
- Provides for outstanding business collaboration.
- Increases trust among business partners.
- Improves the procurement process.
- Provides focused, intuitive, and user-friendly business customer care applications.

Salespeople Benefit from Social Media

Salespeople are beginning to use social media applications that facilitate collaboration. These applications assist them to increase their effectiveness and efficiency in performing their jobs. For a comprehensive overview of how this is done, see Oracle (2008). This Oracle white paper "examines the challenges salespeople face, the growing (use of) Web 2.0 in the enterprise, and the drivers for a new breed of social applications that complement traditional CRM systems to help sales users identify qualified prospects and close additional sales more quickly."

Challenges Facing Salespeople Today

According to Parature (2014), and Fagan (2014), the following are the major challenges facing salespeople today:

- Selling has become harder due to the economic slowdown and stiff global competition.
- There is no effective way to leverage traditional collaboration with other traditional customer support technologies.
- Most traditional applications that support salespeople are not intuitive; therefore, they require too much time and energy from the salespeople who need to use them.
- There are gaps between what salespeople need and what the traditional CRM applications deliver.

The Contribution of Social CRM

According to Parature (2014), Oracle (2008), and Fagan (2014), SCRM can provide capabilities to salespeople that deal with the following challenges:

- **Business collaboration at its best**. This is done by leveraging the collective intelligence of social network members, increasing the interactions, and facilitating innovations. With better collaboration, organizations can empower salespeople with the best in their business network, which will facilitate the collective intelligence and the productivity of the involved community.
- **Focused, intuitive and easy to use applications** (per Oracle 2008). Social enterprise applications

model sales activities capture data as sales representatives conduct their daily tasks, rather than requiring them to enter data afterwards.
- **Contextual data available any place, any time**. Sales representatives per Oracle (2008) "can now have data they need when and where they need them. For example, mashups allow business users to assemble innovative, composite applications from many available sources—spanning Internet and enterprise content—to pull information from RSS feeds, blogs, or other services, and embed them into an application" or a corporate portal.
- **Find better qualified leads, quickly and easily**. According to Oracle (2008) "by analyzing purchasing patterns of existing customers and mining information across the enterprise and public social networks," tools such as Prospector identify what products and services sell best.
- **Improve understanding and trust between salespeople and their business customers**.
- **Convert leads to opportunities with more effective campaigns**. Individual sales representatives can be empowered (per Oracle 2008), "to create and manage their own professional e-mail marketing campaigns, as well as leverage successful campaign templates of peers that have been shared and rated by the broader community."
- **Find the right message to close the sale**. According to Oracle (2008), "by harnessing the collective intelligence of the community, sales representatives can obtain a competitive edge by leveraging sales materials that have been highly rated" (by other salespeople and by customers) in order to close business deals.
- **Enable salespeople to resolve problems and challenges with their business customers**.

Social media tools facilitate sales force automation.

Sales Force Automation Salesforce Inc.'s Chatter

Salespeople constitute a major source of contact with customers (both individuals and businesses). The more computer support they have available, the better, quicker, and more accurate service they can provide to customers. **Sales force automation (SFA)** applications support the selling efforts of a company's sales force, helping salespeople manage leads, prospects, and customers through the sales pipeline. An example of such an application is a wireless device that allows quick communication from outside the company with the corporate intranet. Social media supports new applications.

A major vendor in this area is Salesforce.com, Inc. (**salesforce.com**). The company focuses on helping their business customers build social profiles of their employees and customers. Salesforce Chatter, according to the company, "is the leading enterprise social network that allows teams to sync up and take action, and powers communities to connect like never before." Also, according to Salesforce Inc., its latest technological improvements have made Chatter "a true *social business tool*, with many methods available to chat, share, approve, and otherwise enable the collaborative process." To learn more about the features of Chatter, see **salesforce.com/chatter/overview**. Another addition to Chatter is the ability to include videos to the chats, like in many instant messaging networks (e.g., Yahoo Messenger or Skype) do today. The company's partners also add capabilities (for example, from Reachable Inc.).

Reachable Inc. (reachable.com)

Reachable Inc. uses a social graph to show the relationships among individuals. (They call it an Enterprise Business Graph; see **reachable.com/general/reachable-and-the-enterprise-business-graph**). The tool can be used to discover all connections and relationships in the enterprise. It can be used for predictive analysis.

Field Service Automation

Field service employees, such as sales representatives, are frequently on the road, interacting directly with customers at the customers' places of business. Examples of field service employees who work at customers' sites include repair technicians who work together with a company's maintenance staff. Providing services employees with mobile devices can enhance customer service. Field service automation applications support the customer service efforts of field service reps and service managers. These applications manage customer service requests, service orders, service contracts, service schedules, and service calls. They provide planning, scheduling, dispatching, and reporting features to field service representatives. Examples are industrial wireless devices, such as those provided by Motorola.

Social media tools can facilitate SFA and field service automation as described earlier in the Sony and iRobot cases.

Other Applications

Enterprises need to have good working relationships with their employees, suppliers, and other business partners. They can facilitate these relationships by using private social networks, blogs and wikis, and by deploying RSS and other Web 2.0 tools. Enterprises are also using social media for training, marketing, recruiting, and more. All major vendors provide enterprise applications. For example, Oracle provides Oracle CRM Sales Prospector on Demand, Oracle CRM Sales Campaigns on Demand, and Oracle CRM Sales Library on Demand. For details, see **oracle.com/us/products/applications/social-crm/index.html**. Similar applications are provided by Salesforce, Microsoft, and several other vendors.

7.6 SPECIAL APPLICATIONS AND ISSUES IN SOCIAL CRM

There are many special applications and issues in SCRM. Let us look at the following scenario.

Example: A Lesson in Customer Service

As described in Chap. 6, Groupon featured a discount deal to a restaurant delivery service in Tokyo for the 2010 New Year celebration. The promotion was wildly successful as more than 500 "Groupons" were sold. Unfortunately, the restaurant was not prepared for that level of demand and was unable to accommodate all the orders in time. Deliveries were late, and many of them were in "terrible condition."

Andrew Mason, the CEO of Groupon at the time, accepted the responsibility. He acknowledged that he had contracted with an organization that was not prepared to deal with the volume of the Groupon promotion. Groupon refunded the money to the customers who bought the coupons and gave away vouchers for future business. Groupon also created a video that featured a public apology regarding the incident. The video was sincere and informative, explaining exactly what happened, holding nothing back.

This incident demonstrates one of the issues that social commerce companies may face, and it shows the importance of transparent communication in social media. In this section, we will present several special applications and describe some major deployment issues.

Social Networking Helps Customer Service in Small Companies

Most of the social media examples provided so far in this book have dealt with large companies. What about the small ones? Do they use social media the same way? Obviously, there are some applications the SMEs (small and medium enterprises) cannot afford. However, there are many affordable applications, as illustrated next.

Example

Teusner Wines (**teusner.com.au**) is a small boutique winery (five employees in 2014) in Australia. Using Twitter for a few years, the company's one-person marketing department:

- Initiates online conversations about wine with influential people in the wine business.
- Sends tweets to people the company find talking about Teusner Wines, praising them for trying the wines.
- Starts to build trust with customers via conversations.
- Invites people to tour the winery and taste the wines (resulting in an excellent response).
- Advises potential customers in the United States and Canada where they can purchase the Australian wine.
- Collects real-time feedback from customers.
- Encourages customer-to-customer online conversations.
- Posts customer reviews on Twitter.
- Shares all information with Twitter followers.

All this was done by a tiny company at a minimal financial cost; however, it did take quite a bit of staff time. The company now (2015) is using Instagram, Facebook, and its website for actively marketing its wines online.

For additional examples of small companies and the use of social media, see **socialmediatoday.com/social-customer**, Chap. 11, and an infographic at **socialmediatoday.com/1603731/small-business-guide-social-media-mastery**.

Customer-Touching Applications

As described earlier, *customer-touching applications* are those where customers use interactive computer programs rather than interacting face-to-face with a live representative. The following are several popular customer-touching applications.

Personalized Web Pages and Blogs

Many companies provide customers with tools to create their own individual Web pages (e.g., **my.yahoo.com** and **sites.google.com** and blogs (e.g., **wordpress.com** and **blog.com**).

Social networks do the same. Companies can deliver customized information efficiently (such as product information and warranty information) when the customer logs on to a vendor's Facebook page, or to the customer's personalized page on the vendor's site. Not only can a customer retrieve information from the vendor's site, but the customer can also interact with the vendor. Much of the interaction is facilitated by social media tools.

Web Self-Service

The Web environment provides an opportunity for customers to serve themselves. Known as *Web self-service*, this strategy provides tools for users to perform activities previously done by corporate customer service personnel. Well-known examples of Web self-service are the tracking systems provided by FedEx, USPS, and UPS.

Self-service applications can be used by customers and employees, suppliers, and any other business partners. An example is the self-service provided by Canon's customer support unit (see Consona 2008–2009 for details). In general, Web 2.0 also supports self-service by allowing customers to get help from other customers (e.g., see Libert and Spector 2010).

Self-Configuration, Customization, and Co-design

One of the best ways to provide SCRM to customers is to provide them with the ability to customize products and services. This is especially important for complex products with many possible configuration options. Therefore, many build-to-order vendors, such as Dell and Blue Nile (diamond jewelry), provide customers with tools to self-configure products or services (e.g., "build your own ring"). In addition, social communities, such as Polyvore (see Chap. 6), facilitate self-configuration. Usually, the configured order is transferred directly to production so that production decisions can be based on real time customer demand, expediting the manufacturing process. Customers may seek advice from other customers regarding what to include in a configuration (e.g., see Libert and Spector 2010).

Another aspect is co-design, involving customers in customer service design, as well as in products (e.g., the LEGO Gallery; **lego.com/gallery**). This can be facilitated by crowdsourcing, as we will illustrate in Chap. 8.

Customer-Centric Applications

The fourth Patricia Seybold Group's category, *customer-centric applications*, is synonymous with *CRM analytics*. **CRM analytics** refers to the application of business analytic techniques and business intelligence such as data mining and online analytic processing to CRM applications. In SCRM we use social analytics (see Chap. 10).

Analytics Tools

The main tools used in SCRM analytics are measuring, reporting, and data mining. Managers collect data from social media and other websites and mine them to find marketing opportunities, improve CRM, and solve customers' problems. According to the Web Analytics Association's definition, "Web analytics is the overall term for 'measurement, collection, analysis and reporting of Internet data for purposes of understanding and optimizing Web usage'" (see **digitalanalyticsassociation.org/Files/PDF_standards/ WebAnalyticsDefinitions.pdf**). For details on CRM analytics, see **searchcrm.techtarget.com/definition/CRM-analytics**. For coverage of social commerce analytics, see Chap. 10.

CRM analytics can lead to not only better and more productive customer relations in terms of sales and service, but also to improvement in the planning and analysis of marketing promotions, as well as other improved marketing strategies.

7.7   STRATEGY AND IMPLEMENTATION ISSUES OF SOCIAL CRM

The success or failure of SCRM initiatives depends upon the strategy and the implementation processes. Unfortunately, there is no one recipe for either strategy or implementation since both depend on many variables (see Lacy et al. 2013, Jamieson 2014, and Chaps. 10 and 11). In this section, we will cover some key issues related to both topics.

Social CRM Strategy

The topic of social commerce strategy in general will be described in Chap. 10. Here, we list some basic issues related to SCRM:

- *Strategy for handling negative criticism, a part of reputation management*. This topic was described in Chap. 5. Companies need policies on what is considered negative criticism and how to react to it.
- *Strategy for integrating social media into the traditional CRM*.
- *Strategy for dealing with resistance to change by employees*.
- *Employing reactive or proactive strategies*.
- *Reactive customer service* can be performed, for example, by setting up Twitter listening posts using Tweet Deck (**tweetdeck.com**) or Followerwonk (**follerwonk.com**) to search for conversations with key words relevant to one's company. A company can then give their employees who

are listening to social conversations, guidelines needed for solving problems, so that the employees can directly take care of any issue.
- *Proactive customer service* engages customers before there is a problem, and interacts with customers to improve products and customer service.
- *Controlling customer interactions on Facebook*. Companies need to develop a strategy for controlling customer interactions, both for B2C and B2B.

Example: Bonobos (bonobos.com)

According to Bonobos, a small New York-based online men's clothing company that aims to provide excellent customer experience, used two social media-driven projects:

1. Bonobos formed 1,000-member alpha and beta testing groups solely through Twitter. Before they launch new designs for pants or dress shirts, they use the testing groups to review the products. By using the groups, the company has gained valuable information regarding the customers' preferences. Then, Bonobos transfers that information to their designers.
2. Bonobos also ran blog contests.

Example: Social Commerce Strategy at Threadless

Threadless (**threadless.com**) is a global e-commerce company that produces T-shirts and other merchandise designed by and for its 2.5 million community members. The company is using crowdsourcing (Chap. 8) to get the most out of social media. Threadless uses strategy and software to manage its customer interaction on Facebook (**facebook.com/ threadless**). Specifically, the company's software helps to monitor wall posts and respond to them appropriately. See Swan (2014) for details.

For more on strategy regarding social CRM, see Chap. 10. Note that, since SCRM is an integral part of e-CRM, the strategies for the two are interrelated. For a discussion, see **en. wikipedia.org/wiki/Customer_relationship_management**.

For implementation issues using Salesforce.com products and services, see Taber (2014).

Mobile SCRM

As seen throughout the book, social commerce is facilitated by mobile technologies. This is especially true with social CRM where interactions, sharing, and collaboration can be greatly facilitated by mobile devices. For examples, discussion, strategy, and implementation, see Lacy et al. (2013). For a free e-book *Mobilizing Enterprise Applications: Trends, Best Practices and Strategy Advice*, see Sybase (2011).

For a free e-book on innovative CRM, *Top 5 Trends in Customer Service Innovation* see **img.en25.com/Web/ Pegasystems/%7B0cd45fa8-9c92-4a2c-a137- 9a3e7fdc9606%7D_Top-5-Trends-in-Customer-Service- Innovation-eBook.pdf**. For comprehensive coverage, see **zoho.com/crm/mobile** and Lacy et al. (2013).

SUMMARY

In this chapter, you learned about the following SC topics as they relate to the chapter's learning objectives.

1. **Define CRM, e-CRM, and SCRM.** CRM is a customer service that focuses on building a long-term and sustainable customer relationship. When CRM is supported and delivered electronically, it is called e-CRM. Most CRM programs today are supported electronically and facilitate the flow of information and interactions between customers and vendors, and enable customers' engagement online. CRM is a business strategy and its implementation involves business rules. It is also a technology platform with social characteristics. When the technology platform involves social media (e.g., Web 2.0 tools and social network sites), CRM is referred to as social CRM (SCRM). SCRM provides many benefits for both customers and vendors, which includes an improved relationship between the empowered customers and the vendors, as well as providing better service to customers.

2. **A model for customer interactions.** In this model, the Patricia Seybold Group divides the CRM interactions into four major groups: customer-facing applications, customer-touching applications, customer-centric intelligence applications, and other online networking applications. In each of these, social media can introduce some improvements to the interaction process. For example, in customer-facing applications, one can support customer-enterprise interactions by monitoring customers' conversations on social media platforms and by tweeting to facilitate communication.

3. **The evolution of social CRM.** SCRM evolved from CRM and e-CRM. The evolution can be described along the following five dimensions: The landscape (e.g., structure and focus); the touch points (e.g., the use of social media tools); the business processes (e.g., how to listen to customers); the technology (e.g., socially-oriented tools); and the organizational mindset (e.g., patterns of interactions). This evolution is driven by the explosive use of social network sites, by the rise of the social customer, and by the importance buyers place on social recommendations.

4. **Serving the social customer.** Customers are empowered by social networks; therefore, they can get attention quickly for problem resolution. For example, organizing a Facebook complaint blitz against a company is not difficult. Customers also can make suggestions for improvements and vote on them. Social media allows customers to help themselves and each other, simultaneously reducing merchants' expenses. Customers can become more loyal because they work more closely with vendors. Social networking activities may provide innovative ideas for improved and more efficient customer service (e.g., Twitter can be very helpful). Companies can listen to customers in social network forums, provide easy-to-navigate websites, provide tools for user-generated content and quick problem resolution, and much more.

5. **Social CRM in the enterprise.** Social CRM is also used in the enterprise mainly by salespeople and field service employees. Most applications center on improved communication and collaboration. It helps to increase sales leads. Major vendors, such as Salesforce.com, provide social media features in their standard CRM tools. The use of social media can also facilitate relationships with employees and business partners.

6. **Special SCRM applications and issues.** Many special applications exist. Vendors such as Oracle and Salesforce. com provide applications that harness social media technologies. These are deployed in all segments of the CRM field (see Sect. 7.2). Representative applications include reputation management, SME enablers, Web page personalization, Web self-service and self-configurations, and the use of CRM analytical tools.

7. **Strategy and implementation.** For large-scale SCRM initiatives, strategy and implementation plans are needed. Several issues need to be included; they range from a strategy to handling negative customer comments to dealing with employee resistance to change. These issues are fairly generic and are described in Chaps. 10 and 11.

KEY TERMS

Autoresponder	169
CRM analytics	173
Customer interaction center (CIC)	161
Customer relationship management (CRM)	158
Electronic customer relationship management (e-CRM or CRM 1.0)	158
Sales force automation (SFA)	171
Social customer relationship management (SCRM or CRM 2.0)	158
Social customer	166

REVIEW QUESTIONS

1. Why and how are customers empowered by social networks?
2. Define CRM and e-CRM.
3. Describe social CRM.
4. List the major benefits of SCRM to customers and enterprises.
5. Describe the different ways customers and companies interact (per Patricia Seybold Group).
6. List the five dimensions of the evolution of CRM to SCRM.
7. List the capabilities of SCRM that can help salespeople (including SFA).
8. Describe Cipriani's different dimensions along which CRM has evolved to social CRM.
9. Define social customers and describe their characteristics.
10. Provide some examples of how social customers are properly served.
11. List some SCRM tools.
12. How can social media improve call centers?
13. Describe autoresponding.

TOPICS FOR DISCUSSION AND DEBATES

1. Enter **socialmediatoday.com/social-customer**. Choose five bloggers' posts about SCRM and the social customer; discuss each briefly.
2. Compare how customer service can be provided by a live chat with a person or by a virtual chat that is provided by an avatar (e.g., at ASB Bank's Virtual Branch on Facebook; **apps.facebook.com/asbvirtualbranch** or at Alaska Airlines; **alaskaair.com** "Ask Jenn"). Also check **collegeweeklive.com** (colleges are chatting live now) and Microsoft (**support.microsoft.com/contactus**), which has both live agents online and virtual ("Welcome! I'm an automated service agent available 24/7 to answer your questions about Microsoft Customer Service. Type your question or topic in the space below and click Ask or type '?' to see how I can help you"). Could customer conversations with virtual customer service agents be of equal quality to that with live customer service assistance one day? Debate the issue.
3. Clinique has a comprehensive customer service platform. They offer e-mail, phone service, and live chat. The live chat platform (**clinique.com/customer_service/chatlivenow.tmpl**) has regular live chat, live chat with your photo, and face-to-face live chat using a webcam and speakers. Describe the multichannel service support concept. Comment on the different modes.

4. Enter **altimetergroup.com** and view the webinar "Social CRM Use Cases: 5Ms and Marketing" (**vimeo.com/10788611**), which follows Altimeter Group's 2010 published open research report titled "Social CRM: The New Rules of Relationship Management." (See **slideshare.net/jeremiah_owyang/social-crm-the-new-rules-of-relationship-management**.) Discuss the 5 M's: monitoring, mapping, management, middleware, and measurement.
5. Discuss the five dimensions along which CRM evolved to SCRM, including the major differences in each.
6. Discuss the role of microblogging in SCRM.
7. Discuss the relationship between autoresponding and live chat.
8. Discuss the roles that microblogging (e.g., tweeting) can play in SCRM.
9. Discuss the differences between traditional customers and social customers.
10. Discuss how SCRM handles customer problems.
11. Read Ali's (2013) article and discuss its major conclusions.
12. Enter **reachable.com** and examine all the tool's capabilities. Write a report.
13. Enter **sproutsocial.com** and find its features. Write a summary.

INTERNET EXERCISES

1. Enter **crmbuyer.com/edpick/69895.html** and identify five strategies suggested for improved customer service.
2. Enter **blippy.com** and find the services it provides to customers.
3. View the video "Social Experience Overview" (1.38 minutes) from RightNow Company at **youtube.com/watch?v=hg3-mWGttwA**. Describe how the company's product can help the customer of each participating vendor. Write a summary.
4. Read Oracle's "Best Practices for Creating a Voice of the Customer Service Program Using Oracle RightNow CX Cloud Service" (2012) at **oracle.com/us/products/applications/bespractices-voice-customer-prg-1585083.pdf**. Find out how they measure customer sentiment with SmartSense. Write a report.
5. Enter **gauravbhalla.com** and find ten insights regarding customer-driven strategies. Write a report.
6. Enter Salesforce Radian6 (**salesforcemarketingcloud.com/products/social-media-listening**) and find their activities in the SCRM area. Write a report.
7. Enter **salesforce.com** and identify all SCRM activities supported by the company, especially those related to their Chatter product. View the slide show at

slideshare.net/Salesforce/salesforce-customer-servicebest-practices-25640141. Write a report.

8. Enter **facebook.com/dreamforce** and **salesforce.com/dreamforce**. Find topics that deal with SCRM. Write a summary.

9. Enter **socialtechnologyreview.com** and find out what they offer to vendors in the area of SCRM.

10. Enter Microsoft Dynamics (**microsoft.com/en-us/dynamics/crm.aspx**) and identify all major contributions to SCRM. Write a report.

11. Enter Oracle Social CRM Applications (**oracle.com/us/products/applications/social-crm/index.html**) and find out how Oracle uses its technology to provide social CRM. Write a report.

TEAM ASSIGNMENTS AND PROJECTS

1. **Assignment for the Opening Case**

   Read the opening case and answer the following questions:

   (a) What social media tools and platforms does Sony use?

   (b) How does each tool facilitate customer service?

   (c) What are the major benefits of social CRM to Sony?

   (d) Relate Sony's use of Pinterest to social CRM.

   (e) Enter **community.sony.com**. Find CRM-related activities. Summarize.

   (f) Go to Sony's community and ask a question. Get results. Summarize four experiences.

2. Read Bernoff and Schadler (2010) article "Empowered." Discuss the different tools companies can use to "fight back."

3. Post questions on Facebook, Twitter, YouTube, LinkedIn, Wikianswers, and so on, regarding CRM. Check the quality of answers you get from people in these social networks. Write a report about your experience.

4. Search for a group on a social network that is interested in social CRM. Join the group. Follow the discussions for one month. Each group member concentrates on one topic from this chapter and interacts with the group about this topic. Each member prepares a report, and the group makes a summary presentation for the class.

5. Major CRM vendors (e.g., **salesforce.com**, **oracle.com/us/solutions/crm/overview/index.html**, **sap.com**, **microsoft.com**, **netsuite**, **moxiesoft**, and **lithium.com**) added Web 2.0 tools to their standard CRM packages (consult Diana 2011). Each team (or member) investigates one vendor and writes a report on the finding. A summary of the finding is then presented to the class.

6. Read Sysomos Inc. (2011), and build a strategy for airlines, banks, or a telecom company that targets followers, advocates, and influencers. Comment on each of the four parts of the paper.

REFERENCES

Ali, S. N. "How Does Social CRM Work for Brands?" September 13, 2013. **cygnismedia.com/blog/social-crm-for-brands** (accessed December 2014).

Baker, P. "Social Media Adventures in the New Customer World." April 30, 2015. **crmbuyer.com/story/69895.html** (accessed July 2015).

Beal, V. "What's the difference between CRM and eCRM?" Undated. **ehow.com/info_8098762_difference_between_CRM_eCRM.html**. Accessed Dec 2014

Bernoff, J., and T. Schadler. "Empowered." *Harvard Business Review*, July 2010. **hbr.org/2010/07/empowered/ar** (accessed December 2014).

Boardman, S. "Creating a Lifelong Customer: The Journey from CRM to CXMApril 30, 2013. **information-management.com/news/creating-a-lifelong-customer-the-journey-from-crm-to-cxm-10024347-1.html** (accessed December 2014).

Carr, D. F. "Roomba Robots Listen to Social Media." *InformationWeek*, September 28, 2011.

Chess Media Group (in collaboration with Mitch Lieberman). "Guide to Understanding Social CRM." White Paper, June 2010. **chessmediagroup.com/resources/white-papers/guide-to-understanding-social-crm** (accessed December 2014).

Cipriani, F. "Social CRM: Concept, Benefits, and Approach to Adopt." November 17, 2008. **slideshare.net/fhcipriani/social-crm-presentation-761225** (accessed December 2014).

Consona. "Canon Customers Get Great Service Thanks to Canon ITS and Consona." Consona CRM White Paper, 2008–2009.

Diana, A. "14 Leading Social CRM Applications." March 23, 2011. **informationweek.com/software/social/14-leading-social-crm-applications/d/d-id/1096802?** (accessed December 2014).

Dignan, L. "iRobot Launches New Roomba: Five Innovation Lessons." November 12, 2013. **zdnet.com/irobot-launches-new-roomba-five-innovation-lessons-7000022993** (accessed December 2014).

Doligalski, T. *Internet-Based Customer Value Management*. New York: Springer, 2015.

Eckerle, C. "Social Email Integration: Sony Electronics Nets 3,000 Clickthroughs from Email to "Pin" on Pinterest." Case Study. April 23, 2013. **marketingsherpa.com/article/case-study/sony-nets-3000-clickthroughs-pinterest** (accessed December 2014).

Egeland, B. "One Case for Twitter—Comcast/Salesforce Case Study." *Project Management Tips*, July 25, 2009. **pmtips.net/case-twitter-comcast-salesforce-case-study** (accessed December 2014).

Fagan, L. "Free eBook: How Social CRM Connects You to Customers." April 3, 2014. **blogs.salesforce.com/company/2014/04/free-ebook-social-crm.html** (accessed December 2014).

Greenberg, P. *CRM at the Speed of Light: Social CRM 2.0 Strategies, Tools, and Techniques for Engaging Your Customers*, 4th ed. New York: McGraw-Hill, 2009.

Henschen, D. "From CRM to Social." *InformationWeek*, March 9, 2012.

Holland, A. "How Sony Connects Social Media Monitoring to ROI (and You Can, Too)." December 6, 2011. **raventools.com/blog/how-sony-connects-social-media-monitoring-to-roi-and-you-can-too** (accessed December 2014).

Hootsuite. "OCBC Bank: Investing in Social Customer Service." November 2 2014. **enterpriseinnovation.net/whitepaper/ocbc-bank-investing-social-customer-service**. Accessed Dec 2014

Huba, J. *Monster Loyalty: How Lady Gaga Turns Followers into Fanatics*. New York: Portfolio Hardcover, 2013.

Jack, D. "2013 Forrester Groundswell Entry-Sony Electronics: Support Channels Show Dramatic Improvements in Consumer Engagement and Help Boost Sales." *Lithium Technologies*. August 27, 2013. **lithosphere.lithium.com/t5/lithium-s-view-blog/2013-Forrester-Groundswell-Entry-Sony-Electronics-Support/ba-p/100214** (accessed December 2014).

Jamieson, C.M. *The Small Business Guide to Social CRM*. Birmingham, UK: Packt Publishing, 2014.

Lacy, K. et al. *Social CRM for Dummies*. Hoboken, NJ: John Wiley & Sons, 2013.

Libert, B., and J. Spector. *Crowdsourcing Customer Service: How May We Help We?* Upper Saddle River, NJ: Pearson Education, 2010.

Metz, A. *The Social Customer: How Brands Can Use Social CRM to Acquire, Monetize, and Retain Fans, Friends, and Followers.* New York: McGraw-Hill, 2011.

Minkara, O., and A. Pinder Jr. "Voice of the Customer: Big Data as a Strategic Advantage." April 2014. Aberdeen Group.

Morgan, J. "What Is Social CRM?" November 3, 2010. **socialmediaexaminer.com/what-is-social-crm** (accessed December 2014).

Olson, P. "A Twitterati Calls Out Whirlpool." *Forbes*, September 2, 2009.

Oracle. "It's All about the Salesperson: Taking Advantage of Web 2.0." White Paper, August 2008. **oracle.com/us/products/applications/051279.pdf** (accessed December 2014).

Oracle. "With RightNow, iRobot's World-Class Social Contact Center Successfully Engages the Modern Consumer." 2011. **oracle.com/us/corporate/customers/customersearch/irobot-rightnow-cs-1563785.html** (accessed December 2014).

Parature. *New E-Book Delivers Need-to-Know Social Customer Service Best Practice* (Free). Herdon, VA: Parature (Microsoft), 2014.

Petersen, R. "16 Case Studies That Prove Social CRM." January 13, 2011. **barnraisersllc.com/2011/01/19-case-studies-show-social-media-builds-1-to-1-sales-relationships** (accessed December 2014).

Petersen, R. "21 Experts Define CRM in Their Own Words and Pictures." June 9, 2012. **barnraisersllc.com/2012/06/21-experts-define-crm-words-pictures** (accessed December 2014).

Revoo. "New Automated Review Translation Tool Brings Immediate International Social Commerce Benefits to Sony." Press Release, April 18, 2011. **reevoo.com/pages/press_sony_international_reviews** (accessed July 2015).

RightNow Technologies. "RightNow Helps iRobot Successfully Pioneer a New Market by Listening and Responding to Its Customers." Case Study, 2010. **rightnow.virtuos.com/resources/case-studies/iRobot-Case-Study.pdf** (accessed December 2014).

Roebuck, K. *Social CRM: High-Impact Strategies - What You Need to Know: Definitions, Adoptions, Impact, Benefits, Maturity, Vendors.* Ruislip, Middlesex, UK: Tebbo, 2011.

Shih, C. *The Facebook Era: Tapping Online Social Networks to Market, Sell, and Innovate,* 2nd ed. Upper Saddle River, NJ: Pearson Education Inc., 2011.

Smith, B. "Using Social Media as a Customer Service Tool [Infographic]." *Social Media Today*, May 9, 2013. Available at **beingyourbrand.com/2013/03/17/using-social-media-as-a-customer-service-tool-infographic** (accessed December 2014).

Smith, N., R., et al. *The Social Media Management Handbook: Everything You Need to Know to Get Social Media Working in Your Business.* Hoboken, NJ: John Wiley & Sons, 2011.

Solis, B. "Nissan Embraces Social Media to Improve Customer Experiences and Foster Advocacy." January 30, 2012. **briansolis.com/2012/01/nissan-embraces-social-media-to-improve-customer-experiences-and-foster-advocacy** (accessed December 2014).

Staff Writers. "Facebook Chorus Prompts Qantas to Scrap Instruments Ban." December 30, 2010. **spacedaily.com/reports/Facebook_chorus_prompts_Qantas_to_scrap_instruments_ban_999.html** (accessed December 2014).

Stelzner, M., "Social CRM: How Marketing Can Benefit from Social Media and CRM." July 4, 2014. **socialmediaexaminer.com/social-crm-with-kyle-lacy** (accessed December 2014).

Strauss, J., and R. Frost. *E-Marketing*, 7th ed. Upper Saddle River, NJ: Pearson, 2014.

Swan, S. "Applying Blue Ocean Strategy to Digital Marketing." March 12, 2014. **smartinsights.com/online-brand-strategy/brnd-positioning/blue-ocean-strategy-digital-marketing** (accessed December 2014).

Sybase. *Mobilizing Enterprise Applications: Trends, Best Practices and Strategy Advice*, A free e-book by Sybase (a SAP company), November 2011.

Sysomos, Inc. "Social Media: Leveraging Sentiment and Influence to Develop a Customer Service Strategy." A White Paper, 2011. **social-media-monitor.co.uk/resources/whitepapers/Sysomos-Leverage-Sentiment.pdf** (accessed December 2014).

Taber, D., *Salesforce.com Secrets of Success: Best Practice for Growth and Profitability*, 2nd ed., Upper Saddle River, NJ: Prentice-Hall, 2014.

Taylor, J. "Social CRM Case Study: Sony Europe Creates a Community of Super-Fans." May 14, 2013. **oursocialtimes.com/social-crm-case-study-sony-europe-creates-a-community-of-super-fans** (accessed December 2014).

Valentine, V. "Significant Growth Projected for Social CRM." September 1, 2011. **information-management.com/news/gartner-predicts-social-crm-to-reach-1b-by-2012-10021057-1.html** (accessed December 2014).

Ziff Davis. "Why Social CRM is Important to Business." A White Paper, 2012. **hosteddocs.ittoolbox.com/zd_wp_whysocialcrmis-importanttobusiness_122812.pdf** (accessed December 2014).

Part III

Social Enterprise, Other Applications

The Social Enterprise: From Recruiting to Problem Solving and Collaboration

8

Content

Opening Case: How a Private Enterprise Network
Transformed CEMEX into a Social Business 181

8.1   Social Business and Social Enterprise 182

8.2   Business-Oriented Public Social Networking 185

8.3   Enterprise Social Networks 187

8.4   Online Job Markets and Training
in Social Networks 190

8.5   Managerial Problem Solving, Innovation,
and Knowledge Management 192

8.6   Crowdsourcing: Collective Intelligence
for Problem Solving and Content Creation 194

8.7   Social Collaboration (Collaboration 2.0) 197

References 201

Learning Objectives

Upon completion of this chapter, you will be able to:

1. Define social enterprise and describe its types and benefits.
2. Describe business-oriented public social networks.
3. Explain what enterprise social networks are and what their value is.
4. Discuss the online employment market, including its participants, and benefits.
5. Describe managerial problem solving, knowledge management, and dissemination in social commerce.
6. Describe and discuss online advisory systems.
7. Define crowdsourcing and describe its use in social commerce.
8. Explain how social media enhances collaboration.

OPENING CASE: HOW A PRIVATE ENTERPRISE NETWORK TRANSFORMED CEMEX INTO A SOCIAL BUSINESS

CEMEX (**cemex.com**) is a global building materials company based in Mexico, known primarily for its cement and ready-mix concrete. They do business in over 50 countries, throughout the Americas, Europe, Africa, the Middle East, and Asia, and maintain trade relationships in approximately 108 nations.

The Problem

The global economic slowdown of 2008–2014, and especially the drastic reduction in construction activities, drove CEMEX to try a host of traditional activities for cost reduction and increased productivity. However, this was not enough. In addition, top management was looking for ways to facilitate innovation. Given the company's global nature, top management realized that they needed to improve the company's internal and external collaboration to foster innovation.

Electronic supplementary material The online version of this chapter (doi:10.1007/978-3-319-17028-2_8) contains supplementary material, which is available to authorized users.

The Solution

Recently, many companies have implemented Enterprise 2.0 platforms that include social media tools as well as mechanisms of social network services. CEMEX decided to follow this trend. The company wanted to fully utilize the institutional knowledge possessed by its thousands of employees worldwide and make it available to others whenever needed.

CEMEX created an internal private social collaboration platform called Shift (**cemex.com/whatisshift**), which facilitates innovation, efficiency, and collaboration by letting employees share information and jointly conduct problem solving. Shift integrates some of the best capabilities of social networks with knowledge management (KM) and collaboration techniques (using IBM Global Business Services). Shift includes many internal communities; each is composed of people with similar interests.

The Results

The main result was the major change in the way that people worked together. The workforce became more cooperative; employees helped each other, shared more information and knowledge, were more empowered, and were able to be more mobile. Using in-house networking led to better internal collaboration.

Projects started to move more quickly, with faster time to market; therefore, business processes improved. In short, the company successfully leveraged the collective talents and skills of its employees. One internal community, the "Construction for the 21st Century," was challenged to suggest the strategic topics that CEMEX should focus on to remain a leader in the construction industry. The 400 community members of this 21st Century group responded by proposing innovative ideas, tactics, and strategies addressing the challenge. Overall, Shift drew 5,000 users by the end of its first month. By 2013, Shift had 25,000 users and over 500 groups. By 2014, the stock price of the company increased by over 300 %.

For more results and discussion, see **slideshare.net/soccnx/shifting-the-way-we-work-at-cemex** and Hinchcliffe (2012).

Sources: Based on Garcia et al. (2011), Hinchcliffe (2012), Nerney (2012), and Donston-Miller (2012).

LESSONS LEARNED FROM THE CASE

The CEMEX case illustrates a successful private in-house social network whose major objectives were to foster collaboration among its thousands of employees worldwide and facilitate idea generation via internal

crowdsourcing. Using Web 2.0 tools, collaboration became effective and efficient. A major result was idea generation and the evaluation and implementation of these ideas that facilitated innovation in the company. This is an example of social collaboration (Sect. 8.7). This chapter presents the major activities that social networks support within enterprises and the structure and benefits of public business networks. This chapter also presents the issues of the job market, recruiting and training networking in social innovation and knowledge management, crowdsourcing, and social collaboration.

8.1   SOCIAL BUSINESS AND SOCIAL ENTERPRISE

A major forthcoming trend in social commerce is its move to the enterprise level. This trend is related to the concept of social business. Let us define both terms.

Definitions: Social Business and Social Enterprise

The social enterprise concept has several names, definitions, and explanations. This concept is sometimes confused with the related concept of social business. Generally, one can distinguish between the two concepts that are often used interchangeably. Let us explain.

Social Business

A **social business** is a commercial for-profit or non-profit organization that is designed to achieve some social goal(s) such as improving human well-being, rather than just make a profit. SocialFirms UK (**socialfirmsuk.co.uk**) provides several other definitions of what they call *social enterprise*. They cite the following UK government definition: "A social enterprise is a business with primarily social objectives whose surpluses are reinvested for that purpose in the business or in the community, rather than being driven by the need to deliver profit to shareholders and owners" (see details at **socialfirmsuk.co.uk/faq/faq-what-social-enterprise-and-what-types-are-there**). About.com ("What is Social Media?") distinguishes between two types of social business: one type that describes companies that "aspire to social purposes more than to profit-making," and a seconds type that describes companies that "use social media to advance their business objectives." (See **webtrends.about.com/od/web20/a/social-media.htm**.)

The seconds type is the basis for the *social enterprise*. In summary, we view a *social business* as one that is built mainly around social objective(s), while a *social enterprise* uses social networking to facilitate commercial objectives.

A major organization dedicated to social business (which refers to itself as a "social enterprise"), is the *Social Enterprise Alliance* (**se-alliance.org/what-is-social-enterprise**).

Social Employees

The successful social business needs to empower its employees (e.g., using IBM Connections). For how IBM, AT&T, and other large corporations do this, see Burgess and Burgess (2013).

The Social Enterprise (Enterprise 2.0)

The **social enterprise** refers to the use of social media tools and platforms and conducting social networking activities in organizations, while its major objectives are either commercial or non-profit activities (e.g., the government). For an overview, see Ridley-Duff and Bull (2011).

The concept of the social enterprise has become a buzzword in recent years. Let us see what it is.

Social enterprise applications are spreading rapidly in the industry. They appear under different names, mostly as a social enterprise and Enterprise 2.0. According to Carr (2012), McKinsey (a management consultant company), predicts that the global revenue from social enterprise activities will reach $1 trillion in several years (two thirds of all social commerce value at that time).

Enterprise applications are conducted inside enterprises, on companies' private social networks, or on portals. They also are conducted on public social networks, both business-oriented (e.g., LinkedIn), and general networks, mostly Facebook and Twitter. Major applications are recruitment, collaboration, and problem solving. According to Kern (2012), enterprise social capabilities will facilitate a new type of collaboration, encourage business upgrades, and enable more vendor applications.

According to a 2009 IDC survey (reported by *BusinessWire* 2010), 57 % of U.S. workers in 2009 used social media for business purposes at least once per week. Today, that figure is higher. Corporations are rushing to get involved in several innovative ways, as will be described later in this chapter. Business networks are a core component in the social enterprise.

For additional definitions, characteristics, and discussion on social enterprise, see **centreforsocialenterprise.com/what.html**.

More Complex Definitions

In addition to the above definitions, there are some definitions that are more complex, as illustrated next.

The Social Business Forum's Definition

The Social Business Forum defines *social business* as "an organization that has put in place the strategies, technologies and processes to systematically engage all the individuals of its ecosystem (employees, customers, partners, suppliers) to maximize the co-created value" (**2012.socialbusinessforum.com/what-is-social-business**). The Forum also discusses the implications of this definition and its relevance, across and outside organizations. Note that an efficient creation of value using technology is emphasized.

IBM and IDC's Definition

IDC coined the term *social business* to refer to "those organizations that apply emerging technologies like Web 2.0 accompanied by organizational, cultural, and process changes to improve business performance in an increasingly connected global economic environment" (see IBM 2010 and IDC 2010). The IBM effort concentrates on improved collaboration. The basic idea is that social customers require organizations to significantly change the way they operate, so they can become social businesses. The new structure enables organizations to exploit the opportunities created by the social media environment. IBM is helping organizations become social businesses. (For an example of how they do this, see IBM's A Smarter Planet at **ibm.com/smarterplanet/us/en/?ca=v_smarterplanet**). IBM also has an extensive "social business video library."

Three interesting videos are recommended to better understand social business:
1. "Social PhD: Sandy Carter, IBM: How Do You Become a Social Business?" (1:04 minutes) at **youtube.com/watch?v=OZy0dNQbotg**
2. "How Do You Become a Social Business?" (3:28 minutes) at **youtube.com/watch?v=3Hov0l7SvAo**
3. "Social Business @ IBM" – An Interview with Luis Suarez, Social Computing Evangelist (8:50 minutes) at **youtube.com/watch?v=enudW2gHek0&feature=related**.

Notice that our definition of social enterprise is based on the use of social media tools and platforms. A related topic is *business networks*.

Business Networks

A *business network* refers to a group of people with a professional business relationship; for example, the relationships between sellers and buyers, buyers and suppliers, and professionals and their colleagues, such as the 21st Century Community at CEMEX. In this chapter, we use the term *buyers* to refer to agents buying something for a business (e.g., a purchasing agent). Such a network of people can form **business social networks**, which are business-oriented networks that are built on social relationships and can exist offline or online. For example, public places, such as airports or golf courses, provide opportunities to make new face-to-face business contacts if an individual has good social skills. Similarly, the Internet is also proving to be a good place to network and connect. In this book, we address online networks. The most well-known network is LinkedIn (**linkedin.com**). For a discussion about business social networks, see Bughin and Chui (2013).

Example: Toyo Engineering

Toyo Engineering is a global Japanese corporation. Toyo is working on large number of plant engineering projects in more than 50 countries offering a wide range of diversified technical services for the energy, oil refinement, chemical, pharmaceutical, and food industries. To improve collaboration between global subsidiaries, external business partners, and staff in remote locations, and to enhance communication between project management teams, and engineering, procurement, construction, and other business process units, the company is using social computing solutions from Oracle. Oracle Web Center provides: personalization, search and discovery, enterprise mashups, analytics, and management. For details, see **oracle.com/us/products/middleware/wc-content-customers-in-action-2016601.pdf**.

Types of Business Social Networks

There are three major types of business social networks: (a) *public networks* such as LinkedIn, which are owned and operated by independent companies, and are open to anyone for business networking. The networks connect, for example, sellers and buyers or employers and potential employees; (b) *enterprise private networks*, which operate inside companies, like CEMEX's Shift, in the opening case. These usually restrict membership to employees and sometimes to business partners. An example is USAA, which set up an internal social networking site using Microsoft's Sharepoint, for employees to get to know one another and send internal messages; and (c) *company-owned and hosted enterprise networks* that are controlled by a company but are open to the public, usually for brand-related networking (e.g., Starbucks, Dell).

The Benefits and Limitations of Enterprise Social Networking

Social networking appeals to business users for several reasons. For example, social networking makes it easy to: (a) find people and information about companies, (b) understand the relationships and communication patterns that make a company tick, and (c) create a common culture across large organizations.

The major reasons an organization becomes a social enterprise are that it has the abilities to:

- Improve collaboration inside the enterprise and with business partners
- Facilitate knowledge management (increase access to specialized knowledge)
- Build better customer and employee relationships
- Facilitate recruiting and employee retention
- Increase business and marketing opportunities (e.g., meet new potential business partners and/or customers)
- Reduce operations, communication, and travel costs
- Increase sales and revenue (e.g., more sales leads)
- Improve customer satisfaction
- Reduce marketing and advertising costs
- Improve the performance of employees and organizations
- Foster internal and external relationships
- Collect feedback from employees
- Build an effective workforce
- Improve decision-making capabilities, including forecasting
- "Spy" on competitors (intelligence gathering)
- Find experts and advice (internally and externally)
- Improve customer service and CRM
- Accelerate innovation and competitive advantage

For details of these and other benefits, see Carr (2012), Bughin and Chui (2013), and Sect. 8.2.

Enterprises that use social media extensively can reap the benefits found in the previous list and be transformed into social businesses. For details, see **ibm.com/social-business/us/en**.

Obstacles and Limitations

Some limitations, such as security of information and information pollution, slow down the growth of social enterprising. For details, see Forrester Consulting (2010) and **slideshare.net/norwiz/what-is-enterprise-20**.

How Web 2.0 Tools Are Used by Enterprises

Web 2.0 tools are used in different ways by various corporations. Typical uses are: increasing speed of access to knowledge; reducing communication costs; increasing speed of access to internal exports; decreasing travel costs; increasing employee satisfaction; reducing operational costs; reducing time-to-market for products/services; and increasing the number of successful innovations for new products or services.

For statistics showing which departments in the enterprise use the technology and what specific social media tools are used, see **idc-community.com/groups/it_agenda/social-business/whatarecompaniesdoingwithsocialinitatives-resultsfromthe2013socialbus**. Some of the uses outside the enterprise include recruitment, advice in problem solving, joint design, collaboration on supply chain issues, and marketing communication.

For a comprehensive slide presentation on Enterprise 2.0, see **slideshare.net/norwiz/what-is-enterprise-20**.

8.2 BUSINESS-ORIENTED PUBLIC SOCIAL NETWORKING

Social networking activities are conducted in both public and/or private social networking sites. For example, LinkedIn is a business-oriented public network, whereas Facebook is primarily a public social network used for socially-oriented activities. Facebook, however, allows its members to conduct business-oriented activities. "My Starbucks Idea" (**mystarbucksidea.force.com**) is an example of a company-hosted social network that is open to the public. In contrast, CEMEX's internal social network, Shift (see opening case), is open only to the company's employees and is considered private. In this section, we will concentrate on public social networks.

The following are some examples of business-oriented public social networks:

- **Google +.** Google + ("one Google account for everything"), which began operating in 2011, designated itself as a business-oriented social network. In its first year of operation, it had over 400 million members. In February 2014, it had over 1.15 billion users and 359 million active users (per **socialmediaslant.com/google-plus-traffic-stats-February-2014**). For an overview, see **martinshervington.com/what-is-google-plus** and Brogan (2012).
- **Ryze.** Similar to LinkedIn, Ryze (**ryze.com**), according to its website and About.com, is a business social networking site with a focus on the entrepreneur. Individuals can use Ryze to help build up a personal network and find new jobs, while companies can use Ryze to create a business community. Ryze is especially liked by young professionals, entrepreneurs, and business owners who want to create a networking community for their employees (per **webtrends.about.com/od/profiles/fr/what-is-ryze.htm**).
- **Yammer.** Yammer (**yammer.com**) is a collaborative social software vendor that operates as an enterprise social network. It mainly provides capabilities for collaboration. It is used in over 500,000 leading businesses worldwide, and is considered a socially-oriented communication and collaboration helper. (Microsoft acquired Yammer in 2012, and it is now part of the Microsoft Office Division.) For details, see Sect. 8.3.
- **LinkedIn.** Known as the premier business-oriented network, **linkedin.com** is the most popular network for business, as illustrated in Case 8.1. (See the infographic at **blog.hootsuite.com/social-network-for-work**.) LinkedIn is known primarily as a tool for recruiting and finding jobs (Sect. 8.4 and Martin 2013). LinkedIn shows content and provides customer service in a multitude of languages, including English, Spanish, French, and Tagalog, among others, with a plan for adding other languages in the future.

Case 8.1
SC Application

Linkedin: The Premier Public Business-Oriented Social Network

Let us look at LinkedIn (**linkedin.com**), the world's largest professional network. LinkedIn is a global business-oriented social networking site (offered in over 20 languages), used mainly for professional networking. By November 2014, it had over 332 million registered members in over 200 countries and territories. By 2014, there were 2.1 million different groups, each with a special interest. LinkedIn can be used to find jobs, people, potential clients, service providers, subject experts, and other business opportunities. The company became profitable in 2006; in Q3 2014, revenue was $568 million, an increase of 45 % compared to $393 million in the Q3 2013. According to their full year 2014 guidance, revenue is expected to range between $2.175 billion and $2.180 billion (per **investors.linkedin.com/releasedetail.cfm?ReleaseID=879471**). The company filed for an initial public offering in January 2011 and is one of the best performing on the stock market. A major objective of LinkedIn is to allow registered users to maintain a list of professional contacts (see **en.wikipedia.org/wiki/LinkedIn**), i.e., people with whom they have a professional relationship. The people in each person's network are called *connections*. Users can invite anyone, whether he or she is a LinkedIn user or not, to become a connection. When people join LinkedIn, they create a profile that summarizes their professional accomplishments. This profile makes it easier to be found by recruiters, former colleagues, and others. People can also meet new people and find opportunities for collaboration and marketing (see **linkedin.com/today/post/article/20140830075111-7859692-social-network-101-how-linkedin-works**).

LinkedIn is based on the concept of "degrees of connections." A *contact network* consists of a user's direct connections (called first degree connections), people connected to their first-degree connections (called seconds degree connections), and people connected to the seconds-degree connections (called third degree connections). Degree "icons" appear next to a contact's name. For more about degrees, see "Six Degrees of Separation – LinkedIn Style" at **thedigitalfa. com/d-brucejohnston/six-degrees-of-separation-linkedin-style**. The contact network makes it possible for a professional to gain an introduction, through a mutual, trusted contact, to someone he or she wishes to know. LinkedIn's officials are also members and have hundreds of connections each (see Elad 2014 and **linkedin.com**).

The "gated-access approach," where contact with any professional requires either a preexisting relationship or the intervention of a mutual contact, is intended to build trust among the service's users.

The searchable LinkedIn groups feature allows users to establish new business relationships by joining alumni, industry, professional, or other relevant groups.

LinkedIn is especially useful in helping job seekers and employers find one another. According to Ahmad (2014), 94 % of all U.S. recruiters use LinkedIn to browse for potential candidates. Job seekers can list their résumés, search for open positions, check companies' profiles, and even review the profiles of the hiring managers. Applicants can also make connections with existing contacts who can introduce them to a specific hiring manager. Based on the members' privacy settings, it is even possible for them to see who has looked at their profiles. For details, see **linkedin.com/company/linkedin/careers** and **linkedin.com/directory/jobs**.

Companies can use the site to post available jobs and find and recruit employees, especially those who may not actively be searching for a new position.

Smart Ways to Use Linkedin

LinkedIn is known mostly as a platform for recruitment, job searches, and making connections. However, the network offers many opportunities for marketing, advertising, sales, and more. Members can ask others to write employment or personal references for them. For a list of opportunities, see **linkedintelligence.com/smart-ways-to-use-linkedin**.

LinkedIn Answers, a feature for members to ask questions and let other members provide answers, was discontinued in 2013; however, there are similar options available (see **help. linkedin.com/app/answers/detail/a_id/35227**).

In mid-2008, LinkedIn launched LinkedIn DirectAds (renamed "Ads" in 2011). Ads, which is their version of Google's AdWords, is a self-service, text-based advertising product that allows advertisers to reach a targeted professional audience of their choosing (see their FAQ's at **help. linkedin.com/app/answers/detail/a_id/1015**). For a comparison between DirectAds and AdWords, see **shoutex.com/ linkedin-directads-google-adwords-ppc-1** and **shoutex. com/linkedin-directads-vs-google-adwords-2**. According to a study conducted by HubSpot, LinkedIn has a 'visitor-to-lead' conversion ratio that is 3 times higher than Facebook and Twitter (see **blog.hubspot.com/blog/tabid/6307/ bid/30030/LinkedIn-277-More-Effective-for-Lead-Generation-Than-Facebook-Twitter-New-Data.aspx**).

In 2008, LinkedIn joined forces with the financial news channel CNBC. The deal integrates LinkedIn's networking functionality into CNBC.com, allowing LinkedIn users to share and discuss financial and other news with their professional contacts. Community-generated content from LinkedIn, such as survey and poll results, are broadcasted on CNBC, and CNBC provides LinkedIn with programming, articles, blogs, financial data, and video content. Because of this connection, CNBC is able to draw insights from LinkedIn's global user base to generate new types of business content for CNBC to broadcast. In 2014, LinkedIn acquired Bright.com, which connects prospective employees with employers by using a computer algorithm (the "Bright Score") to find the best fit between a job seeker and a particular job (see **linkedin.com/company/bright.com**).

LinkedIn can also be used for several other marketing strategies such as creating special groups to promote interest in events, purchase paid media space, and following your competitors' online activities (e.g., see Schaffer 2011 and **linkedin.com/about-us**). Note that about 66 % of LinkedIn users are located outside the United States. For example, many users are in Brazil, India, the United Kingdom, and France. Over 1 million teachers use LinkedIn for educational purposes.

As previously mentioned, LinkedIn is a public company. It was an instant success, as the share price almost tripled the first day of trading. In contrast, shares of Monster, a major online recruiting company, plunged more than 60 % during 2011, mainly due to investors' fear that LinkedIn would take business away from Monster.

LinkedIn is constantly adding capabilities to its site. For example, in 2014 the company launched features that help increase local relevance.

Mobile Applications

A mobile version of LinkedIn, launched in February 2008, offers access to most features on the site by using mobile devices. The mobile service is supported in a multitude of languages, including Chinese, English, French, German, Japanese, and Spanish (for mobile devices and supported languages, see **help.linkedin.com/app/answers/detail/a_id/999**). A recent application is the ability to apply for jobs from smartphones and tablets.

Some Resources for Linkedin

The following are some useful resources for using LinkedIn: **blog.linkedin.com, mylinkedinpowerforum.com**, and **linkedin.com/search**.

For LinkedIn success stories, see Elad (2014), Schaffer (2011), and **cbsnews.com/news/linkedin-5-job-search-success-stories**.

Sources: Based on Elad (2014), Schaffer (2011), Bishop (2012), Gowel (2012), Ahmad (2014), and **linkedin. com**.

Questions

1. Enter **linkedin.com** and explore the site. Why do you think the site is so successful?
2. What features are related to recruiting and finding a job?
3. Conduct an investigation to find the company's revenue sources. Prepare a list.
4. Several companies have attempted to clone LinkedIn with little success. Why do you think LinkedIn is dominating?
5. Join the group called "eMarketing Association Network" on LinkedIn (free; it is a private group so you must request to join) and observe their activities regarding social media and e-commerce for one week. Write a report.

Several other international networks that are similar to LinkedIn are Wealink (**wealink.com**) in China, Rediff Pages (**pages.rediff.com**) in India, International High Potential Network (iHipo) (**ihipo.com**) in Sweden, and Moikrug (My Circle; **moikrug.ru**) in Russia.

There are many public business-oriented networks that focus on specific industries or types of professional specialties, some which are discussed next.

Networks for Entrepreneurs

Some business-oriented public networks are focused on entrepreneurial activities. A few examples are listed next.

- **Biznik (biznik.com).** Biznik is a community of entrepreneurs and small business owners dedicated to helping each other by sharing ideas and knowledge. According to **biznik.com/articles/collaboration-beats-the-competition**, "collaboration beats the competition." Their policy is that members must use their real names on the site and Biznik supplements its interactions with face-to-face-meetings.
- **EFactor (efactor.com).** This is the world's largest network of entrepreneurs (over 1 million members in 222 countries across 240 industries; 2014 data) it provides members with knowledge, tools, marketing, and expertise to succeed and make real, trustworthy, and lasting connections. Members connect with like-minded people and with investors.
- **Startup Nation (startupnation.com).** Participants in this community of startup owners and experts are helping others to start and operate new businesses. This is also a forum to grow a business, fund a business, and make connections. Sharing knowledge and ideas is the main objective.
- **Network of Entrepreneurial Women (nentw.com).** This is a grassroots organization for entrepreneurially-minded women. Members can attend events, network, and find programs to help them start and grow small businesses.
- **Inspiration Station (inspiration.entrepreneur. com).** Inspiration Station, a place for entrepreneurs to share inspiring ideas, is one of the best portals for small businesses and start-ups. It has a lot of useful information for business owners. It is also a great community for users to take advantage of, and connect with fellow business owners from around the globe. Inspiration Station is available on Facebook (**facebook.com/inspirationstation**), Twitter (**twitter. com/whatsinspiring**), and Instagram (**instagram. com/whatsinspiring**).
- **SunZu (sunzu.com).** SunZu is a network for people doing business that lets you meet, share, learn, trade, and grow with other business owners. Joining SunZu gives members access to people, learning opportunities, news, updates, business opportunities, and insights (see **sunzu.com/pages/about-sunzu**).

For 20 social networks for business professionals, see Gregory (2012). For 60 social media tools for entrepreneurs (2014), see **inc.com/jeff-haden/60-awesome-social-media-tools-for-entrepreneurs.html**.

8.3 ENTERPRISE SOCIAL NETWORKS

An increasing number of companies have created their own in-house, enterprise social networks. Some of these networks can be private, developed for use only by their employees, former employees, and business partners. Others are open to the public, although these are mostly used by their customers. Private networks are considered to be secured ("behind the firewall"), and are often referred to as *corporate social networks*. Such networks come in several formats, depending on their purpose, the industry, the country, and so forth. For the evolution of the networked enterprise, see Bughin and Chui (2010).

According to Boyd (2008), Scrupski and MacDonald developed a graphical view of Enterprise 2.0, that can be viewed as an overlapping space where Enterprise 2.0 intersects with social media, social collaboration, and digital marketing.

Taxonomy of Social Enterprise Applications

The following terms are frequently used in enterprise networking. Most will be discussed in this chapter.

1. **Networking and community building.** Conducting networking and community building, involving employees, executives, business partners, and customers.
2. **Crowdsourcing.** Gathering ideas, insights, and feedback from crowds (e.g., employees, customers, and business partners; see Sect. 8.2). Salesforce Success Community (**success.salesforce.com**) and My Starbucks Idea (**mystarbucksidea.force.com**) are examples.
3. **Social collaboration.** Collaborative work and problem solving using wikis, blogs, instant messaging, collaborative office documents, and other special purpose Web-based collaboration platforms such as Laboranova (**laboranova.com**).
4. **Social publishing.** This is the creation of user-generated content in the enterprise, which is accessible to all (e.g., **slideshare.net**; **youtube.com**).
5. **Social views and feedback.** Getting feedback and opinions from the enterprise's internal and external communities on specific issues.

Characteristics of Enterprise Social Networks

Enterprise social networks, like any social network, enable employees to create profiles and interact with one another. By encouraging interactions among members, a company can foster collaboration and teamwork, and increase employee satisfaction. The potential benefits of Enterprise

2.0 are described by Tuten (2010) and by Hinchcliffe at **zdnet.com/blog/hinchcliffe**.

For additional information, see the *International Journal of Social and Humanistic Computing*.

An Example of a Private Enterprise Network

In the opening case in Chap. 1, we introduced Starbucks' hosted enterprise network. We also described Sony's and iRobot's hosted enterprise social networks in Chap. 7. Many other companies also have enterprise networks of all kinds. Here is an example of another private network:

Example
The Greater IBM Connection (**ibm.com/ibm/greateribm**) is a global business and professional community ("alumni site") for current and former IBM employees that offers many resources, including a job posting site. Join The Greater IBM Connection community on a variety of social networks (e.g., Facebook, Twitter, LinkedIn). You also can share The Greater IBM Connection with your networks by posting a link to the community and using the hashtags **#greateribm** or **#ibmalumni** in your posts. To find Greater IBMers that share your interests, go to the 'Members' tab of the LinkedIn group and type a keyword that matches your interest (for example, 'social media'). When you find Greater IBMers you would like to connect with, select the 'Connect' button to invite them to connect with you. (See **ibm.com/ibm/greateribm/community_channels.shtml**.) The Greater IBM Connection also has a blog and a private group on LinkedIn.

How Enterprise Social Networking Helps Employees and Organizations

Enterprise social networking can help employees in one or more of the following ways:

1. **Quick access to knowledge, know-how, and "know-who."** As people list their skills, expertise, and experience, enterprise social networks can help simplify the job of locating people with specified knowledge and skills.
2. **Expansion of social connections and broadening of affiliations.** Enterprise social networks help managers and professionals get to know people better by interacting with them in online communities, and by keeping up with their personal information. Such interaction and information about others can decrease the social distance in a company.

3. **Self-branding.** People can become creative in building their profiles the way they want to be known. It helps them promote their personal brand within the corporation.
4. **Referrals, testimonials, and benchmarking.** Enterprise social networks can help employees prepare and display referrals and testimonials about their work and also benchmark them with their colleagues.

Benefits to Organizations

The benefits to organizations, as well as to employees, were presented in Sect. 8.1. In addition, the benefits to employees can develop into benefits to organizations in the long run.

Support Services for Enterprise Social Networks

Businesses can use a variety of services and vendors to support their social networking. Two examples follow.

Example 1: Socialcast

Socialcast (**socialcast.com**), a VMware company, is an online vendor providing internal social network platforms for businesses. Enterprises can use Socialcast to facilitate employees with collaboration and communication with coworkers. In 2014, the company had more than 30,000 customers in 190 countries. The platform connects people to knowledge, ideas, and resources. For details, see **socialcast.com/about**.

Example 2: Socialtext

Socialtext (**socialtext.com**) is an enterprise social software vendor, providing an integrated suite of Web-based applications, including social media tools and platforms. The company also provides Web security services. Businesses can benefit by keeping employees connected to the enterprise strategy and operations. For details, see **socialtext.com/about**.

Yammer: A Social Collaboration Platform

Yammer, Inc. (**yammer.com**) is a Microsoft company. According to its website, Yammer is "an Enterprise Social Network that brings together people, conversations, content, and business data in a single location. With Yammer, you can easily stay connected to coworkers and information, collaborate with team members and make an impact at work. And because Yammer can be easily accessed through a web browser or mobile device, you can connect and collaborate with coworkers anytime, anywhere. More than 200,000 companies worldwide [2014] use Yammer to engage employees, collaborate and innovate. As a platform, Yammer integrates easily with other systems to connect all of your business applications in a single social experience." Yammer is used for communication and collaboration within organizations, or between organizational members and pre-designated groups.

Key Features (compiled from Blair 2011 and from about.yammer.com/product/features).

Yammer's social networks allow users to:
- **Converse using enterprise microblogging.** Start a conversation, read posts, and actively collaborate with coworkers in real time using microblogging.
- **Create profiles.** Report your expertise, work experience, and contact information. You can upload photos, images, and documents. This will help you share information with others, and become easier to find.
- **Manage groups.** Create new groups or join private or public groups, and then discuss issues or collaborate with the group members. Invite team members to join and start collaborating right away.
- **Conduct secure and private messaging.** Create a private dialog with one or multiple coworkers, similar to what you can do on Facebook. Secure the messages with Yammer's security features.
- **Create external networks.** Create external networks for working with business partners.
- **Create a company directory.** Create a directory of all employees.
- **Archive knowledge.** Archive all online conversations to be fully searchable.
- **Use administrative tools.** Keep the Yammer network running smoothly with a suite of features built to increase managerial control.
- **Employ tagging.** Tag the content and message in the company's network to make content easy to search for and organize.
- **Integrate applications.** Install third-party applications into Yammer to increase the functionality of the company's network.
- **Deploy mobile capabilities.** Connect to the company's network from anywhere, at any time. Download free iPhone, Blackberry, Android, and Windows Mobile applications.

How Companies Interface with Social Networking

Enterprises can interface with public and/or private social networks in several ways. The major interfaces, which are shown in Fig. 8.1, are described next.

Fig. 8.1 The major interfaces with social networking

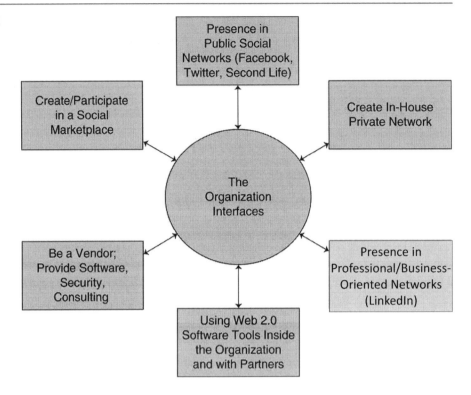

- Use existing public social networks, such as **facebook.com** or virtual worlds, such as **secondlife.com**, to create pages and microcommunities; advertise products or services; and post requests for advice, job openings, and so forth.
- Create an in-house private social network and then use it for communication and collaboration among employees and retirees or with outsiders (e.g., customers, suppliers, designers). Employees can create virtual rooms in their company's social networks where they can deploy applications to share information or collaborate.
- Conduct business activities in a business-oriented or professional social network (e.g., **linkedin** or **sermo.com**; for physicians only).
- Create services for social networks, such as software development, security, consulting services, and more (e.g., Oracle, IBM, Microsoft).
- Use Web 2.0 software tools, mostly blogs, wikis, workspaces, microblogging (Twitter), and team rooms, and create innovative applications for both internal and external users.
- Create and/or participate in a social marketplace such as Fotolia (**us.fotolia.com**).

For a comprehensive report on implementing Enterprise 2.0 at IBM, see Chess Media Group (2012).

8.4 ONLINE JOB MARKETS AND TRAINING IN SOCIAL NETWORKS

A major area of activity in social networks, private and public, relates to human resource management.

Social Recruiting

Finding qualified employees in certain fields may be a difficult task. To accomplish this task, companies pay considerable fees to executive recruiters or third-party online companies such as **monster.com**, **careerbuilder.com**, and **jobthread.com**.

If job seekers are online and active in their search and in posting their résumés, there is a good chance that they will be seen by recruiters. In addition, many so-called passive job seekers are employed and are not actively looking for a new job. Therefore, it is important that both active and passive job seekers maintain a profile online that reflects them in a positive light, especially on LinkedIn and Facebook.

Both recruiters and job seekers are moving to a new recruiting platform—the online social networks—mostly LinkedIn, Facebook, and Twitter (e.g., using TwitJobSearch; **twitjobsearch.com**, a job search engine allowing employers to post job ads on Twitter). Enterprise recruiters are scanning online social networks, blogs, and other resources to identify and find information about potential employees.

Clearly, the electronic job market has benefits, but it can also create high turnover costs for employers by facilitating employees' movements to look for better jobs. In addition, finding candidates online is more complicated than most people think, mostly due to the large number of résumés available in social media sites. To facilitate recruitment, top recruiters are seeking the benefits of Web tools, like interviewing candidates by video from remote locations. They also use social media tools and many social networking sites to help people get hired faster. Some recruiters send Facebook "friend" invitations to candidates whom they have interviewed. However, this can be a controversial practice due to ethical implications (see **archive-org.com/page/3465138/2014-01-04/http://www.naceweb.org/s06122013/social-media-privacy-law.aspx**).

Facebook has many features that help people find jobs (see **jobcast.net** for jobseekers and employers to connect; Social Jobs Partnership [**facebook.com/socialjobs**], a collaboration between Facebook and the U.S. Department of Labor); and Sundberg (2010).

LinkedIn provides a similar service. For an overview and examples, see Sundberg (2011). LinkedIn's search engine can help employers quickly find appropriate candidates. For finding employees (jobs) in other countries, one can use LinkedIn or Xing (**xing.com**). An interesting global recruiting community is EURES (**ec.europa.eu/eures**), which specializes in online recruiting in Europe.

Lately, there has been an increased use of mobile recruiting tools in general, and on Twitter in particular (see Martin 2013), as aids for people who are searching for jobs. The following are possible activities:

(a) Search for posted positions
(b) Follow job search experts
(c) Follow and read about people in your field
(d) Engage, communicate with people, and ask for help
(e) Connect with people at your target companies

For more tips on how to do this, see Scott (2013). For an infographic showing how using social media can help you land a new job, see **mashable.com/2013/01/23/social-media-your-next-job-infographic**.

Recruiting and Job Searching Using Social Networks

Most public social networks, especially those that are business-oriented, facilitate recruiting and job finding. For example, recruiting is a major activity on LinkedIn, and was the driver for the site's development (see Case 8.1, page 181). To be competitive, companies must look at the global market for talent. Luckily, searchers can use global social networking sites to find it. Large companies are using their in-house social networks to find in-house talent for vacant positions. Furthermore, some claim that social media has significantly changed the hiring process (e.g., see Huff

2014). For how to use social media to impress recruiters see Salpeter (2014).

According to a Jobvite survey on social recruiting (2013), 94 % of companies use, or plan to use, social media to recruit and hire new employees, while 78 % have hired a candidate through social media. Of these, 94 % use LinkedIn, 65 % use Facebook, and 55 % use Twitter. Among these, the success rate for hiring is very high on LinkedIn (92 %), moderate on Facebook (24 %), and low on Twitter (14 %). See **web.jobvite.com/rs/jobvite/images/Jobvite_SocialRecruiting2013.pdf**.

As described earlier, LinkedIn, Facebook, MySpace, and Craigslist provide job listings, in competition with online recruiters such as Monster. Many other social networks offer job listings as well. For how to land a job using Facebook, see Morrison (2011). For a comprehensive case study on how to use social media to recruit, see Brouat (2011).

In one example, Salesforce.com (**salesforce.com**), a CRM software company, has partnered with Facebook to allow Salesforce.com customers to build Facebook applications using the Force.com toolkit.

Note that, while over 90 % of recruiters use social networks for seeking and researching qualified candidates, nearly 69 % have rejected candidates due to the content posted on their social network sites, according to a 2011 Reppler study (reported by Bennett 2011). It is important for employees to keep their social media personal information secure (or as private as possible). Another issue for candidates is that many times employers have discovered through social networks that their employees are looking for work elsewhere. For recruiting via gamification, see Greenberg (2014). For a thorough guide to job searching with social media, see Waldman (2013).

Virtual Job Fairs and Recruiting Events

Virtual job fairs offer strategies for quickly finding qualified candidates at a reduced cost. These are done using special vendor sites (e.g., **on24.com**, **expos2.com**, and **brazencareerist.com**), virtual world sites, social networks, or the employers' websites. For an overview, see Martin (2010).

The following are a few examples:

- IBM needed qualified employees for leadership positions in Africa. To quickly attract qualified employees, it used ON24 to conduct a job fair. For the complete story, see **on24.com/case-studies/ibm-job-fair**.
- P&G of Western Europe conducts annual virtual recruiting conferences using INXPO platform. The event is successful and it is used as a model for other European companies. For a complete description, see **inxpo.com/assets/pdfs/CS_P&G.pdf**.

- The state of Michigan periodically conducts virtual career fairs where job seekers and recruiters meet online. The latest ones were held in November 2014. For details, see **michiganvirtualcareerfair.com**.

Virtual job fairs occur frequently in virtual worlds, and may be associated with virtual trade shows, which are described in Chap. 9.

Training Employees

Several companies use enterprise social networking, and virtual worlds in particular, for training purposes. For example, IBM has run management and customer interaction training sessions in Seconds Life. Bernoff and Schadler (2010) provide an example of video training at Black & Decker using user-generated videos posted on YouTube. These videos help reduce training time.

For using social networks to enhance employee learning, see Brotherton (2011) and **unitek.com/training/blog/unitek-education-citrix-training-hands-on-training-in-a-virtual-world**.

Training for Social Media Use

Some businesses are creating training programs to show their employees how the use of social media can be a valuable business tool. Training is done by using traditional training methods and social training tools. In one example, Telstra (**telstra.com.au**), Australia's leading telecommunications and information services company, made social media training mandatory for all its 40,000 plus employees. For details, see **mashable.com/2009/12/16/Telstra-social-media**. For how to conduct social media training, see Schwartzman (2011). For an example of what can be done with social media to conduct effective training, see **trainingmag.com/how-train-employees-using-social-media.**

8.5   MANAGERIAL PROBLEM SOLVING, INNOVATION, AND KNOWLEDGE MANAGEMENT

Managers consistently engage in decision making and problem solving; however, some of the problems are difficult to solve and require specialized knowledge. Thus, a major activity in an organization is discovering and preserving the knowledge of experts for future problem solving. In addition, idea generation is the first major task in a problem-solving process, and it is an essential activity in facilitating innovation. Social media can facilitate all these activities. For an example of *Innovation 2.0*, see Spigit (2011).

Idea Generation and Problem Solving

Bernoff and Li (2008) suggest deployment of social networking for aiding research and development, gaining insight from conversations, and using the input to encourage innovations.

IBM's Innovation Projects and Communities

As a technology leader, IBM has created several innovation centers around the world. It also has several social commerce-oriented projects and communities such as:

- *IBM Jams.* The IBM "Jam" is an Internet-based platform for conducting conversations through brainstorming. Each year, the "Jam" focuses on a different topic. (See **collaborationjam.com**.) In 2011, for example, it was centered around social business (see **ftp.software.ibm.com/ftp/info/social/IBM_Social_Business_Jam_Report.pdf**. In 2013, it was called 'Client Experience Jam.'
- *IBM Connections*. IBM Connections is a social platform for businesses that, according to IBM, "lets you access everyone in your professional network, including your colleagues, customers, and partners."

Problem-Solving Activities

An increasing number of companies use social networking and crowdsourcing (Sect. 8.6) to facilitate problem solving. For an overview, see Liang and Turban (2011/2012).

Here are several examples of problem-solving professional sites:

- HP launched an in-house private social network for their own IT professionals around the world. This network is called "HP Enterprise Business Community" (see **h30499.www3.hp.com**).

  The site offers almost all the features that currently are being offered by public social networks (e.g., Facebook), but is also equipped with HP system management tools. The site offers IT workers a Web platform for troubleshooting and discussing recurrent IT problems. The collected information is entered into a repository of information for future use.
- Some pharmaceutical companies are collaborating with **sermo.com**, a social-networking site, exclusively for licensed physicians. The network provides for interaction and discussion between pharmaceutical professionals and the physicians who use Sermo. Sermo generates revenue by facilitating market research and sharing its content with pharmaceutical companies and clinical research organizations, among others.

Other examples of problem solving social-oriented activities include finding experts and mapping communities of expertise.

Consider the following examples of social networking for *knowledge management* and *expert location*:

- InnoCentive (**innocentive.com**) is a global leader in crowdsourcing innovation problems with over 355,000 registered problem solvers from nearly 200 countries, who compete to provide ideas and solutions to important business, social policy, etc. challenges (for cash rewards -- $5,000 to $1+ million based on the complexity of the problem and nature of the challenge; Data current as of January 2015.)
- Northwestern Mutual Life Insurance Company (**northwesternmutual.com**) created an internal enterprise social network (called Mutualnet) and an internal blog (called (Mutualblog). They also have an internal Yammer account, which is used by over 1,000 employees to have dialog and make connections.
- Caterpillar (**caterpillar.com**) created a knowledge network system for its employees and dealers, and the company markets the software to other companies.

Companies also create *retiree corporate social networks* to keep retirees connected with each other and with the organization where they used to work. Retirees possess a vast source of knowledge that can be tapped for productivity increases and problem solving (e.g., Alumni Connect from SelectMinds; an Oracle Company). With 64 million 'baby boomers' retiring within the next 8 years, preserving their knowledge is critical.

Knowledge Management and Social Networks

Knowledge management (KM) is a process of capturing (or creating) knowledge, storing it, constantly updating it, disseminating it, and using it whenever necessary. This way, knowledge is shared for useful purposes, ranging from problem solving to increased productivity. Most activities in knowledge management can be facilitated by social media tools and platforms.

Knowledge Creation and Sharing

Online communities are a major forum for knowledge creation. For example, social collaboration tools or crowdsourcing can facilitate knowledge creation. This area has several variations. One variety is limited within a single company, such as Knowledge Network at Caterpillar Inc. Another is a public social network whose members are interested in a knowledge management common topic such as knowledge acquisition. Yet another type is a combination of the two. The major purposes of such communities are:

- **Knowledge creation.** The creation of knowledge for a specific problem or area. Individuals are asked to contribute to a solution or offer valuable advice. For example, IBM, GE, and other companies have communities of employees and business partners who contribute to idea generation and problem solving.
- **Knowledge sharing.** Members tell other members where to find knowledge of interest to the community (Currier 2010). Knowledge sharing is supported by tools such as IBM Connections (see IBM Software Group 2011).

Web 2.0 applications help aggregate corporate knowledge and simplify the building of repositories of best practices, as demonstrated by the following example.

Example: IBM's Social Business

IBM has long used communities for idea generation and problem solving. One of its best-known communities is the Innovation Jam, an online brainstorming session which focuses on a different topic each year (e.g., in 2013, it was called the Client Experience Jam; **collaborationjam.com/ IBMJam**). This community of over 150,000 employees and members of business partners tries to help IBM move the latest technologies to the market. IBM has been hosting online brainstorming sessions since 2001. For example, in July 2006, IBM invited employees, partners, and customers to contribute ideas about a certain new product. Within 72 h, more than 50,000 ideas were posted. These ideas were then winnowed down by using sophisticated analytical software. Several ideas generated in this process were implemented, resulting in substantial savings. Sample topics of Innovation Jams include new technologies for water filtration, 3-D Internet, and branchless banking. For more on IBM's Innovation Jams—the process, example of topics, and results, as well as the use of virtual worlds—see Bjelland and Wood (2008) and **collaborationjam.com**.

Virtual meetings where IBM employees can participate in virtual Innovation Jam meetings.

Learning Communities

Social networks and Web 2.0 tools can be used in learning and training as a subset of knowledge sharing. Lenox and Coleman (2010) provide a comprehensive guide explaining how to do this in large libraries. The guide can also be used in other organizations that consider such training. Strong (2013) provides a guide to content brainstorming for 2013.

Online Advice and Consulting

Offering advice and consulting services is an important use of knowledge online. The online advice and consulting field is growing rapidly as tens of thousands of experts of all kinds provide (for a fee or free) their expertise over the Internet. The following are some examples:

- **Social networks.** Several social networks allow users to post questions and get answers. For example, people use the LinkedIn Help Center to ask questions.
- **Medical advice.** Companies such as WebMD (**webmd. com**) and others (e.g., LivePerson (**liveperson.com/ health-medicine**) provide health advice and some consultations with top medical experts, either for free or for a per-minute fee. Consumers can ask specific questions on these sites and get answers from specialists. For example, DoctorSpring (**doctorspring.com**) offers online consultations with health care professionals (fee schedule determined by category), and allows two free follow-up questions. Health advising sites offer specialized advice and tips for travelers, for pet owners, and others. Of special interest is PatientsLikeMe (**patientslikeme.com**), a community where patients discuss their health problems and solutions, with advice and suggestions provided by other members.
- **Gurus.** Several sites provide diversified expert services, some for free. One example is **answers.com** (formerly GuruNet), which is free, and provides businesses with an efficient platform to connect and perform transactions with freelance professionals, locally, nationally, and globally. The community has more than 130 million members on the Web and over 225 million registered users (August 2014).
- Expertise is also available at Elance (**elance.com**). Companies can use this site to find, hire, manage, and pay contractors online. On Elance, companies can gain instant access to tens of thousands of rated and tested professionals who offer technical, marketing, and business expertise. Of special interest is ScientificAmerican.com, which has an "Ask The Experts" section (see **scientificamerican.com/ section/ask-the-experts**), and offers articles by experts on scientific and technological topics. Some other sites that offer information from experts are Yahoo! Answers (**answers. yahoo.com**), Catholic Answers (**forums.catholic.com**), HealthAnswers (**healthanswers.com**), and North Shore Animal League (**animalleague.org/expert-advice**). Some provide answers for free; others charge fees for premium services.

One word of caution about online advice: It is not wise to risk your health, your money, or your legal status on free or even for-fee online advice. Always seek more than one opinion, and carefully check the reputation and the credentials of any advice provider.

Questions and Answers on Social Networks

In a Q&A "answer" function, individuals and companies' employees can post questions. For example, in LinkedIn, you can ask the community a question by using the posting module on the 'Help Forum' or by using the posting module on your homepage to ask your network a question. Additionally, you can use the 'share box' on your home page to ask questions from your connections, everyone on LinkedIn, or even on Twitter. Many other professional networks and their internal groups provide advice and supporting material for help in decision making. These services can be either paid or for free. For example, according to the medical social network Sermo (**sermo. com**; "Social Media Meets Healthcare"), a large online community exclusive to physicians, uses iConsult, an application that "allows physicians to author and discuss urgent and interesting patient cases from any Web- or mobile-enabled device, and based on market tests, be almost assured feedback from multiple colleagues. Typical questions and responses include requested/suggested diagnoses and treatments with the best insights often resulting from collaboration among the doctors" (see **sermo.com/ who-we-are/press-releases-view/3**).

8.6   CROWDSOURCING: COLLECTIVE INTELLIGENCE FOR PROBLEM SOLVING AND CONTENT CREATION

The essentials of crowdsourcing were described in Chap. 2. Listed there, as a major capability, was the facilitation of problem solving.

Crowdsourcing as a Distributed Problem Solving Enabler

Crowdsourcing describes a set of tools, concepts, and methodologies that deal with the process of outsourcing work, including problem solving and idea generation to a *community* of potential solvers known as the 'crowd.'

More than just brainstorming or ideation, crowdsourcing uses proven techniques to focus on the crowd's innovation, creativity, and problem-solving capacity, on topics of vital interest to the host organization. An overview of crowdsourcing is provided in Jeff Howe's video titled "Crowdsourcing" (3:20 minutes) at **youtube.com/watch?v=F0-UtNg3ots**. See also **crowdsourcing.org** and Brabham (2013). Also watch Brabham's video titled "Crowdsourcing as a Model for Problem Solving" (6:12 minutes) at **youtube.com/ watch?v=hLGhKyiJ8Xo**.

Crowdsourcing Categories

Howe (2008) has classified applications of crowdsourcing into the following four categories:

1. **Collective intelligence (or wisdom).** Here, people are solving problems and providing new insights and ideas leading to product, process, or service innovations.
2. **Crowd creation.** Here, people are creating various types of content and sharing it with others (paid or for free). The content may be used for problem solving, advertising, or knowledge accumulation. This can be done by splitting large tasks into small segments (e.g., contributing content to create Wikipedia entries).
3. **Crowd voting.** Here, people are giving their opinions and ratings on ideas, products, or services, as well as evaluating and filtering information presented to them. An example would be voting on *American Idol*.
4. **Crowd support and funding.** Here, people are contributing and supporting endeavors for social causes, which might include volunteering their effort and time, offering donations, and micro-financing.

Chaordix Corp. (**chaordix.com**) classifies crowdsourcing into the following three models:

1. **Secretive.** Individuals submit ideas, and the winner is selected by the company. Ideas are not visible to all participants.
2. **Collaborative.** Individuals submit ideas, the crowd evaluates the ideas, and the crowd picks the winners. Ideas are visible to all participants.
3. **Panel selects.** Individuals submit ideas, the crowd evolves ideas, a panel selects finalists, and the crowd votes for the winner.

A *crowdsortium* is a community of industry practitioners whose mission is to advance the crowdsourcing industry through best practices and education (see **crowdsortium. org**). They view crowdsourcing as an ecosystem.

Crowdsourcing also has the potential to be a problem-solving mechanism for governments and nonprofit use via community participation. Urban and transit planning are prime areas for crowdsourcing. One project used crowdsourcing to encourage public participation in the planning process for the Salt Lake City transit system (from 2008 to 2009). Another notable application of crowdsourcing to government problem solving is the Peer to Patent Community Patent Review project for the U.S. Patent and Trademark Office, see **peertopatent.org**. (This project opens the patent examination process to public participation.)

Progressive companies and organizations now recognize the value of tapping into the wisdom of the crowd to capture the best answers and the most innovative ideas. For a comprehensive coverage, see Chin et al. (2014).

Example

In 2012, the Brazilian furniture company Galatea (**galateacasa.com.br**) tapped the crowd to help design furniture and decide which products to sell. Visitors to their e-commerce site voted on proposed models. For details, see **crowdsourcing.org/document/in-brazil-furniture-store-taps-the-crowds-to-help-decide-product-range/12412**.

The Process of Crowdsourcing

The process of crowdsourcing, which was described briefly in Chap. 2, differs from application to application, depending on the models of the specific problem(s) to be solved and the method used. However, the following steps exist in most enterprise applications, even though the details of the execution differ. The major steps are based on the generic process described in Chap. 2. They are:

1. Identify the task (problem) you want to investigate or accomplish.
2. Select the target crowd.
3. Broadcast the task to the crowd. (Frequently to an unidentified crowd in an open call, as Starbucks and Dell do.)
4. Engage the crowd in accomplishing the task (e.g., idea generation).
5. Collect the user-generated content. (This may include a submission of solutions, voting, new ideas, etc.).
6. Evaluate the quality of submitted material by the management that initiated the request, by experts, or by the crowd.
7. Accept or reject a solution.
8. Compensate the crowd.

The MIT Guide for Collective Intelligence

Malone et al. (2010) conducted a detailed analysis about the use of what they call **collective intelligence (CI)**, which is an application of crowdsourcing for problem solving, idea generation, and innovations. The researchers attempted to answer the question: How can you get the crowds to do what your business needs done?

Successfully Deployed Crowdsourcing Systems: Some Representative Examples

The following are some representative examples of implemented crowdsourcing systems.

- **Dell's IdeaStorm (ideastorm.com)** enables customers to vote on Dell's product features they prefer, including new ones. Dell is using a technically-oriented crowd, such as the Linux community.
- **Procter & Gamble's** researchers post their problems at **innocentive.com** and at **ninesigma.com**, offering cash rewards to problem solvers. P&G uses other crowdsourcing service providers such as **yourencore.com**.
- **Amazon Mechanical Turk (mturk.com)** is a marketplace for distributing large scale work that requires human intelligence. It is limited to large tasks that can be divided (known as HITs—human intelligence tasks) and is posted by companies that need assistance. Then, Amazon arranges workers (the "Mechanical Turk Workers"), each of whom is allocated a small subtask, and is paid when the work is completed. For details, see **mturk.com**.
- **Facebook (facebook.com)** used crowdsourcing to translate its site into more than 65 different languages. The completion of the English to French translated by over 4,000 volunteers only took one day; however, Facebook had to hire a team of professional translators to oversee the whole crowdsourcing process to ensure that the resulting translations were accurate.
- **Goldcorp (goldcorp.com)**, a Canadian mining company, was unable to find sufficient gold. In 2000, the company initiated an open call to the public, providing geological data and $575,000 in prizes to participants with the best methods. Using the submitted ideas, the company discovered $3 billion worth of gold.
- **Frito-Lay (fritolay.com)** used crowdsourcing for designing a successful 2010 Super Bowl advertising campaign (Frito-Lay 2010).
- **Wikipedia (wikipedia.org)** is considered by many to be the "granddaddy" of crowdsourcing, and is certainly the world's largest crowdsourcing project.

Tools for Crowdsourcing

To launch crowdsourcing initiatives, businesses and developers can make use of crowdsourcing tools and platforms, such as NineSigma, InnoCentive, YourEncore, yet2, UserVoice, Get Satisfaction, and IdeaScale.

For related tools for idea generation, see **capterra.com/idea-management-software** and **collaborationproject.org**. For tools for crowdfunding, see *2013 CF Crowdfunding Industry* report. For additional tools for crowdsourcing, see **crowdsourcing.org**.

Crowdfunding and Kickstarter

Raising funds from the crowd for different purposes is gaining popularity with several startups operating in this area. A notable company is Kickstarter. For how they help small businesses, see the 2013 video titled "Small Business: Kickstarter Success" (6:50 minutes) at **youtube.com/watch?v=xudOhEYIwyU**.

Examples of Crowdsourcing

An increasing number of startups are using crowdfunding to initiate their businesses. In Chap. 6 we provided a few examples. Here are three more examples:

- Filmmaker Zach Braff used Kickstarter to raise money for his 2013 film (watch the video "Zach Braff Uses Kickstarter to Get Money for Next Film" (0:51 minutes) at **youtube.com/watch?v=CIyJtcxjWhw**.
- Zach Danger Brown collected over $52,000 on Kickstarter in July 2014 for his 'potato salad' idea. For details, see Root (2014) and a video about how the collection went global at **abcnews.go.com/GMA/video/zach-danger-browns-potato-salad-kickstarter-global-24464503**.
- The digital music phenomenon, Kawehi, is raising money via Kickstarter to promote her music projects in Hawaii. For details, see Russo (2014).

Hypios: A Marketplace for Crowdsourcing

According to its website, Hypios (**hypios.com**) is an open call market for crowdsourcing with over 950,000 experts across the world. As a problem-solving individual or research organization, Hypios combines intelligent crowdsourcing, competency discovery technology, and human outreach to deliver an optimal open problem-solving service. "Seekers" post R&D problems to the network and select a deadline and a price offered for the successful "Solver." The company's partners help formulate the problem, set a reward prize and a deadline. The problem is then posted on the Hypios solving platform and on Facebook (**facebook.com/hypios**). Using its powerful semantic analysis software, Hypios creates a conceptual graph of the problem to extract and suggest relevant keywords. These keywords are then used to search the Web using a competency discovery engine that identifies potential experts. For more information, see **hypios.com/product-services/how-hypios-works-0**.

8.7 SOCIAL COLLABORATION (COLLABORATION 2.0)

One of the major applications of Web 2.0 and social media in the enterprise is in the area of collaboration. Some even equate Web 2.0 with enterprise collaboration (e.g., McAfee 2009). Social collaboration is used for many purposes, an important one being product design.

Supporting Social Collaboration

Collaboration in business can be defined as *"people working with other people toward a common outcome."* For a comprehensive overview of collaboration supported by social media, see Carr (2013). For many images of social collaboration, search Google Images for 'social collaboration.'

Social collaboration refers to people's collaboration within and between communities enabled by social media tools and platforms. The processes help people interact and share information to achieve a common goal. It is also known as *Collaboration 2.0*. Collaboration 2.0 is recognized as a major element in social business that can provide considerable benefits (e.g., see examples in IBM Software Group 2011). For implementation of social collaboration, see Carr (2013).

Social Collaboration (Collaboration 2.0)

Collaboration drives business value up by enabling people to work together more efficiently. Wikis and other social software tools can be used effectively by all types and sizes of enterprises for a wide range of tasks and activities. Collaboration helps with solving business problems and uncovering new opportunities, especially with the help of social media tools (see details in Morgan 2012). Collaboration in social networking is done both internally, among employees from different units working in virtual teams, and externally, when working with suppliers, customers, and other business partners. For example, ccollaboration occurs in forums and other types of groups, and by using wikis and blogs. For details on collaboration in social networks, see Coleman and Levine (2008). For the use of Collaboration 2.0 in the enterprise, see Dortch (2012) and Turban et al. (2015). Social collaboration has several dimensions, as illustrated in Fig. 8.2.

Fig. 8.2 The various dimensions of social collaboration

Some believe that in the future, people will use mostly Web 2.0 tools, rather than e-mail, for collaboration. For a discussion, see The Future Organization at **thefutureorganization.com**.

A large number of Web 2.0 tools are used to support social collaboration. The support is given to idea sharing, communication, working together on the same documents, and more. The Web 2.0 tools range from wikis to virtual worlds. For comprehensive coverage, see Coleman and Levine (2008). Dunay (2014) provides a synopsis of a webinar he moderated on how to use enterprise social networks for internal collaboration.

The development of tools, philosophies, and procedures of social media support for collaboration allows employees and managers to engage much more fully in the collaboration process. Furthermore, social collaboration has improved organizational culture.

Social collaboration is supported mainly by:

- Wikis, blogs, and microblogging (e.g., Twitter)
- Virtual worlds (see Heiphetz and Woodill 2010)
- Collaborative communities (forums and discussion groups)
- Early vintage Web 2.0 technologies
- Crowdsourcing
- Other tools (e.g., Yammer)

Most of the collaboration software vendors are adding Web 2.0 tools to their collaboration suites (e.g., Binfire.com).

Using Blogs and Wikis Inside the Enterprise

In Chap. 2, we provided some examples of blogs and wikis used within enterprises. The use of these tools is expanding rapidly. Ccompanies use blogs and wikis for the following activities:

- Project collaboration and communication
- Process and procedure documentation
- FAQs
- E-learning and e-training
- Forums for new ideas
- Corporate-specific dynamic glossary and terminology
- Collaboration with customers

As you can see, most of the applications in the previous list relate to collaboration. For additional information, you can read various blogs at **zdnet.com/blog/hinchcliffe**.

Using Twitter to Support Collaboration

Twitter is already used extensively in the enterprise to support collaboration. For example, Wagner (2009) describes using Twitter to facilitate the work of focus groups and other collaborative teams. Twitter is used extensively for interaction with customers and prospects as well as conducting market research.

The Role of Mobile Commerce in Social Collaboration

As described in Chap. 6, mobile commerce is growing very rapidly. Most enterprise social applications can be used on wireless devices. This is particularly true for communication and collaboration.

Suites of Social Collaboration Tools

Several companies offer suites of social collaboration tools, either as stand-alone products or as added tools in existing collaboration suites.

What is enterprise collaboration? According to TechTarget, "Enterprise collaboration is a system of communication among corporate employees that may encompass the use of a collaboration platform, enterprise social networking tools, a corporate intranet, and the public Internet" (per **searchcontentmanagement.techtarget.com/definition/enterprise-collaboration-EC**). For why a company needs social collaboration, see **web.esna.com/blog/social-collaboration-at-c-level**.

Example 1: IBM Connections
IBM Connections is a leading social network software platform that provides collaboration tools for creating forums, wikis, and blogs, and new capabilities like advanced social analytics, which enable users to expand their network of connections and engagement. For details, see **ibm.com/software/products/en/conn**.

You can download many free reports at **collaborationjam.com**. IBM also provides the tools needed to support innovation.

Example 2: Cisco WebEx Social Meeting Center
WebEx Meetings offers mobile apps for iPad, iPhone, Android, BlackBerry, Windows Phone, and other devices. For more information, see **webex.com/products/web-conferencing/mobile.html**.

For 10 social networks that aim at improved enterprise social collaboration, see Reisinger (2015).

What is a collaboration platform? According to TechTarget, "a collaboration platform is a category of business software that adds broad social networking capabilities to work processes" (per **searchcontentmanagement. techtarget.com/definition/collaboration-platform**).

Example 3: Laboranova

Under the European Union's Sixth Framework Programme, **laboranova.com** assists professionals who take part in the management and development of innovations. Laboranova's tools and methodologies assist in the areas of team building, knowledge management, and the evaluation of innovations. It consists of a suite of Web 2.0 tools adopted for social innovation and collaboration. The tools include InnoTube (**laboranova.com/ pages/tools/innotube.php?lang=DE**), which operates like a private YouTube for business; and Melodie (**laboranova.com/ pages/tools/melodie.php?lang=DE**), which creates visual maps of concepts or ideas submitted by its users, so that other users can comment or elaborate on the initial ideas.

For a list of the major enterprise collaboration platforms (2013) and their mobile clients (with an infographic), see **zdnet.com/the-major-enterprise-collaboration-platforms- and-their-mobile-clients-7000018519**.

SUMMARY

In this chapter, you learned about the following SC issues as they relate to the chapter's learning objectives.

1. **The social enterprise.** Conducting social networking activities in the enterprise can result in substantial benefits. Two types of business social networks exist: public and private. The private network is company owned; it may have restricted access, or it may be open to the public. The public network (e.g., LinkedIn) is used mainly for recruiting, connections, collaboration, and marketing communication. The private, in-house social enterprise uses Collaboration 2.0, social CRM, social marketing media, and more. You can even "spy" on your competitors (see **entrepreneur.com/article/229350**). All this translates to improved relationships with employees, customers, and business partners. Significant cost reduction, productivity increase, and competitive advantage can be achieved as well.

2. **Business-oriented public social networks.** Following the successful examples of LinkedIn and Xing, many business-oriented public networks were created. Notable networks are Yammer, Viadeo, and Google+. Applications vary from recruiting to market research and advertising. Most notable is F-commerce. One major activity in public networks is external collaboration. Several entrepreneurship networks also exist.

3. **Major enterprise social commerce activities.** Currently, collaboration and communication, as well as community building, are the major activities. In addition, problem solving via idea generation and finding expertise are becoming more and more important. Related to this is knowledge creation and management. Companies recruit, train, and conduct other HRM activities in enterprise networks. In addition, some companies allow P2P activities. Several companies also use the enterprise social network for interactions with customers, suppliers, and other business partners.

4. **The online job market and its benefits.** The online job market is growing rapidly, with thousands of jobs matched with job seekers each day. The major benefits of online job markets for employers are the ability to reach a large number of job seekers at a low cost, provide detailed information online, accept applications online, and even conduct skill tests. In addition, résumés can be checked and matched with positions more quickly by using intelligent software agents. Many job offers are posted on the Internet, helping job seekers to obtain employment. Job seekers can also post their résumés for recruiters to discover. Recruiting via social networks, especially via LinkedIn and Facebook, is growing very rapidly.

5. **Managerial problem solving and knowledge management.** Knowledge has been recognized as an important organizational asset. However, it needs to be properly captured, stored, managed, and shared. Knowledge is critical for many e-commerce and social commerce tasks, and can be shared in different ways; expert knowledge can be provided to non-experts (paid or for free) via a knowledge portal or as a personal service (e.g., via e-mail).

6. **Online advisory systems.** Online advisory systems of all kinds are becoming popular. Some are free, but most charge money. Users must be careful about the quality of the advice. Social networks and portals provide a variety of services. In addition, these systems are in active use with many organizations.

7. **Crowdsourcing and collective intelligence.** Crowdsourcing is used mostly for idea generation, voting, and problem identification. Content creation and division of a big job to small segments (such as translating the Facebook website to many different languages by volunteers) are also supported by crowdsourcing.

8. **Social collaboration.** Many see social collaboration (Collaboration 2.0) as the major activity that social media supports. Activities supported range from joint design to problem solving.

KEY TERMS

Business social network	184
Collective intelligence (CI)	195
Crowdsourcing	194

Knowledge management (KM)   193
Social business   181
Social collaboration (Collaboration 2.0)   197
Social enterprise (Enterprise 2.0)   183

REVIEW QUESTIONS

1. Define a business network and an enterprise social network.
2. List various categories of enterprise applications in social networks.
3. What are the benefits of enterprise social networking for companies? For employees?
4. Define public business-oriented networks. Provide an example.
5. What is an entrepreneur network? Provide two examples.
6. What are the major features and characteristics of effective enterprise social networking?
7. Describe The Greater IBM Connection and Yammer. What are the similarities? What are the differences?
8. List all the ways an organization can interface with social networking.
9. List social networking applications in HRM.
10. How can social networking facilitate problem solving?
11. Why is LinkedIn so useful for job seekers and for employers? List the specific tools provided to job seekers. List the specific tools provided to recruiters.
12. Relate social networking to knowledge management.
13. Describe online advisory services.
14. Relate social networks to providing advice.
15. Define crowdsourcing; provide four examples.
16. List Howe's four categories of applications of crowdsourcing.
17. What are the major benefits of crowdsourcing?
18. Describe the crowdsourcing process.
19. List some issues and concerns regarding crowdsourcing implementation.
20. Describe the tools provided by Kickstarter and Hypios.
21. Define social collaboration.
22. List and describe briefly the major benefits of social collaboration.
23. List several social collaboration tools.
24. Describe The Greater IBM Connection (see **ibm.com/ ibm/greateribm/**).

TOPICS FOR DISCUSSION AND DEBATES

1. How do public business-oriented networks and private enterprise social networks differ?
2. Discuss the potential business use of Twitter in the enterprise (by major categories).
3. What are some of the risks companies may face if they decide to use public social networks?
4. Private enterprise social networking: beneficial or a time-waster? What are the pitfalls of enterprise social networking? Discuss.
5. Review any two Socialcast user case studies at **social-cast.com/customers** and discuss:
   (a) What benefits the companies that embraced Socialcast have realized.
   (b) Lessons learned from these cases.
6. Review the features of Socialtext (**socialtext.com**). Discuss how you would make use of this platform in a small enterprise in (a) retail, (b) manufacturing, and (c) financial services.
7. Would you use **monster.com** or **linkedin.com** for recruiting top managers, or would you rather use a physical office in a traditional agency? Why?
8. Relate IBM's Social Innovation Projects to knowledge management (KM) and social networks.
9. Discuss the role of crowdsourcing in idea generation and market research.
10. How can crowdsourcing reduce risks to merchants?
11. Discuss the business value of social networking. Begin by reading Tom Davenport's post titled "Where's the 'Working' in Social Networking?" at **blogs.hbr. org/2007/10/wheres-the-working-in-social-n**.
12. Read the Bernoff and Schadler (2010) article. Then, discuss the top strategies employed by Sony Corp. Idea generation by employees or customers using crowdsourcing is becoming popular. However, some say that crowdsourcing is only an electronic suggestion box. Others disagree. Discuss.
13. Debate: Some research suggests that the use of public social networks by employees can be good for a business, because employees develop relationships and share information among themselves and with outsiders, which increases productivity and innovation. Others say it is a waste of time and ban the use of Facebook, YouTube, and other such sites in the company during working hours.
14. Debate the pros and cons of the following: In order to control content, Manchester United (UK) does not allow its players to generate any content on its private social network site, nor on public ones (e.g., Facebook). Manchester United has banned its players from using social networking websites. All players news are communicated via its official website, **manutd.com**. Manchester United players are not allowed to maintain personal profiles on social networking websites.
15. Compare and contrast "social collaboration" and "crowdsourcing."

INTERNET EXERCISES

1. Enter the **gillin.com/blog** and find information related to enterprise applications of social commerce technologies. Write a report.
2. Enter **events.brazencareerist.com/recruiting** and watch the video on their home page about the services they provide. Compare the services to the virtual event hosted at **expos2.com**.
3. Enter **xing.com** and identify job-related help features. Prepare a list of support activities offered.
4. Compare what JobServe (**jobserve.com**) and Aspire Media Group (**aspiremediagroup.net**) offer regarding solutions for recruitment. Differentiate services to employees from services to employers. Consult Brouat (2011). Write a report.
5. Identify a difficult business problem. Post the problem on **elance.com**, **linkedin.com**, and **answers.com**. Summarize the suggestions you received to solve the problem.
6. Enter **insight24.com** and **opentext.com/videos** and find the most recent and most popular videos about knowledge management and social media (combined). View three videos on different topics related to this chapter. Prepare a report.
7. Enter **guru.com** and **elance.com** and compare their offerings. On which site would you prefer to post your profile? Why?
8. Enter **mashable.com** and review the latest news regarding crowdsourcing. Write a report.
9. Enter **huddle.com** and view the interactive demo (registration required). In addition, watch the video on the main page. Write a report on social collaboration activities.
10. Enter **eweek.com/videos** and find videos related to social enterprise (business). Watch the most recent two. Write a report.
11. Enter **jivesoftware.com/discover-jive**. Summarize the material related to social business.
12. Enter IBM's Job Referral Program site (**ibm.referrals. selectminds.com**) and write a report about how they use social media for job referrals.

TEAM ASSIGNMENTS AND PROJECTS

1. **Assignment for the Opening Case**

    Read the opening case and answer the following questions:
    (a) Describe the internal and external factors that drive Shift.
    (b) Describe its major benefits.

    (c) Relate the case to Collaboration 2.0 and to crowdsourcing.
    (d) Review Garcia et al. (2011) and watch the supporting videos. Prepare a summary.
2. Have teams explore knowledge management videos and other resources at **portal.brint.com** and **kmworld.com**. In addition, search YouTube and Google for KM videos. Relate them to knowledge management and social media (combined). Prepare a report.
3. Each team is assigned a question-and-answer company (e.g., **answers.com**, **ask.com**). Check the company's features, including social networking/games. Give a presentation.
4. The crowdsourcing model works with designers in this way: (1) A company outlines an area for which they need a design. (2) The company turns the design outline into a competition between amateur and professional designers. (3) The company decides on a winner, either by having the participants vote in the competition (the crowd), or by an executive decision. This is all at little to no cost for the person or company looking for the design. Now, think about the future of the graphic industry in general. What will be the fate of large design firms that are competing for the business of high-profile clients when the clients are now paying tiny, one-time fees to amateur designers? Is using crowdsourcing in your business (or a business you are familiar with) a viable model?
5. Yammer, Huddle, Chatter, and Jive Software are cloud-based social networking services. They are considered very useful, replacing traditional enterprise tools. Investigate the issue and write a report. Begin with Marsan (2011).
6. Each team should initiate a new group on LinkedIn and start some discussions (e.g., try to find some business opportunities).

REFERENCES

Ahmad, I. "How to Boost LinkedIn Engagement [Infographic]." January 3, 2014. **socialmediatoday.com/content/how-boost-linkedin-engagement-infographic** (accessed January 2015).

Bennett, S. "91% of Emploters Use Twitter, Facebook, and LinkedIn to Screen Job Applicants [Infographic]." October 24, 2011. **adweek.com/socialtimes/social-media-job-screening/456574** (accessed July 2015).

Bernoff, J., and C. Li. "Harnessing the Power of the Oh-So-Social Web." *MIT Sloan Management Review*, vol. 49, no. 3, 36-42, Spring 2008.

Bernoff, J., and T. Schadler. "Empowered." *Harvard Business Review*, July–August 2010. **hbr.org/2010/07/empowered/ar/1** (accessed January 2015).

Bishop, J. "Top Five LinkedIn New Year Resolutions for 2012." January 3, 2012. **socialmediatoday.com/content/top-five-linkedin-new-year-resolutions-2012** (accessed January 2015).

Bjelland, O. M., and R. C. Wood. "An Inside View of IBM's 'Innovation Jam.'" *MIT Sloan Management Review*, 50(1), 32-40, 2008.

Blair, K. "How to Use Yammer… And Why You Should Be Using It at Your Business." March 4, 2011. **socialtimes.com/how-to-use-yammer-and-why-you-should-be-using-it-at-your-business_b40658** (accessed January 2015).

Boyd, S. "The Gravitational Pull of Enterprise 2.0." July 10, 2008. **stoweboyd.com/post/857400170/the-gravitational-pull-of-enter-prise-2-0** (accessed January 2015).

Brabham, D.C. *Crowdsourcing.* Cambridge, MA: The MIT Press/MIT Press Essential Knowledge Series, 2013.

Brogan, C. *Google+ for Business: How Google's Social Network Changes Everything.* Upper Saddle River, NJ: Que, 2012.

Brotherton, P. "Social Networks Enhance Employee Learning." *ASTD,* April 19, 2011. **td.org/Publications/Magazines/TD/TD-Archive/2011/04/Social-Networks-Enhance-Employee-Learning** (accessed January 2015).

Brouat, L. "How Deloitte Use Social Media to Recruit [Case Study]." May 26, 2011. **linkhumans.com/blog/how-to-use-social-media-to-recruit-deloitte-case-study**. (Updated on March 28, 2013 by Laurence Hebberd (see **linkhumans.com/case-study/deloitte-update**) (both accessed January 2015).

Bughin, J., and M. Chui. "The Rise of the Networked Enterprise: Web 2.0 Finds Its Payday." *McKinsey Quarterly,* December 2010. **mckinsey.com/insights/high_tech_telecoms_internet/the_rise_of_the_networked_enterprise_web_20_finds_its_payday** (accessed January 2015).

Bughin, J., and M. Chui. "Evolution of the Networked Enterprise: McKinsey Global Survey Results." *McKinsey Quarterly,* March 2013. **mckinsey.com/insights/business_technology/evolution_of_the_networked_enterprise_mckinsey_global_survey_results** (accessed January 2015).

Burgess, C. and M. Burgess. *The Social Employee: How Great Companies Make Social Media Work.* New York: McGraw-Hill, 2013.

BusinessWire. "Social Business Goes Mainstream in the Enterprise, Forcing Cultural and Process Shifts from the Inside Out, IDC Research Finds." January 26, 2010. **businesswire.com/news/home/20100126005084/en/Social-Business-Mainstream-Enterprise-Forcing-Cultural-Process#.VGZxAPnF-So** (accessed January 2015).

Carr, D. F. *Social Collaboration for Dummies.* New York: John Wiley & Sons, 2013.

Carr, D. F. "Why McKinsey Values Social Economy at Up to $1.3 Trillion." July 30, 2012. **informationweek.com/why-mckinsey-values-social-economy-at-up-to-$13-trillion/d/d-id/1105557?** (accessed January 2015).

Chess Media Group. "Implementing Enterprise 2.0 at IBM." Enterprise 2.0 Case Series Report Number 09, May 2012. **chessmediagroup.com/resources/case-studies/implementing-enterprise-2-0-at-ibm/** (accessed January 2015).

Chin, C. M. and T.P. Liang. "What Can Crowdsourcing Do for Decision Support?" *Decision Support Systems* (Fall 2014).

Coleman, D., and S. Levine. *Collaboration 2.0: Technology and Best Practices for Successful Collaboration in a Web 2.0 World.* Cupertino, CA: Happy About Info, 2008.

Currier, G. "Sharing Knowledge in the Corporate Hive." *Baseline,* May/June 2010.

Donston-Miller, D. "Social Business Leader Cemex Keeps Ideas Flowing." November 5, 2012. **informationweek.com/enterprise/social-business-leader-cemex-keeps-ideas-flowing/d/d-id/1107226** (accessed January 2015).

Dortch, M. E. "Working Social: Becoming a Collaborative Enterprise." Ziff Davis, Inc., February 2012. **hosteddocs.ittoolbox.com/zdclbe comingcollaborativeenterprise_020811.pdf** (accessed January 2015)

Dunay, P. "Social Media Organization: What are Best Practices for Internal Collaboration?" January 23, 2014. **socialmediatoday.com/content/social-organization-what-are-best-practices-internal-collaboration** (accessed January 2015).

Elad, J. *LinkedIn for Dummies,* 3rd ed. Hoboken, NJ: Wiley, 2014.

Forrester Consulting. "Social Networking in the Enterprise: Benefits and Inhibitors." June 2010. **cisco.com/web/offer/gist_ty2_asset/SocMednInhib/SocNW_En_TLP.pdf** (accessed January 2015).

Frito-Lay. "Four Consumer-Created Doritos Ads Crash the Super Bowl, Now Face the Pros in Attempt to Win $5 Million Prize." February 7, 2010. **fritolay.com/company/media/media-article/four-consumer-created-doritos-ads-crash-the-super-bowl-now-face-the-pros-in-attempt-to-win-$5-million-prize** (accessed January 2015).

Garcia, J. G., M. A. L. Martinez, and A. San Vicente. "Story: Shift Changes the Way CEMEX Works." A Winner Paper in the 2011 "Management Innovation eXchange Project." July 15, 2011. **managementexchange.com/story/shift-changes-way-cemex-works** (accessed January 2015).

Gowel, D. *The Power in a Link: Open Doors, Close Deals, and Change the Way You Do Business Using LinkedIn.* Hoboken, NJ: Wiley, 2012.

Greenberg, A. "Recruiting Solutions for 2014 - Gamification." December 29, 2013. **recruitingdivision.com/the-recruiting-solutions-for-2014-gamification** (accessed January 2015).

Gregory, A. "20 Social Networking Sites for Business Professionals." August 28, 2012. **sitepoint.com/social-networking-sites-for-business** (accessed January 2015).

Heiphetz, A., and G. Woodill. *Training and Collaboration with Virtual Worlds: How to Create Cost-Saving, Efficient, and Engaging Programs.* New York: McGraw-Hill, 2010.

Hinchcliffe, D. "Social Business Success: CEMEX." February 1, 2012. **zdnet.com/blog/hinchcliffe/social-business-success-cemex/1927** (accessed January 2015).

Howe, J. *Crowdsourcing: Why the Power of the Crowd Is Driving the Future of Business.* New York: Crown Publishing Group, 2008.

Huff, T. "How Social Media Changed the Hiring Process." August 10, 2014. **socialmediatoday.com/content/how-social-media-changed-hiring-process** (accessed January 2015).

IBM Software Group. "The Compelling Returns from IBM Connections in Support of Social Business: Five Stories." Thought Leadership White Paper, New York: IBM Corporation, EPW14010-USEN-00, 2011.

IDC. "Social Business Framework: Using People as a Platform to Enable Transformation." *Insight,* July 2010, IDC #223862, Volume 1 **idc.com/research/images/IDC-Social-Business-Framework-Download.pdf** (accessed January 2015).

Kern, J. "Social Determining Next Generation of Business Applications." July 19, 2012. **information-management.com/news/social-bi-esn-saas-cloud-corum-10022876-1.html** (accessed November 2014).

Lenox, M., and M. Coleman. "Using Social Networks to Create Powerful Learning Communities." *Computers in Libraries,* Vol. 30, No. 7, 12-17, 2010.

Liang-T.P., and E. Turban. "Introduction to the Special Issue: Social Commerce: A Research Framework for Social Commerce." *International Journal of Electronic Commerce,* 16 (2), 5-13, Winter 2011-12.

Malone, T. W., R. Laubacher, and C. Dellarocas. "The Collective Intelligence Genome." *MIT Sloan Management Review,* 21(3), 21-31, 2010.

Marsan, C. D. "Private Social Networks Playing Facebook Role in More Workplaces." October 20, 2011. **networkworld.com/article/2182385/data-center/private-social-networks-playing-facebook-role-in-more-workplaces.html** (accessed January 2015).

Martin, M. "Virtual Career Fair and Job Shadowing Presentation." May 17, 2010. **slideshare.net/michelemmartin/virtual-career-fair-and-job-shadowing-presentation** (accessed January 2015).

Martin, S. "LinkedIn Unveils Mobile Recruiting Tools." October 16, 2013. Retrieved from **usatoday.com/story/tech/2013/10/16/**

linkedin-unveils-mobile-recruiting-tools/2994793/ (accessed January 2015).

McAfee, A. P. *Enterprise 2.0: New Collaborative Tools for Your Organization's Toughest Challenges.* Boston: Harvard Business School Press, 2009.

Morgan, J. *The Collaborative Organization: A Strategic Guide to Solving Your Internal Business Challenges Using Emerging Social and Collaborative Tools.* New York: McGraw-Hill] 2012.

Morrison, A. "How to Land a Job Using Facebook [Infographic]." November 22, 2011. **socialmediatoday.com/anthony-morrison/393105/how-land-job-using-facebook-infographic** (accessed January 2015).

Nerney, C. "Why This Massive Company's Internal Social Network Succeeded Where So Many Fail." December 18, 2012. **citeworld.com/article/2115494/social-collaboration/how-cemex-leveraged-social-and-collaboration-tools-create-culture-innovation.html** (accessed January 2015).

Reisinger, D. "10 Social Networks Aimed at Improving Enterprise Collaboration." January 1, 2015. **eweek.com/cloud/slideshows/10-social-networks-aimed-at-improving-enterprise-collaboration.html** (accessed January 2015).

Ridley-Duff, and M. Bull. *Understanding Social Enterprise: Theory and Practice.* Thousand Oaks, CA: Sage Publications, 2011.

Root, A., "Potato Salad Tops $50k in Pledges." July 8, 2014. **crowdsourcing.org/editorial/potato-salad-tops-50k-in-pledges/32674** (accessed January 2015).

Russo, J. "Talking Story with Kawehi on Her Upcoming Hawaii Tour." July 1, 2014. **mauitime.com/2014/07/01/talking-story-with-kawehi-on-her-upcoming-hawaii-tour** (accessed January 2015).

Salpeter, M., "How to Use Social Media to Impress Recruiters" *AOL Jobs*, October 27, 2014. **jobs.aol.com/articles/2014/10/27/social-media-impress-recruiters** (accessed January 2015).

Schaffer, N. *Maximizing LinkedIn for Sales and Social Media Marketing.* New York: Windmills Marketing, 2011.

Schwartzman, E. "How To: Conduct a Hands-On Social Media Training." June 10, 2011. **blog.ericschwartzman.com/2011/06/how-to-conduct-a-hands-on-social-media-training** (accessed January 2015).

Scott, M. "See How Social Media Can Land You Your Next Job." October 14, 2013. **socialmediatoday.com/content/see-how-social-media-can-land-you-your-next-job** (accessed January 2015).

Spigit. "Nine Keys to Innovation Management 2.0." A White Paper, 2011. **neccf.org/whitepapers/whitepaper-nine-keys.pdf** (accessed January 2015).

Strong, K. "Content Brainstorming Tools for 2013." December 30, 2012. **socialmediatoday.com/content/content-brainstorming-tools-2013** (accessed January 2015).

Sundberg, J. "How Social Media Will Help Your Job Search." September 18, 2011. **socialmediatoday.com/jorgen-sundberg/358886/how-social-media-will-help-your-job-search** (accessed January 2015).

Sundberg, J. "How to Use Facebook to get Hired [5 Ways]." January 12, 2010. **theundercoverrecruiter.com/5-ways-use-facebook-your-job-search** (accessed January 2015).

Turban, E. et al. *Electronic Commerce: A Managerial and Social Networks Perspective,* 8th ed. New York: Springer 2015.

Tuten, T. L. *Enterprise 2.0 [2 volumes]: How Technology, eCommerce, and Web 2.0 Are Transforming Business Virtually.* Westport, CT: Praeger, 2010.

Wagner, M. "Opportunity Tweets." *Informationweek.com Reports*, June 1, 2009.

Waldman, J. *Job Searching with Social Media for Dummies*, 2nd ed. Hoboken, NJ: John Wiley and Sons, 2013.

Innovative Social Commerce Applications: From Social Government to Entertainment and Gaming

9

Contents

Opening Case: Justin Bieber—The Ultimate Story
of Social Media Fame... 205

9.1   Social Media and Commerce in E-Government 207

9.2   B2B Social Networking 210

9.3   Social Commerce: Applications in Virtual Worlds......... 215

9.4   Social Entertainment and Social TV............................ 219

9.5   Social Games, Gaming, and Gamification...................... 222

9.6   Socially Oriented Online Person-to-Person Activities.... 224

References... 228

Learning Objectives

Upon completion of this chapter, you will be able to:

1. Explain how governments use social media.
2. Describe social B2B activities.
3. Describe the commercial applications conducted in virtual worlds.
4. Review entertainment and gaming in social commerce.
5. Describe social gaming.
6. Explain how people can use social media to conduct P2P transactions.

OPENING CASE: JUSTIN BIEBER—THE ULTIMATE STORY OF SOCIAL MEDIA FAME

Justin Bieber, a talented singer and guitar player who was discovered on the Web, has used social media to become what some call the "King of Social Media."

The Problem/Opportunity

Justin Bieber was born in Canada in 1994 and grew up in a very poor family. He was not a musical prodigy, but wanted to become a musician. From a young age, he started practicing his craft, teaching himself to play piano, drums, guitar, and trumpet, and practicing for thousands of hours. This was no small feat. He sang on the streets with a guitar case in front of him, hoping to earn some money. He collected some, but not very much. As he got older, he participated in some small-scale talent competitions. He won some, but this did not provide much money either.

The Solution

In 2007, when Justin turned 13, his mother posted some of his videos on YouTube. In one video, Justin was singing "So Sick," by R&B singer Ne-Yo. Scooter Braun, a music

Electronic supplementary material The online version of this chapter (doi:10.1007/978-3-319-17028-2_9) contains supplementary material, which is available to authorized users.

producer, came across the video by chance. Recognizing Justin's talent, he contacted Bieber and started working with him. However, Braun had difficulty marketing the young singer, so he decided to use social media to help promote him.

Bieber was willing to perform anywhere and sing about almost anything. Therefore, Braun and Justin were able to post a very large number of videos on YouTube during the same time period that the site itself was peaking in popularity. This resulted in a flood of comments on these videos. Shortly thereafter, his music garnered over 10 million views on YouTube. As a result, Braun introduced Justin to Usher, the legendary singer, songwriter, dancer, and actor. Justin signed a contract with Usher and became his protégé. In 2010, the video for his song "Baby," from his debut full-length album *My World 2.0*, was viewed over 408 million times on YouTube, making it the most-watched video of all time (it was overtaken by Psy's *Gangnam Style* in 2012). (See **mtv.com/news/articles/1654090/justin-biebers-baby-bed-intruder-song-most-watched-2010-youtube-videos.jhtml** and **thedailybeast.com/articles/2013/04/23/youtube-s-10-most-watched-videos-ever.html**.) At that time, Braun and Bieber expanded their use of social media even further.

Using Social Media

With Braun's help, Bieber used social media in several creative ways to promote himself. Like other celebrities, Bieber regularly kept in touch with his millions of followers on Twitter, sending them tweets about his plans, new albums, and so forth. For example, on his first visit to Australia, Justin granted an interview to a girl who tweeted that she wanted to meet him. This girl had 90,000 followers in her Justin Bieber fan club, and when she posted the video of the interview on the club's Twitter page, it became a sensation in Australia. In fact, the Australian fans preferred to watch the video rather than read the newspaper articles about the visit. In addition, Justin posted the video and the story on his Facebook page, generating a tremendous response there as well.

In February 2011, Justin's first movie, *Never Say Never*, was released. Braun and Justin used social media to promote the movie, prompting many fans to go to their local theaters to watch the concert film. The promotion included a Web video campaign through JibJab (a digital entertainment studio that distributes original content via many outlets, including a YouTube channel). According to a JibJab press release, the JibJab Web campaign resulted in a record of 2.8 million views from an engaged audience, who subsequently created 400,000 of their own videos within a week. (See **prnewswire.com/news-releases/jibjab-and-paramounts-insurge-pictures-partner-on-record-breaking-justin-bieber-never-say-never-movie-campaign-117063098.html**.)

Unfortunately, social media may sometimes cause damage to someone's reputation as well, and Bieber was no exception. For example, the social media rumor mill had been busy churning out several Bieber stories. One of them, a Web hoax about Justin contracting syphilis, spread via Facebook and became the #1 item on Google Trends in 2010 (see **gawker.com/5563416/how-justin-bieber-caught-a-contagious-syphilis-rumor**). On July 11, 2011, a rumor spread that YouTube would delete Bieber's hit song "Baby" because it had over 1.5 million "dislikes." This false information resulted in millions of tweets to YouTube ("#dontdeletebaby") posting things like "DON'T DELETE BABY! If they do, I'm never going on YouTube again," and "WWIII will start," and the like.

The Results

By early 2015, Bieber had over 72 million Facebook fans (**facebook.com/JustinBieber**), over 5.38 billion views on YouTube (**vidstatsx.com/youtube-top-100-most-subscribed-channels**), over 59.3 million Twitter followers (**twitter.com/justinbieber**), and 108 million "plays" on Myspace. In 2013, he was ranked number two on the list of Forbes' Best-Paid Celebrities under 30 ($58 million). In 2011, he was considered more influential in the social networking sphere than President Obama or the Dalai Lama, according to the social media organization Klout, Inc. (**klout.com**), which calculates its influential index from the number of tweets, pingshots (see Chap. 10), and hits in cyberspace (see **blog.klout.com/2011/01/is-justin-bieber-really-more-influential-than-barack-obama**). A major part of Bieber's appeal stems from his two YouTube channels (**youtube.com/justinbieber** and **youtube.com/user/kidrauhl**). For Justin's awards, statistics, and information on his album sales, see the Wikipedia entries noted in the Sources section and **statistic-brain.com/justin-bieber-statistics**.

Sources: Based on Thomas (2011), Goldstein (2011), Bieber (2010), Antkowiak (2011), **forbes.com/sites/dorothypomerantz/2013/07/22/lady-gaga-tops-forbes-list-of-top-earning-celebrities-under-30**, **forbes.com/profile/justin-bieber**, and **en.wikipedia.org/wiki/Justin_Bieber_discography**.

LESSONS LEARNED FROM THE CASE

First, this case demonstrates that talented performers can be discovered on the Web, especially through videos posted on YouTube. Seconds, with the help of social media, it is possible for people to not only be discovered, but also to advance rapidly in their careers.

(continued)

Social media can direct massive traffic to websites where artists can promote their products and services, and where retailers and others can sell products and services. Third, this is a great example of how social media can facilitate personal relationships and interactions. Fourth, we learned about the power of tweeting. Finally, we learn that even greater success can be achieved when several social media tools are used.

The utilization of social media has facilitated entertainment and its commercial side. This is only one innovative topic covered in this chapter. The other topics are social government, B2B marketing uses of social media, social-oriented virtual worlds, social games, social entertainment, and social P2P (peer-to-peer) activities.

9.1 SOCIAL MEDIA AND COMMERCE IN E-GOVERNMENT

Governments are using social media extensively. We describe briefly the major topics in this section.

Definition and Scope of E-Government

As e-commerce matures and its tools and applications improve, greater attention is given to its use in improving the business of public institutions and governments (country, state, county, city, etc.). **E-government** is the use of information technology in general, and e-commerce in particular, to provide citizens and organizations with more convenient access to government information and services. It also is an efficient and effective way of conducting governments' business transactions with citizens and businesses, and transacting effectively within governments themselves. See Mergel (2012), **w3.org/egov**, and **en.wikipedia.org/wiki/E-Government** for details.

Several major markets fit within this broad definition of e-government: *government-to-citizens* (G2C), *government-to-business* (G2B), *government-to-government* (G2G), and *government-to-employees* (G2E), as well as *internal efficiency and effectiveness* (IEE). Recently, many governments have introduced social government.

E-Government 2.0 (Social Government)

Social government (also known as **government 2.0**) is an emerging field where governments use social media to improve their services to citizens, organizations, and employees, in addition to improving their internal operations. A social government can be viewed as a subset of e-government.

For an 85-slide presentation titled "Local Government to Social Media," see Dawson (2010). *Social government* is a new model for delivering the functions of e-government. For a review of social media use in e-government, see Magro (2012).

Social Government in Action

According to Baumgarten and Chui (2009), government agencies often fail to meet users' needs, despite spending enormous amounts of time and money on Web-based initiatives. By employing Web 2.0 tools, using new business models, and embracing social networks and user participation, government agencies can raise the effectiveness of their online presence and activities. Governments in all levels, from national to local (Black 2013), are using social media and social commerce applications. For extensive coverage on this topic, see NIC Inc. (2010). Government agencies around the world are now experimenting with social media (e.g., India; see Banday and Matto 2013). Governments use social media mainly for collaboration, dissemination of information, e-learning, and citizen engagement. An example is the initiative in New Zealand, where social networking tools are being used extensively by the government, both for internal and external use (see Case 9.1).

Case 9.1
SC Application

Social Networking Initiatives by the New Zealand Government
The New Zealand government is very active in implementing new technologies. As of 2008, it has created a number of e-government social networking initiatives (e.g., see **ssc.govt.nz/bps-initiatives-spotlight**).

Cross-Government Initiatives
Various government agencies and their employees can now work better together due to the implementation of numerous Web 2.0 initiatives.

- **Shared Workspaces.** Specialist groups and networks share experience, expertise, and good practices by utilizing a suite of online tools that supports interagency collaboration and information sharing. Blogs and wikis are the major tools used.
- **E-Initiatives Wiki.** Individuals working on like projects share experience and information through an online library.
- **Principals Electronic Network.** This interactive online community allows school principals and leaders to collaborate through discussion and learn from each other's expertise.

- **Best Practices Forum.** A blog with a goal to impart leadership in order to obtain best practices in significant work programs.
- **Research e-Labs.** Technology, Web trends, and open source software in government are explored in a blog in order to distribute research and case studies.

Public Engagement

Agencies have developed most of the government's social networking initiatives with the aim of engaging with the public. The following are key examples:

- **Policing Act Wiki.** The New Zealand Police implemented a variety of social media initiatives ranging from sharing information on their Twitter feed to collaborating on LinkedIn and Facebook. For example, in 2009, the Queenstown Police gained worldwide notoriety for using Facebook to help catch a burglar (see **policingwithintelligence.blogspot.com/2009/07/new-zealand-police-use-facebook-to-stop.html**). In June 2011, the New Zealand Police received Social Media NZ's "Best Use" award.
- **National Library of New Zealand.** Several initiatives have been created by the National Library of New Zealand (**natlib.govt.nz**), including a blog with categories such as "behind the scenes" and "collections." School services staff in New Zealand provide information to students and libraries about resources and services to support literacy, and more (**natlib.govt.nz/schools**), along with information for librarians on services and digital tools (**natlib.govt.nz/librarians**). Staff also share their views about work progress on the National Library's technology on the Library TechNZ blog (**natlib.govt.nz/blog/categories/library-tech**).
- **Twitter.** In February 2014, The National Library had over 8,000 followers on Twitter (**twitter.com/NLNZ**). This enables the Library to engage patrons online, disseminating information about new collections and exhibits. The people who run NLNZ's Twitter account also post on a Twitter account known as #tbreaktweets. These posts are usually humorous.
- **New Zealand Draft Standards.** Standards New Zealand (**standards.co.nz**) is New Zealand's leading developer and publisher of standards and standards-based solutions. They provide standards solutions on diverse subject areas such as health and disability.
- **Participation Project Wiki.** Established by the State Services Commission, the wiki is a tool for collaborative policy making.
- **ePetitions.** A program created by the Wellington City Council allows anyone the ability to make suggestions (create a petition or sign an open petition) related to Council business, via the Internet (**wellington.govt.nz/have-your-say/epetitions**).

- **Archives New Zealand Audio Visual Wiki.** The public can view films online, discuss them with other users, and add information about the content or context of the films through an Archives of New Zealand initiative (**audiovisual.archives.govt.nz**).
- **Careers New Zealand Outreach.** Careers New Zealand (**careers.govt.nz**) not only joins social networks where they are likely to be influential (e.g., on Facebook), but also actively does social media outreach.
- **Crowdsourcing Images.** The New Zealand Historic Places Trust (**historic.org.nz**) is using Flickr to collect images from the public for its Register of New Zealand's historic places (see **webtoolkit.govt.nz/blog/2013/12/confessions-of-a-social-media-phobe**).
- **Distributing Content on YouTube.** The New Zealand Ministry for Culture and Heritage uses YouTube (**youtube.com/user/ManatuTaonga**) to preserve and promote the country's culture and heritage.
- **Promoting Sports on Facebook.** The Triathlon New Zealand, the national governing body for triathlon, duathlon, and aquathlon, has seen enormous interest and contributions via social media, and raising awareness of the sports.
- **Requesting Data Sets Online.** The New Zealand Department of Internal Affairs (**dia.gov.nz**) provides information online to the public about government services, forms to download (birth certificates, marriage certificates), and publications and reports.

Other Agency-Related Social Media Initiatives

Agencies also use social networking tools to collaborate with nongovernment organizations. Some examples of social media initiatives involve the use of Wikipedia, Facebook, Seconds Life, and online discussion groups.

A New Approach to E-Government

The New Zealand government has implemented an initiative called Rethink Online (for details, see **ict.govt.nz/guidance-and-resources/government-online/rethink-online**). This is a new way for the government to invest in and manage its online channels to attain a more agile strategy, improve the value of financial investments, and achieve better customer experiences. The Rethink Online program consists of four principles, which include coordination, sharing, centrality for users, and collaboration. It also addresses current difficulties in online information and service delivery, and supports government in order to meet people's expectancies as well as the government's ever-changing needs.

Sources: Based on New Zealand Government (2014a, b, c), New Zealand Government State Services Commission (2014), and Fielden and Malcolm (2010).

Questions

1. Given the richness of New Zealand's offerings, do you believe that the portal style of e-government will be replaced by a social networking style?
2. What are the benefits of the internal social networking initiatives?
3. Comment on the initiative's connections to YouTube, Flickr, and Facebook.
4. Why do wikis and blogs play such an important role in many of these initiatives?
5. Which initiatives are related to e-learning? To e-commerce? In what ways?
6. Enter **ict.govt.nz** and identify new initiatives in SC as of January 2015.

Following are three other examples of effective social government.

Example 1: Open Government Places (OGP)

This project connects civil servants and government offices, enabling collaboration throughout communities in the Netherlands. It cuts the red tape and includes a multitude of social media-supported activities. The project won the 2011 Management Innovation eXchange Award. For details, see Spinder (2011).

Example 2: U.S. Cost Guard

Ali (2010) provides an example of how the U.S. Coast Guard uses YouTube, Twitter, and Flickr to disseminate information and discuss their rescue operations. (See also the Coast Guard Social Media's official blog at **coastguard.dodlive. mil/2009/07/official-coast-guard-social-media**.) Notable is FEMA's Twitter feed (previously 'FEMA in Focus'), a channel that provides dissemination of FEMA-related information (see **twitter.com/fema**). Law enforcement agencies use social media (like Facebook and Twitter) to hunt for criminals. (For some examples, see **digitaltrends.com/social-media/the-new-inside-source-for-police-forces-social-networks**.)

Example 3: The FBI

The FBI developed an early-warning system about potential domestic and global threats from material it collected from social networks. It is a kind of market research application (Chap. 10). For details, see BBC News (2012).

The Benefits of Government 2.0

According to a December 2009 Australian government 2.0 task force report (**finance.gov.au/publications/gov20task-forcereport/doc/Government20TaskforceReport.pdf**), embracing government 2.0 can provide the government with the following benefits:

- Improve the quality and responsiveness of services in areas like education, health, public safety, and environmental management, and at the same time deliver these services with greater agility and efficiency.
- Cultivate and harness the enthusiasm of citizens, letting them contribute more fully to their well-being and that of their community.
- Make democracy more participatory and citizens more informed.
- Unlock the immense economic and social value of information and other content held by governments to serve as a platform for innovation.
- Revitalize the public sector and make government policies and services more responsive to people's needs and concerns by:
  (a) Providing governments with social media tools for a much greater level of community engagement
  (b) Allowing the users of government services much greater participation in their design and continual improvement of these services
  (c) Involving communities of interest and practice outside the public sector, which offer unique access to expertise local knowledge, and perspectives, in policy making and delivery
  (d) More successfully attracting and retaining bright, enthusiastic citizens to the public service workforce by making their work less hierarchical, more collaborative, and more intrinsically rewarding.

Some people believe that social networking will replace the current e-government "one-stop" passive portal (e.g., see Vaz 2014). Government initiatives are very diversified with the Web 2.0 approach. For example, many governments have owned islands on Seconds Life (e.g. eGov Island, Coalition Island) on which they present diplomatic issues and promote tourist attractions and investment opportunities. With such initiatives, it is important to have strict security, accountability, and compliance functionality in place, which has proven challenging when implementing wikis and blogs. Government experts encourage employees to experiment with social networking, but suggest that such pilots have to remain very well-focused and somewhat isolated from mainstream processes for at least the first 2 years. For more about what the U.S. government is doing in Seconds Life, see **www. rikomatic.com/betterverse/2009/09/federal-government--in-seconds-life.html**.

Applications and Resources

Politicians use social networking extensively. For example, during the 2008 U.S. presidential election, Democratic candidate Barack Obama created pages on Facebook and LinkedIn, where he made thousands of connections and received hundreds of thousands of responses to his question, "What ideas do you have to keep America competitive in the years ahead?" Many of the responses were very interesting and insightful. President Obama also created an "Obama for America" interest group on LinkedIn.

In addition to the New Zealand Case 9.1, you may look at what is going on in Australia regarding social commerce (see Australian Government 2012).

For an extensive list of resources on social networks in governments, including reports, applications, and policies, see the 2009 Slideshare presentation 'Getting Started in the Social Web: Government 2.0' at **slideshare.net/tamera/getting-started-in-the-social-web-government-20**. For other presentations, search **slideshare.net** for 'social web government 2.0.' E-government software and solutions are provided by most large software vendors (e.g., Adobe, Cisco systems, IBM/Cognos's solutions for government, and Microsoft). For extensive coverage of e-government, see **wisegeek.com/what-is-e-government.htm**.

9.2   B2B SOCIAL NETWORKING

Although a large number of companies conduct social networking that targets individual consumers (B2C), there is also considerable activity in the B2B arena (see Mac 2014). The social B2B potential is huge, and new applications are added daily. See Bodnar and Cohen (2012) and the infographic showing the 2014 B2B social media landscape at **b2bmarketing.net/knowledgebank/social-media-marketing/features/infographic-2014-b2b-social-media-landscape**.

E-Communities in B2B

B2B applications may involve many participants in the supply chain and in nonprofit organizations, business buyers and B2B sellers, service providers, industry associations, and others. In many cases, the B2B market maker can provide typical social network services, such as chat rooms, bulletin boards, and, possibly, personalized Web pages to the community members.

E-communities connect employees, suppliers, distribution channel members, customers, and other business partners and any combination of these. In addition, e-communities offer a powerful resource for e-businesses to leverage online discussions and interactions in order to optimize innovation and responsiveness. It is therefore beneficial to study the tools, methods, and best practices of building and managing B2B e-communities.

B2B e-communities are mostly communities of transactions; as such, members' major interests are trading and business-related information gathering. Many of the communities promote partner relationships.

The Major Opportunities and Benefits of Social Commerce in B2B

Companies that use B2B social networking may have the following opportunities:

- Discover new business partners and build relationships with them (Gillin and Schwartzman 2011).
- Enhance the ability of participants to learn about new technologies, competitors, and the business environment.
- Find more sales leads (see Sysomos Inc. 2011 and Gillin and Schwartzman 2011).
- Post questions and facilitate discussions on LinkedIn by searching the Help Center, asking the community a question through the Help Forum, or by using the posting module on your homepage to ask your network a question. Post questions on other social networks and receive helpful answers.
- Use Instagram to tell the companies' stories (Cohen 2014a).
- Improve participation in industry association activities (including lobbying).
- Create brand awareness.
- Create buzz about upcoming product releases (Gillin and Schwartzman 2011).
- Advertise new and existing products and services.
- Drive traffic to vendors' pages in social networks. Word-of-mouth communication also may increase traffic.
- Create social communities to encourage discussions among business partners (e.g., buyers and suppliers).

MarketingCharts Staff (2014) summarizes B2B Marketing's 2014 Social Media Benchmarketing Report, which found that B2B marketers are focusing their social media efforts on generating sales leads and on pushing sales with branding and positioning as the major objectives. (See **b2bmarketing.net/knowledgebank/social-media-marketing/features/**

infographic-2014-b2b-social-media-landscape for the report and the corresponding 2014 B2B Social Media Landscape infographic.)

For SC opportunities available on LinkedIn, see Schaffer (2011); on Twitter, see Maddox (2010); on Instagram, see Cohen (2014a); and in general, see Jensen (2012).

Most uses of B2B social networking are seen in *enterprise social networking*, which involves private social networks within the enterprise. We discussed this topic in Chap. 8.

Exploiting these opportunities may result in the following benefits (reported by Wiebesick 2011b):

- B2B companies that blog garnered 67 % more leads per month than those who do not.
- 69 % of B2B marketers are shifting their budgets toward social media.
- 41 % of B2B companies acquire customers through Facebook.
- 82 % of B2C companies use social media, while 86 % of B2B companies use social media.
- B2B marketers improve search results aided by social media.

These data are probably higher with the passage of time.

Marketo (undated) lists the following benefits of B2B social media marketing:
- Increases brand awareness
- Builds reputation as a thought leader
- Encourages promoters
- Can improve SEO ranking

For an infographic showing how B2B companies are using social media, see Melin (2013).

Specific Social Networking Activities in B2B

Businesses can use B2B social networking to improve knowledge sharing, collaboration, and collect feedback. Furthermore, social networking sites also may prove beneficial in aiding decision making and problem-solving efforts (e.g., via crowdsourcing).

By the end of 2012, social networking was playing a much more important role in B2B. According to a 2010 study by Regus (reported by Leggatt 2010), both small and large businesses are using social networks quite successfully to find and retain new business. A few highlights of the study include:
- 50–75 % of companies globally use social networks for various networking functions.
- 40 % of businesses worldwide have found new customers via social networks.

- 27 % of companies include social networking activities to both acquire and retain customers in their marketing budget.

The main uses of social networks are keeping in touch with business contacts; meeting with special interest groups; learning useful business intelligence; and organizing, managing, and connecting with customer groups.

Some interesting statistical data are available in a report titled *Social Strategy for B2B Marketing 2011* from GlobalWebIndex (see **slideshare.net/globalwebindex/globalwebindex-b2b-social-media-strategy-2011**). For details, see Cohen (2011).

According to a survey reported by Pardot (2011), social media use among B2B marketers is already very high. However, 30 % are not calculating the return on investment for social media. The survey also ranked Twitter as the most popular social media channel. Other surveys rank LinkedIn as the most popular, followed by Facebook, with Twitter in third place.

According to BIA/Kelsey's U.S. Local Media Annual Forecast (reported by MarketingProfs 2011), B2B advertising on social networking sites will grow from $2.1 billion in 2010 to $8.3 billion by 2015. Other reports attempt to answer the following questions:
- How much will marketers spend on social network advertising aimed at a business audience?
- What types of B2B advertising can businesses do on social network sites?
- Why are companies creating social networks in order to market to business customers, vendors, distributors, and channel partners?
- What are the challenges of developing such networks?

Generating sales leads is one of the major activities of B2B marketing, which can be facilitated by social media.

Usefulness of Social Networking Activities in B2B

According to MarketingCharts Staff (2014), marketing videos on social networks are most effective, followed by images and photos. Social conversations and other engagements are somewhat less effective.

Generating Sales Leads in B2B Social Commerce

Generating sales leads can be a time-consuming and complex challenge; however, it was ranked as the prime area of social B2B activities (MarketingCharts Staff 2014). Using social media, companies can use the following lead generation strategies (per Sysomos Inc. 2011). (See also Matlick 2013.)
- Find and create lead-generation opportunities in the blogosphere.
- Target competitors' customers for highly motivated sales leads.

- Run special offers and promotions that deliver higher conversion rates.

For an infographic, see McTigue (2014). For a discussion about how sales teams generate leads using social media, see Cohen (2014b).

Using the Major Social Networks in B2B

Hallam (2014) provides the following percentages of B2B marketers who use the major social media sites to distribute content: LinkedIn 91 %, Twitter 85 %, Facebook 81 %, YouTube 73 %, Google+ 55 %, Slideshare 40 %, Pinterest 34 %, Instagram 22 %.

The following are few examples of some of these uses.

The Major Social B2B Tools and Platforms

Among the social media tools, Twitter is becoming an important B2B sales platform (e.g., see Viskovich 2013). Thomson (2013) discusses the various social channels which are good for B2B. According to a 2013 survey of B2B buyers in Europe (reported by Rayson 2013), Google+ is the most influential social media networking followed by Facebook and LinkedIn, while Twitter and Pinterest ranked lower. The survey also found that industry forums are the most frequently used social channels. (Friends and networks are the most influential sources of information in B2B buying decisions.) Thus, building your social networks and relationships must be an essential part of your strategy. A special marketplace for B2B social networking is Tradescraper (**tradescraper.com**).

Example

Julig (2013) describes how salespeople in one company use Pinterest to reach a B2B market. The company grew their followers on Pinterest to over 18,000 small businesses in less than 2 years. Their goal is to expand the idea of the brand and think visually. In October 2013, the company had 92 Pinterest boards with over 4,000 pins.

Using LinkedIn in B2B

Some experts believe that the most popular social media marketing channel for B2B marketers is LinkedIn. The IAB has published the B2B Content Marketing Benchmarks, Budgets, and Trends (North America) data for 2014, (see **iab.net/media/file/B2BResearch2014.pdf**). For example, they found that 91 % of B2B marketers use LinkedIn in some way to distribute their content.

Interesting examples of B2B case studies on social media best practices using LinkedIn's marketing solutions are available at **business.linkedin.com/marketing-solutions/social-media-case-studies.html**. The Vestas Inc. case study provided there (at **snap.licdn.com/microsites/content/dam/business/marketing-solutions/global/en_US/site/pdf/cs/linkedin_vestas_case_study_us_en_130314.pdf**) is a comprehensive example (see Internet Exercise #12).

Using Facebook in B2B

There are many possibilities of using Facebook in B2B. Here are a few examples:

- Pickering (2012) suggests using Facebook to (a) build a fan base; (b) share engaging content; (c) capture leads and contact information; (d) make it personal and fun; and (e) reach friends of fans. The author provides several examples of how this is done.
- Johnson (2013) suggests the following: (a) generate content to capture leads; (b) content strategy is the key; (c) concentrate on non-lead generation goals as well; (d) use visuals; and (e) advertise. Johnson (2013) also provides a presentation and free assessment.
- Harper (2014) suggests the following to make Facebook marketing works for B2B: (a) have an understanding of your audience; (b) create and curate thoughtful content; (c) publish updates on your audience's schedule; and (d) target your advertising.

These guides can greatly improve the effectiveness of using Facebook for B2B.

Using Twitter in B2B

Twitter is used extensively in B2C mainly as a communication tool for customer service advertising campaigns, customer engagement platforms, CRM, and market research. Similar uses are evidenced in B2B. More examples are provided in **blog.twilert.com/2014/03/use-twitter-b2b-marketing**. The applications include monitoring conversations for identifying business opportunities, enabling small businesses to engage with potential customers, making contacts with potential customers, and buyers discovering potential suppliers.

Corporate Profiles on Social Networks

LinkedIn and Facebook include substantial information on companies and their individual employees. In fact, employee profiles can be part of a company's brand. For example, in early 2012, IBM had approximately 280,000 employees registered on LinkedIn and Microsoft had around 134,000 as of early 2014. In addition, some sites feature company only profiles, with comments by employees and customers.

Final note: There are less B2B social media applications than B2C ones. However, this situation is changing. For details, see Salesforce Marketing Cloud (2012), and Mac (2014).

B2B Success Stories

BtoB's Interactive Marketing Guide (available at **btobonline.com**; now a part of AdAge) provides the following examples of successful applications:

- **Arketi Group (arketi.com).** Arketi Group created and sponsored a B2B marketing community on LinkedIn, and is known for its 500 ongoing daily discussions.
- **Cisco Systems (cisco.com).** Cisco uses Facebook to aggregate Twitter, Flickr, YouTube, blogs, and RSS feeds from one interface. With about 40,000 fans, daily postings include a video blog (vlog) from the CEO and social events (e.g., Halloween photos).
- **Hewlett-Packard Co. (hp.com).** HP uses *animatics* posted on YouTube to promote renewals of their Care Pack Service agreements (see **youtube.com/watch?v= FIY9VxpIuUM**).
- **Reed Business Information (reedbusiness.com).** Reed Business Information uses LinkedIn-generated content in a community of "Automation and Control Engineering." The community has about 5,000 members that provide expertise to one another, in over 100 discussion groups.
- **Deloitte (deloitte.com).** Deloitte leverages Facebook as a brand-building tool to build its technology innovation strategy.

Another example is that of Pfizer Pharmaceutical Co. Pfizer (**pfizer.com**) developed a social commerce strategy initially internally, among its various units. These efforts were extended to the supply chain (see Dunay 2013). In Pfizer's community, over 25,000 fans are engaged in discussions of how to better serve customers' needs. Pfizer launched an internal intranet platform in 2010, which drew 41,000 unique users who generated 800,000 page views. In 2011, it rose to approximately 60,000 users driving 1.6 million page views. As part of the intranet, Pfizer started a social networking hub, called *My World,* which they developed in partnership with their Business Technology colleagues. *MyWorld* is part of their *PfizerWorld* intranet platform, which is used to engage their colleagues. See **socialmediacases.blogspot. com/2014/04/case-study-enterprise-social-network.html**.

For steps for B2B social media marketing success, see Mac (2014). For case studies, read Simply Zesty's eBook titled "50 Brilliant Social Media B2B Case Studies" (available for purchase at **simplyzesty.com/Blog/Article/ June-2011/50-Brilliant-Social-Media-B2B-Case-Studies**).

For a guide to advanced social media, download Simply Zesty's free e-book "The Giant Free Simply Ebook: An Advanced Guide to Social Media" (available in a 2012 article by Fisher at **simplyzesty.com/Blog/Article/November-2012/**

The-Giant-Free-Simply-Zesty-eBook-An-Advanced-Guide-To-Social-Media-Marketing).

Wiebesick (2011a) provides a slide show of these four examples of success stories:

- Kinaxis (**kinaxis.com**): Increased traffic and leads by creating funny and entertaining videos and posting them on the company blog.
- Archer Technologies (an EMC company): Created an enterprise social network for customers to interact and generate ideas for new products.
- Indium Corp. (**indium.com**): Engineers shared blogs among themselves and with the industry. ("Content is King.")
- Cree, Inc. (**cree.com**): Created an enterprise social network site for engagement, including blogging, YouTube videos, and photo contests.

For more success stories, see Moth (2013).

The following are other examples of significant B2B social commerce activities:

Example 1: American Express-Sponsored Business Travel Social Network

American Express launched an online social network, Business Travel ConneXion (or BTX), **businesstravelconnexion.com**, for the corporate travel industry.

Example 2

Orabrush, Inc. (**orabrush.com**) is a start-up company that makes tongue cleaners that reduce bad breath. The company created funny YouTube videos targeting Walmart employees. In a short time, the company had over 160,000 subscribers on YouTube, and more than 39 million views. In addition, the company advertised on Facebook at a cost of only $28, resulting in 300,000 fans. This publicity convinced some Walmart buyers to try the product, and Orabrush landed a huge contract with Walmart. For details, see Neff (2011).

Social Media Case Studies in Manufacturing

Hallam Internet Limited provides several examples of using social networking in B2B by manufacturers; see **hallaminternet.com/2014/b2b-social-media-case-studies**.

B2B Virtual Trade Shows and Trade Fairs in Virtual Worlds

Trade fairs and trade shows are popular B2B (and sometimes B2C) marketing communication practices. Today, they are becoming popular online.

How Virtual Trade Shows Are Arranged

The structure of a typical trade show (also known as a *trade fair*) often includes a virtual exhibition hall that visitors enter first. Exhibitors can build virtual booths where they present exhibits of their products or services and any related information. Both exhibitors and visitors can create avatars of themselves.

Like their physical counterparts, virtual trade shows can be built for a whole industry, a specialized group within an industry, a group of related companies, a government, or an association. For a comprehensive video on the virtual trade show, see **youtube.com/watch?v=kAFpH5vEhCc**.

Benefits of Virtual Trade Shows

The major benefits of virtual trade shows are:

- The cost of a virtual trade show to the organizers is a fraction of the cost of a real-world trade show. Thus, the participation fees can be much lower, attracting many more exhibitors and attendees.
- Many more attendees can afford to visit due to saving money on travel expenses, accommodations, and registration fees. Additionally, there is no physical space constraint.
- It is possible to have the show as a stand-alone and/or as an extension to a physical trade show.
- More events, entertainment, and interactions can occur in virtual trade shows. Although you cannot get a free cup of coffee, you can, however, get coupons for free coffee and gifts from exhibitors.
- There is no need for organizers to print promotional material.
- There is no carbon footprint to pollute the environment.
- Booths can have superb designs (compared to physical ones), including choice of colors, videos, and so on.

Some trade shows are permanent (always open), whereas others take place once a year. For a discussion and list, see **en.wikipedia.org/wiki/Virtual_tradeshow**. One example is Tradefair Plus+ (**plus.tradefair.com**). For a schematic view of virtual booths and exhibition halls, search Google images for 'virtual trade shows.' For a live demo, see **3d-virtualevents.com**.

For a detailed description of virtual trade shows, see Lindner (2009), and the 'Trade Show Guide' at **trade-show-guide.com/articles/virtualtradeshows.html**.

Example: MarketPlace365

MarketPlace365 (**marketplace365.com/marketing**) is a virtual tradeshow platform that gives companies tools to build virtual trade shows and attract traffic to the shows. For details, see **marketplace365.com/Marketing** and **marketplace365.com/Marketing/features.aspx**.

Note: Social media can be used to support exhibits even in physical trade shows. For more on using social media at trade shows, see Patterson (2012) and download his free 'Social Media Tradeshow Marketing Checklist' at **tradeshowguyblog.com/downloads/Social-Media-Tradeshow-Marketing-Checklist.pdf**.

The Process Used in Virtual Trade Shows

The trade fair participant goes to a specific virtual trade show homepage, typically registering at the site. The participant then visits the virtual exhibit floor. On the virtual exhibit floor, the participant can select a virtual booth, gather information, and engage in "live" interaction (e.g., live chat) and information dissemination. Technologies enable communication through features such as online chat, Web callback, fax, and e-mail. Participants have access to community-building features, such as online discussion boards and online forums that allow collaborations, discussions, and debates. Furthermore, the exhibitors can conduct online surveys. In addition, special speakers or guests can communicate through video-streamed keynote Webcasts. Attendees can also interact with each other through a chat room. Although this enables the event attendees to exchange information in a same-time, different-place mode, it is not as media rich as is the avatar visibility experience available on Seconds Life.

Virtual trade shows can have all the features that you find in a physical trade show, and even more. For example, one of the main reasons for exhibitors to participate in trade fairs is to acquire new leads and contacts. In a virtual trade show, exhibitors can receive attendee leads in real time. A typical attendee report, containing the name of every registered attendee, is made available to all exhibitors. Exhibitors can also access traffic reports of all visitors to each virtual booth. Attendees visiting a booth can drop off an e-business card. The traffic report includes all attendees' names, titles, and relevant contact information, and whether the attendee has requested additional information on any products and services, the company in general, or employment opportunities.

Strategy for B2B Social Networking

Gillin (2010) made several suggestions on how to maximize the value of multiple social marketing channels. Power (2014) provides examples and sources for social media strategy for B2B.

Eventually, companies will be able to use social networking more efficiently. Success stories of five companies—SAP, United Linen (a small laundry service), Forrester Research, Kinaxis, and Expert Laser Services—are discussed by Jensen (2012).

The Future of B2B Social Networking

Marketing users are developing social media and search tools. Businesses must embrace social networking in order to better understand their customers and business partners.

(Note: *B2B marketing* refers to marketing by manufacturers and wholesalers along the sell-side of the supply chain).

For emerging trends in B2B social media marketing, see a slide show presentation at **slideshare.net/BtoBOnline/social-media-reportmay2013**.

9.3 SOCIAL COMMERCE: APPLICATIONS IN VIRTUAL WORLDS

Virtual worlds (see Chap. 2) can be effective platforms for online social interactions, community building, conducting business transactions, and facilitating learning and training (e.g., education). As briefly described in Chap. 2, users can navigate and move around in a virtual world using their avatars, which they can also use for communication and other activities. Virtual worlds also may enable trading in virtual goods, and paying for them with virtual money. For the uses of virtual worlds, see **en.wikipedia.org/wiki/Virtual_world** and **makeuseof.com/tag/what-are-virtual-worlds-what-are-their-uses-makeuseof-explains**. For a list of the major virtual worlds, see **arianeb.com/more3Dworlds.htm**. For using virtual worlds in education, see Angel Learning's 2008 White Paper titled 'The Power of Virtual Worlds in Education: A Seconds Life Primer and Resource for Exploring the Potential of Virtual Worlds to Impact Teaching and Learning,' see **soma.sbcc.edu/Users/Russotti/SL/PowerofVirtual%20WorldsEdu_0708.pdf**.

Businesses can make use of virtual worlds, not just for entertaining their customers and prospects, but also by engaging them in an experience that may be unavailable in the real world. Due to the use of multiple senses in a virtual world, users' experiences can be more fulfilling than in a 2D world, or sometimes even more than in a physical one. For instance, according to a posting on Seconds Life (February 2011), Seconds Life had over 22 million registered user accounts (unique residents) who spent more than 115 million hours a month on the site. As of June 2013, the number of registered users has risen to over 36 million; the equivalent of total time users have spent in Seconds Life is 217,266 days. (See the article and infographic by Reahard 2013). Businesses can leverage features and spaces, as illustrated next, to exploit the opportunities in virtual worlds.

For the business benefits of Seconds Life, see Butler-Borrer (2010). Companies make money in virtual worlds by influencing people to buy virtual items, such as clothes, frequently while playing games. People are spending more and more time in online games. For example, in 2012, online game maker Team Fortress 2 made a half a million dollars from users who were creating content (making hats), which caused their PayPal account to break. Team Fortress 2 was competing against their own userbase. (See **makeuseof.com/tag/virtual-world-millionaires-getting-rich-digital-marketplace**.)

The Features and Spaces of Virtual Worlds

Virtual worlds have a set of properties or features that provide the capabilities where business can be conducted.

The Features That Businesses Can Leverage

- **Shared space.** The virtual world provides many users with the ability to participate simultaneously in activities, engage in discussions, and participate in collaborative activities.
- **3-D visualization (graphical user interface).** The virtual world depicts both 2-D and 3-D images.
- **Immediacy.** Interactions usually occur in real time, and users experience the results of their actions immediately.
- **Interactivity.** Participants can create or modify customized content. They may do so in collaboration with others.
- **Persistence.** Activities in virtual worlds are happening whether members are present or not.
- **Socialization and community formation.** A virtual world provides opportunities for socializing with other users and facilitates group formation of different types (e.g., work teams).

IBM, Walmart, Toyota, Sears, Wells Fargo, and many other large companies have experimented with virtual worlds for testing new designs, customer service, employee training, and marketing communication.

The Landscape of Virtual World Commercial Applications

The potential of virtual worlds is large, particularly when they are integrated with other IT and business systems. A virtual world is particularly attractive to video game players, where sellers can build communities of fans and advertise. Other businesses are using virtual worlds for collaboration, design testing, learning, and relationship building.

Virtual worlds can be viewed as a set of the following multidimensional spaces.

The Spaces in Virtual Worlds

The following are brief descriptions of the major spaces used in virtual worlds:

1. **Social space.** Place where users' avatars (and their owners) can meet, discuss, share information and opinions, and socialize.
2. **Entertainment space.** Place where avatars (and their owners) can play games, watch movies, and attend concerts in a 3-D environment.
3. **Transaction space.** Marketplace where one can conduct business and financial transactions, sell and buy available virtual goods as well as some real goods at a virtual webstore.
4. **Experimental/demonstration space.** Place in the virtual world where real-world environments, products, and services can be simulated for experimentation, demonstration, training, and testing.
5. **Collaboration space.** Place for collaboration, innovation, and new product design and development.
6. **Smart agent space.** Place where software agents can seek information and engage with other agents to fulfill or facilitate transactions for their owners.
7. **Fantasy space.** A dream world where people can do things that are not feasible or not affordable in the real world (e.g., take a trip to the moon or enjoy an expensive cruise).
8. **Educational Space.** Certain places in the virtual world are dedicated to educational activities such as teaching classes, evaluating projects, or learning by doing special projects.

- **Resemblance to the real-world environment.** Businesses can use the technology since it can simulate, and even conduct real world activities (e.g., customer service) more promptly and a low cost (e.g., product design). Additionally, interactions with business partners are easy. It is also a place for attractive advertisements. Users can get a feel of the real world without cost and time constraints (e.g., buy properties, travel).
- **Shopping for virtual goods.** Buying and selling virtual real estate is the major shopping activity in virtual worlds. Users can buy land, develop it, build on it and sell it. Millions of people who cannot afford their dream house (e.g., in developing countries) are satisfied with buying virtual houses. You can also shop for fascinating virtual goods for your avatar or your virtual home on Seconds Life at **secondslife.com/shop**.
- **Attractions for the younger generations.** Today's youth are tomorrow's shoppers. They grew up with computer applications and love games and online entertainment.
- **New means of navigation and discovery.** Virtual worlds enable the creation of visually attractive and unique products that visitors never knew existed.
- **The attributes and capabilities.** These are unique to virtual worlds. First, they are mostly 3-D. Seconds, the worlds are populated with avatars. The virtual worlds are interactive and can be manipulated and changed by users at very low cost.
- **Better online meeting spaces and collaborative platforms.** Virtual worlds provide interesting platforms for collaboration, meetings, discussions, and chatting (e.g., try to chat in 3D at **imvu.com**).
- **Interactive environment for education and training.** Several activities, as shown in Table 9.1, can be used to facilitate training and learning.

One can arrange for the use of one or more of these eight spaces in innovative ways for business, education, medical, political, and other uses. Business applications of virtual worlds are varied and their use depends on the type of business in which a company is engaged, in the organizational objectives, and the target user profiles.

The Major Drivers of Social Commerce in Virtual Worlds

The key factors that drive business applications in virtual worlds are:

The Major Categories of Virtual World Applications

It is common to classify major applications into 18 categories (adapted from Ciaramitaro 2010; Murugesan 2008; Reeves and Read 2009, and **en.wikipedia.org/wiki/ Virtual_world**).

Business Applications in Virtual Worlds

The following are examples of business applications used in virtual worlds.

Table 9.1 The use of virtual worlds to facilitate learning

	Description
Simulation	Users can manipulate simulated scenarios and see results. Creating a virtual business is a popular activity
Distance learning	A virtual world can be used as a place for working, learning, and/or collaborative learning and collaborative problem solving
Class meetings	Learning institutions offer a large number of virtual classes (many in Seconds Life). Students can interact and explore, as well as share and work with teachers, via avatars
Exploration	The virtual world is a good platform for explorative learning. Learners can explore in a way similar to the way they can in the real world. The information is communicated to the user/avatar visually, by text, or via other media
Visualization	Visualization is a key learning enabler. The virtual world can be used to visualize a process. It can be used as a set of data helping with problem analysis and finding solutions
Imaginative scenarios	People can create fantasy objects and scenarios for entertainment
Information dissemination	Many organizations, governments, and universities provide updated interactive information, which can be used to learn geography, public administration, hospitality management, technology, and more

Sources: Based on Murugesan (2008), Terdiman (2008), and **second-slife.com** (accessed January 2015)

1. **Webstores and online sales.** Companies have set up webstores in virtual worlds to enable customers to have a more immersive experience by trying out virtual products, including clothes, cars, or jewelry before they buy them. This is done in a 3-D virtual salesroom. Potential buyers can also conduct research, dress avatars, and sometimes complete a purchase through links that lead them to a secure trading place. For details, see Seconds Life's 'Shop: Learn' page at **secondslife.com/shop/learn**.
2. **Front offices or help desks.** Virtual worlds can act as access points for customer service. The care center is staffed by avatars. This service is available around the clock.
3. **Advertising and product demonstrations.** Marketers and advertisers can place 3D display ads and banners promoting products or services at various locations in virtual worlds to catch the attention of visitors. Consumers also can view demonstrations by avatars on how to install or assemble products such as washing machines or furniture.

There are several advantages for using virtual worlds. Virtual stores allow businesses to reach a variety of demographically diverse customers.

Furthermore, some real world constraints may be reduced or eliminated in virtual worlds. In addition, the cost of experimenting with virtual things is minimal and there is no cost when making errors.

Restrictions and costs that are found in real world situations are further reduced.

For details, see **wiki.secondslife.com/wiki/Advertising_in_Seconds_Life**.

4. **Content creation and distribution.** Virtual worlds can serve as channels for delivering music, games, art, and other forms of interactive content for engaging participants.
5. **Meetings, seminars, and conferences.** Virtual worlds are being used as venues for individuals to virtually meet, participate, and interact through their avatars. Such interactions can reduce the cost and time of conducting real world meetings.
6. **Training.** Virtual worlds can also be used for interactive and/or collaborative training. Trainees can learn by participating in simulations and role-playing. For example, one hotel chain is using virtual lobbies to train receptionists. Other organizations are developing applications that can help them train staff on how to handle emergencies such as accidents and natural disasters. Virtual worlds can also be used for military training (e.g., flight and battlefield simulations). For details, see Heiphetz and Woodill (2010).
7. **Education.** Universities are using virtual worlds as a new immersive and interactive platform that is useful for interacting with students, and even for teaching courses.
8. **Recruiting.** A growing number of organizations, including governments and the military, are recruiting employees via virtual worlds. All recruiting activities, ranging from providing job details to interviewing candidates, are conducted at the recruiter's virtual office. This mode of recruiting is gaining acceptance by technology-savvy graduates and job seekers.
9. **Tourism promotion.** Government tourist boards and tourist operators are using virtual worlds to promote their tourism destinations by providing tourists with 3-D virtual immersive experiences of real places and activities of interest.
10. **Museums and art galleries.** Many artists and agencies are setting up virtual museums and

(continued)

galleries to display their creations and promote sales. They also use virtual worlds to stage musicals and other performances.

11. **Information points.** Virtual worlds are used as sophisticated information kiosks. They can act as extremely powerful, interactive, and dynamic online resources or brochures.

12. **Data visualization and manipulation.** Interactive data visualization and manipulation in the virtual environment is an interesting new application of interest to enterprises and professionals. For instance, the *Glasshouse* software by Green Phosphor (**greenphosphor.com**) allows users to export data from either a spreadsheet or database query to a virtual world and then presents the user with a 3-D representation of the data in a virtual world environment for the user to explore interactively. A user's avatar can then manipulate the visualization of the data by drilling down into it, re-sorting it, or moving it around to view from many different angles.

13. **Renting virtual world land and buildings.** One can earn virtual money by selling or renting buildings and lands in strategic locations in virtual worlds and by engaging in the "real estate" business in the virtual world.

14. **Platform for social science research.** Virtual worlds are also a good platform for conducting experimental social science research to observe how people behave or react (through their avatars) in structured and unstructured situations, and for studying customer behavior in virtual worlds.

15. **Market research.** Using virtual worlds as a platform enables companies to test new products by getting feedback from customers. These insights may give companies a competitive edge.

16. **Platform for design.** In order to receive feedback and opinions, many companies show images of virtual things such as parks and structures, furniture, and avatars to potential customers and designers.

17. **Providing CRM to employees and a platform for socialization.** Companies use virtual worlds to provide CRM to employees and/or customers. For example, several companies have created islands in Seconds Life dedicated solely for use by their employees or for customer care.

18. **Virtual tradeshows.** Virtual tradeshows (sometimes called *virtual trade fairs*), which we described in Sect. 9.2, take place in virtual worlds (see Yu 2010).

Example: Sony's PlayStation Home for a Virtual Community of Gamers

Sony's PlayStation Home (**us.playstation.com/psn/play-station-home**) is a virtual 3-D social gaming platform and a large gathering place and marketplace for owners of PlayStation games. As of 2012, it has attracted about 25 million users worldwide who spend an average of 70 minutes per session (see **digiday.com/publishers/sonys-home-coming-back**). The community of gamers can play hundreds of games, attend different events, and buy many virtual goods.

Note: Unfortunately, Sony closed PlayStation Home on March 31, 2015.

Today, many organizations are looking for ways to conduct virtual meetings in Seconds Life, instead of in the real world.

For examples of how businesses and organizations are using virtual worlds to make the world greener, refer to *The Green Book: An Enterprise Guide to Virtual Worlds*, published by Association of Virtual Worlds (Note: No longer available).

Representative Virtual World Applications Around the Globe

Here are a few other representative examples of virtual world applications (some of which have changed over time):

For additional examples and discussion, see Reeves and Read (2009).

- **Hana City (hanacity.com).** Hana Bank of Korea uses a virtual world to educate its future customers, (children) about home financing investment options.
- **MeetMe (meet-me.jp).** To make your retail shopping experience more exciting, this virtual world takes you shopping (virtually) in Japan.
- **New Belgium Brewing (newbelgium.com).** This brewery provides an interactive tour of the brewery.
- **Aloft (starwoodhotels.com/alofthotels/index. html).** Aloft, the global brand of Starwood hotels and resorts tested the design of its hotels on Seconds Life. The company used the feedback collected from more than a million visitors to create its final design for the hotels.
- **IBM.** IBM is now (2015) selling on Seconds Life. See **kzero.co.uk/blog/ibm-to-take-orders-in-seconds-life**.

Trading Virtual Goods and Properties

There are many business opportunities for buying and selling virtual goods. Sales are conducted by using electronic catalogs, classified advertisements, and auctions (e.g., see **usd.auctions.secondslife.com**). Payments are made with virtual money (e.g., "Linden dollars") that can be converted to real money. The tax and contract/legal issues are not clear (e.g., see **secondslife.com/wiki/Linden_Lab_Official:Required_Tax_Documentation_FAQ** and **secondslife.com/corporate/vat.php**). In 2013, the U.S. Government Accountability office released some guidelines and definitions for a virtual economy and currency (see **cpa2biz.com/Content/media/PRODUCER_CONTENT/Newsletters/Articles_2013/Tax/VirtualEconomy.jsp**).

The major products/services in this category are: land, retail, manufacturing, scripting, fashion, and the adult entertainment industry.

Concerns and Limitations of Commercial Activities in Virtual Worlds

Although virtual worlds were expected to become a major platform for commerce, business, and social activities, they have not yet reached this level. Despite their promise, virtual worlds present several challenges and constraints of which developers, businesses, and individual users must be aware. Virtual worlds such as Seconds Life are not easy to use, and are expensive to build and operate. Software needs to be installed and updated, which is too cumbersome for many users. Additionally, substantial hardware is needed. There are also administrative issues such as legal, taxation, ethics, and reliability. Moreover, there are technology limitations, including reliability and accessibility, and security.

According to **en.wikipedia.org/wiki/Criticism_of_Seconds_Life**, there are occurrences of fraud and violation of intellectual property in Seconds Life. The Seconds Life Community also provides suggestions for dealing with abuse and harassment at **community.secondslife.com/t5/tkb/articleprintpage/tkb-id/English_KB@tkb/article-id/283**.

Virtual worlds are targets for cybercriminals. For instance, Seconds Life has been attacked not only by outsiders, but also by groups of residents who created objects that harass other residents, or disrupt or damage the system.

To protect the users, Seconds Life has increased security.

For a comprehensive history of Seconds Life, see Vitzthum et al. (2011).

For guidelines dealing with the major concerns regarding building and managing businesses in virtual worlds, see Mahar and Mahar (2009).

Note: In 2014, Facebook paid $2 billion for Oculus VR, a virtual reality company. The idea was that, by delivering an altered sense of reality with a social experience, Facebook could give users a more compelling reason to visit regularly (per Kapko 2014).

9.4 SOCIAL ENTERTAINMENT AND SOCIAL TV

The rich media capabilities of Web 2.0 technologies, the ability to engage millions of people who congregate in social networks and who are interested in online entertainment, the availability of innovative social media tools, and the creative and collaborative nature of Web 2.0 all facilitate social entertainment (e.g., *Gangnam Style* was YouTube's most watched video in 2012 and 2013). Web 2.0 tools also are aiding in the proliferation of on-demand entertainment. The most well-known entertainment application is streaming music (e.g., iTunes, Spotify, Pandora, and Google's All Access; **play.google.com/about/music**). The trend today is to stream music on-demand usually for free, which gives listeners the ability to listen to whatever they want, at any time. Jurgensen (2014) provides comprehensive coverage of digital music today and tomorrow, including information about new subscription services, such as Beats Music. Beats Music uses algorithms to discover each user's taste, and recommends songs based on what they learn. Their editorial team consists of music experts. Finally, Facebook and Twitter have entered this area; Facebook has a music app, and in October 2014, Twitter announced its new Audio Card for Android and iOs. This section describes some of the entertainment social networks, as well as other issues related to entertainment in social commerce. Note that, a major issue with such social networks is copyright violations, a topic we discuss in detail in Chap. 11.

Entertainment and Social Networks

A large number of social networks and websites that are using social media tools are fully or partially dedicated to entertainment. Well known examples are Vimeo, Netflix, and MySpace. MySpace has a licensing agreement with Sony, BMG, and other large media companies, that gives its members free access to streaming videos, music, and other entertainment. The following are representative examples of how Web 2.0 applications are used for entertainment.

Mixi

In Japan, Mixi, Inc. (**mixi.jp**) is a highly visited social networking service, even though users must be invited to join. Mixi's goal is to allow users to build friendships with other users who share common interests. As of March 2012, the site had about 27 million members and over 1 million small communities of friends and interests. For details, see **en.wikipedia.org/wiki/Mixi** and **digitalintheround.com/japan-mixi-facebook**.

Last.fm

Last.fm (**last.fm**) is a music discovery service that recommends music to its listeners. In April 2014, Last.fm changed from a streaming radio service to delivering to its customers personalized music via a new music player. Instead of music coming from their own servers, it is piped in from YouTube and VEVO onto the new player. Customers can also listen through Spotify. For details, see **billboard.com/biz/articles/news/digital-and-mobile/6022007/lastfm-pulls-out-of-radio-streaming-plugs-in-youtube** (accessed July 2015).

Web Series and Streaming Movies

Web series are similar to regular, episodic series on TV (e.g., soap operas), but you can only watch them on the Internet. The number of Web series is increasing, and some are already available on DVD. Examples include *Hemlock Grove, House of Cards,* and *Johnny Dynamo.* For more about Web series and other examples, see **webserieschannel.com/web-series-101** and **variety.com/gallery/top-10-web-series-of-2013/#!1/introduction**.

Hulu

Hulu (**hulu.com**) is an ad-supported online video service that offers a selection of hit TV shows, clips, movies and more. Their streaming service offers any current season episode of primetime TV shows from NBC, Fox, Disney (including ABC programs), and other networks and studios. Due to copyright laws, Hulu offers videos only to users in the United States and a few other countries. Hulu provides video in Flash video format. In addition, Hulu offers some TV shows and movies in high definition in a manner similar to Google Sites, Fox Interactive Media, and Yahoo! Sites. Users can manually share videos they like on their Facebook page by using the "Facebook" button. It is not necessary to connect their Hulu and Facebook accounts to do this. Hulu is one of the most popular Internet video sites (**nielsen.com/us/en/newswire/2013/binging-is-the-new-viewing-for-over-the-top-streamers.html**). Hulu offers some of its services free, supported by advertising. It also offers Hulu Plus, which includes premium shows and the ability to watch on more devices, for a monthly fee of $7.99. This service also features limited advertising. For more about their offerings and differences between Hulu and Hulu Plus, click on the "frequently asked questions" tab at **hulu.com/plus** and watch the guided tour on **hulu.com/plus**.

Advertising and subscriptions are the primary social commerce business models for most streaming entertainment sites.

Justin.tv (now Twitch.tv)

According to their website and Wikipedia, **justin.tv** was a website that allowed users to create, share, produce, and watch live streaming videos. This network featured thousands of live channels with over 300 live streams available each month.

In February 2014, the company was renamed Twitch Interactive, Inc. (**twitch.tv**). Twitch Interactive is a site for gaming-related content only.

Funny-or-Die and Cracked.com

According to their website, and Wikipedia, Funny or Die (**funnyordie.com**) is a comedy video website created by actor and comedian Will Ferrell, among others. Like other viral video sites, members of Funny or Die are encouraged to vote on videos that they watch. If they think the video is funny, viewers cast a vote for "Funny." The video then gets a score of the total percentage of people who voted the video "Funny." If the video receives an 80 % or greater "Funny" rating after 100,000 views, it gets an "Immortal" ranking. If the video receives a 20 % or less "Funny" rating after 1,000 views, it "dies" and is relegated to the Crypt section of the site. Cracked.com, another humor website (which includes videos), also uses crowdsourcing to solicit material from the Internet crowd.

Multimedia Presentation and Sharing Sites

Multimedia sharing can be done in several ways, and its purpose is entertainment, advertising, training, and socialization. The following are the major types of sharing, with representative companies:

- **Photography and art sharing.** Flickr, Instagram, Picasa, SmugMug, Photobucket
- **Livecasting.** Livestream (**new.livestream.com**), Skype, Ustream (**ustream.tv**)
- **Music and audio sharing.** ccMixter (**ccmixter.org**), FreeSound (**freesound.org**), Last.fm, MySpace, ReverbNation, The Hype Machine (**hypem.com/popular**)

(continued)

- **Presentation sharing.** SlideSnack, SlideShare, authorSTREAM
- **Media and entertainment platforms.** Kaltura Open Source Video (**corp.kaltura.com/Video-Solutions/Media-and-Entertainment**; **kaltura.org**), Accenture (Media and Entertainment) (**accenture.com/us-en/industry/media-entertainment/Pages/media-entertainment-index.aspx**)
- **Virtual worlds.** Seconds Life, The Sims, Activeworlds, IMVU
- **Game sharing.** Miniclip, Kongregate
- **Mobile social networks**. Path, Line.me
- **Video sharing**. YouTube, Vimeo, Metacafe, Openfilm

Note that many of these have some features of social networks; therefore, they may be referred to as such. In addition, most of the above companies are generating revenue from advertising and/or subscriptions.

Internet TV and Internet Social TV

Two similar streaming technologies are popular on the Web: Internet TV and Internet radio.

Internet TV

Internet TV is the delivery of TV content via the Internet by downloading or streaming videos. The content includes TV shows, sporting events, movies, and other videos. Several video-on-demand and subscription services, such as **netflix.com**, **hulu.com** and **hulu.com/plus**, as well as **amazon.com/Prime-Instant-Video/b?node=2676882011**, offer this service. For a comprehensive description of Internet TV, see **wisegeek.org/what-is-internet-tv.htm**. The major advantage is the ability to select what and when to view content and the ability to do so from computers, tablets, smartphones, and Blu-Ray consoles. Some major players are: Apple TV (**apple.com/appletv**), Roku, Google Chromecast (**google.com/intl/en/chrome/devices/chromecast/**), and Aereo.

Social Television (TV)

Social TV is an emerging social media technology that enables TV viewers who are in different locations to interactively share experiences such as discussions, reviews, tweeting, and recommendations while watching the same show simultaneously. According to WhatIsSocialTelevision.com

(**whatissocialtelevision.com**), social TV is "the union of television and social media" and refers to "the phenomenon of people communicating with each other while watching a TV show or discussing with each other about television content using the Internet as a medium of communication." The communication can be done via texting in social networks, by tweeting (see Samsung 2014), using smartphones, tablets, etc. Social TV combines broadcast television programs and user-generated content with rich social media. Social TV was listed by *MIT Technology Review* (reported by Evangelista 2011) as one of the ten most important emerging technologies of 2010. The editor of *Wired Magazine* named social TV as number three of six important technology trends for 2011 (see **wired.co.uk/news/archive/2011-01/11/david-rowan-predictions-2011**).

Characteristics of Social TV

Social TV has several unique characteristics:

- The possibility of discovering new video content and sharing this discovery with friends.
- Most social TV activities are done in real time by watching content and commenting on it to others, even if the viewers are in different locations.
- Social TV allows people to connect in a unique way with other people who share the same interests.

Social TV is attracting an ample number of viewers. (The number of traditional television viewers is declining due to Internet viewing). Programmers are looking at social media interaction not just as an amplifier of TV programming but as content in its own right (e.g., see Poggi 2012).

Technology and Services of Social TV

A large number of social TV tools and platforms are emerging. According to Rountree (2011), there are three major types of social TV:

1. Using a seconds screen (such as a smartphone, tablet, etc.) or another communication device while watching TV.
2. Using an on-screen experience where information is displayed directly within the TV.
3. Using a personal computer or mobile device to watch TV shows.

These options are not pure social media tools, but they facilitate social interaction revolving around TV programs.

Rountree (2011) and AngelList Social Television Startups (**angel.co/social-television**) provide a list of start-ups in the field (e.g., Kwarter, and YouToo TV). Each start-up and tool has a different capability for specific TV programs. For a list of the most tweeted-about shows of 2014, see **nielsen.com/us/en/insights/news/2014/tops-of-2014-social-tv.html**.

Vendors are interested in social TV mainly as an emerging tool for marketing communication strategies such as increasing brand awareness or conducting market research (e.g., see Proulx and Shepatin 2012). For the future of social TV, see Redniss (2013). Nielsen Corporation monitors audiences on social TV (see **nielsensocial.com**).

Example

In 2011, Pepsi launched a robust community platform powered by Gigya's social technology. The Pepsi Sound Off, a social TV venture, allowed fans of "The X-Factor" (the talent competition reality show) to meet online and interact with others to chat about the contestants and the judges. Interactions occurred mostly in real time.

Internet Radio and Social Radio

Known by several other names, **Internet radio** refers to audio content transmitted live via the Internet. It is a broadcasting service that enables users to listen online to thousands of radio stations (e.g., over 4,000 in Europe; see **listenlive.eu**). The service can broadcast anything that is on the radio stations plus broadcasts from organizations, governments, and even individuals. For details, see Beller (2001) and **radio.about.com/od/listentoradioonline/qt/bl-InternetRadio.htm**. Internet radio has the same copyright issues that apply to Internet TV. Note that, in many cases, there is an agreement between the content creators and the distributors (e.g., Warner Music and Apple reached an iRadio deal in 2013; see **cnet.com/news/apple-reaches-iradio-deal-with-warner-music-suggesting-wwdc-launch** and **apple.com/itunes/itunes-radio**). See also **blogtalkradio.com/beverlymacy**.

Example: Pandora Radio

Pandora is a leading free Internet radio service that delivers music not only from radio stations but also from many other sources. The core of the service is the *Music Genome Project*. According to **pandora.com/about**, the project is a comprehensive analysis of hundreds of musical details on every track. You can drop the name of one of your favorite songs, artists or genres into Pandora, and the Music Genome Project will quickly scan its own entire world of analyzed music to find songs with interesting musical similarities to your choice.

Pandora is actually a music streaming and automated *music recommendation* service that, as of 2015, is available only in the U.S., Australia, and New Zealand. Users can create up to 100 personalized stations that play pre-arranged selections. In February 2014, the company opened up its content submission process to independent artists (see **submit.pandora.com**, **help.pandora.com/customer/portal/articles/24802-information-for-artists-submitting-to-pandora**, and Hockenson 2014). For Pandora's Help Center, see **help.pandora.com**.

Social Radio

An extension of internet radio is **social radio**, which is the integration of Internet radio with social networking activities. It is about listener's choice and control from their news and entertainment sources (e.g., see **socialradio.org/about**).

9.5   SOCIAL GAMES, GAMING, AND GAMIFICATION

A **social game** is a video multiplayer game played on the Internet, mostly in social networks or in virtual worlds. Gamers can play against computers, or against each other. Many social games are "massively" multiplayer online games (known as MMOG or MMO), which are capable of supporting hundreds or thousands of players simultaneously. MMOG players can compete, collaborate, or just interact with other players around the globe. Many game consoles, including the PSP, PlayStation 3, Xbox 360, Nintendo DSi, and Wii, can be played on the Internet. Additionally, mobile devices and smartphones based on such operating systems as Android, iOS, webOS, and Windows Mobile are seeing an increase in the number of available MMO games. Social games are very popular. According to the 2013 State of Online Gaming Report, 44 % of worldwide Internet users play online games (see the report and infographic at **auth-83051f68-ec6c-44e0-afe5-bd8902acff57.cdn.spilcloud.com/v1/archives/1384952861.25_State_of_Gaming_2013_US_FINAL.pdf**), which is over 1.2 billion people (see **venturebeat.com/2013/11/25/more-than-1-2-billion-people-are-playing-games**). Although some games require fees for enhanced features, many are free (see Pearce 2009).

Games on Social Networks

A **social network game** is a video game that is distributed primarily through social networks, and usually involves multiplayers. Social network games may have little or nothing to do with how *social* the games are. However, some games have social components such as educating the public, gift-giving, and helping others, or sharing playing strategies. For an overview, see Humbarger (2011). Social games are embedded within major social networks allowing many users to play together simultaneously. The games are usually simple and easy to learn and play.

For a game to be more social, it should facilitate and encourage engagement and communication about the environment outside the game, run on or be integrated with a social network, and use that network to enhance game playing between players.

Example: Popular Games on Facebook
Players can choose from several thousands of games on Facebook. Some games are played by 50–150 million each. The most popular games each attract tens of millions of players. Facebook's list of popular games for November 2014 includes Candy Crush Saga (the most popular in 2014), Texas HoldEm Poker, Dragon City, FarmVille 2, Pet Rescue Saga, Criminal Case, Farm Heroes Saga, and Words with Friends. (See **gamechitah.com/top-games-on-facebook.html**.)

As of September 2013, the major Facebook developers for games are King, Zynga, Social Point, and Pretty Simple. (See **beforeitsnews.com/science-and-technology/2013/10/top-9-facebook-developer-list-games-September-2013-2-2644806.html**.) Note that people are playing more casino games. For example, see **doubledowninteractive.com/games**. To enhance the game experience, some platforms utilize the players' social graphs.

To learn more about social games, go to **museumstuff.com/learn/topics/Social_network_game**. To find friends and share gaming experiences on the Web, see the following sites: **gamerdna.com**, **raptr.com**, **wegame.en.softonic.com**, **ugamehome.com**, and World of Warcraft (**us.battle.net/wow/en**).

The Business Aspects of Social Games

To understand the variety of games and their properties and commercial possibilities, we suggest you watch the video "Social Media Games: Worldwide Gamification Is the New Paradigm for Life and Business" at **youtube.com/watch?v=xCWsgBHY_VU**. The video presents opportunities for advertising, marketing, and training, among others. It took Facebook 4.5 years to reach the same level of visitors that Zynga reached in 2.5 years. However, Zynga's revenue was overestimated, causing the stock price to decline drastically. As far as revenues, Facebook games provide very little income per person per month. Electronic Arts, Inc., a Zynga competitor, has some games that generate 3–5 times more per game.

Both companies have gone mobile. For example, FarmVille2 for iPad and iPhone are now available. For additional discussion, see Reeves and Read (2009) and Humbarger (2011).

Educational Social Games

Games can also be educational, as the following examples show. Developers have also created environmental apps for kids for iPad and so forth (see **usatoday.com/story/tech/columnist/gudmundsen/2013/09/01/ecology-learning-apps-kids/2700271**). See also **ecogamer.org/environmental-games**.

Example 1: Pollution Reduction Game
The Filipino environmental awareness Facebook game called Alter Space aims to educate people on how to reduce pollution. Specifically, it educates players about the concepts of carbon footprints and cleaner energy, and how they can help achieve a cleaner world.

Example 2: Economic and Finance Game—Empire Avenue
Empire Avenue (**empireavenue.com**) is a social media stock market simulation game where individuals and businesses buy and sell virtual shares from each other. The shares can be of individuals, companies, etc. The share price is based on the shares' trading activity coupled with the players' influence on the major social networks. The trading is done with reward points called *Eaves* and *Vees*. In the game, there are financial data and decision-making capabilities about dividends, number of shares outstanding, and share prices, to name just a few. Empire has many variables within the game. The reward points can also be used as virtual currency to play the Social Market game. Players can interact via popular social networks (e.g., Facebook, Twitter, Instagram) across the Web. The more social the player is, the more virtual currency the player will earn, and the bigger the player's Empire will become. Several major brands are already using this site (e.g., Toyota, AT&T, Audi, and Ford). For details, see Empire Avenue at **businessesgrow.com/2014/01/08/how-empire-avenue-crushed-my-soul/**.

For more on social games, see Reeves and Read (2009) and Pearce (2009).

Gamers Helped Scientists

For decades, scientists were unable to unfold the chemical chain of an enzyme of an AIDS-like virus. However, according to a September 19, 2011 article in the Balita Filipino News (**balita.com**), researchers at the University of Washington used Foldit, a "fun-for-purpose" video game, created by the university. The gamers were divided into groups, and using Foldit, were challenged to compete by using their problem-solving skills to build 3-D models of a protein that scientists had been unable to find for years. The players solved the chemical chain problem accurately in just 3 weeks. (See **balita.com/online-gamers-crack-aids-enzyme-puzzle**.) For more about Foldit ("Solve Puzzles for Science"), see **fold.it/portal**.

Gamification

Social games are played by millions of people. Some social games are designed so that players will connect with vendors or brands in the game environments. This is only one aspect of **gamification**, which refers to the introduction of gaming into social networking. Gamification can also be viewed as the introduction of social networking activities into online games. Our interest is in those applications that are related to social commerce and e-commerce. For more definitions and limitations, see Gamification Wiki (**gamification.org**) and Duggan and Shoup (2013).

Social activities are not new to online gaming. For example, players collectively agree to the rules of the games. In addition, gamers need trust between the players. What is new here is the integration of traditional multiplayer games and social networking. Given that so many people play online games, it is not surprising that vendors are encouraging players (e.g., via rewards) to engage in desired behavior (e.g., problem solving or collaboration). Vendors also use games as advertising platforms.

According to a Lithium (2011) and Florentine (2014), companies can create winning social customer experiences such as increasing loyalty, building trust, accelerating innovation, providing brand engagement, and increasing relevant knowledge.

For commercial possibilities and strategies of social games and gamification, see Radoff (2011), Dignan (2011), and Zichermann and Linder (2013). According to Pedzai (2013), gamification provides a new approach to create sustained engagement between sellers and customers.

For additional information, you can download the e-book titled "The Essential Social Playbook: 3 Steps to Turn Social into Sales," at **powerreviews.com/assets/new/ebooks/powerreviews_essential_social_playbook.pdf**, see **en.wikipedia.org/wiki/Gamification**, and review Walter (2013).

9.6   SOCIALLY ORIENTED ONLINE PERSON-TO-PERSON ACTIVITIES

Many person-to-person (P2P) activities are not related to social media or commerce. However, there is a trend for an increasing number of socially-oriented innovative applications in this field. Here we provide only a few examples. Note that, when individuals trade with other individuals online, they may do so using some social elements. For example, some consider Craigslist to be a socially oriented virtual community. For the impact of P2P on teens, see Paquette (2014).

For information about selling products directly on Facebook, see **new.soldsie.com/blog/selling-facebook-drive-e-commerce-social-media**. For why P2P selling to teens is taking off, see Paquette (2014). P2P is related to the topic of the collaborative (or sharing) economy.

Collaborative (or Sharing) Economy

The **collaborative** (or **sharing) economy** refers to an economic system constructed around the concept of sharing goods and services among the participating people. Also known as 'collaborative consumption,' such systems appear in different forms and frequently use information technologies in their operations. A well-known example is *car sharing*. The essentials of this concept are described by Buczynski (2013).

The major benefits for participants are cost reduction for buyers and ability to sell more for sellers. Societal benefits include reduction of carbon footprints (e.g., in ride sharing), increased recycling, and increased social interactions. For comprehensive coverage, see **en.wikipedia.org/wiki/Sharing_economy**.

Sharing Economy and Social Commerce

Several SC models and companies are based on the concept of the sharing economy. Examples include Uber, connecting riders with drivers; Yerdle, a marketplace for trading used goods; Kickstarter, for crowdfunding; Krrb, a P2P local classified marketplace; and Knok and Love Home Swap for home swapping. Vacation rentals, where home and condo owners provide short term rentals, and home exchanges, where two parties agree to exchange their homes for a short period of time, are also popular examples of the sharing economy (e.g., see Airbnb and HomeAway).

P2P Lending

P2P lending is growing rapidly, enabling people to lend money or other items to each other. During the process, participants also get to know one another. An example of P2P lending is a community of people who rent goods to people in need, usually for the short term.

Some sites have a narrow, obvious focus (like SwapBabyGoods.com), while others are more general like Neighborhood Fruit, which helps people find and share fruit locally. All of the sites are encouraging *collaborative consumption*. Several variations of P2P exist. Some people share cars; others invite travelers to stay in their homes at no cost; others can find a local host when they travel (see Couchsurfing International; **couchsurfing.com**), and many more. Even Google provides a service that connects borrowers and lenders of money.

Social Money Lending

Person-to-person money lending (also known as *peer-to-peer lending* and *social lending*) (abbreviated as *P2P lending*) is lending and borrowing that occurs directly between individuals. Person-to-person lending is usually managed by a third-party company, such as Zopa (in the UK) (**zopa.com**), the pioneer of lending, or Prosper (in the U.S.), **prosper.com**. It involves a community of lenders and borrowers. Another growing area of P2P is a type of *crowdsourcing* known as crowdfunding (Chap. 8), where people raise money mainly from small contributors and investors, both non-profit and for commercial purposes.

The Lending Club

The Lending Club is an online P2P credit marketplace that uses an efficient, transparent, and consumer friendly money lending process. According to **lendingclub.com/public/how-peer-lending-works.action**, the company (which is now on the stock exchange), uses technology to cut expenses and provide qualified borrowers with loans with lower interest rates, lower than they can get in most banks while providing investors with solid returns. The following process is done entirely online:

- "Customers interested in a loan complete a simple application at LendingClub.com" (per Lending Club)
- Lending Club leverages the information, assigns interest rates, and instantly presents a variety of offers to qualified borrowers, who can evaluate options (with no impact to their credit score).
- "Investors ranging from individuals to institutions select loans in which to invest and can earn monthly returns" (per Lending Club)

For a borrower's experience with Lending Club, see Cunningham (2014b). For an investor's review, see Cunningham (2014a).

For an extensive review and analysis, see Frankle (2013).

For more information, see **forbes.com/companies/lending-club**.

Issues in P2P Lending

Several issues are related to P2P lending. Lenders may ask the questions: Is it safe? What is the rate of default? What if Lending Club goes out of business? Am I getting the best income? Borrowers may question the interest rate they pay, the conditions for getting the loans, and how their credit score is determined (see Exercise #7 in 'Team Assignments').

How Peers Use Social Media to Sell to Peers

Individuals are using social networking in many innovative ways to sell to other individuals.

Example #1

How Kawehi became a digital music phenomenon by using social media. Kawehi produces songs and videos with computers and digital instruments. Kawehi formed a core of followers. Here are some of her activities:

- She uses Kickstarter to raise funds for her ventures.
- She uses **bandcamp.com** marketplace to sell her own releases.
- She made videos and posted them on YouTube and Vimeo, thus building a fan base. About half of her fans come from outside the U.S.
- Her most successful music video is "Heart Shaped Box," which was picked up by the digital press, giving her a lot of publicity.
- Her growing fan base comes from her videos.
  For details, see Russo (2014).

Example #2

How the Talbots sold their house by themselves. '*For sale by owner*' has been done for many years, but you can do it much better with the help of social networking. The Talbots did the following to sell their house in Seattle:

- Created a website
- Produced home-tour videos and uploaded them to their website and YouTube.
- Added a 'help us sell our house' link to their blog.
- Posted that their house was for sale on Facebook.
- Got in touch with anyone who typed "move to Seattle" on Twitter.
  For details, see Bankrate.com (2013).

SUMMARY

In this chapter, you learned about the following SC issues as they relate to the chapter's learning objectives.

1. **Social government.** Governments use social media to improve their interactions with the public, to get citizens more involved, to influence citizens, and to improve their internal operations. The variety of possible applications is demonstrated in the New Zealand government case (Case 9.1). Social media facilitates collaboration between governments and citizens and other government partners, as

well as among employees of government agencies. Social governments facilitate more democratization and make citizens more satisfied.

2. **Social B2B.** While most of the attention in social media is given to B2C market activities, social media tools and platforms are used extensively in B2B markets as well. Some areas of action are: finding sales leads, discovering suppliers, organizing group purchasing, conducting virtual trade shows, collaborating on joint projects (such as joint design), and promoting industry activities. Social B2B commerce helps small organizations as well, and it can facilitate B2B global trade. Fostering relationships with business partners is a major objective of social B2B. Finally, social media can facilitate building B2B social strategy.

3. **Business activities in virtual worlds.** An increasing number of business activities are conducted in virtual worlds, most notably in Seconds Life. Popular activities are marketing communication, collaboration, learning and training, trading virtual goods, design testing, and customer service. In addition, there are professional discussions, entertainment and gaming, direct online sales, recruitment, market research activities, and virtual trade shows.

4. **Social commerce and entertainment.** Rich media, user-created content, and groups and subgroups with common interests open many possibilities for a seconds generation of online entertainment. Add to this the wireless revolution and the increased capabilities in mobile devices to support Web 2.0 tools and social networking activities and you will discover a new and exciting world of online entertainment. Social TV, where viewers interact with each other while simultaneously watching TV programs, is an emerging area.

5. **Social games.** Social games are online multiplayer games that are played in social networks, mostly on Facebook. Tens of millions of players play popular games. One source of income for social networks is the selling of virtual goods related to social games. They also make money from paid advertising on some of the games. Games can be educational, but can also be used for training purposes. Most of all, though, players have fun, make friends, and sharpen their competitive skills.

6. **Socially-oriented P2P.** This emerging application area is currently limited to socially lending money, facilitating bartering, and providing services in communities of special interest (e.g., travel, banking, real estate, education). For example, swapping residences while travelling and lending money are two popular activities.

KEY TERMS

Collaborative (or sharing) economy   224
E-government   207
Gamification   224
Internet TV   221
Internet Radio   222
Social games   223
Social government (Government 2.0)   207
Social network games   222
Social radio   222
Social TV   219

REVIEW QUESTIONS

1. Describe the essentials of social government.
2. List five major benefits of social government.
3. What are the major areas of social government in New Zealand?
4. Relate e-communities to B2B.
5. List five major applications of social media in B2B.
6. How can Linkedin, Facebook, and Twitter be used to facilitate B2B?
7. Describe virtual trade shows and list five benefits.
8. What are the major drivers of virtual worlds?
9. What kind of educational and training activities do virtual worlds such as Seconds Life support?
10. What are the major concerns and limitations of virtual worlds? Refer to online resources, including the Social Media & Games Law Blog (**socialgameslaw.com**).
11. Relate entertainment to social commerce.
12. Describe Mixi and Hulu.
13. Relate social networks to streaming music.
14. Describe the ways you watch streaming videos on the Web (videos on-demand).
15. Define social TV.
16. Describe social radio and Pandora.
17. Define social games and describe how they are played in social networks.
18. What are some of the business (commerce) aspects of social games?
19. Describe gamification.
20. What is social P2P?
21. What is P2P lending?

TOPICS FOR DISCUSSION AND DEBATES

1. What are the features of virtual worlds that businesses can make use of in deploying their virtual world applications?
2. From a business application perspective, virtual worlds can be visualized as multidimensional spaces. Briefly describe different dimensions of virtual worlds.
3. Discuss different ways of making real or virtual money in virtual worlds.
4. Discuss some of the opportunities for using social media in B2B.

5. Gamification is attracting the attention of marketers and social networks. Write a status report on this issue.

6. There are several communities for fantasy sports gaming. Identify some and discuss their social features.

7. Some believe that the classical 4P's of marketing (Price, Promotion, Product, and Place) do not apply to B2B. They suggest using the 5C's instead (Context, Creation, Collaboration, Communication, and Competition). Discuss.

8. Groupon has moved to B2B marketing. Find information on how the system works and compare it to B2C daily deals.

9. Examine the online game Grand Theft Auto (**rockstargames.com/grandtheftauto**). Why is it so popular? Identify some social elements.

10. Relate virtual trade shows to virtual job fairs (Chap. 8).

11. Discuss the implication of P2P trading to using real estate brokers and other intermediaries.

12. Discuss how collaborative consumption and P2P companies are changing the e-commerce business models.

13. Discuss the benefits of virtual trade shows to international trade. Write a report.

14. Debate: Will P2P lending hurt the banking industry?

INTERNET EXERCISES

1. Enter **secondslife.com** and find the commercial activities of the following avatars: Fizik Baskerville, Craig Altman, Shaun Altman, FlipperPA Peregrine, and Anshe Chung. Briefly describe what they represent. Relate this to social commerce. Also, check IBM's activities.

2. Enter Mindpix Corporation (**mpixcorporation.us**). Why is it considered an online entertainment service? What are the benefits to viewers? Compare this site to **starz.com**. Also check Strategy& (**strategyand.pwc.com**) (formerly Booz & Co.).

3. Enter **pandora.com**. Find out how you can create and share music with friends. Why is this a social commerce application?

4. Enter **peerform.com**. Describe their P2P lending platform. Compare it to what is offered by **prosper.com**.

5. Enter **abcnews.com** and watch the 5:18 minutes video titled "Social Lending Offers Alternatives" (at **abcnews.go.com/video/playerIndex?id=6123763**). What have you learned from this video?

6. Enter **vevo.com** and **mtv.com**. Check what each site offers. Compare the two.

7. Enter **tvweb360.tv**. What do they offer? With whom do they compete?

8. Enter **thismoment.com** and explain how they use social media to create engaging experiences. Relate it to other vendors that provide similar experiences.

9. Enter **supplegame.com**. Review the site. Relate it to virtual worlds and social commerce.

10. Enter **gaiaonline.com** and find all the socially oriented activities. Write a report.

11. Enter Zopa or Prosper and Lending Club and identify the social elements in their operations.

12. Enter **yukaichou.com/gamification-examples/octalysis-complete-gamification-framework/#.UuzK8vldWSo**. Find Yu-Kai Chou's framework and discuss its value.

13. Enter **business.linkedin.com/content/dam/business/marketing-solutions/global/en_US/site/pdf/cs/linkedin_vestas_case_study_us_en_130314.pdf**. Summarize all the different ways that Vestas is using LinkedIn.

14. Compare the features in the virtual trade shows: InXpo, McLane Company, and IWCE Expo. Write a report.

15. Watch the video at **youtube.com/watch?v=GRnOEKeXsW8** and find a similar video on the same topic (trade show software). Comment on the advantages of virtual trade shows.

TEAM ASSIGNMENTS AND PROJECTS

1. **Assignment for the Opening Case**

   Read the opening case and answer the following questions:

   (a) Explain how viral promotion is used by Justin Bieber. Why is it so successful?

   (b) Summarize the use of YouTube, Twitter, and Facebook by Justin Bieber.

   (c) Find some information on the success of Justin Bieber's publicity derived from *Never Say Never* vs. the success derived from the JibJab promotion.

   (d) Many people consider Justin Bieber to be the "King of Social Media." Do you agree or disagree? Why?

   (e) According to Thomas (2011), Justin Bieber accounts for 3 % of all traffic on Twitter. How do you think this is possible?

   (f) Conduct a search (e.g., blogs) to find any other social media activities that Justin Bieber uses.

   (g) Some say that *Never Say Never* exemplifies the power of social networks that led Justin Bieber to the top. Debate.

   (h) Experts believe that the most important ingredient of Justin Bieber's success is the relationship he created with his fans (read Antkowiak 2011). Comment on this statement.

2. Each group will take one area of collaborative (or shared) consumption and P2P commerce (e.g., money lending, car sharing) and research some activities in this area. (Start with Paquette 2014).

3. What are IBM, Dell,Toyota,Calvin Klein, and Coke doing in SL?
4. Enter **hollywoodtoday.net** and similar websites and check recent information regarding social TV and social commerce. Check information about social TV conferences and summits as well.
5. Check the status and competition in the area of streaming music services (e.g., Spotify, Amazon, Apple, Google, etc.). Write a report.
6. Money lending is going online and becoming social. Companies such as the Lending Club are revolutionizing the process. Investigate all the determining factors (start with Frankle 2013 and Cunningham 2014a and b). Review all the major players including online only banks. Write a report.

REFERENCES

Ali, T. "How Social Media is Changing Government Agencies." May 19, 2010. **mashable.com/2010/05/19/government-agencies-social-media** (accessed January 2015).

Antkowiak, D. "Baby, Oh....What Justin Bieber Taught Me About Social Media." August 16, 2011. **portent.com/blog/social-media/justin-bieber-social-media.htm** (accessed January 2015).

Australian Government. "The AGIMO Government 2.0 Primer." Australian Government: Department of Finance and Deregulation, Version 1.02, February 2012. **webguide.gov.au/web-2-0/gov-2-0-primer** (accessed January 2015).

Banday, M.T., and M.M. Mattoo. "Social Media in e-Governance: A Study with Special Reference to India." *Social Networking*, vol. 2 no. 2, pp. 47-56, 2013. (DOI: 10.4236/sn.2013.22006)

Bankrate.com. "Hot New Way to Sell Your Home? Use Social Media." *The Executive Suite*, September 20, 2013. **thegoldcard.blogspot.com/2013/09/hot-new-way-to-sell-your-home-use.html** (accessed January 2015).

Baumgarten, J., and M. Chui. "E-Government 2.0." *McKinsey & Company Insights & Publications*, July 2009. **mckinsey.com/insights/public_sector/e-government_20** (accessed January 2015).

BBC News. "FBI Plans Social Network Map Alert Mash-Up Application." January 26, 2012. **bbc.co.uk/news/technology-16738209** (accessed January 2015).

Beller, D. "How Internet Radio Works." March 27, 2001. **electronics.howstuffworks.com/internet-radio.htm** (accessed January 2015).

Bieber, J. *Justin Bieber: First Step 2 Forever: My Story*. New York: Harper Collins, 2010.

Black, L. "Social Networks Show Value to Local Governments: Schools, Officials, Leaders Use Social Media as Communication Tool." August 14, 2013. **theleafchronicle.com/article/20130813/NEWS01/308120024/Social-networks-show-value-local-governments** (accessed January 2015).

Bodnar, K., and J. L. Cohen. *The B2B Social Media Book: Become a Marketing Superstar by Generating Leads with Blogging, LinkedIn, Twitter, Facebook, Email, and More*. Hoboken, NJ: Wiley, 2012.

Buczynski, B. *Sharing is Good: How to Save Money, Time and Resources through Collaborative Consumption*. Gabriola Island, BC, Canada: New Society Publishers, 2013.

Butler-Borrer, V. "The Business Benefits of Seconds Life." *It's All Virtual*, March 23, 2010. **allvirtual.me/2010/03/23/business-benefits-of-seconds-life** (accessed January 2015).

Ciaramitaro, B. *Virtual Worlds and E-Commerce: Technologies and Applications for Building Customer Relationships*. New York: Business Science Reference, 2010.

Cohen, J. L. "The 10 Best B2B Instagram Profiles." December 15, 2014(a). **socialmediab2b.com/2014/12/b2b-instagram-profiles-10-best** (accessed January 2015).

Cohen, J. L. "B2B Sales Teams can Use Content Marketing to Generate Leads." July 17, 2014(b). **socialmediab2b.com/2014/07/b2b-sales-content-marketing-generate-leads** (accessed January 2015).

Cohen, J. L. "New Research: 60% of B2B Decision Makers Use Social Media." October 20, 2011. **socialmediab2b.com/2011/10/b2b-social-media-decision-makers-research/** (accessed January 2015).

Cunningham, S. "Lending Club Investor Review: Invest Like a Bank, Earn 5-10 %." September 5, 2014(a), **lendingmemo.com/lending-club-investor-account-review** (accessed January 2015).

Cunningham, S., "Lending Club Review for Borrowers: Low Rates, But is it Legit?" December 23, 2014(b). **lendingmemo.com/lending-club-personal-loan-review** (accessed January 2015).

Dawson, J. "Local Government Guide to Social Media." May 24, 2010. **slideshare.net/jasondawson/local-government-guide-to-social-media** (accessed January 2015).

Dignan, A. *Game Frame: Using Games as a Strategy for Success*. Florence, MA: Free Press, 2011.

Duggan, K., and K. Shoup. *Business Gamification for Dummies (For Dummies; Math & Science)*, Hoboken, NJ: For Dummies, 2013.

Dunay, P. "The Big Brand Theory: How is Social Media Reshaping Pfizer?" August 12, 2013. **socialmediatoday.com/pauldunay/1657956/how-social-media-reshaping-pfizer** (accessed January 2015).

Evangelista, B. "How Social Television Is Gaining in Popularity." January 24, 2011. **sfgate.com/business/article/How-social-television-is-gaining-in-popularity-2531128.php** (accessed January 2015).

Fielden, K., and P. Malcolm. "The Changing Face of Local Egovernment in New Zealand." Paper presented at the Pre-ICIS Workshop: Taking Stock of eGovernment Research, St. Louis, Missouri, December 11, 2010.

Florentine, S. "How Gamification Makes Customer Services Fun." March 3, 2014. **cio.com/article/2378252/consumer-technology/how-gamification-makes-customer-service-fun.html** (accessed January 2015).

Frankle, N., "Lending Club Review for Borrowers and Investors." 2013. **wealthpilgrim.com/lending-club-reviews** (accessed January 2015).

Gillin, P. "B-to-B Firmly in Social Media." April 12, 2010. **adage.com/article/btob/b-b-firmly-social-media/278003/?btob=1#seenit** (accessed January 2015).

Gillin, P., and P. Schwartzman. *Social Marketing to the Business Customer: Listen to Your B2B Market, Generate Major Account Leads, and Build Client Relationships*. Hoboken, NJ: Wiley, 2011.

Goldstein, E. "Justin Bieber: A Social Media Case Study." June 12, 2011. **socialmediatoday.com/eric-goldstein/305692/justin-bieber-social-media-case-study** (accessed January 2015).

Hallam, S. "B2B Social Media Case Studies." *Hallam Internet Limited*, February 28, 2014. **hallaminternet.com/2014/b2b-social-media-case-studies/** (accessed January 2015).

Harper, B. "How to Make Your Facebook Marketing Work for B2B." April 24, 2014. **socialmediaexaminer.com/facebook-marketing-b2b/** (accessed January 2015).

Heiphetz, A., and G. Woodill. *Training and Collaboration with Virtual Worlds: How to Create Cost-Saving, Efficient and Engaging Programs*. New York: McGraw-Hill, 2010.

Hockenson, L. "Updated: Pandora Opens Submission Process to Independent Artists." February 7, 2014. **gigaom.com/2014/02/07/pandora-opens-submission-process-to-independent-artists** (accessed January 2015).

Humbarger, T. "Adding Gamification to Your Community." October 25, 2011. **socialmediatoday.com/content/adding-gamification-your-community** (accessed January 2015).

Jensen, S. "How Do B2B Companies Use Social Media? [Infographic]." November 28, 2012. **unbounce.com/social-media/b2b-social-media** (accessed January 2015).

Johnson, S. "5 Simple Secrets to B2B Lead Generation on Facebook [SlideShare], September 30, 2013. **blog.hubspot.com/marketing/b2b-lead-generation-facebook-secrets-slideshare** (accessed January 2015).

Julig, L. "How Constant Contact Uses Pinterest to Reach a B2B Market." October 16, 2013. **socialmediaexaminer.com/constant-contact-case-study** (accessed January 2015).

Jurgensen, J. "An Ode to Joyful Music Streaming." January 3, 2014 (Updated). **wsj.com/articles/SB100014240527023045916045792 90721300786680** (accessed January 2015).

Leggatt, H. "Survey: Small Businesses Find Success with Social Networking." July 9, 2010. **bizreport.com/2010/07/survey-small-businesses-find-success-with-social-networking.html** (accessed January 2015).

Kapko, M. "What Does a Social-Media-Meets-Virtual-Reality World Look Like?" April 11, 2014. **cio.com/article/2377162/social-media/what-does-a-social-media-meets-virtual-reality-world-look-like-.html** (accessed January 2015).

Lindner, M. "How to Tackle A Virtual Trade Show." July 28, 2009. **forbes.com/2009/07/28/virtual-tradeshow-steps-entrepreneurs-technology-tradeshow.html** (accessed January 2015).

Lithium. "Gamification: Delivering Winning Social Customer Experiences." A White Paper, *Lithium Technologies*, 2011. **lithium.com/pdfs/whitepapers/Lithium-Gamification_bm2DEI6s.pdf** (accessed January 2015).

Mac, A. "5 [Relatively Simple] Steps to B2B Social Media Marketing Success." February 14, 2014. **fastcompany.com/3026450/dialed/5-relatively-simple-steps-to-b2b-social-media-marketing-success** (accessed January 2015).

Maddox, K. "Marketers Working Toward Social, Search Integration." August 16, 2010. **adage.com/article/btob/marketers-working-social-search-integration/279616/?btob=1** (accessed January 2015).

Magro, M. J. "A Review of Social Media Use in E-Government." *Administrative Sciences*, Vol. 2, Issue 2, pp. 148-161, 2012. (doi:10.3390/admsci2020148)

Mahar, J., and S. M. Mahar. *The Unofficial Guide to Building Your Business in the Seconds Life Virtual World: Marketing and Selling Your Product, Services, and Brand In-World.* New York: AMACOM, 2009.

MarketingCharts Staff. "Global B2B Marketers Rate their Most Effective Social Media Post Types" May 1, 2014. **marketingcharts.com/online/global-b2b-marketers-rate-their-most-effective-social-media-post-types-42341** (accessed January 2015).

MarketingProfs. "Social Media Ad Spend to Reach $8.3 Billion by 2015." May 4, 2011. **marketingprofs.com/charts/2011/4977/social-media-ad-spend-to-reach-83-billion-by-2015** (accessed January 2015).

Marketo. "Four Ways that B2B Social Media Marketing Builds Brands and Generates Leads." (undated). **marketo.com/marketing-topics/b2b-social-media-marketing** (accessed January 2015).

Matlick, E., "Back to Basics: What's in a Social Lead?" August 7, 2013. **adage.com/article/btob/back-basics-a-social-lead/289953** (accessed January 2015).

McTigue, J. "Is Social Media an Effective B2B Lead Generation Channel?" March 17, 2014. **kunocreative.com/blog/bid/89603/Is-Social-Media-an-Effective-B2B-Lead-Generation-Channel** (accessed January 2015).

Melin, E. "How B2B Companies Are Using Social Media [Infographic]." October 15, 2013. **spiral16.com/blog/2013/how-b2b-companies-are-using-social-media-infographic** (accessed January 2015).

Mergel, I. *Social Media in the Public Sector: A Guide to Participation, Collaboration and Transparency in the Networked World*, Hoboken, NJ: Jossey-Bass/Wiley, 2012.

Moth, D. "B2B Social: Five Case Studies From Brands Achieving Great Results." October 23, 2013 **econsultancy.com/blog/63646-b2b-social-five-case-studies-from-brands-achieving-great-results/** (accessed January 2015).

Murugesan, S. "Harnessing the Power of Virtual Worlds: Exploration, Innovation, and Transformation—PARTS I & II." *Cutter Business Intelligence Executive Reports* (Cutter Consortium), March and May 2008.

Neff, J. "How Orabrush Got National Walmart Deal with YouTube Videos, $28 in Facebook Ads: Telling Walmart Employees They Have Bad Breath Leads to Distribution in 3,500 Stores." September 20, 2011. **adage.com/article/news/orabrush-national-walmart-deal-youtube-videos/229914** (accessed January 2015).

New Zealand Government. "Guidance and Resources: Government Online: Channels and Touchpoints." (Last updated October 2014a). **ict.govt.nz/guidance-and-resources/government-online/channels-and-touchpoints** (accessed January 2015).

New Zealand Government. "Guidance and Resources: Government Online: Rethink Online." (Last updated November 2014b). **ict.govt.nz/guidance-and-resources/government-online/rethink-online** (accessed January 2015).

New Zealand Government. "Web Toolkit: Social Media." (Last updated July 2014c). **webtoolkit.govt.nz/guidance/social-media** (accessed January 2015).

New Zealand Government State Services Commission. "Better Public Services: Improving interaction with government." September 12, 2014 (last updated December 4, 2014). **ssc.govt.nz/bps-interaction-with-govt** (accessed January 2015).

NIC Inc. "Gov 2.0 - eGovernment Social Media Platform Deployments and Future Opportunities." White Paper, February 8, 2010. **slideshare.net/egov/gov-20-egovernment-social-media-platform-deployments-and-future-opportunities** (accessed January 2015).

Paquette, A. "Why Peer-to-Peer Selling Is Taking Off and What Companies Can Learn From It." July 10, 2014. **mediapost.com/publications/article/229737/why-peer-to-peer-selling-is-taking-off-and-what-co.html** (accessed January 2015).

Pardot. "Many Marketers Don't Measure Social Media Impact." November 3, 2011. **pardot.com/press/many-marketers-dont-measure-social-media-impact** (accessed January 2015).

Patterson, T. "Top Eleven Reasons to Use Social Media at your Next Tradeshow Appearance." June 27, 2012. **socialmediatoday.com/content/top-eleven-reasons-use-social-media-your-next-tradeshow-appearance** (accessed January 2015).

Pearce, C. *Communities of Play: Emergent Cultures in Multiplayer Games and Virtual Worlds.* Boston: The MIT Press, 2009.

Pedzai, C. "Gamification in Social Media for Businesses." *Design and Conquer*, August 12, 2013. **developertodesigner.wordpress.com/2013/08/12/gamification-in-social-media-for-businesses/** (accessed January 2015).

Pickering, B. "How B2B Marketers Are Successfully using Facebook." December 12, 2012. **socialmediaexaminer.com/b2b-marketers-successfully-using-facebook** (accessed January 2015).

Poggi, J. "Social TV Moves Beyond Promotional Role, Becomes Content in Own Right." May 9, 2012 **adage.com/article/special-report-social-tv-conference/social-tv-moves-promotional-role-content/234648** (accessed January 2015).

Power, R., "Creating a Social Media Strategy for B2B Audiences, Products and Services." January 29, 2014. **smartinsights.com/b2b-digital-marketing/b2b-social-media-marketing/creating-social-media-strategy-b2b-audiences-products-services** (accessed January 2015).

Proulx, M., and S. Shepatin, *Social TV: How Marketers Can Reach and Engage Audiences by Connecting Television to the Web, Social Media and Mobile*, Hoboken, NJ: John Wiley & Sons, 2012.

Radoff, J. *Game On: Energize your Business with Social Media Games.* Hoboken. NJ: Wiley, 2011.

Rayson, S. "Research Reveals Most Influential Social Media in B2B Buying." September 16, 2013. **socialmediatoday.com/steve-rayson/1743406/latest-insights-social-media-and-b2b-buying-process** (accessed January 2015).

Reahard, J. "Seconds Life Readies for 10ᵗʰ Anniversary, Celebrates a Million Active Users Per Month," *AOL Tech (Massively by Joystiq)*, June 20, 2013. **massively.joystiq.com/2013/06/20/seconds-life-readies-for-10th-anniversary-celebrates-a-million-a** (accessed January 2015).

Redniss, J. "Where is Social TV Heading in 2014?" December 17, 2013. **adage.com/article/digitalnext/social-tv-heading-2014/245706** (accessed January 2015).

Reeves, B., and J. L. Read. *Total Engagement: Using Games and Virtual Worlds to Change the Way People Work and Businesses Compete.* Boston: Harvard Business School Press, 2009.

Rountree, E. "Social TV 101—The Apps, Tools and Blogs You Need to Know." August 4, 2011. **socialmediaweek.org/blog/2011/08/social-tv-101-the-apps-tools-and-blogs-you-need-to-know/#.UuwOyfldWSq** (accessed January 2015).

Russo, J. "Talking Story with Kawehi on Her Upcoming Hawaii Tour." July 1, 2014. **mauitime.com/2014/07/01/talking-story-with-kawehi-on-her-upcoming-hawaii-tour** (accessed January 2015).

Salesforce Marketing Cloud. *Social Media for B2B: A Beginner's Guide.* Community Ebook (September 2012). **echelonseo.com/wp-content/uploads/2013/02/MarketingCloud_SocialB2B_ebook.pdf** (accessed January 2015).

Samsung. "Social TV Is Here to Stay: Do You Tweet While You Watch?" September 2, 2014. **mashable.com/2014/09/02/social-tv-brandspeak** (accessed January 2015).

Schaffer, N. *Maximizing LinkedIn for Sales and Social Media Marketing* (Windmills Marketing, New York, 2011)

Spinder, K. "Civil Servants Cut through the Red Tape and Share Government Forward." June 1, 2011. **managementexchange.com/story/civil-servants-cut-through-red-tape-and-share-government-forward** (accessed January 2015).

Sysomos Inc. "Generating Sales Leads through the Social Stream." A White Paper, August 30, 2011. **info.marketwire.com/rs/marketwire/images/Sysomos-Social-Stream-Leads.pdf** (accessed January 2015).

Terdiman, D. *The Entrepreneur's Guide to Seconds Life.* Indianapolis, IN: John Wiley & Sons, 2008.

Thomas, K. "Justin Bieber Accounts for 3% of All Traffic on Twitter." November 9, 2011. **techvibes.com/blog/social-media-king-justin-bieber-accounts-for-3-of-all-traffic-on-Twitter-seriously-infographic-2011-11-09** (accessed January 2015).

Thomson, N. "What Social Channels are Good for B2B?" September 6, 2013. **socialmediatoday.com/content/what-social-channels-are-good-b2b** (accessed January 2015).

Vaz, A. "Will Social Networking Mediums Replace Government Websites?" November 7, 2014. **patimes.org/social-networking-mediums-replace-government-run-websites** (accessed July 2015).

Viskovich, J. "Social Selling: Why Twitter is a Powerful B2B Sales Tool." September 16, 2013. **socialmediatoday.com/julio-visko/1743851/why-twitter-powerful-b2b-sales-tool** (accessed January 2015).

Vitzthum, S., A. Kathuria, and B. Konsynski. "Toys Become Tools: From Virtual Worlds to Real Commerce." *Communications of the Association for Information Systems*, Vol. 29, No. 1, Article 21, pp. 379-394, 2011.

Walter, E. "Gamification: Adding Stickiness to your Campaigns." September 9, 2013. **socialmediatoday.com/content/gamification-adding-stickiness-your-campaigns** (accessed January 2015).

Wiebesick, C. "Four B2B Social Media Success Stories: How B2B Companies Can (and Should) Use Social Media." May 24, 2011a. **slideshare.net/cwiebesick/four-b2b-social-media-success-stories-how-b2b-companies-can-and-should-use-social-media** (accessed January 2015).

Wiebesick, C. "Five Awesome B2B Social Media Statistics." August 25, 2011b. **socialmediatoday.com/chad-wiebesick/343431/five-awesome-b2b-social-media-statistics** (accessed January 2015).

Yu, R. "Companies Turn to Virtual Trade Shows to Save Money." January 4, 2010 (Updated January 5, 2010). Retrieved from **usatoday30.usatoday.com/travel/news/2010-01-04-virtual-trade-shows_N.htm** (accessed January 2015).

Zichermann, G., and J. Linder. *The Gamification Revolution: How Leaders Leverage Game Mechanics to Crush the Competition.* New York: McGraw-Hill, 2013.

Part IV

Strategy and Implementation

Strategy and Performance Management in Social Commerce

10

Contents

Opening Case: Social Media-Based Market Research
Helps Del Monte Improve Dog Food 233

10.1   The Strategy-Performance Cycle 235

10.2   Organizational Strategy and Strategic
       Planning for Social Commerce 237

10.3   Justification and ROI in Social Commerce 241

10.4   Market Research in Social Commerce 245

10.5   Metrics and Monitoring Performance 249

10.6   Social Media Analytics and Sentiment Analysis 255

10.7   Improving Performance via Innovation
       and Competitive Analysis 257

References 260

Learning Objectives

Upon completion of this chapter, you will be able to:

1. Describe the strategy-performance cycle and its major elements.
2. Describe the strategic planning process for social commerce.
3. Explain the issues involved in justifying social commerce projects.
4. Explain how market research is conducted to aid social commerce.
5. Describe the use of metrics and monitoring techniques for performance assessment.
6. Describe the process and tools for social media analytics and sentiment analysis.
7. Explain how competitive intelligence and innovations improve social commerce performance.

OPENING CASE: SOCIAL MEDIA-BASED MARKET RESEARCH HELPS DEL MONTE IMPROVE DOG FOOD

The Problem

Del Monte operates in a very competitive global food industry. In addition to manufacturing canned fruits and vegetables for human consumption, Del Monte produces pet food such as Gravy Train, 9 Lives, and Meow Mix. Therefore, using market research, the company constantly looks for innovative ways to increase its competitive edge. The company noticed the fast growth of social media and decided to deploy social media projects "in order to capitalize on social networking as a marketing tool, to help the company get closer to its customers and create the kind of products consumers want" (per Greengard 2008). Their primary goal was to decide the best way to use social media-based market research to support its diverse product line—in this case, dog food.

Electronic supplementary material The online version of this chapter (doi:10.1007/978-3-319-17028-2_10) contains supplementary material, which is available to authorized users.

The Solution

The basic idea was first to connect and collaborate with dog lovers via social networks and then conduct their market research. The corporate IT department was unable to conduct social network research; therefore, the Pet Products Division of Del Monte Foods decided to use Insight Networks, a service launched by MarketTools, Inc., a provider of on-demand online market research (see MarketTools, Inc. 2008 for details).

The first activity conducted using Insight Networks was text analysis—gathering relevant content from over 50 million blogs and analyzing relevant topics of conversation among the target customers. The seconds activity was to create a special online community of dog lovers, where Del Monte could observe interactions and stimulate discussions with the community members. The third activity was on-demand survey research, used to determine the viability of new strategies and ideas (see MarketTools, Inc. 2008.)

Through previous research, Del Monte Pet Products Division identified one segment of the dog owner community as their target, and they wanted to understand that segment more in depth. Del Monte created an online community for dog lovers called "I Love My Dog," where 400 members were chosen to join the private network. In order to connect with millions of dog owners, Insight Networks provided Del Monte Pet Products Division with a direct, interactive connection to their consumers. Using their propriety software, Insight Networks monitors millions of relevant blogs in the blogosphere as well as forums in social networks, in order to identify key ideas in which dog lovers are interested. These ideas were then analyzed in order to predict consumer behavior trends. Such analysis is usually done by using computerized tools such as monitoring consumer interactions, analyzing consumer sentiments, and using social analytics (e.g., see Jayanti 2010).

By utilizing social media, Del Monte can now conduct better market research. The conventional approach was using questionnaires (or focus groups) that were expensive and difficult to fill by qualified participants. Using social media, Del Monte can gather much of the same data faster and at a lower cost. All that is required now is to monitor customer conversations, collect the data, and analyze the vast amount of information. The software provided by MarketTools also facilitates subgroup creation, idea generation, and panel creation.

Del Monte received positive results through their use of Insight Networks. According to Del Monte's senior market research manager, they used the results of the text analysis and communication with the dog lover community to ask questions about which new products to introduce and which products to refine. This method saves Del Monte time and money, helping them focus on products that customers will value most, while helping them gain a new competitive edge. After the market analysis conducted by Insight Networks, Del Monte introduced two new products, with great success. The first was a new variety of Pup-Peroni® dog snacks, with new packaging and a new marketing campaign, which resulted in increased product sales. The other was a new product—Snausages Breakfast Bites™, with sales figures that pleased Del Monte (see MarketTools, Inc. 2008).

The Experiment

The results of the above application were used to help improve the company's dog treat, called Snausages Breakfast Bites. For guidance, Del Monte relied on its dog lovers' social community. By monitoring customer blogs and by posting questions to customers to stimulate discussions, Del Monte used text analysis methods to investigate the relationship between dogs and their owners. Del Monte concluded from the analysis that people who own small dogs would be the major purchasers of Snausages Breakfast Bites. The company also found differences of opinions due to the age of owners. Next, a small sample of the improved dog food was produced and tested in the physical market. As a result of using both social media and traditional market research, the product design decisions were revised. In addition, marketing promotions were modified. Finally, the new approach solidified the community of dog lovers who are happy that their opinions were considered.

The Results

The results of the analysis help Del Monte understand its customers and consequently plan its marketing activities, communication strategies, and customer service applications. The results also help evaluate the success of special marketing campaigns, how well the business processes accomplished the corporate goals, and how to better justify proposed new activities.

Product cycle time was reduced by more than 50 % to only 6 months, and Del Monte was able to develop a better marketing communication strategy. Furthermore, the analysis helped the company better understand customers and their purchasing activities, as well as predicting market trends and identifying and anticipating opportunities. Finally, the quality of the food was improved based on the suggestions of the dog lovers, increasing sales.

Sources: Based on MarketTools, Inc. (2008), Greengard (2008), Jayanti (2010), Big Heart Pet Brands (2012).

LESSONS LEARNED FROM THE CASE

The opening case illustrates that market research can be useful in a competitive market by providing insights for better product development and marketing strategy. In this case, the company collected data online from its socially-oriented customers. One of the first activities MarketTools, Inc. provided was text analysis. By monitoring, collecting, and analyzing relevant content from over 50 million conversations on blogs, MarketTools was able to determine the current topics of conversation among the consumers. The results of the analysis helped Del Monte determine what topics dog owners are most interested in. Using this information, Del Monte was able to improve its dog food and devise new marketing strategies. Online market research, as seen in the case, is related to strategy, planning, performance monitoring, social media analysis, and sentiment analysis; all these topics are addressed in this chapter.

The main focus of this chapter is on the basic steps in creating strategic planning for SC companies. The chapter also presents and discusses issues related to creating an e-strategy to engage in global SC and the opportunities that SC creates for small and medium-sized enterprises (SMEs).

10.1   THE STRATEGY-PERFORMANCE CYCLE

Social media projects, like other projects, are implemented in order to improve *organizational performance*. Companies can view improving performance as a challenge, a requirement for survival, or as a key to profitability and a positive reputation.

In this chapter, we look at performance improvement as a generic cyclical process, which is based on a strategy, metrics, performance assessment, analysis, and innovation. The process, illustrated in Fig. 10.1, involves four major steps: (1) create goals and objectives that express the organizational mission; (2) create the strategy and make plans to attain the goals and objectives; (3) set performance metrics and monitor the performance, then analyze the difference between the two; and (4) develop a corrective strategy.

The remaining portion of this chapter describes the four steps. A brief description of the four steps follows:

Step 1. Organizations exist to accomplish a mission (top box in Fig. 10.1). Any SC project is designed to help attain the goals and objectives. Four major objectives are listed on the right-hand side of the mission box, including the gain of competitive advantage and increased performance. Other goals and objectives relate to specific social commerce projects, and they depend on the specific situation. Examples are:

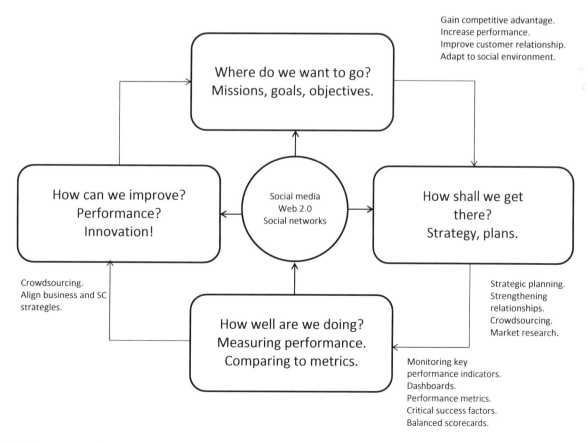

Fig. 10.1   The strategy-performance model

- Facilitate growth
- Increase customer loyalty
- Improve customer relationships and service quality
- Improve partner relationship management
- Generate new business models and facilitate innovation
- Reduce cost

Step 2. Once the goals and objectives are known, an organization needs to decide what to do to attain them. That is, how does the organization get what the organization wants (see right-hand side box in Fig. 10.1). The key activities in this step include strategy formulation and strategic planning (e.g., see Spredfest; **spredfast.com**). Section 10.2 describes these activities as they relate to social commerce.

Note that this step involves the justification of the social commerce initiative(s) (Sect. 10.3). Moreover, this step requires activities such as an analysis of the markets and the competition, which are done via market research (Sect. 10.4).

Step 3. Once the strategy and plans are approved, organizations can proceed and deploy the social commerce program(s). After a few months, it is necessary to assess the program's performance (bottom box of Fig. 10.1); namely, how well the company is performing, with respect to the attainment of its strategy, in terms of the social commerce program, and its contribution to the goals and objectives. This step involves two major activities: (1) setting measurable performance metrics and (2) monitoring, measuring, and comparing performance for these metrics. Several tools are employed here, including generic ones such as balanced scorecards. All these topics are described in detail in Sect. 10.5.

Once the organizations collect performance information, they need to analyze the performance level (quantitatively and qualitatively). This analysis is partially done by using social media analytics, including sentiment analysis. Results of the analysis are presented via reports, tables, and dashboards (see Sect. 10.6).

Step 4. The analysis tells management how well the company performs when it uses social commerce initiatives. Obviously, if the analysis shows negative results, it is necessary to take some corrective action (left box of Fig. 10.1). A key activity here is to use innovations to improve the performance. However, even if the results are good, the organization may take actions that range from providing bonuses to the best performers identified in the analysis to raising the desired levels of employee performance for the future. The primary point is being innovative, because even a good performance can be improved. In addition, techniques such as competitive analysis can be useful (Sect. 10.7).

Note that the process is cyclical. However, at each step, a return to a previous step in order to conduct some modification is possible.

In the remainder of this chapter, we will describe how social media and social networking are related to the four steps (center of Fig. 10.1).

Types of Social Media Projects

In addition to the organizational goals and objectives presented in Step 1, there are goals and objectives that relate to the specific types of social media projects.

In Table 10.1, we present representative types of social commerce projects, along with their potential goals. In addition, Forrester Consulting (2010) identified the major social commerce activities conducted by companies. Their study also identified the strategic goals supported by social media.

For additional information, see **ibm.com/smarterplanet/global/files/us__en_us__socialbusiness__epw14008usen.pdf**.

Note that, these goals are the basis for strategic planning (Sect. 10.2), justification (Sect. 10.3), market research (Sect. 10.4), metrics (Sect. 10.5), and analysis (Sect. 10.6).

To justify SC projects, a company needs to decide which of the goals listed in Table 10.1 and in Sect. 10.1 it wants to attain, and then decide the importance of each goal. This is done by assessing the potential contribution of each specific social commerce project to the attainment of each goal. Note that, the measure of the goals and objectives is intangible, which makes the analysis difficult (see discussion in Sect. 10.3). Other challenges include the plethora of possible performance metrics and the quickly changing nature of social media.

Table 10.1 Major types of social commerce projects and their possible goals

Types of SC project	Possible goals
Social shopping	Increase revenue, acquire new customers, increase customer experience, go global
Marketing communication	Increase brand awareness, increase sales, increase viral marketing, increase customer engagement, reduce customer acquisition cost
Social CRM and customer service	Increase customer satisfaction, increase customer trust and loyalty, increase sellers' reputation, improve public relations
Social enterprise (Enterprise 2.0)	Enable better recruiting, facilitate problem solving and idea generation, facilitate collaboration, improve efficiency, optimize workforce
Crowdsourcing	Increase innovation and collaboration, generate new business models
Entertainment and gaming	Increase users' satisfaction, provide for cross selling, increase awareness, increase advertising income
Social engagement/ reputation management	Increase brand awareness, improve public relations, influence customers to buy

10.2 ORGANIZATIONAL STRATEGY AND STRATEGIC PLANNING FOR SOCIAL COMMERCE

A **strategy** is a framework a business sets forth indicating the direction it plans to take to accomplish its mission and goals. Strategy also outlines the plans and policies that need to be accomplished. According to Mintzberg et al. (2002), **strategic planning** "is an organization's process of defining its strategy, or direction, and making decisions on allocating its resources to pursue this strategy....Strategy has many definitions, but generally involves setting goals, determining actions to achieve the goals, and mobilizing resources to execute the actions. A strategy describes how the ends (goals) will be achieved by the means (resources)." In order to determine the direction of the organization, it is necessary to understand its current position and the possible avenues through which it can pursue a particular course of action. Generally, strategic planning is done for 3–5 years into the future. For a comprehensive discussion about strategy, see Porter (1996).

The **organizational strategy** also expresses the specific plans and policies, of how a business plans to take to achieve its strategy; these policies and plans are referred to as **tactics**. For example, a strategy might be to use crowdsourcing for product improvement, whereas a tactic might be to create a social media page for consumers to post ideas (e.g., Dell and Starbucks do this, as discussed in previous chapters). It is important to note that objectives, strategies, and tactics can exist on many different levels in a company, ranging from high-level corporate strategic planning to a strategy of increasing traffic to a website. Social commerce strategies, including social media marketing and e-commerce strategies need to be aligned with the organization's business strategy and implemented by appropriate departments.

An organizational *strategy* is a comprehensive framework for expressing the manner in which a business plans to achieve its mission, what goals are needed to support it, and what plans and policies will be needed to accomplish these goals. Strategy is also about making decisions on what activities not to pursue and trade-offs between strategic alternatives. An organization's strategy (including EC and SC strategies) starts with understanding where the company is today with respect to its goals, and where it wants to be in the future. Strategies are often related to Porter's competitive forces model.

Porter's 5 Competitive Forces Model and Related Strategies

Companies have used Porter's competitive forces model to develop strategies and tactics for increasing their competitive edge in their industry. The model also demonstrates how IT and SC can enhance competitiveness.

Porter's "5 Forces" model has been used by companies to better compete in their industry. It also illustrates how SC can facilitate a company's competitive advantage. According to Hanlon (2013), the "model helps marketers and business managers to look at the 'balance of power' in a market between different types of organizations...Porter's Five Forces works best when looking at the entire market sector, rather than your own business and a few competitors."

The model recognizes five major forces that may impact a company's position in a given industry. Other forces, including the impact of government, affect all companies in the industry, and therefore may have a less direct impact on the relative success of an individual company within its industry. Although the details of the model differ from one industry to another, its general structure is universal. The five major forces are illustrated in Fig. 10.2.

The model recognizes the following five major forces that affect the degree of competition and, ultimately, the level of profitability, in an industry:

1. Threat of entry of new competitors
2. Bargaining power of suppliers
3. Bargaining power of customers or buyers
4. Threat of substitute products or services
5. Rivalry among existing firms in the industry

The strength of each force is determined by the industry's composition and structure. Existing companies within an industry must watch these forces and need to be ready to protect themselves; alternatively, they can use the forces to improve their position or challenge the leaders in the industry. The definitions and details of the model are provided in Porter (1980) and Hanlon (2013). For an in-depth article on the five forces, along with a video and infographic, see Porter (2008).

Companies identify the forces that influence performance in their marketplace and then develop a strategy to handle the forces. Typical generic strategies are shown in Table 10.2.

In Table 10.2, we first list Porter's three generic strategies (cost leadership, differentiation, and focus (market segmentation, e.g., niche), then we add nine other strategies. Most of these strategies can be facilitated by social media, as shown throughout the book.

Any progressive strategy must consider the Internet. Porter (2001) argues that "a *coherent organizational strategy that includes the Internet is more important than ever before: Many have argued that the Internet renders strategy obsolete. In reality, the opposite is true… it is more important than ever for companies to distinguish themselves through strategy. The winners will be those that view the Internet as a complement to, not a cannibal of, traditional ways of competing.*"

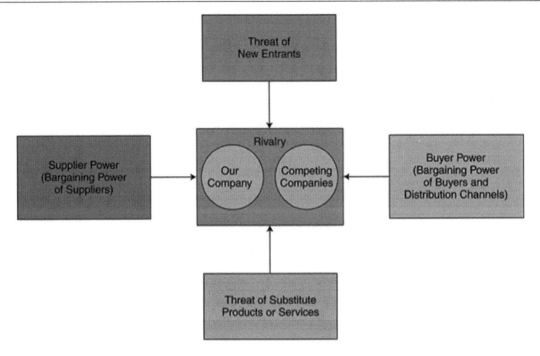

Fig. 10.2 Porter's five forces model

Table 10.2 Strategies for competitive advantage

Strategy	Description
Classic strategies	
Cost leadership	Produce product/service at the lowest cost in the industry
Differentiation	Offer different products, services, or product features
Niche	Select a narrow-scope segment (market niche) and be the best in quality, speed, or cost in that segment
General strategies	
Growth	Increase market share, acquire more customers, or sell more types of products
Alliance	Work with business partners in partnerships, alliances, joint ventures, or virtual companies
Innovation	Introduce new products/services; put new features into existing products/services; develop new ways to produce products/services
Operational effectiveness	Improve the manner in which internal business processes are executed so that the firm performs similar activities better than rivals do
Customer orientation	Concentrate on customer satisfaction
Time	Treat time as a resource, then manage it and use it to the firm's advantage
Entry barriers	Create entry barriers. By introducing innovative products or using EC business models to provide exceptional service, companies can create entry barriers to discourage new competitors
Customer or supplier lock-in	Encourage customers or suppliers to stay with you rather than switching to competitors. Reduce customers' bargaining power by locking them in (e.g., by providing superior customer service)
Increase switching costs	Discourage customers or suppliers from switching to competitors for economic reasons

As an example, travel agencies closed because many were too slow to embrace Internet progress. Porter (2001) has identified several ways that the Internet affects each of the five forces of competitiveness.

The Impact of the Internet on Competitiveness

The Internet's impact on strategic competitiveness and long-term profitability will differ from industry to industry.

Fig. 10.3 The strategic planning process

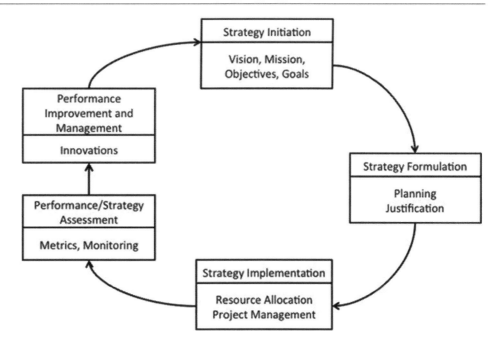

Accordingly, many businesses are taking a focused look at the impact of the Internet and SC on their future. For these firms, social commerce strategy involves the formulation and execution of a vision of how the company intends to do business electronically while deploying social commerce projects, such as those listed in Table 10.2 above.

The Key Elements of a Strategic Planning Process

According to **dummies.com/how-to/content/major-components-of-a-strategic-plan.html**, the major key elements (components) of a strategic plan include a mission statement, a vision statement, values statement, and strategies. In addition, the key elements of a strategic plan are strategic vision; strategy (explaining the value you deliver); strategic plans, goals, and objectives; and strategic plan execution and evaluation.

Strategic planning can also be viewed as maintaining a viable fit between the organization's objectives, resources, and its changing business environment (see Strauss and Frost 2014 for details).

The process of strategic planning will differ depending upon the type of strategy, the implementation method, the size of the firm, and the planning tools and methodologies used. Nevertheless, any strategic planning process has a variation of five major stages, as shown in Fig. 10.3: *initiation, formulation, implementation, assessment, and performance improvement*. For a comprehensive look at the basics of strategic planning, including strategic management and the steps

in strategic planning and management, see **planware.org/strategicplan.htm**, **managementhelp.org/strategicplanning**, and Chap. 13 in Turban et al. (2015).

Strategy Implementation in Social Commerce

Businesses want to be sure they find the right social media strategies, tactics, and plans to achieve their goals and objectives. The best place to start is with the company's objectives, as described in Sect. 10.1. There is a continuum of social media goals, from broad business strategies to specific brand tactics. As you may recall from Chap. 3, the consumer purchasing decision process involves three steps: awareness, attitude, and behavior. These are called the hierarchical stages. Strauss and Frost (2014) developed a scale that indicates which level of the hierarchy affects each goal in the strategy. Note that, many social media tools can facilitate these goals, and that an integrated marketing communication effort can be a very effective strategy over time. For why you need social media strategy, see Dragon (2013). Let us now explore some examples of how businesses implement SC strategies.

Examples of Successful SC Strategies

There are many successful cases of SC strategy implementation and many SC strategic models (e.g., see Sysomos 2011; Radian6 2012; and Shih 2011). A few examples follow.

Example 1: Groupon's Strategy for Growth

Prior to its IPO debut in 2011, Groupon's major strategy was revenue maximization. In order to attain this strategy, Groupon needed to work with as many vendors as possible in each target city. Their tactic was to send special teams to many cities (regardless of cost) to find qualified vendors and convince them to participate in Groupon deals. Groupon then used e-mail and banner ads to promote the special deals provided by the participating merchants. The strategy worked initially with respect to growth. However, the model was not profitable for Groupon. Therefore, Groupon decided to use mobile applications and also have customers search for discounts themselves.

Example 2: Walmart's Strategy for Acquiring New Suppliers and Products

On January 18, 2012, Walmart launched a contest called "Get on the Shelf" to let would-be suppliers pitch their products via YouTube videos. In general, suppliers face intense competition to get their products on any retailer's shelves (especially Walmart's), because in order to add a new product, an old one must be removed or receive fewer facings (rows on the shelf). Consumers watched the YouTube videos, and voted for their favorite products online (similar to an *American Idol* competition). The selected items would be sold at Walmart.com and the most liked brand would be sold at the physical stores. Walmart succeeded by using social media to engage customers and build customer loyalty. For details, see Hayes (2012). In 2011, Walmart began buying social media companies (e.g., privately held social media start-up Kosmix). See Bort (2012). Walmart ran the same type of contest again in 2013, and found entrepreneurs, whose new products are now sold at Walmart.com (see **getontheshelf.walmart.com**).

Example 3: Zynga's Strategy for Dealing with Unpredictable Demand

When Zynga invents a new game for Facebook, they cannot anticipate if there will be 100 million players or only 5 million. Zynga's hybrid cloud strategy (Babcock 2011) helped solve this problem by allowing the company to develop flexibility and speed in their product deployment. This way, Zynga could adapt its capacity to the market's fast-changing demands. In 2013, the company changed its business model to include online gambling in the UK, but decided not to invest money in U.S. real money online gambling, instead preferring to stay focused on free games (see **venturebeat.com/2013/07/25/zynga-exec-explains-why-the-company-is-abandoning-u-s-online-gambling**). Note: Gamers in the UK, but not the U.S., can now use real money to play online poker. It is not clear if the strategy will work. As of 2014, Zynga is struggling to survive.

For ELLE fashion magazine social strategies, see Dragon (2014). For a primer on social media strategies (2013; with infographic), see **digitalinformationworld.com/2014/01/what-marketers-should-and-should-not-do-on-social-media-infographic.html**.

It is important for a company to consider the following issues when planning a successful online SC strategy (condensed from *GoECart.com* 2010 and updated with the authors' experiences).

- Develop an overall e-commerce strategy with clearly defined business goals.
- Show how SC strategy contributes to the e-commerce and overall sales revenue strategy.
- Identify the audiences you want to reach.
- Identify the resources available for SC.
- Decide on appropriate technologies to use.
- Create supportive social culture in the business.
- Effectively market to existing online customers with the support of social media.
- Know how to sell globally as well as locally (if it is cost effective to ship internationally).
- Develop consistent and synchronous online and offline brand strategies ("multichannel" strategies).
- Create a corporate business profile and invite customers to post reviews on public and private social networks.
- Create surveys and two-way communication mechanisms to solicit feedback from customers.
- Develop monitoring and performance assessment plans.

Monaco (2013) provides a comprehensive guide to social media strategy. Additional suggestions on how a company can develop a business-aligned social media and social networking strategy are provided at **ddmcd.com/managing-technology/how-to-develop-a-business-aligned-social-media-social-networ.html**. For the needs and benefits of a social CRM strategy, see Ang (2011).

A Strategy for Successful SC Implementation

To succeed in the implementation of social commerce projects, especially in medium and large companies, a process needs to be properly planned with a deployment strategy. A popular strategy involves four steps:
1. Learn and understand the environment inside and outside the organization.

2. Experiment with a small-scale project so you can observe and learn.
3. Assess the results of the experiment.
4. Develop or abandon the project.

Gombert (2010) proposed similar steps: evaluate opportunities, prepare a plan, engage your audience, and measure results.

Some Other Strategy Issues

There are several strategic issues that companies may need to address when dealing with social commerce. Here are some relevant questions related to these issues.

- Which channel is better for social commerce: Facebook, Twitter, or others? (See **blog.thelettertwo. com/2014/08/12/62-of-consumers-prefer-facebook-over-pinterest-twitter-as-their-social-commerce-channel.**)
- Which social commerce platform drives the most sales? (See **shopify.com/infographics/social-commerce;** with infographics.)
- How do you select a social network site(s) for paid media tactics, or in sales?
- How do you generate constant traffic to your SC site? (For 39 actionable ways to drive traffic to your website (2014), see **forbes.com/sites/ jaysondemers/2014/05/13/39-actionable-ideas-for-driving-traffic-to-your-website**).
- What should small businesses do with social commerce? What should they not do? (See **digitalinfor- mationworld.com/2014/01/what-marketers-should-and-should-not-do-on-social-media-infographic. html**; with infographic.)
- How can you have a sufficient number of fans and friends and encourage them to engage and create and share content? (See **socialmediaexaminer. com/encourage-fans-to-create-share-visual-content.**)

Some Policies and Guidelines

Dozens of experts provide answers to the previous list of questions, as well as to similar strategy questions; they also provide guidelines for success in specific areas of social commerce (e.g., marketing, security, policy). Several examples can be found in Barnes and Barnes (2009). For 57 different social media policies and resources, see **socialmediatoday. com/davefleet/151761/57-social-media-policy-examples-and-resources**. You can also learn from business failures.

For the major elements of social media strategy, see the infographic at **socialmediaonlineclasses.com/social-mediastrategy-chart**. For implications of global marketing strategy, see Berthon et al. (2012).

10.3 JUSTIFICATION AND ROI IN SOCIAL COMMERCE

Justification of social commerce is a multidimensional task. While many people stress the financial justification (ROI and other methods), one also needs to check the technical justification (and feasibility), the organizational fit to social media (e.g., appropriate organizational culture), operational justification, and strategic justification.

An Overview of Justification

Justification of social commerce projects can be very complex.

To illustrate the potential complexity of justification, Brian Solis developed the concept of the *social marketing compass*, which includes a large number of interrelated variables. (See **briansolis.com/2011/01/the-social-compass-is-the-gps-for-the-adaptive-business**, which includes an infographic and explanation of the four "halos" of the social compass.)

To begin with, several areas need to be considered: strategic considerations, technical considerations, and operational considerations. One also needs to manage intangible costs and benefits. On top of that, there are other difficulties in executing justifications.

One important aspect of justification is calculating the rate of return of investments (ROI). For a discussion on how to measure ROI in social commerce, see Blanchard (2011) and Sysomos (2011).

The total cost of SC projects (initial and operations) can be very high due to staff time and cost of potential risks (e.g., very negative social interactions; for example, conversations on social networks). Therefore, it is wise to justify such systems, including the risks. The methodologies available for justification are the same as for any other EC systems and information technology projects. For methodologies and related issues, see Turban et al. (2015). In this section, we cover only the selected topics that are most relevant to social commerce. Specifically, we cover the following topics:

- The justification process
- Some difficulties in conducting justification
- Dealing with intangible costs
- The use of Gartner's hype cycle
- Risk analysis

The SC Justification Process

Justifying large-scale investments involves not only selecting a justification method but also having a plan to execute it. The appropriate process is not simple. According to *Baseline* (2006) and the authors' experiences, the major steps of this process are:

1. Establish an appropriate foundation for analysis with the software vendor (if you use software), and then conduct your ROI analysis.
2. Conduct good research on the relevant metrics and validate them.
3. Justify and document the cost and benefit and the assumptions made regarding data.
4. Document and verify all data used in the calculations. Clarify all assumptions used in the analysis.
5. Do not leave out intangible benefits, including long-term ones. Is the project really improving the company's competitive and strategic advantages?
6. Be careful not to underestimate cost and overestimate benefits (a tendency of many managers).
7. Make supporting figures as realistic as possible and include risk analysis.
8. Involve top management and all important partners, including suppliers and distribution channel members.

The justification process involves the comparison of costs and benefits in a process called *cost–benefit analysis*.

Difficulties in Conducting Cost–Benefit Analysis and Justification

The execution of cost–benefit analysis for social commerce projects can be difficult due to the following obstacles.

Difficulties in Measuring Productivity and Performance Gains

The benefits in cost-benefit analysis are more difficult to measure and assess than costs. See 14 formulas to measure benefits as suggested by Schottmuller (2013), and the considerations companies face with the cost of social media in Nair (2011).

One of the major benefits of using SC is increased productivity, such as with an enterprise social network. However, productivity increases may be difficult to measure, for several reasons. The major reasons are presented next:

Data and Analysis Issues

Data, or the analysis of the data, may hide productivity gains. For example, retailers now use SC to engage customers in proposing and evaluating new products. Knowing what customers think may result in a benefit for the retailers. However, retailers must determine how to measure engagement in order to determine its value.

SC Productivity Gains in One Area May Be Offset by Losses in Other Areas

Another possible difficulty is that SC gains in certain areas of the company may be offset by resultant losses in other areas. For example, a staff member may spend time responding to social media conversations and neglect the creation of new offline marketing communications.

Hidden Costs and Benefits

Some costs and benefits are less visible, or even completely hidden. These need to be determined and considered. Examples of hidden costs or benefits include currency fluctuations; the need to upgrade software over time; and the cost of underestimation or overestimation of benefits (such as increased brand awareness).

Incorrectly Defining What Is Measured

The results of any investment justification depend on what is actually measured. For example, to assess the benefits of SC investment, one should usually look at productivity improvement in the area where the SC project was deployed (e.g., in customer care). However, productivity increase may also result from other factors (e.g., due to a large investment in non-SC projects).

Intangible Cost-Benefit Analysis

Broadly speaking, SC costs and benefits can be classified into two categories: tangible and intangible. *Tangible* costs and benefits are easier to measure. For example, the cost of software (cost) and the amount of labor saved (benefit) are easy to determine. *Intangible* benefits, such as customer satisfaction, improved communication (e.g., by using Twitter), or increased word of mouth, are usually more difficult to measure; thus, it is difficult to determine their value. Therefore, some experts believe that one should not attempt to conduct an ROI study on social media projects (e.g., see Falls and Deckers 2012). This may be correct when the SC projects are small; however, in large projects, not conducting ROI may have negative consequences.

First, let us see what the intangibles are, and then see how companies can handle them.

Intangible Costs and Benefits

Organizations must develop innovative metrics to track down *intangible* costs and benefits as accurately as possible. Intangible costs may include some vague costs; for example, the learning curve of the firm's customer service employees as they attempt to incorporate an SC system that responds to customer inquiries. Another intangible cost may involve having to adapt to changes in certain business processes, such as processing items returned by customers or operating a tracking system for customer complaints.

Handling Intangible Benefits

The first step in dealing with intangible benefits is to define them and, if possible, specify how they are going to be measured.

A straightforward way to deal with intangible benefits is to make *rough estimates* of their monetary values and then conduct an ROI analysis. The simplicity of this approach is attractive; however, in many cases, the simplification assumptions used in these estimates may lead to completely incorrect results. Another way to deal with intangible benefits is to develop a balanced scorecard (Sect. 10.5) for proposed projects. This approach requires listing both tangible and intangible goals and their measures. For an example of how this works, see Person (2013).

The Use of Gartner's Hype Cycle

An important technology that can help in justifying SC projects is Gartner's Hype Cycle (updated annually).

Organizations can use this approach to assess the status of specific SC technologies and tools so they can decide the fate of an SC project before they invest effort and money in cost–benefit analysis and justification.

What Is Gartner's Hype Cycle?

According to Gartner, Inc., the **hype cycle** is a graphic representation of the maturity, adoption, and social application of specific IT and SC tools and how they are potentially relevant to solving real business problems and exploiting new opportunities. The term, developed and used by Gartner Inc., is a similar concept to the marketer's "product life cycle" curve (introduction, growth, maturity, decline). The hype cycle provides a snapshot of the relative maturity of different categories of IT technologies and management-related disciplines. It highlights over-hyped areas versus high impact matured technologies, and provides estimates of how long technologies and trends will take to mature. The Gartner

Hype Cycle's methodology shows how a technology or application will evolve over time. There are many different categories of Gartner hype cycles; each are customized to fit certain industries and technologies; research notes are updated each year (see Gartner, Inc. undated).

Each hype cycle has five overlapping stages that reflect the technology's life cycle, starting with a trigger point, through implementation of technology, and then enduring disillusionment, before finally becoming more mainstream and accepted. The five stages (as compiled from Gartner Inc. (undated) and **whatis.techtarget.com/definition/Gartner-hype-cycle** are:

1. **Technology trigger.** The cycle begins with a breakthrough, public demonstration, product launch, or other event that generates significant media and industry interest.
2. **Peak of inflated expectations.** A phase of over enthusiasm and unrealistic projections during which a flurry of publicized activity by technology and media leaders may result in some successes, but will more likely result in failures as the technology is pushed to its limits. The only businesses that may make money at this stage are conference organizers, consultants, and magazine publishers. Early publicity results can be seen in success stories and some failures (early adopters).
3. **Trough of disillusionment.** The point at which the technology becomes unfashionable and the media abandons the topic because the technology did not live up to its inflated expectations.
4. **Slope of enlightenment.** Focused experimentation and solid hard work by an increasingly diverse range of organizations lead to a true understanding of the technology's applicability, risks, and benefits. Commercial off-the-shelf software methodologies and tools become available to ease the development process. Understanding how the technology works and how it can benefit the enterprise as the technology becomes more widely understood.
5. **Plateau of productivity.** The real-world benefits of the technology are demonstrated and accepted. Tools and methodologies are increasingly stable as they enter their seconds and third generation. The final height of the plateau varies according to whether the technology is broadly applicable or benefits only a niche market. This is the beginning of mainstream adoption, success of broad market applicability, and recognizable relevance.

In addition, the time needed for each technology to reach mainstream adoption (maturity) is indicated on the curve. For example, in July 2011, Gartner estimated that it would take social analytics 2–5 years to reach the mainstream adoption. For details on how several social commerce tools are placed on the hype cycle, see Hodgson (2012).

Application of the Hype Cycle

Gartner Inc. provides an annual report that covers about 80 different hype cycles, evaluating over 2,000 different technologies, services, and trends in over 119 industries. For the 2014 summary, see **gartner.com/newsroom/id/2819918**. Of course, Gartner charges high fees for providing their reports, which include technology trends. The 2013 and 2014 reports cover several SC technologies such as social CRM, microblogging, social analytics, virtual worlds, location-based applications, and collective intelligence.

The 2014 cycle for emerging technologies is described in detail at **gartner.com/newsroom/id/2819918**. The Pew Research Center provides an interesting discussion about several emerging SC and EC technologies in 2014. They also provide an image of the hype cycle of emerging technologies in July 2014. See **pewresearch.org/fact-tank/2014/08/15/chart-of-the-week-the-hype-cycle-of-emerging-technologies**.

The Social Business Power Map

This map, created by Dachis Group, is similar to the hype cycle, but it is completely dedicated to social media and commerce. Dachis Group defines social business "as the distinct process of applying social media to meet business objectives." The map shows the major social media trends from the buzz stage to experimentation, adoption, and maturity. For details, see **stephenslighthouse.com/2010/08/17/the-2010-social-business-landscape**. In 2011, the company launched its *social business index*. In February 2014, Dachis Group was acquired by Sprinklr, a social media analytics firm.

Risk Analysis

Deploying social commerce may involve some potential risks and possibly complex implementation issues. In justifying social commerce projects, one must pay attention to the risk issues related to companies engaged in social commerce activities, as well as to individuals who participate in them. For further discussion, see Thompson et al. (2013) and corresponding summary/infographic at **grantthornton.com/issues/library/survey-reports/advisory/2013/BAS-social-media-survey.aspx**, and Shullich (2012).

The following are representative issues frequently cited by companies:

- Wrong justification data due to the difficulties cited earlier
- Legal risks
- Security threats
- Invasion of privacy
- Social media fraud
- Violation of intellectual property and copyright
- Employee reluctance to participate in social networking
- Data leakage (corporate strategic information)
- Poor or biased quality of user-generated content
- Cyberbullying/cyberstalking and employee harassment
- Misuse and waste of time and other resources (loss of productivity)
- Risk to the company's reputation (loss of credibility) due to user conversations and blog discussion forums (see Chap. 5)

Risk to Users

In addition to risks to the company, there are some possible risks to users, mostly in the areas of fraud and privacy violation. As a result, some users abandon social networks or refrain from their use. For a discussion, see della Cava (2010). For an overview of personal risk and how people can protect themselves, see **netsecurity.about.com/od/newsandeditorial2/a/socialpredators.htm** and Alter (2014).

Conclusion

Because of the difficulties cited earlier, many companies do not measure the value of SC projects. However, this may be a risky approach, since bad projects may be accepted and good ones may be rejected.

Despite all the difficulties, there are many reported ROI studies for successful SC applications. For a list of 166 such cases, see Petersen (2012) and the corresponding 2014 summary at **barnraisersllc.com/2014/04/166-case-studies-prove-social-media-roi**. For an infographic on social media ROI, see Bennett (2013). In addition, many companies and vendors have developed their own ROI methods and calculators. Furthermore, several methodologies for e-commerce are suitable for SC justification. To learn more, see Owen (2013). See also ShopSocially's new A/B Testing Framework, and how it helps e-commerce sites, at **digitaljournal.com/pr/1661430**.

For six steps to measure social media ROI with an infographic, see **mediabistro.com/alltwitter/how-to-measure-social-media-roi_b60174**.

10.4 MARKET RESEARCH IN SOCIAL COMMERCE

Market research involves data collection and analysis of information about consumers and competitors, the results of which are turned into marketing knowledge. Businesses usually hire a market research company to conduct their research, but some businesses do it on their own (per **sbinfocanada.about.com/od/marketing/g/market-research.htm**).

Why Conduct Market Research?

Market research is conducted to understand an organization's markets in order to serve them better than the competition does. Accurate information about consumers and competitors is essential for the development of a successful marketing plan. According to **sbinfocanada.about.com/od/marketing/g/marketresearch.htm**, "market research allows businesses to make decisions that make them more responsive to customers' needs and increase profits." It is important for both start-ups and established businesses to conduct market research. "Small business owners use market research to determine the feasibility of a new business, test interest in new products or services, improve aspects of their businesses, such as customer service or distribution channels, and develop competitive strategies" (per **sbinfocanada.about.com/od/marketing/g/marketresearch.htm**). One major purpose of market research is to provide information for decision making and strategy formulation as part of a business plan and justification. Market research is also conducted to help facilitate competitive intelligence (see Sect. 10.7). Another reason it is used is for justifying requests for funding for marketing plans, such as new product introductions, as well as for other purposes. Market research can be done offline and/or online. In this book, we mostly cover topics associated with online social commerce as related to the generic topic of Internet research. Market research can identify problems and opportunities. For example, see Redsicker (2013).

Social commerce provides superb opportunities to conduct market research. In addition, it is necessary to conduct research on social commerce itself to identify viable SC strategies and tactics. Much of this research is done in social networks and/or by using social software.

Factors such as a person's age, gender, and which websites they use to engage in social networking provide a new opportunity to assess markets, sometimes even in real time. One major area is viral marketing (see Chap. 3).

E-Marketing Research in Brief

Social commerce, as described in Chap. 1, has its roots in e-commerce and e-marketing. Therefore, conducting market research in social commerce includes methods and processes from these two disciplines.

The Major Generic Topics

The following topics are frequently described as being related to Internet-based generic market research:

- Data sources and data collection methods
- Data and information quality
- Learning from (listening to) customers
- Internet social search methodologies and tools
- Support for competitive intelligence
- Internet-based research approaches and methods
- Ethics of online research
- Marketing databases, data and text mining, and data warehouses
- Legal issues and protection of privacy

For comprehensive coverage of these and e-marketing research in general, see Strauss and Frost (2014). For e-commerce market research, see Chap. 9 in Turban et al. (2015). Both books provide additional resources.

For general related information, see Poynter (2011), MarketingSherpa (**marketingsherpa.com**), and Barker et al. (2011). For research in the B2B arena, see Gillin and Schwartzman (2011).

Using Social Networking for Qualitative Market Research

Merchants can easily find customers on social networks and sometimes even see what they are doing online, as well as gather information about their customers' friends. However, it may not be easy to conduct social-oriented market research. An unsolicited message that requests the page owner to follow a link to a survey or comment on a brand will likely be ignored unless it comes from someone the user knows. In this section, we discuss *qualitative* market research in social media, as opposed to *quantitative* survey research.

Example: Mountain Dew
In the past, Mountain Dew's strategy was to target video game lovers and extreme sports enthusiasts, as these individuals tend to drink high-caffeine beverages. However, because the company wanted to unite all of its customers

into one community, Mountain Dew used several "Dewmocracy" contests, which encouraged consumers to choose their next soda flavor. This market research (described next) was conducted for product development purposes.

Although several other food and beverage companies have also used social networks to help choose new product flavors, Mountain Dew did this first by using their most dedicated customers, and then expanding to the public. The first step was to send seven flavors of soda to 50 Dew fanatics. These people were given cameras and asked to make a video of themselves debating the flavors and showing their love for each flavor. Having consumers create videos, was, according to Hespos (2010), "a great idea because they made the social-media effort more personable. Rather than just looking at static images or Tweets, Dew fans could see like-minded fanatics in action. One young man proved his allegiance by brushing his teeth with the soda. After narrowing the seven flavors to three, Mountain Dew turned to its Dew Labs Community, a 4,000-person group of passionate soda fans. Those fans then created nearly every element of the three sodas, including color, name, packaging, and marketing campaigns [an example of crowdsourcing at its best!]. After that process was complete, the three flavors were made available in stores for a limited time, with the general public selecting a winner via online voting" (emphasis added).

According to Hespos (2010), Mountain Dew's SC marketing campaign was different from those at Starbucks and Dell. "Where these two brands set up sites soliciting ideas from all consumers, Dew began its promotion by reaching out to its most dedicated, loyal consumers offline, and then gave that offline community a place to assemble its testimonials and feedback. The Dewmocracy campaign used Facebook, Twitter, and YouTube just like the other campaigns used these social networks to unite consumers through a common interest." The Dewmocracy campaign, like other brands, also used Facebook, Twitter, and YouTube to unite consumers through a common interest. For further details, see Hespos (2010).

According to Mountain Dew's marketing director, the campaign helped to increase the company's social media presence (e.g., an 800,000 increase in Facebook fans from the time they started the campaign), and allowed customers to express themselves about the flavors and feel like they were being heard. The campaigns also generated word-of-mouth buzz and enthusiasm about the brand. (See **adweek.com/news/advertising-branding/what-mountain-dew-learned-dewmocracy-107534**.)

The Process of Conducting Qualitative Market Research for Social Commerce

There are several ways of conducting SC market research, depending upon a company's products, research budget, and research objective. A company may hire a consultant (e.g., Bazaarvoice.com); alternatively, it may join a market research discussion group on LinkedIn and share ideas and best practices, expand their network, research and analyze, and more. Market research is an essential element of the strategy needed for success in social commerce. Decker (2010) and Shih (2011) recommend that marketers go through the following seven-step process:

1. Select social platforms (social networking pages, blogs, forums, etc.) to give people a place online to discuss your products or services.
2. "Let these conversations unfold, but also encourage participation through promotions, contests, ratings and reviews, user-generated content (photo and video) uploads, and whatever else drives social interaction." (Decker 2010)
3. "Analyze the conversations to find out what people are saying and why, to spot trends, and to find out exactly what customers want" (see Sect. 10.6). (Decker 2010)
4. "Deliver products, services, and promotions that meet these wants and needs." (Decker 2010)
5. "Continue to get customer feedback, and integrate these findings with sophisticated analytics and marketing measurement tools to calculate the exact return on investment of social [networking] programs" (emphasis added). (Decker 2010)
6. Use *conversational marketing* as a source for market research. How are consumer conversations and other user-generated content analyzed?
7. Find opportunities for conducting social-based market research.

For additional information, see Rekenthaler (2013).

Learning from Customers: Conversational Marketing

Learning from customers is a major goal of market research. Long before the Internet and the Web, companies collected information *from* customers and *about* customers, and stored it in customer databases. They would use the information to develop marketing communication strategies, and help designers improve product design and customer service. The Internet has provided new opportunities to improve this process by providing both methods and tools.

Companies are starting to utilize Web 2.0 tools to get feedback from customers. This process is referred to as *conversational marketing, learning from customers,* or the *voice of customers* (VOC). In social commerce, customers supply feedback and information via blogs (e.g., see **bloombergmarketing.blogs.com/Bloomberg_marketing**), wikis, Twitter, online forums, chat rooms, and social networking sites (e.g., Facebook). For an illustrative video, go to **vimeo.com/81504169**.

Companies are finding that using social media tools to learn from customers fosters closer customer-vendor relationships. For example, Macy's Inc. quickly removed a metal toothbrush holder from its product line after the product was criticized on several social media channels. Dell and Starbucks allow customers to suggest and vote on improvements to their products. In general, what companies are learning from the customers on social networks is frequently less expensive and yields quicker and possibly better results than the company might learn from using focus groups.

With *enterprise feedback management*, companies are interested not only in collecting information, but also in facilitating the interaction between customers and companies.

Illustrative Examples

Many methods and software products can be used to "listen" to customers. The following are a few examples illustrating how this is done.

Example 1: Cookshack

Barbecue company Cookshack Inc., according to their Barbecue Forum (**forum.cookshack.com/groupee**; archived), "invites customers to ask and answer questions about barbecue sauces, beef smokers, barbecue ovens, and cooking techniques. The community helps (Cookshack) save money by freeing up customer service personnel who used to answer such questions by phone or e-mail. The community also fosters customer loyalty."

Example 2: Del Monte

See the opening case to this chapter.

Methods for Listening to Social Customers

Several methods are available for listening to customers. Some are the same or similar to those described in Sect. 10.5. However, in traditional market research, companies usually listen to customers during a short time period for a well-defined purpose, whereas in social commerce, it is a routine and frequent listening. Representative examples of listening methods to customers are:

- **Polling**. People like to vote (e.g., *American Idol*) and express their preferences (see the Netflix case in Chap. 3). They provide opinions on products, services, and so forth. Voting is also popular on social networks.
- **Blogging**. Bloggers can raise issues or induce others to express opinions.
- **Chatting**. Community members love to chat in public chat rooms. By following the discussions, you can collect current data.
- **Live chat**. Here, you can collect interactive data from customers in real time.
- **Chatterbots**. These can be partially interactive, but quick and inexpensive. Through them, you can analyze logs of communication. In certain cases, people are more honest when they chat with an avatar than talking to a human.
- **Discussion forums**. People that have a common interest join a social media subgroup and use a discussion forum to socialize and exchange opinions.
- **Collective wisdom (intelligence)**. This is a kind of community brainstorming. Researchers can find out what people are debating, agreeing on, or disagreeing with while working jointly on tasks.
- **Find expertise**. Expertise frequently is found via Web 2.0 technologies, many times for free (e.g., the "help forum" on LinkedIn).
- **Folksonomy**. This is a user-generated system of organizing information by social tagging, therefore making data easier to find and access.
- **Data in videos, photos, and other rich media**. Places where these media are shared contribute to valuable data collection.

For further discussion, see Strauss and Frost (2014).

Conducting Market Research Using the Major Social Network Sites

Market research can be conducted by using public social network sites (e.g., Facebook and Twitter), in situations where social software tools are deployed, in social enterprises, and in social presentation sites such as YouTube, Pinterest, and Flickr. For using social media for market research in general, see Nelson (2013). Here are a few representative examples.

Using Facebook for Market Research

Facebook is enabling an increasing number of social commerce activities. Here are some relevant suggestions for merchants conducting market research on Facebook:

> • Get feedback from your Facebook fans (and their friends, if possible) on any promotional campaign, improvement in the product/process, and so on.
> • Test market messages: Provide two or three options and ask fans which one they prefer and why. Do not forget to tell the fans that you love their contributions. Alternatively, see which messages get the highest click-through rate.
> • Use Facebook to recruit users to participate in a survey. Facebook also allows companies to target their audience specifically, based on traditional segmentation variables (e.g., age, gender, etc.).

Note that such an approach must be executed carefully by someone who knows how to do market research; otherwise, you will get a very low response rate.

Example: Conducting Surveys

SurveyMonkey (**surveymonkey.com**) provides software for posting surveys on Facebook or other Web pages. With SurveyMonkey, businesses can easily share surveys on their personal pages with SurveyMonkey's Facebook Collector, or post a survey questionnaire directly on their fan page with their Web Link Collector. For more information, see **surveymonkey.com/mp/facebook.**

Facebook offers an application called Surveys for Facebook (see **facebook.com/simple.surveys**), making it easy for businesses to create and share surveys on their Facebook page. For more information, see **facebooksurvey.net**.

Example: Brown Automotive Group

Brown Automotive Group (BAG) wanted to identify brand advocates among its fans on Facebook and make it easy for them to share their experiences with others. In other words, BAG used WOM to influence people's car purchasing decisions. The fans were invited to connect with BAG by completing an online survey. Based on this, the company identified those fans who were highly satisfied with BAG. (Customers who were not satisfied were contacted by BAG for problem resolution.) BAG contacted the friends of the satisfied friends, directing them to the BAG website to see both special deals as well as customer recommendations. This provided the company with immediate feedback. To read the case study, see **empathica.com/wp-content/uploads/2011/10/Empathica-Browns-Jeep-Chrysler-Dodge-Case-Study.pdf**.

For additional information about conducting marketing research on Facebook, see Silvestre (2012) and Pehrson (2013).

Using Twitter for Market Research

By using Twitter, it is easy to stay instantly updated on many relevant topics. Just follow @marketresearch or **twitter.com/MarketResearch**. The fact that millions of business-oriented people and customers are using Twitter makes it a valuable monitoring tool. Following tweets is a great potential source of new ideas and resources. Here are a few examples of using Twitter for market research (per Harrison 2009) and the authors' experiences:

> • Visit **search.twitter.com** and enter a company's Twitter name. Not only can you monitor what companies are saying on Twitter, you can also legally follow what is said to or about these companies and what are the replies. All this can help competitive intelligence and strategy.
> • Take advantage of the tools that enable you to find people in the industries where your company operates (target industries). Use **search.twitter.com** to monitor industry-specific key words. In addition, check out **twellow.com**, which automatically categorizes a Twitter user into 1–3 industries based on their bio and tweets, and allows users to categorize themselves manually.
> • To monitor your Twitter account, go to **tweetstats.com**. It will provide you with statistical charts showing information such as how many tweets you received during a certain time frame (e.g., day) and whose posts you retweeted. For an example, see **searchenginewatch.com/article/2327748/5-Brilliant-Ways-to-Use-Hashtags-in-Social-Media-Marketing**.

Example: Customer Feedback Using Twitter

An increasing number of companies utilize Twitter to solicit information from customers and interact with them. Several examples can be found at **mashable.com/guidebook/twitter**. For how to advertise on Twitter using their tools, see **business.twitter.com/basics**. To read the success stories of companies who used Twitter to promote their businesses, see **business.twitter.com/success-stories**.

For effective ways to use Twitter for market research, see Washington (2013).

Using LinkedIn for Market Research

There are many ways one can use LinkedIn for market research. One way is to post a question in the "help center" (e.g., solicit advice) regarding the topic in which you are interested. You may get better results if you go to a specific LinkedIn group. Another source for research is the information that people and organizations provide on LinkedIn about themselves. For a slideshow about using LinkedIn for market research, see Outloutl (2013). For a comprehensive list of LinkedIn discussion groups related to market research, go to **quirks.com/resources/market_research_linkedin.aspx**.

Using Virtual Worlds for Conducting Market Research

Using virtual worlds for market research gives researchers a clue about new products or services. This can provide companies with a competitive edge.

Several companies are conducting market research on Seconds Life by presenting a 3-D plan of a product or project they want to test.

Example: Market Research and Product/Service Design

Starwood Hotels constructed a prototype of the new Aloft brand hotels before they appeared in the real world. The company purchased two islands on Seconds Life: Aloft, for the hotel prototype, and Argali, where visitors can view the development project. Working from a preliminary architectural sketch, the designers started the process by roughing out the hotel's layout, furnishings, and textures. These were then refined in response to feedback from the brick-and-mortar architects and from Seconds Life visitors who were invited to assess and critique the design and layout. The company actually built the hotel after implementing the feedback from the Seconds Life residents.

Competitive Surveillance in Social Media

When companies use the previously mentioned techniques to test new products, competitors also see what the company is planning. This is good input for competitive analysis. Companies can also search **brandtags.com** to identify competitive brand images based on descriptive words entered by users. In addition, organizations often review comments and how many "Likes" on their competitors' social networks. Other good sources to find information about the competi-

tion include Google keyword searches for company and executive names, brands, and marketing communication campaign tag lines. Company researchers can follow these links to social media sites. Finally, organizations can search **allfacebook.com/tag/statistics** to find demographics, number of visitors, and many other statistics for millions of Facebook fan pages. These are just a few examples; there are many other ways to use social media for competitive analysis as well (e.g., **unifiedsocial.com**). However, it is important for organizations to realize that while they can test marketing strategies and use competitive surveillance in social media, they are also being watched. For six free analytics tools to help you understand your competitor's Web traffic (2013), see **content.infotrustllc.com/infotrust-blog/bid/180360/6-Free-Analytics-Tools-to-Help-You-Understand-Your-Competitor-s-Web-Traffic**.

10.5 METRICS AND MONITORING PERFORMANCE

The next step in the strategy-performance cycle is to monitor performance and compare it to target objectives. These targets are usually expressed in measurable quantities, such as increasing the number of Facebook fans by a certain percentage, and they usually appear as metrics.

Performance Monitoring and Analysis Cycle

In order to exploit the huge volume of information generated by social media, companies use a process referred to as *social media intelligence* (see the following discussion), because it is similar to business intelligence (see Sharda et al. 2014). The social media intelligence process is illustrated in Fig. 10.4. For the difference between social media monitoring and social intelligence, see **socialbusinessnews.com/listening-look-social-monitoring-vs-social-intelligence**.

As shown in the figure, the process starts by identifying the social media activities that generate the data and information to be studied. Next, a monitoring system is employed to find out what is happening. Several methods and tools exist for this purpose. The monitoring results in various kinds of social data, from text to numbers, can be processed and shown to management via reports and/or dashboards. Many times, however, the collected data need to go through social media analysis techniques (Sect. 10.6), where they are compared to the target metrics, and analyzed, sometimes with the help of scorecards. A special type of analysis is *sentiment analysis* (positive or negative conversations, see Sect. 10.6), which automates the identification and interpretation of subjective information. The results of the analysis

Fig. 10.4 The social media
strategies. *Source*: Strauss and
Frost, E-Marketing 6e p. 312.
Used with permission

Hierarchy Stage	Social Media Strategy
awareness	Raise brand awareness
attitude	Improve favorable perception of a brand/product/service
behavior	Increase customer acquisition
behavior	Maintain customer loyalty
attitude	Create user advocacy and/or advocates
	Gather non-scientific/informal research
	Develop new insights on target market
awareness	Develop/Create Word-of-Mouth and Viral opportunities
awareness	Create buzz on branded experience
awareness	Build incremental reach
behavior	Increase marketing ROI
awareness	Increase consumer conversations about brand
behavior	Drive qualified registrations (newsletter, contests, etc)
awareness	Support a new product launch
behavior	Drive site traffic
behavior	Increase sales

Strategic ... Tactical

are presented to management via dashboard (Sect. 10.6) and notification mechanisms, so management can develop strategies and make decisions. For tools for supporting this cycle, see Dyer (2013).

Social Media Intelligence

According to psychologist Nicholas Humphrey, *social intelligence* refers to the capacity of people "to use very large brains to effectively navigate and negotiate complex social relationships and environments" (per **socialintelligencelab. com/social-intelligence**). The related **social media intelligence** has many definitions. It is generally referred to as the monitoring and collection of online opinions and other social data (such as conversations or reviews) used for guiding corporate decisions and (private and public) actions. For details, see Moe and Schweidel (2014). The process of using social media intelligence is more than just collecting and analyzing social interactions; it also focuses on the ability to find hidden values in the social interactions (and then take appropriate actions based on the findings). Social media intelligence includes tools that companies use to monitor, collect, aggregate, and analyze social data. For information on how to implement social media intelligence, see Harrysson et al. (2012). For a white paper discussing nine insights that drive business sales, see Bazaarvoice (2013).

The remainder of this section addresses measures and methods for organizing, analyzing, and displaying the huge

quantity of social data that are collected by companies (Big Data). First, we present the topic of metrics. Then, we describe the methodology of scorecards. The section ends with a description of social media monitoring. In Sect. 10.6, we introduce social media analytics and sentiment analysis, followed by a brief description of dashboards. For more on social media intelligence, including examples, see **listen-logic.com/2010/04/what-is-social-media-intelligence**.

Using Metrics in Performance Assessment

A **metric** is a specific, measurable standard against which actual performance is compared. Metrics are used to describe many things such as costs, benefits, or the ratio between them. They are used not only for justification but also for measuring actual performance and other economic activities. Metrics can produce very positive results in organizations by *driving behavior* in a number of ways, such as improving performance. According to Person (2013), metrics can:

- Be the basis for specific goals and plans.
- Define the value proposition in business models (see Primer A).
- Communicate a business strategy to the workforce through performance targets.

- Increase accountability when metrics are linked with performance appraisal programs and rewards.
- Align the objectives of individuals, departments, and divisions to the enterprise's strategic objectives.
- Track the performance of SC systems, including usage, types of visitors, page visits, conversion rate, and so forth.
- Assess the health of companies by using tools such as balanced scorecards and performance dashboards.

Social commerce metrics can be tangible or intangible and must be related to goals and objectives, as shown in Table 10.1 (p. 230).

Metrics need to be defined properly, with a clear way to be measured. For example, revenue growth in a company can be measured in total dollars, in percentage change over time, and in market share in the industry where the company operates. Defining the specific measures is critical; otherwise, what the metrics actually measure may be open to different interpretations. For a comprehensive description, see Hoffman and Fodor (2010).

Key Performance Indicators

Metrics are frequently expressed by a set of *key performance indicators* (KPIs), which involve the quantitative expression of some measures of each metric. One metric may have several KPIs.

A **key performance indicator (KPI)** is a quantitative measure commonly used in the industry that expresses the critical success factors of a company, department, or an initiative. Different companies measure success or failure by a different set of KPIs. For example, OrderDynamics (**orderdynamics.com**) conducted a survey to identify the most used KPIs for e-commerce.

These KPIs are continuously monitored by organizations (e.g., via Web analytics, social media, or other methods described in Sect. 10.6).

Examples

In Australia, the government of Victoria is one of the leaders in exploiting the Internet to provide a one-stop service center called "Do It Online" (see **vic.gov.au**). In the United States, the state of California website (**ca.gov**) offers many online social media-oriented services for residents. In both cases, the metric of "waiting time" is used to compare the government 2.0 services against traditional citizen service options. Such comparison is done to justify social media projects.

Using Metrics in Social Commerce

Social media metrics are different from generic e-commerce website metrics because users interact with branded media in several different ways. For an overview, see Lovett (2011), Poston (2012), and Sterne (2010). Unfortunately, there are too many different metrics in social media and commerce. For example, Simply Measured (**simplymeasured.com**) uses over 750 metrics. In addition, measurements can be complex. For example, when an Internet user watches an online video, he or she might spend 10 minutes watching it, but someone else might stop watching after 1 minutes. In addition, if the user uploads, comments on, or shares a branded video, how can this brand engagement be valued? Social media performance metrics, as described in Chap. 5, must capture the richness of user activity online in different areas.

Here are a few examples:

- **Earned media publicity.** This is a message about the company or brand shared with others after an experience with the brand. Metric example: number of blogger posts about the brand or company, or number of users creating a buzz by sending a video link or Facebook widget to their friends.
- **Company owned social media.** These are messages sent through company owned social media channels. Metric example: the number of fans on Starbucks' Facebook page and the weekly number of posts they shared.
- **Paid media.** These are messages on someone else's media channels, rather than those controlled by the company; for example, using offline media like television. Metric example: the number of people who downloaded a placement application on Facebook, or the cost per click on a display ad on a social media site.

For sample metrics in each category, see IAB (2009), Chap. 5, and Strauss and Frost (2014). For a guide to tracking social media metrics, see Lee (2014).

A large number of metrics can be used in social media depending on the area of consideration. In fact, companies are drowning in metric availability and need to carefully select those that measure their social commerce objectives and tactics. For a guide to using social media metrics in non-profit organizations, including social media ROI, what statistics to measure on Facebook and Twitter, and available metrics tools, read the articles and tutorials at **socialbrite.org/sharing-center/metrics**. For a beginner's guide to social media, see **moz.com/beginners-guide-to-social-media**.

Examples

Hoffman and Fodor (2010) and Poston (2012) suggested metrics that are related to marketing. Representative metrics are summarized in the following list:

1. Track traffic for finding leads (e.g., sources, changes over time).
2. Find the average engagement duration (e.g., 4 minutes on a YouTube video).
3. Bounce rate (the percentage of people who leave your site after only viewing one page).
4. Fans on a Facebook page (numbers and their demographic composition).
5. Activity levels (by type).
6. Conversation levels (by type).
7. Brand and company/product health/reputation; positive and negative comments in all social networking activities.
8. Loyalty and sharing: Are members of social groups repeatedly interacting in the network, and sharing opinions, content, and links? How many members participate in discussions about a certain brand? How often do they reshare (e.g., a post)? (Several possible measures can be used here.)
9. Extent of viral activity: For example, sharing tweets and Facebook comments relevant to your company. The speed of resharing (or retweeting) and the number of friends and their friends involved in the resharing.
10. Blog interaction (several measures).

Bernoff and Li (2008) developed success metrics for the social Web in each of the following categories: marketing, sales, customer support, operations, and research and development. Most are quantitative. They also provide the following five categories of *strategic metrics*:

1. "**Listening.** Learn about your customers by paying attention to what they are saying online to one another or directly to you.
2. **Talking.** Communicate with your customers (and fans) by engaging in conversations.
3. **Energizing.** Encourage current customers and fans to spread the word through ratings, reviews, and other positive 'buzz.'
4. **Support.** Help customers solve problems by providing information and online resources like user forums, knowledge bases, and other tools.
5. **Embracing.** Invite customers to generate ideas for new products and services."

Each metric may have several dimensions and measures.

For a comprehensive discussion about social metrics, types of analysis, actions taken, and more, see **personalweb. about.com/od/socialmediaresearch/a/Social-Metrics.htm** and Poston (2012).

Classifying Social Media Metrics

Given the large number of social media metrics, there are several ways to classify them. For example, in Chap. 5, we categorized them as awareness/exposure, brand health, engagement, action, and innovation metrics. Other classifications follow.

1. Jones (2011) uses the following five categories:
   - *Awareness and exposure* (e.g., video views, number of followers)
   - *Share of voice and sentiment* (e.g., number of conversations about a brand versus that of a competitor)
   - *Influence* (e.g., the chance that followers and fans are inspired by messages)
   - *Engagement* (e.g., ratings, retweets, photo views)
   - *Popularity* (e.g., number of "Likes" on a company's Facebook page).
2. Another way to classify metrics is by technology; for example, metrics for Twitter, for Facebook, for e-mail, for videos, and so on.
3. In the marketing arena, one can apply traditional e-marketing metrics (e.g., impressions, click-through rate, cart conversion rate, and attention rate).
4. One can use performance metrics that are related to the balanced scorecard (see description later in this section).
5. Social metrics for business can be implemented. Lasica (2010) provides a list of 10 areas, each with a list of specific metrics: customer engagement, sales and profits, search engine marketing and ranking, traffic and conversation reach, brand sentiment, public outreach, lead generation, customer retention, cost savings, and employee recruitment.
6. The Interactive Advertising Bureau (IAB) provides over 100 metrics in categories such as survey metrics, activity metrics, ROI measurement, and reporting metrics. The reporting metrics are subdivided into general social media metrics, blog metrics, conversation size, size relevance, author credibility, content, and widget and social media applications. Within each category, there are 5–10 specific metrics. For details, see IAB (2009). For tracking these and other metrics, see Lee (2014).

The bottom line is that organizations select the metrics they need for measuring whether or not they reached their social media objectives.

Sources for Social Media Metrics

There are many sources for social media metrics (try a Google search). Here we list some representative examples:

- Guide to social media metrics at **socialbrite.org/sharing-center/metrics**.
- Facebook Insights.
- Books by Sterne (2010), Poston (2012), Lovett (2011), and Blanchard (2011).
- The Interactive Advertisement Bureau (**iab.net**); see IAB (2010).
- Comprehensive coverage at **marketingsherpa.com**.

The large number of available social media metrics poses a challenge for management: which one to use and how. For example, see how Shively (2012) defines 40 different metrics. A practical tool that helps someone make such a determination is the *balanced scorecard*.

Balanced Scorecards (BSC)

One of the best-known and most widely used performance management systems is the balanced scorecard (see **en.wikipedia.org/wiki/Balanced_scorecard**, and the Balanced Scorecard Institute; **balancedscorecard.org**). Kaplan and Norton first articulated this methodology in their 1992 *Harvard Business Review* article "The Balanced Scorecard: Measures That Drive Performance."

The balanced scorecard translates an organization's strategy into a set of objectives, measures, goals, and initiatives in both financial and non financial areas. The non-financial objectives fall into the following three perspectives:

- **Internal business processes.** The processes the organization must succeed at, in order to appease its customers and shareholders.
- **Learning and growth.** How an organization improves its adaptability to changes and its ability to learn so that its mission is achieved.
- **Customers.** How the organization is viewed by its customers with respect to accomplishment of its vision and mission.

Aligning Strategies and Actions

As a strategic management methodology, the balanced scorecard enables an organization to align its actions with its overall strategies as well as with risk analysis (e.g., see Beasley et al. 2006). It accomplishes this task through a series of interrelated steps, although the specific steps involved vary from one project to the next. In social commerce, the process can be depicted in five steps:

1. Identify strategic objectives for each of the three perspectives listed earlier (about 15–25 in all).
2. Identify related measures for each of the strategic objectives; a mix of quantitative and qualitative should be used.
3. Establish goals for all measures.
4. Devise strategic initiatives to accomplish each of the objectives.
5. Link the various strategic objectives through a strategy map.

Note: A **strategy map** is a graphical representation of an organization's strategy. It illustrates how an organization plans to achieve its objectives by delineating the relationships among the objectives across the scorecard's different perspectives.

For specific metrics that are used with the balanced scorecard in the areas of e-marketing and e-business, see Strauss and Frost (2014).

Metrics and Measurements for Social Influence

Setting metrics and measurements for social influence is difficult because influence is mostly subjective; therefore, there is no agreed upon answer on how to accomplish this. However, several vendors offer interesting methodologies and tools to do just that. A major vendor in this area is Klout.com, which developed a proprietary algorithm. The following is an example of how Klout works.

Example

Klout, Inc. (**klout.com**) provides a way for users to build rapport with other users. For example, you can build lists within Klout and give something called +K's, which are tokens of appreciation to someone who has influenced you on a certain topic. Based on your Klout score and influential topics, you are rewarded with "perks" (e.g., discounts, gift cards). Marketers use Klout to find influential bloggers to spread the word about their products. Klout calculates a person's influence from a number of attributes; for example, the number of retweets generated and the amount of engagement they drive from unique individuals. Klout monitors actions and stats from social networks such as Twitter, Google+, Facebook, and LinkedIn (see **klout.com/corp/score**). Since Klout is being criticized for being inaccurate, it is working to improve. In early 2014, Klout changed to a whole new business model. For details, see "The Klout Score" at **klout.com/corp/score**. The Klout Score is a number between 1 and 100 that represents a person's influence. The more influence you have, the higher your score. For example, President Obama's score is 99 and Justin Bieber's is 92. At another site, **triberr. com**, bloggers help other bloggers by developing a community of sharing and support.

11. Brand profiles on social networks such as LinkedIn. com, Facebook.com, and ZoomInfo.com.
12. Web analytics (Sect. 10.6) that will help companies monitor the traffic coming to their own sites.

Monitoring the Social Media Field

The amount of social media data on the Web is increasing exponentially with billions of videos on YouTube, billions of photos on Flickr and Instagram, and endless tweets and other conversations. The problem that companies face is how to monitor the Web for data that are relevant to them. A major area of concern is reputation management. Google offers e-mail *alerts* for any keywords of a user's choice, such as a brand name, or a competitor's brand name, and so forth (see **google.com/alerts**). Users can set up an e-mail alert for the entire Web, including blogs, social networks, vendors' websites, etc. (e.g., see Beal and Strauss 2008).

What and Where to Monitor?

Monitoring is done on all social data in all social platforms and channels. Beal and Strauss (2008) offer these 12 channels for online social media monitoring as it relates to reputation management:

1. Your own content channels—any blogs, comment sections on the company site, or other websites owned by the company that allow user posting.
2. Social media and blogs using Technorati.com alerts and RSS feeds.
3. Google's network of video, news groups, and more (e.g., **news.google.com**).
4. Industry news via e-mail newsletters or competitive site monitoring.
5. Stakeholder conversations that occur on any other website not monitored in other ways.
6. Social communities in the company's industry, such as Tripadvisor.com for the travel industry.
7. Social bookmarking sites such as **delicious.com**, which allow users to tag websites for sharing.
8. Multimedia content such as videos on YouTube and photos on Flickr.
9. Forums and message boards, in Google Groups, LinkedIn, and Yahoo! Groups, and on any website in the company's industry that hosts them.
10. Customer reviews on sites such as Amazon.com (companies that only sell products online).

For additional channels, see Paine (2011). In addition, monitoring can be made simpler with special dashboards (e.g., see Sysomos's Heartbeat social media monitoring dashboard and video at **sysomos.com/products/overview/heartbeat**).

Social Media Monitoring Tools

A large number of tools are available for social media monitoring. For a comprehensive list, see **wiki.kenburbary. com** and Paine (2011). For 50 top tools for social media monitoring, see **socialmediatoday.com/content/50-top-tools-social-media-monitoring-analytics-and-management**. For five social media tools to simplify marketing along with a comprehensive beginner's guide to social media monitoring, see **socialmediaexaminer. com/5-social-media-monitoring-tools-to-simplify-your-marketing**.

A number of social media monitoring services provide data to businesses (e.g., Actionly, Radian6; **salesforcemar-ketingcloud.com/products/social-media-listening**, Visible Technologies, and Oracle; **oracle.com/applications/customer-experience/social/index.html**). Most of these services track online content and then feed summaries and other statistics into dashboards. However, smaller companies can use a variety of free services to conduct monitoring. (For example, Google Alerts, Moreover Technologies, and Yahoo! Alerts monitor news about companies and industries.) Technorati specifically tracks social media sites. Services such as CyberAlert, ChangeDetect, and Bloglovin' all offer ways to track activities in the blogosphere. Some of the monitoring tools provide social media analytics as well. For a list of free tools, see Rayson (2013). For a review and comparison of nine top social media monitoring services, see **social-media-monitoring-review.toptenreviews.com**.

Example of a Comprehensive Tool: Actionly
Actionly (**actionly.com**) is a social media monitoring dashboard and listening platform that is integrated with Google Analytics (see Sect. 10.6). It enables businesses to measure their social media ROI. Users can pull reports to see which of the messages are generating leads, page views, or revenue. To do this, Actionly monitors key words across networks such as Facebook, Twitter, YouTube, and Flickr. Users can view in one dashboard what their customers are saying about them. Actionly's technology also helps analyze social media

conversations, provides sentiment analysis, and finds influencers in social media. For more information on Actionly's integration with Google Analytics, see **actionly.com/support/index.php/category/google-analytics**.

For list of other tools, see Zeevi (2014).

Social media analytics, sentiment analysis, and dashboards are presented next.

10.6 SOCIAL MEDIA ANALYTICS AND SENTIMENT ANALYSIS

The importance of analytics in general has been recognized in the last few years (e.g., see Davenport and Harris 2007 and Fuloria and Iyer 2011).

Analyzing social media data and information is a comprehensive field that utilizes many methods and tools. For comprehensive coverage, see Sponder (2013). We cover only the major ones in this chapter.

Definitions, Importance, and Applications

The umbrella term *social analytics* includes several analysis techniques such as social filtering, social network analysis, sentiment analysis, and opinion mining. Therefore, there are several definitions. **Social media analytics** describes the activities of monitoring and recording, analyzing, and interpreting the results of interactions and associations among people, topics, and ideas. It is the process of gathering data from blogs and social media sites and analyzing that data to make business decisions. These interactions may occur during any social networking activity. The analysis is done on people's opinions, sentiments, reviews, recommendations, and even attitudes and emotions (e.g., see Liu 2012). Social analysis is done frequently in order to check the activities done in communities, what conversations are taking place, and much more. For example, see **bazaarvoice.com/solutions/conversations/intelligence**.

Note that, social media analysis is different from social network analysis, which we presented in Chap. 3.

Social media analytics is crucial for obtaining a strategic understanding of what is taking place in social media, either on the Internet or in private enterprise networks. Johnson (2013) describes the use of social media analysis in market research. Social media analysis usually includes some forms of traditional data analysis, such as data mining (see McCafferty 2010), to create a comprehensive understanding of social consumers. Social media analytics provides the foundation that allows an enterprise to use data to improve its targeted engagements; to optimize social collaboration across multiple business functions, as well as support, loyalty, and advocacy programs; and to enhance customer experience. Social media analytics are most commonly used to gauge customer opinions to support marketing communication, product development, and customer service activities. Social media analytics can help governments better engage and interact with citizens (Ong 2014). For an overview of Web analytics, its benefits, its best practices, its hurdles, and the impact of Google Analytics, see Kaushik (2009) and Peterson (2004).

The Web Analytics Process

According to the Digital Analytics Association, the definition of Web analytics is "the measurement, collection, analysis, and reporting of Internet data for the purposes of understanding and optimizing Web usage" (see **clarku.edu/offices/its/webservices/pdf/web_analytics.pdf**). See also Beasley (2013). Performance data are collected, such as the sites from which visitors came, the pages they viewed while visiting the sites, how long they stayed on those pages, and how they interacted with the site's information. Analytics also reveals what keywords users entered into a search engine prior to arriving at the site. Such data can reveal, for example, the success of SEO methods or advertising campaigns, etc. Because the goal of most SC websites is to increase sales, valuable analysis shows the level of sales increases.

Information about Web analytics is available at **jimnovo.com**. Two of the many Web analytics tools are available at **webtrends.com** and **google.com/analytics**.

Example: Google Analytics

This comprehensive (and free) tool, **google.com/analytics**, can perform many statistical activities (e.g., time-series analysis, cross-sectional analysis, scatter diagrams, trend analysis, ROI, and much more). For details, see England (2013) and **google.com/analytics/features**. Several companies have created tools to supplement Google Analytics. Examples are **sproutsocial.com**, **agencyplatform.com**, **argylesocial.com**, **bazaarvoice.com**, and **actionly.com**.

Social Media Analytics

Social media analytics is a subset of Web analytics that concentrates on social media (see Sponder 2013).

According to Jayanti (2010), Internet consumer conversations facilitate the conducting of market research. Conversation analysis, according to Vittal (2009), also helps companies to "understand emerging issues, follow brand sentiment, benchmark companies against major competitors, detect damaging issues or rumors, spur product development, gather product suggestions, and discover alternate uses and enhancements volunteered by consumers." This requires appropriate analysis. Social analytics was named by Gartner Inc. as one of the top 10 strategic technologies of 2011. For details about social Web analytics, see Ayanso (2014). See also Gartner's Top 10 Tech Trends Through 2015 at **slideshare.net/success_ehs/ gartners-top-10-tech-trends-through-2015** and "Top 10 Strategic Technology Trends for 2014" at **slideshare.net/ ireneventayol/december-10-top-10techtrends2014 dcearley39921**.

Social analytics evaluates interactions and relationships among people, subjects of interest, ideas, and organizations.

Analytics are developed for each social network platform. For example, see **business.pinterest.com/en/ pinterest-analytics**.

Tools for Mining Social Media Activities

There are many ways to analyze social media. Generic e-commerce tools such as Web mining and text mining (e.g., Russell 2013 and Sharda et al. 2014) can be used here as well. Several other tools are also used for data, texting, and Web mining in social media. Comprehensive coverage on social media is provided by Danneman and Heimann (2014). Oracle Cloud (2012) provides a white paper on social media and business intelligence integration.

Example 1
IBM SPSS Modeler is a *predictive analytics software* platform that measures trends in consumer views of products and services as collected from Web 2.0 tools (e.g., blogs and social networks). IBM SPSS Modeler brings predictive intelligence to decisions made by individuals, groups and others in the enterprise. It also analyzes data that is structured (e.g., price, product, location) and unstructured (text, e-mails, social media). The software covers 180 variables and 400,000 industry-specific terms that can be analyzed.

Example 2
Wendy's International uses software (from Clarabridge, Inc.) to analyze hundreds of thousands of relevant customer messages collected each year. Using Clarabridge's text analytics software, Wendy's analyzes comments from its Web-based feedback form, call center notes, e-mails, receipt-based surveys, and social media. Before using Clarabridge's text analytics software, the company used a combination of spreadsheets and keyword searches to analyze the data by a slow and expensive manual process.

Example 3
Compete, Inc. (**compete.com**) specializes in competitive analysis via Web analytics. It provides its customers with a profile of competitors featuring competitive analysis, traffic data and analysis, identification of new threats, and a detailed blog.

Other Web analytic tools are: IBM's Social Business and Social Media Analytics, Sysomos's MAP (Media Analysis Platform), SAS Social Media Analytics; watch their videos at **youtube.com/SASsoftware**, and IBM's SPSS offerings, which includes *sentiment analysis* (see Taft 2012). For social commerce analytics tools for small businesses, see **dirjournal.com/articles/7-social-commerce-analytics-tools-for-small-businesses**. For a list of the top 29 social media analytics software (Fall 2014), see **predictiveanalyticstoday.com/top-social-media-analytics-software**.

Finally, for top 10 social media analytics tools (December 2013), see Hardawar (2013).

Sentiment Analysis and Web 2.0

Sentiment analysis or **opinion mining** refers to a type of analysis that aims to determine the attitude or opinion of a person with respect to a particular issue as expressed in online conversations (e.g., if the opinion is positive, negative, or neutral). For details, see Pang and Lee (2008). Sentiment analysis is measured by techniques such as natural language processing (NLP), computational linguistics, and text analysis.

Automated sentiment analysis is a process of training a computer to identify sentiments within content using NLP. Various sentiment measurement platforms employ different techniques and statistical methodologies to evaluate sentiments, while some use a hybrid system.

IBM Social Sentiment Index
IBM has developed an index that aggregates and gauges public opinions from a range of social media sources. For example, the software identifies the emotional context of a conversation (e.g., between sarcasm and sincerity), and discovers which conversations are important and should be monitored. For details and a video presentation, see **ibm. com/analytics/in/en/conversations/social-sentiment.html**.

For success in sentiment analysis, see Valentine (2014). For how Thomson Reuters is incorporating sentiment analysis gained from Twitter for their market analysis and trading platform, see Lunden (2014). For more information on sentiment analysis including resources and related subjects, see **semantria.com/sentiment-analysis**.

Dashboards in Social Commerce

Once data are analyzed and summarized in tables and charts, they need to be presented to management for decision-making purposes. One popular tool used to do this is a dashboard.

What Is a Dashboard?

A dashboard is a control panel. Its most well-known application is the instrument panel facing a driver of an automobile, or a pilot in an airplane. It usually involves many gauges and indicators. An **information dashboard** (referred to as just a dashboard in this chapter) is a visual display or presentation of data organized in ways easy to read and interpret. The information is presented through gauges, charts, maps, tables, and so forth. It reveals trends and directions of the measured metrics. Dashboards are very popular business tools for use by executives and managers since they visually summarize the most important information (usually KPIs and metrics) and point to deviations from targets, using alerts (e.g., red colors), indicating where actions need to be taken. Dashboards are usually interactive and integrate information from multiple sources. Dashboards may be customized in a multitude of ways, and named accordingly; for example, "the CEO dashboard" is designed for chief executives.

Dashboards can be very colorful. Several dozen examples can be seen when you search Google Images for 'dashboards.'

Social Media Dashboards

Social media dashboard software organizes information from data about a company, brand, or any keyword cited in conversations, from any social media content, and organizes it in one place in images. This makes it easy for companies to monitor conversations and display selected metrics. Several vendors provide dashboards for social media. For an example, see the social media dashboard at **hootsuite.com**. It lets you do more with social media, allowing engagement, listening, analytics, and more.

For five top social media dashboard tools (2014), see **business2community.com/social-media/5-top-social-media-dashboard-tools-manage-social-accounts-01015451**.

For a list of 50 social media tools for monitoring, analytics and management, see Dyer (2013).

10.7 IMPROVING PERFORMANCE VIA INNOVATION AND COMPETITIVE ANALYSIS

The last step in the performance management cycle is to examine the results of the social analytics and take appropriate actions. Three scenarios are possible: (1) performance is in line with expectations, (2) performance exceeds expectations, and (3) performance falls short of expectations.

In this section, we will briefly discuss two topics used to increase productivity (if needed): competitive intelligence and innovation.

Competitive Intelligence for Improving Performance

According to **en.wikipedia.org/wiki/Competitive_intelligence**, **competitive intelligence (CI)** "is the action of defining, gathering, analyzing, and distributing intelligence about products, customers, competitors, and any aspect of the environment needed to support executives and managers in making strategic decisions for an organization." Two key points of this definition are:

1. Competitive intelligence (CI) is an ethical and legal business practice.
2. The focus is on the external business environment related to competition.

Note: The term CI is often viewed as synonymous with competitive analysis; in reality, competitive intelligence involves more than analyzing competitors—it is also about making the organization more competitive relative to its entire business environment and stakeholders. For comprehensive coverage, see Fleisher and Bensoussan (2007) and Strauss and Frost (2014). For further resources, see **entrepreneur.com/encyclopedia/competitive-intelligence**.

For the process of conducting social media competitive analysis, see Stuart (2013) and Hines (2013). For how to create a social media strategy by spying on your competitors, see Hines (2013).

Competitive intelligence in social commerce may involve social intelligence activities, some of which were described in Sects. 10.5 and 10.6.

Innovation in Social Commerce

Innovation in social commerce is similar to any other innovation activity. It is the key to improving performance and may determine the success of social commerce projects, as well as the success of the entire organization and possibly its survival. What is unique today is that the development of philosophy, strategy, and tools of social media enable both management and employees to engage much more fully in the innovation process. Social media also provides management with new sources of innovation, such as the use of crowdsourcing for idea generation and listening to customers' suggestions (and complaints) and using their input for product design or redesign and to improve the way they run their business (for an example of how Pepsi used social media for innovation, see York 2010). For 19 ways to get more customer feedback, see **blog.clientheartbeat.com/customer-feedback**. To learn more about what companies gain from listening to customers, see **yourbusiness.azcentral.com/companies-gain-listening-customer-3055.html**.

Spigit Inc. (2011) provides nine keys to innovation in the social media environment. A summary of the nine key points appears in the following list:

1. Treat innovation as a discipline.
2. Use common, dedicated platforms to increase innovation IQ and strengthen innovation culture.
3. Understand that innovation benefits from a diversity of perspectives.
4. Prevent employee self-censorship of ideas.
5. Create a culture of constant choices.
6. Focus employees' innovation priorities.
7. Recognize innovation as a funnel with valuable leaks.
8. If you cannot measure it, you cannot manage it.
9. Pursue a balanced portfolio of incremental and disruptive innovations.

Finally, for automated review translation tools for global social commerce, see Realwire (2011).

SUMMARY

In this chapter, you learned about the following SC issues as they relate to the chapter's learning objectives.

1. **The strategy-performance cycle.** In order to attain its goals, an organization needs to implement a strategy and plans, as well as monitor its performance levels. Performance needs to be compared to social media metrics using social media analysis. Results are brought to the attention of management via dashboards. At that point, management may need to act. Strategy is related to Porter's 5 competitive forces model, which leads to decision making concerning improved performance. The Internet has a major impact on strategy and competitive analysis.

2. **The strategic planning process.** The strategic planning process includes the tactics that need to be deployed as well as the allocation of organizational resources. There are five stages in the strategy process: initiation, formulation, implementation, assessment, and performance improvement. Companies need to have a strategy concerning the use of social commerce. There are several guidelines for appropriate planning.

3. **Justification of social media projects.** It is difficult to justify social commerce projects due to the intangible nature of many of their benefits. Other difficulties include measuring productivity levels and dealing with inaccurate data. To help with the justification, one can use Gartner's hype cycle to find the maturity of the social media technologies. Finally, risk assessment can be a part of the justification process.

4. **Market research in social commerce.** Market research needs to be conducted as part of the justification and strategic planning. However, it also needs to be done as part of performance improvement. Relevant market research can be done in social network sites and in social software applications (e.g., blogs). Market research can facilitate competitive intelligence. Market research for social commerce is similar to any Internet-related market research. However, the use of communities impacts the process. A major subject of market research is learning from customers (e.g., listening to conversations). Many methods exist for listening to customers (e.g., monitor chatting, polling, blogging, searching for photographs and videos, and encouraging customer engagement on social networks). Other special methods are used to research social networks (e.g., Facebook, Twitter, Instagram, and LinkedIn).

5. **Metrics and monitoring performance.** Monitoring performance and activities in social media can be done in several ways. One common way is to measure performance against metrics (there are hundreds of them in social commerce). For example, one can monitor conversations and other social media activities in order to learn about customer sentiments and then predict performance levels. There are many types of metrics in social commerce; some relate to customers, others to finance. A tool that is used to study these relationships is the balanced scorecard, which emphasizes the major types of metrics (in addition to financials). Metrics can be measured by one or more key performance indicators (KPIs), which are monitored by computerized programs.

6. **Social media analytics and sentiment analysis.** Whatever is monitored in social media needs to be analyzed, which is done mostly by computerized programs due to the huge volume involved (big data). Analysis is conducted by generic tools, such as data and text mining, as well as by statistical tools. In addition, there are methods, referred to as social media analytics, which are developed specifically for social commerce. Google Analytics, IBM SPSS Modeler products, and Webtrends are good examples. A major area of analysis is the use of natural language processing (NPL) to automatically identify and extract subjective information in social media activities.

The analysis of results needs to be presented to management. Since this is time consuming for management, the results are often prepared graphically via computerized dashboards. The dashboards can then present several performance management indications on one page.

7. **Improving performance via innovation.** Performance monitoring and analysis may call management's attention to a need to improve performance. Improvement can be accomplished by several methods (e.g., business process management) as well as via applied innovation. Additionally, conducting competitive intelligence can contribute to increased performance.

KEY TERMS

Competitive intelligence (CI)   257
Hype cycle   243
Information dashboard (dashboard)   257
Key performance indicator (KPI)   251
Metric (s)   249
Organizational strategy   237
Sentiment analysis (opinion mining)   255
Social media analytics   255
Social media intelligence   250
Strategic planning   237
Strategy   235
Strategy map   253
Tactics   237

REVIEW QUESTIONS

1. What is strategy?
2. Describe the strategic planning process.
3. Why is a cyclic approach to strategic planning required?
4. What is a strategy map and how does it help in the strategic planning process?
5. List some of the reasons for justifying an SC investment.
6. Describe the risks of not conducting an SC justification study.
7. What are metrics? What benefits do they offer?
8. Describe KPI.
9. Describe the cyclical use of metrics as it relates to organizational performance.
10. What is Web analytics, and what role does it play in the justification of SC projects?
11. How do organizations measure performance and productivity? What are the difficulties in measuring performance and productivity?
12. Why is it difficult to relate SC investments to organizational performance? List the major reasons.
13. Define tangible costs and benefits.
14. How should management handle intangible benefits?
15. Define Gartner's hype cycle and describe its five stages.
16. Describe how the hype cycle can be used in SC.
17. List some difficulties in SC justification.
18. Describe the balanced scorecard methodology.
19. List and briefly describe three risk factors associated with practicing social commerce.
20. How can a social network be used to conduct market research?
21. How is conversational marketing used for market research?
22. Describe social media analytics.
23. Define and describe social intelligence.
24. Describe sentiment analysis.
25. Define computerized dashboard and explain its use in social media.
26. How is Facebook used for market research?
27. How is Twitter used for market research?

TOPICS FOR DISCUSSION AND DEBATES

1. Your state government is considering an online vehicle registration system. They want to involve the citizens in the process of building a social commerce system for this purpose. Develop a set of SC metrics for assessing the success of a such project.
2. A large company with a large number of products wants to start using social media applications. Discuss the major issues it needs to consider in its deployment strategy.
3. Watch the video titled "Social Media ROI Examples" (4:15 minutes) at **socialnomics.net/2009/11/12/social-media-roi-examples-video**. Identify all the issues related to ROI for social media. Write a report.
4. Watch the video titled "#Socialnomics 2014" by Eric Qualman (3:15 minutes) at **youtube.com/watch?v=zxpa4dNVd3c**. Summarize the major points.
5. Some claim that sentiment analysis is inaccurate and should not be conducted. Others disagree. Debate the issue.
6. What are some of the risks companies may face if they decide to use social commerce?
7. Discuss the business value of enterprise social networking. Begin by reading Brett Bonfield's "Should Your Organization Use Social Networking Sites?" at **ict-knowledgebase.org.uk/socialnetworking**.
8. Debate: A cost–benefit analysis may be inaccurate, so why should a business conduct it?
9. Debate: Should companies build in-house social networks for external activities (e.g., marketing, CRM) or use existing public social networks?
10. There are considerable disagreements regarding Klout and similar companies that measure social influence. Debate the value of such measurements.
11. Discuss the differences between scorecards and dashboards. How are they related?
12. Watch the video titled "How to Measure Social Media ROI" (6:19 minutes) at **youtube.com/watch?v=UhUO 30VRN1M&list=PL142EE084987794BD** and discuss the lessons learned.
13. Read Google (2011) and Rohilla (2013). Explore the topics that are relevant to social media.

INTERNET EXERCISES

1. Survey several online travel agencies (e.g., **travelocity.com, orbitz.com, cheaptickets.com, tripadvisor.com, priceline.com, expedia.com, bestfares.com**) and compare the social strategies of three of them. How do they relate to social media?

2. Enter **digitalenterprise.org/metrics/metrics.html** and read the material about Web analytics. Prepare a report.

3. Enter **sas.com, rocketsoftware.com/brand/rocket-corvu, balancedscorecard.org**, and **cio.com**. Find demos and examples of how to use the various tools and methods to evaluate SC projects. Write a report.

4. Find information about ROI, metrics, and cost–benefit tools as they relate to social commerce. See **bizshifts-trends.com/2014/05/04/redefining-social-media-roi-apply-relevant-metrics-justify-manage-business-case-scrap-traditional-methods**, **matrixsolutions.co.uk, matrixsolutionsglobal.com**, and **matrixgambia.com**. Write a report.

5. Enter **advertising.com**. Find the innovative/scientific methods offered that are related to social commerce.

6. Enter **gillin.com/blog** and find information related to enterprise applications of social commerce technologies. Write a report.

7. Enter **comblu.com**. Explore its products and discuss the role of a social marketing dashboard.

8. Enter **marketresearch.about.com/od/market.research.brand.equity/a/Effective-Use-Of-Twitter-In-Market-Research.htm**. Write a report on what you have learned.

9. Enter **visibletechnologies.com** and identify all products related to this chapter. Summarize the major capabilities of each.

10. Enter **surveymonkey.com** and identify materials related to social media market research. Write a report.

11. Enter **sysomos.com** and find tools and materials for social media monitoring. Write a report.

12. Watch IBM Smarter Commerce's video titled "Advanced Social Analytics Platform" (3:44 minutes) at **youtube.com/watch?v=AxzqyMx0Mm8**. Write a report about the platform's features.

TEAM ASSIGNMENTS AND PROJECTS

1. **Assignment for the Opening Case**
   Read the opening case and answer the following questions.
   (a) How can market research increase the competitive edge of the company?

   (b) Why did the company decide to choose social media to conduct market research?
   (c) Compare the old research methods they used with the social media-based methods. Comment on the differences.
   (d) Comment on the dog food case study.

2. Enter **youtube.com/watch?v=qh1drAg1jdg** and watch the video (8:33 minutes) titled "Gartner Hype Cycle." Write a summary of the major points and complete the included assignment.

3. Conduct a search on the various methods and tools available in the monitoring-metrics-analysis-interpretation activities of social media. Begin your project by checking **quantcast.com, visibletechnologies.com**, and **google.com/analytics**. Prepare a class presentation and a report.

4. The purpose of this exercise is to find how Gatorade's social media Mission Control works. The class reads the articles by Zmuda (2010) and Ostrow (2010) and finds similar sources. Describe how Mission Control conducts its monitoring at Gatorade (what data, when, how). Explain why and how they do sentiment analysis. Write a report. For a free e-book by Salesforce highlighting 10 command centers created by leading organizations, see **exacttarget.com/sites/exacttarget/files/10-Examples-of-Social-Media-Command-Centers.pdf**.

5. Survey the offerings of companies that deal with the topics presented in this chapter (e.g., social media monitoring, analysis and mining, reputation management, sentiment analysis). Start with Google Analytics.

6. In February 2014, Facebook paid $19 billion to acquire mobile messaging start-up WhatsApp. Research the details of the deal and prepare a justification paper for the price paid. Discuss your findings. In addition, research why Snapchat Corp. rejected Facebook's $3 billion bid in 2013.

REFERENCES

Alter, M. "Here Are Some Risks to Consider Before Using Social Media for Your Business." February 20, 2014. **www.accountingweb.com/article/here-are-some-risks-consider-using-social-media-your-business/223082** (accessed January 2015).

Ang, L. "Is SCRM Really a Good Social Media Strategy?" *Journal of Database Marketing & Customer Strategy Management*, vol. 18, 3, 149-153, 2011. (doi:10.1057/dbm.2011.22)

Ayanso, A. *Harnessing the Power of Social Media and Web Analytics (Advances in Social Networking and Online Communities)*, Hershey, PA: IGI Global, 2014.

Babcock, C. "Lessons from FarmVille: How Zynga Uses the Cloud." May 4, 2011. **informationweek.com/it-leadership/lessons-from-farmville-how-zynga-uses-the-cloud/d/d-id/1097546?** (accessed January 2015).

Barker, D. I., M. Barker, and K. T. Pinard. *Internet Research Illustrated (Illustrated (Course Technology))*, 6th ed. Boston, MA: Course Technology, 2011.

Barnes, N.D., and F. R. Barnes. "Equipping Your Organization for the Social Networking Game." *Information Management,* November/December 2009.

Baseline. "How to Calculate ROI." September 6, 2006.

Bazaarvoice. "Social Intelligence: 9 Insights that Drive Business Results." A White Paper, June 15, 2013. **media2.bazaarvoice.com/documents/Bazaarvoice_Whitepaper_Social-Intelligence.pdf** (accessed January 2015).

Beal, A., and J. Strauss. *Radically Transparent: Monitoring and Managing Reputations Online.* Indianapolis, IN: Wiley, 2008.

Beasley, M. *Practical Web Analytics for User Experience: How Analytics Can Help You Understand Your Users.* Burlington, MA: Morgan Kaufmann, 2013.

Beasley, M., A. Chen, K. Nunez, and L. Wright. "Working Hand in Hand: Balanced Scorecards and Enterprise Risk Management." *Strategic Finance,* March 2006. **erm.ncsu.edu/az/erm/i/chan/library/ERMBalScorecardActualFinalStFin06.pdf** (accessed January 2015).

Bennett, S. "10 Amazing Examples of Social Media ROI [Infographic]"September 17, 2013. **mediabistro.com/alltwitter/social-media-roi-examples_b49425** (accessed January 2015).

Bernoff, J., and C. Li. "Harnessing the Power of the Oh-So-Social Web." *MIT Sloan Management Review,* 49(3) Spring, pp. 36-42, 2008.

Berthon, P. R., L. F. Pitt, K. Plangger, and D. Shapiro. "Marketing Meets Web 2.0, Social Media, and Creative Consumers: Implications for International Marketing Strategy." *Business Horizons,* Vol. 55(3), pp. 261-271, May-June 2012. (doi:10.1016/j.bushor.2012.01.007)

Big Heart Pet Brands. "Cats Asked for It by Name: Meow Mix® Jingle Returns!" March 13, 2012. **investors.bigheartpet.com/releasedetail.cfm?releaseid=662524** (accessed January 2015).

Blanchard, O. *Social Media ROI: Managing and Measuring Social Media Efforts in Your Organization.* Indianapolis, IN: Que, 2011.

Bort, J. "Even Walmart is Snapping Up Social Media Companies." January 4, 2012. **businessinsider.com/even-walmart-is-snapping-up-social-media-companies-2012-1** (accessed January 2015).

Danneman, N., and R. Heimann. *Social Media Mining with R.* Birmingham, UK: Packt Publishing, 2014.

Davenport, T. H., and J. G. Harris. *Competing on Analytics: The New Science of Winning.* Boston: Harvard Business School Press, 2007.

Decker, S. "Social Commerce 101: Leverage Word of Mouth to Boost Sales." December 28, 2010. **clickz.com/clickz/column/1711352/social-commerce-101-leverage-word-mouth-boost-sales** (accessed January 2015). (This column was originally published on February 9, 2010 on *ClickZ.*)

della Cava, M. R. "Some Ditch Social Networks to Reclaim Time, Privacy." February 10, 2010 (updated). Retrieved from **usatoday30.usatoday.com/tech/webguide/internetlife/2010-02-10-1Asocialbacklash10_CV_N.htm** (accessed January 2015).

Dragon, R. "The Big Brand Theory: Elle.com Social Strategies." June 16, 2014. **socialmediatoday.com/content/big-brand-theory-ellecom-social-strategies** (accessed January 2015).

Dragon, R. "Why You Need Social Media Strategy." September 9, 2013. **socialmediatoday.com/content/why-you-need-social-media-strategy** (accessed January 2015).

Dyer, P. "50 Top Tools for Social Media Monitoring, Analytics, and Management." May 13, 2013. **socialmediatoday.com/content/50-top-tools-social-media-monitoring-analytics-and-management** (accessed January 2015).

England, R. *The Updated Google Analytics Guide: Your Companion for the Successful Tracking of Your Website Visitors* [Kindle Edition], Seattle, WA: Amazon Digital Services, 2013.

Falls, J., and E. Deckers. *No Bullshit Social Media: The All-Business, No-Hype Guide to Social Media Marketing.* Indianapolis, IN: Pearson Education, 2012.

Fleisher, C., and B. E. Bensoussan. *Business and Competitive Analysis: Effective Application of New and Classic Methods.* Upper Saddle River, NJ: FT Press, 2007.

Forrester Consulting. "Social Networking in the Enterprise: Benefits and Inhibitors." (A commissioned study conducted by Forrester Consulting on behalf of Cisco Systems.) June 2010. **cisco.com/web/offer/gist_ty2_asset/SocMednInhib/SocNW_En_TLP.pdf** (accessed January 2015).

Fuloria, S. and K. Iyer. "Building Sustainable Competitive Advantage with Advanced Analytics." A Cognizant White Paper, June 2011. **cognizant.com/InsightsWhitepapers/Building-Sustainable-Competitive-Advantage-with-Advanced-Analytics.pdf** (accessed January 2015).

Gartner, Inc., "Research Methodologies: Gartner Hype Cycle." (Undated) **gartner.com/technology/research/methodologies/hype-cycle.jsp** (accessed January 2015).

Gillin, P., and P. Schwartzman. *Social Marketing to the Business Customer: Listen to Your B2B Market, Generate Major Account Leads, and Build Client Relationships.* Hoboken, NJ: Wiley, 2011.

GoECart.com. "GoECart CEO Provides Social Networking Tips for Online Merchants During WGCH Business Radio Interview." September 28, 2010. **blog.goecart.com/index.php/goecart-ceo-provides-social-networking-tips-during-interview** (accessed January 2015).

Gombert, P. "4 Steps to Social Media Success." April 29, 2010. **ecommercetimes.com/story/69882.html** (accessed January 2015).

Google. "Maximizing Website Return on Investment: The Crucial Role of High-Quality Search." White Paper WP47-0902, 2011. **static.googleusercontent.com/media/www.google.com/en/us/enterprise/search/files/Google_MaximizingWebsiteROI.pdf** (accessed January 2015).

Greengard, S. "Del Monte Gets Social." July 30, 2008. **baselinemag.com/c/a/Messaging-and-Collaboration/Del-Monte-Gets-Social/** (accessed January 2015).

Hanlon, A. "How to Use Porter's 5 Forces." November 18, 2013. **smartinsights.com/marketing-planning/marketing-models/use-porters-5-forces** (accessed January 2015).

Hardawar, D. "Top 10 Social Media Analytics Tools: The VentureBeat Index." December 20, 2013. **venturebeat.com/2013/12/20/top-10-social-media-analytics-tools-the-venturebeat-index** (accessed January 2015).

Harrison, C. "Good Idea: Using Twitter for Market Research." February 20, 2009. **beingcheryl.com/using-twitter-for-market-research** (accessed January 2015).

Harrysson, M., E. Metayer, and H. Sarrazin. "How 'Social Intelligence' Can Guide Decisions." *McKinsey Quarterly Insights and Publications,* November 2012. **mckinsey.com/insights/high_tech_telecoms_internet/how_social_intelligence_can_guide_decisions** (accessed January 2015).

Hayes, F. "Walmart's Stealth Social Strategy: Pretend This Isn't About Customers." January 18, 2012. **fierceretail.com/retailit/story/wal-marts-stealth-social-strategy-pretend-this-isnt-about-customers** (accessed January 2015).

Hespos, T. "How to Use Social Media to Unite Lonely Customers, Build Brand Loyalty." October 20, 2010. **adage.com/article/digitalnext/social-media-unite-lonely-consumers-build-brand-loyalty/146578** (accessed January 2015).

Hines, K. "How to Create a Social Media Strategy by Spying [sic] your Competitors." December 10, 2013. **socialmediaexaminer.com/social-strategy-competitor-research/** (accessed January 2015).

Hodgson, B. "Social Marketing Tools Hype Cycle." February 8, 2012. **socialmediatoday.com/content/social-marketing-tools-hype-cycle** (accessed January 2015).

Hoffman, D.L., and M. Fodor. "Can You Measure the ROI of Your Social Media Marketing?" *MIT Sloan Management Review,* Fall, 41-49, 2010.

IAB. "Social Media Ad Metrics Definitions." May 2009. **iab.net/media/file/SocialMediaMetricsDefinitionsFinal.pdf** (accessed January 2015).

IAB. *Social Media Buyer's Guide*, February 2010. **iab.net/media/file/IAB_SocialMedia_Booklet.pdf** (accessed January 2015).

Jayanti, R. K. "A Netnographic Exploration: Listening to Online Consumer Conversations." *Journal of Advertising Research*, Vol. 50, No. 2, pp. 181-196. June 2010. DOI: 10.2501/S0021849910091348.

Johnson, B. "Social Media Analysis Tools: The Modern Approach to Market Research." *Pace*, August 1, 2013. **paceco.com/social-media-analysis-tools-market-research** (accessed January 2015).

Jones, R. "5 Ways to Measure Social Media." November 14, 2011. **clickz.com/print_article/clickz/column/2102934/measure-social-media** (accessed January 2015). (This column was originally published on Aug. 22, 2011 on *ClickZ*.)

Kaushik, A. *Web Analytics 2.0*. Hoboken, NJ: Sybex, 2009.

Lasica, J. D. "10 Ways to Measure Social Media for Business." December 15, 2010. **socialmedia.biz/2010/12/15/10-ways-to-measure-social-media-for-business** (accessed January 2015).

Lee, K. "Which Stats Matter: The Definitive Guide to Tracking Social Media Metrics." *Buffer Social*, April 30, 2014. **blog.bufferapp.com/definitive-guide-social-media-metrics-stats/** (accessed January 2015).

Liu, B. *Sentiment Analysis and Opinion Mining (Synthesis Lectures on Human Language Technologies)*. San Rafael, CA: Morgan and Claypool, 2012.

Lovett, J. *Social Media Metrics Secrets*. Hoboken, NJ: Wiley & Sons, 2011.

Lunden, I. "Thomson Reuters Taps Into Twitter for Big Data Sentiment Analysis." February 3, 2014. **techcrunch.com/2014/02/03/twitter-raises-its-enterprise-cred-with-thomson-reuters-sentiment-analysis-deal** (accessed January 2015).

MarketTools, Inc. "Del Monte Turns to Dog Owners to Unleash Innovation." Case Study, May 2008. **classmatandread.net/565media/DelMonte.pdf** (accessed January 2015).

McCafferty, D. "IT Management Slideshow: Mining Social Media for Customer Trends." May 20, 2010. **cioinsight.com/c/a/IT-Management/Mining-Social-Media-for-Customer-Trends-887009** (accessed January 2015).

Mintzberg, H., et al. *The Strategy Process: Concepts, Contexts, Cases*. Upper Saddle River, NJ: Prentice-Hall, 4th ed., 2002.

Moe, W.W., and D.A. Schweidel. *Social Media Intelligence*. Cambridge, MA: Cambridge University Press, 2014.

Monaco, S. *Insightful Knowledge: An Enlightened View of Social Media Strategy & Marketing*. Tulsa, OK: Total Publishing and Media, 2013.

Nair, M. "Understanding and Measuring the Value of Social Media." *Journal of Corporate Accounting & Finance*, Vol. 22(3), pp. 45-51. March/April 2011.

Nelson, R. "How to Use Social Media for Market Research." March 19, 2013. **socialmediatoday.com/content/how-use-social-media-market-research** (accessed January 2015).

Ong, K. "Social Media Analytics can Help Governments Listen to Citizens Better." February 11, 2014. **enterpriseinnovation.net/article/social-media-analytics-can-help-governments-listen-citizens-better-679448892** (accessed January 2015).

Oracle Cloud. "Social Media & Business Intelligence: Creating the Integrated Customer Hub." An Oracle White Paper, September 2012. **oracle.com/us/products/social-media-and-bi-1845281.pdf** (accessed January 2015).

Ostrow, A. "Inside Gatorade's Social Media Command Center." June 15, 2010. **mashable.com/2010/06/15/gatorade-social-media-mission-control** (accessed January 2015).

Outloutl. "Using LinkedIn for Market Research." (Slideshow and Presentation Transcript), March 12, 2013. **slideshare.net/outloutl/market-research-deck-for-slide-share** (accessed January 2015).

Owen, M. "Social Media ROI: A Data-Driven Case Study." October 17, 2013. **econsultancy.com/blog/63598-social-media-roi-a-data-driven-case-study#i.1kqxmyn18yyfd2** (accessed January 2015).

Paine, K. D. *Measure What Matters: Online Tools for Understanding Customers, Social Media, Engagement, and Key Relationships*. Hoboken, NJ: Wiley, 2011.

Pang, B., and L. Lee. "Opinion Mining and Sentiment Analysis." *Foundation and Trends in Information Retrieval*, vol. 2, nos. 1-2, pp. 1-135, 2008. (doi: http://dx.doi.org/10.1561/1500000011)

Pehrson, M. "How to Use Facebook to Do Market Research for Your Digital Products [Video]." May 8, 2013. **thefutureofink.com/facebook-market-research** (accessed January 2015).

Person, R. *Balanced Scorecards and Operational Dashboards with Microsoft Excel*, 2nd edition. Hoboken, NJ: Wiley, 2013.

Petersen, R. "166 Case Studies Prove Social Media Marketing ROI." (free e-book), *BarnRaisers Group*, 2012. Available to download at **barnraisersllc.com**.

Peterson, E.T. *Web Analytics Demystified: A Marketer's Guide to Understanding How Your Web Site Affects Your Business*. United States: Celilo Group Media and CaféPress, 2004. (Also available as a free e-book at **webanalyticsdemystified.com/community.asp#books**.)

Porter, M. E. "What is Strategy?" *Harvard Business Review on Point Article*, November-December, 1996.

Porter, M. E. *Competitive Strategy: Techniques for Analyzing Industries and Competitors*. New York: The Free Press, 1980.

Porter, M. E. "Strategy and the Internet." *Harvard Business Review*, pp. 62-79, March 2001.

Porter, M. E. "The Five Competitive Forces That Shape Strategy." *Harvard Business Review*, June 2008.

Poston, L. *Social Media Metrics for Dummies*. Hoboken, NJ: John Wiley & Sons, 2012.

Poynter, R. *The Handbook of Online and Social Media Research: Tools and Techniques for Market Researchers*. Hoboken, NJ: Wiley, 2011.

Radian6. "30 Ideas for Your 2012 Social Media Plan." Community e-Book, January 18, 2012. View as a slideshow at **slideshare.net/Radian6/30-ideas-for-your-2012-social-media-plan** (accessed January 2015).

Rayson. "Free Tools to Track the Secrets of Social Shares." September 4, 2013. **socialmediatoday.com/content/free-tools-track-secrets-social-shares** (accessed January 2015).

Realwire. "New Automated Review Translation Tool Brings Immediate International Social Commerce Benefits to Sony." April 18, 2011. **realwire.com/releases/New-automated-review-translation-tool-brings-immediate-international-social-commerce-benefits-to-Sony** (accessed January 2015).

Redsicker, P. "New Facebook Marketing Research Shows What Works." October 9, 2013 **socialmediaexaminer.com/new-facebook-marketing-research** (accessed January 2015).

Rekenthaler, D., Jr. "The Value of Visitor Identification: Selling to Buyer 2.0 in the Information Age." White Paper by Demandbase, Inc., July, 2013. **demandbase.com/assets/Uploads/ValueOfVisitorIdentification-DemandbaseWhitePaper.pdf** (accessed January 2015).

Rohilla, S. "Tips to Maximize Your Return on Investment." February 14, 2013. **socialmediatoday.com/content/tips-maximize-your-return-investment** (accessed January 2015).

Russell, M. A. *Mining the Social Web: Data Mining Facebook, Twitter, LinkedIn, Google+, GitHub and More*, 2nd ed. Sebastopol, CA: O'Reilly Media, 2013.

Schottmuller, A. "Social Media ROI: 14 Formulas to Measure Social Media Benefits." February 21, 2013. **searchenginewatch.com/**

article/2249515/Social-Media-ROI-14-Formulas-to-Measure-Social-Media-Benefits (accessed January 2015).

Sharda, R., et al. *Business Intelligence: A Managerial Perspective on Analytics*, 3rd ed. Upper Saddle River, NJ: Pearson Education, 2014.

Shih, C. *The Facebook Era: Tapping Online Social Networks to Market, Sell, and Innovate,* 2nd ed. Upper Saddle River, NJ: Prentice Hall, 2011.

Shively, K. "40 Key Social Media Metrics Defined." December 20, 2012. **simplymeasured.com/blog/2012/12/20/40-key-social-media-metrics-defined** (accessed January 2015).

Shullich, R. "Risk Assessment of Social Media." A White Paper, SANS Institute, 2012. **sans.org/reading-room/whitepapers/risk management/risk-assessment-social-media-33940** (accessed January 2015).

Silvestre, T. "7 Ways to Use Facebook to Find and Research Your Target Market." March 27, 2012. **thewordchef.com/2012/03/target-market-research-facebook/** (accessed January 2015).

Spigit. "Nine Keys to Innovation Management 2.0." A White Paper, May 2011. **neccf.org/whitepapers/whitepaper-nine-keys.pdf** (accessed January 2015).

Sponder, M. *Social Media Analytics: Effective Tools for Building, Interpreting, and Using Metrics.* New York: McGraw-Hill, 2013.

Sterne, J. *Social Media Metrics: How to Measure and Optimize Your Marketing Investment (New Rules Social Media Series).* Hoboken, NJ: Wiley, 2010.

Strauss, J., and R. Frost. *E-Marketing*, 7th ed. New York: Pearson/Prentice Hall, 2014.

Stuart, A. "How to Conduct a Social Media Competitive Analysis." *SwellPath Blog*, January 31, 2013. **swellpath.com/2013/01/conducting-a-social-media-competitive-analysis** (accessed January 2015).

Sysomos. "Building the Business Case for Social Media: A Guidebook to the Benefits of Social Media and How to Sell It to the C-Suite." A White Paper, 2011. **info.marketwire.com/rs/marketwire/images/Sysomos-Social-Media-Business-Case.pdf** (accessed January 2015).

Taft, D. K. "IBM Bolsters Social Business Play with Analytics." January 16, 2012. **eweek.com/c/a/IT-Infrastructure/IBM-Bolsters-Social-Business-Play-With-Analytics-609927/** (accessed January 2015).

Thompson, T., J. Hertzberg, and M. Sullivan. "Social Media Risks and Rewards." A Grant Thornton White Paper, September 2013. **grantthornton.com/~/media/content-page-files/advisory/pdfs/2013/ADV-social-media-survey.ashx** (accessed January 2015).

Turban, E., et al. *Electronic Commerce: A Managerial and Social Networks Perspective, 8th edition.* New York: Springer, 2015.

Valentine, S. *Sentiment Analysis 19 Success Secrets—19 Most Asked Questions on Sentiment Analysis—What You Need to Know.* Australia: Emereo Publishing, 2014.

Vittal, S. "The Forrester Wave: Listening, Platforms, Q1 2009." *Forrester Group Reports*, 2009.

Washington, R. "5 Most Effective Ways to Use Twitter for Market Research." July 9, 2013. **blog.marketresearch.com/blog-home-page/bid/313512/5-Most-Effective-Ways-to-Use-Twitter-for-Market-Research** (accessed January 2015).

York, E. B. "Building the Next FourSquare? Pepsi Would Like a Few Words." June 8, 2010. **adage.com/article/digital/building-foursquare-pepsi-a-words/144327/** (accessed January 2015).

Zeevi, D. "11 Best Social Media Management Tools." July 31, 2014. **blog.dashburst.com/best-social-media-management-tools** (accessed January 2015).

Zmuda, N. "What's a Sport? Gatorade Redefines to Broaden Target." April 12, 2010. **adage.com/article/news/a-sports-drink-pepsi-s-gatorade-broadens-target/143217** (accessed January 2015).

Implementing Social Commerce Systems

11

Content

Opening Case: Domino's Employees Post Vulgar
Videos on YouTube.. 265

11.1 Social Commerce Implementation Issues..................... 267

11.2 Security and Fraud Protection in
Social Commerce 268

11.3 Issues of Legality, Privacy, Cyberbullying,
and Ethics.. 272

11.4 Technological Issues 276

11.5 Employee-Related Implementation Issues 278

11.6 Organizational Issues and the Impacts
of Social Commerce.. 279

11.7 Other Implementation Issues 281

11.8 Successes, Failures, and Lessons Learned.................... 283

11.9 The Future of Social Commerce................................... 284

References.. 287

Learning Objectives

Upon completion of this chapter, you will be able to:

1. Describe the major issues in the social commerce implementation landscape.
2. Discuss the security and fraud protection issues in social commerce.
3. Describe legal, privacy, security, and cyberbullying issues.
4. Describe the major technological issues including integration, systems development, and software and vendor selection.
5. Discuss the major employee-related implementation issues ranging from wasting time to participation, and the related guidelines and policies.
6. Discuss organizational impacts including transformation to social business.
7. Discuss implementation issues related to SMEs and risk management.
8. Discuss the major success and failure factors, policies and guidelines, and adoption of social commerce.
9. Describe the future of social commerce.

OPENING CASE: DOMINO'S EMPLOYEES POST VULGAR VIDEOS ON YOUTUBE

Domino's Pizza is a global company with 11,700 stores worldwide (May 2015 data). The company is a world leader in pizza delivery with a significant business in home delivery pizza. Domino's pioneered practices including online ordering and expanded product variety, such as hot sandwiches. The company had a good reputation until 2009.

Electronic supplementary material The online version of this chapter (doi:10.1007/978-3-319-17028-2_11) contains supplementary material, which is available to authorized users.

The Problem (The Incident)

In April 2009, during a slow workday at the Conover, NC, Domino's Pizza franchise, two employees, Kristy Hammonds and Michael Setzer, created five prank videos and posted them on YouTube. The video went viral, amassing millions of views. These videos, which Hammonds filmed, featured Setzer engaged in a variety of acts of food contamination, including putting slices of cheese up his nose and then on a sandwich and spreading nasal mucus on a sandwich. Over the course of the video, numerous orders were tampered with before being boxed up for unsuspecting customers who had no idea what had taken place. These videos would obviously be problematic from any standpoint, but the fact that they featured Domino's employees in uniform engaged in these acts clearly represented a significant problem for the company. Furthermore, during the longest video by the pair of workers, titled "Domino's Pizza Special Ingredients," Hammonds jokes during the contamination of the food (seemingly intended for delivery to an identified customer) about this being "business as usual" and that's how they "roll" at Domino's.

Six hours after being posted, the videos were featured on the consumer advocacy site Consumerist (**consumerist. com**). According to Peeples and Vaughn (2009), Consumerist readers alerted Domino's to the situation and helped pinpoint Hammonds and Setzer and the store where they worked. However, the damage had already been done, even though YouTube pulled the videos; the links continued to spread rapidly across the Internet due to people downloading and reposting on numerous other sites. The precise number of times the videos were viewed is unknown; however, by the Wednesday following the release of the videos all five had trended to the top results on YouTube, and one of the videos had already been viewed over a million times (Peeples and Vaughn 2009). The reactions by customers were exceptionally rapid (there was a "tidal wave of public disgust" (see **brian-solis.com/2009/04/dominos-effect**), with the online research site YouGov.com (**today.yougov.com/opi**) reporting that Domino's reputation had trended to negative. Even though the videos were pulled by Wednesday because of a copyright claim from Hammonds, they continued to damage the Domino's brand, with many stores rapidly losing business.

The Solution (The Company's Response)

Domino's was unprepared for this disaster; according to VP of Corporate Communications Tim McIntyre, the company was in the process of putting together a social media communications team, and was within a week of launch at the time of the incident. Consumerist readers assisted Domino's in tracking down the perpetrators using a geolocation tech-nique to identify the location from which the videos were uploaded. Using this information, the firm identified the perpetrators rapidly and Domino's immediately fired them, requiring them to write a letter explaining the videos. Domino's also threatened legal action, after ascertaining that no contaminated food had actually been served to customers. Domino's also shared information about this process with the Consumerist site, garnering positive reactions from the site's readers, as well as those on Domino's own website. In addition, the company posted an apology on the site, detailing the process they used. (The employees were arrested later and charged with a felony).

Perhaps the most effective action that was taken by Domino's, involved CEO Patrick Doyle making a video, apologizing for the situation and saying that the two employees have been fired and arrested. This video, which was uploaded to YouTube under the same keywords used in the vulgar videos, offered a simple message to viewers who had seen the original videos. By using the same keywords, people searching for the damaging videos would be shown links to the apology video instead. The key message was: We (Domino's) did not do this. We are sorry. And Domino's wants to earn your trust back. This video was highly effective, given that it offered a direct response to both Domino's customers and to others who had seen the videos, and it also explained what Domino's was doing about the problem. Domino's also expedited its social media expansion plans by immediately starting a corporate Twitter account, giving customers direct access to the company's top management and offering a way to directly respond to customers concerned about the videos, as well as any other issues. Domino's is now actively participating in social media by doing everything from social CRM to sharing promotions with its online social community.

The Results

Domino's immediate reaction was similar to what we described in Chap. 5 (reputation management), but the company also implemented other measures. One of the most obvious points is that Domino's did not have an active social media monitoring system in place, which is an absolute necessity for such a large retailer. According to McIntyre, the incident gave Domino's the impetus to start a social media communications and monitoring program (see Chap. 10). This program started with a presence on Twitter and Facebook and was followed by an orderly entry into other online avenues, including using individual Twitter feeds for senior management; hiring a social media specialist in order to manage and maintain an up-to-date social media presence, identifying potential issues; and refining their use of real-time social listening and monitoring software. Domino's also started practicing proactive customer interactions via social media, expanding their initial success with direct customer engagement and using social media as a means of rebuilding their brand and maintaining communications. Today, Domino's has an active presence on Facebook and Twitter as well as an official YouTube channel, in addition to active listening strategies in other social media sites.

Note that some social media gurus give "high marks" to Domino's about their response (see **usatoday30.usatoday. com/money/industries/food/2009-04-15-kitchen-pr-dominos-pizza_N.htm?POE=click-refer**).

Sources: Based on Clifford (2009), Jacques (2009), Peeples and Vaughn (2009), and Domino's Pizza (undated).

LESSONS LEARNED FROM THE CASE

We can learn several lessons about the use of social media from the opening case. The first and most obvious is that employees are all spokespeople for the brand; therefore, they should all be trained in social media use (and misuse) to make them aware of the potential damage caused by the use of negative brand videos. A seconds lesson is that reputation-management response should use the same social media channels, allowing the company to specifically target the desired audience. Third, whether implementing social media or not, a company needs to explicitly monitor activities (Chap. 10) and be ready to respond immediately in case of a crisis, given the speed of content spreading on social media and the potential for damage. This should include the use of real-time social media monitoring and specialist knowledge of social media. The final lesson that can be learned is that, in the social media world, companies do not have the luxury of long response times that may exist in more traditional media. Instead, firms must immediately respond to this type of crisis in order to be effective. For social analytics tactics that can be deployed ahead of a crisis, see Hemann and Burbary (2013). The Domino's incident demonstrates several issues involving social media implementation: security, employee behavior, company policies regarding social media, and technology issues, all of which, and several other issues, are the subjects of this chapter.

11.1 SOCIAL COMMERCE IMPLEMENTATION ISSUES

Once organizations formulate and complete a social commerce strategy, they need to carry out the agreed upon strategy and tactics in what is referred to as *implementation*.

What Is Implementation?

Implementation is the process of carrying out, executing, or practicing a business plan. As such, implementation encompasses all the activities involved in getting the social commerce system operating properly, including installation, running, testing, and making necessary changes and updates. Although the word *deployment* is sometimes used to mean implementation, some view deployment as just one activity in the implementation process, as we do in this book.

The Implementation Process and Its Major Issues

The implementation process depends on what system is put in place. For example, the process for conducting social media marketing differs from that used for conducting enterprise recruiting using LinkedIn. Nevertheless, there are similar activities in many types of applications. Additionally, several managerial and technical activities and issues exist in most of the applications, which are briefly described next.

The Major Issues and Activities of Social Commerce Implementation

In Chap. 10, we introduced some activities related to implementation, such as developing justification and improving processes. Here, we deal with a slew of other issues, which are summarized in Fig. 11.1. In the figure, we marked the section numbers in this chapter where the specific issues are presented. Management needs to consider these issues, since they may determine the success of failure of social commerce. Note that some of the issues relate to the limitations and risks of social commerce.

For implementation issues related to marketing activities on Facebook and Twitter, and for social enterprise tactics, see the 115-slide show presentation titled "Social Media Implementation" at **slideshare.net/fated82/social-media-implementation-slides**.

Implementation Activities

Here, we present a brief description of the major implementation issues. For additional discussion, see Safko (2012) and Chui et al. (2009). For a comprehensive presentation, see Wollan et al. (2011).

Justification/Economics

The first issue is to find out if you need to get involved in a social commerce project(s). Then you must justify

Fig. 11.1 The major
implementation issues of social
commerce

your need. This issue is part of strategy formulation, and was discussed in Chap. 10 under the heading "The SC Justification Process."

Security Issues

Public social networks run on the unprotected Internet, and consequently suffer from security problems ranging from poor data protection to denial of service (DoS) and other attacks by hackers. These issues are discussed in Sect. 11.2.

Legal, Privacy, Cyberbullying, and Ethical Issues

These issues are critical to the success of social commerce. They are discussed in Sect. 11.3.

Technological Issues

Social commerce uses a computerized system; therefore, its implementation depends upon the hardware, software, networks, website design, and other related issues presented in Sect. 11.4.

Employee-Related Issues

Employee-related issues include assuring the quality of the user-generated content, overcoming their reluctance to participate, preventing them from wasting time surfing the Internet during working hours, and more (see Sect. 11.5).

Organizational Readiness and Impacts of Social Commerce

Issues such as how to organize the SC unit within an enterprise and how to deal with changing business processes, as well as other changes influenced by social commerce adoption, are all part of the implementation considerations. In addition, potential impacts on marketing, manufacturing, and people need to be addressed. Furthermore, some technical issues, such as connecting to other information systems, need to be addressed. These are all described in Sect. 11.6.

Other Implementation Issues

There are several other implementation issues, some of which are generic. Representative examples are provided in Sect. 11.7. A major issue is the use of social networks in SMEs.

Critical Success Factors

Section 11.8 deals with some of the critical success factors related to implementing social commerce projects. This includes learning from both successes and failures.

11.2   SECURITY AND FRAUD PROTECTION IN SOCIAL COMMERCE

It seems that hackers and criminals are in love with social networks, as social networks frequently are subject to social engineering attacks (e.g., phishing). Therefore, users' activities such as disclosing confidential and sensitive information on publicly accessible, or even internally shared workspaces, may result in security breaches, with possible losses suffered by both participating consumers and merchants. For an overview, see Wohlgemuth et al. (2014). For a white paper, see Dinerman (2011).

Major security issues are discussed next.

Social Engineering and Fraud

Social engineering occurs when criminals use psychology to persuade unsuspecting people to disclose personal information about themselves, in order to allow the criminals to gain unauthorized access into the user's computer, to collect confidential information for use in illegal activities. The social engineers (hackers) may also attempt to gain access to the user's computer in order to install malicious software

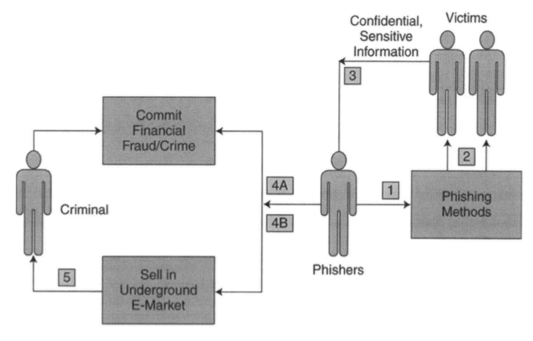

Fig. 11.2 Social engineering: from phishing to financial fraud and crime

that will give them control over the user's computer. The major social engineering attack method is phishing several methods. Typically, a phisher sends an e-mail that appears to come from a legitimate source, for example, *pretexting* (e.g., an e-mail allegedly sent from a friend asking for money), and *diversion theft* (when a social engineer convinces a courier company that she/he is the real recipient of the package but it should be "rerouted" to another address, whereupon the social engineer accepts the package). The information that is obtained from a victim, is frequently used for committing crimes (e.g., sabotaging the network), mostly for financial gain, or for posting advertisements (e.g., the social engineer creates a problem in the network and poses as a security consultant offering to help). The growth rate of vulnerabilities and the volume of e-mails result in increasing social engineering activities. For a comprehensive discussion and examples, see **webroot.com/us/ en/home/resources/tips/online-shopping-banking/ secure-what-is-social-engineering**. A typical social engineering process is shown in Fig. 11.2.

As you can see in the figure, phishers (or other criminals) obtain confidential information by using methods ranging from hacking to physical theft of information. The stolen information (e.g., credit card numbers, users' identity) is used by the thieves to commit fraud for financial gain, or it is sold in the underground Internet marketplace to another set of criminals, who then use the information to conduct financial crimes. For details, see Goodchild (2012). In this section, we will describe how phishing, which is a subset of social engineering, is conducted.

Social Phishing

In the field of computer security, **phishing** is defined as a fraudulent process of acquiring confidential information, such as credit card or banking details, from unsuspecting computer users. According to **webroot.com/us/en/home/ resources/tips/online-shopping-banking/secure-what-is-social-engineering**, "a phisher sends an e-mail, IM, comment, or text message that appears to come from a legitimate, popular company, bank, school, or institution." However, such site is corrupted. Once the user enters the corrupted website, he or she may be tricked into submitting confidential information (e.g., being asked to "update" his or her profile). Sometimes phishers install malware to facilitate the extraction of information. For an interesting novel that "cries out an alarm about cyber security," read *"Marlins Cry A Phishing Story"* by Swann (2012). The process of Web-based phishing is illustrated in Fig. 11.3

For a discussion of what phishing is and how to recognize it, see **ehow.com/how_7350964_recognize-phishing.html**. EMC/RSA (2014) provides comprehensive coverage of phishing with statistics and forecasts. Also see RSA Monthly Fraud Report (September 2014) at **emc.com/collateral/ fraud-report/rsa-online-fraud-report-0914.pdf**.

Example: Using Fake Netflix

Casti (2014a) describes a phishing scam on Netflix's brand where users were tricked into contacting phony customer service representatives and handing over personal data. This has led to copycat scammers. Scammers have targeted other

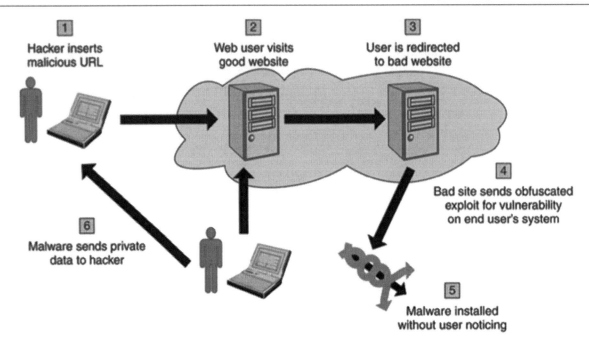

1. Hacker inserts malicious URL
2. Web user visits good website
3. User is redirected to bad website
4. Bad site sends obfuscated exploit for vulnerability on end user's system
5. Malware installed without user noticing
6. Malware sends private data to hacker

Fig. 11.3 How phishing is accomplished

companies, such as AT&T and Comcast, by attracting users to fake websites via phony sponsored ads. Another typical scam that is preying on trusting customers is where targeted users will see a phony webpage similar to the Netflix login page (e.g., via a link in a phishing e-mail, pop-up ad, etc.). When a user enters their Netflix account information into the fake site, they see a message that their Netflix account has been suspended due to "unusual activity" and then are provided with a fake "customer service" number for the customer to call. When the user calls that number, a "representative" recommends purchasing and downloading "Netflix support software," which is actually remote login software that gives the scammers complete access to the user's computer, for example, banking information, lists of passwords, etc. Casti (2014b).

Selling stolen information, like selling any stolen goods, can be profitable and difficult to stop. Unfortunately, potential e-commerce customers list "the potential risk of fraud," and "the mistrust of online merchants that you do not know" as their primary reasons for not shopping online.

Note that, as companies try to expand their e-businesses in countries where the legal systems are underdeveloped, opportunities for fraud expand, making it difficult to conduct EC and social commerce activities.

There are several different kinds of phishing. One of them, is *spear phishing*, which occurs when attackers target specific individuals by gaining personal data about them through information they share on the Internet, such as on social networks. Spear phishing is more dangerous than regular phishing

because the scammers are targeting specific people or organizations, rather than millions of unknown individuals.

Social Media Makes Social Engineering Easy

Social engineering attack tactics have become more diversified with SC (e.g., see Teller 2012 and Ruble 2013). In the past, social engineers used mostly e-mails to extract information from their victims. Now, however, social media sites that contain valuable information are major targets for new attack methods. More users are taking advantage of Web 2.0 applications such as social networking sites, blogs, wikis, and tweeting. As a result, malware authors, identity thieves, and other criminals are exploiting the vulnerabilities in the applications' security, see Mello (2013).The most popular sites, such as Facebook and Twitter, are attacked most frequently.

Social networking sites are vulnerable and fertile areas for hackers and con artists to gain a user's trust, according to the following study by Danish-owned IT security company CSIS.

Example: The CSIS Security Group Research (csis.dk)
Dennis Rand, a security and malware researcher at CSIS designed the following experiment:
1. Using the name "John Smith," he created a fake profile on LinkedIn.com.
2. He selected thousands of people at random, inviting them to join his network.

3. He targeted several companies and posed on their enterprise social network as an ex-employee.
4. Many existing employees of these companies, who were included in the randomly selected sample, accepted the invitation, creating a network of over a thousand trusted members for Rand.
5. Rand communicated with the members, thereby collecting their e-mail addresses. He harvested confidential data from some of the members. He also sent links (e.g., recommendations to videos), some of which were clicked on by the recipients.

The objective of the experiment was to study the potential security risks in using social networks. For example, messages may include links to malware in attachments which may be opened since they come from trusted friends. Some social networks do not even encourage users to select strong passwords and change them periodically. At the end of the experiment, Rand sent an e-mail to all participating members, explaining the purpose of the experiment. Then he closed the "John Smith" profile. See Rand (2007) for details.

For phishing attacks on social networks, see Lemos (2014).

How Hackers Are Attacking Social Networks

Hackers are exploiting the trusted environment of social networks that contain personal information (especially Facebook) to launch different types of social engineering attacks, e.g., stealing passwords (see Chumley 2013). There is a growing trend among hackers to use social networking sites as platforms for stealing users' personal data.

Examples
Here are some examples of security problems in social networking:

- Users may unknowingly insert malicious code into their profile page, or even their list of friends.
- Many anti-spam social networking-related solutions cannot differentiate between legitimate and criminal requests to connect to a network.
- Facebook and other popular social networking sites offer free, useful, attractive applications. These applications may have been built by developers who used weak security.
- Twitter users are targeted by phishing, hacking, and spamming (Cluley 2014).
- Scammers may create a fake profile on a social network and use it in a phishing scam.

For the top 5 social media scams, see Norton (undated).

Spam in Social Networks and in the Web 2.0 Environment

Social networks attract spammers due to the large number of potential recipients and the less secured Internet and social network platforms. Spammers like to attack Facebook in particular. Another problem area is blog spam.

Automated Blog Spam
Bloggers are spammed by automatically generated advertisements (some real and some fake) for items ranging from herbal Viagra to gambling vendors. Blog writers can use software tools to ensure that a human, and not an automated system, posts comments on their blogs.

Examples
Some examples of spam attacks in social networks (social spam) are:

- In January 2009, Twitter became a target for a hacker who hijacked the accounts of 33 high-profile users (including President Obama), sending out fake messages in their names.
- Instant messaging in social networks is frequently vulnerable to spam attacks.
- Cluley (2014) describes how Twitter users are being attacked by phishing attacks and spammers.

Defending Social Commerce Systems

In addition to standard protection of information systems and EC security systems, one needs to pay special attention to social commerce application protection. The major areas are:

Protecting Against Phishing

Because there are many phishing methods, there are many defense methods as well. Illustrative examples are provided by Wood (2013) and the FTC Consumer Information at **consumer.ftc.gov/articles/0003-phishing** and **scamwatch.gov.au**. For risk and fraud insights, see **sas.com/en_us/insights/risk-fraud.html**. For a comprehensive discussion and infographic on how and why social engineering works, including examples (e.g., phishing, hoaxes), see DuPaul (2013). For an overview and analysis of global threat activity, see Symantec Corporation (2014). Another resource to consult is the

Anti-Phishing Working Group (APWG); this "worldwide coalition unifying the global response to cybercrime across industry, government and law-enforcement sectors."

Protection Against Spam

Sending spam that disguises a sales pitch to look like a personal e-mail in order to bypass filters, violates the U.S. Controlling the Assault of Non-Solicited Pornography and Marketing (CAN-SPAM) Act of 2003. The Act makes it a crime to send commercial e-mail messages with false or misleading message headers or misleading subject lines. However, many spammers hide their identity to escape detection by using hijacked PCs, or spam zombies, to send spam.

Protecting Against Spyware

In response to the emergence of spyware, security companies are continuously inventing new antispyware software. Antispyware laws, available in many jurisdictions, usually target any malicious software that is installed without the knowledge of users. The U.S. Federal Trade Commission advises consumers about spyware infections and protection. For details and resources, see **ftc.gov/news-events/media-resources/identity-theft-and-data-security/spyware-and-malware**.

The Anti-Spyware Coalition is a group comprised of anti-spyware software companies and public interest groups, which is committed to combating the rise of unwanted spyware. The combined experience of the members gives consumers better ways to defend their computers against unwanted intruders, improves communications, and offers proposals for strengthening anti-spyware technology (see **antispywarecoalition.org**).

Fraud in Social Commerce

Social commerce is infested with fraudulent activities conducted by sellers, buyers, and computer criminals. Social commerce has some unique aspects that make it a prime target for fraud. For example, using fake profiles on LinkedIn or Facebook, criminals can manipulate innocent buyers and sellers to commit fraud. Further, social networks are attractive targets to phishing and identify theft. An important issue in fraud is the sales of counterfeit items both in P2P and in some B2C transactions. For Alibaba's problem with counterfeiters and their repair strategy, see Chen (2014). For more details about the CAN-SPAM Act, see **spamlaws.com/federal/can-spam.shtml**.

Fraud Protection

It is necessary to protect both sellers and buyers (consumers) against fraud they may commit against each other. In their special annual online fraud reports, CyberSource (2012 and 2013) describes the problem of payment fraud committed by buyers, which has cost merchants several billions of dollars annually. The reports cover the areas of detection, prevention, and management of online fraud. The reports also list tools for automatic screening of credit cards. The world's first online platform to fight Internet fraud was launched in China in 2014. According to McCoy (2014), the system is used to verify consumer complaints, and if they are legitimate, Internet users will be notified of the scam websites.

According to Trulioo (2014), the following are common measures: card verification, address verification, profile database, rule-based filters, and automated transaction scoring. Trulioo suggested including a social login as an added security measure.

11.3   ISSUES OF LEGALITY, PRIVACY, CYBERBULLYING, AND ETHICS

Several important legal, privacy, and ethical issues are related to social commerce implementation. Here, we provide only some representative examples.

Legal Issues

The introduction of social commerce may create a host of legal issues already relevant to computer systems. According to Saper (2009), the following are some legal issues related to social media:

- Employees (and students) freely copying or using UGC, what they see on the Internet, including copyrighted material;
- Posting of inappropriate or offensive content on company bulletin boards or blogs (see the opening case);
- Discrimination in hiring employees through Internet job postings;
- Badmouthing a company on personal blogs;
- Using Facebook or other social networks, including those in-house, to discriminate against or harass fellow employees;
- Requirements for backing up electronic communications in the event of litigation;

- Management forcing employees to use the in-house social network;
- Electronic communications policies;
- Employees' expectations of privacy on their office computers or in their e-mail, and social media profiles.

View the slide show "Managing Legal Risks in Social Media" by Manishin (2010) at **slideshare.net/gmanishin/social-media-managing-legal-risks**.

Intellectual Property and Copyright: Violations

Social media is built on a free and open Internet. However, violations of intellectual property laws, intentionally or unintentionally in user-generated content, are fairly common (see Case 11.1). For example, not requesting or receiving permission from individuals and organizations while creating content about them or using content created by these individuals, is a common phenomenon and may become a significant legal liability. Barnes and Barnes (2009) point to legal risks related to copyright and trademarks as well as to the inappropriate use of data.

Millennial consumers, also known as Generation Y (born in the 1980s and early 1990s), like companies that distribute social media content, such as Google, Facebook, and Amazon, more than they like the companies that produce and package the content and insist on being paid for doing so. Case 11.1 illustrates the controversy over users' free Internet access to information against the intellectual property rights of content creators presented online.

Case 11.1
SC Application

Internet Blackout against Anti-piracy Laws
On January 18, 2012, Wikipedia led an Internet "blackout." For 24 h, users attempting to access Wikipedia pages were met with a blank screen and a statement beginning, "Imagine a world without free knowledge." Wikipedia indicated they were making the website unavailable for a 24-h period to protest against two acts that were being debated in the U.S. Congress at the time. Protests and outcry against the Stop Online Piracy Act (SOPA) and Protect Intellectual Property Act (PIPA) had been growing in online and real-life communities, and Wikipedia led the way in shutting off site access for a day. Notably, however, Wikipedia's blackout was not complete—the blank screen carrying its protest message also informed users that they could access Wikipedia during the "blackout" via mobile devices. Facebook voiced opposition to SOPA and PIPA, but did not participate in any blackout or shutdown that day. Google took part in its own anti-SOPA/PIPA protest, blacking out its own logo on the Google search page and providing a link to an online petition against the Acts. Twitter—the largest social microblogging site—did not join Wikipedia's voluntary shutdown.

The U.S. Anti-piracy Bills: SOPA and PIPA
The Stop Online Piracy Act (SOPA) was a bill under consideration in the U.S. House of Representatives, and the Protect Intellectual Property Act (PIPA) was the analogous bill under consideration in the U.S. Senate. Both acts were intended to reduce online piracy. In particular, the bills sought to combat the illegal online distribution of downloaded films and other media when that media was hosted on a foreign server. If these bills were approved, anyone found to have streamed copyrighted media on more than ten occasions and without the copyright holder's express permission could face a jail sentence of up to 5 years and pay a large fine. This provision of the bills concerns Wikipedia, as the site could have been held liable for copyright infringement by other external sites to which users linked Wikipedia content. Further, SOPA and PIPA would have forbidden advertisers, ISPs, and companies processing payments from dealing with any individual or website alleged to have infringed a copyright.

For and Against Protest Viewpoints
Wikipedia's protest found many supporters, and sites from Reddit to Google joined Wikipedia in a show of solidarity—or so it seemed. All the sites taking part in the protest had a lot to lose if SOPA/PIPA had been passed, as they could have been made vulnerable to legal actions relating to third-party copyright infringements. The fact is that there is no realistic means of policing or monitoring information on their sites. Individuals and websites that joined the protests did so, believing in the freedom of users to access information on the Internet. However, sites were undoubtedly also acting out of self-interest, jumping on the hot topic of the day to generate Web traffic and revenue for themselves. Opinions against the Wikipedia-led protest centered on the right of intellectual property owners to protect their work, or alternatively, on the idea that Wikipedia's protest went about things the wrong way. Undoubtedly, copyright infringements are commonplace in the world of social media, having knock-on effects on creators of copyrighted material and the economy as a whole.

Implications of the Incident
In the twenty-first century, content is often distributed rather than sold in a physical format. This has enabled great creative freedom for everyone, from musicians to filmmakers, and rappers to violinists. Technology has become more affordable, and access to digital distribution has widened. Independent musicians, for example, can sell their music on

iTunes through distributors such as CDBaby for about $50. This represents a real bargain in comparison to the costs of creating CDs for distribution. The digital revolution has opened up the world of media for unprecedented sharing. However, this opening has come with a reduction in overall content quality due to the lack of third-party editing. Andrew Keen's 2007 book, *The Cult of the Amateur: How Today's Internet Is Killing Our Culture,* argues that increased access to content creation has generated situations in which the Internet is awash with poor-quality media, opinions taken as facts, and a dilution of real knowledge and expertise. Open access to copyrighted material can also make it more difficult for creative professionals to earn their living doing the work they love. Perhaps an album, which a musician has spent 5 years making, should not be freely distributed without that musician's consent, partly because he or she cannot earn a living from that freely distributed work. Finally, the role of large corporations like Apple and Amazon in controlling media distribution cannot be underestimated. Amazon, iTunes, and similar content distribution channels commonly take up to half of all proceeds as a sales commission. Distribution through a large corporation is expensive for the copyright holder; however, it is often worth it for the broader distribution the company provides. In a market where millennial consumers are accustomed to paying low prices—or nothing—for digital media, making a living as a creative professional becomes more difficult, and our culture suffers as a result. The protest led by Wikipedia was successful in raising awareness of two particular pieces of proposed legislation, but not in changing the landscape of the twenty-first century digital world.

Sources: Based on BBC (2012), Hais and Winograd (2012), and Keen (2007).

Questions

1. What did Wikipedia's blackout accomplish?
2. Has Wikipedia damaged its reputation in the process?
3. How can we keep a free and open Internet while protecting the intellectual property rights and copyrights of social media content?

Privacy Issues in Social Commerce

Privacy means different things to different people. In general, **privacy** is the right to be left alone and free from unwanted intrusions or disturbances in one's private life or affairs. Privacy has long been a legal, ethical, and social issue in many countries. Today, every state in the United States, as well as many other countries, recognizes the right to privacy, either by statute or by common law. The definition of privacy can be interpreted quite broadly. However, the following two rules have been followed fairly closely in past court deci-

sions: (1) The right to privacy is not absolute—privacy must be balanced against the needs of society and (2) The public's right to know is superior to the individual's right to privacy. These two rules show why it is difficult, in some cases, to determine and enforce privacy regulations. Online privacy issues have their own characteristics and policies. One area where privacy may be jeopardized is discussed next.

Invasion of Privacy

Due to hacking attacks and the policy of some social media sites (notably Facebook) to collect and sell members' information to advertisers, there have been many reported cases of invasion of privacy. For example, in May 2010, *IT World* reported that an employee who disclosed his sexual orientation on Facebook – a fact that was previously unknown to his employer – was fired when the employer discovered the Facebook post. Facebook's insufficient security and weak commercial use of private data (Facebook controls the use and display of content published on its platform) has been cited in many other cases as the cause of invasion of privacy. However, it is worth noting that Facebook is constantly improving the security and privacy protection on its site. For guidelines to protect privacy in SC, see Johansson (2013).

Collecting Information About Individuals

Implementing social commerce may require individual employee or customer data. In the past, the complexity of collecting, sorting, filing, and accessing cases was a built-in protection against misuse of private information. It was simply too expensive, cumbersome, and complex to invade a person's privacy in many cases. The Internet, in combination with large-scale databases and social networks, has created entirely new techniques for accessing and using personal data. The inherent power of systems that are able to access vast amounts of data can be used to invade privacy or misuse the information. On the other hand, having such information may benefit a company or even society. For example, by matching records using a computer program, it is possible to eliminate or reduce fraud, crime, corporate mismanagement, and so on. However, what price must the individual pay in terms of loss of privacy so that a company can fight fraud more efficiently? People's private information may aid in perfectly matching people with products, but their privacy may be violated.

The Web and Information Collection

The Internet offers a number of methods to collect private information from individuals. Here are some of the ways it can be done:

- Reading an individual's social media profile and postings
- Looking up an individual's profile in a social network
- Reading an individual's e-mails, blogs, or discussion board postings
- Wiretapping employees' wireline and wireless communications
- Conducting surveillance on employees
- Asking an individual to complete a website registration
- Recording an individual's actions using cookies or spyware as he or she navigates the Web

Mobile User Privacy

Many users are unaware that their private information can be tracked through a mobile smartphone or other cellphone. For example, Sense Networks' platforms are built upon the use of data from cellphone companies that track each phone as it moves from one cell tower to another, from GPS-enabled devices that transmit users' locations, and from mobile devices transmitting information at Wi-Fi hotspots. Such data can be used in location-based systems, for example. Note: Location-powered behavioral targeting builds user profiles, which incorporate behavioral attributes from location data.

What happens when LinkedIn, Facebook, Twitter, or Foursquare provide the ability for a GPS-enabled mobile device user to dynamically share its location status with others? Will businesses begin to take advantage of these capabilities to build applications, enabling GPS tracking of different kinds and support personnel, by leveraging the location status capabilities already available in their mobile devices? What are the privacy implications? Who will be held responsible or legally liable for unforeseen harm resulting from so much awareness and connectivity? Clear rules for social media sites are needed to govern what social media can do with the massive amount of personal data they collect, and how they inform their users about their practices.

Cyberbullying

According to **stopybullying.gov**, **cyberbullying** is "bullying that takes place using electronic technology." Electronic technology includes devices and equipment such as cell phones, computers, and tablets as well as communication

tools including social media sites, text messages, chat, and websites. Examples of cyberbullying include inappropriate text messages or e-mails, rumors sent by e-mail or posted on social networking sites, and embarrassing pictures, videos, websites, or fake profiles (per **stopbullying.gov/cyberbullying/what-is-it/index.html**). For more information, see **cyberbullying.us** and **stopcyberbulling.org**.

Cyberbullying Through Social Media

Cyberbullying through various social media outlets is on the rise because we are a civilization dependent on social media of communication. It is easy to hide behind a computer and post hurtful comments (per **socialnomics.net/2011/05/15/cyber-bullying-rises-but-social-media-fights-back**). Typical forms of cyberbullying include: (1) harassing another person; (2) exploiting someone in a sexual or violent manner; and (3) dissemination of false information that can cause mental or physical harm to others. According to **nobullying.com/bullying-statistics-2014**, one study shows that seven out of ten young people have been victims of cyberbullying.

The MySpace Example

In 2008, a jury convicted a woman for her role in a mean-spirited Internet hoax that apparently drove a 13-year-old girl to commit suicide. The woman, Lori Drew, upset that a teen named Megan Meier was spreading rumors about her daughter, created a MySpace account for a fictitious 16-year-old boy and then sent flirtatious messages from him to the teenage neighbor. After 4 weeks of flirting with Megan, the fictitious boy sent her a message that the world would be a better off place without her, and other MySpace members who were linked to the "Josh Evans" profile also began to send her negative messages. Subsequently, Meier committed suicide. According to the prosecution, this was a clear case of "cyberbullying," but the case hinged on an unprecedented and highly questionable application of the Computer Fraud and Abuse Act. The jury chose not to extend the law. As a result, felony conspiracy charges were dropped, and Drew was convicted of a misdemeanor violation. See **en.wikipedia.org/wiki/United_States_v._Lori_Drew**.

A similar case is that of the suicide of the popular 17-year-old soccer star Alexis Pilkington, who took her life following vicious taunts on Facebook. See Long and Gross (2010).

Ethics in Social Commerce

Several ethical issues are related to social commerce. Representative ethical issues that may be of interest in SC implementations include the following:

- Accuracy of computer-generated recommendations
- Ethics in social commerce websites and application design
- Invasion of individuals' privacy (e.g., by advertisers or e-mail spam)
- Use of intellectual property, including reports and expertise, without permission from, or payments to, the creators
- Accuracy of user-generated content
- Use of corporate computer resources for non-work-related purposes

Personal values constitute a major factor in the issue of ethical social commerce. An important ethical issue is human judgment; even though it may be subjective, it is frequently a key factor in social support and recommendations. Human judgment may lead to unethical decision making; for example, should an organization employ productivity-savings procedures that are not 100 % accurate? Another ethical issue is the use of knowledge extracted from people; for example, should a company compensate an employee who contributed special knowledge that was used for improving organizational efficiency? This issue is related to the motivation to participate in social commerce activities. It is also related to privacy and copyright. Should people be informed as to who contributed certain knowledge? Companies should provide an ethical code for those involved in social commerce.

11.4 TECHNOLOGICAL ISSUES

A large number of technological issues relate to the deployment of social networking. (*Deployment*, which refers to the introduction of new technology into an organization, is a major aspect of implementation.) Here are some issues to consider.

Social Commerce Systems Integration

Several options exist for an organization to integrate social commerce functionality into its information systems environment. Examples are: (1) adding collaborative technologies and tools; (2) integrating e-commerce data and applications with social networks; (3) connecting to third-party social media modules; and (4) using third-party system development platforms. The following sections describe how the Facebook platform can be used for the implementation of social commerce systems.

A Facebook Platform

Facebook created a platform that allows websites and apps to share information about users allowing vendors to target customers on one-to-one basis to tailor offers, features, and services to each one's interest and taste—even if that individual has never visited the vendors' sites before. See more at **developers.facebook.com/docs**, **mashable.com/2010/04/21/facebook-open-graph**, and **developers.facebook.com/docs/opengraph/overview**.

Open Graph

Facebook's social graph describes people and the interactions they have regarding everything they care about. In 2010, Facebook introduced an early version of "open graph," an extension of the social graph (Chap. 3), via the open graph protocol. The open graph protocol enables developers to integrate their pages into the social graph.

Social Plug-Ins

Facebook has developed plug-ins that websites and apps can deploy to make it easy for users to see information about (and from) their Facebook friends. Users can share things with their friends without leaving Facebook. One example is the "Like" button on each website, which allows users to "Like" content on a website and share it with their Facebook friends. (See **developers.facebook.com/docs/plugins/like-button**.)

Social Commerce Tools

Businesses can use a wide range of social media tools to get more interactive and facilitate engagement—in other words, to communicate and exchange information with customers. Businesses are increasingly using these tools to implement social commerce. See **blog.interactiveinsightsgroup.com** for more details. Several tools were presented in Chap. 2. Here is a description of some tools, set forth by Sommer (2010), that can be useful for social commerce:

- **Really Simple Syndication (RSS).** RSS is a syndication format that allows websites and blogs to distribute their updated, dynamic content as feeds to users.
- **Photo sharing.** Photo sharing tools allow users to upload and post their photographs online to share them with other users.
- **Podcasts.** A podcast is a digital audio clip that is distributed via the Internet for playback on a user's

computer or portable media device such as an MP3 player or an iPod.

- **Social news.** Social news sites allow users to submit Web pages and articles and have other users vote on them, with the number of votes determining which articles are presented on the social news site (e.g., Digg.com).
- **Video sharing.** Video sharing allows users to upload and share videos to video sharing websites such as YouTube.

Acquisition of Social Commerce Systems

In general, the information system acquisition issue is not simple, especially when medium- and large-scale projects are involved. The acquisition approach depends on the business type, the product line, and the budget, as well as the functionality of the social commerce system. A simple social commerce system with a few key components can be developed with HTML, Java, or another programming language. Companies can deploy social commerce using commercial packages, which are purchased or leased from an application service provider (ASP), or from a site builder. Larger or special social commerce applications can be developed in-house

or their development can be outsourced, as Del Monte did (Chap. 10). Building medium to large applications requires extensive integration with existing information systems, such as corporate databases, intranets, and enterprise and other application programs. Therefore, although the process of building social commerce systems can vary, in many cases, it tends to follow a fairly standard format. Figure 11.4 shows the major steps needed to develop a typical social commerce application.

Managing the Development Process

The development process illustrated in Fig. 11.4 can be fairly complex, and must be managed properly. For medium-to-large applications, a project team is usually created to manage the process and the vendors. Collaboration with business partners is also critical. Projects can be managed using project management software (see examples of various project management software at **en.wikipedia.org/wiki/Comparison_of_project_management_software** and reviews of the top project management software at **capterra.com/project-management-software**). Best practice management also includes periodic evaluations of system performance. Standard project management techniques and tools are useful for this task (see **project-management.com**). Finally, do not rule out the possibility that implementing a

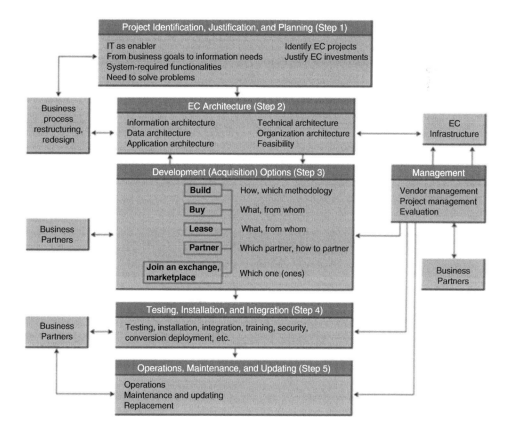

Fig. 11.4 The social commerce application development process

social commerce project may require the restructuring of one or more business processes. For a social media starter kit, see Carter (2013). For a software platform for SC, see **jivesoftware.com**.

11.5 EMPLOYEE-RELATED IMPLEMENTATION ISSUES

As illustrated in the opening case, there are several social commerce-related issues that involve employees. Representative examples are provided next.

Non-work-Related Use of Social Media

Employees are tempted to use social media while at work for non-work-related purposes. This use can be higher than work-related uses of the Internet. This problem has several dimensions. For example, social media can be used to harass other employees, which poses a legal threat to a company. Social media can also be used to conduct illegal gambling activities. Last, but not least, is the time employees waste surfing non-work-related websites, including social networks.

Employee Reluctance or Resistance to Participate

Employee resistance or reluctance to use enterprise social media applications, or contribute to them, can be a serious problem. Based on the experience of using wikis in a university administration context, issues such as sufficient user training, resource availability, and skills to support technology should be considered when planning for social commerce deployment.

Quality of Content and Biases of User-Generated Content

Any user-generated content, including contributions to Wikipedia, providing online advice, and generating feedback can be of poor quality or biased. An interesting research topic is how to judge the quality of user-generated content.

Data Leakage and Loss of Data

It is very easy for employees to post confidential information about their company, regardless of its nature—be it unwittingly or deliberately—in a blog or on a social media site. Data leakage can lead to losses related to litigation, fines, or even imprisonment of company officials.

Transferring Data

While social networks can be advantageous to support social CRM, the data related to individuals may not be secure. Thus, it would not be difficult for an untrusted or inexperienced employee to transfer proprietary information to a competitor (intentionally or unintentionally) using a network of friends/business colleagues on a social network site. For example, after having built up an extended network of friends/business colleagues through a social media site, it would not be difficult for an employee to take the company's entire sales database with him.

Social Media Management at Work

Social media, when used in a corporate setting, represents a mix of rewards (e.g., business opportunities) and risks for a company. The following are some guidelines that organizations might undertake to properly deal with such a mix of rewards and risks (per Osterman Research 2011).

Develop Social Media Policies

An organization should develop detailed and thorough policies that focus on establishing acceptable use of social media. In addition, the policies must specify which functions and features are permitted, which are not permitted, and so forth.

Monitor Content

An organization should deploy procedures and technologies that will monitor social media. To prevent malware infections from social media—protect pages with real-time monitoring and removal of all unwanted content. There is a need to protect against generated malware, and to prevent potentially libelous comments, trade secrets, or other inappropriate content from being sent externally. This chapter's opening case illustrates how inappropriate social media content shared by employees can damage a company's brand. For a discussion of polices, see **jeffbullas.com/2013/10/22/what-is-the-right-social-media-policy-for-your-company**. For a list of social media policies and guidelines for corporations, non profits and media companies, see **socialmedia.biz/social-media-policies**. Socialmedia.biz also provides best practices for developing a social media policy, at **socialmedia.biz/social-media-policies/best-practices-for-developing-a-social-media-policy**.

Archive Social Media Content

An organization should determine the extent to which formal and informal communications are being sent and received via social media.

11.6 ORGANIZATIONAL ISSUES AND THE IMPACTS OF SOCIAL COMMERCE

Limited statistical data or empirical research on the organizational impact of social commerce is rarely available because the field is relatively new. Therefore, the discussion in this section is based primarily on expert opinions, logic, and only some actual data.

Existing and emerging Web technologies are offering organizations unprecedented opportunities to rethink strategic business models, processes, and relationships. The discussion here is also based in part on the generic model of Bloch et al. (1996), who approached the impact of e-marketplaces on organizations in general, from a value-added point of view. Their model divides the impact of e-marketplaces into three major categories: *improving direct marketing, transforming organizations*, and *redefining orga-*

nizations. This section briefly examines each of these impacts as applied to social commerce. For the impact on social commerce using Twitter, see Mohd and Uwandu (2013).

Improving Marketing and Sales Revenue

For digital products—software, music, books/other text, photo images, and videos—the changes brought about by social media are dramatic. These are already delivered in huge volumes over the Internet. New marketing models, such as group buying, increase sales potential, as described in Chap. 6. The potential impacts of social media marketing on marketing and sales are summarized in Table 11.1.

Many of the changes may impact marketing with a provision of a competitive advantage over those that use only traditional direct-sales methods.

Transforming Organizations and Work

A seconds impact is the transformation of organizations to become social businesses. This topic is championed by IBM, which helps companies transform themselves to become social businesses (e.g., see **ibm.com/software/collaboration/**

Table 11.1 The changing face of marketing

	Old model—mass marketing	New model—one-to-one and customization
Relationships with customers	Customer is mostly a passive recipient	Customer is an active content co-producer
Customer needs	Only articulated	Articulated and inferred
Segmentation	Mass market and target segments	Target marketing is to individuals Segments looking for customized solutions and segmented targets; one-to-one targets
Product and service offerings	Product line and brand extensions and modification	Customized products, personalized services
New product development	Marketing and R&D drive new product development	R&D focuses on developing the platforms that allow consumers to customize based on customer engagement and input
Branding	Traditional branding and co-branding	The customer's name as the brand (e.g., My Brand or Brand 4 ME) Brand image is shaped by customer's opinion online
Pricing	Fixed prices and discounting	Customers influence pricing (e.g., via blogs or social network participation, tweeting, and group buying) Dynamic pricing used for various customer segments
Communications	One way "interrupt" marketing communications, such as advertising	Integrated, interactive, and customized marketing communication, education, and entertainment; use of avatars as chat bots
Advertising	TV, newspapers, billboards	Innovative, viral, on the Web, social ads, wireless devices
Distribution	Traditional retailing and direct marketing	Direct (online) distribution via social marketing and innovative models
Basis of competitive advantage	Marketing power	Marketing finesse and "capturing" the customer as a "partner" while integrating marketing, operations, market research, CRM, and R&D
Communities	Discounts to members in physical communities	Discounts to members of social networks and groups

Sources: Based on Evans (2012) and Shih (2011)

social/business). IBM sells software for social businesses and provides several interesting white papers on the topic. Here, we look at five key topics: *organizational learning, changing the nature of work, restructuring business processes, change management,* and *the structure of the social commerce unit.* For a framework for research on social media and business transformation, see Aral et al. (2013).

Technology and Organizational Learning

Rapid progress in social commerce will force a Darwinian struggle: To survive, companies will have to learn and quickly adapt to the new technologies. This struggle will offer them an opportunity to experiment with new products, services, and business models, which may lead to strategic and structural changes. An example is the newspaper industry, where losses, bankruptcies, and consolidations are regular events. These changes transform the way in which business is done. We believe that as social commerce progresses, it will have a large and long-lasting impact on the strategies and operations of many organizations and industries.

In summary, corporate change must be planned for and managed. Before getting it right, organizations may have to struggle with different experiments and learn from their mistakes.

The Changing Nature of Work

The nature of some work has been restructured already by the Social Web. For example, recruiting is moving to social networks and video ads are reshaping advertising. Crowdsourcing is an important tool for improved design and idea generation (Chap. 8). The upheaval brought on by changes due to social commerce creates new opportunities and new risks, and is forcing people to think about their careers and salaries in new ways.

The social age company will have to view its core of essential workers as its most valuable asset. Human capital and social capital are as important as physical assets. Therefore, companies will have to constantly provide employees with all means needed to expand their capabilities. For details, see Boutros and Purdie (2013).

Restructuring Business Processes

By using technology and reorganization tools, a company can prepare a work analysis of its operations, including interactions and transactions with its business partners, then devise an improved organizational structure and business processes that are an alternative to the existing ones. Such solutions may include new job descriptions and workflows. Several technologies, including *business process reengineering* and *business process management,* are available for such restructuring. **Business process reengineering (BPR)** is a methodology for conducting a comprehensive redesign of an enterprise's processes, and **business process management (BPM)** is (1) a method for business restructuring that combines workflow systems and redesign methods, covering three types of interactions: people-to-people, systems-to-systems, and systems-to-people; and (2) a holistic management approach focused on aligning all aspects of an organization with the wants and needs of its customers and partners. It promotes business effectiveness and efficiency, while striving for innovation, flexibility, and integration with technology. For more details, see vomBrocke and Rosemann (2015), and Dumas et al. (2013).

Change Management

Implementing a social commerce project, especially if it involves major restructuring, introduces changes to organizations that must be managed properly. **Change management** "is a structured approach to shifting/transitioning individuals, teams, and organizations from a current state to a desired future state. It is an organizational process aimed at empowering employees to accept and embrace changes in their current business environment" (per Rajput et al. 2012). According to **change-management.com/tutorial-defining-change-management.htm**, a commonly accepted definition of change management is "the process, tools, and techniques to manage the people-side of change to achieve the required business outcome.... Change management incorporates the organizational tools that can be utilized to help individuals make successful personal transitions resulting in the adoption and realization of change."

A formal organizational *change management* should begin, according to Rajput et al. (2012), "with a systematic diagnosis of the current situation in order to determine both the need for change and the capability to change. The objectives, content, and process of change should all be specified as part of a Change Management plan." In addition, a "successful change management is more likely to occur if the following are included" (per Rajput et al. 2012):

- "Benefits management and realization to define measurable stakeholder aims, create a business case for their achievement (which should be continuously updated), and monitor assumptions, risks, dependencies, costs, return on investment, benefits and cultural issues affecting the progress of the associated work.

> • Effective communications that inform various stakeholders of the reasons for the change (Why?), the benefits of successful implementation (What is in it for us, and you?) as well as the details of the change (When? Where? Who is involved? How much will it cost? etc.).
> • Devise an effective education, training and/or skills upgrading scheme for the organization.
> • Counter resistance from the employees of companies and align them to overall strategic direction of the organization.
> • Provide personal counselling (if required) to alleviate any change-related fears.
> • Monitoring of the implementation and fine-tuning as required."

For additional information, see Boutros and Purdie (2013). For a comprehensive guide to generic change management, see Cameron and Green (2012).

How to Organize a Social Commerce Unit in a Company

If a company is engaged in social commerce, it may have several full-time employees working in this area. The question is how to organize a social commerce unit. The best organizational structure depends on factors such as:

> • The absolute and relative size of the social commerce workforce
> • The nature of the social commerce projects (e.g., marketing, recruiting)
> • The existing organizational structure of the company
> • Whether or not the company is a pure-play Internet company (only existing online)
> • The nature of the products/services sold by the company
> • The internal politics of the organization
> • The budget of the social commerce workforce

These factors need to be considered. Most likely, the social commerce unit will be a part of the marketing department. Large retailers (e.g., McDonald's) have an independent social commerce department.

For how social entrepreneurship works, see Bornstein and Davis (2010).

11.7 OTHER IMPLEMENTATION ISSUES

Several other topics are related to implementation. Examples are:

> • Adoption of technology.
> • Implementation of B2B social networks.
> • The issues of social software selection, adoption, and usage patterns (see **searchunified-communications.techtarget.com/feature/Socialize-Comparing-enterprise-social-software-vendors**).
> • Corporate culture and social commerce project implementation.
> • Information flow.
> • Implementation in small and medium companies.
> • Risk factors and their analysis.

Here we will discuss the last two topics only. For other topics, see Shih (2011) and Safko (2012).

Implementation Issues in SMEs

Most of the social commerce implementation examples provided here and in other books involve large companies. The same is true of success stories provided by software vendors. An interesting question is: What are small and medium enterprises doing in social commerce? According to several reports (e.g., Leggatt 2010), even small companies can succeed in social commerce. We demonstrate this via the following examples.

Examples: Small Businesses Conducting Social Commerce on Facebook

Here are four examples of how small businesses are using social media (see Lai 2011):
• The photographer and owner of Studio Seven, Lydia Schuster, started her business solely on the belief that Facebook would work for her. She had more than 600 Facebook friends and had always received positive feedback about the photos she posted on her personal Facebook page. She then started her Facebook business page; to attract customers, she offered some incentives, such as the first person who reviewed a new photo would get a photo sitting at no charge. As her reputation grew, she started acquiring more fans, and her photos received thousands of votes. Schuster said she thinks that people today look on photographers' Facebook pages instead of

on professional websites. (See **facebook.com/ studiosevenMo?sk=photos**).

- Portland Nursery (**portlandnursery.com**) is doing some philanthropy work online. This includes a social voting photo contest and an online matching donation program, which includes promoting the campaign via e-mail and Facebook (see **prweb.com/releases/prweb2011/10/ prweb8875301.htm**).
- Virginia McCoskrie, owner of Smockingbirds, started a weekly giveaway on her Facebook page. People need to comment on photos in order to enter their name into a drawing. Since she started the drawing, she has gained more people as fans of her business page, and her business has grown dramatically (see **smockingbirdsgifts. com/about-us**).
- Center Court Office Supplies uses its Facebook page to update its customers on what is new in the store and about any promotions being offered. The company is able to decide on promotions and run them quickly. Networking has helped the small store (see **facebook.com/ centercourtoffice**).

For a beginner's guide to social media for small businesses, see **socialmediaexaminer.com/social-media-guide-small-businesses**. For a discussion on the usefulness of social media for small businesses, see **forbes.com/sites/ michaelfertik/2014/08/21/is-social-media-worth-it-for-small-businesses**. For how small businesses are using social media (with an infographic), see **blog.hootsuite.com/how-small-businesses-are-using-social-media**. For 20 social media marketing solutions for small businesses, see **businessnewsdaily.com/5782-social-media-marketing.html**. For a comprehensive guide to implementing a small business social media strategy, see **investopedia.com/university/ implementing-small-business-social-media-strategy**.

Some Strategy Issues for SMEs

There are several strategic issues that SMEs may need to address. Here are some related questions, some of which apply to large companies as well.

- Which is better for social media marketing: Facebook, Twitter, or others?
- How do you select a social media site(s) on which to advertise or sell?
- Do you need an internal private network? Why or why not?
- How do you generate constant traffic to your social commerce site? See five ways of doing so at **ecommerce-weekly.com/tips/5-tips-to-increase-traffic-to-your-e-commerce-site**. For seven strategies to increase traffic, see **postcron.com/en/blog/e-commerce-7-strategies-increase-traffic-visibility-sales**.

- How can social media work for small businesses? How can a company with a page in a social network have a sufficient number of fans and friends and have these people participate?

For a discussion on these questions, see Macarthy (2013) and Gratton and Gratton (2012).

A Small Number of Followers

One of the biggest challenges for almost all brands is the number of followers garnered by the brand. Unless a brand has a national reputation like Starbucks, Coca-Cola, and McDonald's, it may not be easy for the brand to acquire millions of fans. Hiring a consultant to help is not a bad idea, but it may be expensive for small and even some medium companies. Reading books, surfing the Internet, and posting questions asking what to do on Yahoo's "Answers" and other Q&A sites, can help. Another way to draw traffic is to build a "thought leaders within their niche" and show your expertise in social media by answering questions on Q&A sites, reviewing books on your specialty, writing blogs, and posting slide show presentations and videos on YouTube.

Risk Factors and Analysis

Although social commerce presents many opportunities for organizations, its deployment may involve some potential risks and possible complex implementation issues (Steinhart 2009). Concerns and issues are related to both companies engaged in social commerce activities and to individuals who participate in them.

Interfacing with social media is not without risks. Aligning a product or a company with sites where content is user-generated and has not been checked or filtered, may introduce some risk. A company is a good candidate for social commerce if it has positive customer relationships and strong positive feedback, and if it is willing to have customers share this feedback, whether it is good or bad. If, however, the company worries about what its customers might say, the business may not be ready for social commerce.

Another potential risk is a bias due to a few contributors submitting most of the content. For example, in an analysis of thousands of submissions over a 3-week period on the site Digg.com, the *Wall Street Journal* reported that one-third of the stories that made it to Digg's homepage were submitted by 30 contributors (out of 900,000 registered members), and that a single user on Netscape was responsible for 13 % of all stories that reached the most popular list the top posts on that site. Such distribution may result in bias in any user-generated content, see **wsj.com/articles/ SB117106531769704150**.

11.8 SUCCESSES, FAILURES, AND LESSONS LEARNED

Many vendors, consultants, and experts try to assist companies to succeed in deploying social commerce. Here are some representative issues and sources for further study.

A Strategy for Social Commerce Implementation Success

To succeed in implementing a social commerce project, especially in medium and large companies, an implementation process needs to be properly planned with a deployment strategy. A popular deployment strategy involves four steps: (1) Learn and understand the environment inside and outside the organization; (2) Experiment with a small-scale project so you can observe and learn before taking a large risk; (3) Assess the results of the experiment; and (4) Develop or abandon the project.

Similar steps are proposed by Gombert (2010): Evaluate opportunities, prepare a plan, engage your audience, and measure results. For some guidelines, see Wollan et al. (2011).

There are many ways to execute the previous strategy (Shih 2011). For example, a strategy that integrates social media with e-commerce can drive revenue growth, expand brand awareness, and increase customer loyalty and satisfaction.

Some Policies and Guidelines

It is useful for a company that is engaged in social commerce to have guidelines and policies regarding SC technologies. Several examples can be found at Macarthy (2013), and at Giordano (2014). For 57 different social media policies and resources, see **socialmediatoday.com/content/57-social-media-policy-examples-and-resources** and Gratton and Gratton (2012). For guidelines to getting a business on the top social network sites, including Facebook and Twitter, see Williams and Klein (2014).

Learning from Failures

One can learn from both success stories (available at many vendors' websites) and failures.

Example: Walmart's In-House Social Network
In 2006, Walmart launched a social network similar to MySpace in order to target younger consumers. The company hired professional actors to pose as teens on the site; however, the actors were "not–so–hip" and young people were not impressed. In addition, in an attempt to avoid potential lawsuits, Walmart allowed parents to control page content, which turned off the young viewers. Walmart pulled down the site after a short time. (See **blogherald.com/2006/10/02/wal-marts-attempts-at-copying-myspace-go-down-in-flames**.) Today, Walmart actively uses Pinterest, Facebook, Twitter, and Google+. For guidelines, see **corporate.walmart.com/social-media-guidelines**.

For other examples of failures, download the free white paper "5 Biggest Blunders to Avoid with Enterprise Social Software" at **socialtext.com/solutions/wp-social-software-blunders.php**. For the example of Starbucks' Foursquare failure, see Teicher (2010). For 13 brand and enterprise social media mistakes, see **solutions/wp-social-software-blunders.php**.

For 15 lessons of failing social media strategies, see Liubarets (2013).

Adoption Strategies

Many companies, consultants, vendors, and researchers provide tips, guidelines, and recipes for success. For example, Dion Hinchcliffe offers adoption strategies at **ebizq.net/blogs/enterprise/2011/09/five_emergent_strategies_for_social_business.php**.

Revenue Generation Strategies in Social Commerce

The success of social commerce depends on the ability to generate revenue and on the ability to solve problems. The following are some interesting ways social media generates revenue (see the social commerce business models in Chap. 1 and Primer A for a more complete list):

1. Offer premium service to individuals for a monthly or per-service fee.
2. Partner with organizations that pay a monthly service fee.
3. Create affiliations with physical venues where members can meet (e.g., **meetup.com**). Physical venues, such as coffee shops, may have to pay a fee to be affiliated with social media.

Increased Revenue and Its Benefits

Web 2.0 tools can generate revenue growth, user growth, and increased resistance to competition in indirect ways, which, in turn, leads to increased subscriptions, advertising, and commission revenue.

11.9   THE FUTURE OF SOCIAL COMMERCE

Many researchers and consultants are speculating on the future of SC (e.g., **adage.com/article/the-media-guy/reasons-google-exploding-hurt-facebook/228851**, Shih (2011), and **siliconprairienews.com/2010/07/lava-row-s-nathan-wright-predicts-future-of-social-media**). The predictions are diverse, ranging from "SC will dominate EC" to "it is a buzz word and will disappear soon." The problem is that there are many drivers of SC. Tzeng (2014) lists ten statistics that drive the future. These include *consumer trust*, *better shopping experience*, *future markets,* and the *future of e-commerce* in general. Given the popularity of Facebook, Twitter, Pinterest, YouTube, social games, social shopping, and social advertising, it is difficult to side with the pessimistic predictions. It looks as if mobile social commerce will be a major area of growth. Also, several of the social shopping and social collaboration models could be very successful. In the enterprise area, there is a trend to have a "social as a service" rather than as an application approach (due to the influence of cloud computing). For stats and trends of social commerce in the U.S. (2014) looking ahead to 2015—or projecting trends in 2015, see **adweek.com/socialtimes/social-commerce-stats-trends/500895?red=at**.

Creation of Jobs

Social commerce and media companies are creating a huge number of jobs with many opportunities emerging. As of 2015, skilled SC employees have been in large demand, commanding very high starting salaries.

IBM's Watson, Smart Computing and Social Commerce

There are many opinions on what the future of SC will be. Instead of presenting them, we decided to end this chapter by looking at IBM's Watson supercomputer's cognitive technology. In February 2011, IBM's Watson won a *Jeopardy* 3-day tournament against two world champions. This was a great achievement for what IBM calls Social Business and Smart Computing. Aided by intelligent systems such as IBM's Pure Systems, Watson will be able to do much more. According to **ibm.com/smarterplanet/us/en/ibmwatson**, Watson may assist people in the following social commerce-related tasks:

- **Personal investment advisor.** There is no need to conduct research any longer. All you have to do is to state your investment goals and Watson will make recommendations after checking all the needed input data. Given what goals you have, Watson can figure out what you need, recommending what to buy or sell. Upon your approval, Watson can conclude the deal for you.
- **Language translator.** In SC, in order to exploit global opportunities, we sometimes need language translation for introducing websites to people who understand other languages. We need it also for translating a natural human language to a language that a computer can understand. Today's automatic machine translation is not optimal, but it is improving. Computer systems, such as IBM's Watson, have powerful natural language processors that are getting even better with time, and thus providing better machine translation.
- **Customer service.** Providing technical support is critical for success (e.g., see the iRobot case in Chap. 7). Watson's intelligence will enable automatic guides for people who need help, taking them through all the necessary steps. The service will be consistent, top quality, and available in real time.
- **Q&A service.** Watson will provide the best answers to any business, medical, legal, or personal question you have. It can answer any question and subsequent subquestions.
- **Matchmaking.** Watson can match sellers and buyers, products and markets, job seekers and job offers, partners to bartering, P2P lending participants or any other match you can think of. For example, Watson will be able to find you a contact who will fit your stated goals.
- **Other applications.** Engagement advisor or discovery advisor, in industries such as healthcare, finance, retail, and the public sector. see **ibm.com/smarterplanet/us/en/ibmwatson/implement-watson.html**. Watson, a Smarter Planet innovation, is related to IBM's Smarter Commerce activities (see **ibm.com/smarterplanet/us/en/smarter_commerce/overview**; for a full description, see Lawinski (2011) and **ibm.com/smarterplanet/us/en/ibmwatson/offerings.html**).

Conclusion

The commercial aspects of social networking are rapidly increasing. Facebook is making billions in revenue and profits. Social commerce is continuously changing the face of marketing (including advertising), customer service, marketing research, collaboration and more. For a discussion, see Fallon (2014), and Sickles (2014).

Overall, Quora (**quora.com/what-is-the-future-of-social-commerce**) predicts the total market of SC to be $14 billion in 2015 (up from $9 billion in 2014), a 55 % increase. Yet, it is only 5 % of the total e-commerce 2015 estimate. But with a growth rate four times that of e-commerce, the future is very bright.

SUMMARY

In this chapter, you learned about the following SC topics as they relate to the chapter's learning objectives.

1. **The major issues of social commerce implementation.** Four major categories exist for implementation: justification and economics (cost–benefit); acquiring and/or developing the social commerce systems; assurance of organizational readiness and performance of necessary restructuring, training, and so forth; and cultivating the necessary success factors while avoiding the mistakes. The process of implementing social commerce, and the issues involved, are similar to those of e-commerce and IT. The issues can be divided into technical issues (e.g., security, systems integration, scalability, appropriate design) and nontechnical issues (e.g., justification, employee resistance to contribute and use social networking, lack of management support, lack of resources, risk mitigation, and training). Companies need to conduct a cost–benefit analysis of each project, including risk mitigation. Implementation is an important step in corporate strategy toward social networking and social media participation.

2. **Internet fraud, phishing, and spam.** A large variety of Internet crimes exist. Notable examples are identity theft and misuse, stock market fraud, get-rich-quick scams, malware, and phishing. Personal information is acquired from people by persuasion (e.g., masquerading as a trustworthy entity) and tricks, and that information is then sold to criminals who use it to commit financial crimes, such as fraudulently transferring money to fake accounts. A related area is the use of unsolicited advertising or sales via spam.

3. **Legal, privacy, and ethical issues.** Issues of privacy, ethics, and legal exposure may seem tangential to running a business, but ignoring them puts a company at risk for issues such as offending customers and disrupting operations. Social commerce operations are subject to various types of intellectual property (IP) laws. IP law provides companies with ways to be compensated for damages or misuse of their property rights. A social commerce company needs a well-established principle of protecting customer privacy: Notify customers before collecting their personal information; inform them about content and so on; obtain consent regarding the type and extent of disclosures; make sure the data are accurate and securely managed; and apply some method of enforcement and remedy to deter privacy breaches. In this manner, the company can avoid litigation and gain the long-term trust of customers.

4. **The major technological issues.** The major technological issues include the integration of the SC system with other information systems (including supply chain-related systems), the platforms provided by social networks, the major support software tools, and the alternative for systems acquisition.

   Because of their cost and complexity, large social commerce sites need to be developed in a systematic fashion. The development of a social commerce site should proceed in steps. First, a social commerce application portfolio is defined based on an organization's strategy. Seconds, the social commerce architecture is created. Third, a decision needs to be made whether to build, buy, or outsource the development. Fourth, the system is installed, tested, and deployed. Finally, the system goes into operation and maintenance mode, with changes being made continuously to ensure the system's continuing success.

5. **The major employee-related issues.** These major issues are: (1) employees using social media sites for non-work-related uses during working hours, and how to control such use, (2) employee reluctance to participate and contribute to the use of social media, and (3) the quality of employee-generated content, and data leakage by employees (intentional or unintentional). Related to these problems are solutions that include content monitoring, social media conduct policies, and the deployment of management controls.

   Companies should expect organizational changes in all functional areas once e-commerce reaches momentum. Change is particularly evident in the financial services sector, where additional services are continuously offered online. Social marketing and shopping are other areas with major potential changes (especially in F-commerce). E-procurement is changing the purchasing business processes, while affiliate programs are changing the paradigm of marketing and business partnerships, and social CRM is changing customer service.

6. **Organizational impacts.** The topics in this category include improving marketing and sales, transforming a traditional business to a social one, developing organizational learning, restructuring of business processes, conducting change management, and organizing a social commerce unit in the enterprise.

7. **Other implementation issues.** Several other implementation issues need to be considered. For example, the issue of deploying SC systems in SMEs is important. This includes the role of social networks and the strategy to be adopted. Another issue is how to increase the number of fans or followers in a social network. Next is the issue of risks.

   There are several potential risks in deploying social commerce projects in organizations and/or when using public social networks. The major risks and concerns are invasion of privacy, opening the gate for hackers, misuse of time and computing resources, revealing an organization's confidential information, introducing inappropriate or inaccurate content, the possibility of negative reviews, and the possibility of biased content by a few contributors (including bloggers) who supply a large portion of SC content.

8. **Successes and failures of social commerce.** Strategies for the successes of, and ideas on how to eliminate failures in, social commerce implementation are essential. One area to consider is the use of appropriate policies and guidelines. Also important are the adoption strategies and the revenue generation strategies.

9. **The future of social commerce.** Social commerce is growing rapidly both as an addition to traditional EC and IT and as a standalone field. A major area of growth is that of mobility both within the enterprise and in sales. A special area of growth involves intelligent and smart socially-based computing. This expansion will occur via social networks and in innovative SC apps.

KEY TERMS

Business process management (BPM)	280
Business process reengineering (BPR)	280
Change management	280
Cyberbullying	275
Phishing	269
Privacy	274
Social engineering	268

REVIEW QUESTIONS

1. Why is the implementation of social commerce so complex?
2. What are the major elements of social commerce implementation? (Consult Fig. 11.1.)
3. What factors determine the deployment and adoption of social commerce?
4. Define social engineering and phishing.
5. What are the employee-related issues of social commerce implementation and use?
6. List the major social commerce system development and acquisition options.
7. Describe how Facebook and Twitter serve as social commerce platforms.
8. Name and briefly describe the most commonly used social commerce tools and platforms.
9. Describe how social commerce improves direct marketing.
10. Describe how social commerce transforms organizations.
11. Discuss the need for change management in deploying social commerce projects to e-businesses.

TOPICS FOR DISCUSSION AND DEBATES

1. Discuss the need to restructure business processes and how to do so.
2. Consider how a hacker might trick people into divulging their personal user IDs and account passwords. What are some of the ways that a hacker might accomplish this? What crimes can be committed with such information?
3. Discuss some of the difficulties encountered in eliminating online financial fraud and phishing.
4. What are some of the risks companies may face if they decide to use public social networks?
5. How can we fight online piracy on open and free social commerce systems?
6. Debate: Should employee communication via social media be monitored?
7. Watch the video "Paid Social Media Jobs" (at **slicksocialmediajobs.com/paid-social-media-jobs-videos**). Also, go to **marketplace.paidsocialmediajobs.com**. Identify the best SC employment opportunities (jobs). Write a summary.
8. Debate: Employees should not be allowed to surf social networks during work hours.

INTERNET EXERCISES

1. Visit **business.com/starting-a-business** and find some of the SC opportunities available to small businesses. Also visit the website of the Small Business Administration (SBA) office in your area. Summarize recent SC-related topics for SMEs.
2. Conduct research on small businesses and their use of the Internet for SC. Visit sites such as **microsoft.com/en-us/business** and **uschamber.org**. In addition, enter **google.com** or **yahoo.com** and type "small businesses + social commerce." Use your findings to write a report on current small business SC issues.
3. You want to set up an ethical blog. Find sites that deal with bloggers' code of ethics. Also find a suggested guide to publishing a blog. Make a list of the top 10 ethical issues for blogging.
4. Find the status of the latest Internet-related copyright legislation. Write a report.
5. Conduct a Google search to learn how to prohibit unsolicited e-mail. Describe how your privacy is protected.
6. Enter **scambusters.org** and identify and list the antifraud and anti-scam provided.
7. Enter three social business software platforms (e.g., **jivesoftware.com**) and compare their features. Write a report.
8. Enter **staysafeonline.org**. Find information on protection against spam, phishing, etc. in social networks. Write a report.

TEAM ASSIGNMENTS AND PROJECTS

1. **Assignment for the Opening Case**
   Read the opening case. Find some new material about the social commerce activities at Domino's Pizza. Answer the following questions:
   (a) What appears to be the business problem facing Domino's in this case?
   (b) Why did Domino's choose to apologize on YouTube? Should the company have provided a press release instead?
   (c) How effective was the YouTube apology?
   (d) What impact did the incident have on Domino's social media policy?
   (e) Comment on how the Internet and social media platforms have changed crisis communications.
   (f) What did you learn about social media adoption from the case?
2. The class will set up a store on Facebook. For a tutorial, see **youtube.com/watch?v=HQh-f1IYSg4** and read the accompanying article at **creatingawebstore.com/how-to-create-a-facebook-store-in-minutes.html**. In addition, see **apps.facebook.com/aradium**. You can use the application from Ecwid (**ecwid.com/payvment**) or from Bigcommerce (go to **support.bigcommerce.com/questions/1127/How+can+I+setup+SocialShop+2+to+sell+on+Facebook%3 F**). Have several members place products there while others shop. Emphasize SC-oriented applications (such as voting and 'Like'). Write a report on your experience.
3. Read two Symantec white papers: (1) "The Risks of Social Networking" (at **symantec.com/content/en/us/enterprise/media/security_response/whitepapers/the_risks_of_social_networking.pdf**) and (2) "The Rise of PDF Malware" (at **symantec.com/content/en/us/enterprise/media/security_response/whitepapers/the_rise_of_pdf_malware.pdf**). Prepare a summary of both and describe how they relate to each other.
4. Each team is assigned to one method of fighting online fraud that is related to social commerce. Each method should deal with a different type of fraud (e.g., in banking; see IBM's ZTIC), identifying suspicious e-mails, dealing with cookies in Web browsers, protecting credit cards, securing wireless networks, installing anti-phishing protection for your browser with a phishing filter, and so forth.
5. Watch the video "Can Social Media Drive Social Change? Should It?" at **youtube.com/watch?v=s2zhhDrJ8Ik** and debate the issue in class. Write a report.
6. Watch the 7:18 minutes video at **youtube.com/watch?v=5iR8kJU85tU** about legal, social, ethical, and other issues related to this chapter. Find additional information about the topics discussed in the video.

REFERENCES

Aral, S., C. Dellarocas, and D. Godes. "Social Media and Business Transformation: A Framework for Research." *Information Systems Research*, March 2013. Published online January 14, 2013, **dx.doi.org/10.1287/isre.1120.0470**. Accessed Nov 2104

Barnes, N.D., and F. R. Barnes. "Equipping Your Organization for the Social Networking Game." *Information Management,* November/December 2009. **content.arma.org/IMM/Libraries/Nov-Dec_2009_PDFs/IMM_1109_equipping_your_organization_for_social_networking.sflb.ashx**. Accessed October 2014

BBC. "Wikipedia Joins Blackout Protest at US Anti-Piracy Moves." January 18, 2012. **bbc.com/news/technology-16590585**. Accessed October 2014

Bloch, M., Y. Pigneur, and A. Segev. "Leveraging Electronic Commerce for Competitive Advantage: A Business Value Framework." *Proceedings of the Ninth International Conference on EDI-IOS*, June 10-12, 1996, Bled, Slovenia.

Bornstein, D. and S. Davis, *Social Entrepreneurship: What Everyone Needs to Know.* New York: Oxford University Press, 2010.

Boutros, T., and T. Purdie. *The Process Improvement Handbook: A Blueprint for Managing Change and Increasing Organizational Performance*. New York: McGraw-Hill Professional, 2013.

Cameron, E., and M. Green, *Making Sense of Change Management: A Complete Guide to the Models, Tools and Techniques of Organizational Change, Third Edition*, Philadelphia, PA: Kogan Page Limited, 2012.

Carter, G., *The Social Media Starter Kit: The Simplified Guide to Getting Started in Social Media Marketing & SEO*, [Kindle Edition], Durham, NC: Bull City Publishing, 2013.

Casti, T. "Phishing Scam Targeting Netflix May Trick You With Phony Customer Service Reps." March 3, 2014a. (Updated April 17, 2014.) **huffingtonpost.com/2014/03/03/netflix-phishing-scam-customer-support_n_4892048.html**. Accessed October 2014.

Casti, T. "Scammers are Targeting Netflix Users Again, Preying on the Most Trusting Among Us." April 17, 2014b. **huffingtonpost.com/2014/04/17/netflix-comcast-phishing-_n_5161680.html**. Accessed October 2014

Chen, L.Y. "Alibaba Shakes Off Counterfeit Label Smoothing Path to U.S. IPO." March 18, 2014. **bloomberg.com/news/2014-03-18/alibaba-shakes-off-counterfeit-label-smoothing-path-to-u-s-ipo.html**. Accessed October 2014

Chui, M., A. Miller, and R.P. Roberts. "Six Ways to Make Web 2.0 Work." February 2009. **mckinsey.com/insights/business_technology/six_ways_to_make_web_20_work**. Accessed October 2014

Chumley, C.K. "Hack Attack: 2 Million Facebook, Twitter Passwords Stolen." December 5, 2013. **washingtontimes.com/news/2013/dec/5/hack-attack-2-million-facebook-twitter-passwords**. Accessed October 2014

Clifford, S. "Video Prank at Domino's Taints Brand." April 15, 2009. **nytimes.com/2009/04/16/business/media/16dominos.html**. Accessed October 2014

Cluley, G. "Phishing and Diet Spam Attacks Hit Twitter Users." January 9, 2014. **grahamcluley.com/2014/01/phishing-diet-spam-attacks-hit-twitter-users**. Accessed October 2014

CyberSource. *13th Annual 2012 Online Fraud Report*, CyberSource Corporation (2012).

CyberSource. *14th Annual 2013 Online Fraud Report*, CyberSource Corporation (2013).

Dinerman, B. "Social Networking and Security Risks." *GFI White Paper*, 2011. **gfi.com/whitepapers/Social_Networking_and_Security_Risks.pdf**. Accessed October 2014

Domino's Pizza. "About Domino's." (Undated.) **biz.dominos.com/web/about-dominos-pizza** (accessed July 2015)

Dumas, M., M. La Rosa, J. Mendling, and H. Reijers. *Fundamentals of Business Process Management*, New York: Springer, 2013.

DuPaul, N. "Hacking the Mind: How & Why Social Engineering Works." March 6, 2013. **veracode.com/blog/2013/03/hacking-the-mind-how-why-social-engineering-works**. Accessed October 2014

EMC/RSA. "2013 A Year in Review." Report # JAN RPT 0114, *RSA Monthly Fraud Report*, January 2014. **emc.com/collateral/fraud-report/rsa-online-fraud-report-012014.pdf**. Accessed October 2014

Evans, D. *Social Media Marketing: An Hour a Day*, 2nd edition. Hoboken, NJ: Sybex (Wiley), 2012.

Fallon, N. "The Future of Social Commerce: Shopping on Twitter, Pinterest and Beyond." April 30, 2014. **businessnewsdaily.com/6318-future-of-social-commerce.html**. Accessed October 2014

Giordano, C. "14 Social Media Resolutions for 2014." December 21, 2013. **socialmediatoday.com/content/14-social-media-resolutions-2014**. Accessed October 2014

Goodchild, J. "Social Engineering: The Basics." December 20, 2012. **csoonline.com/article/2124681/security-awareness/social-engineering-the-basics.html**. Accessed October 2014

Gombert, P. "4 Steps to Social Media Success." April 29, 2010. **ecommercetimes.com/story/69882.html**. Accessed October 2014

Gratton, S.-J., and A. Gratton, *Zero to 100,000: Social Media Tips and Tricks for Small Businesses*. (Que Biz-Tech Series), Indianapolis, IN: Que and Pearson Education, 2012.

Hais, M., and M. Winograd. "Crowdsourcing the Congress: Wikipedia's Blackout Bomb." January 22, 2012 (Updated March 23, 2012). **huffingtonpost.com/michael-hais-and-morley-winograd/sopa-blackout_b_1222318.html?ref=fb&src=sp&comm_ref=false**. Accessed October 2014

Hemann, C. and K. Burbary. *Digital Marketing Analytics: Making Sense of Consumer Data in a Digital World*. (Que Biz-Tech Series), Indianapolis, IN: Que Publishing, 2013.

Jacques, A. "Domino's Delivers During Crisis: The Company's Step-by-Step Response After a Vulgar Video Goes Viral." *The Public Relations Strategist*, August 17, 2009. **prsa.org/Intelligence/TheStrategist/Articles/view/8226/102/Domino_s_delivers_during_crisis_The_company_s_step#.VC3CI_ldWSp**. Accessed October 2014

Johansson, M. "9 Ways to Maintain (Some) Privacy on Social Media and the Web." October 14, 2013. **socialmediatoday.com/content/9-ways-maintain-some-privacy-social-media-and-web**. Accessed October 2014

Keen, A. *The Cult of the Amateur: How Today's Internet Is Killing Our Culture*. New York: Crown Business Publishing, (Doubleday/Random House), 2007.

Lai, L. "Facebook Lessons for E-Business Startups." *World Academy of Science, Engineering and Technology*, Issue 60, pp. 774-778, 2011. **waset.org/journals/waset/v60/v60-146.pdf**. Accessed Nov 2014

Lawinski, J. "Companies Spend on Security Amid Mobile and Social Threats." September 14, 2011. **baselinemag.com/c/a/Security/Companies-Spend-On-Security-Amid-Mobile-and-Social-Threats-293839/**. Accessed October 2014

Leggatt, H. "Survey: Small Businesses Find Success with Social Networking." July 9, 2010. **bizreport.com/2010/07/survey-small-businesses-find-success-with-social-networking.html**. Accessed October 2014

Lemos, R. "Phishing Attacks Increasingly Focus on Social Networks, Studies Show." *eWeek*, July 1, 2014.

Liubarets, T. "15 Ways to Make Your Social Media Strategy Complete Fail." *Business2 Community*, September 5, 2013. **smallbusiness.yahoo.com/advisor/15-ways-social-media-strategy-complete-fail-030942525.html**. Accessed October 2014

Long, C. and S. Gross. "Alexis Pilkington Facebook Horror: Cyberbullies Harass Teen Even After Suicide." May 24, 2010. **huffingtonpost.com/2010/03/24/alexis-pilkington-faceboo_n_512482.html**. Accessed October 2014

Macarthy, A. *500 Social Media Marketing Tips: Essential Advice, Hints and Strategy for Business: Facebook, Twitter, Google+, YouTube, Instagram, Pinterest, LinkedIn, and More! (Updated Fall 2014)* Swansea, UK: CreateSpace Independent Publishing Platform, 2013.

Manishin, G. "Managing Legal Risks in Social Media." September 30, 2010. **slideshare.net/gmanishin/social-media-managing-legal-risks**. Accessed October 2014

McCoy, J., "World's First Online Platform to Fight Internet Fraud is Launched (in China)." May 7, 2014. **socialmediatoday.com/content/worlds-first-online-platform-fight-internet-fraud-launched-china**. Accessed October 2014

Mello, J.P., Jr. "Social Media, Mobile Phones Top Attack Targets." September 25, 2013. **csoonline.com/article/2134010/mobile-security/social-media--mobile-phones-top-attack-targets.html**. Accessed October 2014

Mohd, F., and N. F. Uwandu. "A Study on the Impact of Social Media in Social Commerce Using Twitter as a Case Study." *Proceedings of the International Conference on Multimedia and Human Computer Interaction,* Toronto, Ontario, Canada, vol. 1, July 18-19, 2013. **researchgate.net/publication/257933151_a_study_on_the_impact_of_social_media_in_social_commerce_using_twitter_as_a_case_study**. Accessed October 2014

Norton. "Top 5 Social Media Scams." *Symantec Corp.,* (undated). **us.norton.com/yoursecurityresource/detail.jsp?aid=social_media_scams**. Accessed October 2014

Osterman Research. "The Risks of Social Media and What Can Be Done to Manage Them." White Paper, June 2011. **static.pseupdate.mior.ca.s3.amazonaws.com/media/links/The_Risks_of_Social_Media_and_What_Can_be_Done_to_Manage_Them.pdf**. Accessed October 2014

Peeples, A., and C. Vaughn. "Domino's 'Special' Delivery: Going Viral through Social Media (Parts A & B)." *Arthur W. Page Society Case Study Competition in Corporate Communications*, 2009. **awpagesociety.com**. Accessed October 2014

Rajput, S., S. Singh, and P. Singh. "Business Strategy, Change Management and Organizational Development." *VSRD International Journal of Business & Management Research*, Vol. 2(2), 2012. **vsrdjournals.com/MBA/Issue/2012_02_Feb/Web/6_Shubhangi_Rajput_Sharma_595_Research_Communication_Feb_2012.pdf**. Accessed October 2014

Rand, D. "Research Paper: Threats When Using Online Social Networks." CSIS Security Group, May 16, 2007; updated October 19, 2007. **csis.dk/downloads/LinkedIn.pdf**. Accessed October 2014

Ruble, K. "Hackers Attack Facebook, Twitter, and Other Social Media Databases." *Guardian Liberty Voice*, December 4, 2013. **guardianlv.com/2013/12/hackers-attack-facebook-twitter-and-other-social-media-databases**. Accessed October 2014

Safko, L. *The Social Media Bible: Tactics, Tools, and Strategies for Business Success, Third Edition*. Hoboken, NJ: Wiley, 2012.

Saper, D. "An Introduction to Legal Issues Surrounding Social Media." Slide Show, *Saper Law*, May 27, 2009. **slideshare.net/DaliahSaper/legal-implications-of-social-media**. Accessed October 2014

Shih, C. *The Facebook Era: Tapping Online Social Networks to Market, Sell, and Innovate*, 2nd ed. Upper Saddle River, NJ: Pearson/Prentice Hall, 2011.

Sickles, K. "The Future of Social Commerce" *1 World Sync*, September 9, 2014. **blog.1worldsync.com/en/future-social-commerce**. Accessed December 2014

Sommer, L., "Social Media for Rotary District 9940." New Zealand, May 2010

Steinhart, M. "Web 2.0: Worth the Risk?" A Secure Computing White Paper, 2009. **itoamerica.com/media/pdf/secure_coomputing/ worth_the_risk.pdf**. Accessed October 2014

Swann, C. T. *Marlins Cry a Phishing Story.* Spokane, WA: Cutting Edge Communications, Inc., 2012.

Symantec Corporation. "Internet Security Threat Report 2014." 2013 Trends, Vol. 19, April 2014. **symantec.com/security_response/ publications/threatreport.jsp**. Accessed October 2014

Teicher, D. "What Marketers Can Learn from Starbucks' Foursquare Stumble." July 27, 2010. **adage.com/article/digitalnext/ marketers-learn-starbucks-foursquare-stumble/145108/**. Accessed October 2014

Teller, T. "Social Engineering: Hacking the Human Mind." March 29, 2012. **forbes.com/sites/ciocentral/2012/03/29/social-engineering- hacking-the-human-mind**. Accessed October 2014

Trulioo. "Social Login as an Added Measure for E-Commerce Fraud." May 13, 2014. **trulioo.com/blog/2014/05/13/social- login-as-an-added-measure-for-e-commerce-fraud**. Accessed December 2014

Tzeng, E. "10 Stats Driving the Future of Social Commerce." October 2, 2014. **blog.gigya.com/10-stats-driving-the-future-of-social- commerce**. Accessed December 2014

vomBrocke, J., and M. Rosemann (Eds.) *Handbook on Business Process Management 1 and 2*, 2nd ed., New York: Springer, 2015.

Williams, C., and R. Klein, *Getting Your Business Easily on The Top 8 Social Sites: Take Your Business on Sites Like Facebook, Twitter, Google+, and Others in Less Than a Day!* (Kindle Edition: NY: Market My Market, 2014.)

Wohlgemuth, S., S. Sackmann, N. Sonchara, A.M. Tjon. "Security and Privacy in Business Networking." *Electronic Markets*, vol. 24, Issue 2, 81-88, June 2014.

Wollan, R., et al. *The Social Media Management Handbook: Everything You Need To Know To Get Social Media Working In Your Business.* Hoboken, NJ: Wiley, 2011.

Wood, P. "Phishing on Social Networks: What's the Value of Your Small Biz Twitter Account?" May 16, 2013. **symantec.com/con- nect/blogs/phishing-social-networks-what-s-value-your-small- biz-twitter-account**. Accessed December 2014

Appendix: Recommended Resources for Social Commerce

PART A: COMPREHENSIVE WEBSITES

Part A includes only upper level URLs for each source. The sources in this part are very comprehensive, including articles, videos, white papers, blogs, and so forth. You enter these sites and then search for the topic and the type of the resources you need. For example: "social CRM-white papers," or "crowdsourcing-case studies." You can use Google of course to do the same, but you may get better results using our list. Note that some of the sites also cover topics other than social commerce.

answers.com/topic/social-commerce
bazaarvoice.com
bizreport.com
brint.com
cioinsights.com
ecommerce-guide.com
ecommercetimes.com
volusion.com
shopify.com
fluid.com
entrepreneur.com
forrester.com
ibm.com/social
internet.com
internetretailer.com
linkedin.com/groups (several groups discussing SC)
marketingconversations.com
mashable.com
moz.com
powerreviews.com/resources
practicalecommerce.com
searchcio.techtarget.com
securityweek.com
shop.org
shoppost.com
shopvisible.com

socialmediatoday.com
socialmediaexaminer.com
socialtechonologyreview.com
techcrunch.com/social
techrepublic.com
zdnet.com/blog/hinchcliffe

PART B: MORE SPECIFIC SITES

The resources in this list are more specific than in Part A, sometimes dedicated to one topic.

informationweek.com/events: Webcasts news, analysis, advice, and free library for IT and SC.

techtarget.com: A useful content search and creation for case studies, Webcasts, news, and white papers on SC, EC, and IT.

searchcio.com: Helps you find many topics.

siliconvalley.com: A place for news, community opinions, SC companies, links, and more.

gartner.com/it: Mostly IT resource center, but some SC.

bitpipe.com: Comprehensive SC and IT resources.

eseminarslive.com: Large collection of Webcasts, videos, events, and more on technology topics including security, mobility, and cloud computing.

cio.com/white-papers: Index of white papers by topic offered by CIO.com.

thesocialmediaguide.com: A social media glossary.

lithium.com: An integrated social platform (analysis, community, measurement—for customer connection.

socialmediasecurity.com: Podcasts on different topics, blog, videos, guides and research.

socialtext.com: Socialtext is an endless source of Web social enterprise products/services.

socialcast.com: A customer case stories, enterprise platform for connecting people to knowledge, ideas, and resources.

thesocialmediaguide.com: A social media guide for small businesses.

E. Turban et al., *Social Commerce: Marketing, Technology and Management*, Springer Texts in Business and Economics, DOI 10.1007/978-3-319-17028-2, © Springer International Publishing Switzerland 2016

crowdsourcing.org: Leading source of crowdsourcing and crowdfunding information. Includes a directory of over 2,000 websites.

slideshare.net: Salesforce desk slide show about social customers (2013).

slideshare.net: Comprehensive slideshow (178 slides) about transforming retail into social commerce.

ibm.com/socialbusiness/us/en/learn.html?Ink=sbnav: The characteristics of a social business, the IBM POV (download).

digitalintelligencetoday.com: A comprehensive online resource for news, comment and analysis in the field of social commerce and media.

fastcompany.com: Guides, case studies (see the BMW case), videos, evaluations, articles, infographics, statistics, and much more.

bloomberg.com: Bloomberg Business week; hundreds of news items, blog items, regarding social media and commerce.

toprankblog.com: Articles and more on social media marketing, strategy, blogs, search, and more.

exacttarget.com/products/social-media-marketing: Products, case studies, Radian6, demo, resources.

socialmediaexaminer.com/getting-started: An easy guide for businesses to start using social media.

digitalintelligencetoday.com: A psychology blog for digital marketers.

mashable.com/social media: Extensive coverage, guides, social media, news, companies, articles, videos, and so forth.

simplyzesty.com: The most comprehensive blog, viral videos, tips, and useful social media resources. See video at **youtube.com/user/SimplyZesty**.

zdnet.com/topics/social+commerce: Collection of news articles, blog posts, white papers, case studies, videos and comments relating to social media and commerce.

smartinsights.com/ecommerce/social-commerce: Resources, strategy, blog and more.

gigya.com/resource-library: A collection of e-books, webinars, case studies and more.

hongkiat.com/blog/free-ebooks-social-media-marketers: 20 free e-books on social media marketing.

socialmediaB2B.com: Exploring the impact of social media on B2B.

e-commerce-europe.eu/website: Facts, figures, and articles.

digitalmarketingdepot.com: Comprehensive resource center.

Primer A: E-Commerce Basics

Contents

1 Electronic Commerce: Definitions and Concepts 293

2 The Content and Framework of the Field 294

3 The Types of E-Commerce Transactions 296

4 Capabilities, Benefits, Limitations, and Drivers
   of E-Commerce 297

5 Electronic Commerce Business Models 299

6 Resources for E-Commerce 302

Note: This Primer was extracted from Turban et al. 2015.

1. ELECTRONIC COMMERCE: DEFINITIONS AND CONCEPTS

The field of electronic commerce (EC) is diversified and has several definitions.

Defining Electronic Commerce

A common definition of *electronic commerce (EC)* is the process of buying, selling, transferring, or exchanging products, services, and/or information via computer networks, mostly the Internet and intranets. For an overview, see **en.wikipedia.org/wiki/E-commerce**. EC is often confused with e-business.

What Is E-Business

Some people view the term *commerce* as describing only buying and selling transactions conducted between business partners. If this definition of commerce is used, the term *electronic commerce* would be fairly narrow. Thus, many use the term *e-business* instead. *E-business* refers to a broader definition of EC, not just the buying and selling of goods and services, but doing all kinds of business transactions online, such as servicing customers, collaborating with business partners, conducting e-learning, and supporting electronic transactions within an organization. In this primer, we use the broadest meaning of electronic commerce, which is basically equivalent to the broadest definition of e-business. The two terms will be used interchangeably throughout the primer.

E. Turban et al., *Social Commerce: Marketing, Technology and Management*, Springer Texts in Business and Economics, DOI 10.1007/978-3-319-17028-2, © Springer International Publishing Switzerland 2016

Table A.1 Classifications of E-commerce

Activity	Combination number							
	1	2	3	4	5	6	7	8
Ordering, payment	P	D	D	D	D	P	P	P
Order fulfillment	P	D	D	P	P	D	P	D
Delivery (shipment)	P	D	P	P	D	D	D	D
Type of EC	Non EC	Pure EC	Partial EC					

P = Physical; D = Digital

Major EC Concepts

Several concepts are frequently used in conjunction with EC. The major ones are as follows:

Pure Versus Partial EC

EC can be either pure or partial, depending on the nature of its three major activities: ordering and payments, order fulfillment, and delivery to customers. Each activity can be physical or digital. Thus, there are eight possible combinations as shown in Table A.1. If all activities are digital, we have pure EC, if none are digital, we have no EC, otherwise, we have partial EC.

If there is at least one digital dimension, we consider the situation EC, but only partial EC. For example, purchasing a computer from Dell's website or a book from Amazon.com is partial EC, because the merchandise is physically delivered. However, buying an e-book from Amazon.com or a software product from Buy.com is pure EC, because ordering, processing, and delivery to the buyer are all digitally accomplished. Note that many companies operate in partial EC. For example, Jaguar has a 3-D application for self-configuration of cars online, prior to ordering (see Vizard 2013). For a video titled "Introduction to E-Commerce," see **plunkettresearch. com/video/ecommerce**.

EC Organizations

Purely physical organizations (companies) are referred to as *brick-and-mortar (old economy) organizations*, whereas companies that are engaged only in EC are considered *virtual (pure-play) organizations*. *Click-and-mortar (click-and-brick) organizations* are those that conduct some EC activities, usually as an additional marketing channel. Gradually, many brick-and-mortar companies are changing to click-and-mortar ones (e.g., Walmart, Target).

Electronic Markets and Networks

EC can be conducted in an *electronic market (e-marketplace)* where buyers and sellers meet online to exchange goods, services, money, or information. Any individual company or even a person can also open a webstore selling products or services. Electronic markets are connecting sellers and buyers via the Internet or via its counterpart within organizations, an *intranet*. An *intranet* is a corporate or government internal network that uses Internet tools, such as Web browsers, and Internet protocols. Another EC computer environment is an *extranet*, a network that uses the Internet to link intranets of several organizations in a secure manner (see **en. wikipedia.org/wiki/Extranet**).

2. THE CONTENT AND FRAMEWORK OF THE FIELD

To illustrate the content of the EC field, let us look at Dell Computers.

Dell is selling computers online in several ways. Most of Dell's sales are either business-to-consumer (B2C) or business-to-business (B2B). In B2C, online transactions are made between businesses and individual consumers, such as when a person purchases a dress at **net-a-porter.com** or a computer at Dell. In B2B, businesses make online transactions with other businesses, such as when Dell sells to businesses or purchases materials from suppliers. For more types see Turban et al. (2015).

AN EC FRAMEWORK

The EC field is a diverse one, involving many activities, organizational units, and technologies. Therefore, a framework that describes its contents can be useful. Figure A.1 introduces one such framework.

As shown in the figure, there are many EC applications (top of the figure), several of which are illustrated throughout the Primer (see Plunkett et al. 2014). To execute these applications, companies need the right information, infrastructure, and support services. Figure A.1 shows that EC applications are supported by an infrastructure and by the following five support areas (shown as pillars in the figure):

- **People.** Sellers, buyers, intermediaries, information systems and technology specialists, other employees, and any other participants comprise an important support area.

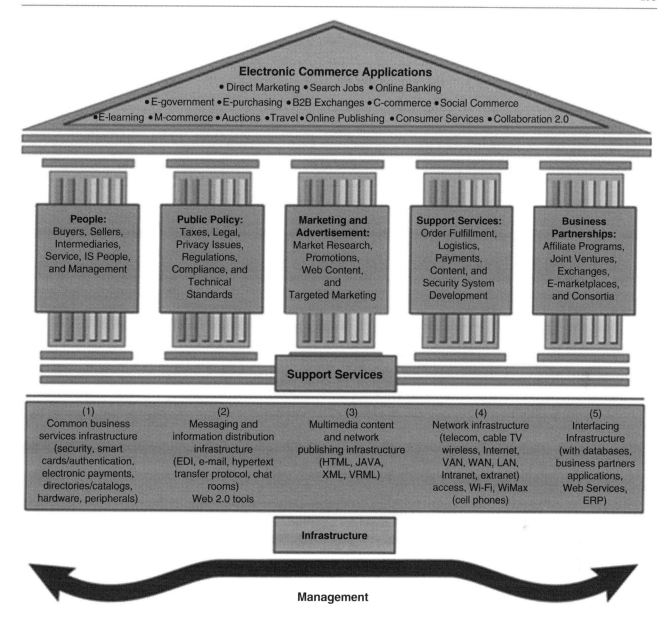

Fig. A.1 A framework for electronic commerce

- **Public policy.** Legal and other policy and regulatory issues, such as privacy protection and taxation, are determined by governments. Included as part of public policy is the issue of technical standards, which are established by governments and/or industry-mandated policy-making groups. Compliance with regulations is an important issue.
- **Marketing and advertising.** Like any other business, EC usually requires the support of marketing and advertising. This is especially important in B2C online transactions, in which the buyers and sellers usually do not know each other.

- **Support services.** Many services are needed to support EC. These range from content creation to payments to order delivery.
- **Business partnerships.** Joint ventures, exchanges, and business partnerships of various types are common in EC. These occur frequently throughout the *supply chain* (i.e., the interactions between a company and its suppliers, customers, and other partners).

The infrastructure for EC is shown at the bottom of the figure and it describes the hardware, software, and networks used in EC. All of these components require good *management practices*. This means that companies need to plan, organize, motivate, devise strategy, and restructure processes, as needed, to optimize the business use of EC models and strategies.

3. THE TYPES OF E-COMMERCE TRANSACTIONS

A common classification of EC is by the nature of the transactions or the relationship among the participants. The major types of EC transactions are listed below.

Business-to-Business (B2B)

All the participants in *business-to-business (B2B)* e-commerce are either businesses or other organizations (see Wirthwein and Bannon 2014). Today, about 85 % of EC volume is B2B. For Dell, the entire wholesale transactions are B2B. Dell buys almost all of its parts through e-commerce, and sells its products to businesses (and individuals) using e-commerce.

Business-to-Consumer (B2C)

Business-to-consumer (B2C) EC includes retail transactions of products or services, from businesses to individual shoppers. The typical shopper at Amazon.com is an individual. B2C is also called *e-tailing*.

Business-to-Business-to-Consumer (B2B2C)

In *business-to-business-to-consumer (B2B2C)* EC, a business provides some product or service to a client business. The client business maintains its own customers, who may be its own employees or business partners, to whom the product or service is provided. An example is **godiva.com**. The company sells chocolates directly to business customers. Those businesses may then give the chocolates as gifts or sell them to employees or to other businesses. Godiva may mail the chocolate directly to the recipients (with compliments of…).

Consumer-to-Business (C2B)

The *consumer-to-business (C2B)* category includes individuals who use the Internet to offer products or services to business (e.g., a consumer may offer to buy an airline ticket at a certain price, or higher). Then a seller may accept or reject the offer. (Priceline administers this type of C2B.)

Intrabusiness EC

The *intrabusiness EC* category includes all internal EC organizational activities that involve the exchange of goods, services, or information among various units and individuals in that organization. Activities can range from selling corporate products to one's employees, to online training, and to collaborative design efforts.

Business-to-Employees (B2E)

The *business-to-employees (B2E)* category is a subset of the intrabusiness group in which an organization delivers services, information, or products to individual employees. A major category of employees is *mobile employees*, such as field representatives or repair services that go to customers. EC support to such employees is also called *business-to-mobile employees (B2ME)*.

Consumer-to-Consumer (C2C)

In the *consumer-to-consumer (C2C)* category (sometimes refered to as person-to-person, P2P) consumers transact directly with other consumers. Examples of C2C include individuals selling residential property, cars, and so on in online classified ads. EBay's auctions and sales are mostly C2C, and so are the classified ads at Craigslist. The advertising of personal services over the Internet and the online selling of knowledge and expertise are other examples of C2C.

Collaborative Commerce

When individuals or groups communicate or collaborate online, they may be engaged in *collaborative commerce (c-commerce)*. For example, business partners in different locations may design a product together using collaborative software and online procedures.

E-Government

In *e-government EC*, a government entity buys or provides goods, services, or information from or to businesses (G2B) or from or to individual citizens (G2C). Governments can deal also with other governments (G2G).

The previous categories are summarized in Fig. A.2.

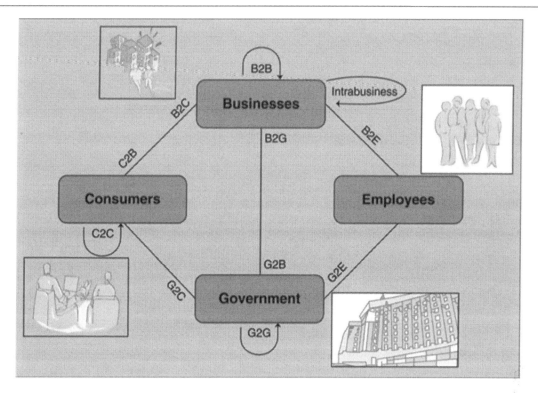

Fig. A.2 Categories of e-commerce transactions

The Interdisciplinary Nature of EC

Because EC is a relatively new field, it is just now developing its theoretical and scientific foundations. From just the brief overview of the EC framework and classification, you can probably see that EC is related to several different disciplines. The major academic EC disciplines include the following: *accounting, business law, computer science, consumer behavior, economics, engineering, finance, human resource management, management, management information systems, marketing, public administration,* and *robotics.*

4. CAPABILITIES, BENEFITS, LIMITATIONS, AND DRIVERS OF E-COMMERCE

EC initiatives play an increasing role in supporting innovations and strategies that help companies to compete and flourish, especially companies that want to be proactive and introduce changes rather than be reactive and respond to them. What makes EC suitable for such a role is a *set of capabilities* which are presented next.

The Capabilities of E-Commerce

The essential capabilities that drive EC are the ability to:

- Provide efficient and effective business transactions.
- Provide global reach for selling, buying, or finding business partners.
- Conduct business anytime, from anywhere, in a convenient way. For example, there were about 2 billion smartphones in use in 2015 in the world. For comprehensive statistics and descriptions see Mobithinking (2014).
- Disseminate information rapidly, frequently in real time.
- Compare prices.
- Customize products and personalize services.
- Use rich media in advertisement, entertainment, and social networking.
- Receive experts' and other users' advice quickly.
- Collaborate in different ways, both internally and externally.
- Share information and knowledge.
- Increase productivity and performance, reduce costs, and compress time (e.g., by having smarter applications).
- Fing information about vendors, products, and competitors easily and quickly.

Table A.2 The benefits of E-commerce

Benefit	Description
Benefits to organizations	
Global reach	Quickly locating customers and/or suppliers at reasonable cost worldwide
Cost reduction	Lower cost of information processing, storage, and distribution
Facilitate problem solving	Solve complex problems that have remained unsolved
Supply chain improvements	Reduce delays, inventories, and cost
Business always open	Open 24/7/365; no overtime or other costs
Customization/personalization	Make order for customer preference
Ability to innovate, use new business models	Facilitate innovation and enable unique business models
Lower communication costs	The Internet is cheaper then VAN private lines
Efficient procurement	Saves time and reduces costs by enabling e-procurement
Improved customer service and relationship	Direct interaction with customers, better CRM
Help SME to compete	EC may help small companies to compete against large ones by using special business models
Lower inventories	Using customization inventories can be minimized
Lower cost of distributing digitizable product	Delivery online can be 90 % cheaper
Provide competitive advantage	Innovative business models
Benefits to consumers	
Inventory	Huge selection to choose from (vendor, products, styles)
Ubiquity	Can shop any time from any place
Self configuration	Can self-customize products
Find bargains	Use comparison engine
Real time delivery	Download digital products
No sales tax	Sometimes; changing
Enable telecommuting	Can work or study at home or any place
Social interaction	In social networks
Find unique items	Using online auctions, collectible items can be found
Comfortable shopping	Shop at your leisure without pushy sales clerks bothering you
Benefits to society	
Enable telecommuting	Facilitate work at home; less traffic, pollution
More public services	Provided by e-government
Improved homeland security	Facilitate domestic security
Increased standard of living	Can buy more and cheaper goods/services
Close the digital divide	Allow people in rural areas and developing countries to use more services and purchase what they really like

Because EC technology is improving over time and decreasing in cost, its comparative advantage over manual systems is continuously increasing, further contributing to the growth of EC.

Benefits and Limitations of Electronic Commerce

Few innovations in human history encompass as many benefits as EC does. The global nature of the technology, the opportunity to reach hundreds of millions of people, its interactive nature, the variety of possibilities for its use, and the resourcefulness and rapid growth of its supporting infrastructures, especially the Web, result in many potential benefits to organizations, individuals, and society. These benefits are just starting to materialize, but they will increase significantly as EC expands. It is not surprising that some maintain that the EC revolution is as profound as the change that accompanied the Industrial Revolution. The major benefits are summarized in Table A.2.

The Limitations and Barriers of EC

Barriers to EC can be classified as either technological or non technological. The technological ones are declining with time.

The major barriers to EC are: (1) resistance to new technology; (2) implementation difficulties; (3) security

Fig. A.3 Major drivers of EC

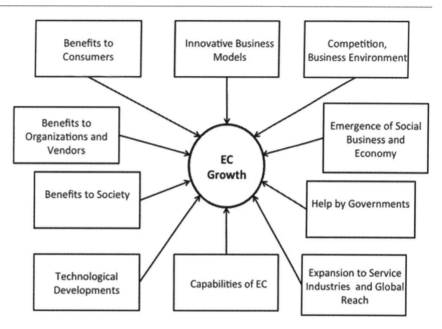

concerns; (4) lack of technology skills by buyers; (5) lack of potential customers; (6) cost; (7) insufficient bandwidth; (8) cultural barriers; and (9) an incomplete set of standards. The barriers can be classified into: sectoral barriers (e.g., government, private sector, international organizations); enterprise internal barriers (e.g., poor security, lack of technical knowledge, incomplete B2B interface, and lack of time and resources); external barriers (e.g., lack of government support); cultural barriers; organizational differences; international trade barriers; and lack of EC standards. These limitations need to be addressed when implementing EC.

Drivers of E-Commerce

The tremendous explosion of EC can be explained by its drivers and characteristics, benefits, and by changes in the business environment.

Although EC is only about 20 years old, it is expected to have non-stoppable growth and expand consistently into new areas of our life. The question is why? What drives EC?

The Major Drivers of EC

EC is driven by many factors depending on the industry, company, and application involved. The major drivers are shown in the self-explanatory Fig. A.3.

5. ELECTRONIC COMMERCE BUSINESS MODELS

One of the major characteristics of EC is that it enables the creation of new business models. A *business model* is a method of doing business by which a company can generate revenue to sustain itself. A model also spells out where the company is positioned in the value chain; that is, by what activities the company adds value to the product or service it supplies.

Note that, the January-February 2011 issue of *Harvard Business Review* is dedicated to business model innovations (five articles), including several topics related to e-commerce.

THE STRUCTURE AND PROPERTIES OF BUSINESS MODELS

Several different EC business models are possible, depending on the company, the industry, and so on.

A comprehensive business model is composed of the following elements:

- A description of the *customers* to be served and the company's relationships with these customers, including what constitutes value from the customers' perspective (*customers' value proposition*).

- A description of all *products* and *services* the business will offer and the markets in which they will be sold.
- A description of the *business process* that is required to make and deliver the products and services including distribution and marketing strategies.
- A list of the *resources* required and the identification of which ones are available, which will be developed in-house, and which will need to be acquired (including human resources).
- A description of the organization's *supply chain*, including *suppliers* and other *business partners*.
- A list of the major competitors, their market share, and strengths/weaknesses.
- The competitive advantage offered by the business model.
- The anticipated organizational changes and any resistance to change.
- A description of the revenues expected (*revenue model*), anticipated costs, sources of financing, and estimated profitability (*financial viability*).

Models also include a *value proposition,* which is an analysis of the benefits of using the specific model (tangible and intangible), for both customers and organization. A detailed discussion of and examples of business models and their relationship to business plans is presented at **en.wikipedia. org/wiki/Business_model**.

This Primer presents two of a model's elements: *revenue models* and *value propositions*.

Revenue Models

A revenue model outlines how an organization, or an EC project, will generate revenue. It includes costs as well.

SALES

Companies generate revenue from selling merchandise or services on their websites. For example, Amazon. com and Godiva that sell products online.

TRANSACTION FEES

A company receives a commission based on the volume of transactions made. For example, when a homeowner sells a house, he or she typically pays a transaction fee to the broker. The higher the value of the sale, the higher the total transaction fee. Alternatively, transaction fees can be levied *per transaction*. With online stock trades, for example, there is usually a fixed fee per trade, regardless of the volume.

SUBSCRIPTION FEES

Customers pay a fixed amount, usually monthly, to get some type of service. An example would be the Internet access fee. Thus, the Internet provider's primary revenue model is subscription fees (fixed monthly payments).

ADVERTISING FEES

Companies charge others for allowing them to place a banner or other ad on their sites.

AFFILIATE FEES

Companies receive commissions for referring customers to others' websites. A good affiliate program is available at Amazon.com.

LICENSING FEES

Another revenue source is licensing fees (e.g., see **progress.com/datadrect**). Licensing fees can be assessed as a monthly or annual fee or a per usage fee. Microsoft receives fees from each workstation that uses Windows NT, for example.

OTHER REVENUE SOURCES

Some companies allow people to play online games for a fee or to watch a sports competition in real time for a fee (e.g., see **espn.go.com**).

A company uses its *revenue model* to describe how it will generate revenue and its *business model* to describe the *process* it will use to do so. The Internet allows for innovative revenue models.

The revenue model can be part of the value proposition or it may supplement it.

Value Proposition

Business models also include a value-proposition statement. A *value proposition* refers to the benefits, including the intangible, non-quantitative ones, that a company can derive from using the model. In B2C EC, for example, a value proposition defines how a company's product or service fulfills the needs of customers. The *value proposition* is an important part of the marketing plan of any product or service.

Functions of a Business Model

Business models have the following functions or objectives:

- Describe the major business processes of a company.
- Describe the business's (the venture's) positioning within the value network linking suppliers and customers (includes identification of potential complementary companies and competitors). Also, describe the supply and value chains.
- Formulate the venture's competitive strategy and its long-range plans.
- Articulate a customer value proposition.
- Identify a market segment (who will use the technology for what purpose).
- Specify the revenue-generation process; where the company will operate.
- Define the venture's specific value chain structure.
- Estimate the cost structure and amount, and the profit potential.

Typical EC Business Models

There are many types of EC business models. Examples and details of EC business models can be found in Rappa (2010), **slideshare.net/kaiser2009/e-businessmodels-ppt**, and Turban et al. (2015). The following four common models followed by some less common ones (# 5–18) are:

1. **Online direct marketing.** The most obvious model is that of selling products or services online. Sales may be from a *manufacturer* to a customer, eliminating intermediaries or physical stores (e.g., Dell Computer), or from *retailers* to consumers, making distribution more efficient (e.g., Walmart online). This model is especially efficient for digitizable products and services (those that can be delivered electronically). This model has several variations and it uses different mechanisms (e.g., auctions). It is practiced in B2C (where it is called *e-tailing*) and in several B2B types of EC (e.g., e-procurement, e-wholesale).

2. **Electronic tendering systems.** Large organizational buyers, private or public, usually make large-volume or large-value purchases through a *tendering (bidding) system*, also known as a *reverse auction*. Such tendering can be done online, saving time and money. Pioneered by General Electric Corp., e-tendering systems are gaining popularity. Indeed, several government agencies mandate that most of their procurement *must* be done through e-tendering.

3. **Electronic marketplaces and exchanges.** Electronic marketplaces existed in isolated applications for decades (e.g., stock and commodities exchanges). But as of 1996, hundreds of e-marketplaces (old and new) have introduced new methods and efficiencies to the trading process. If they are well organized and managed, e-marketplaces can provide significant benefits to both buyers and sellers. Of special interest are vertical marketplaces that concentrate on one industry.

4. **Viral marketing.** According to the viral marketing model, people use e-mail and social networks for spreading word-of-mouth advertising. Thus, an organization can increase brand awareness, or even generate sales, by inducing people to send influencing messages to other people or to recruit friends to join certain programs. It is basically Web-based *word-of-mouth* advertising, and it is popular in social networks.

5. **Name your own price.** Pioneered by Priceline.com, the name-your-own-price model allows buyers to set the price they are willing to pay for a specific product or service. Priceline.com will try to match a customer's request with a supplier willing to sell the product or service at that price. This model is also known as a *demand-collection model*.

6. **Find the best price.** According to this model, also known as a search engine model, a customer specifies a need and then an intermediate company, such as Hotwire.com, matches the customer's need against a database, locates the lowest price, and submits it to the consumer. The potential buyer then has 30–60 minutes to accept or reject the offer. A variation of this model is available for purchasing insurance: A consumer can submit a request

for insurance to Insweb.com and receive several quotes. Many companies employ similar models to show *price comparisons* and find the lowest price. For example, consumers can go to **eloan.com** to find the best interest rate for auto or home loans. A well-known company in this area is Shopping.com.

7. **Affiliate marketing.** Affiliate marketing is an arrangement whereby a marketing partner (a business, an organization, or even an individual) refers consumers to a selling company's website. The referral is done by placing a banner ad or the logo of the selling company on the affiliated company's website. Whenever a customer who was referred to the selling company's website makes a purchase there, the affiliated partner receives a commission (which may range from 3 to 15 %) of the purchase price. In other words, by using affiliate marketing, a selling company creates a virtual commissioned sales force. Pioneered by CDNow, the concept is now employed by thousands of retailers and manufacturers. For example, Amazon.com has over one million affiliates, and even tiny Cattoys.com offers individuals and organizations the opportunity to put its logo and link on their websites to generate commissions.

8. **Group purchasing.** In the offline world of commerce, discounts are usually available for purchasing large quantities. So, too, EC has spawned the concept of demand aggregation, wherein a third party finds individuals or small-to-medium enterprises (SMEs), aggregates their small orders to attain a large quantity, and then negotiates (or solicits a tender offer) for the best deal. Thus, using the concept of group purchasing, a small business, or even an individual, can get a discount. This model is also known as the *volume-buying model*. One leading aggregator is Letsbuyit.com. Online purchasing groups are also called e-co-ops. Group purchasing is now associated with social commerce with companies such as Groupon.

9. **Online auctions.** Almost everyone has heard of eBay, the world's largest online auction site. Several hundred other companies, including Amazon.com and Yahoo!, also conduct online auctions. In the most popular type of auction, online shoppers make consecutive bids for various goods and services, and the highest bidders get the items auctioned. E-auctions come in different shapes and use different models. For example, eBay is using over 40,000 "assistants" in a model where the assistants perform the order fulfillment function.

10. **Product and service customization.** With customization, a product or service is created according to the buyer's specifications. Customization is not a new model, but what is new is the ability to quickly configure customized products online for consumers at costs not much higher than their non customized counterparts. Dell is a good example of a company that customizes PCs for its customers; Nike will customize their shoes for you.

11. **Information brokers (infomediaries).** Information brokers provide privacy, trust, matching, search, content, and other services (e.g., **bizrate.com**, **google.com/products**).

12. **Bartering.** Companies use bartering to exchange surpluses they do not need for things that they do need. A market maker arranges such exchanges (e.g., **webbarter.com** or **tradeaway.com**).

13. **Deep discounting.** Companies such as Half.com and Groupon.com offer products and services at deep discounts, as much as 50 % off the retail price.

14. **Membership.** A popular offline model, in which only members get a discount, also is being offered online (e.g., **netmarket.com**).

15. **Value-chain integrators.** This model offers services that aggregate information-rich products into a more complete package for customers, thus adding value. For example, Carpoint.com provides several car buying–related services, such as financing and insurance.

16. **Value-chain service providers.** These providers specialize in a supply chain function such as logistics (**ups.com**) or payments (**paypal.com**).

17. **Supply chain improvers.** One of the major contributions of EC is in the creation of new models that change or improve supply chain management. Most interesting is the conversion of a linear supply chain, which can be slow, expensive, and error prone, into a hub.

18. **Negotiation.** The Internet offers negotiation capabilities between individuals (e.g., **ioffer.com**) or between companies. Negotiation can also be facilitated by intelligent software agents.

6. RESOURCES FOR E-COMMERCE

E-Commerce Journal (**ecommerce-journal.com**): Source for news, events, etc., about e-commerce.

Electronic Resource Guide: (**libguides.rutgers.edu/ecommerce**): Offers resources and links to Internet statistics—see ClickZ Stats, Nielsen/NetRatings, U.S. Census Bureau, and comScore.

Social Computing Journal (**socialcomputingjournal.com**): Open forum with articles on the Internet, social commerce, collective intelligence, and all things Web 2.0.

webopedia.com: Online encyclopedia dedicated to computer technology.

whatis.techtarget.com/definition: Detailed definitions of most e-commerce and other technological topics.

This Primer was extracted from Turban et al. (2015). Many more resources are listed in the various chapters of that book.

References

Plunkett, J. W., et al., (ed.) *Plunkett's E-Commerce & Internet Business Almanac 2014. (Plunkett's E-Commerce and Internet Business Almanac).* Houston, TX: Plunkett Research Ltd., 2014.

Rappa, M. "Business Models on the Web." January 17, 2010. **digitalenterprise.org/models/models.html** (accessed January 2015).

Turban, E., et al. Electronic Commerce: A Managerial and Social Networks Approach, 8th ed. New York: Springer, 2015.

Vizard, M. "Jaguar Launches Virtual Shopping Experiences." *CIO Insight*, June 5, 2013.

Wirthwein, C., and J. Bannon. *The People Powered Brand: A Blueprint for B2B Brand and Culture Transformation.* Ithaca, NY: Paramount Market Publishing, Inc., 2014.

Primer B: E-Marketing Basics

Content

1 What Is E-Marketing? 305

2 Markets... 306

3 Market Research 306

4 E-Marketing Management and Business Models.............. 307

5 Creating Value: Product and Price.................................... 308

6 Distributing Products.. 310

7 Communicating Value: IMC 310

8 Building Value: CRM.. 312

1. WHAT IS E-MARKETING?

E-marketing is the result of information technology applied to traditional marketing. Applying this to the American Marketing Association's definition of marketing, e-marketing is the *use of information technology* for the "marketing activity, set of institutions, and processes for creating, communicating, delivering, and exchanging offerings that have value for customers, clients, partners, and society at large." Electronic marketing is only one part of an organization's e-business activities. E-marketing is also called Internet marketing, Web marketing, or online marketing.

E-marketing reaches far beyond the Web. First, many e-marketing technologies exist without the Web, including software and hardware used in customer relationship management, supply chain management, and electronic data interchange arrangements pre-dating the Web. For example, when you call a company to complain about a product, the information might be stored in a database and automatically sent over the Internet to marketing managers and product development teams. Seconds, non-Web Internet communications such as e-mail, Internet telephony like Skype, social media like Facebook, and text messaging are effective avenues for marketing communication. Third, the Internet delivers text, video, audio, and graphics to many more information-receiving appliances than simply personal computers (PCs). These forms of digital content also go over the Internet infrastructure to the television, smartphones, tablets (like the iPad) and even the refrigerator or automobile. Finally, offline electronic data-collection devices, such as bar code scanners and databases, receive and send data about customers and products over a secure internal network, called an Intranet.

It is helpful to think of it this way: Content providers create digital text, video, audio, and graphics to send over the Internet infrastructure to users who receive it as information, entertainment, or communication on many types of appliances. As marketers think outside of the Web, they find many new possibilities for creating products that provide

E. Turban et al., *Social Commerce: Marketing, Technology and Management*, Springer Texts in Business and Economics,
DOI 10.1007/978-3-319-17028-2, © Springer International Publishing Switzerland 2016

value and communicate in ways that build relationships with customers.

E-marketing affects traditional marketing in two ways. First, it increases efficiency and effectiveness in traditional marketing functions. Seconds, the technology of e-marketing transforms many marketing strategies. This transformation also results in new business models that add customer value and/or increase company profitability, such as the highly successful Craigslist, Facebook, Twitter, and Google Ad Sense advertising models.

In this primer we include a basic introduction to traditional marketing, and discuss ways that information technology enhances and changes traditional offline marketing strategies and tactics. Along the way we'll introduce a lot of terminology that will help you understand the field.

2. MARKETS

E-marketing is only effective if an organization's target markets use the Internet. Most government agencies, non-profit organizations, and businesses use the Internet for business purposes. However, only 87 % of U.S. adults use the Internet. It would not benefit a company to use e-marketing tactics if its markets were mostly in the 13 % of Americans who don't use the Internet. The less-connected groups tend to be older, less educated, in ethnic minority groups, do not have children, live in rural areas, and have a lower income (according to research from Pew Research Internet Project 2014).

Also, only 42.3 % of the world's population in 233 countries uses the Internet (3,035,749,340 people). Many countries have fewer than 50 % of the population using the Internet. Asia has the largest number of users (1,386.2 million), but North America has the highest penetration rate at 87.7 % (Internet World Stats 2014). China has 642.3 million users but that represents only 47.4 % of the population. Without major shifts, some countries may not ever achieve high levels of Internet adoption among individual consumers, although high cell phone adoption may change this picture eventually. This is important to know as e-marketers chase international markets.

Marketers also want to know what their prospective and current customers do online. Table A.3 shows that e-mail is

Table A.3 Internet usage data

Activity	Percent of internet users doing it
Send or read e-mail	92
Use a social network	72
Use a search engine to find information	91
Do online banking	61
Get news online	74
Buy a product online	71

Source: Pew Internet Research Project (March 2011–May 2014)

far from dead and it is still a good way to reach target markets. However, younger generations use social networking and text messaging more often than e-mail, so again, marketing tactics depend on specific target market behavior.

Both individual and business buyers are more demanding than ever because they are just one click away from a plethora of global competitors, all vying for their business. As well, the Internet's social media provide a communication platform where individual product comments can spread like wildfire in a short time and quickly either enhance or damage a brand image. This phenomenon is only one part of a trend that has been growing for years because of the Internet—the power balance has finally shifted from companies to individuals and this has huge implications for marketing strategies and tactics.

3. MARKET RESEARCH

Marketers use both primary and secondary research for understanding their markets. The Nielsen Company recruits a panel of over 200,000 people and measures their Internet usage behavior at over 30,000 sites, then sells this to site owners and advertisers as secondary research (Nielsen 2014). Marketers conduct quantitative primary research online through panels and survey research and also via their Web server logs that capture every click from site visitors (Web analytics). Qualitative online research involves creative experiments of online ads (e.g., which one got the most clicks to the advertiser's site), online focus groups, and observation (e.g., monitoring conversation in social networks). This information helps organizations to design strategies and tactics that meet marketing objectives. For an example, see Fig. A.4. This shows how Purina PetCare turned data into information and knowledge for advertising decision making. It is important to recall that data need careful analysis and insight to be actionable.

Survey research response rates are declining, making it more difficult to collect market information both on and off line. Some other issues with Internet marketing research include:

1. Respondents are increasingly upset at getting unsolicited e-mail requesting survey participation.
2. Some researchers "harvest" e-mail addresses from Internet forums and groups without permission. Perhaps, this practice is analogous to gathering names from a telephone book, but some people object because consumers are not posting with the idea of being contacted by marketers.
3. Some companies conduct "surveys" for the purpose of building a database for later solicitation. Ethical marketers clearly mark the difference between marketing research and marketing promotion and do not sell under the guise of research.

Fig. A.4 From data to decision at Nestlé Purina PetCare Company

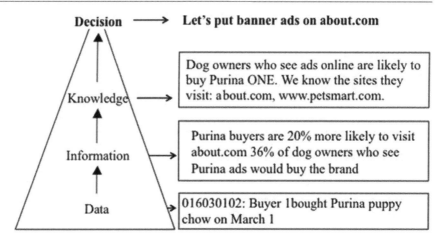

Decision ⟶ **Let's put banner ads on about.com**

Knowledge ⟶
> Dog owners who see ads online are likely to buy Purina ONE. We know the sites they visit: about.com, www.petsmart.com.

Information ⟶
> Purina buyers are 20% more likely to visit about.com 36% of dog owners who see Purina ads would buy the brand

Data
> 016030102: Buyer 1bought Purina puppy chow on March 1

4. Privacy of user data is a huge issue in this medium, because it is relatively easy and profitable to send electronic data to others via the Internet.

These and other concerns prompted ESOMAR®, the European Society for Opinion and Marketing Research, to include guidelines for Internet research in its International Code of Marketing and Social Research Practice. ESOMAR has more than 4,900 members in 130 countries (see **boa** Also, the U.S. Marketing Research Association has a code of Marketing Research ethics regarding honesty, professionalism, fairness, and confidentiality of respondents that help to support the marketing research profession as marketers conduct online research (see **marketingresearch.org/code**).

Real-time profiling and real-space primary data collection are two other important research techniques.

Real-time profiling occurs when special software tracks a user's movements through a website, then compiles and reports on the data at a moment's notice. Also known as "tracking user clickstream in real time," or "behavioral targeting," this approach allows marketers to analyze consumer online behavior and make instantaneous adjustments to site promotional offers and Web pages. For example, if you look at a particular book on Amazon.com but don't buy it, you might see that book presented to you on the Amazon home page on your next visit.

Real-space primary data collection refers to technology-enabled approaches to gather information offline that is subsequently stored and used in marketing databases to be used for e-marketing. The most important real-space techniques are bar code scanners and credit card terminals at brick-and-mortar retail stores, although computer entry by customer service reps while talking on the telephone with customers might also be included here. Offline data collection is important for e-marketing because these data, when combined with online data, paint a complete picture of consumer behavior for individual retail firms. Smart card and credit card readers, interactive point of sale machines (iPOS), and bar code scanners are mechanisms for collecting real-space consumer data.

4. E-MARKETING MANAGEMENT AND BUSINESS MODELS

Armed with data about an organization's customers, competitors, and market conditions, marketing managers write objectives and strategies for achieving them. Marketing objectives generally include goals for acquiring new customers and increasing revenue or market share. An objective usually includes a measurable task and time frame. For example: "Increase sales on our website by 15 % within 12 months."

Next, the company designs strategies to achieve its objectives. *E-marketing strategy* is the design of marketing strategy that capitalizes on the organization's electronic or information technology capabilities to reach specified objectives. In essence, e-marketing strategy is where technology strategy and marketing strategy wed.

For example, a Mexican hotel chain, with many hotel properties in South America, maintains a sophisticated, large customer database. It is able to send customized e-mails by customer segments, such as, customers who are high value, recent visitors, or who booked through a travel agent. By targeting special offers to relevant customers, it has increased hotel bookings and profits. This relevant targeting keeps customers happy and supports the company's customer relationship management e-marketing strategy—ultimately supporting the corporate growth strategy. In this example, the objectives were to increase hotel bookings and profits; the strategy was to target high value recent hotel visitors and the key e-marketing tactic was to send special e-mails to these visitors.

E-Marketing Contributes to Business Models

The term *business model* is often mentioned in print and by executives. A *business model* is a method by which the organization sustains itself in the long term and includes its value

Table A.4 E-marketing contributes to the E-business model

E-marketing increases benefits
- Online mass customization (different products and messages to different stakeholders)
- Personalization (giving stakeholders relevant information)
- 24/7 convenience
- Self-service ordering and tracking
- One-stop shopping
- Learning, engaging, and communicating with customers on social networking sites

E-marketing decreases costs
- Low-cost distribution of communication messages (e.g., e-mail)
- Low-cost distribution channel for digital products
- Lowers costs for transaction processing
- Lowers costs for knowledge acquisition (e.g., research and customer feedback)
- Creates efficiencies in supply chain (through communication and inventory optimization)
- Decreases the cost of customer service

E-marketing increases revenues
- Online transaction revenues such as product, information, advertising, and subscription fees; or commission/fee on a transaction or referral
- Adds value to products/services and increases prices (e.g., online FAQ and customer support)
- Increases the customer base by reaching new markets
- Builds customer relationships and, thus, increases current customer spending (share of wallet)

proposition for partners and customers as well as its revenue streams. This description is in line with the *marketing concept*, which suggests that the social and economic justification for an organization's existence is the satisfaction of customer wants and needs while meeting organizational objectives. Business partners might include supply chain members such as suppliers, wholesalers, and retailers, or firms with which the company joins forces to create new brands (such as the Microsoft and NBC alliance to create MSNBC).

Organizations deliver stakeholder value through e-business models by using digital products and processes. Whether online or offline, the value proposition involves knowing what is important to the customer or partner and delivering it better than other organizations. *Value* encompasses the customer's perceptions of the product's benefits, specifically its attributes, brand name, and support services. Subtracted from benefits are the customer costs involved in acquiring the product, such as monetary, time, energy, and psychic costs. Like customers, partners evaluate value by determining whether the partnership provides more benefits than costs. This concept is shown as follows:

$$\text{Value} = \text{Benefits} - \text{Costs}$$

Information technology usually increases benefits and lowers costs to stakeholders. For example, consumers can search for the lowest price product online without leaving home. Conversely, it can decrease value when websites are complex, information is hard to locate, and technical difficulties interrupt data access or shopping transactions. Table A.4 lists e-marketing activities that contribute to a company's e-business models.

Now we move to the marketing mix. Product, price, place, and promotion (known as the 4 Ps) combine with information technology to create value for customers. Figure A.5 demonstrates how these tools blend to create both transactions and customer relationships.

5. CREATING VALUE: PRODUCT AND PRICE

Never has competition for online customer attention and dollars been fiercer. To succeed, firms must employ strategies—grounded in solid marketing principles—that result in customer value. What is value? First, it is the entire product experience. It starts with a customer's first awareness of a product, continues at all customer *touch points* (including the website experience, e-mail from a firm, and much more), and ends with the actual product usage and post purchase customer service. It even includes the compliments a consumer gets from friends while whipping out that iPad, or the fun she has when messaging friends on Skype or Facebook. Seconds, value is defined wholly by the mental beliefs and attitudes held by customers. Regardless of how favorably the firm views its own products, it is the customers' perceptions that count. Third, value involves customer expectations; if the actual product experience falls short of their expectations, customers will be disappointed. Fourth, value is applied at all

Fig. A.5 Marketing mix and CRM strategies and tactics for relational and transactional outcomes

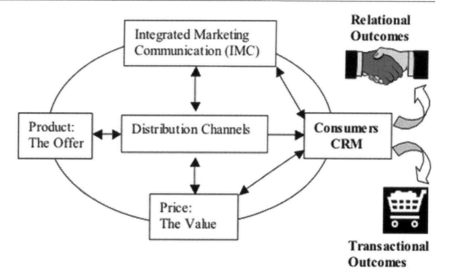

price levels. Both a $0.05 micropayment for an online article in a news archive and a $2 million e-commerce computer application can provide value.

Marketers must make five general product decisions that comprise its bundle of benefits to meet customer needs: attributes, branding, support services, labeling, and packaging. Except for physical packaging, all of these can be converted from atoms to bits for online delivery:

- *Product attributes* include overall quality and specific features, such as, color, size, download speed, and so forth. *Benefits*, on the other hand, are the same features from a user perspective (i.e., what will the attribute do to solve problems or meet needs and wants?). For example, users can download media, music, software, and other digital products from the Web or a mobile app. Perhaps the most important benefit is mass customization (e.g., Pandora radio combines songs from many different artists as desired by customers).

- A *brand* includes a name (McDonald's), a symbol (golden arches), or other identifying information, but is much more than that. It is a perception in the mind of the customer about the promised benefits. Tangible and service products, companies, people (politicians/sports figures), vacation destinations and ideas can all be branded. Brand names can generate trust in consumers if they deliver on the promise. E-marketing issues with branding include the selection of Facebook page and domain names (URLs), and the need to monitor brand mentions online for possible reputation damage.

- Customer *support services*, both during and after the purchase, are a critical component in the organization's value proposition. Companies design support services when designing the product. The topic of customer service online is so important that it morphed into the topic of customer relationship management (CRM) and now social CRM.

- Product *labels* identify brands, sponsoring firms, product ingredients, and often provide instructions for use. Labels on tangible products create product recognition and influence decision behavior at the point of purchase. For online services, the "label" might include terms of product usage, product features, and other information on websites. For example, when users download iTunes software for organizing their iPod music, they can first read the "label" to discover how to install and use the software. In addition, many companies have extensive legal information about copyright use on their Web pages.

In the narrowest sense, *price* is the amount of money charged for a product or service. More broadly, price is the sum of all the values (such as money, time, energy, and psychic cost) that buyers exchange for the benefits of having or using a good or service. For example, beside the dollars, is your price higher to drive to a physical bookstore or to search and find that book online? Online you might have to pay additional shipping costs but less time cost. E-marketers work this out as they decide which products to offer online and how to price them.

In addition, the increasing power of buyers means control over pricing in some instances—such as with online product bidding. The Internet's properties also allow for *price transparency*—the idea that both buyers and sellers can view competitive prices for items sold online. This feature is available at shopping agent sites that compare prices among many online retailers, such as **shopzilla.com**. Online auctions are another interesting e-marketing pricing tactic, especially in B2B markets where excess supplies exist (such as a company trying to unload a lot of excess wire).

Information technology complicated pricing strategies and changed the way marketers use this tool, especially in online markets. Some expenses are lower online, such as, self-service order processing by customers, digital media that do not need to be produced in physical copies and less overhead costs without physical retail stores. Others are higher, such as, technology, Web page design, and shipping costs.

A final consideration for pricing involves payment methods. Credit card companies and PayPal charge fees to sellers for each transaction. This electronic money is convenient for both buyers and sellers but also lowers company profit and opens the door to potential fraud and credit card database hacking.

6. DISTRIBUTING PRODUCTS

A *distribution channel* is a group of interdependent firms that work together to transfer product and information from the supplier to the consumer. It is composed of the following participants:

- **Producers:** Manufacturers and their suppliers, such as those who grow the raw ingredients.
- **Intermediaries:** Firms that match buyers and sellers and mediate the transactions among them (e.g., wholesalers, agents and retailers). For example Expedia.com is an online travel agent.
- **Buyers:** Consumers or business users of the product or service.

There are many successful e-marketing business models involving product distribution:

- *Content sponsorship* occurs when companies create websites, attract a lot of traffic, and sell advertising.
- The online *broker* creates a market in which buyers and sellers negotiate and complete transactions. Brokers typically charge the seller and/or buyer a transaction fee, but they don't represent either party for providing exchange and negotiation services. For example E*Trade brokers the stock market online and Autobytel allows customers to receive bids from qualified car dealers on vehicles available in their area without first phoning or visiting the dealer.
- *Agents do* represent either the buyer or the seller depending on who pays their fee. Expedia is paid commissions by hotels and airlines for booking travelers. *Affiliate programs* pay commissions to website owners for customer referrals (such as the Amazon affiliates who show books and other merchandise on their websites).
- *Online retailing* is one of the most visible e-business models and the subject of this book. A huge part of *e-commerce*, merchants set up webstores and sell to businesses and consumers.

Note that there are many e-marketing tactics behind the scenes of these distribution models. For example, when online retailers send a physical product to a buyer, FedEx or another shipper will provide tracking information to both buyer and seller via the Internet. Another important aspect of product distribution involves multichannel marketing—the use of more than one sales channel, such as Web, mobile, brick and mortar store, and catalog. Most large traditional retailers are multichannel marketers because they also sell products online.

7. COMMUNICATING VALUE: IMC

Integrated marketing communication (IMC) is a cross-functional process for planning, executing, and monitoring brand communications designed to profitably acquire, retain, and grow customers. IMC is cross-functional because every touch point that a customer has with a firm or its agents helps to form brand images. For example, a Home Depot retail customer might buy and use a product from the website, then e-mail, Facebook message or call 1-800 to complain about a problem, and finally return the product to the brick-and-mortar retail store. Every contact with an employee, a website, a Facebook post, a blog comment about the product, a YouTube video, a magazine ad, a catalog, the physical store facilities, and so forth helps the customer form an image of the company brand.

IMC strategy begins with a thorough understanding of target markets, the brand, its competition, and many other internal and external factors. Then marketers select specific Marketing Communication (MarCom) tools to achieve their communication objectives and media for reaching target markets. During and after implementation, they measure execution effectiveness, make needed adjustments, and re-evaluate the results.

MarCom consists of both planned and unplanned messages between firms and customers, as well as those among customers. Companies use planned messages when trying to inform or persuade their target stakeholders, such as the owned and paid media in Chaps. 4 and 5 of this book. Unplanned messages include things such as word of mouth among consumers and publicity in media (earned media).

Using innovative technologies, e-marketers can enhance the *effectiveness* (reaching the target market with little wasted coverage) and *efficiency* (low cost) of traditional MarCom in many interesting ways. Online marketing communication can be used for *brand communication* (to build brand awareness and create a favorable brand image) or to elicit a *direct response* in the form of a transaction, customer engagement, or some other behavior (such as website registration, social media "like"/comment post, or e-mail inquiry). Brand communication works at the awareness and attitude levels (heads and hearts) of the Social Commerce Brand Decision Process model, also called the *hierarchy of effects model*, while direct-response communication primarily works at the behavioral level (do something). Advertising can be used for both branding and direct response, while marketing public relations aims to build brand images, and sales promotion, direct marketing, and personal selling primarily attempt to solicit a direct response (see Chap. 4 for definitions of these tools).

Advertising

There are many types of online advertising and below are just a few (recall that this is paid for space in someone else's media property):

- **Display ads**. These contain more graphics and white space than text, and include traditional banners and many additional sizes.
- **Mobile ad**. An SMS text or multi-media message sent to a cell phone.
- **Map ad**. Text or graphics linked from, and appearing in or over, a location on an electronic map such as on Google Maps.
- **Pop-up**. A new window, which opens in front of the current one, displaying an advertisement, or entire Web page.
- **Contextual ads.** Ad servers, such as Google's Double-Click, maintain an inventory of ads from clients and serve them into websites as appropriate users are viewing particular pages.
- **E-mail advertising**. This is generally just a few sentences of text embedded in another firm's e-mail content.
- **Sponsorships**. Also called advertorials, these integrate editorial content and advertising, such as when Kraft Foods pays for space to put recipes on a food website.

Advertising is purchased using one of two main models (or a hybrid of both). *Cost per thousand impressions*, known by all media buyers as CPM, charges the advertiser based on the number of users who are exposed to an ad online. It is calculated: (ad cost/number of impressions)/1,000. For example, an online ad costing $500 and reaching 30,000 users would have a CPM of $16.67. The seconds model is *cost-per-click (CPC)*, which charges advertisers based on the number of click-throughs to the advertiser's Web property. CPC is also known as cost-per-action (CPA) and is performance based. CPC/CPA are the pricing models used most often by website owners.

Other pricing models include cost per engagement (CPE) for actions such as number of votes, views, ratings, or submission of branded user-generated content and cost per install (CPI) for a widget or application on a social network or mobile device.

Marketing Public Relations

Marketing public relations (MPR) includes brand-related activities and nonpaid, third party media coverage to positively influence target markets and generate earned media. MPR activities using Internet technology include the website content itself, online events, blogs, communities, and other social media and many ways to build a buzz online. These are owned media.

Online Sales Promotions

Sales promotion activities include coupons, discounts, rebates, product sampling, contests, sweepstakes, and premiums (free or low-cost gifts). Of these promotion types, only sampling, discounts, and contests/sweepstakes/games are widely used on the Internet. For example, some sites allow users to sample digital products prior to purchase: software companies provide free downloads of fully functional demo versions of their software and iTunes or Amazon offer a portion of the song for free listening.

Direct Marketing

These e-marketing tactics include *e-mail marketing*, *text messaging* (also called *short message services—SMS), multimedia message services (MMS)*, and *instant messaging (IM)*.

E-mail is still the Internet's killer application: It has not been replaced by RSS feeds, blogs, or social networking, in spite of the many people predicting its demise. Instead, marketers integrate e-mail with social media, such as sending an article excerpt in e-mail and linking to the full article on a blog, or offering customers the choice of receiving information via an e-mail newsletter, RSS feed, Twitter feed. E-mail has several advantages over postal direct mail. First, it requires no postage or printing charges. Seconds, e-mail offers an immediate and convenient avenue for direct response; in fact, e-mail often directs users to websites using hyperlinks. Third, and perhaps most important, e-mail can be automatically individualized to meet the needs of specific users—beyond just using a name in the e-mail.

Opt-in means that users check a box to receive e-mail from a company. *Opt-out* means they have to uncheck a box to not get the mail. E-marketers use both techniques but opt-in techniques are more considerate of customers and produce better results. They are part of a bigger traditional marketing strategy called *permission marketing*.

Search Marketing

Search engine optimization (SEO) is the act of altering a website and incoming links so that it does well in the organic, crawler-based listings of search engines. Also called natural search, this involves HTML meta-tags and the titles and text on the Web page itself. Search engines figure out how to categorize the page based on the content, relevance, popularity, and about 200 other variables. *Paid search* is when advertisers buy keywords that appear as sponsored links on search engine results pages, such as the Google AdWords program (this is advertising).

Inbound marketing refers to being found online, versus interrupting users while they are consuming content, such as with a television ad or display ad on a website or social network. SEO is a key tool for assuring that target markets find the marketer's products.

IMC Performance Metrics

E-marketers are drowning in data, yet they need to assess the effectiveness of their IMC campaigns. The bottom line is that they want to see whether (1) their marketing objectives were achieved, and (2) to what extent the various IMC tactics contributed. For marketing objectives involving sales or market share growth internal records and secondary data about competitive sales will help.

IMC tactics are a different story. We presented some key metrics at the end of Chap. 5, regarding awareness/exposure, brand health, engagement, action, and innovation. The metrics selected by e-marketers depend on what they are trying to achieve, however, some of the most common IMC metrics follow:

- *E-mail* response rates, database growth (more customer information) and return on investment.
- *Website* analytics tell e-marketers how people found the site, how long they stay on it and how they move through the site. If it is a retailer, they want to know *conversion rate* (how many site visitors purchased) and cost per order (the cost to acquire that customer/dollars spend on orders).
- *Sales promotion* metrics include number of coupons redeemed, contest entries, or number of sample downloads (such as music samples).
- *Marketing public relations* metrics might include number of video views for a viral video or other viral content and the size and sentiment of earned media discussion. Companies also measure the number subscribing to RSS feeds, number of "Likes" on Facebook pages, Twitter followers, comments to blog posts, and much more.
- *Share of voice* is the brand's advertising weight expressed as a percentage of a defined market segment's messages during a specified time period.
- *Advertisers* want to know the CPC (Cost per Click), CPA (Cost per Action), CPE (Cost per Engagement) and CPI (Cost per Installation) for performance-based advertising. They normally use CPM prior to purchasing advertising to evaluate its efficiency; however, they will also double-check this as the ad runs.

Marketers monitor their selected metrics very frequently because two of the Internet's strengths are that (1) these are easy to measure, and (2) IMC tactics can change in minutes if something is not working as expected.

8. BUILDING VALUE: CRM

Customer relationship management (CRM) is a philosophy, strategy, and process. It involves acquiring, retaining and growing customer value. It is grounded in customer data and conversations, and facilitated by technology. The benefits of CRM include increased revenue from better prospect targeting, increased wallet share with current customers, and retaining customers for longer periods of time. These benefits are quantified through databases that help companies understand their customers better and use this knowledge to build loyalty and optimize lifetime value. CRM tactics can also decrease costs, resulting in greater profitability.

An organization using relationship marketing focuses on wallet share more than market share. *Wallet share* is the amount of sales a firm can generate from one customer and, thus, reflects a focus on retention and growth rather than an acquisition focus (market share). For instance, Amazon wants to sell books, music, household appliances, and more to each customer. Relationship marketing differentiates individual customers based on need rather than differentiating products for target groups—such as buyers of novels by a particular author.

CRM is facilitated online by cookie files, WEB analytics, databases (and mining them for information on customer buying patterns), collaborative filtering, behavioral targeting, and many other techniques discussed throughout this book.

E-marketers use numerous metrics to assess the Internet's value in delivering CRM performance—among them are ROI (Return on Investment), cost savings, revenues, customer satisfaction, and especially the contribution of each CRM tactic to these measures. Other important metrics include customer retention rates, average order value (AOV) and *customer lift*—increased response or transaction rates. Finally, organizations want to understand the customer *lifetime value (LTV)* to the company so they know how much to invest in retention versus acquisition tactics.

Note: Most of this material is an excerpt from Strauss and Frost (2014).

References

"Internet World Stats." 2014. **internetworldstats.com**. Accessed January 2015

Nielsen "Online Measurement Methodology" **nielsen.com/us/en/solutions/measurement/online.html**. Accessed January 2015.

Pew Internet Research Project. "Usage over Time Tip Sheet." see excel spreadsheet. (March 2011 – May 2014.) **pewinternet.org/data-trend/internet-use/internet-use-over-time**. Accessed January 2015.

Strauss, J., and R. D. Frost. *E-Marketing,* seventh edition. Upper Saddle NJ : Pearson, Inc, 2014.

Glossary

Advergaming These are (1) games featuring a company's product or (2) the integration of advertisements into video games, especially computer-based ones: both promote a company's product or a service

Advertising "Any paid form of non-personal presentation and promotion of ideas, goods, or services by an identified sponsor" (Kotler and Armstrong 2011)

Autoresponders Automated e-mail reply systems

Avatars Animated representations of humanlike movements and behaviors depicted as 2-D or 3-D graphical representations that populate virtual worlds

Behavioral targeting The one-to-one targeting of ads to consumers base on individuals' Web-browsing behavior, such as search history

Blog A personal website, or part of a website, open to the public, where the owners expresses their feelings, opinions, information, and expertise

Business model The method (or plan) implemented by a company to meet the customer's needs, and by which a company generates revenue and creates value

Business-oriented social networks Also known as *professional social networks*, are networks whose primary objective is to facilitate business activities and connections. They are built on social relationships and can exist offline or online

Business process management (BPM) (1) A method for business restructuring that combines workflow systems and redesign methods, covering three types of interactions: people-to-people, systems-to-systems, and systems-to-people; and (2) a holistic management approach focused on aligning all aspects of an organization with the wants and needs of its customers and partners. It promotes business effectiveness and efficiency, while striving for innovation, flexibility, and integration with technology

Business process reengineering (BPR) A methodology for conducting a comprehensive redesign of an enterprise's processes

Change management "Is a structured approach to shifting/transitioning individuals, teams, and organizations from a current state to a desired future state. It is an organizational process aimed at empowering employees to accept and embrace changes in their current business environment" (per Rajput et al. 2012)

Collaborative filtering Using proprietary formulas that automatically connects the preferences and activities of many customers that have similar characteristics to predict the preferences of new customers and to recommend products to them

Collaborative (or sharing) economy An economic system constructed around the concept of sharing goods and services among the participating people. Also known as 'collaborative consumption'

Collective intelligence (CI) An application of crowdsourcing for problem solving, idea generation, and innovations

Communal shopping A method of shopping where consumers enlist friends and other people they trust to advise them on what products to shop for

Competitive intelligence (CI) "The action of defining, gathering, analyzing, and distributing intelligence about products, customers, competitors, and any aspect of the environment needed to support executives and managers in making strategic decisions for an organization" (**en.wikipedia.org/wiki/Competitive_intelligence** accessed January 2015)

Content marketing "A marketing technique of creating and distributing valuable, relevant, and consistent content to attract and acquire a clearly defined audience—with the objective of driving profitable consumer action…. It is an *ongoing process* that is best integrated into your overall marketing strategy, and it focuses on *owning media*, not renting it" (Content Marketing Institute)

Cookies Small files sent from a website and stored in a designated area in your computer. They allow companies to save certain information for future use

CRM analytics The application of business analytic techniques and business intelligence such as data mining and online analytic processing to CRM applications

Crowdsourcing Describes a set of tools, concepts, and methodologies that deal with the process of outsourcing

E. Turban et al., *Social Commerce: Marketing, Technology and Management*, Springer Texts in Business and Economics,
DOI 10.1007/978-3-319-17028-2, © Springer International Publishing Switzerland 2016

work, including problem solving and idea generation to a *community* of potential solvers known as the 'crowd'

Customer engagement (CE) "The engagement of customers with one another, with a company, or a brand. The initiative for engagement can be either consumer- or company-led and the medium of engagement can be on or offline" (per Wikipedia)

Customer interaction center (CIC) A comprehensive customer service entity in which enterprises take care of customer service issues communicated through various contact channels (**searchcrm.techtarget.com/definition/contact-center** accessed January 2015)

Customer relationship management (CRM) An approach that focuses on acquiring customers and building long-term and sustainable relationships that add value to the customers as well as the organizations

Cyberbullying "Bullying that takes place using electronic technology" (**stopybullying.gov** accessed January 2015)

Direct marketing "Direct connections with carefully targeted individual consumers to both obtain and immediate response and cultivate lasting customer relationships—the use of direct mail, the telephone, direct response television, e-mail, the Internet, and other tools to communicate directly with specific customers" (Kotler and Armstrong 2011)

Earned media When customer conversations become the channel

E-government The use of information technology in general, and e-commerce in particular, to provide citizens and organizations with more convenient access to government information and services

Electronic customer relationship management (e-CRM or CRM 1.0) The electronically delivered set of tools that helps manage CRM

Enterprise 2.0 Using Web 2.0 tools in the workplace

Folksonomy (collaborative tagging, social tagging) The practice and method of collaboratively creating, classifying, and managing tags to annotate and categorize content

Gamification The introduction of gaming into social networking

Hype cycle A graphic representation of the maturity, adoption, and social application of specific IT and SC tools and how they are potentially relevant to solving real business problems and exploiting new opportunities

Inbound marketing A marketing strategy that relates to being found by customers, as opposed to "interrupt" marketing

Information dashboard A visual display or presentation of data organized in ways easy to read and interpret

Internet radio Audio content transmitted live via the Internet. It is a broadcasting service that enables users to listen online to thousands of radio stations

Internet TV The delivery of TV content via the Internet by downloading or streaming videos

Key performance indicator (KPI) A quantitative measure commonly used in the industry that expresses the critical success factors of a company, department, or an initiative

Knowledge management (KM) A process of capturing (or creating) knowledge, storing it, constantly updating it, disseminating it, and using it whenever necessary. This way, knowledge is shared for useful purposes, ranging from problem solving to increased productivity

Mashup Combination of two or more websites into a single websites that provides the content of both sites (whole or partial) to deliver a novel product to consumers

Metric A specific, measurable standard against which actual performance is compared. Metrics are used to describe many things such as costs, benefits, or the ratio between them

Microblogging A form of blogging that allows users to write short messages (or an image, or embedded video) and publish them, to be viewed either by anyone or by a restricted group that can be chosen by the users. These messages can be submitted by a variety of means, including text messaging from cell phones, instant messaging, e-mail, MP3, or just on the Web

Mobile social networking Social networking where members interact with one another using cellphones or other mobile devices

Online customer engagement "Is qualitatively different from offline engagement as the nature of the customer's interactions with a brand, company and other customers differ on the internet. Discussion forums or blogs, for example, are spaces where people can communicate and socialize in ways that cannot be replicated by any offline interactive medium" (per Wikipedia)

Organizational strategy Expresses the specific plans and policies, a business plan to take to achieve its strategy

Owned media These carry communication messages from the organization to Internet users on channels that are owned and, thus, at least partially controlled by the company

Paid Media When the brand pays to leverage social media properties. Also called advertising

Performance metric A measure of the organization's performance on activities designed to achieve specific objectives (also called "Web Analytics" for the online environment)

Personalization The matching of services, products, and/or marketing communication content to individuals, based on their preferences

Personal selling "Personal interactions between a customer's and the firm's sales force for the purpose of making sales and building customer relationships" (Kotler and Armstrong 2011)

Phishing A fraudulent process of acquiring confidential information, such as credit card or banking details, from unsuspecting computer users

Privacy The right to be left alone and free from unwanted intrusions or disturbances in one's private life or affairs

Public relations "Building good relations with the company's various publics by obtaining favorable publicity, building up a good corporate image, and handling or heading off unfavorable rumors, stories, and events" (Kotler and Armstrong 2011)

QR codes Barcodes that appear as many black modules arranged as a square grid on a white background. They are now an exciting extension of offline paid media that engages Internet users (see **en.wikipedia.org/wiki/QR_code** accessed January 2015)

Reputation management systems Various predefined criteria for processing complex data to report reputation

RSS (*Really Simple Syndication*) A family of Web feed formats used to publish frequently updated content such as blog entries, news headlines, audio, and video, in a standardized format

Sales force automation (SFA) Applications that support the selling efforts of a company's sales force, helping salespeople manage leads, prospects, and customers through the sales pipeline

Sales promotion "Short-term incentives to encourage the purchase or sale of a product or service" (Kotler and Armstrong 2011)

Search engine optimization (SEO) The process of improving the visibility of a company or a brand on the results page displayed by a search engine

Sentiment analysis (opinion mining) A type of analysis that aims to determine the attitude or opinion of a person with respect to a particular issue as expressed in online conversations (e.g., if the opinion is positive, negative, or neutral)

Social ad "An online ad that incorporates user interactions that the consumer has agreed to display and be shared. The resulting ad displays these interactions along with the user's persona (picture and/or name) within the ad content" (Interactive Advertising Bureau 2009)

Social bookmarking A method for Internet users to organize, store, manage, and search for bookmarked URLs of resources online with the help of metadata

Social business "A business that embraces networks of people to create business value" (per **ibm.com/smarterplanet/global/files/us__en_us__socialbusiness__epw14008usen.pdf** accessed July 2015)

Social capital The value created by connections among individuals and within social networks. It highlights the value of social relations and the role of cooperation. It also helps to get economic results

Social collaboration People's collaboration within and between communities enabled by social media tools and platforms

Social commerce (SC) E-commerce transactions delivered via social media

Social computing A type of computing that includes an interaction of computers and social behavior

Social customer relationship management (SCRM or CRM 2.0) CRM supported by social media (e.g., Web 2.0 tools, social network sites, as demonstrated in the opening case), which are designed to engage customers in conversations, sharing and other interactions in order to provide benefits to all participants and increase trust

Social customers These customers are usually members of social networks. They share opinions about products, services, and vendors; do social shopping; and understand their rights, and they know how to use the wisdom and power of the crowds and communities to their benefit

Social engineering When criminals use psychology to persuade unsuspecting people to disclose personal information about themselves, in order to allow the criminals to gain unauthorized access into the user's computer, to collect confidential information for use in illegal activities

Social enterprise The use of social media tools and platforms and conducting social networking activities in organizations while its major objectives are either commercial or non-profit activities (e.g., the government)

Social game A video multiplayer game played on the Internet, mostly in social networks or in virtual worlds

Social government (government 2.0) An emerging field where governments use social media to improve their services to citizens, organizations, and employees, in addition to improving their internal operations. A social government can be viewed as a subset of e-government

Social graph A diagram that illustrates the interconnections among people, groups, and organizations in a social network

Social influence "The change in behavior that one person causes in another, intentionally or unintentionally, as a result of the way the changed (persons) perceive themselves in relationship to the influencer, other people and society in general" (see **changingminds.org/explanations/theories/social_influence.htm**)

Social marketplace A marketplace that uses social media tools for conducting activities, such as the buying and selling of products, services, and resources

Social media Online text, image, audio, and video content created by users using Web 2.0 platforms and tools, which people use for social interactions and conversations, mainly to share opinions, experiences, insights, and perceptions

Social media analytics Describes the activities of monitoring and recording, analyzing, and interpreting the results of interactions and associations among people, topics, and ideas. It is the process of gathering data from blogs and social media sites and analyzing that data to make business decisions

Social media intelligence The monitoring and collection of online opinions and other social data (such as conversations or reviews) used for guiding corporate decisions and (private and public) actions

Social media marketing (SMM) The use of social networking and social media as marketing communication and marketing tools (McAfee, A. *Enterprise 2.0: New Collaborative Tools for Your Organization's Toughest Challenges.* Boston: Harvard Business School Press, 2009)

Social network A social structure that describes a virtual community. It is composed of nodes (which are generally individuals, groups, or organizations) that are tied by one or more specific types of interdependencies, such as values, visions, ideas, financial exchange, friendship, kinship, dislike, or trade. The structures can range from simple to very complex

Social network analysis (SNA) A method for analyzing social networks. It involves the mapping and measuring of both relationships and information flows among groups, organizations, and other connected entities in social networks (see Scott and Carrington 2011)

Social network game A video game that is distributed primarily through social networks, and usually involves multiplayers

Social network sites Web-based services that allow individuals to join a social network (community) and perform social media activities, including interaction, sharing, and building profiles

Social networking The act of exchanging information, private or public, through various forms of networks technology, such as the Internet, cellphones, and other devices and services, using social media tools, Apps, or networks

Social networks services (SNSs) Also known as social networks sites such as LinkedIn or Facebook, provide a Web space for people to build their homepages, which the service organizations host for free. They also provide basic communication and other support tools (e.g., blogs, e-mail, and chatting capabilities) for conducting different activities

Social radio The integration of Internet radio with social networking activities

Social shopping Online shopping done with social media tools and platforms

Social software A range of software tools that allow users to interact and share data and other media

Social support One's perception of being cared for, receiving responses, and being helped by people in their social group

Social TV An emerging social media technology that enables TV viewers who are in different locations to interactively share experiences such as discussions, reviews, tweeting, and recommendations while watching the same show simultaneously

Social web "A set of social relations that link people through the World Wide Web"

Software application (App) A piece of software (usually small) that is run on the Internet, or on an intranet on your computer, or on your wireless device, such as the iPhone and iPad. Apps are designed for end users. Numerous Apps are available for social media

Strategic planning "An organization's process of defining its strategy, or direction, and making decisions on allocating its resources to pursue this strategy....Strategy has many definitions, but generally involves setting goals, determining actions to achieve the goals, and mobilizing resources to execute the actions. A strategy describes how the ends (goals) will be achieved by the means (resources)" (per Mintzberg et al. 1996)

Strategy A framework indicating the direction a business is planning to accomplish its mission and goals. Strategy also outlines the plans and policies that need to be accomplished

Strategy map A graphical representation of an organization's strategy

Tactics The specific plans and policies, a business plan to take to achieve its strategy

Tag A key word or term assigned to a piece of information (such as an Internet bookmark, digital image, video clip, or any computer document)

Tweets Short text-based posts (up to 140 characters) posted to Twitter

Twitter A free microblogging service that allows its users to send and read other users' updates. An online social networking and microblogging service that enables its users to send messages and read other users' messages and updates

User-generated content (UGC) Various kinds of media content that are produced by end users and are publicly available

User profile Describes customer preferences, behaviors, and demographics

Viral blogging When bloggers conduct viral marketing activities by leveraging the power of the blog community to spread content

Viral marketing A word-of-mouth (WOM) method by which people tell others (frequently their friends) about a product they like or dislike. Passing marketing messages to gain exponential visibility

Viral marketing (viral advertising) "Any marketing technique that induces websites or users to pass on a marketing message to other sites or users, creating a potentially exponential growth in the message's visibility and effect" (see **whatis.techtarget.com**)

Viral video A video that is spread rapidly through the process of online information sharing

Virtual community A community in which the interaction takes place over a computer network, mostly the Internet

Virtual economy An emerging economy existing in several virtual worlds, where people exchange virtual goods frequently related to an Internet game or a virtual business

Virtual goods Computer images of real or imaginary goods

Virtual presence (telepresence) Being present via intermediate technologies, usually radio, telephone, television or the Internet

Virtual world A 3-D computer-based simulated environment built and owned by its residents (the community)

Vlog (or video blog) A blog with video content

Web 2.0 O'Reilly viewed this term as describing a seconds generation of Internet-based tools and services. Some properties cited by O'Reilly were: user-generated content, online collaboration and information, and sharing data interactively

Widgets Mini Web applications that are used to distribute or share content throughout the social Web, downloaded to a mobile device or desktop, or accessed on a Website or blog" (Interactive Advertising Bureau 2010)

Wiki (wikilog) A tool that allows users the easy creation and editing of any number of interlinked Web pages via a Web browser, using a simplified markup language or a WYSIWYG text editor (What You See Is What You Get)

Word of mouth Oral communication that passes information from person to person (per **investopedia.com/terms/w/word-of-mouth-marketing.asp** accessed January 2015)

Index

A

Advergaming (in-game advertising), 87
Advertising, 4, 24, 49, 76, 105, 128, 156, 184, 210, 234, 269, 295, 306, 313
Autoresponder, 169, 170, 313
Avatars, 39–41, 86, 147, 161, 169, 176, 214–218, 227, 245, 279, 313

B

Behavioral targeting, 10, 55, 57, 68, 82, 91, 275, 307, 312, 313
Blog, 4, 24, 49, 76, 100, 131, 156, 186, 207, 232, 270, 291, 310, 313
Business model, 15–17, 20, 29, 30, 34, 40–42, 109, 128–129, 131, 133, 138, 139, 141, 142, 144, 148, 150, 152, 158, 207, 220, 227, 234, 236, 238, 248, 251, 279, 280, 283, 298–302, 306–308, 310, 313
Business process management (BPM), 256, 280, 313
Business process reengineering (BPR), 280, 313
Business social network, 36, 184, 185, 199
Business-oriented social networks, 33, 35–36, 41, 185, 313

C

CE. *See* Customer engagement (CE)
Change management, 280–281, 285, 286, 313
CIC. *See* Customer interaction center (CIC)
Collaborative (or sharing) economy, 224, 313
Collaborative filtering, 48, 49, 55–57, 68, 108, 312, 313
Collective intelligence (CI), 4, 14, 29, 30, 37, 171, 194–196, 242, 302, 313
Competitive intelligence (CI), 243, 246, 255, 256, 313
Content marketing, 8, 83–85, 212, 313
Cookie, 56, 67, 91, 119, 135, 245, 275, 287, 312, 313
CRM. *See* Customer relationship management (CRM)
CRM analytics, 173–175, 313
Crowdfunding, 37, 39, 41, 42, 146, 196, 224, 225, 292
Crowdsourcing, 10, 14, 16, 19, 24, 26, 29, 37–39, 41, 42, 63, 67, 109, 122, 137, 138, 150, 161, 162, 173, 174, 181, 182, 188, 192–196, 198–201, 208, 211, 220, 225, 234, 235, 244, 255, 280, 291, 292, 313–314
Customer engagement (CE), 20, 31, 60–62, 99–124, 144, 145, 212, 234, 250, 256, 266–267, 279, 310, 314
Customer interaction center (CIC), 61, 116, 160–161, 174, 175, 192, 266–267, 314
Customer relationship management (CRM), 10, 18–19, 80, 84, 85, 97, 111, 155–177, 184, 191, 199, 212, 218, 234, 238, 242, 257, 266, 278, 279, 285, 291, 298, 305, 307, 309, 312–315
Cyberbullying, 242, 268, 272–276, 314

D

Direct marketing, 82, 94, 95, 156, 279, 301, 310, 311, 314

E

E-government, 207–210, 296, 298, 314, 315
Earned media, 58, 83–85, 88, 95, 101–104, 116, 118–120, 123, 124, 249, 310–312, 314
Electronic customer relationship management (e-CRM or CRM 1.0), 158, 314
Enterprise 2.0, 9, 11–13, 16, 19, 182, 183, 185, 188, 190, 234, 314, 316

G

Gamification, 191, 223, 224, 314

H

Hype cycle, 239, 241–242, 256, 258, 314

I

Inbound marketing, 25, 85, 94, 312, 314
Information dashboard (dashboard), 255, 314
Internet radio, 221, 222, 314, 316
Internet TV, 91, 221–222, 314

K

Key performance indicator (KPI), 249, 256, 314
Knowledge management (KM), 32, 182, 184, 193, 199–201, 314

M

Metric, 43, 61, 63, 77, 79, 92, 94, 95, 99–124, 233, 234, 240, 241, 247–253, 255–258, 312, 314
Microblogging, 8, 14, 26, 29–32, 34, 41, 43, 58, 60, 79, 83, 85–87, 93, 95, 106, 169, 189, 190, 198, 242, 273, 314, 316
Mobile social networking, 36, 37, 221, 314

O

Online customer engagement, 61, 314
Organizational strategy, 235–239, 280, 281, 314
Owned media, 83–85, 88, 95, 97, 101, 311, 314

P

Paid media, 83–85, 88, 90, 95, 101, 102, 104, 108, 114, 115, 123, 186, 239, 249, 310, 314, 315

Performance metric, 79, 94, 95, 118, 122, 123, 233, 234, 249, 250, 312, 314

Personal selling, 82, 94, 95, 310, 314

Personalization, 24, 29, 31, 40, 48, 49, 51, 54–57, 63, 69, 87, 132, 136, 138, 140, 144, 167, 173, 175, 184, 210, 220, 222, 279, 297, 298, 308, 314

Phishing, 268–272, 285–287, 315

Privacy, 16, 19, 30, 36, 57, 69, 105, 115–116, 139, 145, 149, 151, 186, 191, 242, 243, 268, 272–276, 285–286, 295, 302, 307, 315

Public relations, 11, 31, 82, 94, 95, 101, 103, 190, 234, 310–312, 315

Q

QR codes, 108–109, 120, 122, 123, 315

R

Reputation management systems, 30, 115–116, 122, 315

S

Sales force automation (SFA), 161, 171–172, 315

Sales promotion, 11, 16, 82, 85, 86, 88, 89, 94, 95, 111, 310–312, 315

Search engine optimization (SEO), 114, 116–118, 122, 211, 253, 311, 312, 315

Sentiment analysis (opinion mining), 156, 161, 233, 234, 247, 248, 252–258, 315

SEO. *See* Search engine optimization (SEO)

SFA. *See* Sales force automation (SFA)

SMM. *See* Social media marketing (SMM)

SNA. *See* Social network analysis (SNA)

SNSs. *See* Social network services (SNSs)

Social ads, 88, 90–91, 94, 95, 279, 284, 315

Social business, 9–11, 15, 16, 19, 41, 158, 172, 181–184, 192, 193, 197, 201, 242, 254, 279, 280, 284, 286, 292, 315

Social capital, 8, 33, 49, 64, 66–68, 280, 315

Social collaboration (Collaboration 2.0), 41, 182, 188, 193, 197–199, 201, 253, 284, 315

Social commerce (SC), 5, 23, 49, 79, 101, 131, 157, 182, 207, 233, 267, 291, 302, 310, 315

Social computing, 5–9, 18, 40, 183, 184, 302, 315

Social customer, 18–19, 131, 132, 150, 155–177, 183, 224, 245, 292, 315

Social customer relationship management (SCRM or CRM 2.0), 158–169, 171–177, 315

Social engineering, 268–271, 315

Social enterprise (Enterprise 2.0), 183, 234

Social games, 18–19, 29, 34, 147, 151, 207, 222–224, 226, 284, 315

Social government (government 2.0), 205–228, 315

Social graph, 33, 63–66, 68, 84, 111, 116, 144, 172, 223, 276, 315

Social influence, 14, 17, 49, 64, 66, 68, 69, 107, 251–253, 257, 315

Social media, 3, 25, 54, 75, 100, 131, 155, 182, 205, 231, 266, 291, 305, 314

Social media analytics, 233, 234, 242, 247, 248, 252–256, 316

Social media intelligence, 247, 248, 316

Social media marketing (SMM), 5, 10–12, 18, 19, 28, 37, 42, 59, 62, 78, 79, 90, 94, 95, 115–117, 131, 142, 160, 210–213, 215, 235, 246, 258, 267, 279, 282, 292, 316

Social network, 4, 25, 48, 77, 100, 128, 156, 182, 206, 231, 268, 297, 306, 313

Social network analysis (SNA), 64, 65, 253, 316

Social network games, 222–223, 316

Social network services (SNSs), 5, 17, 33, 116, 182, 194, 210, 312

Social network sites, 10, 12, 27, 28, 33–35, 40, 64–65, 86, 102, 132, 144, 158, 161, 166, 168, 175, 191, 200, 213, 239, 245–247, 256, 278, 315, 316

Social psychology, 8, 19, 49, 51, 63–66, 68, 111

Social radio, 222, 316

Social software, 9, 12, 19, 30, 32, 34, 132, 136, 185, 189, 197, 243, 245, 256, 281, 283, 316

Social support, 8, 10, 14, 18, 19, 49, 51, 63, 66–67, 133, 276, 316

Social TV, 219–222, 226, 228, 316

Social Web, 5–7, 18–19, 49, 88, 156, 157, 210, 250, 254, 280, 316, 317

Software application (app), 28–29, 88, 256, 316

Strategic planning, 233–239, 256, 316

Strategy, 8, 28, 51, 76, 100, 128, 158, 189, 208, 232, 267, 292, 296, 307, 313

Strategy map, 251, 316

T

Tactics, 10, 30, 53, 54, 58, 66, 78–80, 86, 92, 94, 95, 104, 105, 114, 115, 117–118, 120, 122, 124, 182, 235, 237–239, 243, 249, 256, 267, 270, 306, 307, 309–312, 316

Tweet, 4, 6, 16, 31–32, 51, 55, 58, 68, 76, 79–82, 86–88, 93–95, 103, 106, 107, 112, 113, 116, 120–122, 140, 149, 150, 157, 173–176, 206, 207, 221, 222, 244, 246, 250, 252, 270, 279, 316

Twitter, 4, 25, 55, 76, 100, 129, 156, 183, 206, 239, 266, 306, 316

U

User profile, 32, 55–56, 81, 216, 275, 316

User-generated content (UGC), 6–8, 16, 18, 19, 26, 28–30, 82, 101, 109, 113, 120, 122, 133, 175, 188, 195, 221, 242, 244, 268, 272, 273, 276, 278, 282, 311, 316, 317

V

Video blog (vlog), 29, 30, 60, 92, 121, 213, 317

Viral blogging, 59–60, 106, 122, 316

Viral marketing (viral advertising), 12, 18, 58–60, 69, 87, 105–107, 122, 124, 234, 243, 301, 316, 317

Viral video

    communal shopping, 132, 313

    social marketplace, 5, 41, 143–144, 150, 190, 315

    social shopping, 6, 8, 12, 15–17, 19, 51, 55, 56, 63, 64, 108, 127–152, 166, 234, 284, 315, 316

    virtual economy, 147, 219, 317

    virtual goods, 28, 144–150, 215, 216, 218, 219, 226, 317

Virtual world, 9, 17, 26, 29, 34, 39, 41, 82, 83, 86, 93, 95, 120, 147, 150, 190–193, 198, 207, 215–219, 221, 222, 226, 227, 242, 247, 313, 315, 317

W

Web 2.0, 5, 7–10, 12, 13, 18, 19, 26, 28–30, 33, 40–42, 59, 76, 91, 132, 149, 158, 161, 162, 168, 171–173, 175, 177, 182–185, 190, 193, 197–199, 207, 209, 219, 226, 244, 245, 254, 270, 271, 283, 302, 314, 315, 317

Widgets, 16, 88, 94, 249, 250, 311, 317

Wiki (wikilog), 5–7, 25, 26, 28, 30–32, 34, 39, 53, 56, 60–61, 63, 65, 66, 86, 91, 101, 103, 105, 108, 142, 143, 147, 148, 156, 158, 174, 185, 206–208, 214–217, 219, 220, 224, 251, 252, 255, 275, 277, 293, 294, 300, 313, 315, 317

Word of mouth (WOM), 8, 14, 15, 19, 30–32, 49, 51–54, 57–61, 68, 84, 87, 100, 103, 105–108, 110, 122, 131, 140, 144, 160, 162, 210, 240, 244, 246, 301, 310, 316, 317